WORD STUDIES

IN THE

NEW TESTAMENT

BY

MARVIN R. VINCENT, D.D.

BALDWIN PROFESSOR OF SACRED LITERATURE IN UNION THEOLOGICAL SEMINARY
NEW YORK.

VOLUME I

THE SYNOPTIC GOSPELS
ACTS OF THE APOSTLES
EPISTLES OF PETER, JAMES, AND JUDE

WORD STUDIES IN THE NEW TESTAMENT
4 Volume Set

Hendrickson Publishers
P.O. Box 3473
Peabody, MA 01961-3473

Printed in the United States of America

ISBN 0-917006-30-5

PREFACE.

New-Testament commentaries are so numerous, and, many of them, so good, that a new essay requires some explanation. The present work is an attempt in a field which, so far as I am aware, is not covered by any one book, though it has been carefully and ably worked by many scholars. Taking a position midway between the exegetical commentary and the lexicon and grammar, it aims to put the reader of the English Bible nearer to the stand-point of the Greek scholar, by opening to him the native force of the separate words of the New Testament in their lexical sense, their etymology, their history, their inflection, and the peculiarities of their usage by different evangelists and apostles.

The critical student of the Greek Testament will, therefore, find himself here on familiar, and often on rudimental, ground, and will understand that the book has not been prepared with any design or expectation of instructing him. It has in view, first of all, those readers whose ignorance of Greek debars them from the quickening contact of the original words, and to whom is unknown the very existence of those tracks which the Greek scholar threads with unconscious ease and in clear light.

No scholar will maintain that such a task is rendered superfluous by even the most idiomatic and accurate translation. The most conscientious and competent translator is fettered by difficulties inherent in the very nature of a translation. Something must exhale in the transfer from one language to another; something which is characteristic in proportion to its subtlety. Reading an author in a translation is like hearing through a telephone. The words may reach the ear distinctly, but the quality of the most familiar voice is lost. In translation, as in exchange of money, transfer often necessitates breaking up—the destruction of the original symbol, in order to embody its contents in the symbols of another tongue. A particular coin of one country may have no exact representative in a coin of another country; and the difference must be made out with small change. A single Greek word often requires two or three words for its reproduction in English, and even then the partial equivalent must be made good by comment or paraphrase. There are, besides, certain features of every language, and particularly of every dead language, which defy transfer by any process—embodiments of a subtle play of perception or of thought which has vanished, like the characteristic expression from a dead face, and which, though it may give some hint of itself to an English mind, eludes the grasp of an English formula.

Difficulties like these can be met only by the study of individual words. The translator is compelled to deal mainly with the contents of sentences and periods; to make the forms of thought subordinate to the substance. A translation which should literally reproduce the idiomatic structure of its original would be a monstrosity. If the thought is to circulate freely and familiarly in Anglo-Saxon society, and to do its best work upon Anglo-Saxon minds, it must assume the Anglo-Saxon dress. It must modify or abandon its native habits. It cannot be continually thrusting into notice its native antecedents, and the forms of the life which evolved it. It must be naturalized throughout. Hence the translator is compelled to have mainly in view his own audience; to expound the message rather than to flatter the nationality of the messenger. He cannot stop to show his reader how each constituent word of the original sentence is throbbing with a life of its own, and aglow with the fascination of a personal history. This is rather the work of the commentator; and not of the commentator who explains the meaning and the relation of verses and chapters, but of one who deals with words in detail, and tells their individual stories.

For a language is not made to order and out of hand. It is a growth out of a people's life; and its words are not arbitrary symbols fixed by decree or by vote, but are struck out, as needed, by incidents and crises. They are the formulas in which new needs and first impressions of external facts spontaneously voice themselves, and into which social customs run. Hence language becomes more picturesque as we recede toward its earlier forms. Primitive speech is largely figurative; primitive words are pictures. As the language becomes the expression of a more conventional and artificial life, and of a deeper and more complex thought, new words are coined representing something more subjective and subtle; and the old words, as they become pressed into the new service and stretched to cover a wider range of meaning, lose their original sharpness of outline. They pass into conventional symbols in the multiform uses of daily speech; they become commonplace factors of a commonplace present, and remain historic only to lexicographers and philologists. None the less, these words forever carry hidden in their bosom their original pictures and the mark of the blow which struck each into life; and they will show them to him who lovingly questions them concerning their birth and their history.

These remarks apply in a peculiar manner to the Greek language, which was the outgrowth of a national character at once poetic and passionate, logical and speculative, and which was shaped by an eventful and romantic history and by a rich and powerful literature. The words of a language which traverses the period from Homer to Aristotle, from Marathon to Leuctra; which told the stories of Herodotus, carried the mingled fire and logic of Demosthenes, voiced the tremendous passion of Oedipus, and formulated the dialectic of Plato and the reasoning of Aristotle, must enfold rare treasures; and the more as we follow it into its later development under the contact of Oriental thought, which fused it in the alembic of Alexandria, ran the new combination into the mould of the Septuagint, and added the last element necessary to constitute it the bearer of the Gospel message. The highest testimony to the resources of this wonderful tongue is furnished in its exquisite sensitiveness to the touch of the new faith, and its ready adaptation to the expression of the new truth. Its contact with the fresh, quickening ideas of the Gospel seemed to evoke from it a certain deep-lying quality, overlaid till then by the baser moral conceptions of Paganism, but springing up in prompt response to the summons of Christian thought and sentiment. Yet even the words which lent themselves so readily to the new and higher message of Christianity could not abjure their lineage or their history. They bore the marks of the older and less sacred burdens they had carried. In the histories of its choicest words, Christianity asserts itself as a redeemer of human speech. The list of New-Testament words lifted out of ignoble associations and uses, and mitred as ministers of sacred truth, is a long and significant one; and there are few more fascinating lines of study than this, to which Archbishop Trench long ago directed English readers in his "Study of Words" and his "New-Testament Synonyms."

The biblical student may therefore profitably combine two distinct lines of study; the one directed at the truth of scripture in mass, the other at the medium or vehicle of the truth in detail. A thorough comprehension of scripture takes in the warp no less than the woof. Labor expended upon etymologies, synonyms, and the secrets of particles and tenses, upon the wide range of pictures and hints and histories underlying the separate words and phrases of the New Testament, is not thrown away, and issues in a larger result than the mere accumulation of curious lore. Even as nature fills in the space between the foreground and the background of her landscapes with countless details of form and color, light and shadow, so the rich details of New-Testament words, once apprehended, impart a depth of tone and a just relation and perspective to the salient masses of doctrine, narrative, and prophecy. How much is habitually lost to the English student through the use of one and the same term in rendering two words which the writer selected with a clear recognition of a distinction between them. How often a picture or a bit of history is hidden away in a word, of which a translation gives and can give no hint. How many distinctive characteristics of a writer are lost in a translation. How often, especially in the version of 1611, the marvellous play of the Greek tenses, and the nicely-calculated force of that potent little instrument, the article, are utterly overlooked. As the reader steps securely over the carefully-fitted pavement laid for him by modern revisers, he does not even guess at the rare and beautiful things lying beneath almost every separate block.

Can the reader who knows no Greek be put in possession of these treasures? Not of all; yet certainly of a goodly share of them. It has seemed to me that the following results might be reached:

1. Where a word has a history, he may learn it, and may be shown through what stages the word has attained its present meaning, and how its variations have successively grown out of each other. Illustrations are furnished by such words as "humility," "meekness," "blessed."

2. He may be shown, in part, at least, the peculiar form in which a thought comes to a Greek mind; or, in other words, he may form some acquaintance with Greek idioms. Thus, to take some very simple instances, he can easily see how, when

he thinks of his food as set *before* him on the table, the Greek thinks of it as set *beside* him, and writes accordingly; or how his idea of *sitting down* to the table comes to the Greek as *reclining;* or he can understand how, when Luke says, "we came *the next day*," the idea of the next or second day comes to him in the form of an adjective qualifying *we*, so that he thinks of himself and his companions as *second-day men*. Sometimes, when two languages develop a difference of idiom in their classical usage, the classical idiom of the one reappears in the vulgar dialect of the other. The spirit of numerous Greek words or phrases, even in the New Testament, could be reproduced most faithfully by English expressions which have been banished from polite diction.

3. He can be shown the picture or the figure hidden away in a word. See, for example, the note on *compel*, Matt. v. 41.

4. He may learn something of Greek synonyms. He may be shown how two different Greek words, rendered by the same English word, represent different sides or phases of the same idea, and why each word is used in its own place. Thus, the word "net" occurs in both Matt. iv. 18 and Matt. xiii. 47; but the Greek word is different in each verse, and either word would have been inappropriate in the place of the other.

5. He may be shown how two English words, having apparently no connection with each other, are often expressed by the same Greek word; and he may be put in possession of the connecting idea. He does not suspect that "bosom," in Luke vi. 38, and "creek" or "bay," in Acts xxvii. 39, are one and the same word; or that there is any connection between the "winding up" of Ananias' body (Acts v. 6) and Paul's assertion that the time is "*short*" (1 Cor. vii. 29).

6. He may be made to understand the reasons for many changes of rendering from an older version, which, on their face, seem to him arbitrary and useless.

7. He can be taught something of the characteristic usage of

words and phrases by different authors, and may learn to detect, even through the English version, certain differences of style. (See the Introductions to the different books.)

8. He can be shown the simpler distinctions between the Greek tenses, and the force of the Greek article; and how the observance of these distinctions adds to the vigor and liveliness of the translation.

Much valuable matter of this kind is contained in commentaries; and in some popular commentaries considerable prominence is given to it, notably in the two admirable works of Dr. Morison on Matthew and Mark. But it is scattered over a wide surface, and is principally confined to commentaries prepared for the critical student; while very much lies hidden in lexicons and etymological treatises, and in special essays distributed through voluminous periodicals. I have collected and sifted a large amount of this material from various and reliable sources, and have applied it to the treatment of the words as they occur, verse by verse, divesting it of technicalities, and trying to throw it into a form suited to the students of the English Bible.

I had these so prominently in view at the beginning that I seriously contemplated the entire omission of Greek words. On further thought, however, I decided that my plan might, without detriment to the original purpose, be stretched so as to include beginners in the study of the Greek Testament, and certain college-bred readers who have saved a little Greek out of the wreck of their classical studies. For the convenience of such I have inserted the original words wherever it seemed expedient; but always in parentheses and with the translation appended. The English reader may therefore be assured that any value which the book may have for him will not be impaired by the presence of the unfamiliar characters. He has but to pass them over, and to confine his attention to the English text.

It is evident that my purpose relieves me of the duty of the exegesis of passages, save in those cases where the word under consideration is the point on which the meaning of the entire passage turns. The temptation to overstep this limit has been constantly present, and it is not impossible that I may have occasionally transgressed. But the pleasure and the value of the special study of words will, I think, be enhanced for the student by detaching it from the jungle of exegetical matter in which, in ordinary commentaries, it is wellnigh lost.

A few words should be said respecting a name which the title of this book will at once suggest to New-Testament students—I mean Bengel. The indebtedness of all workers in this field to John Albert Bengel it is not easy to overstate. His well-known "Gnomon," which still maintains a high and honorable rank among commentaries after the lapse of nearly a century and a half, was the pioneer in this method of treating scripture. My own obligations to him are very great for the impulse to this line of study which I received in translating the "Gnomon" more than twenty-five years ago; more for that, indeed, than for any large amount of help in the present work. For his own labors have contributed to the great extension of his special line of study since the appearance of the "Gnomon" in 1742. The entire basis of New-Testament philology and textual criticism has been shifted and widened, and many of his critical conclusions, therefore, must be either modified or rejected. His work retains its value for the preacher. He must always stand pre-eminent for his keen and deep spiritual insight, and for that marvellously terse and pithy diction with which, as with a master-key, he so often throws open by a single turn the secret chambers of a word; but for critical results the student must follow later and surer guides.

As to materials, let it suffice to say that I have freely used whatever I have found serviceable. The book, however, is not a compilation. My plan has compelled me to avoid lengthy discussions and processes, and to confine myself mostly to the statement of results. In order to avoid encumbering the pages with a multitude of references, I have appended a list of the sources on which I have drawn; and the names of other authors not mentioned there will be found appended to quotations.

I have not attempted textual criticism. I have followed principally the text of Westcott and Hort, comparing it with Tischendorf's eighth edition, and commonly adopting any reading in which the two agree. It is, perhaps, scarcely necessary to say that the very literal and often uncouth renderings which frequently occur are given merely in order to throw sentences or phrases as nearly as possible into their Greek form, and are not suggested for adoption as versions. Each word or passage commented upon is cited first according to the authorized version.

My task has been a labor of love, though pursued amid the numerous distractions and varied duties of a city pastorate. I hope to complete it in due time by an additional volume containing the writings of John and Paul.

It is said that there was discovered, some years ago, in one of our Western States, a magnificent geode, which, on being broken, disclosed a mass of crystals arranged in the form of a cross. It will be a great joy to me if, by this attempt to break the shell of these words of life, and to lay bare their hidden jewels, I may help a Bible-student here and there to a clearer vision of that cross which is the centre and the glory of the Gospel.

MARVIN R. VINCENT.

COVENANT PARSONAGE, NEW YORK, October 30, 1886.

PREFACE TO SECOND EDITION.

In this second edition a number of errors in the Scripture references have been corrected, together with sundry typographical mistakes in the Greek text, such as misplaced accents, omitted breathings, etc. A few changes have also been made in accordance with the suggestions of my reviewers. For many of the corrections in the Greek text I am under great obligations to my old friend Dr. Henry Drisler, of Columbia College, whose invaluable aid it would never have occurred to me to ask in such a matter of literary drudgery, but who voluntarily, and most kindly, furnished me with a list of the errors noted by him in his perusal of the volume.

New York, December 10, 1888.

LIST OF AUTHORS AND EDITIONS.

Angus, Joseph: Commentary on the Epistle of Jude. New York, 1883.

Apocrypha, Greek and English. Bagster, London, 1871.

Abbot, Edwin A.: Article "Gospels," in Encyclopaedia Britannica. 9th edition.

Arnold, W. T.: Roman Provincial Administration. London, 1879.

Autenrieth, Géorg: Homeric Dictionary. New York, 1880.

Augustine: Sermon on the Mount. Edited by Trench. 3d edition. London, 1869.

Alford, Henry: Greek Testament. 5 vols. London, 1857–61.

Becker, W. A.: Gallus. Translated by F. Metcalfe. London, 1849.

Becker, W. A.: Charicles. New edition. London, 1854.

Barrow, Isaac: Sermons. 3 vols. London, 1861.

Butler, Joseph: Sermons. Bohn, London, 1855.

Bosworth, Joseph, and Waring, G.: Gothic and Anglo-Saxon Gospels, with the Versions of Wycliffe and Tyndale. 2d edition. London, 1874.

Bengel: Gnomon Novi Testamenti. Edited by Steudel. Tübingen, 1855.

Bengel: Gnomon Novi Testamenti. Auslegung in fortlaufenden Anmerkungen von C. F. Werner. 2 vols. Stuttgart, 1853.

Bengel: Gnomon Novi Testamenti. Translated by C. T. Lewis and M. R. Vincent. 2 vols. Philadelphia, 1860.

Burgon, John W.: Letters from Rome to Friends in England. London, 1862.

Bruce, Alexander B. : The Parabolic Teaching of Jesus. New York, 1883.

Bryennios, Philotheos : The Teaching of the Twelve Apostles. Translated and edited by Roswell D. Hitchcock and Francis Brown. New York, 1885.

Bryennios, Philotheos : The Same. Edited by Philip Schaff. New York, 1886.

Cox, Samuel : The Book of Job. London, 1880.

Cox, Samuel : An Expositor's Note-Book. London, 1872.

Cox, Samuel : Biblical Expositions. London, 1874.

Cadena, Mariano Velazquez de la : Pronouncing Dictionary of the Spanish and English Languages. New York, 1882.

Cheyne, T. K. : The Prophecies of Isaiah. 2d edition. 2 vols. London, 1882.

Clarke, Mrs. Cowden : Concordance to Shakespeare. London, 1879.

Conybeare, W. J., and Howson, J. S. : Life and Epistles of St. Paul. 2 vols. London, 1856.

Cremer, Hermann : Biblico-Theological Lexicon of New Testament Greek. Edinburgh, 1878.

Crosby, Howard : The New Testament, Old and New Versions. New York, 1884.

Curtius, Ernst : History of Greece. 5 vols. London, 1868.

Cook, F. C. : Commentary on First Peter, in Speaker's Commentary. New York.

Davies, S. S. : St. Paul in Greece, in series "The Heathen World and St. Paul." London.

Döllinger, John J. J. : The Gentile and the Jew. Translated by N. Darnell. 2 vols. London, 1862.

Dixon, Hepworth ; The Holy Land. 2 vols. London, 1865.

Davidson, Samuel : Introduction to the Study of the New Testament. 2d edition. 2 vols. London, 1882.

De Wette, W. M. L. : Kurzgefasstes Exegetisches Handbuch zum Neuen Testament. 4th edition. 5 vols. Leipzig, 1857.

De Wette, W. M. L. : Die Heilige Schrift. 4th edition. Heidelberg, 1858.

Delitzsch, Franz: Commentary on Job, "Clark's Theological Library." 2 vols. Edinburgh, 1869.

Di Cesnola, Louis P.: Cyprus; its Ancient Cities, Tombs, and Temples. New York, 1878.

Edwards, Thomas C.: Commentary on First Corinthians. London, 1885.

Edersheim, Alfred: Life and Times of Jesus the Messiah. 2 vols. London, 1883.

Edersheim, Alfred: The Temple; its Ministry and Services at the Time of Jesus Christ. Boston, 1881.

Edersheim, Alfred: Sketches of Jewish Social Life in the Days of Christ. London, 1876.

Expositor. 1st and 2d series. 20 vols. London, 1875–84.

Ellicott, Charles J.: Commentary on the Epistles of Paul. 2 vols. Andover, 1872.

Eadie, John: The English Bible. 2 vols. London, 1876.

Eastwood, J., and Wright, W. Aldis: The Bible Word-Book. New York, 1874.

Englishman's Greek Concordance to the New Testament. New York, 1859.

Findlay, Alexander G.: Classical Atlas. London.

Farrar, Frederic W.: The Life of Christ. 2 vols. New York, 1874.

Farrar, Frederic W.: The Life and Work of St. Paul. 2 vols. London, 1879.

Farrar, Frederic W.: The Messages of the Books. London, 1885.

Farrar, Frederic W.: Greek Syntax. London, 1876.

Farrar, Frederic W.: Language and Languages. New York, 1878.

Fuerst, Julius: Hebrew and Chaldee Lexicon to the Old Testament. Translated by S. Davidson. 4th edition. London, 1871.

Ford, James: The Gospel of St. Luke Illustrated. London, 1851.

Grote, George: History of Greece. 8 vols. London, 1862.

Godet, F.: Commentary on the Gospel of St. Luke. 3d edition. 2 vols. Edinburgh, 1879.

Gibbon, Edward: Decline and Fall of the Roman Empire. 8 vols. London, 1838.

Grimm, C. L. Willibald: Wilke's Clavis Novi Testamenti. 2d edition. Leipzig, 1879.

Grimm, C. L. Willibald: The Same. Translated, revised, and enlarged by Joseph H. Thayer. New York, 1887.

Gloag, Paton J.: Critical and Exegetical Commentary on the Acts of the Apostles. 2 vols. Edinburgh, 1870.

Gloag, Paton J.: Commentary on the Epistle of James. New York, 1883.

Geikie, Cunningham: The Life and Words of Christ. 2 vols. in one. New York, 1880.

Goebel, Siegfried: The Parables of Jesus. Edinburgh, 1883.

Gladstone, W. E.: Studies on Homer and the Homeric Age. 3 vols. Oxford, 1858.

Grimm, Wilhelm and Jacob: Deutsches Wörterbuch. 6 vols. Leipzig, 1854–73.

Howson, J. H.: The Metaphors of St. Paul. New York, 1871.

Hackett, Horatio B.: Commentary on the Acts of the Apostles. Boston, 1858.

Hobart, William K.: The Medical Language of St. Luke. London, 1882.

Herzog, J. J., and Plitt, G. L.: Real Encyklopädie für Protestantische Theologie und Kirche. 2d edition. 16 vols. Leipzig, 1877–85.

Herodotus. Translated by George Rawlinson. 4 vols. London, 1858.

Huther, John Edward; Kritisch Exegetisches Handbuch über den 1 Brief des Petrus, den Brief des Judas, und den 2 Brief des Petrus. 2d edition. Göttingen, 1859.

Huther, John Edward: Kritisch Exegetisches Handbuch über den Brief des Jakobus. Göttingen, 1858.

Jameson, Mrs.: History of our Lord. 2d edition. 2 vols. London, 1865.

Jameson, Mrs.: Sacred and Legendary Art. 4th edition. 2 vols. London, 1863.

Jelf, William Edward: A Grammar of the Greek Language. 2 vols. Oxford, 1851.

Jowett, B.: The Dialogues of Plato, translated into English. 2d edition. 5 vols. Oxford, 1875.

Josephus: The Jewish War. Translated by Traill. London, 1868.

Kypke, George David: Observationes Sacrae in Nov. Foed. Libros. 2 vols. in one. Breslau, 1755.

Lange, J. P.: Critical, Doctrinal, and Homiletical Commentary. New York.

Lightfoot, J. B.: St. Paul's Epistle to the Galatians. London, 1866.

Lightfoot, J. B.: St. Paul's Epistle to the Philippians. London, 1869.

Lightfoot, J. B.: St. Paul's Epistles to the Colossians and Philemon. London, 1875.

Lightfoot, J. B.: On a Fresh Revision of the New Testament. 2d edition. New York, 1873.

Liddon, Henry P.: The Divinity of our Lord and Saviour Jesus Christ. London, 1867.

Liddell, Henry G., and Scott, Robert: Greek-English Lexicon. 7th edition. New York, 1883.

Liddell, Henry G.: History of Rome. 2 vols. London, 1855.

Lumby, J. Rawson: Commentary on Second Peter, in Speaker's Commentary. New York.

Lumby, J. Rawson: Commentary on Jude, in Speaker's Commentary. New York.

Lewin, Thomas: The Life and Epistles of St. Paul. 2 vols. New York, 1875.

Lewis, Charlton T., and Short, Charles A.: New Latin Dictionary. Oxford and New York, 1879.

Lucas, Newton Ivory: Deutsch-Englisches Wörterbuch. Bremen, 1868.

Lardner, Nathaniel: Works. 5 vols. London, 1815.

Merivale, Charles: History of the Romans under the Empire. 2d edition of Vols. I.–III. 7 vols. London, 1852–62.

Meyer, Heinrich W. H : Commentaries on Matthew, Mark, Luke Acts. New York, 1884.

Mommsen, Theodor : History of Rome. Translated by Dickson. 4 vols. London, 1867.

Morison, James : A Practical Commentary on the Gospel according to St. Matthew. Boston, 1884.

Morison, James : A Practical Commentary on the Gospel according to St. Mark. Boston, 1882.

McClintock, John, and Strong, James : Cyclopaedia of Biblical, Theological, and Ecclesiastical Literature. 10 vols. New York, 1867–81.

Mansel, Henry L. : The Gnostic Heresies of the First and Second Centuries. Edited by J. B. Lightfoot. London, 1875.

Newman, J. H. : Callista. London.

Northcote, J. S., and Brownlow, W. R. : Roma Sotterranea. London, 1869.

Old Testament. Revision of 1885. Cambridge.

Parker, J. H.: Primitive Fortifications of Rome. 2d ed. London.

Palgrave, William Gifford : Central and Eastern Arabia. London, 1873.

Plutarch : Lives. Translated by A. H. Clough. 5 vols. Boston, 1859.

Phrynichus : Eclogae Nominum et Verborum Atticorum. Edited by C. A. Lobeck. Leipzig, 1820.

Porter, J. L. : Handbook for Syria and Palestine. New edition. 2 vols. London, 1868.

Plumptre, E. H. : St. Paul in Asia Minor, in series "The Heathen World and St. Paul." London.

Plumptre, E. H. : The Spirits in Prison, and Other Studies on the Life after Death. New York, 1885.

Revisers' Text of the Greek Testament. Oxford, 1881.

Reynolds, Henry R. : John the Baptist. London, 1874.

Robinson, Edward : Greek and English Lexicon of the New Testament. New York, 1859.

Robinson, Edward : Harmony of the Gospels in Greek. Revised by M. B. Riddle. Boston, 1885.

Riddle, M. B., and Schaff, Philip: Commentary on the Gospel of Mark. New York, 1879.

Riddle, M. B., and Schaff, Philip: Commentary on the Gospel of Luke. New York, 1879.

Rawlinson, George: Ancient Monarchies. 2d edition. 3 vols. New York, 1871.

Rawlinson, George: History of Ancient Egypt. 2 vols. London and New York, 1881.

Ruskin, John: Modern Painters. 5 vols. New York, 1862.

Scott, Robert: Commentary on the Epistle of James, in Speaker's Commentary. New York.

Schaff, Philip: Encyclopaedia of Religious Knowledge. 3 vols. New York, 1882–83.

Schaff, Philip, and Riddle, M. B.: Commentary on the Gospel of Matthew. New York, 1879.

Schaff, Philip: History of the Christian Church. Vols. I., II. New York, 1882.

Stirling, William: Annals of the Artists of Spain. 3 vols. London, 1848.

Salmond, S. D. F.: Commentary on First and Second Peter. New York, 1883.

Stormonth, J.: Etymological and Pronouncing Dictionary of the English Language. Edinburgh, 1877.

Septuagint. According to the Vatican edition. Bagster, London.

Skeat, Walter W.: Etymological Dictionary of the English Language. Oxford, 1882.

Stier, Rudolph: The Words of the Lord Jesus. 8 vols. Edinburgh, 1855.

St. John, J. A.: History of the Manners and Customs of Ancient Greece. 3 vols. London, 1842.

Schmidt, J. H. H.: Synonymik der Griechischen Sprache. 4 vols. Leipzig, 1876–86.

Smith, James: The Voyage and Shipwreck of St. Paul. 3d edition. London, 1866.

Smith, William: Dictionary of Greek and Roman Biography and Mythology. 3 vols. London and Boston, 1849.

Smith, William : Dictionary of Greek and Roman Geography. 2 vols. Boston, 1854.

Smith, William : Dictionary of Greek and Roman Antiquities Edited by Anthon. New York, 1855.

Stanley, Arthur P. : The Epistles of St. Paul to the Corinthians 4th edition. London, 1876.

Stanley, Arthur P. : Sinai and Palestine. New York, 1863.

Stanley, Arthur P. : The Jewish Church. 3 vols. New York, 1864–76.

Stanley, Arthur P. : Sermons and Essays on the Apostolic Age. Oxford and London, 1874.

Scrivener, Frederick H. : A Plain Introduction to the Criticism of the New Testament. 2d edition. Cambridge and London, 1874.

Trench, Richard C. : Synonyms of the New Testament. 8th edition. London, 1876.

Trench, Richard C. : Notes on the Miracles of our Lord. 2d American edition. New York, 1862.

Trench, Richard C. : Notes on the Parables of our Lord. 2d American edition. New York, 1862.

Trench, Richard C. : Studies in the Gospels. New York, 1867.

Trench, Richard C. : On the Study of Words. New York, 1856.

Trench, Richard C. : Proverbs and their Lessons. 5th edition. London, 1861.

Trench, Richard C. : On the Authorized Version of the New Testament. New York, 1873.

Trench, Richard C. : English, Past and Present. 13th edition. London, 1886.

Trench, Richard C. : Select Glossary of English Words. 5th edition. London, 1879.

Theologische Studien und Kritiken.

Tholuck, A. : The Sermon on the Mount. Edinburgh, 1874.

Thomson, William M. : The Land and the Book. London, 1870.

Thomson, William M. : The Land and the Book. 3 vols. New York, 1880–86.

Thoms, John A. : Concordance to the Revised Version of the New Testament. New York, 1883.

Tischendorf, Constantine: Novum Testamentum Graece. 8th edition. Leipzig, 1878.

Tregelles, S. P.: An Account of the Printed Text of the Greek New Testament. London, 1854.

Westcott, Brooke Foss: Introduction to the Study of the Gospels. 5th edition. London, 1875.

Westcott, Brooke Foss, and Hort, Fenton J. A.: The New Testament in the Original Greek. American edition. New York, 1881.

Westcott, Brooke Foss: The Epistles of St. John. London, 1883.

Winer, G. B.: Grammar of New Testament Greek. 8th English edition. Edited by W. F. Moulton. Edinburgh, 1877.

Wilkinson, Gardner: The Ancient Egyptians. 7 vols. London, 1837–41.

Wilkinson, Gardner: Modern Egypt and Thebes. 2 vols. London, 1843.

Zeschwitz, Gerhard von: Profangräcität und Biblischer Sprachgeist. Leipzig, 1859.

ABBREVIATIONS.

A. V. Authorized Version.
Apoc. Apocalypse.
Cit. Cited.
= Equivalent to.
Expn. Explanation.
Lit. Literally.
Rev. Revised Version of the New Testament.
Rev. O. T. Revised Version of the Old Testament.
Sept. Septuagint Version of the Old Testament.
Sqq. Following.
Synop. Synoptists.
Tex. Rec. Received Text.
Tynd. Tyndale's Version of the New Testament.
Vulg. Vulgate or Latin Translation of the New Testament.
Wyc. Wycliffe's Version of the New Testament.

The phrase "only here in New Testament" refers to Greek words only.

THE GOSPEL ACCORDING TO MATTHEW.

INTRODUCTION.

Concerning Matthew personally we know very little. He was a son of Alphæus, a brother of James the Little, possibly a brother of Thomas Didymus. The only facts which the gospels record about him are his call and his farewell feast. He had been a publican or tax-collector under the Roman government; an office despised by the Jews because of the extortions which commonly attended it, and because it was a galling token of subjection to a foreign power. When called by Christ, Matthew forsook at once his office and his old name of Levi. Tradition records of him that he lived the life of an ascetic, on herbs and water. There is a legend that after the dispersion of the apostles he travelled into Egypt and Ethiopia preaching the Gospel; that he was entertained in the capital of Ethiopia in the house of the eunuch whom Philip baptized, and that he overcame two magicians who had afflicted the people with diseases. It is further related that he raised the son of the king of Egypt from the dead, healed his daughter Iphigenia of leprosy, and placed her at the head of a community of virgins dedicated to the service of God; and that a heathen king, attempting to tear her from her asylum, was smitten with leprosy, and his palace destroyed by fire.

According to the Greek legend he died in peace; but according to the tradition of the Western Church he suffered martyrdom.

Mrs. Jameson ("Sacred and Legendary Art") says: "Few churches are dedicated to St. Matthew. I am not aware that he is the patron saint of any country, trade, or profession, unless it be that of tax-gatherer or exciseman; and this is perhaps the reason that, except where he figures as one of the series of evangelists or apostles, he is so seldom represented alone, or in devotional pictures. When he is portrayed as an evangelist, he holds a book or a pen; and the angel, his proper attribute and attendant, stands by, pointing up to heaven or dictating, or he holds the inkhorn, or he supports the book. In his character of apostle, St. Matthew frequently holds a purse or money-bag, as significant of his former vocation."

Matthew wrote, probably in Palestine, and evidently for Jewish Christians. There are two views as to the language in which his gospel was originally composed: one that he wrote it in Hebrew or Syro-Chaldaic, the dialect spoken in Palestine by the Jewish Christians; the other that he wrote it in Greek. The former theory is supported by the unanimous testimony of the early church; and the fathers who assert this, also declare that his work was translated into Greek. In that case the translation was most probably made by Matthew himself, or under his supervision. The drift of modern scholarship, however, is toward the theory of a Greek original. Great uncertainty prevails as to the time of composition. According to the testimony of the earliest Christian fathers, Matthew's gospel is the first in order, though the internal evidence favors the priority of Mark. Evidently it was written before the destruction of Jerusalem (A.D. 70). "Had that event preceded the writing of the synoptic gospels and the epistles of St. Paul, nothing is more certain than that it must have been directly mentioned, and that it must have exercised an immense influence on the thoughts and feelings of the apostles and evangelists. No writer dealing with the topics and arguments and prophecies with which they are constantly occupied, could possibly have failed to appeal to the tremendous sanction which had been given to all their views by God himself, who thus manifested his providence in human history, and showed all things by the quiet light of inevitable circumstances" (Farrar, "Messages of the Books").

Matthew's object was to exhibit the Gospel as the fulfilment of the law and the prophecies; to connect the past with the present; to show that Jesus was the Messiah of the Jews, and that in the Old Testament the New was prefigured, while in the New Testament the Old was revealed. Hence his gospel has a more decidedly Jewish flavor than any other of the synoptics. The sense of Jewish nationality appears in the record of Christ's words about the "lost sheep of the house of Israel" (xv. 24); in the command not to go into the way of the Gentiles nor into the villages of the Samaritans (x. 5); in the prophecy that the apostles shall sit as judges in "the regeneration" (xix. 28). Also in the tracing of the genealogy of our Lord no further back than to Abraham; in the emphasis laid on the works of the law (v. 19; xii. 33, 37); and in the prophecy which makes the end of Israel contemporaneous with the "consummation of the age" (xxiv. 3, 22; x. 23).

On the other hand, a more comprehensive character appears in the adoration of the infant Jesus by the Gentile magi; in the prophecy of the preaching of the Gospel of the kingdom to all the world (xxiv. 14), and the apostolic commission to go to all nations (xxviii. 19); in the commendation of the faith of a Gentile above that of Israel (viii. 10–12; compare the story of the Syrophœnician woman, xv. 28); in the use of the word "Jews," as if he were outside the circle of Jewish nationality; in the parables of the laborers in the vineyard (xx. 1–16), and of the marriage of the king's son (xxii. 1–14); in the threat of taking away the kingdom from Israel (xxi. 43), and in the value attached to the moral and religious element of the law (xxii. 40; xxiii. 23). The genealogy of Jesus contains the Gentile names of Rahab the Canaanite, and Ruth the Moabitess. To Matthew Jesus is alike the Messiah of the Jew and the Saviour of the world.

It being his task to show how the law and the prophets were fulfilled in Christ, his allusions are frequent to the Old Testament scriptures. He has upward of sixty references to the Old Testament. His citations are of two classes: those which he quotes himself as fulfilled in the events of Christ's life, such as i. 23; ii. 15, 18; iv. 15, 16; and those which are a part of the discourse of his different characters, such as iii. 3; iv. 4, 6,

7, 10; xv. 4, 8, 9. He exhibits the law of Christ, not only as the fulfilment of the Mosaic law, but in contrast with it, as is illustrated in the Sermon on the Mount. Yet, while representing the new law as gentler than the old, he represents it, at the same time, as more stringent (see v. 28, 32, 34, 39, 44). His gospel is of a sterner type than Luke's, which has been rightly styled "the Gospel of universality and tolerance." The retributive element is more prominent in it. Sin appeals to him primarily as the violation of law; and therefore his word for iniquity is ἀνομία, *lawlessness,* which occurs nowhere else in the Gospels. He alone records the saying, "Many are called, but few are chosen" (xxii. 14), and, as Professor Abbot has acutely remarked, the distinction between *the called* (κλητοί) and *the chosen* (ἐκλεκτοί) is the more remarkable, because Paul uses the two words almost indifferently, and Luke, although he too has the parable of the unworthy guests, has not ventured to use κλητοί in Matthew's disparaging signification (Art. "Gospels," in Encyclop. Britannica). To him, also, is peculiar the record of the saying that "Whosoever shall break one of the least commandments, and teach men so, shall be called least in the kingdom of heaven" (v. 19). To continue the quotation from Professor Abbot, "Matthew, more than the rest of the evangelists, seems to move in evil days, and amid a race of backsliders, among dogs and swine, who are unworthy of the pearls of truth; among the tares sown by the enemy; among fishermen who have to cast back again many of the fish caught in the net of the Gospel. The broad way is ever in his mind, and the multitude of those that go thereby, and the guest without the wedding garment, and the foolish virgins, and the goats as well as the sheep, and those who even cast out devils in the name of the Lord, and yet are rejected by him because they work 'lawlessness.' Where Luke speaks exultantly of joy in heaven over one repentant sinner, Matthew, in more negative and sober phrases, declares that it is not the will of the Father that one of the little ones should perish; and as a reason for not being distracted about the future, it is alleged that 'sufficient for the day is the evil thereof.' The condition of the Jews, their increasing hostility to the Christians, and the wavering or retrogression of many Jewish converts when the hostility became intensified shortly before and during the siege of Jerusalem—this may well explain one side of Matthew's gospel; and the other side (the condemnation of 'lawlessness') might find an explanation in a reference to Hellenizing Jews, who (like some of the Corinthians) considered that the new law set them free from all restraint, and who, in casting aside every vestige of nationality, wished to cast aside morality as well. Viewed in the light of the approaching fall of Jerusalem, and the retrogression of great masses of the nation, the introduction into the Lord's Prayer of the words 'Deliver us from the evil,' and the prediction that 'by reason of the multiplying of lawlessness the love of many shall wax cold,' will seem not only appropriate, but typical of the character of the whole of the First Gospel."

As related to the other synoptical gospels, Matthew's contains fourteen entire sections which are peculiar to him alone. These include ten parables: The Tares; the Hid Treasure; the Pearl; the Draw-net; the Unmerciful Servant; the Laborers in the Vineyard; the Two Sons; the Marriage of the King's Son; the Ten Virgins, and the Talents. Two miracles: The Cure of Two Blind Men, and the Coin in the Fish's Mouth. Four events of the infancy: The Visit of the Magi; the Massacre of the Infants; the Flight into Egypt, and the Return to Nazareth. Seven incidents connected with the Passion and the Resurrection: the Bargain and Suicide of Judas; the Dream of Pilate's Wife; the Resurrection of the Departed Saints; the Watch at the Sepulchre; the Story of the Sanhedrim, and the Earthquake on the Resurrection Morning. Ten great passages of our Lord's discourses: Parts of Sermon on the Mount (v.–vii.); the Revelation to Babes; the Invitations to the Weary (xi. 25–30); Idle Words (xii. 36, 37); the Prophecy to Peter (xvi. 17–19); Humility and Forgiveness (xviii. 15–35); Rejection of the Jews (xxi. 43); the Great Denunciation (xxiii.); the Discourse about Last Things (xxv. 31–46); the Great Commission and Promise (xxviii. 18–20).

Hence Matthew's is pre-eminently the *didactic* Gospel, one-quarter of the whole being occupied with the actual words and discourses of the Lord.

Matthew is less characteristic in style than in arrangement and matter. The orderly, business-like traits which had been fostered by his employment as a publican, appear in his methodical arrangement and grouping of his subject. His narrative is more sober and less graphic than either Mark's or Luke's. The picture of our Lord's life, character, and work, as Teacher, Saviour, and Messianic King, is painted simply, broadly, and boldly, but without minute detail, such as abounds in Mark. His diction and construction are the most Hebraistic of the synoptists, though less so than those of John's gospel. The following Hebrew peculiarities are to be noted: 1. The phrase, *Kingdom of Heaven* (*βασιλεία τῶν οὐρανῶν*), which occurs thirty-two times, and is not found in the other evangelists, who use *Kingdom of God*. 2. *Father in Heaven*, or *Heavenly Father* (ὁ πατὴρ ὁ ἐν οὐρανοῖς: ὁ πατὴρ ὁ οὐράνιος). This occurs fifteen times in Matthew, only twice in Mark, and not at all in Luke, xi. 2 being a false reading. 3. *Son of David*, seven times in Matthew, three in Mark, three in Luke. 4. *The Holy City* (Jerusalem), in Matthew only. 5. *The end of the world*, or *consummation of the age* (ἡ συντέλεια τοῦ αἰῶνος), in Matthew only. 6. *In order that it might be fulfilled which was spoken* (ἵνα or ὅπως πληρωθῇ τὸ ῥηθέν), eight times in Matthew, and not elsewhere in this form. This is Matthew's characteristic formula. 7. *That which was spoken* (τὸ ῥηθέν), twelve times; *It was spoken* (ἐῤῥήθη), six times. Not elsewhere used of scripture, for Mark xiii. 14 is a false reading. Matthew always uses *that which was spoken* (τὸ ῥηθέν) when quoting scripture himself. In other quotations he has *It is written* (γέγραπται), like the other evangelists. He never uses the singular γραφή (properly *a passage of scripture*). 8. *And behold* (καὶ ἰδού), in narrative, twenty-three times; in Luke, sixteen. 9. *Heathen* (ἐθνικός), in Matthew only. 10. *To swear in* (ὀμνύειν ἐν, i.e., *by*), thirteen times, in Matthew and Apoc. x. 6.

A number of words condemned by the grammarians as unclassical or as slang are employed by Mark, and a few of these may be found in Matthew, such as μονόφθαλμος, *having one eye*; κολλυβισταί, *money-changers*; κοράσιον, *maid*; ῥαφίς, a *needle*. He also uses some Latinisms, three at least in common with

Mark: πραιτώριον, *prætorium;* κῆνσος, *tribute;* φραγελλόω, *to scourge*; also κουστωδία, *guard*, peculiar to him alone.

He frequently uses the words *to come or go* (προσέρχομαι, πορέυω) after the oriental manner, to expand his narrative; as, *when the tempter came he said* (iv. 3); *a centurion came beseeching* (viii. 5); *a scribe came and said* (viii. 19); *the disciples of John came, saying* (ix. 14). The former of these verbs (προσέρχομαι) occurs fifty-one times, while in Mark it is found but six times, and in Luke, ten. The word ὄναρ, *a dream*, is used by him alone in the New Testament, and always in the phrase κατ' ὄναρ, *in a dream.* It occurs six times. Τάφος, *a tomb*, is also peculiar to him, the other evangelists using μνῆμα or μνημεῖον, the latter being used also by Matthew. ὁ λεγόμενος, *who is called*, is a favorite expression in announcing names or surnames (i. 16; x. 2; xxvi. 3, 14). He adds *of the people* to *scribes* or *elders* (ii. 4; xxi. 23; xxvi. 3, 47; xxvii. 1). He writes, *into the name* (εἰς τὸ ὄνομα), where the other evangelists have ἐν, *in*, or ἐπί, *upon* (x. 41, 42; xviii. 20; xxviii. 19). His favorite particle of transition is τότε, *then*, which occurs ninety times, to six in Mark and fourteen in Luke (ii. 7; iii. 5; viii. 26; xi. 20, etc.). There are about a hundred and twenty words which are used by him alone in the New Testament. Two instances occur of a play upon words: ἀφανίζουσι φανῶσι, they make their real faces *disappear*, in order that they may *appear* (vi. 16); κακοὺς κακῶς, he will *evilly* destroy those *evil* husbandmen" (xxi. 41).

The writer is utterly merged in his narrative. The very lack of individuality in his style corresponds with the fact that, with the single exception of the incident of his call and feast, he does not appear in his gospel, even as asking a question. It has been suggested that traces of his old employment appear in the use of the word *tribute-money*, instead of *penny*, and in the record of the miracle of the coin in the fish's mouth; but the name "Matthew the publican" serves rather to emphasize his obscurity. The Jew who received the Messiah he portrayed could never lose his disgust for the office and class which he represented. A gospel written by a publican would seem least of all adapted to reach the very people to whom it was addressed.

Whether or not the perception of this fact may have combined to produce this reticence, with the humility engendered by his contemplation of his Lord, certain it is that the evangelist himself is completely hidden behind the bold, broad masses in which are depicted the Messiah of Jewish hope, the Saviour of mankind, the consummate flower of the ancient law, and the perfect life and unrivalled teaching of the Son of David.

THE GOSPEL ACCORDING TO MATTHEW.

SUPERSCRIPTION.

The Gospel (*εὐαγγέλιον*). Signifies originally *a present given in return for joyful news.* Thus Homer makes Ulysses say to Eumæus, "Let this *reward* εὐαγγέλιον be given me for my good news" (Od., xiv. 152). In Attic Greek it meant (in the plural) *a sacrifice for good tidings.* Later it comes to mean *the good news itself*—the joyful tidings of Messiah's kingdom. Though the word came naturally to be used as the title of books containing the history of the good tidings, in the New Testament itself it is never employed in the sense of a written book, but always means *the word preached.*

According to (*κατά*). This is not the same as the phrase Gospel *of* Matthew. The Gospel is God's, not Matthew's nor Luke's; and is substantially one and the same in all the evangelists' writings. The words "according to," therefore, imply a generic element in the Gospel which Matthew has set forth in his own peculiar style. The meaning is, *the good tidings of the kingdom, as delivered or represented by Matthew.*

Matthew (*Ματθαῖον*). The names Matthew and Levi denote the same person (Matt. ix. 9; Mark ii. 14; Luke v. 27). The name Levi is wanting in all lists of the apostles, but Matthew is named in all these lists. The Jews marked decisive changes in their life by a change of name (compare Simon and Peter; Saul and Paul); so that it is evident that Levi, after his call to the apostolate, styled himself Matthew, a contracted form of the

Hebrew Mattathias, meaning *gift of God;* a name reproduced in the Greek *Theodore* (θεός, God; δῶρον, a gift). This name so completely displaced the old one that it is anticipated by Matthew himself in ch. ix. 9, where he is called Matthew; whereas Mark and Luke, in narrating his call, more correctly style him Levi (Mark ii. 14; Luke v. 27); while in their lists of the apostles (Mark iii. 18; Luke vi. 15; Acts i. 13) they rightly call him Matthew.

CHAPTER I.

Ver. 1. **Christ** (Χριστός). Properly an adjective, not a noun, and meaning *anointed* (χρίω, to anoint). It is a translation of the Hebrew *Messiah*, the king and spiritual ruler from David's race, promised under that name in the Old Testament (Ps. ii. 2; Dan. ix. 25, 26). Hence Andrew says to Simon, "We have found the Messiah, which is, being interpreted, Christ (John i. 41; compare Acts iv. 27; x. 38; xix. 28). To us "Christ" has become a proper name, and is therefore written without the definite article; but, in the body of the gospel narratives, since the identity of Jesus with the promised Messiah is still in question with the people, the article is habitually used, and the name should therefore be translated "*the* Christ." After the resurrection, when the recognition of Jesus as Messiah has become general, we find the word beginning to be used as a proper name, with or without the article. In this passage it omits the article, because it occurs in the heading of the chapter, and expresses the evangelist's own faith in Jesus as the Messiah.

Anointing was applied to kings (1 Sam. ix. 16; x. 1), to prophets (1 Kings xix. 16), and to priests (Exod. xxix. 29; xl. 15; Lev. xvi. 32) at their inauguration. "The Lord's anointed" was a common title of the king (1 Sam. xii. 3, 5; 2 Sam. i. 14, 16). Prophets are called "Messiahs," or anointed ones (1 Chron. xvi. 22; Ps. cv. 15). Cyrus is also called "the Lord's Anointed," because called to the throne to deliver the Jews out of captivity (Isa. xlv. 1). Hence the word "Christ" was representative of our Lord, who united in himself the offices of king, prophet, and priest.

It is interesting to see how anointing attaches to our Lord in other and minor particulars. Anointing was an act of hospitality and a sign of festivity and cheerfulness. Jesus was anointed by the woman when a guest in the house of Simon the Pharisee, and rebuked his host for omitting this mark of respect toward him (Luke vii. 35, 46). In the Epistle to the Hebrews (i. 8, 9), the words of the Messianic psalm (xlv. 7) are applied to Jesus, "God, even thy God, hath anointed thee with the oil of gladness above thy fellows."

Anointing was practised upon the sick (Mark vi. 13; Luke x. 34; Jas. v. 14). Jesus, "the Great Physician," is described by Isaiah (lxi. 1, 2; compare Luke iv. 18) as *anointed* by God to bind up the broken-hearted, and to give the mournful the *oil of joy* for mourning. He himself anointed the eyes of the blind man (John ix. 6, 11); and the twelve, in his name, "anointed with oil many that were sick, and healed them" (Mark vi. 13).

Anointing was practised upon the dead. Of her who brake the alabaster upon his head at Bethany, Jesus said, "She hath anointed my body aforehand for the burying" (Mark xiv. 8; see, also, Luke xxiii. 56).

The Son (*υἱός*). The word *τέκνον* (*child*) is often used interchangeably with *υἱός* (*son*), but is never applied to Christ. (For *τέκνον*, see on 1 John iii. 1.) While in *τέκνον* there is commonly implied the passive or dependent relation of the children to the parents, *υἱός* fixes the thought on the person himself rather than on the dependence upon his parents. It suggests individuality rather than descent; or, if descent, mainly to bring out the fact that the son was worthy of his parent. Hence the word marks the filial relation as carrying with it privilege, dignity, and freedom, and is, therefore, the only appropriate term to express Christ's sonship. (See John i. 18; iii. 16; Rom. viii. 29; Col. i. 13, 15.) Through Christ the dignity of sons is bestowed on believers, so that the same word is appropriate to Christians, *sons of God*. (See Rom. viii 14; ix. 26; Gal. iii. 26; iv. 5, 6, 7.)

6. **David the king** (*τὸν Δαυεὶδ τὸν βασιλέα*, "*the* David, *the* king"). Both words are thus emphasized: *the* David from whom Christ, if he were the Messiah, *must* have descended; *the* king with whom the Messiah's genealogy entered upon the kingly dignity. In this genealogy, where the generations are divided symmetrically into three sets of fourteen, the evangelist seems to connect the last of each set with a critical epoch in the history of Israel: the first reaching from the origin of the race to the commencement of the monarchy ("David *the king*"); the second, from the commencement of the monarchy to the captivity in Babylon; the third and last, from the captivity to the coming of "*the* Christ." The same emphatic or demonstrative use of the article occurs with the name of Joseph (ver. 16), marking his peculiar relation to Jesus as the husband of Mary: *the* Joseph, the husband of Mary.

18. **Espoused** (*μνηστευθείσης*: Rev., *betrothed;* Tyn., *maryed*). The narrative implies a distinction between betrothal and marriage. From the moment of her betrothal a woman was treated as if actually married. The union could be dissolved only by regular divorce. Breach of faithfulness was regarded as adultery, and was punishable with death (Deut. xxii. 23, 24), and the woman's property became virtually that of her betrothed, unless he had expressly renounced it; but, even in that case, he was her natural heir.

19. **Not willing** (*μὴ θέλων*)—**was minded** (*ἐβουλήθη*). These two words, describing the working of Joseph's mind, and evidently intended to express different phases of thought, open the question of their distinctive meanings in the New Testament, where they frequently occur (*θέλω* much oftener than *βούλομαι*), and where the rendering, in so many cases by the same words, furnishes no clue to the distinction. The original words are often used synonymously in cases where no distinction is emphasized; but their use in other cases reveals a radical and recognized difference. An interchange is inadmissible when the greater force of the expression requires *θέλειν*. For instance, *βούλεσθαι* would be entirely inappro-

priate at Matt. viii. 3, "*I will*, be thou cleansed;" or at Rom. vii. 15.

The distinction, which is abundantly illustrated in Homer, is substantially maintained by the classical writers throughout, and in the New Testament.

Θέλειν is the stronger word, and expresses a *purpose* or *determination* or *decree*, the execution of which is, or is believed to be, in the power of him who wills. **Βούλεσθαι** expresses *wish*, *inclination*, or *disposition*, whether one desires to do a thing himself or wants some one else to do it. **Θέλειν**, therefore, denotes the *active resolution*, the *will urging on to action*. **Βούλεσθαι** is to *have a mind*, to *desire*, sometimes a little stronger, running into the sense of *purpose*. **Θέλειν** indicates the *impulse* of the will; **βούλεσθαι**, its *tendency*. **Βούλεσθαι** can always be rendered by **θέλειν**, but **θέλειν** cannot always be expressed by **βούλεσθαι**.

Thus, Agamemnon says, "I *would not* (**οὐκ ἔθελον**) receive the ransom for the maid (*i.e.*, I *refused* to receive), because I greatly *desire* (**βούλομαι**) to have her at home" (Homer, "Il.," i. 112). So Demosthenes: "It is fitting that you should *be willing* (**ἐθέλειν**) to listen to those who *wish* (**βουλομένων**) to advise" ("Olynth.," i. 1). That is to say, It is in your power to *determine* whether or not you will listen to those who *desire* to advise you, but whose power to do so depends on your consent. Again: "If the gods *will* it (**θέλωσι**) and you *wish* it (**βούλησθε**)" (Demosth., "Olynth.," ii. 20).*

In the New Testament, as observed above, though the words are often interchanged, the same distinction is recognized. Thus, Matt. ii. 18, "Rachael *would not* (**ἤθελε**) be comforted;" obstinately and positively refused. Joseph, having the right and power under the (assumed) circumstances to make Mary a public example, *resolved* (**θέλων**) to spare her this exposure. Then the question arose—What should he do? On this *he thought*,

---

* A full discussion of the classical usage would require an essay. The critical student is referred to the article βούλεσθαι in Schmidt's Synonymik der Griechischen Sprache, vol. iii., p. 602. See, also, the art, θέλω, in Grimm's Clavis Nov. Test. His classification of meanings, however, needs careful revision.

and, having thought (ἐνθυμηθέντος), his mind *inclined* (tendency), *he was minded* (ἐβουλήθη) to put her away secretly.

Some instances of the interchanged use of the two words are the following: Mark xv. 15, "Pilate *willing*" (βουλόμενος); compare Luke xxiii. 20, "Pilate *willing*" (θέλων). Acts xxvii. 43, "The centurion *willing*" (βουλόμενος); Matt. xxvii. 17, "Whom *will ye* that I release" (θέλετε); so ver. 21. John xviii. 39, "*Will ye* that I release" (βούλεσθε); Matt. xiv. 5, "When he *would* have put him to death" (θέλων). Mark vi. 48, "He *would* have passed by them" (ἤθελε); Acts xix. 30, "Paul *would* have entered" (βουλομένου). Acts xviii. 27, "He *was disposed* to pass" (βουλομένου). Tit. iii. 8, "I *will* that thou affirm" (βούλομαι). Mark vi. 25, "I will that thou give me" (θέλω), etc., etc.

In the New Testament θέλω occurs in the following senses:

1. *A decree or determination of the will.* (*a*) Of God (Matt. xii. 7; Rom. ix. 16, 18; Acts xviii. 21; 1 Cor. iv. 19; xii. 18; xv. 38). (*b*) Of Christ (Matt. viii. 3; John xvii. 24; v. 21; xxi. 22). (*c*) Of men (Acts xxv. 9). Festus, having the power to gratify the Jews, and *determining* to do so, says to Paul, who has the right to decide, "*Wilt thou* go up to Jerusalem?" John vi. 67, Others of the disciples had decided to leave Jesus. Christ said to the twelve, "*Will* ye also go away?" Is that your *determination?* John vii. 17, If any man *sets his will, is determined* to do God's will. John viii. 44, The lusts of your father your will *is set to do.* Acts xxiv. 6.

2. A *wish or desire.* Very many of the passages, however, which are cited under this head (as by Grimm) may fairly be interpreted as implying something stronger than a wish; notably Mark xiv. 36, of Christ in Gethsemane. Our Lord would hardly have used *what thou wilt* in so feeble a sense as that of a *desire* or *wish* on God's part. Mark x. 43, "Whosoever *will* be great," expresses more than the *desire* for greatness. It is the *purpose* of the life. Matt. xxvii. 15, It was given to the Jews to decide what prisoner should be released. Luke i. 62, The name of the infant John was referred to Zacharias' decision. John xvii. 24, Surely Christ does more than *desire* that those whom the Father has given him shall be with him.

Luke ix. 54, It is for Jesus to *command* fire upon the Samaritan villages if he so wills. (See, also, John xv. 7; 1 Cor. iv. 21; Matt. xvi. 25; xix. 17; John xxi. 22; Matt. xiii. 28; xvii. 12.) In the sense of *wish* or *desire* may fairly be cited 2 Cor. xi. 12; Matt. xii. 38; Luke viii. 20; xxiii. 8; John xii. 21; Gal. iv. 20; Matt. vii. 12; Mark x. 35.

3. *A liking* (Mark xii. 38; Luke xx. 46; Matt. xxvii. 43). (See note there.)

Βούλομαι occurs in the following senses:

1. *Inclination* or *disposition* (Acts xviii. 27; xix. 30; xxv. 22; xxviii. 18; 2 Cor. i. 15).

2. Stronger, with the idea of *purpose* (1 Tim. vi. 9; James i. 18; iii. 4; 1 Cor. xii. 11; Heb. vi. 17).

In most, if not all of these cases, we might expect θέλειν; but in this use of βούλομαι there is an implied emphasis on the element of *free choice* or *self-determination*, which imparts to the *desire* or *inclination* a *decretory* force. This element is in the human will by *gift* and *consent*. In the divine will it is *inherent*. At this point the Homeric usage may be compared in its occasional employment of βούλομαι to express determination, but only with reference to the gods, in whom to *wish* is to *will*. Thus, "Whether Apollo *will* (βούλεται) ward off the plague" ("Il.," i. 67). "Apollo *willed* (βούλετο) victory to the Trojans" ("Il.," vii. 21).

To make a public example (δειγματίσαι). The word is kindred to δείκνυμι, *to exhibit, display, point out*. Here, therefore, to expose Mary to public shame (Wyc., *publish* her; Tyn., *defame* her). The word occurs in Coloss. ii. 15, of the victorious Saviour displaying the vanquished powers of evil as a general displays his trophies or captives in a triumphal procession. "He made a show of them openly." A compound of the same word (παραδειγματίζω) appears in Heb. vi. 6, "They crucify the Son of God afresh, and *put him to an open shame*."

21. **Shalt call**. Thus committing the office of a father to Joseph. The naming of the unborn Messiah would accord with popular notions. The Rabbis had a saying concerning the six

whose names were given before their birth: "Isaac, Ishmael, Moses, Solomon, Josiah, and the name of the Messiah, whom may the Holy One, blessed be His name, bring quickly in our days."

Jesus (*Ἰησοῦν*). The Greek form of a Hebrew name, which had been borne by two illustrious individuals in former periods of the Jewish history—Joshua, the successor of Moses, and Jeshua, the high-priest, who with Zerubbabel took so active a part in the re-establishment of the civil and religious polity of the Jews on their return from Babylon. Its original and full form is *Jehoshua*, becoming by contraction *Joshua* or *Jeshua*. Joshua, the son of Nun, the successor of Moses, was originally named *Hoshea* (*saving*), which was altered by Moses into *Jehoshua* (*Jehovah* (*our*) *Salvation*) (Num. xiii. 16). The meaning of the name, therefore, finds expression in the title *Saviour*, applied to our Lord (Luke i. 47; ii. 11; John iv. 42).

Joshua, the son of Nun, is a type of Christ in his office of *captain* and *deliverer* of his people, in the military aspect of his saving work (Apoc. xix. 11–16). As God's revelation to Moses was in the character of a law-giver, his revelation to Joshua was in that of the Lord of Hosts (Josh. v. 13, 14). Under Joshua the enemies of Israel were conquered, and the people established in the Promised Land. So Jesus leads his people in the fight with sin and temptation. He is the leader of the faith which overcomes the world (Heb. xii. 2). Following him, we enter into rest.

The priestly office of Jesus is foreshadowed in the high-priest Jeshua, who appears in the vision of Zechariah (ch. iii.; compare Ezra ii. 2) in court before God, under accusation of Satan, and clad in filthy garments. Jeshua stands not only for himself, but as the representative of sinning and suffering Israel. Satan is defeated. The Lord rebukes him, and declares that he will redeem and restore this erring people; and in token thereof he commands that the accused priest be clad in clean robes and crowned with the priestly mitre.

Thus in this priestly Jeshua we have a type of our "Great High-Priest, touched with the feeling of our infirmities, and in all points tempted and tried like as we are;" confronting Satan in the wilderness; trying conclusions with him upon the victims of his malice—the sick, the sinful, and the demon-ridden. His royal robes are left behind. He counts not "equality with God a thing to be grasped at," but "empties himself," taking the "form of a servant," humbling himself and becoming "obedient even unto death" (Philip. ii. 6, 7, Rev.). He assumes the stained garments of our humanity. He who "knew no sin" is "made to be sin on our behalf, that we might become the righteousness of God in him" (2 Cor. v. 21). He is at once priest and victim. He pleads for sinful man before God's throne. He will redeem him. He will rebuke the malice and cast down the power of Satan. He will behold him "as lightning fall from heaven" (Luke x. 18). He will raise and save and purify men of weak natures, rebellious wills, and furious passions—cowardly braggarts and deniers like Peter, persecutors like Saul of Tarsus, charred brands—and make them witnesses of his grace and preachers of his love and power. His kingdom shall be a kingdom of priests, and the song of his redeemed church shall be, "unto him that loveth us, and loosed us from our sins by his own blood, and made us to be a kingdom, to be *priests* unto his God and Father; to him be the glory and the dominion forever and ever. Amen" (Apoc. i. 5, 6, in Rev.).

It is no mere fancy which sees a suggestion and a foreshadowing of the *prophetic* work of Jesus in the economy of salvation, in a third name closely akin to the former. *Hoshea*, which we know in our English Bible as Hosea, was the original name of Joshua (compare Rom. ix. 25, Rev.) and means *saving*. He is, in a peculiar sense, the prophet of grace and salvation, placing his hope in God's personal coming as the refuge and strength of humanity; in the purification of human life by its contact with the divine. The great truth which he has to teach is the love of Jehovah to Israel as expressed in the relation of *husband*, an idea which pervades his prophecy, and which is generated by his own sad domestic experience. He foreshadows Jesus in his pointed warnings against sin, his repeated offers of divine mercy, and his patient, forbearing love, as manifested in his dealing with an unfaithful and dissolute wife, whose soul he succeeded in rescuing from sin and death (Hosea i.–iii.). So long as he lived, he was one continual, living prophecy of the tenderness of God toward sinners; a picture of God's love for us when alien from him, and with nothing in us to love. The faithfulness of the prophetic teacher thus blends in Hosea, as in our Lord, with the compassion and sympathy and sacrifice of the priest.

He (αὐτὸς). Emphatic; and so rightly in Rev., "For *it is He* that shall save his people."

Their **sins** (ἁμαρτιῶν). Akin to ἁμαρτάνω, *to miss a mark;* as a warrior who throws his spear and fails to strike his adversary, or as a traveller who misses his way.* In this word, therefore, one of a large group which represent sin under different phases, sin is conceived as *a failing and missing the true end and scope of our lives, which is God.*

22. **Through** the prophet (διὰ). So the Rev. rightly, instead of *by.* In quotations from the Old Testament, the writers habitually use the preposition διὰ (*through*) to denote the *instrumentality* through which God works or speaks, while they reserve ὑπὸ (*by*) to express the primary agency of God himself. So here the prophecy in ver. 23 was spoken *by* the Lord, but was communicated to men *through* his prophet.

23. **The** virgin (ἡ παρθένος). Note the demonstrative force of the article, pointing to a particular person. Not, *some virgin or other.*

They shall call (καλέσουσιν.) In ver. 21, it is *thou shalt call.* The original of Isaiah (vii. 14) has *she shall call;* but Matthew generalizes the singular into the plural, and quotes the prophecy in a form suited to its larger and final fulfilment: *men shall call* his name Immanuel, as they shall come to the practical knowledge that God will indeed dwell with men upon the earth.

Immanuel (Hebrew, *God is with us*). To protect and save. A comment is furnished by Isa. viii. 10, "Devise a device, but it shall come to naught; speak a word, but it shall not stand, for

* See Homer, "Iliad," ix., 501; Sophocles, "Oedipus Tyrannus," 621.

with us is God." Some suppose that Isaiah embodied the purport of his message in the names of his children: *Maher-shalal-hash-baz* (*speed-prey*), a warning of the coming of the fierce Assyrians; *Shear-Jashub* (*a remnant shall return*), a reminder of God's mercy to Israel in captivity, and *Immanuel* (*God is with us*), a promise of God's presence and succor. However this may be, the promise of the name is fulfilled in Jesus (compare "Lo, I am *with you* alway," Matt. xxviii. 20) by his helpful and saving presence with his people in their sorrow, their conflict with sin, and their struggle with death.

24. **The** or **his sleep** (τοῦ ὕπνου). The force of the definite article; *the* sleep in which he had the vision. So Rev., "Arose from *his* sleep."

CHAPTER II.

1. **Bethlehem.** Hebrew, *House of Bread*, probably from its fertility. The birthplace of him who calls himself *the Bread of Life* (John vi. 35), and identified with the history of his human ancestry through Ruth, who was here married to Boaz, and was the ancestress of David (i. 5, 6), and through David himself, who was born there, and anointed king by Samuel (compare Luke ii. 11, *city of David*).

Wise men, or *Magi* (μάγοι). Wycliffe renders *kings.* A priestly caste among the Persians and Medes, which occupied itself principally with the secrets of nature, astrology, and medicine. Daniel became president of such an order in Babylon (Dan. ii. 48). The word became transferred, without distinction of country, to all who had devoted themselves to those sciences, which were, however, frequently accompanied with the practice of magic and jugglery; and, under the form *magician*, it has come to be naturalized in many of the languages of Europe. Many absurd traditions and guesses respecting these visitors to our Lord's cradle have found their way into popular belief and into Christian art. They were said to be kings, and three in number; they were said to be representatives of the three families of Shem, Ham, and Japhet, and therefore one of them is pictured as an Ethiopian; their names are given as Caspar, Balthasar, and Melchior, and their three skulls, said to have been discovered in the twelfth century by Bishop Reinald of Cologne, are exhibited in a priceless casket in the great cathedral of that city.

2. **The east** (ἀνατολή). Literally, *the rising*. Some commentators prefer to render *at its rising*, or *when it rose*. In Luke i. 78, the word is translated *dayspring*, or *dawn*. The kindred verb occurs in Matt. iv. 16, "light *did spring up*" (ἀνέτειλεν).

4. **All the chief priests.** We should expect only *one* chief priest to be mentioned; but the office had become a lucrative one, and frequently changed hands. A rabbi is quoted as saying that the first temple, which stood about four hundred and ten years, had only eighteen high-priests from first to last; while the second temple, which stood four hundred and twenty years, had more than three hundred high-priests. The reference here is not to a meeting of the Sanhedrim, since the elders, who are not mentioned, belonged to this; but to an extraordinary convocation of all the high-priests and learned men. Besides the high-priest in actual office, there might be others who had been his predecessors, and who continued to bear the name, and in part the dignity. It may possibly have included the heads of the twenty-four courses of priests.

6. **Land of Judah.** To distinguish it from Bethlehem in the territory of Zebulon.

Shall be shepherd of (ποιμανεῖ), from ποιμήν, *a shepherd*. So Rev., rightly, instead of *shall rule*. The word involves the whole office of the shepherd—guiding, guarding, folding, as well as feeding. Hence appropriate and often applied to the guides and guardians of others. Homer calls kings "the shepherds of the people." To David the people said, "The Lord said to thee, Thou shalt *feed* (as a shepherd) my people Israel" (2 Sam. v. 2; compare Ps. lxxviii. 70–72). God is often called a shepherd (Gen. xlviii. 15; Ps. xxiii. 1; lxxvii. 20; lxxx. 1; Isa. xl. 11; Ezek. xxxiv. 11–31). Jesus calls himself *the good shepherd* (John x. 11). Peter, who is bidden by Jesus to *shepherd* his sheep (John xxi. 16, ποίμαινε, Rev., *tend*), calls him the *Shepherd of Souls* (1 Pet. ii. 25), and the *Chief Shepherd* (1 Pet. v. 4); and in the Epistle to the Hebrews (xiii. 20), he is styled *the great Shepherd of the sheep*. In Apoc. ii. 27, *rule* is literally to *shepherd* (compare xix. 15); but Christ will shepherd his enemies, not with the pastoral crook, but with a sceptre of iron. Finally, Jesus will perpetuate this name and office in heaven among his redeemed ones, for "the *Lamb*, which is in the midst of the throne, *shall be their shepherd* (Apoc. vii. 17, Rev.). In this verse the word *governor* is in harmony with the idea of shepherding, since the word ἡγούμενος originally means one who *goes before*, or *leads the way*, and suggests Christ's words about the good shepherd in John x. 3, 4: "He calleth his own sheep by name, and leadeth them out. . . . He goeth before them, and the sheep follow him."

Inquired diligently (ἠκρίβωσεν). Better *learned accurately*. The verb is formed from ἄκρος, *at the point* or *end*. The idea is, therefore, he *ascertained to the last point;* denoting the exactness of the information rather than the diligence of the search for it. Compare ver. 8, "Search out *carefully*" (ἀκριβῶς). So the Rev. for *diligently*.

What time the star appeared (τὸν χρόνον τοῦ φαινομένου ἀστέρος). Lit., *the time of the appearing star*. Herod asks, "*How long does the star make itself visible since its rising in the East?* rather than "*At what time did it appear?*"

12. **Being warned** (χρηματισθέντες). The verb means *to give a response to one who asks or consults:* hence, in the passive, as here, *to receive an answer*. The word therefore implies that the wise men had sought counsel of God; and so Wycliffe, "*And answer taken in sleep.*"

16. **The children** (τοὺς παῖδας). *Male* children, as is indicated by the masculine form of the article, and so Rev.

23. **The prophets.** Note the plural, as indicating not any one prediction in particular, but a summary of the import of several prophetic statements, such as Ps. xxii. 6, 8; lxix. 11, 19; Isa. liii. 2, 3, 4.

A Nazarene. A term of contempt (compare John i. 46, and vii. 52). The very name of Nazareth suggested insignificance. In Hebrew it meant *sprout* or *shoot*. The name is prophetically given to the Messiah (Isa. xi. 1). In Isa. x. 33, 34, the fate of Assyria is described under the figure of the felling of a cedar-forest. The figure of the tree is continued at the opening of ch. xi. concerning the Jewish state. The cedar throws out no fresh suckers, but the oak is a tree "in which, after the felling, a stock remaineth" (Isa. vi. 13; compare Job xiv. 9). There is a future then for Israel, represented by the oak. "There shall come forth a shoot from the stock of Jesse, and a twig from his roots shall bear fruit." As David sprang from the humble family of Jesse, so the Messiah, the second David, shall arise out of great humiliation. The fact that Jesus grew up at Nazareth was sufficient reason for his being despised. He was not a lofty branch on the summit of a stately tree; not a recognized and honored son of the royal house of David, now fallen, but an insignificant *sprout* from the roots of Jesse; a Nazarene, of an upstart sprout-town.

CHAPTER III.

1. **In those days.** The phrase is indefinite, but always points back to a preceding date; in this case to the date of the settlement of the family at Nazareth. "In those days," *i.e.*, some time during the nearly thirty years since that settlement.

John. Hebrew, meaning *God has dealt graciously*. Compare the German *Gotthold*.

Came (*παραγίνεται*). Rev., *cometh*. The verb is used in what is called the *historical present*, giving vividness to the narrative, as Carlyle ("French Revolution"): "But now also the National Deputies from all ends of France *are* in Paris with their commissions." "In those days *appears* John the Baptist."

Preaching (*κηρύσσων*). See on 2 Pet. ii. 5.

Wilderness (*τῇ ἐρήμῳ*). Not suggesting absolute barrenness but unappropriated territory affording free range for shepherds and their flocks. Hepworth Dixon ("The Holy Land") says, "Even in the wilderness nature is not so stern as man. Here and there, in clefts and basins, and on the hillsides, grade on grade, you observe a patch of corn, a clump of olives, a single palm."

2. **Repent** (*μετανοεῖτε*). A word compounded of the preposition *μετά*, *after*, *with*; and the verb *νοέω*, *to perceive*, and to *think*, as the result of perceiving or observing. In this compound the preposition combines the two meanings of *time* and *change*, which may be denoted by *after* and *different*; so that the whole compound means *to think differently after*. *Μετάνοια* (*repentance*) is therefore, primarily, an *after-thought*, *different* from the former thought; then, a *change of mind* which issues in *regret* and in *change of conduct*. These latter ideas, however, have been imported into the word by scriptural usage, and do not lie in it etymologically nor by primary usage. *Repentance*, then, has been rightly defined as "Such a virtuous alteration of the mind and purpose as begets a like virtuous change in the life and practice." *Sorrow* is not, as is popularly conceived, the primary nor the prominent notion of the word. Paul distinguishes between *sorrow* (*λύπη*) and *repentance* (*μετάνοια*), and puts the one as the outcome of the other. "Godly *sorrow* worketh *repentance*" (2 Cor. vii. 10).

The kingdom of heaven. Lit., *the kingdom of the heavens* (*ἡ βασιλεία τῶν οὐρανῶν*). An expression peculiar to Matthew. The more usual one is *the kingdom of God*. It is a kingdom of heaven because its origin, its end, its king, the character and destiny of its subjects, its laws, institutions, and privileges—all are heavenly. In the teaching of Christ and in the apostolic writings the kingdom of the Messiah is the actual consummation of the prophetic idea of the rule of God, without any national limitation, so that participation therein rests only on faith in Jesus Christ, and on the moral renewal which is conditioned by the same. It is the combination of all rights of Christian citizenship in this world, and eternal blessedness in the next. All its senses are only different sides of the same great idea—the subjection of all things to God in Christ.

Voice. John's personality is thrown into shadow behind Christ. "What would be the duty of a merely human teacher of the highest moral aim, entrusted with a great spiritual mission and lesson for the benefit of mankind? The example of St. John Baptist is an answer to this inquiry. Such a teacher would represent himself as a mere 'voice,' crying aloud in the moral wilderness around him, and anxious, beyond aught else, to shroud his own insignificant person beneath the majesty of his message" (Liddon, "Our Lord's Divinity").

6. **Were baptized** (*ἐβαπτίζοντο*). See on Mark vii. 4.

Confessing their sins (*ἐξομολογούμενοι τὰς ἁμαρτίας αὐτῶν*). The words imply: 1. That confession was connected with baptism. They were baptized *while in the act of confessing*. 2. An *open* confession, not a private one to John (*ἐξ*, compare Acts xix. 18; Jas. v. 16). 3. An *individual* confession; possibly a *specific* one. (See Luke iii. 10–15.)

9. **These stones.** Pointing, as he spoke, to the pebbles on the beach of the Jordan.

10. **Is laid** (*κεῖται*). Not, *is applied*, as "She *layeth* her hands to the spindle" (Prov. xxxi. 19), but *is lying*.

Is hewn down and cast. The present tense is graphic, denoting what is to happen at once and certainly.

11. **To bear.** Compare to *unloose*, Mark i. 7. John puts himself in the position of the meanest of servants. To *bear* the sandals of their masters, that is, to bring and take them away, as well as to fasten or to take them off, was, among the Jews, Greeks, and Romans, the business of slaves of the lowest rank.

12. **Fan, floor** (Wyc. has *corn-floor*). The picture is of a farmer at his threshing-floor, the area of hard-beaten earth on which the sheaves are spread and the grain trodden out by animals. His *fan*, that is his *winnowing-shovel* or *fork*, is in his hand, and with it he throws up the mingled wheat and chaff against the wind in order to separate the grain.*

Throughly cleanse (διακαθαριεῖ). *Throughly* (retained by Rev.) obsolete form of *thoroughly*, is the force of the preposition διά (*through*). In that preposition lies the picture of the farmer beginning at one side of the floor, and working *through* to the other, cleansing as he goes.

The whole metaphor represents the Messiah as separating the evil from the good, according to the tests of his kingdom and Gospel, receiving the worthy into his kingdom and consigning the unworthy to destruction (compare Matt. xiii. 30; 39–43; 48–50).

14. **Forbad** (διεκώλυεν). The A. V., following Wyc. and Tynd., misses the meaning of the verb. As in so many instances, it overlooks the force of the imperfect tense, which expresses past action, either in progress or in process of conception, in the agent's mind. John did not forbid Jesus, but *had it in mind* to prevent him: *was for hindering him.* Hence Rev., properly, *would have hindered him.* Again, the preposition (διά) intensifies the verb, and represents *strong* feeling on John's part. He was moved to *strenuous* protest against Jesus' baptism by him.

16. **As a dove** (ὡσεὶ περιστερὰν). In the form of a dove, and not, as some interpret, referring merely to the *manner* of the descent—swiftly and gently as a dove (compare Luke iii. 22 "*In*

* *Floor*, ἅλωνα, properly a *circular* space. Used also of *the disk* of the sun or moon, or of *a halo*, which is a transcript of the Greek word.

a bodily form, as a dove"). The dove was an ancient symbol of purity and innocence, adopted by our Lord in Matt. x. 16. It was the only bird allowed to be offered in sacrifice by the Levitical law. In Christian art it is the symbol of the Holy Spirit, and that in his Old Testament manifestations as well as in those of the New Testament. From a very early date the dove brooding over the waters was the type of the opening words of Genesis. An odd fresco on the choir-walls of the Cathedral of Monreale, near Palermo, represents a waste of waters, and Christ above, leaning forward from the circle of heaven with extended arms. From beneath him issues the divine ray along which the dove is descending upon the waters. So Milton:

> "Thou from the first
> Wast present, and with mighty wings outspread
> Dove-like sat'st brooding on the vast abyss
> And mad'st it pregnant."

In art, the double-headed dove is the peculiar attribute of the prophet Elisha. A window in Lincoln College, Oxford, represents him with the double-headed dove perched upon his shoulder. The symbol is explained by Elisha's prayer that a double portion of Elijah's *spirit* might rest upon him.

It has been asserted that, among the Jews, the Holy Spirit was presented under the symbol of a dove, and a passage is cited from the Talmud: "The Spirit of God moved on the face of the waters like a dove." Dr. Edersheim ("Life and Times of Jesus the Messiah") vigorously contradicts this, and says that the passage treats of the supposed distance between the upper and the lower waters, which was only three finger-breadths. This is proved by Gen. i. 2, where the Spirit of God is said to brood over the face of the waters, "just as a dove broodeth over her young without touching them." "Thus the comparison is not between the Spirit and the dove, but between the *closeness* with which a dove broods over her young without touching them, and the supposed proximity of the Spirit to the lower waters without touching them." He goes on to say that the dove was not the symbol of the Holy Spirit, but of Israel. "If, therefore, *rabbinic* illustration of the descent of the Holy

Spirit with the visible appearance of a dove must be sought for, it would lie in the acknowledgment of Jesus as the ideal typical Israelite, the representative of his people."

CHAPTER IV.

1. **The Devil** (τοῦ διαβόλου). The word means *calumniator, slanderer*. It is sometimes applied to men, as to Judas (John vi. 70); in 1 Tim. iii. 11 (*slanderers*); and in 2 Tim. iii. 3, and Tit. ii. 3 (*false accusers*). In such cases never with the article. *The* Devil, Satan, the god of this world (ὁ διάβολος), is always with the article and never plural. This should be distinguished from another word, also wrongly rendered *devil* in the A. V.—δαίμων, and its more common neuter form δαιμόνιον, both of which should be translated *demon*, meaning the unclean spirits which possessed men, and were cast out by Christ and his apostles. The Rev., unfortunately, and against the protest of the American revisers, retains *devil* for both words, except in Acts xvii. 18, where it renders as A. V. *gods*.

The **Son** of God. By its position in the sentence *Son* is emphatic. "If thou standest to God in the relation of *Son*."

Bread (ἄρτοι). Lit., *loaves* or *cakes*. So Wyc., *loaves*. These stones were perhaps those "silicious accretions," which assume the exact shape of little loaves of bread, and which were represented in legend as the petrified fruits of the cities of the plain. By a similar fancy certain crystallizations on Mount Carmel and near Bethlehem are called "Elijah's melons," and the "Virgin Mary's peas;" and the black and white stones found along the shores of the Lake of Galilee have been transformed into traces of the tears of Jacob in search of Joseph. The very appearance of these stones, like the bread for which the faint body hungered, may have added force to the temptation. This resemblance may have been present to Christ's mind in his words at Matt. vii. 9.

4. **It is written** (γέγραπται). The perfect tense. "It *has been* written, and *stands* written." The first recorded words of Jesus after his entrance upon his ministry are an assertion of the authority of scripture, and that though he had the fulness of the Spirit. When addressing man, our Lord seldom quoted scripture, but said, *I say* unto you. In answer to Satan he says, *It is written.*

5. **Taketh** (παραλαμβάνει). The preposition παρά (*with, by the side of*), implies *taketh along with himself*, or *conducteth.* It is the same word which all three evangelists use of our Lord's taking his chosen apostles to the Mount of Transfiguration (Matt. xvii. 1; Mark ix. 2; Luke ix. 28).

The holy city. Matthew alone calls Jerusalem by this name, in accordance with the general intent of his gospel to connect the old economy with the new.

Pinnacle of the temple (τὸ πτερύγιον τοῦ ἱεροῦ). *Pinnacle,* from the Latin *pinnaculum,* a diminutive of *pinna* or *penna* (*a wing*), is a literal translation of πτερύγιον, which is also a diminutive (*a little wing* or *winglet*). Nothing in the word compels us to infer that Christ was placed on the top of a tower or spire, which is the popular meaning of pinnacle. The word may be used in the familiar English sense of the wing of a building. Herod's temple had two wings, the northern and southern, of which the southern was the higher and grander; that being the direction in which the chief enlargement of the temple area made by Herod was practicable. That enlargement, according to Josephus, was effected by building up walls of solid masonry from the valley below. At the extremity of the southern side of the area, was erected the "royal portico," a magnificent colonnade, consisting of a nave and two aisles, running across the entire space from the eastern to the western wall. Josephus further says, that "while the valley of itself was very deep, and its bottom could scarcely be seen when one looked down from above, the additional vastly high elevation of the portico was placed on that height, insomuch that, if any one looked down from the summit of the roof, combining the two altitudes in one stretch of vision, he would be giddy, while his sight could not reach to such an immense depth." This, in comparison with the northern wing, was so emphatically *the* wing of the temple as to explain the use of the article here, as a well-known locality. The scene of the temptation may have been (for the whole matter is mainly one of conjecture) the roof of this portico, at the southeastern angle, where it joined Solomon's Porch, and from which the view into the Kedron valley beneath was to the depth of four hundred and fifty feet.

The word *temple* (ἱερόν, lit., *sacred place*) signifies the whole compass of the sacred inclosure, with its porticos, courts, and other subordinate buildings; and should be carefully distinguished from the other word, ναός, also rendered *temple*, which means the temple itself—the "Holy Place" and the "Holy of Holies." When we read, for instance, of Christ teaching in the *temple* (ἱερόν) we must refer it to one of the temple-porches. So it is from the ἱερόν, the court of the Gentiles, that Christ expels the money-changers and cattle-merchants. In Matt. xxvii. 51, it is the veil of the ναός which is rent; the veil separating the holy place from the holy of holies. In the account of Zacharias entering into the *temple* of the Lord to burn incense (Luke i. 9), the word is ναός, the holy place in which the altar of incense stood. The people were "without," in the forecourts. In John ii. 21, *the temple of his body*, ἱερόν would be obviously inappropriate.

6. **In** their hands (ἐπὶ). *On* their hands (so Rev.) is more correct, and gives a different picture from the A. V. *in:* lifted *on* their hands, as on a litter or platform.

7. **Again** (πάλιν). Emphatic, meaning *on the other hand*, with reference to Satan's *it is written* (ver. 6); as if he had said, "the promise which you quote must be explained by another passage of scripture." Archbishop Trench aptly remarks, "In that '*It is written again*' of Christ, lies a great lesson, quite independent of that particular scripture which, on this occasion, he quotes, or of the use to which he turns it. There lies in it

the secret of our safety and defence against all distorted use of isolated passages in holy scripture. Only as we enter into the unity of scripture, as it balances, completes, and explains itself, are we warned against error and delusion, excess or defect on this side or the other. Thus the retort, '*It is written again*,' must be of continual application; for indeed what very often are heresies but one-sided, exaggerated truths, truths rent away indeed from the body and complex of the truth, without the balance of the counter-truth, which should have kept them in their due place, co-ordinated with other truths or subordinated to them; and so, because all such checks are wanting, not truth any more, but error."

12. **Was cast into prison** (*παρεδόθη*). The verb means, first, to *give*, or *hand over* to another. So, to *surrender* a city or a person, often with the accompanying notion of treachery. The Rev., therefore, rightly renders, *was delivered up*.

16. The people **which sat** (*ὁ καθήμενος*); Wyc., *dwelt*. The article with the participle (lit., *the people, the one sitting*) signifying something characteristic or habitual: the people *whose characteristic it was* to sit in darkness. This thought is emphasized by repetition in a stronger form; *sitting in the region and shadow of Death*. Death is personified. This land, whose inhabitants are spiritually dead, belongs to Death as the realm of his government.

17. **To preach** (*κηρύσσειν*). Originally, *to discharge the duty of a herald* (*κήρυξ*); hence to *cry out, proclaim* (see on 2 Pet. ii. 5). The standing expression in the New Testament for the proclamation of the Gospel; but confined to the *primary announcement* of the message and facts of salvation, and not including *continuous instruction in the contents and connections of the message*, which is expressed by *διδάσκειν* (*to teach*). Both words are used in Matt. iv. 23; ix. 35; xi. 1).

18. **The sea** (*τὴν θάλασσαν*). The small lake of Gennesaret, only thirteen miles long and six wide in its broadest part,

is called *the sea*, by the same kind of popular usage by which Swiss and German lakes are called *See;* as the *Königsee*, the *Trauensee.* So, also, in Holland we have the *Zuyder Zee.* The Latin *mare* (*the sea*) likewise becomes *meer* in Holland, and is used of a lake, as *Haarlemmer Meer;* and in England, *mere*, as appears in *Windermere*, *Grasmere*, etc.

A net (ἀμφίβληστρον). From ἀμφὶ, *around*, and βάλλω, *to throw.* Hence the *casting*-net, which, being cast over the shoulder, spreads into a *circle* (ἀμφὶ). The word is sometimes used by classical Greek writers to denote a garment which *encompasses* the wearer. In ver. 20, the word *net* again occurs, but representing a different Greek word (δίκτυον) which is the general name for all kinds of nets, whether for taking fish or fowl. Still another word occurs at Matt. xiii. 47, σαγήνη, the *draw*-net. See farther on that passage.

21. **Mending** (καταρτίζοντας). Not necessarily *repairing;* the word means *to adjust*, to "*put to rights.*" It may mean here *preparing* the nets for the next fishing.

23, 24. **Sickness, Disease, Torments, Taken, Lunatic.** The description of the ailments to which our Lord's power was applied gains in vividness by study of the words in detail. In ver. 23, the Rev. rightly transposes *sickness* and *disease*; for νόσος (A. V., *sickness*) carries the notion of something severe, dangerous, and even violent (compare the Latin *noceo*, *to hurt*, to which the root is akin). Homer always represents νόσος as the visitation of an angry deity. Hence used of the plague which Apollo sent upon the Greeks ("Iliad," i. 10). So Sophocles ("Antigone," 421) calls a whirlwind θείαν νόσον (*a divine visitation*). *Disease* is, therefore, the more correct rendering as expressing something stronger than *sickness* or *debility*. *Sickness*, however, suits the other word, μαλακίαν. The kindred adjective, μαλακός, means *soft*, as a couch or newly-ploughed furrow, and thus easily runs into our invidious moral sense of *softness*, namely, *effeminacy* or *cowardice*, and into the physical sense of *weakness, sickness.* Hence the word emphasizes the idea of *debility* rather than of violent suffering or danger.

In ver. 24 we have, first, a general expression for ailments of all kinds: *all that were sick* (lit., *all who had themselves in evil case; πάντας τοὺς κακῶς ἔχοντας*). Then the idea of *suffering* is emphasized in the word *taken* (*συνεχομένους*), which means literally *held-together* or *compressed;* and so the Rev. *holden* is an improvement on *taken*, in which the A. V. has followed Wyc. and Tyn. The word is used of the multitude *thronging* Christ (Luke viii. 45). Compare, also, "how am I *straitened* (Luke xii. 50); and I *am in a strait* (Philip i. 23). Then follow the *specific forms* of suffering, the list headed again by the inclusive word *νόσοις*, *diseases*, and the *καὶ* following having the force of *and particularly.* Note the word *torments* (*βασάνοις*). *Βάσανος* originally meant the "Lydian stone," or touchstone, on which pure gold, when rubbed, leaves a peculiar mark. Hence, naturally, a *test;* then a test or trial by *torture.* "Most words," says Professor Campbell ("On the Language of Sophocles") "have been originally metaphors, and metaphors are continually falling into the rank of words," used by the writer as mere vehicles of expression without any sense of the picturesque or metaphorical element at their core. Thus the idea of a *test* gradually passes entirely out of *βάσανος*, leaving merely the idea of *suffering* or *torture.* This is peculiarly noticeable in the use of this word and its derivatives throughout the New Testament; for although suffering as a test is a familiar New Testament truth, these words invariably express simply torment or pain. Wycliffe renders, "They offered to him all men having evil, taken with divers sorrows and torments;" and Tyndale, "All sick people that were taken with divers diseases and gripings." *Lunatic*, or *moon-struck*, (*σεληνιαζομένους*), is rendered by Rev. *epileptic*, with reference to the real or supposed influence of the changes of the moon upon the victims of epilepsy.

CHAPTER V.

1. **A mountain** (τὸ ὄρος). The Rev. recognizes the force of the definite article, and renders "*the* mountain," that particular mountain in the place where Jesus saw the multitudes. The mountain itself cannot be identified. Delitzsch calls the Mount of Beatitudes "The Sinai of the New Testament."

When he was set (καθίσαντος), following Tyndale. Rev., more literally, *when he had sat down* (compare Wyc., *when he had sete*). After the manner of the rabbis, he seated himself ere he began to teach.

2. **Taught** (ἐδίδασκεν). The imperfect signifies *began to teach.*

3. **Blessed** (μακάριοι). As this word and its cognates occur at least fifty-five times in the New Testament, it is important to understand its history, which is interesting because it is one of those numerous words which exhibit the influence of Christian association and usage in enlarging and dignifying their meaning. It is commonly rendered *blessed*, both in the A. V. and Rev., and that rendering might properly be given it in every instance.

Its root is supposed to be a word meaning *great*, and its earlier meaning appears to be limited to *outward* prosperity; so that it is used at times as synonymous with *rich*. It scarcely varies from this meaning in its frequent applications to the Grecian gods, since the popular Greek ideal of divine blessedness was not essentially moral. The gods were *blessed* because of their power and dignity, not because of their holiness. "In general," says Mr. Gladstone ("Homer and the Homeric Age") "the chief note of deity with Homer is emancipation from the restraints of moral law. Though the Homeric gods have not yet ceased to be the vindicators of morality upon earth, they have personally ceased to observe its rules, either for or among themselves. As compared with men, in conduct they are generally characterized by superior force and intellect, but by inferior morality."

In its peculiar application to the dead, there is indicated the despair of earthly happiness underlying the thought of even the cheerful and mercurial Greek. Hence the word was used as synonymous with *dead*. Only the dead could be called truly blessed. Thus Sophocles ("Œdipus Tyrannus"):

> "From hence the lesson learn ye
> To reckon no man happy till ye witness
> The closing day; until he pass the border
> Which severs life from death, unscathed by sorrow."

And again ("Œdipus at Colonus"):

> "Happiest beyond compare,
> Never to taste of life:
> Happiest in order next,
> Being born, with quickest speed
> Thither again to turn
> From whence we came."

Nevertheless, even in its pagan use, the word was not altogether without a moral background. The Greeks recognized a prosperity which waited on the observance of the laws of natural morality, and an avenging Fate which pursued and punished their violation. This conception appears often in the works of the tragedians; for instance, in the "Œdipus Tyrannus" of Sophocles, where the main motive is the judgment which waits upon even unwitting violations of natural ties. Still, this prosperity is external, consisting either in wealth, or power, or exemption from calamity.

With the philosophers a moral element comes definitely into the word. The conception rises from outward propriety to inward correctness as the essence of happiness. But in all of them, from Socrates onward, virtue depends primarily upon knowledge; so that to be happy is, first of all, to know. It is thus apparent that the Greek philosophy had no conception of *sin* in the Bible sense. As virtue depended on knowledge, sin was the outcome of ignorance, and virtue and its consequent happiness were therefore the prerogative of the few and the learned.

The biblical use of the word lifted it into the region of the spiritual, as distinguished from the merely intellectual, and besides, intrusted to it alone the task of representing this higher conception. The pagan word for happiness (*εὐδαιμονία, under the protection of a good genius or daemon*) nowhere occurs in the New Testament nor in the Scriptures, having fallen into disrepute because the word *daemon*, which originally meant a deity, good or evil, had acquired among the Jews the bad sense which we attach to *demon*. Happiness, or better, *blessedness*, was therefore represented both in the Old and in the New Testament by this word *μακάριος*. In the Old Testament the idea involves more of outward prosperity than in the New Testament, yet it almost universally occurs in connections which emphasize, as its principal element, a sense of God's approval founded in righteousness which rests ultimately on love to God.

Thus the word passed up into the higher region of Christian thought, and was stamped with the gospel signet, and laden with all the rich significance of gospel blessedness. It now takes on a group of ideas strange to the best pagan morality, and contradictory of its fundamental positions. Shaking itself loose from all thoughts of outward good, it becomes the express symbol of a happiness identified with pure character. Behind it lies the clear cognition of sin as the fountain-head of all misery, and of holiness as the final and effectual cure for every woe. For knowledge as the basis of virtue, and therefore of happiness, it substitutes faith and love. For the aristocracy of the learned virtuous, it introduces the truth of the Fatherhood of God and the corollary of the family of believers. While the pagan word carries the isolation of the virtuous and the contraction of human sympathy, the Gospel pushes these out with an ideal of a world-wide sympathy and of a happiness realized in ministry. The vague outlines of an abstract good vanish from it, and give place to the pure heart's vision of God, and its personal communion with the Father in heaven. Where it told of the Stoic's self-sufficiency, it now tells of the Christian's poverty of spirit and meekness. Where it hinted at the Stoic's self-repression and strangling of emotion, it now throbs with a holy sensitiveness, and with a monition to rejoice with them that rejoice, and to weep with them that weep. From the pagan word the flavor of immortality is absent. No vision of abiding rest imparts patience and courage amid the bitterness and struggle of life; no menace of the destiny of evil imposes a check on human lusts. The Christian word *blessed* is full of the light of heaven. It sternly throws away from itself every hint of the Stoic's asserted right of suicide as a refuge from human ills, and emphasizes something which thrives on trial and persecution, which glories in tribulation, which not only endures but conquers the world, and expects its crown in heaven.

The poor (*οἱ πτωχοὶ*). Three words expressing *poverty* are found in the New Testament. Two of them, *πένης* and *πενιχρός*, are kindred terms, the latter being merely a poetic form of the other, and neither of these occurs more than once (Luke xxi. 2; 2 Cor. ix. 9). The word used in this verse is therefore the current word for *poor*, occurring thirty-four times, and covering every gradation of want; so that it is evident that the New Testament writers did not recognize any nice distinctions of meaning which called for the use of other terms. Luke, for instance (xxi. 2, 3), calls the widow who bestowed her two mites both *πενιχρὰν* and *πτωχὴ*. Nevertheless, there is a distinction, recognized by both classical and ecclesiastical writers. While *ὁ πένης* is one of narrow means, one who "earns a scanty pittance," *πτωχός* is allied to the verb *πτώσσειν*, *to crouch* or *cringe*, and therefore conveys the idea of *utter* destitution, which abjectly solicits and lives by alms. Hence it is applied to Lazarus (Luke xvi. 20, 22), and rendered *beggar*. Thus distinguished, it is very graphic and appropriate here, as denoting the *utter spiritual destitution*, the consciousness of which precedes the entrance into the kingdom of God, and which cannot be relieved by one's own efforts, but only by the free mercy of God. (See on 2 Cor. vi. 10; viii. 9.)

4. **They that mourn** (*πενθοῦντες*). Signifying grief *manifested;* too deep for concealment. Hence it is often joined with *κλαίειν*, *to weep audibly* (Mark xvi. 10; James iv. 9).

Shall be comforted. See on John xiv. 16.

5. **The meek** (*οἱ πραεῖς*). Another word which, though never used in a bad sense, Christianity has lifted to a higher plane, and made the symbol of a higher good. Its primary meaning is *mild, gentle*. It was applied to inanimate things, as light, wind, sound, sickness. It was used of a horse; *gentle*.

As a human attribute, Aristotle defines it as *the mean between stubborn anger and that negativeness of character which is incapable of even righteous indignation:* according to which it is tantamount to *equanimity*. Plato opposes it to fierceness or cruelty, and uses it of humanity to the condemned; but also of the conciliatory demeanor of a demagogue seeking popularity and power. Pindar applies it to a king, *mild* or *kind* to the citizens, and Herodotus uses it as opposed to anger.

These pre-Christian meanings of the word exhibit two general characteristics. 1. They express *outward conduct* merely. 2. They contemplate relations to *men only*. The Christian word, on the contrary, describes an *inward* quality, and that as related primarily to *God*. The *equanimity, mildness, kindness*, represented by the classical word, are founded in self-control or in natural disposition. The Christian *meekness* is based on *humility*, which is not a natural quality but an outgrowth of a renewed nature. To the pagan the word often implied *condescension*, to the Christian it implies *submission*. The Christian quality, in its manifestation, reveals all that was best in the heathen virtue—mildness, gentleness, equanimity—but these manifestations toward men are emphasized as outgrowths of a spiritual relation to God. The *mildness* or *kindness* of Plato or Pindar imply no sense of inferiority in those who exhibit them; sometimes the contrary. Plato's demagogue is kindly from self-interest and as a means to tyranny. Pindar's king is condescendingly kind. The meekness of the Christian springs from a sense of the inferiority of the creature to the Creator, and especially of the *sinful* creature to the *holy* God. While, therefore, the pagan quality is redolent of *self-assertion*, the Christian quality carries the flavor of *self-abasement*. As toward God, therefore, meekness accepts his dealings without murmur or resistance as absolutely good and wise. As toward man, it accepts opposition, insult, and provocation, as God's permitted ministers of a chastening demanded by the infirmity and corruption of sin; while, under this sense of his own sinfulness, the meek bears patiently "the contradiction of sinners against himself," forgiving and restoring the erring in a spirit of meekness, considering himself, lest he also be tempted (see Gal. vi. 1–5). The ideas of forgiveness and restoration nowhere attach to the classical word. They belong exclusively to Christian meekness, which thus shows itself allied to love. As ascribed by our Lord to himself, see on Matt. xi. 29. Wyc. renders "Blessed be *mild* men."

6. **Shall be filled** (χορτασθήσονται). A very strong and graphic word, originally applied to the feeding and fattening of animals in a stall. In Apoc. xix. 21, it is used of the filling of the birds with the flesh of God's enemies. Also of the multitudes fed with the loaves and fishes (Matt. xiv. 20; Mark viii. 8; Luke ix. 17). It is manifestly appropriate here as expressing the *complete satisfaction* of spiritual hunger and thirst. Hence Wycliffe's rendering, *fulfilled*, is strictly true to the original.

7. **The merciful.** See on Luke i. 50.

9. **The peacemakers** (οἱ εἰρηνοποιοί). Should be held to its literal meaning, peace-*makers*; not as Wyc., *peaceable men.* The *founders* and *promoters* of peace are meant; who not only *keep* the peace, but seek to bring men into harmony with each other. Tynd. renders, the *maintainers of peace.*

13. **Have lost his savour** (μωρανθῇ). The kindred noun (μωρός) means *dull, sluggish;* applied to the mind, *stupid* or *silly;* applied to the taste, *insipid, flat.* The verb here used of salt, *to become insipid,* also means *to play the fool.* Our Lord refers here to the familiar fact of salt losing its pungency and becoming useless. Dr. Thompson ("The Land and the Book") cites the following case: "A merchant of Sidon, having

farmed of the government the revenue from the importation of salt, brought over a great quantity from the marshes of Cyprus —enough, in fact, to supply the whole province for many years. This he had transferred to the mountains, to cheat the government out of some small percentage of duty. Sixty-five houses were rented and filled with salt. Such houses have merely earthen floors, and the salt next the ground was in a few years entirely spoiled. I saw large quantities of it literally thrown into the road to be trodden under foot of men and beasts. It was 'good for nothing.'"

15. **A bushel** (*τὸν μόδιον*). Rev., rightly, "*the* bushel;" since the definite article is designed to indicate a familiar object—*the* grain-measure which is found in every house.

A candlestick (*τὴν λυχνίαν*). Rev., *the stand.* Also a part of the furniture of every house, and commonly but one in the house: hence the article. The word, which occurs four times in the Gospels and eight times elsewhere, means, in every case, not a candlestick, but a lamp-stand. In Heb. ix. 2, the golden "candlestick" of the tabernacle is called **λυχνία**; but in the description of this article (Exod. xxv. 31, 39), we read, "Thou shalt make the seven *lamps* thereof;" and in Zech. iv. 2, where the imagery is drawn from the sanctuary, we have a "candlestick" with a bowl on the top of it, "and his seven *lamps* thereon, and seven pipes (for the oil) to the lamps which are upon the top thereof."

16. **So** shine (*οὕτως*). Often misconceived, as if the meaning were, "Let your light shine *in such a way that* men may see," etc. Standing at the beginning of the sentence, it points back to the illustration just used. "*So,*" even as that lamp just mentioned, let *your* light shine. Wycliffe has apparently caught this correct sense: *So shine your light before men.*

17. **To destroy** (*καταλῦσαι*). Lit., *to loosen down, dissolve;* Wyc., *undo.*

18. **Jot, tittle** (ἰῶτα, κεραία). *Jot* is for *jod*, the smallest letter in the Hebrew alphabet. *Tittle* is the little bend or point which serves to distinguish certain Hebrew letters of similar appearance. Jewish tradition mentions the letter *jod* as being irremovable; adding that, if all men in the world were gathered to abolish the least letter in the law, they would not succeed. The guilt of changing those little hooks which distinguish between certain Hebrew letters is declared to be so great that, if such a thing were done, the world would be destroyed.

22. **Hell-fire** (τὴν γέενναν τοῦ πυρός). Rev., more accurately, *the hell of fire*. The word *Gehenna*, rendered *hell*, occurs outside of the Gospels only at James iii. 6. It is the Greek representative of the Hebrew *Ge-Hinnom*, or Valley of Hinnom, a deep, narrow glen to the south of Jerusalem, where, after the introduction of the worship of the fire-gods by Ahaz, the idolatrous Jews sacrificed their children to Molech. Josiah formally desecrated it, "that no man might make his son or his daughter pass through the fire to Molech" (2 Kings xxiii. 10). After this it became the common refuse-place of the city, into which the bodies of criminals, carcasses of animals, and all sorts of filth were cast. From its depth and narrowness, and its fire and ascending smoke, it became the symbol of the place of the future punishment of the wicked. So Milton:

> "The pleasant valley of Hinnom, Tophet thence
> And black Gehenna called, the type of hell."

As fire was the characteristic of the place, it was called *the Gehenna of fire*. It should be carefully distinguished from Hades (ᾅδης), which is never used for the place of punishment, but for the *place of departed spirits*, without reference to their moral condition. This distinction, ignored by the A. V., is made in the Rev.

25. **Agree with** (ἴσθι εὐνοῶν). Lit., *be well-minded towards;* inclined to satisfy by paying or compromising. Wyc., *Be thou consenting to.*

Officer (ὑπηρέτῃ). Denoting a subordinate official, as a herald or an orderly, and in this sense applied to Mark as the "minister" or attendant of Paul and Barnabas (Acts xiii. 5). It furnishes an interesting instance of the expansion of a word from a limited and special meaning into a more general one; and also of the influence of the Gospel in lifting words into higher and purer associations. Formed with the verb ἐρέσσω, to *row*, it originally signified *a rower*, as distinguished from a soldier, in a war-galley. This word for a *galley-slave* comes at last, in the hands of Luke and Paul, to stand for the noblest of all offices, that of *a minister of the Lord Jesus* (Luke i. 2; Acts xxvi. 16; 1 Cor. iv. 1).

29. **Offend** (σκανδαλίζει). The word *offend* carries to the English reader the sense of *giving offence, provoking*. Hence the Rev., by restoring the picture in the word, restores its true meaning, *causeth to stumble*. The kindred noun is **σκάνδαλον**, a later form of **σκανδάληθρον**, the stick in a trap on which the bait is placed, and which springs up and shuts the trap at the touch of an animal. Hence, generally, a *snare*, a *stumbling-block*. Christ's meaning here is: "If your eye or your hand serve as an obstacle or trap to ensnare or make you fall in your moral walk." How the *eye* might do this may be seen in the previous verse. Bengel observes: "He who, when his eye proves a stumbling-block, takes care not to see, does in reality blind himself." The words *scandal* and *slander* are both derived from *σκάνδαλον*; and Wyc. renders, "If thy right eye *slander* thee." Compare Æschylus, "Choephori," 301, 372.

40. **Coat, cloke** (χιτῶνα, ἱμάτιον). The former, the shirt-like under-garment or *tunic*; the latter, the *mantle*, or ampler over-garment, which served as a covering for the night, and therefore was forbidden by the Levitical law to be retained in pledge over night (Exod. xxii. 26, 27). To yield up this without resistance therefore implies a higher degree of concession.

41. **Shall compel thee to go** (ἀγγαρεύσει). This word throws the whole injunction into a picture which is entirely lost

to the English reader. A man is travelling, and about to pass a post-station, where horses and messengers are kept in order to forward royal missives as quickly as possible. An official rushes out, seizes him, and forces him to go back and carry a letter to the next station, perhaps to the great detriment of his business. The word is of Persian origin, and denotes the *impressment* into service, which officials were empowered to make of any available persons or beasts on the great lines of road where the royal mails were carried by relays of riders.

42. **Borrow** (*δανίσασθαι*). Properly, to borrow at interest.

43. **Neighbor** (*τὸν πλησίον*). Another word to which the Gospel has imparted a broader and deeper sense. Literally it means the one *near* (so the Eng., *neighbor* = *nigh-bor*), indicating a mere *outward* nearness, *proximity*. Thus a neighbor might be an enemy. Socrates (Plato, "Republic," ii., 373) shows how two adjoining states might come to want each a piece of its neighbor's (*τῶν πλησίον*) land, so that there would arise war between them; and again (Plato, "Theaetetus," 174) he says that a philosopher is wholly unacquainted with his next-door neighbor, and does not know whether he is a man or an animal. The Old Testament expands the meaning to cover *national* or *tribal* fellowship, and that is the sense in our Lord's quotation here. The Christian sense is expounded by Jesus in the parable of the Good Samaritan (Luke x. 29 sqq.), as including the whole brotherhood of man, and as founded in love for man, as man, everywhere.

CHAPTER VI.

1. **Of** your Father (*παρὰ*). The A. V. implies the *source* of the reward; but the preposition means *with*, *by the side of*; so that the true sense is, *reserved for you and awaiting you by the side of your Father*. Rev., rightly, *with*.

2. **Sound a trumpet** (*σαλπίσῃς*). There seems to be no trace of any such custom on the part of almsgivers, so that the

expression must be taken as a figurative one for making a display. It is just possible that the figure may have been suggested by the "trumpets" of the temple treasury—thirteen trumpet-shaped chests to receive the contributions of worshippers. (See on Luke xxi. 2.)

Have their reward (ἀπέχουσιν). The preposition ἀπὸ indicates receipt *in full*. Rev. renders *they have received*, so that there is nothing more to receive. So Wyc., *They have received their meed.*

6. **Closet** (ταμιεῖον). See on Luke xii. 3.

7. **Use vain repetitions** (βατταλογήσητε). A word formed in imitation of the sound, *battalogein:* properly, to *stammer;* then to *babble* or *prate*, to repeat the same formula many times, as the worshippers of Baal and of Diana of Ephesus (1 Kings xviii. 26; Acts xix. 34) and the Romanists with their paternosters and aves.

12. **Debts** (ὀφειλήματα). So, rightly, A. V., and Rev. (compare Luke xi. 4). Sin is pictured as a *debt*, and the sinner as a *debtor* (compare Matt. xviii. 28, 30). Accordingly the word represents sin both as a *wrong* and as *requiring satisfaction.* In contrast with the prayer, "Forgive us our debts," Tholuck ("Sermon on the Mount") quotes the prayer of Apollonius of Tyana, "O ye gods, give me the things which are owing to me."

Forgive (ἀφήκαμεν). Lit., to *send away*, or *dismiss.* The Rev. rightly gives the force of the past tense, *we have forgiven;* since Christ assumes that he who prays for the remission of his own debts has already forgiven those indebted to him.*

13. **Temptation** (πειρασμόν). It is a mistake to define this word as only *solicitation to evil.* It means *trial* of any kind,

* The tense is the aorist, denoting completed action at an indefinite past time, and so, strictly, *forgave;* but where any effect of the action expressed by the aorist remains, we are justified in rendering it by a perfect; and so Rev.

without reference to its moral quality. Thus, Gen. xxii. 1 (Sept.), "God did *tempt* Abraham;" "This he said to *prove* him" (John vi. 6); Paul and Timothy *assayed* to go to Bithynia (Acts xvi. 7); "*Examine* yourselves" (2 Cor. xiii. 5). Here, generally of all situations and circumstances which furnish an occasion for sin. We cannot pray God not to tempt us to sin, "for God cannot be tempted with evil, neither tempteth he any man" (James i. 13).

14. **Trespasses** (παραπτώματα). The Lord here uses another word for *sins*, and still another (ἁμαρτίας) appears in Luke's version of the prayer, though he also says, "every one that is *indebted* to us." There is no difficulty in supposing that Christ, contemplating sins in general, should represent them by different terms expressive of different aspects of wrong-doing (see on Matt. i. 21). This word is derived from παραπίπτω, to *fall* or *throw one's self beside.* Thus it has a sense somewhat akin to ἁμαρτία, of *going beside a mark, missing.* In classical Greek the verb is often used of *intentional* falling, as of *throwing one's self upon* an enemy; and this is the prevailing sense in biblical Greek, indicating *reckless* and *wilful* sin (see 1 Chron. v. 25; x. 13; 2 Chron. xxvi. 18; xxix. 6, 19; Ezek. xiv. 13; xviii. 26). It does not, therefore, imply palliation or excuse. It is a conscious violation of right, involving guilt, and occurs therefore, in connection with the mention of forgiveness (Rom. iv. 25; v. 16; Col. ii. 13; Eph. ii. 1, 5). Unlike παράβασις (*transgression*), which contemplates merely the objective violation of law, it carries the thought of sin as affecting the sinner, and hence is found associated with expressions which indicate the consequences and the remedy of sin (Rom. iv. 25; v. 15, 17; Eph. ii. 1).

16. **Ye fast** (νηστεύητε). Observe the force of the present tense as indicating action *in progress: Whenever ye may be fasting.*

Of a sad countenance (σκυθρωποί). An uncommon word in the New Testament, occurring only here and at Luke xxiv. 17.

Trench ("Studies in the Gospels") explains it by the older sense of the English *dreary*, as expressing the downcast look of settled grief, pain, or displeasure. In classical Greek it also signifies *sullenness* and *affected gravity*. Luther renders, *Look not sour*.

Disfigure (ἀφανίζουσιν). The idea is rather *conceal* than *disfigure*. There is a play upon this word and φανῶσιν (*they may appear*) which is untranslatable into English: they *conceal* or *mask* their true visage that they may *appear* unto men. The allusion is to the outward signs of humiliation which often accompanied fasting, such as being unwashed and unshaven and unanointed. "Avoid," says Christ, "the squalor of the unwashed face and of the unkempt hair and beard, and the rather anoint thy head and wash thy face, so as to *appear* (φανῇς) not unto men, but unto God as fasting." Wycliffe's rendering is peculiar: *They put their faces out of kindly terms.*

19. **Lay not up treasures** (μὴ θησαυρίζετε). Lit., *treasure not treasures*. So Wyc., *Do not treasure to you treasures*. The beautiful legend of St. Thomas and Gondoforus is told by Mrs. Jameson ("Sacred and Legendary Art"): "When St. Thomas was at Caesarea, our Lord appeared to him and said, 'The king of the Indies, Gondoforus, hath sent his provost, Abanes, to seek for workmen well versed in the science of architecture, who shall build for him a palace finer than that of the Emperor of Rome. Behold, now I will send thee to him.' And Thomas went, and Gondoforus commanded him to build for him a magnificent palace, and gave him much gold and silver for the purpose. The king went into a distant country and was absent for two years; and St. Thomas, meanwhile instead of building a palace, distributed all the treasures among the poor and sick; and when the king returned he was full of wrath, and he commanded that St. Thomas should be seized and cast into prison, and he meditated for him a horrible death. Meantime the brother of the king died, and the king resolved to erect for him a most magnificent tomb; but the dead man, after that he had been dead four days, suddenly arose and sat upright, and

said to the king, 'The man whom thou wouldst torture is a servant of God; behold, I have been in Paradise, and the angels showed to me a wondrous palace of gold and silver and precious stones; and they said, 'This is the palace that Thomas, the architect, hath built for thy brother, King Gondoforus.' And when the king heard these words, he ran to the prison, and delivered the apostle; and Thomas said to him, 'Knowest thou not that those who would possess heavenly things have little care for the things of this earth? There are in heaven rich palaces without number, which were prepared from the beginning of the world for those who would purchase the possession through faith and charity. Thy riches, O king, may prepare the way for thee to such a palace, but they cannot follow thee thither.'"

Rust (βρῶσις). That which *eats;* from the verb βιβρώσκω, *to eat.* Compare *corrode*, from the Latin *rodo*, *to gnaw.*

Doth corrupt (ἀφανίζει). Rev., *consume.* The same word which is used above of the hypocrites *concealing* their faces. The rust *consumes*, and therefore *causes to disappear.* So Wyc., *destroyeth.*

Break through (διορύσσουσιν). Lit., *dig through*, as a thief might easily penetrate the wall of a common oriental house of mud or clay. The Greek name for a burglar is τοιχωρύχος, *a wall-digger.* Compare Job xxiv. 16, "In the dark they dig through houses." Also Ezek. xii. 5. Wyc., *Thieves delve out.*

22. **Single** (ἁπλοῦς). The picture underlying this adjective is that of a piece of cloth or other material, neatly folded *once*, and without a variety of complicated folds. Hence the idea of *simplicity* or *singleness* (compare *simplicity* from the Latin *simplex; semel, once; plicare, to fold*). So, in a moral sense, *artless, plain, pure.* Here *sound*, as opposed to *evil* or *diseased.* Possibly with reference to the double-mindedness and indecision condemned in ver. 24.

Full of light (φωτεινὸν). Bengel says, "As if it were all eye."

23. **In thee—darkness.** Seneca, in one of his letters, tells of an idiot slave in his house, who had suddenly become blind. "Now, incredible as the story seems, it is really true that she is unconscious of her blindness, and consequently begs her attendant to go elsewhere because the house is dark. But you may be sure that this, at which we laugh in her, happens to us all; no one understands that he is avaricious or covetous. The blind seek for a guide; *we* wander about without a guide."

"Seeing falsely is worse than blindness. A man who is too dim-sighted to discern the road from the ditch, may feel which is which; but if the ditch appears manifestly to him to be the road, and the road to be the ditch, what shall become of him? False seeing is unseeing, on the negative side of blindness" (Ruskin, "Modern Painters").

24. **The other** (ἕτερον). Implying distinction in *quality* rather than *numerical* distinction (ἄλλος). For example, "whoever smiteth thee on thy right cheek, turn to him *the other* (τὴν ἄλλην); *i.e.*, the other one of the two (Matt. v. 39). At Pentecost, the disciples began to speak with *other* (ἑτέραις) tongues; *i.e.*, *different* from their native tongues. Here the word gives the idea of two masters of distinct or opposite character and interests, like God and Mammon.

Hold to (ἀνθέξεται). The preposition ἀντί, *against*, indicates holding to the one master as *against* the other. He who is for God must be against Mammon.

25. **Take no thought** (μὴ μεριμνᾶτε). The cognate noun is μέριμνα, *care*, which was formerly derived from μερίς, *a part*; μερίζω, *to divide*; and was explained accordingly as a *dividing* care, distracting the heart from the true object of life. This has been abandoned, however, and the word is placed in a group which carries the common notion of *earnest thoughtfulness*. It may include the ideas of *worry* and *anxiety*, and may empha-

size these, but not necessarily. See, for example, "*careth* for the things of the Lord" (1 Cor. vii. 32). "That the members should have the same *care* one for another" (1 Cor. xii. 25). "Who will *care* for your state?" (Phil. ii. 20). In all these the sense of *worry* would be entirely out of place. In other cases that idea is prominent, as, "the *care* of this world," which chokes the good seed (Matt. xiii. 22; compare Luke viii. 14). Of Martha; "Thou art *careful*" (Luke x. 41). *Take thought*, in this passage, was a truthful rendering when the A. V. was made, since *thought* was then used as equivalent to *anxiety* or solicitude. So Shakspeare ("Hamlet"):

> "The native hue of resolution
> Is sicklied o'er with the pale cast of *thought*."

And Bacon (Henry VII.): "Hawis, an alderman of London, was put in trouble, and died with *thought* and anguish." Somers' "Tracts" (in Queen Elizabeth's reign): "Queen Catherine Parr died rather of *thought*."

The word has entirely lost this meaning. Bishop Lightfoot ("On a Fresh Revision of the New Testament") says: "I have heard of a political economist alleging this passage as an objection to the moral teaching of the sermon on the mount, on the ground that it encouraged, nay, commanded, a reckless neglect of the future." It is uneasiness and worry about the future which our Lord condemns here, and therefore Rev. rightly translates *be not anxious*. This phase of the word is forcibly brought out in 1 Peter, v. 7, where the A. V. ignores the distinction between the two kinds of care. "Casting all your *care* (μέριμναν, Rev., *anxiety*) upon Him, for He *careth* (αὐτῷ μέλει) for you," with a fatherly, tender, and provident care."

CHAPTER VII.

3. **Beholdest** (βλέπεις). Staring at *from without*, as one who does not see clearly.

Considerest (κατανοεῖς). A stronger word, *apprehendest from within*, what is already there.

Mote (κάρφος). A. V. and Rev. The word *mote*, however, suggests *dust*; whereas the figure is that of a minute *chip* or *splinter*, of the same material with the beam. Wyc. renders *festu*, with the explanation, *a little mote*. In explaining the passage it is well to remember that the obstruction to sight is of the same material in both cases. The man with a great *beam* in his eye, who therefore can see nothing accurately, proposes to remove the little splinter from his brother's eye, a delicate operation, requiring clear sight. The figure of a splinter to represent something painful or annoying is a common oriental one. Tholuck ("Sermon on the Mount") quotes from the Arabic several passages in point, and one which is literally our Lord's saying: "How seest thou the splinter in thy brother's eye, and seest not the cross-beam in thine eye?"

Beam (δοκὸν). A log, joist, rafter; indicating a *great* fault.

5. **See clearly** (διαβλέψεις). The preposition διά, *through*, giving the sense of *thoroughness*. Compare the simple verb βλέπεις (*beholdest*), ver. 3. With the beam in thine eye thou *starest* at thy brother's little failing. Pull out the beam; then thou shalt *see clearly*, not only the fault itself, but how to help thy brother get rid of it.

To cast out (ἐκβαλεῖν). The Lord's words assume that the object of scrutiny is not only nor mainly *detection*, but *correction*. Hence thou shalt see clearly, not the mote, but to *cast out* the mote.

6. **That which is holy** (τὸ ἅγιον). *The holy thing*, as of something commonly recognized as sacred. The reference is to the meat offered in sacrifice. The picture is that of a priest throwing a piece of flesh from the altar of burnt-offering to one of the numerous dogs which infest the streets of Eastern cities.

Pearls before swine (μαργαρίτας ἔμπροσθεν τῶν χοίρων). Another picture of a rich man wantonly throwing handfuls of small pearls to swine. Swine in Palestine were at best but half-tamed, the hog being an unclean animal. The wild boar haunts the Jordan valley to this day. Small pearls, called by jewellers *seed-pearls*, would resemble the pease or maize on which the swine feed. They would rush upon them when scattered, and, discovering the cheat, would trample upon them and turn their tusks upon the man who scattered them.

Turn (*στραφέντες*). The Rev. properly omits *again*. The word graphically pictures the quick, sharp turn of the boar.

Rend (*ῥήξωσιν*). Lit., *break;* and well chosen to express the peculiar character of the wound made by the boar's tusk, which is not a *cut*, but a long *tear* or *rip*.

9. **Bread, a stone** (*ἄρτον, λίθον*). Rev. for *bread* reads *loaf*, which is better. On the resemblance of certain stones to cakes of bread, see on Matt. iv. 3.

13. **Strait gate** (*στενῆς πύλης*). Rev., *narrow*. A remarkable parallel to this passage occurs in the "Pinax" or "Tablet" of Cebes, a writer contemporary with Socrates. In this, human life, with its dangers and temptations, is symbolically represented as on a tablet. The passage is as follows: "Seest thou not, then, a little door, and a way before the door, which is not much crowded, but very few travel it? This is the way which leadeth into true culture."

Leadeth (*ἀπάγουσα*). Lit., leadeth *away*, from death, or, perhaps, from the broad road. Note that the gate is not at the *end*, but at the *beginning* of the road.

16. **Ye shall know** (*ἐπιγνώσεσθε*). The compound verb indicates *full* knowledge. Character is *satisfactorily* tested by its fruits.

22. Have we **not** (*οὐ*). That form of the negative is used which expects an affirmative answer. It therefore pictures both the self-conceit and the self-deception of these persons. "Surely we have prophesied," etc.

23. **Profess** (*ὁμολογήσω*). The word which is used elsewhere of open confession of Christ before men (Matt. x. 32; Rom. x. 9); of John's public declaration that he was not the Christ (John i. 20); of Herod's promise to Salome in the presence of his guests (Matt. xiv. 7). Here, therefore, of Christ's *open, public* declaration as Judge of the world. "There is great authority in this saying," remarks Bengel.

24 sqq. **I will liken him,** etc. The picture is not of two men deliberately selecting foundations, but it contrasts one who carefully chooses and prepares his foundation with one who builds at hap-hazard. This is more strongly brought out by Luke (vi. 48): "Who digged and went deep, and laid a foundation upon the rock" (Rev.). Kitto ("Pictorial Bible") says: "At this very day the mode of building in Christ's own town of Nazareth suggests the source of this image. Dr. Robinson was entertained in the house of a Greek Arab. The house had just been built, and was not yet finished. In order to lay the foundations he had dug down to the solid rock, as is usual throughout the country here, to the depth of thirty feet, and then built up arches." The abrupt style of ver. 25 pictures the sudden coming of the storm which sweeps away the house on the sand: "Descended the rain, and came the floods, and blew the winds."

27. **Great was the fall of it.** The conclusion of the Sermon on the Mount. "Thus," remarks Bengel, "it is not necessary for every sermon to end with consolation."

28. **Were astonished** (*ἐξεπλήσσοντο*). From *ἐκ*, *out of*, and *πλήσσω*, *to strike*. Often to drive one out of his senses by a sudden shock, and therefore here of *amazement*. They were *astounded*. We have a similar expression, though not so strong: "I was *struck* with this or that remarkable thing."

29. **He taught** (*ἦν διδάσκων*). *He was teaching*. This union of the verb and participle emphasizes the idea of *duration* or *habit* more than the simple tense.

CHAPTER VIII.

6. **Tormented** (*βασανιζόμενος*). See on *torments*, Matt. iv. 24.

7. **Heal** (*θεραπεύσω*). So A. V. and Rev. The word, however, originally means *to attend*, and to *treat medically*. The centurion uses another and stronger word, *shall be healed* (*ἰαθήσεται*). Luke, who as a physician is precise in the use of medical terms, uses both words in one verse (ix. 11). Jesus *healed* (*ἰᾶτο*) all who had need of *treatment* (*θεραπείας*). Still, Luke himself does not always observe the distinction. See on Luke v. 15.

9. **Also** (*καὶ*). Omitted in A. V., but very important. "I *also* am a man under authority," as well as thou. (Tynd., *I also myself*). The centurion compares the Lord's position with his own. Christ had authority over disease. The centurion *also* was in authority over soldiers. As the centurion had only to say to a soldier "Go!" and he went, so Christ had only to say to disease "Go!" and it would obey him.

11. **Shall sit down** (*ἀνακλιθήσονται*). Lit., *recline*. The picture is that of a banquet. Jews as well as Romans reclined at table on couches.

12. **The outer** (*τὸ ἐξώτερον*). The Greek order of words is very forcible. "They shall be cast forth into the darkness, *the outer* (darkness). The picture is of an illuminated banqueting chamber, *outside* of which is the thick darkness of night.

13. **Was healed** (*ἰάθη*). Note that the stronger word of the centurion (ver. 8) is used here. Where Christ *tends*, he *heals*.

14. **Sick of a fever** (*πυρέσσουσαν*). Derived from *πῦρ*, fire. Our word *fever* comes through the German *feuer*.

17. **Bare** (ἐβάστασεν). This translation is correct. The word does not mean "he *took away*," but "he *bore*," as a burden laid upon him. This passage is the corner-stone of the faith-cure theory, which claims that the atonement of Christ includes provision for *bodily* no less than for *spiritual* healing, and therefore insists on translating "took away." Matthew may be presumed to have understood the sense of the passage he was citing from Isaiah, and he could have used no word more inadequate to express his meaning, if that meaning had been that Christ *took away* infirmities.

20. **Holes** (φωλεοὺς). Wyc. has *ditches*, with *burrows* in explanation.

Nests (κατασκηνώσεις). Only here and in the parallel, Luke ix. 58. *Nests* is too limited. The word, derived from σκηνή, *a tent*, has the more general meaning of *shelter* or *habitation*. In classical Greek it is used of an *encampment*. The nest is not to the bird what the hole is to the fox, a *permanent dwelling-place*, since the bird frequents the nest only during incubation. The Rev. retains *nests*, but puts *lodging-places* in the margin.

24. **Tempest** (σεισμὸς). Lit., *shaking*. Used of an earthquake. The narrative indicates a *sudden* storm. Dr. Thomson ("Land and Book") says: "Such winds are not only violent, but they come down suddenly, and often when the sky is perfectly clear. . . . To understand the causes of these sudden and violent tempests we must remember that the lake lies low—six hundred and eighty feet below the sea; that the mountainous plateau of the Jaulân rises to a considerable height, spreading backward to the wilds of the Haurân, and upward to snowy Hermon; that the water-courses have worn or washed out profound ravines and wild gorges, converging to the head of this lake; and that these act like great funnels to draw down the cold winds from the mountains."

28. **The tombs** (μνημείων). Chambers excavated in the mountain, which would afford a shelter to the demoniac.

Chandler ("Travels in Asia Minor") describes tombs with two square rooms, the lower containing the ashes, while in the upper, the friends performed funeral rites, and poured libations through a hole in the floor. Dr. Thomson ("Land and Book") thus describes the rock-cut tombs in the region between Tyre and Sidon: "They are nearly all of the same form, having a small chamber in front, and a door leading from that into the tomb, which is about six feet square, with niches on three sides for the dead." A propensity to take up the abode in the tombs is mentioned by ancient physicians as a characteristic of madmen. The Levitical uncleanness of the tombs would insure the wretches the solitude which they sought. Trench ("Notes on the Miracles") cites the following incident from Warburton ("The Crescent and the Cross"): "On descending from these heights I found myself in a cemetery whose sculptured turbans showed me that the neighboring village was Moslem. The silence of night was now broken by fierce yells and howlings, which I discovered proceeded from a naked maniac who was fighting with some wild dogs for a bone. The moment he perceived me he left his canine comrades, and bounding along with rapid strides, seized my horse's bridle, and almost forced him backward over the cliff."

Fierce (*χαλεποὶ*). Originally, *difficult, hard.* Hence hard to manage; intractable.

32. **A steep place** (*τοῦ κρημνοῦ*). Much better *the steep* (Rev.). Not an overhanging precipice, but a steep, almost perpendicular declivity, between the base of which and the water was a narrow margin of ground, in which there was not room for the swine to recover from their headlong rush. Dr. Thomson ("Land and Book") says: "Farther south the plain becomes so broad that the herd might have recovered and recoiled from the lake." The article localizes the steep as in the vicinity of the pasture.

CHAPTER IX.

9. **Receipt of custom** (τελώνιον). Rev., *place of toll*. Wyc., *tolbooth*, toll-booth, or toll-cabin, which is an excellent word, though obsolete. Sitting *at*, is, literally, sitting *on:* the elevated platform or bench which was the principal feature of the toll-office, as in modern custom-bazaars, being put for the whole establishment. This customs-office was at Capernaum, the landing-place for the many ships which traversed the lake or coasted from town to town; and this not only for those who had business in Capernaum, but for those who would there strike the great road of eastern commerce from Damascus to the harbors of the West. Cicero, in his oration on the Consular Provinces, accuses Gabinius, the pro-consul of Syria, of relieving the Syrians and Jews of some of their legitimate taxes, and of ordering the small buildings to be taken down, which the publicans had erected at the approaches to bridges, or at the termination of roads, or in the harbors, for the convenience of their slaves and collectors.

16. **New** (ἀγνάφου). From ἀ, *not*, and γνάπτω, *to card* or *comb wool;* hence to *dress* or *full cloth*. Therefore Rev. renders more correctly *undressed* cloth, which would shrink when wet, and tear loose from the old piece. Wyc. renders *rude*. Jesus thus pictures the combination of the old forms of piety peculiar to John and his disciples with the new religious life emanating from himself, as the patching of an old garment with a piece of unfulled cloth, which would stretch and tear loose from the old fabric and make a worse rent than before.

17. **Bottles** (ἀσκούς). Rev., rightly, *wine-skins*, though our word *bottle* originally carried the true meaning, being a bottle of *leather*. In Spanish, *bota* means a *leather bottle*, a *boot*, and a *butt*. In Spain wine is still brought to market in pig-skins. In the East, goat-skins are commonly used, with the rough side inward. When old, they break under the fermentation of the wine.

18. **Is even now dead** (*ἄρτι ἐτελεύτησεν*). The literal force of the aorist tense is more graphic. *Just now died.*

20. **Hem** (*κρασπέδου*). Rev., *border.* The fringe worn on the border of the outer garment, according to the command in Num. xv. 38. Dr. Edersheim ("Life and Times of Jesus") says that, according to tradition, each of the white fringes was to consist of eight threads, one of them wound round the others; first seven times, with a double knot; then eight times with a double knot; then eleven times with a double knot; and, lastly, thirteen times. The Hebrew characters representing these numbers formed the words *Jehovah One.*

23. **Minstrels** (*αὐλητὰς*). More correctly, as Rev., *flute-players*, hired or volunteering as mourners.

Making a noise (*θορυβούμενον*). Rev., *tumult.* Representing the loud screaming and wailing by the women. It is the word used in Acts xvii. 5: "Set the city in *an uproar.*"

32. **Dumb** (*κωφὸν*). The word is also used of *deafness* (Matt. xi. 5; Mark vii. 32; Luke vii. 22). It means *dull* or *blunted.* Thus Homer applies it to the earth; the *dull, senseless* earth ("Iliad," xxiv., 25). Also to a *blunted* dart ("Iliad," xi., 390). The classical writers use it of speech, hearing, sight, and mental perception. In the New Testament, only of hearing and speech, the meaning in each case being determined by the context.

36. **Fainted** (*ἦσαν ἐσκυλμένοι*). Rev., better, *were distressed.* Note the verb with the participle, denoting their *habitual* condition. The word orginally means to *flay, rend,* or *mangle.* Æschylus uses it of the tearing of dead bodies by fish ("Persae," 577). As appropriate to the figure of sheep, it might be rendered here *fleeced.* Wyc., *they were travailed.*

Scattered (*ἐῤῥιμμένοι*). So A. V. and Rev. The word is the perfect participle passive of *ῥίπτω, to throw* or *cast,* and means *thrown down, prostrated.* So Wyc., *lying.* It is not the *dispersion* one from another, but their *prostration* in themselves that is meant. They have cast themselves down for very weariness.

38. **Send forth** (ἐκβάλῃ). So A. V. and Rev. But the word is stronger: *thrust out, force them out,* as from urgent necessity.

CHAPTER X.

1. **The disciples** (τοὺς μαθητὰς). *The* or *his*, referring to them as already chosen, though he nowhere relates their choosing. See Mark iii. 14; Luke vi. 13.

2. **Apostles** (ἀποστόλων). Compare *disciples*, ver. i. *Apostles* is the official term, used here for the first time. They were merely *learners* (*disciples*, μαθηταὶ) until Christ gave them authority. From ἀποστέλλω, *to send away.* An apostle is *one sent forth.* Compare John xiii. 16 and Rev., *one that is sent.* Cremer ("Biblico-Theological Lexicon") suggests that it was the rare occurrence of the word in profane Greek that made it all the more appropriate as the distinctive appellation of the twelve. Compare Luke vi. 13; Acts i. 2. Also, John xvii. 18, *I have sent.* The word is once used of Christ (Heb. iii. 1), and in a very general sense to denote any one sent (2 Cor. viii. 23; Philip. ii. 25).

4. **The Canaanite** (ὁ Καναναῖος). Rev., *Cananaean.* The word has nothing to do with Canaan. In Luke vi. 15; Acts i. 13, the same apostle is called *Zelotes.* Both terms indicate his connection with the Galilaean Zealot party, a sect which stood for the recovery of Jewish freedom and the maintenance of distinctive Jewish institutions. From the Hebrew *kanná, zealous;* compare the Chaldee *kanán*, by which this sect was denoted.

5. **Judas Iscariot** (ὁ Ἰσκαριώτης). The article distinguishes him from others of the name of Judas (compare John xiv. 22).

Iscariot is usually explained as a compound, meaning *the man of Kerioth*, with reference to his native town, which is given in Joshua (xv. 25) as one of the uttermost cities of Judah toward the coast of Edom southward.

In the four catalogues of the apostles (here; Mark iii. 16; Luke vi. 14; Acts i. 13) Simon Peter always stands first. Here expressly; "*first* Simon." Notice that Matthew names them *in pairs*, and compare Mark vi. 7, "sent them forth *two and two*." The arrangement of the different lists varies; but throughout, Peter is the leader of the first four, Philip of the second, and James, son of Alphaeus, of the third.

6. **The lost sheep** (*τὰ πρόβατα τὰ ἀπολωλότα*). The Greek order throws the emphasis on *lost;* the sheep, *the lost ones.* Bengel observes that Jesus says *lost* oftener than *led astray.* Compare xviii. 12, 14.

9. **Brass** (*χαλκὸν*). Properly *copper.* A decending climax. Copper would be as unnecessary as gold.

10. **Staves** (*ῥάβδους*). But the proper reading is *staff*, (*ῥάβδον*.)

The workman is worthy, etc. Ver. 11, **There abide,** etc. "The Teaching of the Twelve Apostles," a tract discovered in 1873 in the library of the monastery of the Most Holy Sepulchre at Constantinople, by Bryennios, Metropolitan of Nicomedia, is assigned to the date of 120 A.D., and by some scholars is placed as early as 100 A.D. It is addressed to Gentile Christians, and is designed to give them practical instruction in the Christian life, according to the teachings of the twelve apostles and of the Lord himself. In the eleventh chapter we read as follows: "And every apostle who cometh to you, let him be received as the Lord; but he shall not remain except for one day; if, however, there be need, then the next day; but if he remain three days, he is a false prophet. But when the apostle departeth, let him take nothing except bread enough till he lodge again, but if he ask money, he is a false prophet." And again (ch. xiii.): "Likewise a true teacher, he also is worthy like the workman, of his support. Every first-fruit, then, of the products of wine-press and threshing-floor, of oxen and sheep, thou shalt take and give to the prophets, for they are your high-priests. . . . If thou makest a baking of bread, take the first of it and give according to the commandment. In like manner, when thou openest a jar of wine or oil, take the first of it and give to the prophets; and of money and clothing, and every possession, take the first, as may seem right to thee, and give according to the commandment."

12. **When ye come into** (*εἰσερχόμενοι*). The Greek indicates more distinctly the simultaneousness of the entrance and the salutation: *as ye are entering*. Rev., *as ye enter*. So of the departure, *as ye are going forth* (*ἐξερχόμενοι*, ver. 14).

14. **Shake off** (*ἐκτινάξατε*). "The very dust of a heathen country was unclean, and it defiled by contact. It was regarded like a grave, or like the putrescence of death. If a spot of heathen dust had touched an offering, it must at once be burnt. More than that, if by mischance any heathen dust had been brought into Palestine, it did not and could not mingle with that of 'the land,' but remained to the end what it had been—unclean, defiled and defiling everything to which it adhered." The apostles, therefore, were not only to leave the house or city which should refuse to receive them, "but it was to be considered and treated as if it were heathen, just as in the similar case mentioned in Matt. xviii. 17. All contact with such must be avoided, all trace of it shaken off" (Edersheim, "Jewish Social Life in the Days of Christ"). The symbolic act indicated that the apostles and their Lord regarded them not only as unclean, but as entirely responsible for their uncleanness. See Acts xviii. 6.

16. **I send you forth** (*ἐγὼ ἀποστέλλω*). Cognate to the word *ἀπόστολος* (*apostle*). The *I* is emphatic: "It is *I* that send you forth."

Wise (φρόνιμοι). So A. V. and Rev. Denoting prudence with regard to their own safety. Wyc., *wary*.

Harmless (ἀκέραιοι). Lit., *unmixed, unadulterated.* Used of wine without water, and of metal without alloy. Hence *guileless.* So Luther, *without falsity.* Compare Rom. xvi. 19; Philip. ii. 15. They were to imitate the serpent's *wariness*, but not his *wiliness.* "The presence of the wolves demands that ye be *wary;* the fact that ye are my apostles (compare "*I* send you") demands that ye be *guileless*" (Dr. Morison on Matthew).

17. **Of men** (τῶν ἀνθρώπων). Lit., "*the* men," already alluded to under the term *wolves.*

19. **Take no thought** (μὴ μεριμνήσητε). Rev., *Be not anxious.* See on vi. 25.

In that hour (ἐν ἐκείνῃ τῇ ὥρᾳ). Very precise. "In *that selfsame* hour." Bengel remarks: "Even though not before. Many feel most strongly their spiritual power when the hour comes to impart it to others."

25. **Beelzebub** (βεελζεβοὺλ, *Beelzebul*). There is a coarse witticism in the application of the word to Christ. Jesus calls himself "the Master of the house," and the Jews apply to him the corresponding title of the Devil, Heb., *Beelzebul, Master of the dwelling.* (The phrase reappears in German, where the Devil is sometimes called *Herr vom Haus.* See Goethe, "Faust," sc. xxi.). Dr. Edersheim's explanation, though ingenious, seems far-fetched. He says that *szebuhl*, in Rabbinic language, means, not any ordinary dwelling, but specifically *the temple;* so that Beelzebul would be *Master of the Temple*, an expression having reference to the claims of Jesus on his first purification of the temple. He then conceives a play between this word and *Beelzibbul*, meaning *Lord of idolatrous sacrifice*, and says: "The Lord of the temple was to them the chief of idolatrous worship; the representative of God, that of the

worst of demons. *Beelzebul* was *Beelzibbul.* What, then, might his household expect at their hands?" ("Life and Times of Jesus").

27. **Preach** (κηρύξατε). Better Rev., *proclaim.* See on Matt. iv. 17.

29. **Sparrows** (στρουθία). The word is a diminutive, *little sparrows*, and carries with it a touch of tenderness. At the present day, in the markets of Jerusalem and Jaffa, long strings of little birds, sparrows and larks, are offered for sale, trussed on long wooden skewers. Edersheim thinks that Jesus may have had reference to the two sparrows which, according to the Rabbins, were used in the ceremonial of purification from leprosy (Lev. xiv. 49–54).

Shall not fall. A Rabbinic legend relates how a certain Rabbi had been for thirteen years hiding from his persecutors in a cave, where he was miraculously fed; when he observed that when the bird-catcher laid his snare, the bird escaped or was caught, according as a voice from heaven proclaimed "Mercy" or "Destruction." Arguing that if even a sparrow cannot be caught without heaven's bidding, how much more safe was the life of a son of man, he came forth.

32. **Confess me** (ὁμολογήσει ἐν ἐμοὶ). A peculiar but very significant expression. Lit., "Confess *in* me." The idea is that of confessing Christ out of a state of oneness with him. "Abide in me, and being in me, confess me." It implies identification of the confessor with the confessed, and thus takes confession out of the category of mere formal or verbal acknowledgment. "Not every one that *saith* unto me, 'Lord! Lord!' shall enter into the kingdom of heaven." The true confessor of Christ is one whose faith rests in him. Observe that this gives great force to the corresponding clause, in which Christ places himself in a similar relation with those whom he confesses. "I will confess *in* him." It shall be as if I spoke abiding in him. "I in them and thou in me, that they may be

perfected into one, and that *the world may know* that thou hast sent me, and hast loved them as thou hast loved me" (John xvii. 23).

34. **To send** (*βαλεῖν*). Lit., *to throw* or *cast.* By this word the expectancy of the disciples is dramatically pictured, as if he represented them as eagerly looking up for peace as something to be flung down upon the earth from heaven. Dr. Morison gives the picture thus: "All are on tiptoe of expectation. What is it that is about to happen? Is it the reign of peace that is just about to be inaugurated and consummated? Is there henceforth to be only unity and amity? As they muse and debate, lo! a sword is flung into the midst."

35. **Set at variance** (*διχάσαι*). Lit., *part asunder.* Wyc., *to depart* = *part.*

Daughter-in-law (*νύμφην*). So A. V. and Rev.; but the full force is lost in this rendering. The word means *bride,* and though sometimes used in classical Greek of any married woman, it carries a notion of comparative youth. Thus in Homer, "Odyssey," iv., 743, the aged nurse, Euryclea, addresses Penelope (certainly not a bride) as *νύμφα φίλη* (*dear bride*), of course as a term of affection or petting. Compare "Iliad," iii., 130, where Iris addresses Helen in the same way. The radical and bitter character of the division brought into households by the Gospel is shown by the fact of its affecting domestic relations in their very freshness. The newly-married wife shall be set at variance with her mother-in-law. Wycliffe's rendering is peculiar: *And the son's wife against the wife's or husband's mother.*

38. **His cross** (*τὸν σταυρὸν αὐτοῦ*). This was no Jewish proverb, crucifixion not being a Jewish punishment; so that Jesus uses the phrase anticipatively, in view of the death which he himself was to die. This was one of those sayings described in John xii. 16, which the disciples understood not at the first, but the meaning of which was revealed in the light of later

events. The figure itself was borrowed from the practice which compelled criminals to bear their own cross to the place of execution. *His* cross: his own. All are not alike. There are different crosses for different disciples. The English proverb runs: "Every cross hath its inscription"—the name of him for whom it is shaped.

39. **Findeth** (*εὑρὼν*). The word is really a past participle, *found*. Our Lord looked back in thought to each man's past, and forward to its appropriate consummation in the future. Similarly, *he who lost* (*ἀπολέσας*). Plato seems to have foreshadowed this wonderful thought. "O my friend! I want you to see that the noble and the good may possibly be something different from saving and being saved, and that he who is truly a man ought not to care about living a certain time: he knows, as women say, that we must all die, and therefore he is not fond of life; he leaves all that with God, and considers in what way he can best spend his appointed term" ("Gorgias," 512). Still more to the point, Euripides:

"Who knows if life be not death, and death life?"

CHAPTER XI.

1. **Commanding** (*διατάσσων*). The preposition *διά* has a distributive force: giving to each his appropriate charge.

Their cities (*αὐτῶν*). The towns of those to whom he came —the Galilaeans. Compare iv. 23.

2. **Two** of his disciples (*δύο*). But the correct reading is *διά*, *by*. He sent by his disciples. So Rev.

3. **Thou.** Emphatic. Art *thou* "the Coming One?"—a current phrase for the Messiah.

5. **The lame walk.** Tynd., *The halt go.*

6. **Be offended** (σκανδαλισθῇ). See on ch. v. 29. Rev., *shall find none occasion of stumbling.* Compare Wyc., *shall not be slandered.*

7. **As they departed** (τούτων δὲ πορευομένων). Rev., more literal and better, *as these went their way ;* or while they, John's disciples, were departing: thus giving the *simultaneousness* of Jesus' words with the act of departure.

To see (θεάσασθαι). Rev., *to behold.* *θεᾶσθαι*, like *θεωρεῖν*, expresses the calm, continuous contemplation of an object which remains before the spectator. Compare John i. 14. Another verb is used in Christ's repetition of the question, vv. 8, 9; *ἰδεῖν* in the ordinary sense of seeing. The more earnest expression suits the first question.

12. **Suffereth violence** (βιάζεται). Lit., *is forced, overpowered, taken by storm.* Christ thus graphically portrays the intense excitement which followed John's ministry; the eager waiting, striving, and struggling of the multitude for the promised king.

The violent take it by force (βιασταὶ ἁρπάζουσιν αὐτήν). This was proved by the multitudes who followed Christ and thronged the doors where he was, and would have *taken him by force* (the same word) and made him a king (John vi. 15). The word *take by force* means literally *to snatch away, carry off.* It is often used in the classics of *plundering.* Meyer renders, *Those who use violent efforts, drag it to themselves.* So Tynd., *They that make violence pull it unto them.* Christ speaks of believers. They seize upon the kingdom and make it their own. The Rev., *men of violence*, is too strong, since it describes a class of *habitually* and *characteristically* violent men; whereas the *violence* in this case is the result of a special and exceptional impulse. The passage recalls the old Greek proverb quoted by Plato against the Sophists, who had corrupted the

Athenian youth by promising the easy attainment of wisdom : *Good things are hard.* Dante has seized the idea:

> "*Regnum coelorum* (the kingdom of heaven) suffereth violence
> From fervent love, and from that living hope
> That overcometh the divine volition;
> Not in the guise that man o'ercometh man,
> But conquers it because it will be conquered,
> And conquered, conquers by benignity."
>
> *Parad.*, xx., 94–99.

14. **If ye will** (εἰ θέλετε). More correctly, Rev., *If ye are willing* or *disposed.* For there would naturally be an unwillingness to receive the statement about John's high place, in view of John's imprisonment.

16. **Children** (παιδίοις). Diminutive, *little* children. The Rev. Donald Fraser gives the picture simply and vividly: "He pictured a group of little children playing at make-believe marriages and funerals. First they acted a marriage procession; some of them piping as on instruments of music, while the rest were expected to leap and dance. In a perverse mood, however, these last did not respond, but stood still and looked discontented. So the little pipers changed their game and proposed a funeral. They began to imitate the loud wailing of eastern mourners. But again they were thwarted, for their companions refused to chime in with the mournful cry and to beat their breasts. . . . So the disappointed children complained: 'We piped unto you and ye did not dance; we wailed, and ye did not mourn. Nothing pleases you. If you don't want to dance, why don't you mourn? . . . It is plain that you are in bad humor, and determined not to be pleased'" ("Metaphors in the Gospels"). The issue is between the Jews (*this generation*) and the children of wisdom, v. 9.

Market-places (ἀγοραῖς). From ἀγείρω, to *assemble.* Wyc., renders *cheepynge;* compare *cheapside, the place for buying and selling;* for the word *cheap* had originally no reference to *small* price, but meant simply *barter* or *price.* The primary conception in the Greek word has nothing to do with buying and selling. *'Αγορά* is *an assembly;* then *the place of assembly.* The idea of a place of *trade* comes in afterward, and naturally, since trade plants itself where people habitually gather. Hence the Roman Forum was devoted, not only to popular and judicial assemblies, but to commercial purposes, especially of bankers. The idea of trade gradually becomes the dominant one in the word. In Eastern cities the markets are held in bazaars and streets, rather than in squares. In these public places the children would be found playing. Compare Zech. viii. 5.

17. **Mourn** (ἐκόψασθε). Lit., *beat* or *strike* (the breast), as in oriental funeral lamentations.

20. **Mighty works** (δυνάμεις). The supernatural works of Christ and his apostles are denoted by six different words in the New Testament, exhibiting these works under different aspects and from different points of view. These will be considered in detail as they occur. Generally, a miracle may be regarded: 1. As a *portent* or prodigy (τέρας); as Acts vii. 36, of the wonders shown by Moses in Egypt. 2. As a *sign* (σημεῖον), pointing to something beyond itself, a mark of the power or grace of the doer or of his connection with the supernatural world. So Matt. xii. 38. 3. As an exhibition of God's glory (ἔνδοξον), Luke xiii. 17; *glorious things.* 4. As a *strange* thing (παράδοξον), Luke v. 26. 5. As a *wonderful* thing (θαυμάσιον), Matt. xxi. 15. 6. As a *power* (δύναμις); so here: a *mighty* work.

22. **But** (πλὴν). Better Rev., *howbeit,* or as Wyc., *nevertheless.* Chorazin and Bethsaida did *not* repent; therefore a woe lies against them; *nevertheless* they shall be more excusable than you who have seen the mighty works which were not done among them.

25. **Answered.** In reply to something which is not stated.

I thank (ἐξομολογοῦμαι). Compare Matt. iii. 6, of *confessing* sins. Lit., *I confess.* I recognize the justice and wisdom of thy doings. But with the dative, as here (σοι, *to thee*), it means to *praise*, with an undercurrent of *acknowledgment;* to *confess* only in later Greek, and with an accusative of the object. Rev. gives *praise* in the margin here, and at Rom. xiv. 11. Tynd., *I praise.*

Prudent (συνετῶν). Rev., *understanding;* Wyc., *wary.* From the verb συνίημι, to *bring together*, and denoting that peculiarity of mind which brings the simple features of an object into a whole. Hence *comprehension, insight.* Compare on Mark xii. 33, *understanding* (συνέσεως). *Wise* (σοφῶν) and *understanding* are often joined, as here. The general distinction is between productive and reflective wisdom, but the distinction is not always recognized by the writer.

27. **Are delivered** (παρεδόθη). More lit., *were* delivered, as of a single act at a given time, as in this case, where the Son was sent forth by the Father, and clothed with authority. Compare xxviii. 18.

Knoweth (ἐπιγινώσκει). The compound indicating *full* knowledge. Others behold only in *part*, "through a glass, darkly."

28. **Labor and are heavy-laden** (κοπιῶντες καὶ πεφορτισμένοι). The first an active, the second a passive participle, exhibiting the active and passive sides of human misery.

Give rest (ἀναπαύσω). Originally *to make to cease;* Tynd., *ease;* Wyc., *refresh.* The radical conception is that of *relief.*

29. **Yoke** (ζυγόν). "These words, as recorded by St. Matthew, the Evangelist of the Jews, must have sunk the deeper into the hearts of Christ's Jewish hearers, that they came in their own old, familiar form of speech, yet with such contrast of spirit. One of the most common figurative expressions of the time was that of the yoke for submission to an occupation or obligation. Very instructive for the understanding of the figure is

this paraphrase of Cant. i. 10: 'How beautiful is their neck for bearing the yoke of thy statutes; and it shall be upon them like the yoke on the neck of the ox that plougheth in the field and provideth food for himself and his master.'

"The public worship of the ancient synagogue commenced with a benediction, followed by the *shema* (*Hear, O Israel*) or creed, composed of three passages of scripture: Deut. vi. 4–9; xi. 13–21; Num. xv. 37–41. The section Deut. vi. 4–9, was said to precede xi. 13–21, so that we might take upon ourselves the yoke of the kingdom of heaven, and only after that the yoke of the commandments. The Saviour's words must have had a special significance to those who remembered this lesson; and they would now understand how, by coming to the Saviour, they would first take on them the yoke of the kingdom of heaven, and then that of the commandments, finding this yoke easy and the burden light" (Edersheim, "Life and Times of Jesus," and "Jewish Social Life").

Meek (*πραΰς*). See on Matt. v. 5.

Lowly (*ταπεινός*). The word has a history. In the classics it is used commonly in a bad and degrading sense, of meanness of condition, lowness of rank, and cringing abjectness and baseness of character. Still, even in classical Greek, this is not its universal usage. It is occasionally employed in a way which foreshadows its higher sense. Plato, for instance, says, "To that law (of God) he would be happy who holds fast, and follows it in all *humility* and order; but he who is lifted up with pride, or money, or honor, or beauty, who has a soul hot with folly, and youth, and insolence, and thinks that he has no need of a guide or ruler, but is able himself to be the guide of others, he, I say, is left deserted of God" ("Laws," 716). And Aristotle says: "He who is worthy of small things, and *deems himself so*, is wise" ("Nich. Ethics," iv., 3). At best, however, the classical conception is only *modesty, absence of assumption*. It is an element of wisdom and in no way opposed to self-righteousness (see Aristotle above). The word for the Christian virtue of *humility* (*ταπεινοφροσύνη*), was not used before the Christian era, and is distinctly an outgrowth of the Gospel. This virtue is based upon a correct estimate of our actual littleness, and is linked with a sense of sinfulness. True greatness is holiness. We are little because sinful. Compare Luke xviii. 14. It is asked how, in this view of the case, the word can be applied to himself by the sinless Lord? "The answer is," says Archbishop Trench, "that *for the sinner* humility involves the confession of sin, inasmuch as it involves the confession of his true condition; while yet for the unfallen creature the grace itself as truly exists, involving for such the acknowledgment, not of *sinfulness*, which would be untrue, but of *creatureliness*, of absolute dependence, of having nothing, but receiving all things of God. And thus the grace of humility belongs to the highest angel before the throne, being as he is a creature, yea, even to the Lord of Glory himself. In his human nature he must be the pattern of all humility, of all creaturely dependence; and it is only *as a man* that Christ thus claims to be *lowly;* his human life was a constant living on the fulness of his Father's love; he evermore, as man, took the place which beseemed the creature in the presence of its Creator" ("Synonyms," p. 145). The Christian virtue regards man not only with reference to God, but to his fellow-man. *In lowliness of mind each counting other better than himself* (Philip. ii. 3, Rev.). But this is contrary to the Greek conception of *justice* or *righteousness*, which was simply "his own to each one." It is noteworthy that neither the Septuagint, the Apocrypha, nor the New Testament recognize the ignoble classical sense of the word.

Ye shall find (εὑρήσετε). Compare *I will give you* and *ye shall find.* The rest of Christ is twofold—*given* and *found.* It is given in pardon and reconciliation. It is found under the yoke and the burden; in the development of Christian experience, as more and more the "strain passes over" from self to Christ. "No other teacher, since the world began, has ever associated *learn* with *rest.* 'Learn of me,' says the philosopher, 'and you shall find restlessness.' 'Learn of me,' says Christ, 'and you shall find rest'" (Drummond, "Natural Law in the Spiritual World").

30. **Easy** (χρηστὸς). Not a satisfactory rendering. Christ's yoke is not *easy* in the ordinary sense of that word. The word means originally, *good*, *serviceable*. The kindred noun, χρηστότης, occurring only in Paul's writings, is rendered *kindness* in 2 Cor. vi. 6; Tit. iii. 4; Gal. v. 22; Eph. ii. 7 (Rev.), and *goodness*, Rom. ii. 4 (Rev.). At Luke v. 39, it is used of old wine, where the true reading, instead of *better*, is *good* (χρηστός), mellowed with age. Plato (" Republic," 424) applies the word to education. " *Good* nurture and education (τροφὴ γὰρ καὶ παίδευσις χρηστὴ) implant *good* (ἀγαθὰς) constitutions; and these *good* (χρησταὶ) constitutions improve more and more;" thus evidently using χρηστός and ἀγαθός as synonymous. The three meanings combine in the word, though it is impossible to find an English word which combines them all. Christ's yoke is *wholesome, serviceable, kindly.* " Christ's yoke is like feathers to a bird; not loads, but helps to motion" (Jeremy Taylor).

CHAPTER XII.

1. **Time** (καιρῷ). Rev., *season*. The word implies a *particular* time; as related to some event, a *convenient*, *appropriate* time; absolutely, a particular point of time, or a particular season, like spring or winter.

Corn (σπορίμων). From σπείρω, *to sow*. Properly, as Rev., *corn-fields*.

2. **What is not lawful.** "On any ordinary day this would have been lawful; but on the Sabbath it involved, according to the Rabbinic statutes, at least two sins, viz., plucking the ears, which was reaping, and rubbing them in their hands (Luke vi. 1), which was sifting, grinding, or fanning. The Talmud says: 'In case a woman rolls wheat to remove the husks, it is considered as sifting; if she rubs the heads of wheat, it is regarded as threshing; if she cleans off the side-adherencies, it is sifting out fruit; if she bruises the ears, it is grinding; if she throws them up in her hand, it is winnowing'" (Edersheim, "Life and Times of Jesus").

6. **One greater** (μείζων). The correct reading makes the adjective neuter, so that the right rendering is *something greater* (Rev., in margin). The reference is, of course, to Christ himself (compare vv. 41, 42, where the neuter πλεῖον, *more* (so Rev., in margin), is used in the same way). Compare, also, John ii. 19, where Christ speaks of his own body as a *temple*. The indefiniteness of the neuter gives a more solemn and impressive sense.

10. **Is it lawful?** (εἰ ἔξεστιν). The εἰ can hardly be rendered into English. It gives an indeterminate, hesitating character to the question: *I would like to know if*, etc.

13. **Stretch forth thy hand.** The arm was not withered.

20. **Flax.** The Hebrew is, literally, *a dimly burning wick he shall not quench* (Isa. xlii. 3). The quotation stops at the end of the third verse in the prophecy; but the succeeding verse is beautifully suggestive as describing the Servant of Jehovah by the same figures in which he pictures his suffering ones—*a wick* and a *reed*. "He shall not burn dimly, neither shall his spirit be crushed." He himself, partaking of the nature of our frail humanity, is both a lamp and a reed, humble, but not to be broken, and the "light of the world." Compare the beautiful passage in Dante, where Cato directs Virgil to wash away the stains of the nether world from Dante's face, and to prepare him for the ascent of the purgatorial mount by girding him with a rush, the emblem of humility:

> "Go, then, and see thou gird this one about
> With a smooth rush, and that thou wash his face,
> So that thou cleanse away all stain therefrom.
> For 'twere not fitting that the eye o'ercast
> By any mist should go before the first
> Angel, who is of those of Paradise.
> This little island, round about its base,
> Below there, yonder, where the billow beats it,
> Doth rushes bear upon its washy ooze.
> No other plant that putteth forth the leaf,
> Or that doth indurate, can there have life,
> Because it yieldeth not unto the shocks.
> . . . . . .

> There he begirt me as the other pleased;
> O marvellous! for even as he culled
> The humble plant, such it sprang up again
> Suddenly there where he uprooted it."
>
> *Purg.*, i., 94–105, 133–137.

26. **He is divided** (ἐμερίσθη. Lit., "*he was divided.*" If he is casting *himself* out, there must have been a previous division.

28. **Is come unto you** (ἔφθασεν ἐφ' ὑμᾶς). The verb is used in the simple sense *to arrive at* (2 Cor. x. 14; Philip. iii. 16), and sometimes *to anticipate* (1 Thess. iv. 15). Here with a suggestion of the latter sense, which is also conveyed by the Rev., "come *upon.*" It has come upon you before you expected it.

29. **Of a strong man** (τοῦ ἰσχυροῦ). Rev. rightly gives the force of the article, *the* strong man. Christ is not citing a general illustration, but is pointing to a specific enemy—Satan. How can I despoil Satan without first having conquered him?

Goods (σκεύη). The word originally means a *vessel*, and so mostly in the New Testament. See Mark xi. 16; John xix. 29. But also *the entire equipment of a house, collectively: chattels, house-gear.* Also the baggage of an army. Here in the sense of *house-gear*. Compare Luke xvii. 31; Acts xxvii. 17, of the gear or tackling of the ship. Rev., *lowered the gear.*

32. **The Holy Spirit** (τοῦ πνεύματος τοῦ ἁγίου). *The Spirit —the holy.* These words define more clearly the *blasphemy against the Spirit*, ver. 31.

35. **Bringeth forth** (ἐκβάλλει). But the translation is feeble. The word means *to throw* or *fling out.* The good or evil things come forth out of the *treasure* of the heart (34). "Out of the *abundance* of the heart the mouth speaketh." The issues of the heart are *thrown* out, as if under pressure of the abundance within.

36. **Idle** (ἀργὸν). A good rendering. The word is compounded of ἀ, *not*, and ἔργον, *work*. An idle word is a *non-working* word; an *inoperative* word. It has no legitimate work, no office, no business, but is morally useless and unprofitable.

39. **Adulterous** (μοιχαλὶς). A very strong and graphic expression, founded upon the familiar Hebrew representation of the relation of God's people to him under the figure of marriage. See Ps. lxxiii. 27; Isa. lvii. 3 sqq.; lxii. 5; Ezek. xxiii. 27. Hence idolatry and intercourse with Gentiles were described as adultery; and so here, of moral unfaithfulness to God. Compare James iv. 4; Apoc. ii. 20 sqq. Thus Dante:

> "Where Michael wrought
> Vengeance upon the proud adultery."
> *Inf.*, vii., 12.

40. **The whale** (τοῦ κήτους). A general term for a sea-monster.

41. **Shall rise up** (ἀναστήσονται). Rev., *stand up*. Come forward as witnesses. Compare Job xvi. 9, Sept.; Mark xiv. 57. There is no reference to rising from the dead. Similarly *shall rise up*, ver. 42. Compare Matthew xi. 11; xxiv. 11.

A greater (πλεῖον). Lit., something *more*. See on ver. 6.

49. **Disciples** (μαθητὰς). Not the *apostles* only, but all who followed him in the character of *learners*. The Anglo-Saxon renders *learning knights*.

CHAPTER XIII.

2. **Shore** (αἰγιαλὸν). Rev., *beach*, that over which the *sea* (ἅλς) *rushes* (ἀΐσσει). The word for *shore*, ἀκτή, on which the sea *breaks* (ἄγνυμι), is never used in the New Testament. Wyc., *brink*.

3. **Parables** (*παραβολαῖς*). From *παρά*, *beside*, and *βάλλω*, *to throw*. A parable is a form of teaching in which one thing is *thrown beside* another. Hence its radical idea is *comparison*. Sir John Cheke renders *biword*, and the same idea is conveyed by the German *Beispiel*, a *pattern* or *example*; *bei*, *beside*, and the old high German *spel*, *discourse* or *narration*.

The word is used with a wide range in scripture, but always involves the idea of *comparison*:

1. Of *brief sayings*, having an oracular or proverbial character. Thus Peter (Matt. xv. 15), referring to the words "If the blind lead the blind," etc., says, "declare unto us this *parable*." Compare Luke vi. 39. So of the patched garment (Luke v. 36), and the guest who assumes the highest place at the feast (Luke xiv. 7, 11). Compare, also, Matt. xxiv. 32; Mark xiii. 28.

2. Of *a proverb*. The word for *proverb* (*παροιμία*) has the same idea at the root as *parable*. It is *παρά*, *beside*, *οἶμος*, a *way* or *road*. Either a *trite*, *wayside* saying (Trench), or *a path by the side of the high road* (Godet). See Luke iv. 23; 1 Sam. xxiv. 13.

3. Of a *song* or *poem*, in which an example is set up by way of comparison. See Micah ii. 4; Hab. ii. 6.

4. Of a word or discourse which is *enigmatical* or *obscure* until the meaning is developed by application or comparison. It occurs along with the words *αἴνιγμα*, *enigma*, and *πρόβλημα*, *a problem*, something *put forth* or *proposed* (*πρό*, *in front*, *βάλλω*, *to throw*). See Ps. xlix. (Sept. xlviii.) 4; lxxviii. (Sept. lxxvii.) 2; Prov. i. 6, where we have *παραβολήν*, *parable*; *σκοτεινὸν λόγον*, *dark saying*; and *αἰνίγματα*, *enigmas*. Used also of the sayings of Balaam (Num. xxiii. 7, 18; xxiv. 3, 15).

In this sense Christ uses parables *symbolically* to expound the *mysteries* of the kingdom of God; as utterances which conceal from one class what they reveal to another (Matt. xiii. 11–17), and in which familiar facts of the earthly life are used figuratively to expound truths of the higher life. The unspiritual do not link these facts of the natural life with those of the supernatural, which are not discerned by them (1 Cor. ii. 14), and therefore they need an interpreter of the relation between the two. Such symbols assume the existence of a law common to the natural and spiritual worlds under which the symbol and the thing symbolized alike work; so that the one does not merely resemble the other superficially, but stands in actual coherence and harmony with it. Christ formulates such a law in connection with the parables of the Talents and the Sower. "To him that hath shall be given. From him that hath not shall be taken away." That is a law of morals and religion, as of business and agriculture. One must *have* in order to *make.* Interest requires capital. Fruit requires not only *seed* but *soil.* Spiritual fruitfulness requires *an honest and good heart.* Similarly, the law of growth as set forth in the parable of the Mustard Seed, is a law common to nature and to the kingdom of God. The great forces in both kingdoms are *germinal,* enwrapped in small seeds which unfold from within by an inherent power of growth.

5. A parable is also an *example* or *type;* furnishing a *model* or a *warning;* as the Good Samaritan, the Rich Fool, the Pharisee and the Publican. The element of comparison enters here as between the particular incident imagined or recounted, and all cases of a similar kind.

The term parable, however, as employed in ordinary Christian phraseology, is limited to those utterances of Christ which are marked by a complete figurative history or narrative. It is thus defined by Goebel ("Parables of Jesus"). "A narrative moving within the sphere of physical or human life, not professing to describe an event which actually took place, but expressly imagined for the purpose of representing, in pictorial figure, a truth belonging to the sphere of religion, and therefore referring to the relation of man or mankind to God."

In *form* the New Testament parables resemble the *fable.* The distinction between them does not turn on the respective use of rational and irrational beings speaking and acting. There are fables where the actors are human. Nor does the fable always deal with the impossible, since there are fables in which an animal, for instance, does nothing contrary to its nature. The distinction lies in the *religious* character of the New Testament parable as contrasted with the *secular* character of the fable.

While the parable exhibits the relations of man to God, the fable teaches lessons of worldly policy or natural morality and utility. "The parable is predominantly symbolic; the fable, for the most part, typical, and therefore presents its teaching only in the form of example, for which reason it chooses animals by preference, not as symbolic, but as typical figures; never symbolic in the sense in which the parable mostly is, because the higher invisible world, of which the parable sees and exhibits the symbol in the visible world of nature and man, lies far from it. Hence the parable can never work with fantastic figures like speaking animals, trees," etc. (Goebel, condensed).

The parable differs from the allegory in that there is in the latter "an interpenetration of the thing signified and the thing signifying; the qualities and properties of the first being attributed to the last," and the two being thus blended instead of being kept distinct and parallel. See, for example, the allegory of the Vine and the Branches (John xv.) where Christ at onee identifies himself with the figure: "I am the true vine." Thus the allegory, unlike the parable, carries its own interpretation with it.

Parable and proverb are often used interchangeably in the New Testament; the fundamental conception being, as we have seen, the same in both, the same Hebrew word representing both, and both being enigmatical. They differ rather in extent than in essence; the parable being a proverb expanded and carried into detail, and being necessarily figurative, which the proverb is not; though the range of the proverb is wider, since the parable expands only one particular case of a proverb. (See Trench, "Notes on the Parables," Introd.)

3. **A sower** (*ὁ σπείρων*). Rev., *the* sower. Generic, as representing a class.

To sow (*τοῦ σπείρειν*). "According to Jewish authorities, there was twofold sowing, as the seed was either cast by the hand or by means of cattle. In the latter case, a sack with holes was filled with corn and laid on the back of the animal, so that, as it moved onward, the seed was thickly scattered" (Edersheim, "Life and Times of Jesus").

4. **By the wayside.** Dean Stanley, approaching the plain of Gennesareth, says: "A slight recess in the hillside, close upon the plain, disclosed at once, in detail and with a conjunction which I remember nowhere else in Palestine, every feature of the great parable. There was the undulating cornfield descending to the water's edge. There was the trodden pathway running through the midst of it, with no fence or hedge to prevent the seed from falling here and there on either side of it or upon it; itself hard with the constant tramp of horse and mule and human feet. There was the 'good' rich soil which distinguishes the whole of that plain and its neighborhood from the bare hills elsewhere descending into the lake, and which, where there is no interruption, produces one vast mass of corn. There was the rocky ground of the hillside protruding here and there through the cornfields, as elsewhere through the grassy slopes. There were the large bushes of thorn—the *nabk*, that kind of which tradition says that the crown of thorns was woven—springing up, like the fruit-trees of the more inland parts, in the very midst of the waving wheat" ("Sinai and Palestine").

5. **Stony places.** Not ground covered with loose stones, but a hard, rocky surface, covered with a thin layer of soil.

7. **Sprang up.** The seed, therefore, fell, not among *standing* thorns, but among those beneath the surface, ready to spring up.

Trench ("Parables") cites a striking parallel from Ovid, describing the obstacles to the growth of the grain:

> "Now the too ardent sun, now furious showers,
> With baleful stars and bitter winds combine
> The crop to ravage; while the greedy fowl
> Snatch the strown seeds; and grass with stubborn roots,
> And thorn and darnel plague the ripening grain."
>
> *Metamorphoses*, v., 486.

8. **A hundred-fold.** Mentioned as something extraordinary. Compare Gen. xxvi. 12. Herodotus (i., 93) says of Babylonia, "In grain it is so fruitful as to yield commonly two-hundred-fold; and when the production is the greatest, even three-hundred-fold."

11. **Mysteries** (μυστήρια). From μύω, to *close* or *shut*. In classical Greek, applied to certain religious celebrations to which persons were admitted by formal initiation, and the precise character of which is unknown. Some suppose them to have been revelations of religious secrets; others of secret politico-religious doctrines; others, again, scenic representations of mythical legends. In this latter sense the term was used in the Middle Ages of miracle-plays—rude dramas representing scenes from scripture and from the apocryphal gospels. Such plays are still enacted among the Basque mountaineers. (See Vincent, "In the Shadow of the Pyrenees.")

A mystery does not denote an *unknowable* thing, but one which is withdrawn from knowledge or manifestation, and which cannot be known without special manifestation of it. Hence appropriate to the things of the kingdom of heaven, which could be known only by revelation. Paul (Philip. iv. 12) says, "I am *instructed* (μεμύημαι) both to be full and to be hungry," etc. But Rev. gives more correctly the force of *instructed*, by rendering *I have learned the secret:* the verb being μυέω (from the same root as μυστήρια) *to initiate into the mysteries.*

14. **Is fulfilled** (ἀναπληροῦται). Rather of something in progress: *is being fulfilled* or *in process of fulfilment.*

15. **Is waxed gross** (ἐπαχύνθη). Lit., *was made fat.* Wyc., *enfatted.*

Are dull of hearing (τοῖς ὠσὶν βαρέως ἤκουσαν). Lit., *They heard heavily with their ears.*

They have closed (ἐκάμμυσαν), κατά, *down*, μύω, *to close*, as in μυστήρια above. Our idiom shuts *up* the eyes. The

Greek shuts them *down*. The Hebrew, in Isa. vi. 10, is *besmear*. This insensibility is described as a punishment. Compare Isa. xxix. 10; xliv. 18; in both of which the closing of the eyes is described as a judgment of God. Sealing up the eyes was an oriental punishment. Cheyne ("Isaiah") cites the case of a son of the Great Mogul, who had his eyes sealed up three years by his father as a punishment. Dante pictures the envious, on the second cornice of Purgatory, with their eyes sewed up:

> "For all their lids an iron wire transpierces,
> And sews them up, as to a sparhawk wild
> Is done, because it will not quiet stay."
>
> *Purg.*, xiii., 70–72.

Be converted (ἐπιστρέψωσιν). Rev., *turn again; ἐπί, to* or *toward, στρέφω, to turn;* with the idea of their turning *from* their evil *toward* God.

19. **When any one heareth.** The rendering would be made even more graphic by preserving the *continuous* force of the present tense, as exhibiting action in progress, and the simultaneousness of Satan's work with that of the gospel instructor. "While any one *is hearing*, the evil one *is coming* and *snatching away*, just as the birds do not wait for the sower to be out of the way, but are at work while he is sowing.

He which received seed (ὁ σπαρείς). Lit., and much better, Rev., *He that was sown;* identifying the *seed* of the figure with the *man* signified.

21. **Dureth for a while** (πρόσκαιρός ἐστιν). Rev., *endureth*. Lit., *is temporary:* thus bringing out the *quality* of the hearer. He is *a creature of circumstances*, changing as they change. Wyc., *is temporal*, with explanation, *lasteth but a little time.*

For (δὲ). Rev. better, *and*, for the following clause does not give a reason for the temporariness, but adds something to the description of the hearer.

Tribulation (θλίψεως). θλίβω, to *press* or *squeeze*. Tribulation is perhaps as accurate a rendering as is possible, being derived from *tribulum*, the threshing-roller of the Romans. In both the idea of *pressure* is dominant, though θλῖψις does not convey the idea of *separation* (as of corn from husk) which is implied in *tribulatio*. Trench cites, in illustration of θλῖψις, *pressure*, the provision of the old English law, by which those who wilfully refused to plead had heavy weights placed on their breasts, and so were pressed and crushed to death ("Synonyms of the New Testament").

23. **Understandeth** (συνιείς). See on xi. 25, *prudent*. The three evangelists give three characteristics of the good hearer. Matthew, *he understandeth* the word; Mark, *he receiveth it;* Luke, *he keepeth it*.

24. **Put he forth** (παρέθηκεν). But this would be rather the translation of προβάλλω, from which πρόβλημα, a *problem*, is derived, while the word here used means rather to *set before* or *offer*. Often used of meals, to *serve up*. Hence, better, Rev., *set he before them*. See on Luke ix. 16.

25. **Sowed** (ἐπέσπειρεν). The preposition ἐπί, *upon*, indicates sowing *over* what was previously sown. Rev., "sowed *also*."

33. **Leaven** (ζύμῃ). Wyc., *sour dough*, as German *Sauerteig*. From ζέω, *to boil* or *seethe*, as in fermentation. The English *leaven* is from the Latin *levare*, to raise, and appears in the French *levain*.

35. **I will utter** (ἐρεύξομαι). The verb, in which the sound corresponds to the sense (*ereuxomai*), means originally to *belch*, to *disgorge*. Homer uses it of the sea *surging* against the shore ("Iliad," xvii., 265). Pindar of the *eruption* of Aetna ("Pyth.," i., 40). There seems to lie in the word a sense of *full, impassioned* utterance, as of a prophet.

From the foundation (ἀπὸ καταβολῆς). "It is assumed by the Psalmist (Ps. lxxviii. 2) that there was a hidden meaning in

God's ancient dealings with his people. A typical, archetypical, and prefigurative element ran through the whole. The history of the dealings is one long Old Testament parable. Things long *kept secret*, and that were hidden indeed in the depths of the divine mind from before the foundation of the world, were involved in these dealings. And hence the evangelist wisely sees, in the parabolic teaching of our Lord, a real culmination of the older parabolic teaching of the Psalmist. The culmination was divinely intended, and hence the expression *that it might be fulfilled*" (Morison on Matthew).

43. **Shine forth** (*ἐκλάμψουσιν*). The compound verb with *ἐκ*, *forth*, is designedly used to express a *dissipating* of darkness which has hidden: a bursting into light. The righteous shall *shine forth* as the sun from behind a cloud. The mixture of evil with good in the world obscures the good, and veils the true glory of righteous character. Compare Dan. xii. 3.

47. **Net** (*σαγήνῃ*). See on Matt. iv. 18. The only occurrence of the word in the New Testament. A long *draw-net*, the ends of which are carried out and drawn together. Through the transcription of the word into the Latin *sagena* comes *seine*. From the fact of its making a great sweep, the Greeks formed a verb from it, *σαγηνεύω*, *to surround and take with a drag-net*. Thus Herodotus (iii., 149) says: "The Persians *netted* Samos." And again (vi., 31), "Whenever they became masters of an island, the barbarians, in every single instance, *netted* the inhabitants. Now, the mode in which they practise this netting is the following: Men join hands, so as to form a line across from the north coast to the south, and then march through the island from end to end, and hunt out the inhabitants." Compare Isa. xix. 8: "Those who spread nets on the face of the waters shall languish." Also, Hab. i. 15–17, where the Chaldaean conquests are described under this figure.

Gathered of every kind. Compare the graphic passage in Homer ("Odyssey," xxii., 384–389) of the slain suitors in the halls of Ulysses.

"He saw that all had fallen in blood and dust,
Many as fishes on the shelving beach,
Drawn from the hoary deep by those who tend
The nets with myriad meshes. Poured abroad
Upon the sand, while panting to return
To the salt sea, they lie till the hot sun
Takes their life from them."

48. **Sat down.** Implying deliberation in the assortment.

52. **Which is instructed unto the kingdom of heaven.** *Instructed* μαθητευθεὶς. Rev., *who hath been made a disciple to the kingdom*, etc. The kingdom of heaven is personified. The disciples of Christ are disciples of that kingdom of which he is the representative.

Which (ὅστις). The pronoun marks the householder as belonging to a class and exhibiting the characteristic of the class: *a householder—one of those who* bring forth, etc.

Bringeth forth (ἐκβάλλει). Lit., *flingeth forth.* See on xii. 35. Indicating his *zeal* in communicating instruction and the *fulness* out of which he speaks.

CHAPTER XIV.

1. **Tetrarch.** A ruler of a fourth part. Archelaus had obtained two-fourths of his father's dominions, and Antipas (this Herod) and Philip each one-fourth.

The fame (ἀκοὴν). Better as Rev., *report.* Lit., *hearing.*

3. **Put him in prison** (ἐν φυλακῇ απέθετο). Lit., "*put* him *away* or *aside*" (ἀπὸ). This prison was the fortress of Machaerus on the east side of the Dead Sea, almost on a line with Bethlehem, above the gorge which divided the Mountains of Abarim from the range of Pisgah. Perched on an isolated cliff at the end of a narrow ridge, encompassed with deep ravines, was the citadel. At the other end of this ridge Herod built a great wall, with towers two hundred feet high at the

corners; and within this inclosure, a magnificent palace, with colonnades, baths, cisterns, arsenals—every provision, in short, for luxury and for defence against siege. The windows commanded a wide and grand prospect, including the Dead Sea, the course of the Jordan, and Jerusalem. In the detached citadel, probably in one of the underground dungeons, remains of which may still be seen, was the prison of John. "We return through what we regard as the ruins of the magnificent castle-palace of Herod, to the highest and strongest part of the defences—the eastern keep or the citadel, on the steep slope, one hundred and fifty yards up. The foundations of the walls all around, to the height of a yard or two above the ground, are still standing. As we clamber over them to examine the interior, we notice how small this keep is: exactly one hundred yards in diameter. There are scarcely any remains of it left. A well of great depth, and a deep, cemented cistern, with the vaulting of the roof still complete, and—of most terrible interest to us—two dungeons, one of them deep down, its sides scarcely broken in, 'with small holes still visible in the masonry where staples of wood and iron had once been fixed!' As we look down into its hot darkness, we shudder in realizing that this terrible keep had, for nigh ten months, been the prison of that son of the free wilderness, the bold herald of the coming kingdom, the humble, earnest, self-denying John the Baptist" (Edersheim, "Life and Times of Jesus").

6. **Birthday** (*γενεσίοις*). Though some explain it as the anniversary of Herod's accession. The custom of celebrating birthdays by festivities was not approved by the strict Jews; but it is claimed that the Herodian princes adopted the custom. The Roman satirist, Persius, alludes to a festival known as "Herod's Day," and pictures a banquet on that occasion.

"But when
Comes Herod's day, and on the steaming panes
The ranged lamps, festooned with violets, pour
The unctuous cloud, while the broad tunny-tail
Sprawled o'er the red dish swims, and snowy jars
Swell with the wine."

Sat. v., 180–183.

Before (ἐν τῷ μέσῳ.) Rev., *in the midst.* Wyc., *leaped in the middle.*

7. **He promised** (ὡμολόγησεν.) Lit., *confessed;* conveying the idea of acknowledging the obligation of his oath. Salome had degraded herself to perform the part of an *almeh* or common dancer, and could claim her reward.

8. **Being before instructed** (προβιβασθεῖσα). Wyc., *monestid*, with *warned* in explanation. Both wrong. Rev., rightly, *being put forward.* Compare Acts xix. 33, where the right meaning is, *they pushed Alexander forward* out of the crowd; and not as A. V., *drew out.* The correct rendering slightly relieves Salome of the charge of wanton cruelty, and throws it wholly upon Herodias.

Here (ὧδε). She demanded it *on the spot*, before Herod should have had time to reflect and relent; the more so, as she knew his respect for John (compare *was sorry*, ver. 9). The circumstances seem to point to Machaerus itself as the scene of the banquet; so that the deed could be quickly done, and the head of the Baptist delivered while the feast was still in progress.

In a charger (ἐπὶ πίνακι). The Revisers cannot be defended in their retention of this thoroughly obsolete word. A *charge* is originally a *burden;* and a *charger* something *loaded.* Hence, *a dish.* Wyc., *dish.* Tynd., *platter.*

9. **The oath's sake** (διὰ τοὺς ὅρκους). But the A. V. puts the apostrophe in the wrong place. The word is plural, and the Rev. rightly renders *for the sake of his oaths.* It is implied that Herod in his mad excitement had confirmed his promise with *repeated* oaths.

11. **To the damsel** (τῷ κορασίῳ). Diminutive, the *little girl.* Luther gives *mägdlein, little maid.*

13. **On foot** (πεζῇ). Rev., *by land* in margin, which is better; for the contrast is between Jesus' journey *by ship* and that of the multitude *by land.*

15. **Desert** (ἔρημος). In the Greek order standing first as emphatic. The dominant thought of the disciples is *remoteness* from supplies of food. The first meaning of the word is *solitary;* from which develops the idea of *void, bereft, barren.* Both meanings may well be included here. Note the two points of emphasis. The disciples say, *Barren is the place.* Christ answers, *No need have they to go away.*

Give (δότε). The disciples had said, "Send them away *to buy for themselves.*" Christ replies, *Give ye.*

19. **Brake.** As the Jewish loaves were thin cakes, a thumb's breadth in thickness, and more easily broken than cut.

20. **Were filled** (ἐχορτάσθησαν). See on Matt. v. 6.

Baskets (κοφίνους). Wyc., *coffins,* a transcription of the Greek word. Juvenal, the Roman satirist, describes the grove of Numa, near the Capenian gate of Rome, as being "let out to the Jews, whose furniture is a *basket* (*cophinus*) and some hay" (*for a bed*), "Sat." iii., 14. These were small hand-baskets, specially provided for the Jews to carry levitically clean food while travelling in Samaria or other heathen districts. The word for *basket* used in relating the feeding of the *four* thousand (Matt. xv. 37) is σπυρίς, *a large provision-basket* or *hamper,* of the kind used for letting Paul down over the wall at Damascus (Acts ix. 25). In Matt. xvi. 9, 10, Christ, in alluding to the two miracles, observes the distinctive term in each narrative; using κοφίνους in the case of the five thousand, and σπυρίδας in the other. Burgon ("Letters from Rome") gives a drawing of a wicker basket used by the masons in the cathedral at Sorrento, and called *cóffano.* He adds, "Who can doubt that the basket of the gospel narrative was of the shape here represented, and that the denomination of *this* basket exclusively has lingered in a Greek colony, where the Jews (who once carried the *cophinus* as a personal equipment) formerly lived in great numbers?"

22. **Constrained.** Implying the disciples' reluctance to leave him behind.

24. **Tossed** (*βασανιζόμενον*). Rev., better, *distressed.* See on Matt. iv. 24.

26. **A spirit** (*φάντασμα*). Of which our word *phantasm* is a transcription. Rev., rather stiffly, *apparition.* Wyc., *phantom.*

29. **To go to** (*ἐλθεῖν πρὸς*). But some of the best texts read *καὶ ἦλθεν πρὸς*, *and went toward.*

30. **He was afraid.** "Although," says Bengel, "a fisherman and a good swimmer" (John xxi. 7).

32. **Ceased** (*ἐκόπασεν*). A beautiful word. Lit., *grew weary;* sank away like one who is weary.

36. **Were made perfectly whole** (*διεσώθησαν*). The preposition *διά*, *through* or *thorough*, indicates *complete* restoration. The Rev. omits *perfectly*, because *whole*, in itself, implies completeness.

CHAPTER XV.

1. **Transgress** (*παραβαίνουσιν*). Lit., *to step on one side.*

2. **Wash not their hands.** Washing *before* meals was alone regarded as a *commandment;* washing *after* meals only as a *duty.* By and by the more rigorous actually washed between the courses, although this was declared to be purely voluntary. The distinctive designation for washing after meals

was *the lifting of the hands;* while for washing before meat a term was used which meant, literally, *to rub.* If "holy," *i.e.*, sacrificial food was to be partaken of, a complete immersion of the hands, and not a mere "uplifting" was prescribed. As the purifications were so frequent, and care had to be taken that the water had not been used for other purposes, or something fallen into it that might discolor or defile it, large vessels or jars were generally kept for the purpose (see John ii. 6). It was the practice to draw water out of these with a kind of ladle or bucket—very often of glass—which must hold at least one and a half egg-shells (compare *draw out now*, John ii. 8). The water was poured on both hands, which must be free of anything covering them, snch as gravel, mortar, etc. The hands were lifted up so as to make the water run to the wrist, in order to insure that the whole hand was washed, and that the water polluted by the hand did not again run down the fingers. Similarly, each hand was rubbed with the other (the fist), provided the hand that rubbed had been affused; otherwise, the rubbing might be done against the head, or even against a wall. But there was one point on which special stress was laid. In the "first affusion," which was all that originally was required when the hands were not levitically "defiled," the water had to run down to the wrist. If the water remained short of the wrist, the hands were not clean. See on Mark vii. 3 (Edersheim, "Life and Times of Jesus").

3. **Also** (*καὶ*). The significance of this little word must not be overlooked. Christ admits that the disciples had transgressed a *human* injunction, but adds, "Ye *also* transgress, and in a much greater way." "Whether the disciples transgress or not, you are the greatest transgressors" (Bengel). The one question is met with the other in the same style. Luther says, "He places one wedge against the other, and therewith drives the first back."

4. **Die the death** (*θανάτῳ τελευτάτω*). The Hebrew idiom is, *he shall certainly be executed.* The Greek is, lit., *let him come to his end by death.*

5. **It is a gift** (δῶρον). Rev., *given to God.* The picture is that of a churlish son evading the duty of assisting his needy parents by uttering the formula, *Corban, it is a gift to God.* "Whatever that may be by which you might be helped by me, is not mine to give. It is vowed to God." The man, however, was not bound in that case to give his gift to the temple-treasury, while he was bound not to help his parent; because the phrase did not necessarily dedicate the gift to the temple. By a quibble it was regarded as something like *Corban*, as if it were laid on the altar and put entirely out of reach. It was expressly stated that such a vow was binding, even if what was vowed involved a breach of the law.

6. **Have made of none effect** (ἠκυρώσατε). Rev., *made void; ἀ, not, κῦρος, authority.* Ye have deprived it of its authority.

7. **Well** (καλῶς). Admirably.

8. **Is far** (ἀπέχει). Lit., *holds off from me.*

19. **Out of the heart.** Compare Plato. "For all good and evil, whether in the body or in human nature, originates, as he declared, in the soul, and overflows from thence, as from the head into the eyes; and therefore, if the head and body are to be well, you must begin by curing the soul. That is the first thing" ("Charmides," 157).

Thoughts (διαλογισμοὶ). Lit., *reasonings* (compare Mark ix. 33, Rev.), or *disputings* (Philip. ii. 14), like the captious questioning of the Pharisees about washing hands.

21. **Coasts** (μέρη). Lit., and better, as Rev., *parts.*

22. **Out of the same coasts** (ἀπὸ τῶν ὁρίων ἐκείνων). Lit., as Rev., *from those borders; i.e.*, she crossed from Phœnicia into Galilee.

Cried (ἐκραύγασεν). With a loud, *importunate* cry: from behind. Compare *after*, ver. 23.

Me. Making her daughter's misery her own.

Grievously vexed with a devil (κακῶς δαιμονίζεται). Lit., *is badly demonized.* Sir J. Cheke, *very evil devilled.*

23. **Send her away.** With her request granted; for, as Bengel exquisitely remarks, "Thus Christ was accustomed to send away."

26. **Children's** (τῶν τέκνων). Bengel observes that while Christ spoke severely to the Jews, he spoke honorably of them to those without. Compare John iv. 22.

Dogs (κυναρίοις). Diminutive: *little dogs.* In ver. 27, Wyc. renders *the little whelps*, and Tynd., in both verses, *whelps.* The picture is of a family meal, with the pet house-dogs running round the table.

Their masters. The children are the masters of the little dogs. Compare Mark vii. 28, "*the children's* crumbs."

30. **Cast them down** (ἔρριψαν). Very graphic. Lit., *flung* them down; not carelessly, but *in haste*, because so many were coming on the same errand.

32. **I will not** (οὐ θέλω). The A. V. might easily be mistaken for the simple future of the verb *send.* But two verbs are used: the verb *I will* expressing Jesus' *feeling* or *disposition.* The Greek order is, *and to send them away fasting I am not willing.* Therefore Rev. is better: *I would not.*

Faint (ἐκλυθῶσιν). Lit., *be unstrung or relaxed.*

34. **Little fishes** (ἰχθύδια). Diminutive. The disciples make their provision seem as small as possible. In ver. 36 the diminutive is not used.

35. **On the ground** (ἐπὶ τὴν γῆν). Compare Mark viii. 6. On the occasion of feeding the five thousand, the multitude sat down on *the grass* (ἐπὶ τοὺς χόρτους), Matt. xiv. 19. It was then the month of flowers. Compare Mark vi. 39, *the green grass*, and John vi. 10, *much grass*. On the present occasion, several weeks later, the grass would be burnt up, so that they would sit on the ground.

Gave thanks. According to the Jewish ordinance, the head of the house was to speak the blessing only if he himself shared in the meal; yet if they who sat down to it were not merely guests, but his children or his household, then he might speak it, even if he himself did not partake.

37. **Baskets** (σπυρίδας). See on Matt. xiv. 20.

CHAPTER XVI.

2. **Fair weather** (εὐδία). Colloquial. Looking at the evening sky, a man says to his neighbor, "Fine weather:" and in the morning (ver. 3), "Storm to-day" (σήμερον χειμών).

3. **Lowering** (στυγνάζων). The verb means to *have a gloomy look*. Dr. Morison compares the Scotch *gloaming* or *glooming*. Cranmer, *the sky is glooming red*. The word is used only here and at Mark x. 22, of the young ruler, turning from Christ with his face overshadowed with gloom. A. V., *he was sad*. Rev., *his countenance fell*.

9, 10. Note the accurate employment of the two words for *basket*. See on xiv. 20.

15. **Thou art the Christ.** Compare on i. 1. Note the emphatic and definite force of the article in Peter's confession, and also the emphatic position of the pronoun (σὺ, *thou*): "*Thou* art *the* anointed, *the* Son of *the* God, *the* living."

17. **Blessed** (μακάριος). See on ch. v. 3.

18. **Thou art Peter** (σὺ εἶ Πέτρος). Christ responds to Peter's emphatic *thou* with another, equally emphatic. Peter says, "*Thou* art the Christ." Christ replies, "*Thou* art Peter." Πέτρος (*Peter*) is used as a proper name, but without losing its meaning as a common noun. The name was bestowed on Simon at his first interview with Jesus (John i. 42) under the form of its Aramaic equivalent, *Cephas*. In this passage attention is called, not to the giving of the name, but to its meaning. In classical Greek the word means a *piece of rock*, as in Homer, of Ajax throwing a *stone* at Hector ("Iliad," vii., 270), or of Patroclus grasping and hiding in his hand a jagged *stone* ("Iliad," xvi., 734).

On this rock (ἐπὶ ταύτῃ τῇ πέτρᾳ). The word is feminine, and means a *rock*, as distinguished from a *stone* or a *fragment of rock* (πέτρος, above). Used of a *ledge of rocks* or a *rocky peak*. In Homer ("Odyssey," ix., 243), the *rock* (πέτρην) which Polyphemus places at the door of his cavern, is a mass which two-and-twenty wagons could not remove; and the rock which he hurled at the retreating ships of Ulysses, created by its fall a wave in the sea which drove the ships back toward the land ("Odyssey," ix., 484). The word refers neither to *Christ* as a *rock*, distinguished from *Simon*, a *stone*, nor to *Peter's confession*, but to *Peter himself*, in a sense defined by his previous confession, and as enlightened by the "Father in Heaven."

The reference of πέτρα to Christ is forced and unnatural. The obvious reference of the word is to Peter. The emphatic *this* naturally refers to the nearest antecedent; and besides, the metaphor is thus weakened, since Christ appears here, not as the *foundation*, but as the *architect:* "On this rock *will I build*." Again, Christ is the great foundation, the "chief corner-stone," but the New Testament writers recognize no impropriety in applying to the members of Christ's church certain terms which are applied to him. For instance, Peter himself (1 Pet. ii. 4), calls Christ a *living stone*, and, in ver. 5, addresses the church as *living stones*. In Apoc. xxi. 14, the names of the twelve apostles appear in the twelve foundation-stones of the heavenly city; and in Eph. ii. 20, it is said, "Ye are built upon the foundation of *the apostles and prophets* (*i.e.*, *laid* by the apostles and prophets), Jesus Christ himself being the chief corner-stone."

Equally untenable is the explanation which refers πέτρα to Simon's confession. Both the play upon the words and the natural reading of the passage are against it, and besides, it does not conform to the fact, since the church is built, not on *confessions*, but on *confessors*—living men.

"The word πέτρα," says Edersheim, "was used in the same sense in Rabbinic language. According to the Rabbins, when God was about to build his world, he could not rear it on the generation of Enos, nor on that of the flood, who brought destruction upon the world; but when he beheld that Abraham would arise in the future, he said: 'Behold, I have found a *rock* to build on it, and to found the world,' whence, also, Abraham is called a rock, as it is said: 'Look unto the rock whence ye are hewn.' The parallel between Abraham and Peter might be carried even further. If, from a misunderstanding of the Lord's promise to Peter, later Christian legend represented the apostle as sitting at the gate of heaven, Jewish legend represents Abraham as sitting at the gate of Gehenna, so as to prevent all who had the seal of circumcision from falling into its abyss" ("Life and Times of Jesus").

The reference to Simon himself is confirmed by the actual relation of Peter to the early church, to the Jewish portion of which he was a foundation-stone. See Acts, i. 15; ii. 14, 37; iii. 12; iv. 8; v. 15, 29; ix. 34, 40; x. 25, 26; Gal. i. 18.

Church (*ἐκκλησίαν*), *ἐκ*, *out*, *καλέω*, to *call* or *summon*. This is the first occurrence of this word in the New Testament. Originally *an assembly of citizens, regularly summoned.* So in New Testament, Acts xix. 39. The Septuagint uses the word for the congregation of Israel, either as summoned for a definite purpose (1 Kings viii. 65), or for the community of Israel collectively, regarded as a congregation (Gen. xxviii. 3), where *assembly* is given for *multitude* in margin. In New Testament, of the congregation of Israel (Acts vii. 38); but for this there is more commonly employed *συναγωγή*, of which *synagogue* is a transcription; *σύν*, together, *ἄγω*, *to bring* (Acts xiii. 43). In Christ's words to Peter the word *ἐκκλησία* acquires special emphasis from the opposition implied in it to the synagogue. The Christian community in the midst of Israel would be designated as *ἐκκλησία*, without being confounded with the *συναγωγή*, the Jewish community. See Acts v. 11; viii. 1; xii. 1; xiv. 23, 27, etc. Nevertheless *συναγωγή* is applied to a Christian assembly in James ii. 2, while *ἐπισυναγωγή* (*gathering or assembling together*) is found in 2 Thess. ii. 1; Heb. x. 25. Both in Hebrew and in New Testament usage *ἐκκλησία* implies more than a collective or national unity; rather a community based on a special religious idea and established in a special way. In the New Testament the term is used also in the narrower sense of a single church, or a church confined to a particular place. So of the church in the house of Aquila and Priscilla (Rom. xvi. 5); the church at Corinth, the churches in Judea, the church at Jerusalem, etc.

Gates of hell (*πύλαι ᾅδου*). Rev., *Hades*. Hades was originally the name of the god who presided over the realm of the dead—Pluto or Dis. Hence the phrase, *house of Hades*. It is derived from *ἀ*, *not*, and *ἰδεῖν*, *to see*; and signifies, therefore, the *invisible land*, the realm of shadow. It is the place to which all who depart this life descend, without reference to their moral character.

By this word the Septuagint translated the Hebrew *Sheol*, which has a similar general meaning. The classical *Hades* embraced both good and bad men, though divided into *Elysium*, the abode of the virtuous, and *Tartarus*, the abode of the wicked. In these particulars it corresponds substantially with *Sheol;* both the godly and the wicked being represented as gathered into the latter. See Gen. xlii. 38; Ps. ix. 17; cxxxix. 8; Isa. xiv. 9; lvii. 2; Ezek. xxxii. 27; Hos. xiii. 14. Hades and Sheol were alike conceived as a definite place, lower than the world. The passage of both good and bad into it was regarded as a *descent*. The Hebrew conception is that of a place of darkness; a cheerless home of a dull, joyless, shadowy life. See Ps. vi. 5; xciv. 17; cxv. 17; lxxxviii. 5, 6, 10; Job x. 21; iii. 17–19; xiv. 10, 11; Eccl. ix. 5. Vagueness is its characteristic. In this the Hebrew's faith appears bare in contrast with that of the Greek and Roman. The pagan poets gave the popular mind definite pictures of Tartarus and Elysium; of Styx and Acheron; of happy plains where dead heroes held high discourse, and of black abysses where offenders underwent strange and ingenious tortures.

There was, indeed, this difference between the Hebrew and the Pagan conceptions; that to the Pagan, Hades was the final home of its tenants, while *Sheol* was a temporary condition. Hence the patriarchs are described (Heb. xi. 16) as looking for a better, heavenly country; and the martyrs as enduring in hope of "a better resurrection." Prophecy declared that the dead should arise and sing, when Sheol itself should be destroyed and its inmates brought forth, some to everlasting life, and others to shame and contempt (Isa. xxvi. 19; Hos. xiii. 14; Dan. xii. 2). Paul represents this promise as made to the fathers by God, and as the hope of his countrymen (Acts xxvi. 7). God was the God of the dead as well as of the living; present in the dark chambers of Sheol as well as in heaven (Ps. cxxxix. 8; xvi. 10). This is the underlying thought of that most touching and pathetic utterance of Job (xiv. 13–15), in which he breathes the wish that God would hide him with loving care in Hades, as a place of temporary concealment, where he will wait patiently, standing like a sentinel at his post, awaiting the divine voice calling him to a new and happier life. This, too, is the thought of the familiar and much-disputed passage, Job xix. 23–27. His *Redeemer*, *vindicator*, *aven-*

ger, shall arise after he shall have passed through the shadowy realm of Sheol. "A judgment in Hades, in which the judge will show himself his friend, in which all the tangled skein of his life will be unravelled by wise and kindly hands, and the insoluble problem of his strange and self-contradicting experience will at last be solved—*this* is what Job still looks for on that happy day when he shall see God for himself, and find his *Goel* (vindicator) in that Almighty Deliverer" (Cox, "Commentary on the Book of Job").

In the New Testament, Hades is the realm of the dead. It cannot be successfully maintained that it is, in particular, the place for sinners (so Cremer, "Biblico-Theological Lexicon"). The words about Capernaum (Matt. xi. 23), which it is surprising to find Cremer citing in support of this position, are merely a rhetorical expression of a fall from the height of earthly glory to the deepest degradation, and have no more bearing upon the moral character of Hades than the words of Zophar (Job xi. 7, 8) about the perfection of the Almighty. "It is high as *heaven*—deeper than *Sheol*." Hades is indeed coupled with Death (Apoc. i. 18; vi. 8; xx. 13, 14), but the association is natural, and indeed inevitable, apart from all moral distinctions. Death would naturally be followed by Hades in any case. In Apoc. xx. 13, 14, the general judgment is predicted, and not only Death and Hades, but the sea give up their dead, and only those who are not written in the book of life are cast into the lake of fire (ver. 15). The rich man was in Hades (Luke xvi. 23), and *in torments*, but Lazarus was also in Hades, "in Abraham's bosom." The details of this story "evidently represent the views current at the time among the Jews. According to them, the Garden of Eden and the Tree of Life were the abode of the blessed. . . . We read that the righteous in Eden see the wicked in Gehenna and rejoice; and similarly, that the wicked in Gehenna see the righteous sitting beatified in Eden, and their souls are troubled (Edersheim, "Life and Times of Jesus"). Christ also was in Hades (Acts ii. 27, 31). Moreover, the word γέεννα, *hell* (see on Matt. v. 22), is specially used to denote the place of future punishment.

Hades, then, in the New Testament, is a broad and general

conception, with an idea of *locality* bound up with it. It is the condition following death, which is blessed or the contrary, according to the moral character of the dead, and is therefore divided into different realms, represented by *Paradise* or *Abraham's bosom*, and *Gehenna*.

The expression *Gates of Hades* is an orientalism for the court, throne, power, and dignity of the infernal kingdom. Hades is contemplated as a mighty city, with formidable, frowning portals. Some expositors introduce also the idea of the *councils* of the Satanic powers, with reference to the Eastern custom of holding such deliberations in the gates of cities. Compare the expression *Sublime Porte*, applied to the Ottoman court. The idea of a *building* is maintained in both members of the comparison. The kingdom or city of Hades confronts and assaults the church which Christ will build upon the rock. See Job xxxviii. 17; Ps. ix. 13; cvii. 18; Isa. xxxviii. 10.

19. **Keys** (κλεῖδας). The similitude corresponding to *build*. The church or kingdom is conceived as a house, of which Peter is to be the steward, bearing the keys. "Even as he had been the first to utter the confession of the church, so was he also privileged to be the first to open its hitherto closed gates to the Gentiles, when God made choice of him, that, through his mouth, the Gentiles should first hear the words of the Gospel, and at his bidding first be baptized" (Edersheim, "Life and Times of Jesus").

Bind—loose (δήσῃς—λύσῃς). In a sense common among the Jews, of *forbidding* or *allowing*. No other terms were in more constant use in Rabbinic canon-law than those of *binding* and *loosing*. They represented the *legislative* and *judicial* powers of the Rabbinic office. These powers Christ now transferred, and that not in their pretension, but in their reality, to his apostles; the first, here, to Peter, as their representative, the second, after his resurrection, to the church (John xx. 23, Edersheim). "This legislative authority conferred upon Peter can only wear an offensive aspect when it is conceived of as possessing an arbitrary character, and as being in no way determined by the ethical influences of the Holy Spirit, and when it is regarded as being of an absolute nature, as independent of any connection with the rest of the apostles. Since the power of binding and loosing, which is here conferred upon Peter, is ascribed (Matt. xviii. 18) to the apostles generally, the power conferred upon the former is set in its proper light, and shown to be of necessity a power of a collegiate nature, so that Peter is not to be regarded as exclusively endowed with it, either in whole or in part, but is simply to be looked upon as first among his equals" (Meyer on Matt. xvi. 19; xviii. 18).

21. **From that time began** (ἀπὸ τότε ἤρξατο). He had not shown it to them before.

Must (δεῖ). It was *necessary* in fulfilment of the divine purpose. See Matt. xxvi. 54; Heb. viii. 3; Luke xxiv. 26.

Suffer. This first announcement mentions his passion and death generally; the second (xvii. 22, 23), adds his betrayal into the hands of sinners; the third (xx. 17–19), at length expresses his stripes, cross, etc.

Elders and chief priests and scribes. A circumstantial way of designating the *Sanhedrim*, or supreme council of the Jewish nation.

22. **Took** (προσλαβόμενος). Not, *took him by the hand*, but *took him apart to speak with him privately*. Meyer renders, correctly, *after he had taken him to himself*. "As if," says Bengel, "by a right of his own. He acted with greater familiarity after the token of acknowledgment had been given. Jesus, however, reduces him to his level."

Began. For Jesus did not suffer him to continue.

Be it far from thee (ἵλεώς σοι.) Rev., in margin, *God have mercy on thee*. In classical usage, of the gods as *propitious*, *gracious* toward men, in consideration of their prayers and sacrifices. The meaning here is, *may God be gracious to thee.*

Shall not be (*οὐ μὴ ἔσται*). The double negative is very forcible: "Shall *in no case* be." Rev. renders it by *never.*

23. **Turned** (*στραφεὶς*). Not *toward* Peter, but away from him.

Get thee behind me. See iv. 10.

Offence (*σκάνδαλον*). Rev., better, *stumbling-block.* See on v. 29. Not, *thou art offensive*, but *thou art in my way.* Dr. Morison, "Thou art not, as before, a noble block, lying in its right position as a massive foundation-stone. On the contrary, thou art like a stone quite out of its proper place, and lying right across the road in which I must go—lying as a stone of stumbling."

Savourest not (*οὐ φρονεῖς*). Rev., better, *mindest not.* Thy thoughts and intents are not of God, but of men. *Savourest* follows the Vulgate *sapis*, from *sapere*, which means 1st, *to have a taste or flavor of:* 2d, *to have sense or discernment.* Hence used here as the rendering of *φρονεῖν*, *to be minded.* Thus Wyc., 1 Cor. xiii., 11, "When I was a child I *savoured* (*ἐφρόνουν*) as a child." The idea is, strictly, *to partake of the quality or nature of.*

26. **Gain—lose** (*κερδήσῃ—ζημιωθῇ*). Note that both words are in the past (aorist) tense: "*if he may have gained or lost.* The Lord looks back to the details of each life as the factors of the final sum of gain or loss. For *lose*, Rev. gives *forfeit.* The verb in the active voice means *to cause loss or damage.* Often in the classics, of *fining* or *mulcting* in a sum of money. Compare 2 Cor. vii. 9.

Soul (*ψυχὴν*) Rev., *life*, with *soul* in margin. This will be specially considered in the discussion of the psychological terms in the Epistles.

In exchange (*ἀντάλλαγμα*). Lit., *as an exchange.*

CHAPTER XVII.

1. **Taketh** (παραλαμβάνει). Rev. gives the force of the preposition παρά, taketh *with* him.

Apart (κατ' ἰδίαν). Not said of the *mountain*, as isolated, but of the *disciples;* so that they might be alone with him. Compare Mark ix. 2, *apart by themselves* (κατ' ἰδίαν μόνους: lit., *apart alone*).

2. **He was transfigured** (μετεμορφώθη), μετά, denoting *change* or *transfer*, and μορφή, *form*. This latter word denotes the *form* regarded as the distinctive nature and character of the object, and is distinguished from σχῆμα, the changeable, outward *fashion:* in a man, for instance, his gestures, clothes, words, acts. The μορφή partakes of the *essence* of a thing; the σχῆμα is an *accident* which may change, leaving the *form* unaffected. Compare Mark xvi. 12; Christ "appeared in another *form*" (μορφή), and 1 Cor. vii. 31: "the *fashion* (σχῆμα) of the world passeth away." The distinction passes into the verbs compounded with these two nouns. Thus, Rom. xii. 2, "Be not *conformed* to this world," is μὴ συσχηματίζεσθε; *i.e.*, be not fashioned according to the fleeting *fashion* of this world. So Rev., *fashioned.* See, also, 2 Cor. xi. 13, 14, 15, where the changes described are changes in outward semblance. False apostles appeared in the outward fashion of apostles of Christ; Satan takes on the outward appearance of an angel. All these changes are in the *accidents* of the life, and do not touch its inner, essential *quality*. On the other hand, a change in the *inner* life is described as a change of μορφή, never of σχῆμα. Hence, Rom. xii. 2, "Be ye *transformed* (μεταμορφοῦσθε); the change taking place by the renewing of the *mind.* Compare Rom. viii. 29; 2 Cor. iii. 18; Philip. iii. 21; and see, further, on Philip. ii. 6, 7.

Why, then, it may be asked, is a compound of μορφή employed in this description of the transfigured Saviour, since the change described is a change in his outward appearance? It may be answered, because a compound of σχῆμα, expressing merely a change in the aspect of Christ's person and garments, would not express the deeper truth of the case, which is, that the visible change gets its real character and meaning from that which is *essential* in our Lord—his divine nature. A foreshadowing or prophecy of his true *form*—his distinctive character—comes out in his transfiguration. He passes over into a form identified, so far as revealed, with the divine quality of his being, and prophetic of his revelation "as he is" (1 John iii. 2), in the glory which he had with the Father before the world was (John xvii. 5). In truth, there is a deep and pregnant hint in the use of this word, which easily escapes observation, and which defies accurate definition. The profound and overwhelming impression upon the three disciples was due to something besides the shining of Christ's face and garments, and the presence of Moses and Elijah; and was deeper and subtler than the effect of all these combined. There was a fact and a power in that vision which mere radiance and the appearance of the dead patriarchs could not wholly convey: a revelation of Deity breaking out in that glorified face and form, which appealed to something deeper than sense, and confirmed the words from heaven: *This is my beloved Son.*

The same truth is illustrated in the use of μορφή in Mark xvi. 12, where it is said that Jesus appeared *in a different form* (ἐν ἑτέρᾳ μορφῇ) after his resurrection. The accidents of figure, face, pierced hands and feet, were the same; but an indefinable change had passed upon him, the characteristic of which was that it prefigured his passing into the condition peculiar and appropriate to his essential spiritual and divine being.

4. **Let us make** (ποιήσωμεν). But the best texts read, ποιήσω, *I will make*, which is more characteristic of Peter. He would erect the booths himself.

Three **tabernacles** (σκηνάς). *Tents* or *booths*, out of the brushwood lying near. Peter realized that it was night, and was for preparing shelters into which the heavenly visitants might retire after their interview.

9. **Vision** (*ὅραμα*). The spectacle.

11. **Cometh.** Elijah cometh first. An abstract statement expressing the fact that Elijah's coming precedes in time the coming of the Messiah. It is a point of Jewish chronology; just as a teacher of history might say to his pupils, "The Saxons and Danes precede the Normans in England." Elijah had already come in the person of John the Baptist.

15. **Is lunatic** (*σεληνιάζεται*). Rev., *epileptic*. The A. V. preserves the etymology of the word (*σελήνη*, *the moon*), but *lunatic* conveys to us the idea of *demented;* while the Rev. *epileptic* gives the true character of the disease, yet does not tell us the fact contained in the Greek word, that epilepsy was supposed to be affected by the changes of the moon. See on Matt. iv. 24.

17. **Perverse** (*διεστραμμένη*). Wyc., *wayward.* Tynd., *crooked; διά, throughout; στρέφω, to twist. Warped.*

20. **Unbelief** (*ἀπιστίαν*). But the better reading is *ὀλιγοπιστίαν, littleness of faith.* Hence Rev., *Because of your little faith.*

24. **They that received tribute-money** (*οἱ τὰ δίδραχμα λαμβάνοντες*). Rev., *They that received the half-shekel.* Every male Israelite of age, including proselytes and manumitted Jews, was expected to pay annually for the temple-service a half-shekel or *didrachm*, about thirty-five cents. This must be paid in the ancient money of Israel, the regular half-shekel of the treasury; and the money-changers, therefore, were in demand to change the current into the temple coin, which they did at a rate of discount fixed by law, between four and five cents on every half-shekel. The annual revenue to the money-changers from this source has been estimated at nearly forty-five thousand dollars; a very large sum in a country where a laborer received less than twenty cents for a day's work, and where the good Samaritan left about thirty-three cents at the

inn for the keeping of the wounded man. Jesus attacked a very powerful interest when he overthrew the tables of the money-changers.

25. **Yes** (ναί). Indicating that Jesus had paid the tax on former occasions.

Prevented (προέφθασεν). Rev., rather awkwardly, but following Tynd., *Spake first to him. Prevent*, in its older sense, *to anticipate*, *get before*, was a correct translation. Compare Shakspeare:

> "So shall my anticipation *prevent* your discovery."
> *Hamlet*, ii., 1.

Out of this grew the secondary meaning, *to hinder*. By *getting before* another, one *hinders* him from accomplishing his purpose. This meaning has supplanted the other. Wyc. renders *came before him*. The meaning is that Jesus did not wait for Peter to tell him of the demand of the collectors. He *anticipated* him in speaking about it.

Custom or **tribute** (τέλη ἢ κῆνσον). Rev. gives *toll* for *custom*. *Toll* is duty upon goods; *tribute*, tax upon individuals. Κῆνσος, *tribute*, is merely a transcription of the Latin *census*, which means, first, a *registration* with a view to taxation, and then the tax itself.

Strangers (ἀλλοτρίων). Not *foreigners*, but others than those of their own families; their *subjects*. In other words, Does a king tax his own children or his subjects?

27. **Hook** (ἄγκιστρον). The only mention in the New Testament of fishing with a hook. A single fish is wanted.

A piece of money (στατῆρα). The A. V. is very inadequate, because Christ names a definite sum, the *stater*, which is a literal transcription of the Greek word, and represents two didrachmas, or a *shekel*. Hence Rev., *a shekel*.

CHAPTER XVIII.

1. The Rev. inserts *then* after *who*, thus restoring the Greek *ἄρα*, which the A. V. overlooks. *Who then? Who, as things stand.* Since one of our number has been doubly honored in being called "the rock," and in being appointed to take part in a special miracle, who *then* is greatest?

3. **Be converted** (*στραφῆτε*). The word *converted* has acquired a conventional religious sense which is fundamentally truthful, but the essential quality of which will be more apparent if we render literally, as Rev., *except ye turn.* The picture is that of turning round in a road and facing the other way.

Shall not enter (*οὐ μὴ εἰσέλθητε*). But the double negative is very forcible, and is given in Rev. *in nowise.* So far from being greatest in the kingdom of heaven, ye shall not so much as *enter.*

4. **As this little child.** Not, as this little child *humbles himself*, but, shall make himself humble as this little child *is* lowly; shall willingly become by spiritual process what the child is by nature.

5. **In my name** (*ἐπὶ τῷ ὀνόματί μου*). Lit., *upon* my name; *on the ground of*, or *on account of; for my sake.*

6. **A millstone** (*μύλος ὀνικὸς*). Two kinds of millstones were in use; the one turned by hand, the other, and larger, by an ass (*ὄνος*). Here Jesus says an *ass-millstone;* or, as Rev., *a great millstone;* Wyc., *millstone of asses.*

12. **Leave upon the mountains.** The text here is disputed. Both A. V. and Rev. follow a text which reads: "Doth he not, leaving the ninety and nine, go into the mountains?" Rather join *leave* with *on the mountains*, and read, "Will he not leave the ninety and nine upon (ἐπὶ, *scattered over*) the mountains, and go," etc. This also corresponds with ἀφήσει, *leaving*, *letting out*, or *letting loose*.

13. **If so be** (ἐὰν γένηται). If it should so come to pass. God's grace is not irresistible.

14. **The will of your Father** (θέλημα ἔμπροσθεν τοῦ πατρὸς ὑμῶν). Though some read *my* Father (μοῦ). Lit., *There is not a will before your* (my) *Father*. So Wyc., *It is not will before your Father*. Meyer paraphrases, *There is not before the face of God any determination having as its object that one of these*, etc.

15. **Go** (ὕπαγε). Do not wait for him to come to you.

Tell him his fault (ἔλεγξον). Rev., *shew* him. The verb means, first, to *test*, *try*, *search out;* therefore, to *cross-examine* with a view of convincing or refuting; thence to *rebuke* or *chide*. The Rev. *shew* is better than *tell*, which implies merely *naming* the fault; whereas the injunction is, go and *prove* to him how he has erred. Wyc., *reprove*, with *snub* as explanation.

16. **In the mouth** (ἐπὶ στόματος). Better Rev., "*at* the mouth," or on the testimony of.

19. **Shall agree** (συμφωνήσουσιν). From σύν, *together*, and φωνή, *sound* or *voice*. Transcribed in our word *symphony*. It has so far lost its distinctive character as a concord of *voices* as to be used for agreement in the deeper and more inward sense.

Concerning anything that they shall ask (περὶ παντὸς πράγματος οὗ ἐὰν αἰτήσωνται). The literal rendering is, if any thing, stronger: *Everything, whatever it be, for which they may have asked.* Wyc., *Shall consent of everything whatever they shall ask.* Tynd., *Shall agree in any manner thing whatsoever they shall desire.* The word πρᾶγμα, *thing*, is used like the Latin *res;* a *matter, affair, business*, with the meaning at bottom of something to be *done*, since it is cognate to the verb πράσσω, *to do.* *Shall be done*, however, is γενήσεται, *it shall come to pass.*

20. **In my name** (εἰς τὸ ἐμὸν ὄνομα). Lit., "*into* my name." When two or three are drawn together *into* Christ as the common centre of their desire and faith.

22. **Seventy times seven** (ἑβδομηκοντάκις ἑπτά).* It was a settled rule of Rabbinism that forgiveness should not be extended more than three times. Even so, the practice was terribly different. The Talmud relates, without blame, the conduct of a rabbi who would not forgive a very small slight of his dignity, though asked by the offender for thirteen successive years, and that on the day of atonement; the reason being that the offended rabbi had learned by a dream that his offending brother would attain the highest dignity; whereupon he feigned himself irreconcilable, to force the other to migrate from Palestine to Babylon, where, unenvied by him, he might occupy the chief place (Edersheim). It must, therefore, have seemed to Peter a stretch of charity to extend forgiveness from three to seven times. Christ is not specifying a number of times greater than the limit of seven. He means that there is to be *no* limit. "Forgiveness is *qualitative*, not *quantitative*."

---

* It is uncertain whether this means four hundred and ninety times, or seventy-seven times. Those who maintain the latter, claim that the expression is derived from the Septuagint, Gen. iv., 24. Authorities, however, do not agree on the rendering of the Hebrew in that passage. Meyer says it cannot possibly mean anything else than seventy-seven, while Bunsen renders seven times seventy, and Grotius *septuagies et id ipsum septies*, "seventy times and that seven times over." The point, however, is unimportant, for, as Dr. Morison observes, "So far as the *spirit* of our Saviour's answer is concerned, both enumerations are right."

23. **A certain king** (ἀνθρώπῳ βασιλεῖ). Lit., a *man*, a *king*. The kingdom of heaven is like unto a *human* king.

Take account of his servants (συνᾶραι λόγον μετὰ τῶν δούλων αὐτοῦ). The rendering of the A. V. is loose and inadequate, and might be taken to mean *to reckon the number of his servants*. The verb συνᾶραι is compounded of σύν, *with*, and αἴρω, *to take up*, and means literally *to take up together*, *i.e.*, *cast up*, as an *account*. The A. V. also overlooks the force of μετὰ,* *with*. Therefore, Rev., better, *make a reckoning with his servants*.

24. **Which owed him** (ὀφειλέτης). Lit., *a debtor* of ten thousand talents.

Ten thousand talents. An enormous sum; about twelve millions of dollars.

25. **To be sold.** According to the law of Moses: Ex. xxii. 3; Lev. xxv. 39, 47.

28. **Found.** Either went in search of him, as he himself had been sought out by his lord, or came upon him accidentally in the street.

A hundred pence (ἑκατὸν δηνάρια). Less than a millionth part of his own debt.

Took him by the throat (αὐτὸν ἔπνιγεν). Lit., *throttled*. Wyc., *strangled*. Compare *were choked*, Mark v. 13. Creditors often dragged their debtors before the judge, as the Roman law allowed them to do, holding them by the throat. Thus Livy (iv. 53), relates how, a difficulty having arisen between the consul Valerius and one Menenius, the tribunes put an end to the contest, and the consul ordered into prison (*collum torsisset, twisted the neck*) the few who appealed. And Cicero ("Pro Cluentio," xxi.): "Lead him to the judgment-seat with twisted neck (*collo obtorto*)." Compare Cicero, "In C. Verrem," iv., 10.

What thou owest (εἴ τι ὀφείλεις). Lit., *If thou owest anything.* Not that the creditor is uncertain about the *fact* of the debt, though some uncertainty about the exact amount may be implied. This would agree with *found*, in the sense of coming upon accidentally. Compare Matt. xiii. 44. He came suddenly upon him and recognized him as a debtor, though not certain as to the amount of his debt. Meyer remarks, "The *if* is simply the expression of a pitiless logic. If thou owest anything (as thou dost) pay!" The word *pay* (ἀπόδος) is emphatic in position.

29. **Besought** (παρεκάλει). The imperfect has the force of *earnestly* besought.

30. **Went** (ἀπελθὼν). Lit. went *away:* dragging the other with him to judgment.

31. **Told** (διεσάφησαν). More than merely *narrated.* The verb is from διά, *throughout*, and σαφέω, to *explain.* They explained the circumstances throughout.

Their Lord (τῷ κυρίῳ ἑαυτῶν). Lit., "their *own* Lord;" as befitted their position, and as a mark of their confidence in him.

34. **To the tormentors** (βασανισταῖς). Livy pictures an old centurion complaining that he was taken by his creditor, not into servitude, but to a workhouse and torture, and showing his back scarred with fresh wounds (ii., 23).

CHAPTER XIX.

1. **Coasts** (ὅρια). Better Rev., *borders;* though it is easy to see how the translation *coasts* arose, *coast* being derived from the Latin *costa, a side*, and hence a *border* generally, though now applied to the sea-side only.

3. **Tempting.** See on Matt. vi. 13.

For every cause. The *temptation* turned upon the dispute dividing the two great Rabbinical schools, the one of which (that of Hillel) held that a man might divorce his wife for any reason which rendered her distasteful to him; and the other (that of Shammai) that divorce was allowable only in case of unchastity. The querists would be anxious to know which side Jesus espoused.

5. **Shall cleave** (κολληθήσεται). Lit., *shall be glued.*

Shall be one flesh (ἔσονται εἰς σάρκα μίαν). Lit., "*into* one flesh;" Wyc., *two in one flesh.*

6. **What** (ὃ). Not *those.* Christ is contemplating, not the *individuals*, but the *unity* which God cemented; and so Wyc., *that thing that God enjoined; i.e.*, knit together. The aorist tense (denoting the occurrence of an event at some past time, considered as a momentary act) seems to refer to the original ordinance of God at the creation (ver. 4).

7. **Writing** (βιβλίον). Rev., *bill.* The word is a diminutive of βίβλος, which originally means the inner bark of the papyrus, used for writing, then a book or roll of this bark; hence a *paper*, *bill.*

8. **Because of** (πρὸς). Rev., *for:* having regard to.

It was not so (οὐ γέγονεν οὕτως). The A. V. is commonly understood to mean, *it was not so in the beginning.* But that is not Christ's meaning. The verb is in the perfect tense (denoting the continuance of past action or its results down to the present). He means: Notwithstanding Moses' permission, the case *has not been* so from the beginning until now. The original ordinance has never been abrogated nor superseded, but continues in force.

9. **Except for fornication** (μὴ ἐπὶ πορνείᾳ). Lit., *not on account of fornication.*

10. **The case** (*αἰτία*). Not the *relation* of the man to his wife, nor *the circumstances, the state of the case. Αἰτία* refers to *cause* (ver. 3), and the meaning is, if the matter stands thus with reference to the *cause* which the man must have for putting away his wife.

14. **Suffer** (*ἄφετε*). Lit., *leave alone.* Compare Mark xiv. 6; xv. 36; Luke xiii. 8. Sir J. Cheke: *Let these children alone.*

17. **Why callest thou me good?** (*τί με λέγεις ἀγαθόν*). But the true reading is, *τί με ἐρωτᾷς περὶ τοῦ ἀγαθοῦ*; *Why askest thou me concerning the good?*

There is none good but one, that is God (*οὐδεὶς ἀγαθὸς εἰ μὴ εἷς ὁ Θεός*). But the reading is, *εἷς ἐστὶν ὁ ἀγαθός*, *One there is who is good.* The saying of Christ appears especially appropriate in the light of the Rabbinic apothegm, "There is nothing else that is good but the law."

24. **Camel — through a needle's eye** (*κάμηλον διά τρύπηματος ῥαφίδος*). See on Mark x. 25; Luke xviii. 25. Compare the Jewish proverb, that a man did not even in his dreams see an elephant pass through the eye of a needle. The reason why the camel was substituted for the elephant was because the proverb was from the Babylonian Talmud, and in Babylon the elephant was common, while in Palestine it was unknown. The Koran has the same figure: "The impious shall find the gates of heaven shut; nor shall he enter there till a camel shall pass through the eye of a needle." Bochart, in his history of the animals of scripture, cites a Talmudic passage: "A needle's eye is not too narrow for two friends, nor is the world wide enough for two enemies." The allusion is not to be explained by reference to a *narrow gate* called a *needle's eye.*

26. **This** (*τοῦτο*). Not the salvation of *rich* men, but salvation in general. It is in answer to the question, *who can be*

saved? Man cannot save himself nor his fellow. God only can save him.

27. **We.** Emphatic, in contrast with the young ruler.

28. **Have followed.** "Peter had said *together* the words *we have left, we have followed.* Jesus replies to them *separately;* for the latter was peculiar to the apostles, the former common to them with others" (Bengel).

In the regeneration. The final restitution of all things. To be construed with *ye shall sit.*

Shall sit (καθίσῃ). Or *shall have taken his seat,* which brings out more vividly the solemn inauguration of Christ's judgment.

29. **Every one** (πᾶς). Compare 2 Tim. iv. 8, "to *all* them that love his appearing." "Not only apostles, nor ought Peter to have inquired only concerning them" (Bengel). The promise hitherto restricted to the apostles now becomes general.

A hundred-fold (ἑκατονταπλασίονα). But many very high authorities read πολλαπλασίονα, *manifold.* So Rev. in margin. Compare Mark x. 30, where there is added "houses and brethren," etc. Also the Arabic proverb: "Purchase the next world with this; so shalt thou win both."

CHAPTER XX.

1. **For** (γάρ). Explaining and confirming xix. 30.

Early in the morning (ἅμα πρωῒ). *Along with the dawn.* "Here (at Hamadan, in Persia), we observed every morning, before the sun rose, that a numerous band of peasants were collected, with spades in their hands, waiting to be hired for the day to work in the surrounding fields. This custom struck me as a most happy illustration of our Saviour's parable, particularly when, passing by the same place late in the day, we found others standing idle, and remembered his words, 'Why stand ye here all the day idle?' as most applicable to their situation; for on putting the very same question to them, they answered us, 'Because no man hath hired us.'" (Morier, "Second Journey through Persia," cited by Trench, "Parables.")

2. **For a penny** (ἐκ δηναρίου). A *denarius*, the chief silver coin of the Romans at this time, and of the value of about seventeen cents. We must remember to reckon according to the rate of wages in that day. A denarius was regarded as good pay for a day's work. It was the pay of a Roman soldier in Christ's time. In almost every case where the word occurs in the New Testament it is connected with the idea of a liberal or large amount. Compare Matt. xviii. 28; Mark vi. 37; Luke vii. 41; John xii. 5.

For a penny is, literally, *out of* or *on the strength of* a penny; the payment being that on the strength of which the agreement was made. The agreement arose *out of* the demand on the one hand and the promise on the other.

10. **Every man a penny** (τὸ ἀνὰ δηνάριον). Lit., *the sum amounting in each case to a penny; or a penny apiece*. *'Ανά* is distributive. Wyc., *each one by himself a penny.*

12. **Heat** (καύσωνα). Rev., *the scorching heat.* The word is from *καίω, to burn.* It refers to the dry, scorching heat borne by the east wind. Compare Job xxvii. 21; Hos. xiii. 15. The wind blows from the Arabian desert, parching, dry, exciting the blood, and causing restlessness and sleeplessness. It seldom brings storms, but when it does, they are doubly destructive. During harvest the corn cannot be winnowed if the east wind blows, for it would carry away both chaff and corn. In Pharaoh's dream (Gen. xli. 6) the ears are blasted by it: Jonah's gourd is withered by it (Jon. iv. 8), and the vine in Ezekiel's parable of the Babylonian captivity is blighted by it (Ezek. xvii. 10).

13. **One.** Representing the whole body.

Friend (ἑταῖρε). Lit., *companion, comrade.*

14. **Take** (ἆρον). Lit., as Rev., *take up*, as if the money had been laid down for him on a table or counter.

I will give (θέλω δοῦναι). But, as in other cases in the A. V., this may be mistaken for the simple future of the verb; whereas there are two verbs. Therefore, Rev., rightly, *It is my will to give.* See on Matt. xv. 32.

21. **Grant** (εἰπὲ). Lit., *speak; i.e.*, with authority. Compare "*command* these stones," Matt. iv. 3; "*bid* you," Matt. xxiii. 3. Rev., *command.*

26. **Will be great** (θέλῃ εἶναι). See on ver. 14. Rev. *would be.*

Minister (διάκονος). **Servant,** ver. 27 (δοῦλος). Δοῦλος, perhaps from δέω, *to bind*, is the *bondman*, representing the permanent *relation* of servitude. Διάκονος, probably from the same root as διώκω, *to pursue*, represents a servant, not in his relation, but in his *activity*. The term covers both slaves and hired servants. The attendants at the feast at Cana (John ii. 5) are called διάκονοι. In the epistles διάκονος is often used specifically for a *minister of the Gospel* (1 Cor. iii. 5; 2 Cor. iii. 6; Eph. iii. 7). The word *deacon* is, moreover, almost a transcription of it (Philip. i. 1; 1 Tim. iii. 8, 12). It is applied to Phoebe (Rom. xvi. 1).

28. **A ransom for many.** Compare Sophocles, "Oed. Col.," 488.

> "For one soul working in the strength of love
> Is mightier than ten thousand to atone."

30. **That Jesus passed by** (ὅτι Ἰησοῦς παράγει). The ὅτι is equivalent to quotation marks. They heard the crowd cry *Jesus is passing!*

CHAPTER XXI.

1. **Bethphage.** House of figs.

2. **A colt with her.** The Lord does not separate the colt from its dam.

3. **The Lord** (ὁ κύριος). From κῦρος, *supreme power, authority*. Hence κύριος, *one having authority, lord, owner, ruler*. In classical Greek, used of the gods, and in inscriptions applied to different gods, as Hermes, Zeus, etc.; also of the head of the family, who is *lord* (κύριος) of the wife and children (1 Sam. i. 8, Sept.); while to the slaves he is δεσπότης. In the Pauline writings, however, the master of slaves is called both δεσπότης (1 Tim. vi. 1, 2; Tit. ii. 9; 1 Pet. ii. 18), and κύριος (Eph. vi. 9; Col. iv. 1).

In the Septuagint it is used by Sarah of her husband (Gen. xviii. 12; compare 1 Pet. iii. 6). Joseph is called *lord* of the country (Gen. xlii. 33), and is addressed by his brethren as *my lord* (xlii. 10). It is applied to God (Gen. xviii. 27; Ex. iv. 10). In the New Testament it is a name for God (Matt. i. 20, 22, 24; ii. 15; Acts xi. 16; xii. 11, 17; Apoc. i. 8). As applied to Christ, it does not express his divine nature and power. These are indicated by some accompanying word or phrase, as *my God* (John xx. 28); *of all* (Acts x. 36); *to the glory of God the Father* (Philip. ii. 11); *of glory* (1 Cor. ii. 8); so that, as a title of Christ, *Lord* is used in the sense of *Master* or *Ruler*, or in address, *Sir* (Matt. xxii. 43, 45; Luke ii. 11; vi. 46; John xiii. 13, 14; 1 Cor. viii. 6). *Ὁ κύριος, the Lord*, is used of Christ by Matthew only once (xxi. 3) until after the resurrection (xxviii. 6). In the other gospels and in the Acts it occurs far oftener. Nevertheless, in the progress of Christian thought in the New Testament, the meaning develops toward a specific designation of the divine Saviour, as may be seen in the phrases *Jesus Christ our Lord, Our Lord Jesus Christ, Our Lord, Jesus our Lord.*

5. **Daughter of Sion.** Jerusalem. Compare *daughter of Babylon* for the city of Babylon (Ps. cxxxvii. 8; Isa. xlvii. 1); *daughter of Tyre* for the city or people of Tyre (Ps. xlv. 12); *daughter of my people* (Isa. xxii. 4).

Sitting (ἐπιβεβηκὼς). Lit., *having gone upon*, or *mounted*. Rev., *riding*.

Foal of an ass (υἱὸν ὑποζυγίου). Lit., *son of a beast-of-burden*. Ὑποζύγιον, from ὑπό, *beneath*, ζυγός, *a yoke*. Wyc., *son of a beast-under-yoke*. The phrase emphasizes the humble state of Jesus. He is mounted, not on a stately charger with embroidered and jewelled housings, nor even on an ass for the saddle, the Eastern ass being often of great beauty and spirit, and in demand for this purpose. He rides on a common beast-of-burden, furnished with the every-day garments of his disciples.

Garments (ἱμάτια). Outer garments. See on Matt. v. 40.

7. **Set him thereon.** But the preferable reading is ἐπεκάθισεν, *he took his seat upon*.

A very great multitude (ὁ πλεῖστος ὄχλος). The A. V. is wrong. The reference is not to the *size*, but to the *proportionate part* of the multitude which followed him. Hence Rev., correctly, *The most part of the multitude*.

Their garments (ἑαυτῶν). Lit., "their *own* garments." The disciples spread their garments on the beasts; the multitude strewed *their own* garments in the way. Dr. Edward Robinson, cited by Dr. Morison, speaking of the inhabitants of Bethlehem who had participated in the rebellion of 1834, says: "At that time, when some of the inhabitants were already imprisoned, and all were in deep distress, Mr. Farrar, then English consul at Damascus, was on a visit to Jerusalem, and had rode out with Mr. Nicolayson to Solomon's Pools. On their return, as they rose the ascent to enter Bethlehem, hundreds of people, male and female, met them, imploring the consul to interfere in their behalf, and afford them his protection; and all at once, by a sort of simultaneous movement, they spread their garments in the way before the horses."

The variation of tenses is not preserved in the English versions. *Spread their garments*, aorist tense, denoting one definite act. *Cut down*, *spread in the way*, imperfects, denoting continued action. As Jesus advanced, they *kept cutting* branches and *spreading* them, and the multitude *kept crying*.

9. **Hosanna.** *O save!*

10. **Was moved** (ἐσείσθη). *Moved* is hardly strong enough. It is *shaken* as by an earthquake. Rev., *stirred*. As Morison happily observes, "a profounder ground-swell of feeling."

12. **The money-changers** (κολλυβιστῶν). From κόλλυβος, *the rate of exchange*. These changers sat in the temple, in the court of the Gentiles, to change the foreign coins of pilgrims into the shekel of the sanctuary for payment of the annual tribute. See on Matt. xvii. 24.

13. **Thieves** (λῃστῶν). Rev., correctly, *robbers*. See on Matt. xxvi. 55; Luke x. 30.

16. **Say** (λέγουσιν). The Rev. is more graphic, *are saying*. While the songs and shouts are rising, the priests turn angrily to Christ with the question, "Hearest thou what these are saying?"

Thou hast perfected (κατηρτίσω). The same word as at Matt. iv. 21, where it is used of adjusting or mending nets. Its secondary meaning is to *furnish completely*, *equip*; hence to *perfect*. Thou hast provided the perfection of praise. The quotation from Ps. viii. 2, follows the Septuagint, and not the Hebrew, which is, "Thou hast *founded* strength."

19. **A fig-tree** (συκῆν μίαν). Lit., *one single* fig-tree. Rev., in margin.

Presently (παραχρῆμα). *Presently*, in popular speech, has acquired something of a future force. I will do such a thing *presently* means, I will do it, not *immediately*, but *soon*. The rendering here was correct in the older English sense of *instantly*. So constantly in Shakspeare:

"PROSPERO. Go, bring the rabble,
O'er whom I gave thee pow'r, here, to this place.
ARIEL. Presently?
PROS. Ay, with a twink.
AR. Before you can say 'come,' and 'go,'
And breathe twice; and cry 'so so;'
Each one tripping on his toe
Will be here." *Tempest*, iv., 1.

Compare ver. 20. "How did the fig-tree *immediately* wither away?" Rev.

29. **Repented** (μεταμεληθεὶς). This is a different word from that in Matt. iii. 2; iv. 17; μετανοεῖτε, *Repent ye*. Though it is fairly claimed that the word here implies all that is implied in the other word, the New Testament writers evidently recognize a distinction, since the noun which corresponds to the verb in this passage (μεταμέλεια) is not used at all in the New Testament, and the verb itself only five times; and, in every case except the two in this passage (see ver. 32), with a meaning quite foreign to repentance in the ordinary gospel sense. Thus it is used of Judas, when he brought back the thirty pieces (Matt. xxvii. 3); of Paul's not regretting his letter to the Corinthians (2 Cor. vii. 8); and of God (Heb. vii. 21). On the other hand, μετανοέω, *repent*, used by John and Jesus in their summons to repentance (Matt. iii. 2; iv. 17), occurs thirty-four times, and the noun μετάνοια, *repentance* (Matt. iii. 8, 11), twenty-four times, and in every case with reference to that change of heart and life wrought by the Spirit of God, to which remission of sins and salvation are promised. It is not impossible, therefore, that the word in this passage may have been intended to carry a different shade of meaning, now lost to us. Μεταμέλομαι, as its etymology indicates (μετά, *after*, and μέλω, *to be an object of care*), implies an *after-care*, as contrasted with the *change of*

mind denoted by *μετάνοια*. Not sorrow for moral obliquity and sin against God, but annoyance at the consequences of an act or course of acts, and chagrin at not having known better. "It may be simply what our fathers were wont to call *hadiwist* (had-I-wist, or known better, I should have acted otherwise)" (Trench). *Μεταμέλεια* refers chiefly to single acts; *μετάνοια* denotes the repentance which affects the whole life. Hence the latter is often found in the imperative: *Repent ye* (Matt. iii. 2; iv. 17; Acts ii. 38; iii. 19); the former never. Paul's recognition of the distinction (2 Cor. vii. 10) is noteworthy. "Godly sorrow worketh *repentance* (*μετάνοιαν*) unto salvation," a salvation or repentance "which bringeth no regret on thinking of it afterwards" (*ἀμεταμέλητον*). There is no occasion for one ever to *think better* of either his repentance or the salvation in which it issued.

33. **Hedged it round about** (*φραγμὸν αὐτῷ περιέθηκεν*). Rev., more literally, *set a hedge about it;* possibly of the thorny wild aloe, common in the East.

Digged a wine-press (*ὤρυξεν ληνὸν*). In Isa. v. 1, 2, which this parable at once recalls, the Hebrew word rendered by the Septuagint and here *digged*, is *hewed out*, *i.e.*, from the solid rock. "Above the road on our left are the outlines of a winefat, one of the most complete and best preserved in the country. Here is the upper basin where the grapes were trodden and pressed. A narrow channel cut in the rock conveyed the juice into the lower basin, where it was allowed to settle; from there it was drawn off into a third and smaller basin. There is no mistaking the purpose for which those basins were excavated in the solid rock" (Thomson, "Land and Book").

A tower (*πύργον*). For watchmen. Stanley ("Sinai and Palestine") describes the ruins of vineyards in Judea as enclosures of loose stones, with the square gray tower at the corner of each. Allusions to these watching-places, temporary and permanent, are frequent in Scripture. Thus, "*a booth in a vineyard*" (Isa. i. 8). "The earth moveth to and fro like a *hammock*" (so Cheyne on Isa.; A. V., *cottage;* Rev., *hut*), a vineyard-watchman's deserted hammock tossed to and fro by the storm (Isa. xxiv. 20). So Job speaks of a *booth* which the keeper of a vineyard runneth up (xxvii. 18), a hut made of sticks and hung with mats, erected only for the harvest season on the field or vineyard, for the watchman who spreads his rude bed upon its high platform, and mounts guard against the robber and the beast. In Spain, where, especially in the South, the Orient has left its mark, not only upon architecture but also upon agricultural implements and methods, Archbishop Trench says that he has observed similar temporary structures erected for watchmen in the vineyards. The *tower* alluded to in this passage would seem to have been of a more permanent character (see Stanley above), and some have thought that it was intended not only for watching, but as a storehouse for the wine and a lodging for the workmen.

Let it out (*ἐξέδετο*). "There were three modes of dealing with land. According to one of these, the laborers employed received a certain portion of the fruits, say a third or a fourth of the produce. The other two modes were, either that the tenant paid a money-rent to the proprietor, or else that he agreed to give the owner a definite amount of the produce, whether the harvest had been good or bad. Such leases were given by the year or for life; sometimes the lease was even hereditary, passing from father to son. There can scarcely be a doubt that it is the latter kind of lease which is referred to in the parable: the lessees being bound to give the owner a certain amount of fruits in their season" (Edersheim, "Life and Times of Jesus"). Compare ver. 34, and Mark xii. 2, "that he might receive *of* the fruits" (*ἀπὸ τῶν καρπῶν*).

37. **They will reverence** (*ἐντραπήσονται*). The verb literally means to *turn toward;* hence to *give heed to, pay respect to.*

41. **He will miserably destroy those wicked men** (*κακοὺς κακῶς ἀπολέσει αὐτούς*). There is a play upon the words which the A. V. misses and the Rev. preserves by rendering "*miser-*

ably destroy those *miserable* men." So the Rheims version: "The *naughty* men will he bring to *naught*." Tynd., "He will *evil* destroy those *evil* persons." The order of the Greek words is also striking: *Miserable men, miserably he will destroy them.*

Which (οἵτινες). The compound Greek pronoun marks the character of the new husbandmen more distinctly than the simple *which*; husbandmen *of such a character* that, or *belonging to that class* of honest men who will give him his due.

44. **Shall be broken** (συνθλασθήσεται). The verb is stronger: *broken to pieces*; so Rev.

Grind him to powder (λικμήσει αὐτόν). But the A. V. misses the picture in the word, which is that of the *winnowing-fan* that separates the grain from the chaff. Literally it is, *will winnow him.* Rev., *scatter him as dust.*

CHAPTER XXII.

2. **Made a marriage** (ἐποίησεν γάμους). But the phrase refers to the *marriage-feast*, rather than to the marriage-ceremony. In Esther ix. 22, the word is used of feasting without any reference to a marriage. Rev., *a marriage-feast.*

3. **To call them that were bidden** (καλέσαι τοὺς κεκλημένους). Perhaps an unconscious play on the words, lost in both A. V. and Rev., *to call the called.* This was according to the Oriental custom of sending a messenger, after the invitations have been issued, to notify the invited guests that the entertainment is prepared. Thus Esther invites Haman to a banquet on the morrow, and, at the actual time, the chamberlain comes to bring him to the feast (Esth. v. 8; vi. 14).

4. **Dinner** (ἄριστον). Not the principal meal of the day, but a *noon-breakfast*; *luncheon.*

Fatlings (σιτιστὰ). From σῖτος, *corn*, *grain*, or *food* generally. Properly animals especially *fed up* or *fatted* for a feast.

5. **Made light of it** (ἀμελήσαντες). Not in the sense of *jeering*. They simply gave it no heed.

His farm (ἴδιον ἀγρόν). Rev., his *own* farm; bringing out the contrast between his selfish interest and the respect due to his king. Compare 2 Chron. xxx. 10.

7. **Armies** (στρατεύματα). Not in our grand sense of armies, but *troops*, *soldiers*. Compare Luke xxiii. 11, where the word is rendered *men of war*; Rev., *soldiers*.

9. **Highways** (διεξόδους). Literally, the word means *a way out through*; *passage*, *outlet*, *thoroughfare*. The idea of *crossings* grows out of the junction of the smaller cross-ways with the trunk roads.

10. **Was furnished** (ἐπλήσθη). The Greek is stronger; *was filled*: so Rev.

11. **To see** (θεάσασθαι). Rev., somewhat stiffly, *behold*; but the idea is correct, as the verb denotes *careful seeing*, *looking intently*, *inspection*. See on Matt. xi. 7.

12. **Not having** (μὴ ἔχων). It is hardly possible to convey the subtle sense of the negative particle (μὴ) to the English reader. A different word for *not* (οὐκ) is used in the preceding verse, expressing an *outward*, *objective* fact which attracted the king's notice. The man had *not* (οὐκ) a wedding garment. When the king addresses the guest, he is thinking not so much of the *outward token* of disrespect, as of the guest's *mental attitude* toward the proprieties of the occasion. It is as if he had said, "What were you thinking of, where was your respect for me and for my guests, when you allowed yourself to come hither *not* (μὴ) having the proper garment, as you knew you ought to have?" It implies, as Dr. Morison observes, that the

man was conscious of the omission when he entered, and was intentionally guilty of the neglect. This distinction between the two negative particles rests on the law of the Greek language, according to which *οὐ* and its compounds stand where something is to be denied as a *matter of fact*, and *μή* and its compounds when something is to be denied as a matter of *thought*.

He was speechless (*ἐφιμώθη*). Lit., *he was muzzled* or *gagged*. It is used of muzzling the ox (1 Tim. v. 18), and is addressed by Christ to the demon (Mark i. 25), and to the raging sea (Mark iv. 39). Peter uses it of putting the ignorant and foolish to silence (1 Pet. ii. 15).

The outer darkness. See on Matt. viii. 12.

15. **Entangle** (*παγιδεύσωσιν*). From *παγίς*, a *trap* or *snare*. Better, therefore, Rev., *ensnare*.

19. **Tribute-money** (*νόμισμα τοῦ κήνσου*). Lit., *the current coin of tribute*, which was paid not in Jewish but in Roman money. See on ch. xvii. 25, *tribute*.

A penny. See on Matt. xx. 2.

20. **Image and superscription** (*εἰκὼν καὶ ἐπιγραφή*). Images on coins were not approved by the Jews. Out of respect to this prejudice none of the earlier Herods had his own image impressed on them. Herod Agrippa I., who murdered James and imprisoned Peter, introduced the practice. The coin shown to Christ must either have been struck in Rome, or else was one of the Tetrarch Philip, who was the first to introduce the image of Caesar on strictly Jewish coins.

24. **Shall marry** (*ἐπιγαμβρεύσει*). From *γαμβρός*, a word used in classical Greek to denote any one connected by marriage: a brother-in-law, father-in-law, even a bridegroom. The word is appropriate here because it refers to marriage between marriage-relatives.

34. **Put to silence** (ἐφίμωσεν). There is a kind of grim humor in the use of this word: he had *muzzled* the Sadducees. Compare ver. 12.

36. **Which is the great commandment** (ποία ἐντολὴ μεγάλη). The A. V. and Rev. alike miss the point of this question, which is: *which kind of command is great in the law?* That is, what kind of a commandment must it be to constitute it a great one? Not, which commandment is greatest as compared with the others? The scribes declared that there were 248 affirmative precepts, as many as the members of the human body; and 365 negative precepts, as many as the days in the year; the total being 613, the number of letters in the Decalogue. Of these they called some *light* and some *heavy*. Some thought that the law about the fringes on the garments was the greatest; some that the omission of washings was as bad as homicide; some that the third commandment was the greatest. It was in view of this kind of distinction that the scribe asked the question; not as desiring a declaration as to which commandment was greatest, but as wanting to know the *principle* upon which a commandment was to be regarded as a *great* commandment.

38. **The great and first.** With the definite article.

39. **A second.** The article omitted. So Rev.

CHAPTER XXIII.

2. Moses' **seat** (καθέδρας). Or *chair*, as Wyc., in allusion to the practice of teachers sitting.

5. **To be seen** (πρὸς τὸ θεαθῆναι). See **vi. 1,** where the same word occurs. The scribes and Pharisees deport themselves with a view to being *contemplated* as actors in a theatre; so that men may fix their gaze upon them admiringly.

Phylacteries—Borders of their garments (φυλακτήρια—κράσπεδα). Phylacteries, called by the Rabbis *tephillin*, *prayer-fillets*, were worn on the left arm, toward the heart, and on the forehead. They were capsules containing on parchment these four passages of Scripture: Ex. xiii. 1–10; xiii. 11–16; Deut. vi. 4–9; xi. 13–21. That for the head was to consist of a box with four compartments, each containing a slip of parchment inscribed with one of the four passages. Each of these slips was to be tied up with well-washed hair from a calf's tail; lest, if tied with wool or thread, any fungoid growth should ever pollute them. The phylactery of the arm was to contain a single slip, with the same four passages written in four columns of seven lines each. The black leather straps by which they were fastened were wound seven times round the arm and three times round the hand. They were reverenced by the Rabbis as highly as the scriptures, and, like them, might be rescued from the flames on a Sabbath. They profanely imagined that God wore the *tephillin*.

The Greek word transcribed *phylacteries* in our versions is from φυλάσσω, to *watch* or *guard*. It means originally a *guarded post*, a *fort*; then, generally, a *safeguard* or *preservative*, and therefore an *amulet*. Sir J. Cheke renders *guards*. They were treated as such by the Rabbis. It is said, for instance, that the courtiers of a certain king, intending to kill a Rabbi, were deterred by seeing that the straps of his phylacteries shone like bands of fire. It was also said that they prevented all hostile demons from injuring any Israelite. See on Matt. ix. 20, for *borders*.

6. **The uppermost rooms** (πρωτοκλισίαν). Rev., more correctly, the *chief place*, the foremost *couch* or uppermost place on the divan.

7. **Rabbi.** My master. In addressing Jesus, διδάσκαλος (*teacher*) answers to *Rabbi*. Compare John i. 39; Luke ii. 46.

9. **Father** (πατέρα). Aimed at those who courted the title *Abba*, or *Father*. Compare the title *Papa—Pope*.

10. **Masters** (καθηγηταί). Lit., *leaders*.

13. **Hypocrites** (ὑποκριταί). From ὑποκρίνω, to *separate gradually;* so of *separating the truth* from a mass of falsehood, and thence to *subject to inquiry*, and, as a result of this, to *expound* or *interpret* what is elicited. Then, to *reply to inquiry*, and so to answer *on the stage*, to *speak in dialogue*, to *act*. From this the transition is easy to *assuming*, *feigning*, *playing a part*. The hypocrite is, therefore, etymologically, an *actor*.

Against (ἔμπροσθεν). Very graphic. The preposition means *before*, or *in the face of*. They shut the door in men's faces.

18. **He is guilty** (ὀφείλει). In the rendering of this word the A. V. seems to have been shaped by the earlier and now obsolete sense of *guilt*, which was probably a *fine* or *payment*. Compare Anglo-Saxon *gyld*, a *recompense*, and German *geld*, *money*. There is a hint of this sense in Shakspeare, Henry IV. (Second Part), Act iv., Sc. 4:

> "England shall double *gild* his treble *guilt*,"

where the play upon the words hovers between the sense of *bedeck* and *recompense*. Wyc. renders *oweth*, and Tynd., *he is debtor*. Rev., *he is a debtor*.

23. **Ye Tithe** (ἀποδεκατοῦτε). ἀπό, *from*, δεκατόω, *to take a tenth*. *Tithe* is *tenth;* also in older English, *tethe*, as *tethe hest*, the tenth commandment. A *tething* was a district containing ten families.

Mint (ἡδύοσμον). ἡδύς, *sweet*, ὀσμή, *smell*. A favorite plant in the East, with which the floors of dwellings and synagogues were sometimes strewn.

Anise—Cummin (ἄνηθον—κύμινον). Rev. renders *anise*, *dill* in margin. Used as condiments. The tithe of these plants would be very small; but to exact it would indicate scrupulous conscientiousness. The Talmud tells of the ass of a certain Rabbi which had been so well trained as to refuse corn of which the tithes had not been taken.

Faith (πίστιν). Rather *faithfulness*, as in Rom. iii. 3, Rev. Gal. v. 22, Rev.

24. **Strain at** (διυλίζοντες). διά, *thoroughly* or *through*, and ὑλίζω, to *filter* or *strain*. Strain *at* is an old misprint perpetuated. Hence the Rev. correctly, as Tynd., *strain out*. Insects were ceremonially unclean (Lev. xi. 20, 23, 41, 42), so that the Jews strained their wine in order not to swallow any unclean animal. Moreover, there were certain insects which bred in wine. Aristotle uses the word *gnat* (κώνωπα) of a worm or larva found in the sediment of sour wine. "In a ride from Tangier to Tetuan I observed that a Moorish soldier who accompanied me, when he drank, always unfolded the end of his turban and placed it over the mouth of his *bota*, drinking through the muslin to strain out the gnats, whose larvæ swarm in the water of that country" (cited by Trench, "On the Authorized Version").

Swallow (καταπίνοντες). The rendering is feeble. It is *drink down* (κατά); *gulp*. Note that the camel was also unclean (Lev. xi. 4).

25. **Platter** (παροψίδος). παρά, *beside*, ὄψον, *meat*. A side-dish, with the accompanying sense of something *dainty;* later, as here, the dish itself as distinguished from its contents.

Excess (ἀκρασίας). ἀ, *not*, κράτος, *power*. Hence conduct which shows a want of power over one's self: *incontinence* or *intemperance*.

27. **Whited sepulchres** (τάφοις κεκονιαμένοις). Not the rock-tombs, belonging mostly to the rich, but the graves covered with plastered structures. In general, cemeteries were outside of cities; but any dead body found in the field was to be buried on the spot where it had been discovered. A pilgrim to the Passover, for instance, might easily come upon such a grave in his journey, and contract uncleanness by the contact (Num. xix. 16). It was therefore ordered that all sepulchres

should be whitewashed a month before Passover, in order to make them conspicuous, so that travellers might avoid ceremonial defilement. The fact that this general whitewashing was going on at the time when Jesus administered this rebuke to the Pharisees gave point to the comparison. The word κεκονιαμένοις (*whitened*, from κόνις, *dust*) carries the idea of whitening with a *powder*, as *powdered lime*.

29. **Tombs of the prophets.** By this name are called four monuments at the base of the Mount of Olives, in the valley of Jehoshaphat; called at present the tombs of Zechariah, Absalom, Jehoshaphat, and St. James. Two of them are monoliths cut out of the solid rock; the others are merely excavations, with ornamental portals. "They appear," says Dr. Thomson, "to be quite extensive, consisting of winding or semicircular galleries, passing under the mountain more than a hundred feet from east to west, and terminating in a rotunda about eighty feet from the entrance. There is no authority for the name which they commonly bear." Possibly they were in sight of our Lord when he spoke, and were pointed to by him. The reference would be all the more telling, if, as has been conjectured, the Pharisees were engaged in constructing the tombs of Zechariah and Absalom at the time that the Lord addressed them, and that the chambered sepulchres of James and Jehoshaphat, lying between those two, were the sepulchres which they were garnishing at their entrances.

35. **Temple** (ναοῦ). Rev., rightly, *sanctuary*. See on Matt. iv. 5. Zechariah was slain between the temple proper and the altar of burnt-offering, in the priests' court.

37. **Hen** (ὄρνις). Generic: *bird* or *fowl;* but *hen* is used generically of the mother-bird of all species.

CHAPTER XXIV.

1. **Went out and departed from the temple** (ἐξελθὼν ἀπὸ τοῦ ἱεροῦ ἐπορεύετο). Rev., better: *Went out from the temple and was going on his way. The temple*, ἱεροῦ, not ναοῦ: the whole of the buildings connected with the temple, all of which, including the ναός, or *sanctuary*, and the porches and courts, constituted the ἱερόν. See on Matt. iv. 5.

3. **Coming** (παρουσίας). Originally, *presence*, from παρεῖναι, *to be present.* In this sense in Philip. ii. 12; 2 Cor. x. 10. Also *arrival*, as in 1 Cor. xvi. 17; 2 Cor. vii. 6, 7; 2 Thess. ii. 9; 2 Pet. iii. 12. Of the second coming of Christ: James v. 8; 1 John ii. 28; 2 Pet. iii. 4; 1 Thess. iv. 15.

Of the world (αἰῶνος). Rather *the existing, current age.* They do not ask the signs of the Messiah's coming at the end of *all* time, to judge the world.

4. **Deceive** (πλανήσῃ).) Lit., *lead astray*, as Rev.

5. **In my name** (ἐπὶ τῷ ὀνόματί μου). Lit., *on* my name, *i.e.*, on the strength of; resting their claims on the name Messiah.

12. **Shall abound** (πληθυνθῆναι). Lit., *shall be multiplied.* See Acts vi. 1, 7; vii. 17; ix. 31; Heb. vi. 14.

Of many (τῶν πολλῶν). The A. V. in omitting the definite article, misses the force of Christ's saying. It is not the love of *many people* only that shall be chilled, but of *the* many, *the majority, the great body.*

Wax cold (ψυγήσεται). The verb means originally *to breathe* or *blow;* and the picture is that of spiritual energy blighted or chilled by a malign or poisonous wind.

14. **World** (τῇ οἰκουμένῃ). Lit., *the inhabited.* The whole habitable globe. Rev., in margin, *inhabited earth.*

15. **Abomination of desolation** (βδέλυγμα τῆς ἐρημώσεως). The cognate verb, *βδελύσσομαι*, means *to feel a nausea or loathing for food:* hence used of disgust generally. In a moral sense it denotes an object of moral or religious repugnance. See 2 Chron. xv. 8; Jer. xiii. 27; Ezek. xi. 21; Dan. ix. 27; xi. 31. It is used as equivalent to *idol* in 1 Kings xi. 17; Deut. vii. 26; 2 Kings xxiii. 13. It denotes anything in which estrangement from God manifests itself; as the eating of unclean beasts, Lev. xi. 11; Deut. xiv. 3; and, generally, all forms of heathenism. This moral sense must be emphasized in the New Testament use of the word. Compare Luke xvi. 15; Apoc. xvii. 4, 5; xxi. 27. It does not denote mere physical or æsthetic disgust. The reference here is probably to the occupation of the temple precincts by the idolatrous Romans under Titus, with their standards and ensigns. Josephus says that, after the burning of the temple the Romans brought their ensigns and set them over against the eastern gate, and there they offered sacrifices to them, and declared Titus, with acclamations, to be emperor.

17. **Him which is on the house-top** (ὁ ἐπὶ τοῦ δώματος). From roof to roof there might be a regular communication, called by the Rabbis "the road of the roofs." Thus a person could make his escape passing from roof to roof, till, at the last house, he would descend the stairs on the outside of the house, but within the exterior court. The urgency of the flight is enhanced by the fact that the stairs lead into this court. "Though you must pass by the very door of your room, do not enter to take anything out. Escape for your life."

22. **Should be shortened** (ἐκολοβώθησαν). Rev., *had been shortened.* A very picturesque word. The verb is, literally, *to dock, to cut off, leaving a stump*, as a limb. Wyc., *abridged.* As a fact, various causes did combine to shorten the siege. Herod Agrippa was stopped in his work of strengthening

the walls by orders from the emperor; the Jews, absorbed in their party strifes, had totally neglected preparations to stand a siege; the magazines of corn and provisions were burnt before the arrival of Titus. Titus arrived suddenly, and the Jews voluntarily abandoned parts of the fortification. Titus himself confessed that God was against the Jews, since otherwise neither his armies nor his engines would have availed against their defences.

24. **Signs and wonders** (σημεῖα καὶ τέρατα). See on Matt. xi. 20. The two words often joined in the New Testament. See John iv. 48; Acts ii. 22; iv. 30; 2 Cor. xii. 12. The words do not denote different classes of supernatural manifestations, but these manifestations regarded from different points of view. The same miracle may be a *mighty work*, or a *glorious work*, regarded with reference to its power and grandeur; or a *sign* of the doer's supernatural power; or a *wonder*, as it appeals to the spectator. *Τέρας* (derivation uncertain) is a miracle regarded as a *portent* or *prodigy*, awakening amazement. It most nearly corresponds, therefore, to the etymological sense of the word *miracle* (Lat., *miraculum, a wonderful thing*, from *mirari, to wonder*).

26. **In the desert—Secret chambers.** Rev., *wilderness—inner chambers.* Both retired places, indicating that the false Messiahs will avoid public scrutiny.

27. **Shineth** (φαίνεται). Rev., better, *is seen.* The coming of the Lord will be a plain, unmistakable fact, like the lightning which lightens both ends of the heaven at once, and is seen of all. It will not be connected with some particular place, but will manifest itself and be recognized over the whole world. Compare Apoc. i, 7: "Every eye shall see him."

28. **Carcase** (πτῶμα). From πίπτω, *to fall.* Originally *a fall*, and thence *a fallen body; a corpse.* Compare Lat. *cadaver*, from *cado, to fall.* See Mark vi. 29; Apoc. xi. 8. On the saying itself, compare Job xxxix. 30.

Eagles (ἀετοί). Rev. puts *vultures* in margin. The griffon vulture is meant, which surpasses the eagle in size and power. Aristotle notes how this bird scents its prey from afar, and congregates in the wake of an army. In the Russian war vast numbers were collected in the Crimea, and remained until the end of the campaign in the neighborhood of the camp, although previously scarcely known in the country.

30. **Mourn** (κόψονται). Stronger: *beat their breasts in anguish.*

31. **With a great sound of a trumpet** (μετὰ σάλπιγγος φωνῆς μεγάλης). Some read *with a great trumpet.* The blowing of trumpets was anciently the signal for the host of Israel on their march through the desert. It summoned to war, and proclaimed public festivals, and marked the beginnings of months; Num. x. 1–10; Ps. lxxxi. 3. Hence the symbolism of the New Testament. Jehovah's people shall be summoned before their king by sound of trumpet. Compare the proclamation of Christ as king at the trumpet of the seventh angel, Apoc. xi. 15.

32. **A parable** (τὴν παραβολήν). More strictly, *the* parable which she has to teach. Rightly, therefore, Rev., *her* parable.

Branch (κλάδος). From κλάω, *to break.* Hence *a young slip or shoot,* such as is broken off for grafting. Such were the "branches" which were cut down and strewed in the Lord's path by the multitudes (Matt. xxi. 8).

40. **Shall be taken—left.** Both verbs are in the present tense, which makes the saying more lively. *One is taken and one is left.* So Rev.

41. **The mill** (τῷ μύλῳ). The ordinary hand-mill with a handle fixed near the edge of the upper stone, which is turned by two women.

42. **What hour.** Later texts, however, read ἡμέρᾳ, *day*. ποίᾳ ἡμέρᾳ, *in what kind of a day*, whether a near or a remote one. Similarly ver. 43: ἐν ποίᾳ φυλακῇ, *in what kind of a watch*, whether a night or a morning watch.

43. **Would come** (ἔρχεται). Rev., *was coming*. But the present is graphically thrown in as in vv. 40, 41: *is* coming or *cometh*.

Broken up (διορυγῆναι). Rev., *broken through*. See on Matt. vi. 19. Wyc., *undermined*.

45. **In due season** (ἐν καιρῷ). At the regular hours which his Lord observes when at home; and not delaying because he thinks that his Lord delayeth his coming (ver. 48), but doing his duty in its appointed time.

CHAPTER XXV.

1. **Lamps** (λαμπάδας). Lit., *torches*. Probably a short, wooden stem held in the hand, with a dish at the top, in which was a piece of cloth dipped in oil or pitch.

3. **They that were foolish** (αἵτινες μωραί). Read αἱ γὰρ μωραὶ, *for the foolish*. The *for* justifies the epithet *foolish* in the preceding verse.

5. **Slumbered and slept** (ἐνύσταξαν καὶ ἐκάθευδον). *Slumbered* is, literally, *nodded*. Note the variation of tense. *Nodded* is aorist, denoting a transient act, the *initial stage* of slumber. *They dropped their heads*. *Slept* is imperfect, of *continuous* slumber.

6. **There was a cry made** (κραυγὴ γέγονεν). Rev., *there is a cry*. The verb is in the perfect tense, representing the past event as perpetuated in the present result, and hence is rendered by the English present. A great and decisive change was the

result of the cry. No more sleeping, waiting, or silence. *There is a cry*, and behold the awaking, the bustle, the trimming of lamps and the running to the oil-vendors.

To meet him (*εἰς ἀπάντησιν*). The translation can hardly convey the meaning of the Greek phrase, which implies *a custom* or *familiar ceremony*. Come forth *unto meeting*.

7. **Then all those virgins arose** (*τότε ἠγέρθησαν πᾶσαι αἱ παρθένοι ἐκεῖναι*). The Greek order is expressive. *Then arose all the virgins, those former ones.* Those (*ἐκεῖναι*) a pronoun of remoter reference, and emphatic by its position at the end of the sentence.

Trimmed (*ἐκόσμησαν*). From *κοσμός*, *order*, and meaning *to put in order* or *arrange*. Tynd., *prepared*. Trench ("Parables") quotes from Ward ("View of the Hindoos"), describing a marriage ceremony in India: "After waiting two or three hours, at length near midnight it was announced, as in the very words of Scripture, 'Behold the bridegroom cometh; go ye out to meet him.' All the persons employed now lighted their lamps, and ran with them in their hands to fill up their stations in the procession. Some of them had lost their lights, and were unprepared, but it was then too late to seek them, and the cavalcade moved forward."

Their lamps (*ἑαυτῶν*). Lit., "their *own* lamps;" emphasizing the *personal* preparation in contrast with the foolish, who depended for supply on their fellows.

8. **Are gone out** (*σβέννυνται*). The A. V. misses the graphic force of the continuous present, denoting something in progress. They see the flame waning and flickering, and cry, *Our lamps are going out!* So Rev.

9. **Not so, lest,** etc. (*μήποτε οὐ μὴ ἀρκέσῃ*). The Greek does not give the blunt negative of the A. V. It is a more courteous form of refusal, making the reason for refusing to supply the

place of the negative. *Give us of your oil,* say the foolish. The wise reply, *Lest perchance there be not by any means* (οὐ μὴ, the double negative) *enough.* The Rev. gives it very happily. *Peradventure there will not be enough,* etc.

10. **And while they went** (ἀπερχομένων). A present participle, and very graphic: *while they are going away.*

They that were ready (αἱ ἕτοιμοι). Lit., *the ready* or *prepared ones.*

To the marriage (γάμους). Marriage-*feast,* as Matt. xxii. 2, 3, 4; and so Rev.

11. **Lord, lord.** Applying directly to the bridegroom, whose will was supreme, now that he had arrived at the bride's residence.

14. **Travelling** (ἀποδημῶν). The sense is more nearly *about to travel,* like our *going abroad.*

15. **Several** ability (ἰδίαν). Lit., his *own* or *peculiar* capacity for business.

16. **Straightway** (εὐθέως). Connected with the beginning of this verse, instead of with the end of ver. 15: *Straightway he that had received,* etc., indicating promptness on the servant's part.

Traded with them (ἠργάσατο ἐν αὐτοῖς). Lit., *wrought* with them. The virgins *wait,* the servants *work.*

Made (ἐποίησεν). Not made *them,* as A. V. The word is used in our sense of *make money.* Wyc. and Tynd., *won.* Geneva, *gained.* Some read ἐκέρδησεν, *gained,* as in ver. 17.

24. **Hard** (σκληρὸς). Stronger than the *austere* (αὐστηρός) of Luke xix. 21 (see there), which is sometimes used in a good

sense, as this never is. It is an epithet given to a surface which is at once dry and hard.

Strawed (διεσκόρπισας). Rev., *didst scatter*. Not referring to the sowing of seed, for that would be saying the same thing twice. The *scattering* refers to the *winnowing* of the loosened sheaves spread out upon the threshing-floor. "The word," as Trench observes "could scarcely be applied to the measured and orderly scattering of the sower's seed. It is rather the *dispersing, making to fly* in every direction." Hence used of the pursuit of a routed enemy (Luke i. 51); of the prodigal scattering his goods; *making the money fly*, as we say (Luke xv. 13); of the wolf scattering the sheep (Matt. xxvi. 31). Wyc., *spread abroad*.

25. **That is thine** (τὸ σόν). The Greek is more concise, and is better given by Rev., *Lo, thou hast thine own*.

26. **Slothful.** With no more trouble than he expended in digging, he might have gone to the exchangers. The verse should be read interrogatively, *Didst thou indeed know this of me?* Thou shouldst then have acted with the promptness and care which one observes in dealing with a hard master. To omit the interrogation is to make the Lord admit that he was a hard master.

27. **Put** (βαλεῖν). Lit., *throw* or *fling down*, as one would throw a bag of coin upon the exchanger's table.

Exchangers (τραπεζίταις). Taking their name from the *table* or *counter* at which they sat (τράπεζα). The Jewish bankers bore precisely the same name.

Usury (τόκῳ). A very graphic word, meaning first *childbirth*, and then *offspring*. Hence of interest, which is the *produce* or *offspring* of capital. Originally it was only what was paid for the *use* of money; hence *usury;* but it became synonymous with *extortionate* interest. Rev., better, *with interest*.

The Jewish law distinguished between *interest* and *increase.* In Rome very high interest seems to have been charged in early times. Practically usury was unlimited. It soon became the custom to charge monthly interest at one per cent. a month. During the early empire legal interest stood at eight per cent., but in usurious transactions it was lent at twelve, twenty-four, and even forty-eight. The Jewish bankers of Palestine and elsewhere were engaged in the same undertakings. The law of Moses denounced usury in the transactions of Hebrews with Hebrews, but permitted it in dealing with strangers (Deut. xxiii. 19, 20; Ps. xv. 5).

32. **All the nations** (*πάντα τὰ ἔθνη*). The whole human race; though the word is generally employed in the New Testament to denote *Gentiles* as distinguished from Jews.

Separate **them** (*αὐτοὺς*). Masculine, while the word *nations* is neuter. Nations are regarded as gathered *collectively;* but in contemplating the act of separation the Lord regards the *individuals.*

The sheep from the goats (or *kids*, so Rev. in margin). "The bald division of men into sheep and goats is, in one sense, so easy as not to be worth performing; and in another sense it is so hard as only to be possible for something with supernatural insight" (John Morley, "Voltaire"). Goats are an appropriate figure, because the goat was regarded as a comparatively worthless animal. Hence the point of the elder son's complaint in the parable of the Prodigal: *Not so much as a kid* (Luke xv. 29). The diminutive (*ἐρίφια*) expresses contempt.

33. **Goats** (*ἐρίφια*). Diminutive. Lit., *kidlings.* The sheep and goats are represented as having previously pastured together. Compare the parables of the Tares and the Net.

On the right (*ἐκ δεξιῶν*). Lit., *from* the right side or parts. The picture to the Greek reader is that of a row, beginning at the judge's right hand.

35. **Ye took me in** (συνηγάγετέ με). Tynd., *I was harbourless and ye lodged me.* The preposition σύν implies *along with.* Ye took me *with you* into the household circle.

36. **Visited** (ἐπεσκέψασθε). Lit., *Ye looked upon.** Our word *visit* is from the Latin *viso*, *to look steadfastly at*, and thence to visit. We retain the original thought in the popular phrases *go to see one*, and *to look in upon one.*

40. **The least.** The word in the Greek order is emphatic: One of these my brethren, *the least.* So Rev., *even these least.*

CHAPTER XXVI.

2. **Is betrayed** (παραδίδοται). The present tense expresses here something which, though future, is as good as present, because already determined, or because it must ensue in virtue of an unalterable law. Thus the passover *is* (γίνεται): it must come round at the fixed season. The Son of Man *is* betrayed according to the divine decree. Compare ver. 24.

3. **Palace** (αὐλὴν). But the word never means *palace* in the New Testament. It is the *court*, the open court or hall, forming the centre of an oriental building, and often used as a meeting-place. Rev., *court.* Wyc., *hall.*

7. **An alabaster box** (ἀλάβαστρον). Rev., *cruse; flask* in margin. Lit., *an alabaster*, just as we call a drinking-vessel made of glass *a glass.* Luther renders *glass.* It was a kind of cruet, having a cylindrical form at the top. Pliny compares these vessels to a closed rosebud, and says that ointments are best preserved in them.

8. **To what purpose is this waste?** Wyc., *Whereto this loss?* Tynd., *What needed this waste?* See on John xii. 3.

10. **When Jesus understood it** (γνοὺς δὲ ὁ Ἰησοῦς). The A. V. implies that some time elapsed before Jesus was aware

* Hebraistically, of *gracious* visitation. Comp. Luke vii. 16; Heb. ii. 6.

of the disciples' complaint. But the statement is that Jesus perceived it *at once.* Rev., rightly, *Jesus perceiving it.*

Good work (καλὸν). Lit., *beautiful,* but in a moral sense: an excellent, morally beautiful deed.

15. **What will ye give?** (τί θέλετέ μοι δοῦναι;) Rather, *What are ye willing to give me?* It brings out the *chaffering* aspect of the transaction. So Rev.

They covenanted with him for (ἔστησαν αὐτῷ). But the meaning is, *they weighed unto him;* or, very literally, *they placed for him* (in the balance). Although coined shekels were in circulation, weighing appears to have been practised, especially when considerable sums were paid out of the temple-treasury.

Thirty pieces of silver (τριάκοντα ἀργύρια). Matthew refers to Zech. xi. 12. These pieces were shekels of the sanctuary, of standard weight, and therefore heavier than the ordinary shekel. See on Matt. xvii. 24. Reckoning the Jerusalem shekel at seventy-two cents, the sum would be twenty-one dollars and sixty cents. This was the price which, by the Mosaic law, a man was condemned to pay if his ox should gore a servant (Exod. xxi. 32). Our Lord, the sacrifice for men, was paid for out of the temple-money, destined for the purchase of sacrifices. He who "took on him the form of a servant" was sold at the legal price of a slave.

18. **Such a man** (τὸν δεῖνα). The indefiniteness is the Evangelist's, not our Lord's. He, doubtless, described the person and where to find him.

20. **He sat down** (ἀνέκειτο). But this rendering misses the force of the imperfect tense, which denotes something in progress. The Evangelist says *he was sitting* or reclining, introducing us to something which has been going on for some time.

22. **Began** to say (ἤρξαντο). Denoting the commencement of a series of questions; one after the other (*every one*) saying, *Is it I?*

Is it I? (μήτι ἐγώ εἰμι). The form of the negative expects a negative answer. "*Surely I am not the one.*"

23. **The dish** (τρυβλίῳ). Wyc., *platter*. A dish containing a broth made with nuts, raisins, dates, figs, etc., into which pieces of bread were dipped.

25. **Which betrayed** (ὁ παραδιδοὺς). The article with the participle has the force of an epithet: *The betrayer*.

28. **Testament** (διαθήκης). From διατίθημι, *to distribute; dispose of*. Hence of the disposition of one's property. On the idea of disposing or arranging is based that of *settlement* or *agreement*, and thence of *a covenant*. The Hebrew word of which this is a translation is primarily *covenant*, from a verb meaning *to cut*. Hence the phrase, to *make a covenant*, in connection with dividing the victims slain in ratification of covenants (Gen. xv. 9–18). *Covenant* is the general Old Testament sense of the word (1 Kings xx. 34; Isa. xxviii. 15; 1 Sam. xviii. 3); and so in the New Testament. Compare Mark xiv. 24; Luke i. 72; xxii. 20; Acts iii. 25; vii. 8. Bishop Lightfoot, on Gal. iii. 15, observes that the word is never found in the New Testament in any other sense than that of *covenant*, with the exception of Heb. ix. 15–17, where it is *testament*. We cannot admit this exception, since we regard that passage as one of the best illustrations of the sense of *covenant*. See on Heb. ix. 15–17. Render here as Rev., *covenant*.

Is shed (ἐκχυννόμενον). The present participle, *is being shed*. Christ's thought goes forward to the consummation.

29. **New** (καινὸν). Another adjective, νεόν, is employed to denote *new* wine in the sense of *freshly-made* (Matt. ix. 17; Mark ii. 22; Luke v. 37, 38, 39). The difference is between

newness regarded in point of *time* or of *quality*. The *young*, for instance, who have *lately* sprung up, are **νέοι** or **νεώτεροι** (Luke xv. 12, 13). The *new* garment (Luke v. 36) is contrasted as to *quality* with a worn and threadbare one. Hence **καινοῦ**. So a *new* heaven (2 Pet. iii. 13) is **καινὸς**, contrasted with that which shows signs of dissolution. The tomb in which the body of Jesus was laid was **καινὸν** (Matt. xxvii. 60); in which no other body had lain, making it ceremonially unclean; not *recently* hewn. Trench ("Synonyms") cites a passage from Polybius, relating a stratagem by which a town was nearly taken, and saying "we are still *new* (**καινοί**) and *young* (**νέοι**) in regard of such deceits." Here **καινοί** expresses the *inexperience* of the men; **νέοι**, their *youth*. Still, the distinction cannot be pressed in all cases. Thus, 1 Cor. v. 7, "Purge out the old leaven that ye may be a *new* (**νέον**) lump;" and Col. iii. 10, "Put on the new (**νέον**) man," plainly carry the sense of *quality*. In our Lord's expression, "drink it *new*," the idea of quality is dominant. All the elements of festivity in the heavenly kingdom will be of a new and higher quality. In the New Testament, besides the two cases just cited, **νέος** is applied to *wine*, to the *young*, and once to *a covenant*.

30. **Sung a hymn.** Very probably tne second part of the Jewish *Hallel* or *Hallelujah*, embracing Ps. cxv., cxvi., cxvii., cxviii.

They went out. In the original institution of the Passover it was enjoined that no one should go out of his house until morning (Exod. xii. 22). Evidently this had ceased to be regarded as obligatory.

32. **I will go before you.** The thought links itself with what Christ had just said about the shepherd and the sheep. Compare John x. 4. I will go before you, as a shepherd before his flock.

34. **Before the cock crow.** A little more graphic if the article is omitted, as in the Greek. Before *a single cock* shall

be heard, early in the night, thou shalt deny me. Dr. Thomson ("Land and Book") says that the barn-door fowls "swarm round every door, share in the food of their possessors, are at home among the children in every room, roost overhead at night, and with their ceaseless crowing are the town-clock and the morning-bell to call up sleepers at early dawn."

35. **Though I should die** (*κἂν δέῃ με ἀποθανεῖν*). The A. V. misses the force of *δέῃ*: "Though *it should be necessary* for me to die." Wyc., "*If it shall behove me to die.*" Rev., excellently, "Even if I *must die.*"

36. **Gethsemane.** Meaning *oil-press.* Beyond the brook Kedron, and distant about three-quarters of a mile from the walls of Jerusalem. Dean Stanley says of the olive-trees there: "In spite of all the doubts that can be raised against their antiquity, the eight aged olive-trees, if only by their manifest difference from all others on the mountain, have always struck the most indifferent observers. They will remain, so long as their already protracted life is spared, the most venerable of their race on the surface of the earth. Their gnarled trunks and scanty foliage will always be regarded as the most affecting of the sacred memorials in or about Jerusalem; the most nearly approaching to the everlasting hills themselves in the force with which they carry us back to the events of the gospel history" ("Sinai and Palestine").

40. **What!** It is hardly possible to convey the exact force of the Greek *οὕτως*, *thus* or *so.* The idea is, "are ye *thus* unable, or *so utterly* unable to watch?"

45. **The hour is at hand.** He probably heard the tramp and saw the lanterns of Judas and his band.

47. **One of the twelve.** Repeated in all three evangelists, in the narratives both of the betrayal and of the arrest. By the time Matthew's Gospel was written, the phrase had become a stereotyped designation of the traitor, like *he that betrayed him.*

A great multitude. The Sanhedrin had neither soldiery nor a regularly-armed band at command. In John xviii. 3, Judas receives a *cohort* of soldiers and officers from the chief priests and Pharisees. Part of the band would consist of this regularly-armed cohort, and the rest of a crowd armed with cudgels, and embracing some of the servants of conspicuous men in the Sanhedrin.

49. **Kissed him** (κατεφίλησεν). The compound verb has the force of an *emphatic, ostentatious* salute. Meyer says *embraced and kissed.* The same word is used of the tender caressing of the Lord's feet by the woman in the Pharisee's house (Luke vii. 38), of the father's embrace of the returned prodigal (Luke xv. 20), and of the farewell of the Ephesian elders to Paul (Acts xx. 37).

50. **Wherefore art thou come?** (ἐφ' ὃ πάρει). The interrogation of the A. V. is wrong. The expression is elliptical and condensed. Literally it is, *that for which thou art here;* and the mind is to supply *do* or *be about.* The Lord spurns the traitor's embrace, and says, in effect, "Enough of this hypocritical fawning. Do what you are here to do." So Rev., *Do that for which thou art come.*

51. **The servant** (τὸν δοῦλον). The article marks the special servant; the *body*-servant.

Ear (ὠτίον). A diminutive in form but not in sense; according to a Greek popular usage which expressed parts of the body by diminutives; as ῥίνια, *the nostrils;* ὀμμάτιον, *the eye;* σαρκίον, *the body.* Peter aimed his blow at the servant's head, but missed.

52. **Put up again.** Peter was still brandishing his sword.

53. **Twelve legions of angels.** Compare the story of Elisha at Dothan (2 Kings vi. 17).

55. **A thief** (ληστὴν). Better Rev., *a robber*. See John x. 1, 8; and Luke xxiii. 39–43. It is more than a petty stealer; rather one with associates, who would require an armed band to apprehend him. Hence the propriety of the reference to swords and staves.

I sat (ἐκαθεζόμην). The imperfect tense, denoting something *habitual*. I was *accustomed* to sit.

63. **I adjure thee.** I call upon thee to swear. The high-priest put Christ upon oath.

That (ἵνα). *In order that;* signifying the design with which he adjured the Lord.

64. **Thou hast said.** An affirmation. You have spoken the truth. What thou hast asked me is the fact. Compare ver. 25.

Nevertheless (πλὴν). *However.* Apart from my affirmation, you shall see for yourself.

66. **Guilty of death** (ἔνοχος θανάτου). Rev., *worthy* of death. See on Matt. xxiii. 18. ἐν, *in*, ἔχω, *to hold.* The idea is, literally, *holden of death; in bonds* to *death.*

67. **Buffet** (ἐκολάφισαν). With the fist.

Smote with the palms of their hands. All expressed by one word, ἐράπισαν, from ῥαπίς, a *rod*, and meaning to smite with *rods*, not with the *palms.* The same word is employed Matt. v. 39. It came to mean generally *to strike.*

69. **A damsel** (μία παιδίσκη). Lit., *one* damsel, because the writer has in mind a second one (ver. 71).

71. **Gone out.** Through fear of being further questioned.

72. **The man.** As if he did not know Jesus' name.

74. **To curse** (*καταθεματίζειν*). A new development of profanity. Hitherto he had merely *sworn.* Now he adds *imprecation;* invoking curses on himself if the case be not as he says.

CHAPTER XXVII.

3. **Repented himself** (*μεταμεληθεὶς*). See on Matt. xxi. 29.

What is that to us? They ignore the question of Christ's innocence. As to Judas' sin or conscience, that is *his* matter. *Thou wilt see to that.*

5. **In the temple.** But the best reading is *εἰς τὸν ναόν*, *into the sanctuary.* He cast the pieces over the barrier of the enclosure which surrounded the *sanctuary*, or temple proper, and within which only the priests were allowed, and therefore *into* the sanctuary.

6. **It is not lawful.** In such cases the Jewish law provided that the money was to be restored to the donor; and if he insisted on giving it, that he should be induced to spend it for something for the public weal. This explains the apparent discrepancy between Matthew's account and that in the book of Acts (i. 18). By a fiction of the law the money was still considered to be Judas', and to have been applied by him to the purchase of the potter's field.

Scarlet (*κοκκίνην*). From *κόκκος*, *cochineal*, which grew in several parts of Greece. Garments of this color would seem to have been rare among the orientals. Herodotus relates that the admiration of Darius, then an officer in the army, was excited by the scarlet cloak of a Samian exile, who, on his offering to purchase it, presented it to him, and was afterward richly rewarded when Darius came to the throne (iii. 139).

28. **Robe** (χλαμύδα). The short military cloak which kings and emperors as well as soldiers wore.

32. **Compelled to go** (ἠγγάρευσαν). See on Matt. v. 41. Rev. has *impressed* in margin.

33. **Golgotha.** An Aramaic word, *Gulgoltha*, = the Hebrew, *Gulgoleth*, and translated *skull* in Judg. ix. 53; 2 Kings ix. 35. The word *Calvary* comes through the Latin *calvaria*, meaning *skull*, and used in the Vulgate. The New Testament narrative does not mention a mount or hill. The place was probably a rounded elevation. The meaning is not, as Tynd., *a place of dead men's skulls*, but simply *skull*.

34. **Wine** (οἶνον). The older texts read ὄξος, *vinegar*. The compound of wine and gall was intended as a stupefying draught.

36. **Watched** (ἐτήρουν). Or, to give the force of the imperfect tense, *kept watch*. This was to prevent the infliction of wanton cruelties, and also to prevent what sometimes happened, the taking down and restoring of the victim.

37. **Accusation** (αἰτίαν). Lit., *cause*, and so rendered by Wyc. Tynd., *cause of his death*. The word *accusation* is compounded with the Latin *causa*, a *cause*. It is the cause of his condemnation and suffering.

38. **Thieves** (λησταί). Rev., *robbers*. See on Matt. xxvi. 55.

42. **He saved others,** etc. The Greek order is, *Others he saved; himself he cannot save.*

43. **If he will have him** (εἰ θέλει αὐτόν). Rev., correctly, *If he desireth him:* i.e., *If he likes him.* Compare Ps. xviii. (Sept. xvii.) 19; *because he delighted in me* (ἠθέλησέ με), Ps. xli. (Sept. xl.) 11 (τεθέληκάς με).

36. **Ninth hour.** "Early on Friday afternoon the new course of priests, of Levites, and of the 'stationary men' who were to be the representatives of all Israel, arrived in Jerusalem, and having prepared themselves for the festive season went up to the temple. The approach of the Sabbath, and then its actual commencement, were announced by threefold blasts from the priests' trumpets. The first three blasts were blown when one-third of the evening-sacrifice service was over, or about the ninth hour; that is, about 3 P.M. on Friday" (Edersheim, "The Temple").

48. **Vinegar** (ὄξους). Sour wine; the *posca* or ordinary drink of the Roman soldiers.

Gave him to drink (ἐπότιζεν). The imperfect tense implies *was in the act of giving*, or *about to give*. At this point the Jews standing near interposed, saying, *Let be* (ἄφες)! "Stop! Do not give him the drink. Let us see if Elijah will come to his aid."

50. **Yielded up the ghost** (ἀφῆκε τὸ πνεῦμα). Lit., *dismissed his spirit*. Rev., *yielded up his spirit*. The fact that the evangelists, in describing our Lord's death, do not use the neuter verb, ἔθανεν, *he died*, but *he breathed out his life* (ἐξέπνευσε, Mark xv. 37), *he gave up his spirit* (παρέδωκε τὸ πνεῦμα, John xix. 30), seems to imply a *voluntary* yielding up of his life. Compare John x. 18. Augustine says, "He gave up his life *because* he willed it, *when* he willed it, and *as* he willed it."

51. **The veil of the temple.** According to the Rabbis this was a handbreadth in thickness, and woven of seventy-two twisted plaits, each plait consisting of twenty-four threads. It was sixty feet long and thirty wide. Two of them were made every year, and according to the exaggerated language of the time it needed three hundred priests to manipulate it. This veil was the one which covered the entrance to the holy of holies, and not, as has been asserted, the veil which hung before the main entrance to the sanctuary. The holy of holies contained only a large stone, on which the high-priest sprinkled

the blood on the day of atonement, occupying the place where the ark with the mercy-seat had stood.

54. **The Son of God.** But there is no article. The words must not be construed as a recognition of Christ's divine sonship. They were uttered by a pagan soldier in his own sense of *a demigod* or *hero*. Yet they may have taken color from the fact that the soldiers had heard from the chief priests and others that Christ had claimed to be God's son.

55. **Which** had followed (αἵτινες). Denoting a class: who were *of the body of women* that had followed him.

56. **Magdalene** (ἡ Μαγδαληνὴ). Neither Mary of Bethany (Matt. xxvi. 6–13) nor the woman who had been a sinner (Luke vii. 37–48). The word denotes merely her *town: She of Magdala.*

57. **When even was come.** The Hebrews reckoned two evenings, an earlier and a later. The former began midway between noon and sunset, or at three o'clock in the afternoon. The latter began at sunset, six o'clock. The reference here is to the earlier evening, though the time may have been well on toward the beginning of the later. The preparations had to be hurried because the Sabbath would begin at sunset.

60. **New** tomb (καινῷ). See on Matt. xxvi. 29. Not *newly hewn*, but *fresh*, undefiled by anybody.

A great stone. Though in the Jews' sepulchres in general there were doors hung on hinges, the grooves and perforations for which may still be seen. Joseph's tomb may have been differently constructed, or else was in an unfinished state.

63. **We remember** (ἐμνήσθημεν). Lit., *we remembered: i.e.*, it occurred to us: we have just remembered, and have come to tell you before it shall be too late.

That deceiver (ἐκεῖνος ὁ πλάνος). The pronoun *that* is very picturesque; being used of distant objects, and therefore here as pointing to one who is out of the way and far removed. *Πλάνος*, *deceiver*, is akin to *πλανάω*, *to wander;* and hence a *vagabond impostor.*

64. **Error** (πλάνη). Not, as many render, *deceit* or *imposture,* referring to πλάνος above; but the error on the *people's* part. The last error, namely, the false impression that he has risen from the dead, will be worse than the first error—the impression made by his impostures that he was the Messiah.

65. **Ye have** (ἔχετε). Or, as some render, imperatively: *Have a guard!* Rev., in margin, *take.*

66. **Sealing the stone and setting a watch** (σφραγίσαντες τὸν λίθον, μετὰ τῆς κουστωδίας). Lit., *having sealed the stone with the watch.* Rev., *Sealing the stone, the guard being with them.* This is rather awkward, but the rendering rightly corrects the A. V. The idea is that they sealed the stone in the presence of the guard, and then left them to keep watch. It would be important that the guard should witness the sealing. The sealing was performed by stretching a cord across the stone and fastening it to the rock at either end by means of sealing clay. Or, if the stone at the door happened to be fastened with a cross beam, this latter was sealed to the rock.

CHAPTER XXVIII.

3. **Countenance** (εἰδέα). Rev., more correctly, *appearance.* The word occurs nowhere else in the New Testament. It does not refer to the face alone, but to the general aspect. Wyc., *looking.*

As lightning. In effulgence. Each evangelist's account of the resurrection emphasizes different particulars. Matthew alone notes the outward glory, the earthquake, the agency of the angel, and the impotence of the military and priestly power to crush the new faith. He only notices the adoration of the risen Lord before his ascension, and traces to its origin the calumny current among the Jews to this day.

7. **He goeth before you** (προάγει). He is in the act of going. See on Matt. xxvi. 32.

9. **All hail** (χαίρετε). The ordinary Greek form of salutation.

12. **Large money** (ἀργύρια ἱκανὰ). Lit., *sufficient money.* Enough to bribe them to invent a lie.

14. **We will persuade** (πείσομεν). i.e., *satisfy* or *appease.* Compare Gal. i. 10. "Do I *conciliate* men or God?"

Secure you (ὑμᾶς ἀμερίμνους ποιήσομεν). Lit., *make you without care.* The word *secure,* however, is, etymologically, a correct rendering. It is from the Latin *se* = *sine, without,* and *cura, care.* It has passed into the popular meaning to *make safe.* Compare 1 Cor. vii. 32. "I would have you to be *free from cares*" (Rev.).

17. **Worshipped** (προσεκύνησαν). As in ver. 9. Prostrated themselves. The first time that the disciples are described as doing so.

18. **Came to.** Verse 17 evidently describes the impression made by seeing him at a distance. Possibly from feelings of modesty they had not ventured close to him. Jesus now approaches and addresses them.

Spake—saying (ἐλάλησεν—λέγων). Two different words are here used to express speech, with a nice distinction which can hardly be conveyed without paraphrase. The verb λαλεῖν is used of speaking, in contrast with or as a breaking of silence, voluntary or imposed. Thus the dumb man, after he was healed, *spake* (ἐλάλησεν); and Zacharias, when his tongue was loosed, *began to speak* (ἐλάλει). In the use of the word the writer contemplates the *fact* rather than the *substance* of speech. Hence it is used of God (Heb. i. 1), the point being, not *what* God said, but the fact that he spake to men. On the contrary, λέγειν refers to the *matter* of speech. The verb originally means to *pick out*, and hence to use words *selected* as appropriate expressions of thought, and to put such words together in orderly discourse. Here, then, we have Jesus first *breaking silence* (ελάλησεν), and then *discoursing* (λέγων).

Power (ἐξουσία). Better, *authority*, as Rev.

Is given (ἐδόθη). Lit., *was given*, by the divine decree.

19. **Teach** (μαθητεύσατε). Rev., rightly, *make disciples of*.

In the name (εἰς τὸ ὄνομα). Rev., correctly, "*into* the name." Baptizing *into* the name has a twofold meaning. 1. *Unto*, denoting *object* or *purpose*, as εἰς μετάνοιαν, *unto repentance* (Matt. iii. 11); εἰς ἄφεσιν ἁμαρτιῶν, *for the remission of sins* (Acts ii. 38). 2. *Into*, denoting *union* or *communion with*, as Rom. vi. 3, "baptized *into* Christ Jesus; *into* his death;" *i.e.*, we are brought by baptism into fellowship with his death. Baptizing into the name of the Holy Trinity implies a spiritual and mystical union with him. *Εἰς*, *into*, is the preposition commonly used with *baptize*. See Acts viii. 16; xix. 3, 5; 1 Cor. i. 13, 15; x. 2; Gal. iii. 27. In Acts ii. 38, however, Peter says, "Be baptized *upon* (ἐπὶ) the name of Jesus Christ; and in Acts x. 48, he commands Cornelius and his friends to be baptized *in* (ἐν) the name of the Lord. To be baptized *upon* the name is to be baptized on the confession of that which the name implies: *on the ground of* the name; so that the name Jesus, as the contents of the faith and confession, is the ground upon which the becoming baptized rests. *In* the name (ἐν) has reference to the *sphere* within which alone true baptism is accomplished. The *name* is not the mere *designation*, a sense which would give to the baptismal formula merely the force of a *charm*. The *name*, as in the Lord's Prayer ("Hallowed be thy name"), is the expression of the sum total of the divine Being: not his *designation* as God or Lord, but the formula in which all his attributes and characteristics are summed up. It is equivalent to his *person*. The finite mind can deal with him only through his name; but his name is of no avail detached from his nature. When one is baptized into the name of the Trinity, he professes to acknowledge and appropriate God in all that he is and in all that he does for man. He recognizes and depends upon God the Father as his Creator and Preserver; receives Jesus Christ as his only Mediator and Redeemer, and his pattern of life; and confesses the Holy Spirit as his Sanctifier and Comforter.

Alway (*πάσας τὰς ἡμέρας*). Lit., *all the days*. Wyc., *in all days*.

20. **End of the world** (*συντελείας τοῦ αἰῶνος*). Rev., in margin, and lit., *consummation of the age*. The current age is meant; and the *consummation* is coincident with the second coming of Christ, after the Gospel shall have been proclaimed throughout the world. "The Saviour's mind goes no farther; for after that, evangelizing work will cease. No man, after that, will need to teach his neighbor, saying, 'Know the Lord'" (Jer. xxxi. 34) (Morison "On Matthew").

LIST OF GREEK WORDS USED BY MATTHEW ONLY.

ἀγγεῖον, vessel, xiii., 48 ; xxv., 4
ἄγκιστρον, hook, xvii., 27
ἀθῷος, innocent, xxvii., 4, 24
αἱμοῤῥοέω, having an issue of blood, ix., 20
αἱρετίζω, choose, xii., 18
ἀκμήν, yet, xv., 16
ἀκριβόω, inquire diligently, ii., 7, 16
ἀναβιβάζω, draw up, xiii., 48
ἀναίτιος, blameless, xii., 5, 7
ἄνηθον, anise, xxiii., 23
ἀπάγχομαι, hang one's self, xxvii., 5
ἀπονίπτω, wash, xxvii., 24
βάρ, son, xvi., 17
βαρύτιμος, very precious, xxvi., 7
βασανιστής, tormentor, xviii., 34
βαττολογέω, use vain repetitions, vi., 7
βιαστής, violent, xi., 12
βροχή, rain, vii., 25, 27
δάνειον, debt, xviii., 27
δεῖνα (ὁ), such a man, xxvi., 18
δέσμη, bundles, xiii., 30
διακωλύω, forbid, iii., 14
διαλλάττομαι, be reconciled, v., 24
διασαφέω, tell, xviii., 31
δίδραχμον, half-shekel, xvii., 24
διέξοδος, parting of the highways, xxii., 9
διετής, two years old, ii., 16
διστάζω, doubt, xiv., 31 ; xxviii., 17
διϋλίζω, strain through, xxiii., 24
διχάζω, set at variance, x., 35
ἑβδομηκοντάκις, seventy times, xviii., 22
ἔγερσις, resurrection, xxvii., 53
ἐθνικός, Gentile, v., 47 ; vi., 7 ; xviii., 17
ειδέα, countenance, xxviii., 3
ειρηνοποιός, peacemaker, v., 9
ἐκλάμπω, shine forth, xiii., 43
Ἐμμανουήλ, Emmanuel, i., 23
ἐμπορία, merchandise, xxii., 5
ἐμπρήθω, burn up, xxii., 7
ἐξορκίζω, adjure, xxvi., 63
ἐξώτερος, outer, viii., 12 ; xxii., 13 ; xxv., 30
ἐπιγαμβρεύω, marry, xxii., 24
ἐπικαθίζω, to set upon, xxi., 7
ἐπιορκέω, forswear, v., 33
ἐπισπείρω, sow upon, xiii., 25
ἐρεύγομαι, utter, xiii., 35
ἐρίζω, strive, xii., 19
ἐρίφιον, goat, kid, xxv., 33
ἑταῖρος, fellow, friend, xi., 16 ; xx., 13 ; xxii., 12 ; xxvi., 50
εὐδία, fair weather, xvi., 2
εὐνοέω, agree, v., 25
εὐνουχίζω, make a eunuch, xix., 12
εὐρύχωρος, broad, vii., 13
ζιζάνια, tares, xiii., 25–40
Ἠλί, my God, xxvii., 46
θαυμάσιος, wonderful, xxi., 15
θεριστής, reaper, xiii., 30, 39
θρῆνος, lamentation, ii., 18
θυμόομαι, to be wroth, ii., 16
ἰῶτα, jot, v., 18
καθά, as, xxvii., 10
καθηγητής, master, xxiii., 8, 10
καταμανθάνω, consider, vi., 28

καταναθεματίζω, curse, xxvi., 74
καταποντίζομαι, sink, be drowned, xiv., 30; xviii., 6
κῆτος, whale, xii., 40
κουστωδία, watch, guard, xxvii., 65, 66; xxviii., 11
κρυφαῖος, secret, vi., 18
κύμινον, cummin, xxiii., 23
κώνωψ, gnat, xxiii., 24
μαλακία, sickness, iv., 23; ix., 35; x., 1
μεῖζον, the more, xx., 31
μεταίρω, depart, xiii., 53; xix., 1
μετοικεσία, carrying away, i., 11, 12, 17
μίλιον, mile, v., 41
μισθόομαι, hire, xx., 1, 7
μύλων, mill, xxiv., 41
νόμισμα, tribute-money, xxii., 19
νοσσιά, brood, xxiii., 37
οἰκέτεια, household, xxiv., 25
οἰκιακός, belonging to the house, x., 25, 36
ὄναρ, dream, i., 20; ii., 12, 13, 19, 22; xxvii., 19
οὐδαμῶς, by no means, ii., 6
παγιδεύω, ensnare, xxii., 15
παραθαλάσσιος, upon the sea-coast, iv., 13
παρακούω, neglect, xviii., 17
παρομοιάζω, to be like unto, xxiii., 27
παροψίς, platter, xxiii., 25
πλατύς, wide, vii., 13
πολυλογία, much-speaking, vi., 7
προφθάνω, forestall, xvii., 25
πυῤῥάζω, to be red or fiery, xvi., 2, 3
ῥακά, Raca, v., 22
ῥαπίζω, smite, v., 39; xxvi., 67
σαγήνη, drag-net, xiii., 47
σεληνιάζομαι, to be lunatic, iv., 24; xvii., 15.
σιτιστός, fatling, xxii., 4
στατήρ, stater; piece of money, xvii., 27
συναίρω, take (a reckoning), xviii., 23, 24; xxv., 19
συνάντησις, meeting, viii., 34
συναυξάνομαι, grow together, xiii., 30
συντάσσω, appoint, xxvi., 19; xxvii., 10
τάλαντον, talent, xviii., 24; xxv., 15–28
ταφή, burial, xxvii., 7
τελευτή, end (in sense of death), ii., 15
τραπεζίτης, exchanger, xxv., 27
τρύπημα, eye (of a needle), xix., 24
τυφόω, to smoke, xii., 20
φράζω, declare, xiii., 36; xv., 15
φυλακτήριον, phylactery, xxiii., 5
φυτεία, plant, xv., 13
χλαμύς, robe, xxvii., 28, 31
ψευδομαρτυρία, false witness, xv., 19; xxvi., 59.
ψύχομαι, wax cold, xxiv., 12

THE GOSPEL ACCORDING TO MARK.

INTRODUCTION.

Mark the Evangelist is, by the best authorities, identified with John Mark, the son of Mary. The surname Mark was adopted for use among the Gentiles; Mark (*Marcus*) being one of the commonest Latin names (compare *Marcus Tullius Cicero*, *Marcus Aurelius*), as John was one of the commonest Hebrew names. Mark was a cousin of Barnabas, and was, from a very early period, the intimate friend and associate of Peter (Acts xii. 11–17), who affectionately refers to him as "my son" at the close of his first epistle. The general opinion of the fathers, as well as that of modern authorities, is that Mark drew the great mass of his materials from the oral discourses of Peter. This opinion was perpetuated in Christian art, in representations of Peter seated on a throne with Mark kneeling before him and writing from his dictation; Mark sitting and writing, and Peter standing before him, with his hand raised, dictating; and Peter in a pulpit, preaching to the Romans, and Mark taking down his words in a book (see Mrs. Jameson, "Sacred and Legendary Art," i., 149).

This opinion finds support in the evidences of Peter's influence upon the style of this Gospel. The restlessness and impetuosity of Mark's disposition, of which we have hints in his forsaking Paul and Barnabas at Perga (Acts xiii. 13; xv. 38), in his subsequent readiness to join them on the second missionary journey (Acts xv. 39), and, if the tradition be accepted, in his rushing into the street on the night of Christ's arrest, clad only in a linen sheet (Mark xiv. 51, 52), would naturally be in sympathy with the well-known character of Peter. Peter was a man of observation and action rather than of reflection; impulsive and impetuous. "When we assume," says Dr. Morison, "that Mark drew directly from the discoursings of St. Peter, then we understand how it comes to pass that it is in his pages that we have the most particular account of that lamentable denial of his Lord of which the apostle was guilty. On no other person's memory would the minute particulars of the prediction, and of its unanticipated fulfilment, be so indelibly engraven. It is also noteworthy that, while the very severe rebuke which our Lord administered to St. Peter in the neighborhood of Caesarea Philippi is faithfully and circumstantially recorded in Mark's pages, the splendid eulogium and distinguishing blessing, which had been previously pronounced, are, as it were, modestly passed by. Doubtless the great apostle would not be guilty of making frequent or egotistic references to such marks of distinction" ("Commentary on Mark").

Unlike the other gospels, Mark's narrative is not subordinated to the working out of any one idea. Matthew's memoirs turn on the relation of Christ to the law and the prophets. He throws a bridge from the old economy to the new. His is the Gospel as related to the past, the Gospel of Christianity regarded as the fulfilment of Judaism. Luke exhibits Jesus as a Saviour, and expounds the freeness and universality of the Gospel, and the sacredness of humanity. John wrote that men might believe that Jesus is the Christ, and might have life in him. While Matthew and Luke deal with his offices, John deals with his person. John carries forward the piers of Matthew's bridge toward that perfected heavenly economy of which his Apocalypse reveals glimpses. In Matthew Jesus is the Messiah; in John, the *Eternal Word.* In Matthew he is the fulfiller of the law; in John he foreshadows the grander and richer economy of the Spirit.

Mark, on the other hand, is a chronicler rather than a historian. His narrative is the record of an observer, dealing with the facts of Christ's life without reference to any dominant conception of his person or office. Christ's portrait is drawn "in the clearness of his present energy;" not as the fulfilment of the past, as by Matthew, nor as the foundation of the future, as by John. His object is to portray Jesus in his daily life, "in the awe-inspiring grandeur of his human personality, as a man who was also the Incarnate, the wonder-working Son of God." Hence his first words are the appropriate keynote of his Gospel: "The beginning of the Gospel of Jesus Christ, the Son of God."

Such a narrative might have been expected from Peter, with his keen-sightedness, his habit of observation, and his power of graphically describing what he was so quick to perceive. There is, of course, less room for the exhibition of these traits in his epistles, though they emerge even there in certain peculiar and picturesque words, and in expressions which reflect incidents of his personal association with Christ. Those brief epistles contain over a hundred words which occur nowhere else in the New Testament. Certain narratives in the Book of Acts record incidents in which Peter was the principal or the only apostolic actor, and the account of which must have come from his own lips; and these narratives bear the marks of his keen observation, and are characterized by his picturesque power. Such are the accounts of the healing of the cripple at the temple-gate (iii.); of Ananias and Sapphira (v.); of Peter's deliverance from prison (xii.); of the raising of Dorcas (ix.); and of the vision of the great sheet (x.). In these, especially if we compare them with narratives which Luke has evidently received from other sources, we are impressed with the picturesque vividness of the story; the accurate notes of time and place and number; the pictorial expressions, the quick transitions; the frequent use of such words as *straightway*, *immediately*; the substitution of dialogue for narrative, and the general fulness of detail.

All these characteristics appear in Mark's Gospel, and are justly regarded as indicating the influence of Peter, though comparatively few of the same words are employed by both; a fact which may be, in great part, accounted for by the difference between a hortatory epistle and a narrative. The traces of Peter's quick perception and dramatic and picturesque power are everywhere visible in Mark. While Matthew fully records the discourses of our Lord, Mark pictures his deeds. Hence, while Matthew gives us fifteen of his parables, Mark reproduces only four, and that in a condensed form. "Mark does not wear the flowing robes of Matthew. His dress is 'for speed succinct.' Swift-paced, incisive, his narrative proceeds straight to the goal, like a Roman soldier on his march to battle." His Gospel is the Gospel of the present, not of the past. His references to the Old Testament, with the exception of i. 2, 3, are quotations occurring in the discourses of Christ, or cited by others. They belong, as Canon Farrar observes, "to the narrative, not to the recorder" (xv. 28 is an interpolation). The word νόμος, *law*, never occurs in Mark nor in Peter.

Mark's is, therefore, pre-eminently the pictorial Gospel: the Gospel of detail. "There is," says Canon Westcott, "perhaps not one narrative which he gives in common with Matthew and Luke, to which he does not contribute some special feature." Thus he adds to John the Baptist's picture of loosing the shoe-latchet another touch, in the words *to stoop down* (i. 7). He uses a more graphic term to describe the opening of the heavens at Christ's baptism. According to Matthew and Luke the heavens *were opened* (ἀνεῴχθησαν); Mark depicts them as *rent asunder* (σχιζομένους; i. 10). Matthew and Luke represent Jesus as *led* (ἀνήχθη) into the wilderness to be tempted; Mark as *driven* (ἐκβάλλει); adding, *He was with the wild beasts;* to which some detect a reference in Peter's comparison of the devil to a *roaring lion* (1 Pet. v. 8). He gives a realistic touch to the story of James and John forsaking their employment at the call of Jesus, by adding that they left their father *with the hired servants* (i. 20). After the discourse from the boat to the multitude upon the shore, Mark alone tells us that the disciples sent away the multitude, and throws in the little details, they took him *as he was;* and *there were with them other little ships* (iv. 36). His account of the storm which followed is more vivid than Matthew's or Luke's. He pictures the waves *beating* into the boat, and the boat beginning *to fill;* notes the steersman's cushion at the stern on which the sleeping Lord's head reposed (iv. 37, 38); and throws the awaking by the disciples and the stilling of the tempest into a dramatic form by the distressful question, *Master, carest thou not that we perish?* and the command to the sea as to a raging monster, *Peace! Be still!* (iv. 38, 39).

In the narrative of the feeding of the five thousand, only Mark relates the Saviour's question, *How many loaves have ye? Go and see* (vi. 38). An oriental crowd abounds in color, and to Mark we are indebted for the gay picture of the crowds arranged on the *green* grass, in companies, like *flower-beds* with their varied hues. He alone specifies the division of the two fishes *among them all* (vi. 39, 41). He tells how Jesus, walking on the sea, *would have passed by* the disciples' boat; he expresses their cry of terror at Christ's appearance by a stronger word than Matthew, using the compound verb **ἀνέκραξαν** where Matthew uses the simple verb **ἔκραξαν**. He adds, *they all saw him* (vi. 48–50). When Jesus descends from the mount of transfiguration, it is Mark that fills out the incident of the disciples' controversy with the bystanders by relating that *the scribes* were questioning with them. He notes the amazement which, for whatever reason, fell upon the people at Jesus' appearance, their running to salute him, and his inquiry, *What question ye with them?* (ix. 14, 16). Mark gives us the bystanders' encouragement of Bartimeus when summoned by Jesus, and tells how *he cast off his outer garment* and *leaped up* (x. 49, 50). He alone relates the *breaking* of the alabaster by the woman (xiv. 3), and Christ's taking the little child *in his arms* after he had set him in the midst (ix. 36).

In the account of the two demoniacs of Gadara, Matthew (viii.) relates that they were met coming out of the tombs, and that they were exceeding fierce, so that no one could pass that way. Mark mentions only one demoniac, but adds that *he had his dwelling* in the tombs (*κατοίκησιν εἶχεν*, stronger than Luke's *abode*, *ἔμενεν*); that the attempt had been made to fetter him, but that he had broken the fetters; and that he was day and night in the tombs and in the mountains, crying and cutting himself with stones (v. 3–6). In the interview with the lawyer who desired to know what kind of a commandment was great in the law, Matthew (xxii. 34–40) ends the dialogue with Jesus' answer to this question. Mark gives the lawyer's reply and his enlargement upon Jesus' answer, the fact that Jesus observed that he answered discreetly, and his significant words, *Thou art not far from the kingdom of God.*

It is interesting to compare the account of Herod's feast and John the Baptist's murder as given by Matthew and Mark respectively. Mark alone mentions the great banquet and the rank of the guests. He adds the little touches of Salome's *entering in* and delighting *the guests*. He throws Herod's promise and Salome's request into dialogue. Where Matthew says simply, *He promised with an oath to give her whatsoever she should ask*, Mark gives it, *Ask of me whatsoever thou wilt, and I will give it thee. And he sware unto her, whatsoever thou shalt ask of me, I will give it thee, unto the half of my kingdom*. The whole narrative is more dramatic than Matthew's. Matthew says that Salome was *put forward* by her mother. Mark pictures her *going out*, and details her conversation with Herodias, and her *entering in* again *with haste*, and demanding the horrible boon *forthwith*. Mark also enlarges upon Herod's regret: he was *exceeding* sorry; and where Matthew notes merely his compliance with the damsel's request, Mark lets us into his feeling of unwillingness to refuse her. Mark, too, emphasizes the promptness of the transaction. Salome demands the Baptist's head *forthwith;* Herod sends the executioner *straightway*. Mark alone mentions the *executioner*. While the dialogue is not peculiar to Mark, it is to be noted that it is characteristic of Peter's style, so far, at least, as can be inferred from the stories in the book of Acts, of Ananias and Sapphira (v. 3–9), Cornelius (x.), and Peter's deliverance from prison (xii.).

Mark is peculiarly minute and specific as to details of persons, times, numbers, and places; a feature in which, also, he resembles Peter (compare Acts ii. 15; vi. 3; iv. 22; v. 7, 23; xii. 4). Thus, *of persons*, "They entered into the house of *Simon* and *Andrew* with *James* and *John*" (i. 29): "*Simon* and *they that were with him* followed after him" (i. 36): "In the days of *Abiathar* the high-priest" (ii. 26): "The *Pharisees* took counsel with the *Herodians*" (iii. 6): "The woman was a *Greek, a Syro-Phenician* by nation" (vii. 26). Compare, also, xi. 11;

xiii. 3; xv. 21. *Of places:* "A multitude from *Galilee* and *Judaea*," etc. (iii. 7, 8): The demoniac proclaimed his recovery in *Decapolis* (v. 20): Jesus departed "from the border of *Tyre* and came through *Sidon* unto the *Sea of Galilee*, through the midst of the borders of *Decapolis*" (vii. 31). Compare viii. 10; xi. 1; xii. 41; xiv. 68. *Of number:* The paralytic was "borne of *four*" (ii. 3): The swine were about *two thousand* (v. 13): The twelve were sent out *two and two* (vi. 7): The people sat down by *hundreds* and *fifties* (vi. 40): "Before the cock crow *twice* thou shalt deny me *thrice*" (xiv. 30). *Of time:* Jesus rose up *in the morning, a great while before day* (i. 35): "The *same day, when the even was come*" (iv. 35). Compare xi. 11; xiv. 68; xv. 25.

But Mark does not confine himself to mere *outward* details. He abounds in strokes which bring out the *feeling* of his characters. He uses six different words expressive of fear, wonder, trouble, amazement, extreme astonishment. The compound ἐκθαμβεῖσθαι, *greatly amazed, affrighted* (ix. 15; xvi. 5, 6) occurs nowhere else in the New Testament. Thus the look and emotion of our Lord are portrayed: "*He looked round about* on them *with anger, being grieved* at the hardness of their heart" (iii. 5): "*He looked round about* on them which sat round about him, and said, Behold my mother," etc. (iii. 34): "*He looked round about*" to see who had touched him in the crowd (v. 32): "*He marvelled* because of their unbelief" (vi. 6): *He looked* on the young ruler and *loved* him (x. 21): He was *moved with compassion* toward the leper (i. 41): *He sighed deeply in his spirit* (viii. 12).

Similarly Mark depicts the tender compassion of the Lord. A beautiful hint of his delicate and loving appreciation of an ordinary need closes the story of the healing of the ruler's daughter. In their joy and wonder at her miraculous restoration, the friends would naturally forget the immediate practical demand for food, of which the Lord promptly reminds them by his command *that something should be given her to eat* (v. 43). Luke notes the same circumstance. In like manner his appreciation of his disciples' weariness appears in the words, "Come ye yourselves apart into a desert place and rest awhile" (vi. 31).

He is *moved with compassion* toward the multitude because they are as sheep without a shepherd (vi. 34): he is touched with the need and fatigue of the many who had *come from far* (viii. 3): he shows his interest in the condition of the epileptic lad by inquiring into the history of his case (ix. 21): he is *much displeased* at the disciples' rebuke of those who are bringing the young children to him (x. 14).

In like manner Mark describes the mental and emotional states of those who were brought into contact with Christ. Those who witnessed the miracle of the loaves *understood not*, and *their heart was hardened* (vi. 52): the disciples were perplexed, *questioning among themselves what the rising again from the dead should mean* (ix. 10): they *were amazed* at his words about a rich man entering into the kingdom of heaven (x. 24): a sudden and mysterious awe fell upon them in their journey to Jerusalem (x. 32): Pilate *marvelled* at Jesus being already dead, and sent for the centurion in order to ask *whether he had been any while dead* (xv. 44). Compare i. 22, 27; v. 20, 42; vi. 20; vii. 37; xi. 18. He depicts the interest excited by the words and works of Christ; describing the crowds which flocked to him, and their spreading abroad the fame of his power (i. 28, 45; ii. 13; iii. 20, 21; iv. 1; v. 20, 21, 24; vi. 31; vii. 36).

We find in Mark certain peculiarly forcible expressions in our Lord's language, such as, "*To them that are without*" (iv. 11); "Ye *leave* the commandment of God, and *hold fast* the tradition of men" (vii. 8); "This *adulterous and sinful* generation" (viii. 38); "*Be set at nought*" (ix. 12); "*Quickly* to speak evil of me" (ix. 39); "Shall receive *brethren and sisters and mothers*," etc., "*with persecutions*" (x. 30).

His narrative *runs*. His style abounds in quick transitions. The word εὐθέως, *straightway*, occurs in his Gospel something like forty times. He imparts vividness to his narration by the use of the present tense instead of the historic (i. 40, 44; ii. 3, sq.; xi. 1, 2, 7; xiv. 43, 66). He often defines his meaning by coupling similar words or phrases. Beelzebub is called by two names (iii. 22), and by a third (iii. 30): The sick are brought *at even, when the sun did set* (i. 32): The blasphemer *hath no more forgiveness*, but is *guilty of an eternal sin* (iii. 29): He spake *with many parables*, and *without a parable he spake not* (iv. 33, 34). Compare iii. 5, 27; v. 26; vi. 25; vii. 21. He employs over seventy words which are found nowhere else in the New Testament. We find him preserving the identical Aramaic words uttered by the Lord. In his Gospel alone occur *Boanerges* (iii. 17); *Talitha cumi* (v. 41); *Korban* (vii. 11); *Ephphatha* (vii. 34); and *Abba* (xiv. 36). Writing for Romans we find him transferring certain Latin words into Greek, such as *legio, legion* (v. 9); *centurio, κεντυρίων, centurion*, which elsewhere is ἑκατόνταρχος–χης (xv. 39); *quadrans, farthing* (xii. 42); *flagellare, to scourge* (xv. 15); *speculator, executioner* (vi. 27); *census, tribute* (xii. 14); *sextarius, pot* (vii. 4); *praetorium* (xv. 16). Three of these, *centurio, speculator*, and *sextarius* are found in his Gospel only. He always adds a note of explanation to Jewish words and usages.

His style is abrupt, concise, and forcible; his diction less pure than that of Luke and John. Besides irregularities of construction which cannot be explained to the English reader, he employs many words which are expressly forbidden by the grammarians, and some of which are even condemned as slang. Such are ἐσχάτως ἔχει, *is at the point of death* (v. 23); κράββατος, *bed* (ii. 4, 9, 11, 12); μονόφθαλμος, *with one eye* (ix. 47); κολλυβισταί, *money-changers* (xi. 15); κοράσιον, *maid* (v. 41); ὁρκίζω, *I adjure* (v. 7); ῥάπισμα, *a blow of the hand* (xiv. 65); ῥαφίδος, *needle* (x. 25).

I have described the characteristics of Mark at some length, because they lie peculiarly in the line of the special purpose of this book, which deals with individual words and phrases, and with peculiarities of diction, rather than with the exegesis of passages. Of this Gospel it is especially true that its peculiar flavor and quality cannot be caught without careful verbal study. It is a gallery of word-pictures. Reading it, even in the familiar versions, we may discover that it is, as Canon Westcott remarks, "essentially a transcript from life;" but nothing short of an insight into the original and individual words will reveal to us that the transcript itself is alive.

THE GOSPEL ACCORDING TO MARK.

CHAPTER I.

1. **Beginning** (ἀρχὴ), without the article, showing that the expression is a kind of title. It is the beginning, not of his book, but of the facts of the Gospel. He shows from the prophets that the Gospel was to begin by the sending forth of a forerunner.

3. **A voice** (φωνὴ). No article as A. V. and Rev., "*the* voice." It has a sort of exclamatory force. Listening, the prophet exclaims, *Lo! a voice.*

4. **John did baptize** (ἐγένετο Ἰωάννης ὁ βαπτίζων). Lit., *John came to pass or arose who baptized.* Rev., *John came who baptized.*

Baptism of repentance (βάπτισμα μετανοίας). A baptism the characteristic of which was repentance; which involved an obligation to repent. We should rather expect Mark to put this in the more dramatic form used by Matthew: *Saying, Repent ye!*

5. **There went out** (ἐξεπορεύετο). The imperfect tense signifies, *there kept going out.*

The river. Peculiar to Mark.

Confessing. See on Matt. iii. 6.

6. **With camels' hair** (τρίχας καμήλου). Lit., *hairs.* Not with a camel's skin, but with a vesture woven of camels' hair. Compare 2 Kings 1, 8.

Wild honey. "The innumerable fissures and clefts of the limestone rocks, which everywhere flank the valleys, afford in their recesses secure shelter for any number of swarms of wild bees; and many of the Bedouin, particularly about the wilderness of Judaea, obtain their subsistence by bee-hunting, bringing into Jerusalem jars of that wild honey on which John the Baptist fed in the wilderness" (Tristram, "Land of Israel"). Wyc., *honey of the wood.*

7. **To stoop down.** A detail peculiar to Mark.

And unloose. Compare *to bear;* Matt. iii. 11.

10. **Straightway.** A favorite word with Mark. See Introduction.

Opened (σχιζομένους). Lit., as Rev., *rent asunder:* much stronger than Matthew's and Luke's ἀνεῴχθησαν, *were opened.*

11. **Thou art my beloved son.** The three synoptists give the saying in the same form: *Thou art my son, the beloved.*

12. **Driveth him** (ἐκβάλλει). Stronger than Matthew's ἀνήχθη, *was led up,* and Luke's ἤγετο, *was led.* See on Matt. ix. 38. It is the word used of our Lord's expulsion of demons, Mark i. 34, 39.

The Wilderness. The place is unknown. Tradition fixes it near Jericho, in the neighborhood of the Quarantania, the precipitous face of which is pierced with ancient cells and chapels, and a ruined church is on its topmost peak. Dr. Tristram says that every spring a few devout Abyssinian Christians are in the habit of coming and remaining here for forty days, to keep their Lent on the spot where they suppose that our Lord fasted and was tempted.

13. **With the wild beasts.** Peculiar to Mark. The region just alluded to abounds in boars, jackals, wolves, foxes, leopards, hyenas, etc.

15. **The time** (ὁ καιρὸς). That is, the *period* completed by the setting up of Messiah's kingdom. Compare *the fulness of the time*, Gal. iv. 4.

Repent. See on Matt. iii. 2; xxi. 29. Mark adds, *and believe in the Gospel.*

16. **Casting a net** (ἀμφιβάλλοντας). See on Matt. iv. 18. Mark here uses, more graphically, only the verb, without adding *net.* Lit., *throwing about* in the sea. Probably a fisherman's phrase, like *a cast, a haul.*

17. **To become** (γενέσθαι). An addition of Mark.

19. **A little farther.** Added by Mark.

Mending. See on Matt. iv. 21.

20. **With the hired servants.** Peculiar to Mark. It may imply that Zebedee carried on his business on a larger scale than ordinary fishermen.

22. **He taught** (ἦν διδάσκων). The finite verb with the participle denoting something continuous: *was teaching.*

23. **Straightway.** At the conclusion of his teaching.

With an unclean spirit (ἐν πνεύματι ἀκαθάρτῳ). Lit., "*in* an unclean spirit." Ἐν (*in*) has the force of *in the power of.* Dr. Morison compares the phrases *in drink, in love.*

24. **Us.** Me and those like me. "The demons," says Bengel, "make common cause."

The Holy One of God. The demon names him as giving to the destruction the impress of hopeless certainty.

25. **Hold thy peace** (φιμώθητι). Lit., *be muzzled* or *gagged.* See on Matt. xxii. 12.

26. **Had torn** (σπαράξαν). Rev., *tearing*, *convulsions* in margin. Luke has *had thrown him down in the midst.* Mark adds the crying out with a loud voice.

27. **They questioned among themselves** (συνζητεῖν πρὸς ἑαυτοὺς). Stronger than Luke, who has *they spake together.* Tynd., *They demanded one of another among themselves.*

30. **Lay sick of a fever** (κατέκειτο πυρέσσουσα). *Κατά, prostrate.* Mark adds, *they tell him of her.* Luke, *they besought him for her.* Mark, *he came to her.* Luke, *he stood over her.* Mark only, *he took her by the hand and raised her up.*

32. **At even, when the sun did set.** An instance of Mark's habit of coupling similar words or phrases.

That were sick. See on Matt. iv. 23, 24.

34. **Devils** (δαιμόνια). The Rev., unfortunately, and against the protest of the American committee, retains *devils* instead of rendering *demons.* See on Matt. iv. 1. The New Testament uses two kindred words to denote the evil spirits which possessed men, and which were so often cast out by Christ: *δαίμων*, of which *demon* is a transcript, and which occurs, according to the best texts, only at Matt. viii. 31; and *δαιμόνιον*, which is not a diminutive, but the neuter of the adjective *δαιμόνιος*, *of, or belonging to a demon.* The cognate verb is *δαιμονίζομαι to be possessed with a demon*, as in Mark i. 32.

The derivation of the word is uncertain. Perhaps *δαίω, to distribute*, since the deities allot the fates of men. Plato derives it from *δαήμων*, *knowing or wise.* In Hesiod, as in Pythagoras, Thales, and Plutarch, the word *δαίμων* is used of men of the golden age, acting as tutelary deities, and forming the link between gods and men. Socrates, in Plato's "Cratylus," quotes Hesiod as follows: "*Socrates:* You know how Hesiod uses the word? *Hermogenes:* Indeed I do not. *Soc.:* Do you not remember that he speaks of a golden race of men who came first? *Her.:* Yes, I know that. *Soc.:* He says of them,

> 'But now that fate has closed over this race,
> They are holy demons upon earth,
> Beneficent, averters of ills, guardians of mortal men.'"

After some further conversation, Socrates goes on: "And therefore I have the most entire conviction that he called them *demons*, because they were δαήμονες (*knowing* or *wise*). Now, he and other poets say truly that, when a good man dies, he has honor and a mighty portion among the dead, and becomes a demon, which is a name given to him signifying wisdom. And I say, too, that every wise man who happens to be a good man is more than human (δαιμόνιον) both in life and death, and is rightly called a demon." Mr. Grote ("History of Greece") observes that in Hesiod demons are "invisible tenants of the earth, remnants of the once happy golden race whom the Olympic gods first made—the unseen police of the gods, for the purpose of repressing wicked behavior in the world." In later Greek the word came to be used of any departed soul.

In Homer δαίμων is used synonymously with θεός and θεά, *god and goddess*, and the moral quality of the divinity is determined by the context: but most commonly of the *divine power* or *agency*, like the Latin *numen*, the deity considered as a *power* rather than as a *person*. Homer does not use δαιμόνιον substantively, but as an adjective, always in the vocative case, and with a sorrowful or reproachful sense, indicating that the person addressed is in some astonishing or strange condition. Therefore, as a term of reproach—*wretch! sirrah! madman!* ("Iliad," ii., 190, 200; iv., 31; ix., 40). Occasionally in an admiring or respectful sense ("Odyssey," xiv., 443; xxiii., 174); *Excellent stranger! noble sir!* Homer also uses δαίμων of one's *genius* or attendant spirit, and thence of one's *lot* or *fort-*

une. So in the beautiful simile of the sick father ("Odyssey," v., 396), "Some malignant genius has assailed him." Compare "Odyssey," x., 64; xi., 61. Hence, later, the phrase κατὰ δαίμονα is nearly equivalent to *by chance*.

We have seen that, in Homer, the bad sense of δαιμόνιος is the prevailing one. In the tragedians, also, δαίμων, though used both of good and bad fortune, occurs more frequently in the latter sense, and toward this sense the word gravitates more and more. The undertone of Greek thought, which tended to regard no man happy until he had escaped from life (see on Matt. v. 3, *blessed*), naturally imparted a gloomy and forbidding character to those who were supposed to allot the destinies of life.

In classical Greek it is noticeable that the abstract τὸ δαιμόνιον fell into the background behind δαίμων, with the development in the latter of the notion of a *fate* or *genius* connected with each individual, as the demon of Socrates; while in biblical Greek the process is the reverse, this doctrine being rejected for that of an overruling personal providence, and the strange gods, "obscure to human knowledge and alien to human life," taking the abstract term uniformly in an evil sense.

Empedocles, a Greek philosopher, of Sicily, developed Hesiod's distinction; making the demons of a mixed nature between gods and men, not only the link between the two, but having an agency and disposition of their own; not immortal, but long-lived, and subject to the passions and propensities of men. While in Hesiod the demons are all good, according to Empedocles they are both bad and good. This conception relieved the gods of the responsibility for proceedings unbecoming the divine nature. The enormities which the older myths ascribed directly to the gods—thefts, rapes, abductions—were the doings of bad demons. It also saved the credit of the old legends, obviating the necessity of pronouncing either that the gods were unworthy or the legends untrue. "Yet, though devised for the purpose of satisfying a more scrupulous religious sensibility, it was found inconvenient afterward when assailants arose against paganism generally. For while it abandoned as indefensible a large portion of what had once been genuine faith, it still retained the same word *demons* with an entirely altered signification. The Christian writers in their controversies found ample warrant among the *earlier* pagan authors for treating all the gods as demons; and not less ample warrant among the *later* pagans for denouncing the demons generally as evil beings" (Grote, "History of Greece").

This evil sense the words always bear in the New Testament as well as in the Septuagint. Demons are synonymous with *unclean spirits* (Mark v. 12, 15; iii. 22, 30; Luke iv. 33). They appear in connection with Satan (Luke x. 17, 18; xi. 18, 19); they are put in opposition to the Lord (1 Cor. x. 20, 21); to the faith (1 Tim. iv. 1). They are connected with idolatry (Apoc. ix. 20; xvi. 13, 14). They are special powers of evil, influencing and disturbing the physical, mental, and moral being (Luke xiii. 11, 16; Mark v. 2–5; vii. 25; Matt. xii. 45).

33. **All the city was gathered together at the door.** Peculiar to Mark.

35. **A great while before day** (ἔννυχα). Lit., *while it was in the night.* The word is peculiar to Mark.

36. **Followed after** (κατεδίωξαν). The word found only in Mark. Simon and his companions, as well as the people of the city, seem to have been afraid lest he should have permanently left them. Hence the compound verb indicates that they followed him *eagerly; pursued* him as if he were fleeing from them. Simon, true to his nature, was foremost in the pursuit: *Simon, and they that were with him.*

37. **All.** All the people of Capernaum, all *are seeking* thee. The continuous present tense. So Rev., better than A. V. The *all* is peculiar to Mark.

38. **Towns** (κωμοπόλεις). Lit., *village-towns*, suburban towns.

41. **Moved with compassion.** Only Mark.

43. **Strictly charged** (ἐμβριμησάμενος). Rev., *sternly*, in margin. The word is originally *to snort*, as of mettlesome horses. Hence, to *fret*, or *chafe*, or be otherwise strongly moved; and then, as a result of this feeling, to *admonish* or *rebuke urgently*. The Lord evidently spoke to him *peremptorily*. Compare *sent him out* (ἐξέβαλεν); lit., *drove* or *cast* him out. The reason for this charge and dismissal lay in the desire of Jesus not to thwart his ministry by awaking the premature violence of his enemies; who, if they should see the leper and hear his story before he had been officially pronounced clean by the priest, might deny either that he had been a leper or had been truly cleansed.

45. **The city.** Properly, as Rev., *a* city; any city.

CHAPTER II.

1. **It was noised** (ἠκούσθη). Lit., *it was heard.*

That he was in the house (ὅτι εἰς οἶκόν ἐστιν). The ὅτι, *that*, is recitative, introducing the report in the direct form. *It was reported—he is in the house!* The preposition *in* is literally *into*, carrying the idea of the motion preceding the stay in the house. "*He has gone into* the house, and is there." But the best texts read ἐν οἴκῳ, *in the house.* The account of this rumor is peculiar to Mark.

He preached (ἐλάλει). Lit., *spake*, as Rev. Imperfect tense. He was speaking when the occurrence which follows took place.

3. **Borne of four.** A detail peculiar to Mark.

4. **Come nigh unto him** (προσεγγίσαι). The word does not occur elsewhere in the New Testament. But some read προσενέγκαι, *bring him unto him.* So Rev., in margin.

They uncovered (ἀπεστέγασαν). The only use of the word in New Testament.

Broken it up (ἐξορύξαντες). Lit., *scooped it out.* Very graphic and true to fact. A modern roof would be *untiled* or *unshingled;* but an oriental roof would have to be *dug* to make such an opening as was required. A composition of mortar, tar, ashes, and sand is spread upon the roofs, and rolled hard, and grass grows in the crevices. On the houses of the poor in the country the grass grows more freely, and goats may be seen on the roofs cropping it. In some cases, as in this, stone slabs are laid across the joists. See Luke v. 19, where it is said they let him down *through the tiles;* so that they would be obliged, not only to dig through the grass and earth, but also to pry up the tiles. Compare Ps. cxxix. 6.

The bed (κράβαττον). One of Mark's Latin words, *grabatus*, and condemned by the grammarians as inelegant. A rude pallet, merely a thickly padded quilt or mat, held at the corners, and requiring no cords to let it down. They could easily reach the roof by the steps on the outside, as the roof is low; or they could have gone into an adjoining house and passed along the roofs. Some suppose that the crowd was assembled in an upper chamber, which sometimes extended over the whole area of the house. It is not possible accurately to reproduce the details of the scene. Dr. Thomson says that Jesus probably stood in the *lewan* or reception-room, a hall which is entered from the court or street by an open arch; or he may have taken his stand in the covered court in front of the house itself, which usually has open arches on three sides, and the crowd was around and in front of him.

6. **Reasoning** (διαλογιζόμενοι). The word *dialogue* is derived from this, and the meaning literally is, that *they held a dialogue* with themselves.

8. **Perceived** (ἐπιγνοὺς). The preposition ἐπί gives the force of *fully.* He was not only *immediately* aware of their thought, but *clearly* and *fully* aware.

9. **Walk** (περιπάτει). Lit., *walk about.*

10. **Power** (ἐξουσίαν); or better, *authority*, as Rev., in margin. The word is derived from ἔξεστι, *it is permitted* or *lawful.* It combines the ideas of *right* and *might.* Authority or *right* is the dominant meaning in the New Testament.

13. **Resorted—taught** (ἤρχετο—ἐδίδασκεν). The imperfects are graphic—*kept coming, kept teaching.*

14. See on Matt. ix. 9.

15. **His house.** Levi's. See Luke v. 29.

16. **Scribes and Pharisees.** But the best texts read γραμματεῖς τῶν Φαρισαίων, *scribes of the Pharisees.* So Rev. Scribes belonging to the sect of the Pharisees. They had followed him into the hall where the company were seated. This hall answered to the *k'hāwah* of Arabian houses, which is thus described by William Gifford Palgrave: "The *k'hāwah* was a long, oblong hall about twenty feet in height, fifty in length, and sixteen or thereabouts in breadth. The walls were covered in a rudely decorative manner with brown and white wash, and sunk here and there into small triangular recesses, destined to the reception of books, lamps, and other such like objects. The roof was of timber, and flat; the floor was strewn with fine, clean sand, and garnished all round alongside of the walls with long strips of carpet, upon which cushions, covered with faded silk, were disposed at suitable intervals. In poorer houses, felt rugs usually take the place of carpets" ("Central and Eastern Arabia").

17. **They that are whole** (οἱ ἰσχύοντες). Lit., *they that are strong.* See on Luke xiv. 30, *was not able;* and 2 Pet. ii. 11, *power.*

No need. The Greek order throws the emphasis on these words: *No need have they that are strong of a physician.*

Wyc., *Whole men have no need to a leech, but they that have evil.*

18. **And of the Pharisees.** But the *of* is wrong. Read as Rev., *John's disciples and the Pharisees.*

Used to fast (ἦσαν νηστεύοντες). The A. V. refers to the fact as a *custom;* but Mark means that they *were observing a fast at that time.* Hence the use of the participle with the finite verb. Rev., correctly, *were fasting.* The threefold repetition of the word *fast* is characteristic of Mark. See Introduction.

19. **Children of the bride-chamber** (υἱοὶ τοῦ νυμφῶνος). More correctly as Rev., *sons.* It is noteworthy that Christ twice uses a figure drawn from marriage in his allusions to John the Baptist, the ascetic. Compare John iii. 29. The sons of the bride-chamber are different from the groomsmen. They are the guests invited to the bridal. The scene is laid in Galilee, where groomsmen were not customary, as in Judaea. Hence there is no mention of them in the account of the marriage at Cana. In Judaea there were at every marriage two groomsmen or *friends of the bridegroom.* See on John iii. 29.

20. **Then—in those days.** The proper reading is ἐν ἐκείνῃ τῇ ἡμέρᾳ, *in that day.* So Rev. Another of Mark's double expressions: *then—in that day.*

21. **Seweth** (ἐπιῤῥάπτει). A word found in Mark only. Matthew (ix. 16) and Luke (v. 36) use ἐπιβάλλει, *throweth upon,* as we speak of *clapping* a patch upon.

23. **He went** (αὐτὸν παραπορεύεσθαι). Lit., *went along beside,* along the stretches of standing grain. Matthew and Luke use διά, *through,* as Mark does, but not παρά.

Began, as they went, to pluck (ἤρξαντο ὁδὸν ποιεῖν τίλλοντες). Lit., *began to make a way plucking the ears.* This does not mean that the disciples broke a way for themselves through the standing corn by plucking the ears, for in that event they would have been compelled to break down the stalks. They could not have made a way by plucking the heads of the grain. Mark, who uses Latin forms, probably adopted here the phrase *iter facere*, *to make a way*, which is simply *to go*. The same idiom occurs in the Septuagint, Judges xvii. 8; **ποιῆσαι ὁδὸν αὐτοῦ**, *as he journeyed*. The offence given the Pharisees was the *preparation* of food on the Sabbath. Matthew says *to eat*, stating the *motive*, and Luke, *rubbing with their hands*, describing the *act*. See on Matt. xii. 2. The Rev. rightly retains the rendering of the A. V.

25. **Had need.** Mark adds this to the *was an hungered*, which is in both Matthew and Luke. The analogy lay in the *necessity*. The *had need* is generic; the *was hungry* is specific, describing the peculiar character of the need.

26. **The shewbread** (*τοὺς ἄρτους τῆς προθέσεως*). Lit., *the loaves of proposition*, i.e., the loaves which were *set forth* before the Lord. The Jews called them the *loaves of the face*, i.e., *of the presence of God*. The bread was made of the finest wheaten flour that had been passed through eleven sieves. There were twelve loaves, or cakes, according to the number of tribes, ranged in two piles of six each. Each cake was made of about five pints of wheat. They were anointed in the middle with oil, in the form of a cross. According to tradition, each cake was five hand-breadths broad and ten long, but turned up at either end, two hand-breadths on each side, to resemble in outline the ark of the covenant. The shewbread was prepared on Friday, unless that day happened to be a feast-day that required sabbatical rest; in which case it was prepared on Thursday afternoon. The renewal of the shewbread was the first of the priestly functions on the commencement of the Sabbath. The bread which was taken off was deposited on the golden table in the porch of the sanctuary, and distributed among the outgoing and incoming courses of priests (compare *save for the priests*). It was eaten during the Sabbath, and in the temple itself, but

only by such priests as were Levitically pure. This old bread, removed on the Sabbath morning, was that which David ate.

27. **For** man (διά). *On account of*, or *for the sake of*. This saying is given by Mark only.

CHAPTER III.

1. **A withered hand** (ἐξηραμμένην τὴν χεῖρα). More correctly Rev., *his hand withered.* The participle indicates that the withering was not congenital, but the result of accident or disease. Luke says his *right hand.*

2. **They watched** (παρετήρουν). Imperfect tense. *They kept watching.* The compound verb, with παρά, *by the side of*, means to *watch carefully* or *closely*, as one who dogs another's steps, keeping *beside* or *near* him. Wyc., *They aspieden him:* i.e., *played the spy.* On τηρέω, *to watch*, see on John xvii. 12.

He would heal (θεραπεύσει). Future tense: *whether he will heal*, the reader being placed at the time of the watching, and looking forward to the future.

3. **Stand forth** (ἔγειρε εἰς τὸ μέσον). Lit., *rise into the midst.* So Wyc., *Rise into the middle.* Tynd., *Arise and stand in the midst.*

5. **Being grieved** (συλλυπούμενος). Why the compound verb, with the preposition σύν, *together with?* Herodotus (vi., 39) uses the word of *condoling with another's misfortune.* Plato ("Republic," 462) says, "When any one of the citizens experiences good or evil, the whole state will either rejoice or sorrow *with him* (ξυλλυπήσεται). The σύν therefore implies Christ's *condolence* with the moral misfortune of these hard-hearted ones. Compare the force of *con*, in *condolence.* Latin, *con, with, dolere, to grieve.*

Hardness (πωρώσει). From πῶρος, a *kind of marble*, and thence used of a *callus* on fractured bones. *Πώρωσις* is originally the process by which the extremities of fractured bones are united by a *callus*. Hence of *callousness*, or *hardness* in general. The word occurs in two other passages in the New Testament, Rom. xi. 25; Eph. iv. 18, where the A. V. wrongly renders *blindness*, following the Vulgate *caecitas*. It is somewhat strange that it does not adopt that rendering here (Vulgate, *caecitate*) which is given by both Wyc. and Tynd. The Rev. in all the passages rightly gives *hardening*, which is better than *hardness*, because it hints at the *process* going on. Mark only records Christ's feeling on this occasion.

7. **Withdrew.** Mark alone notes no less than eleven occasions on which Jesus retired from his work, in order to escape his enemies or to pray in solitude, for rest, or for private conference with his disciples. See i. 12; iii. 7; vi. 31, 46; vii. 24, 31; ix. 2; x. 1; xiv. 34.

A great multitude (πολὺ πλῆθος). Compare ver. 8, where the order of the Greek words is reversed. In the former case the *greatness* of the mass of people is emphasized; in the latter, the *mass of people itself*.

8. **He did** (ἐποίει). Imperfect tense. Others read ποιεῖ, *he is doing*. In either case the tense has a continuous force: what things he *was doing* or *is doing*. Note in vv. 7, 8, Mark's accurate detail of places. See Introduction. The reasons for our Lord's withdrawing into a boat, given with such minuteness of detail in vv. 9–11, are also peculiar to Mark.

10. **Pressed upon** (ἐπιπίπτειν). Lit., *fell* upon.

Plagues (μάστιγας). Lit., *scourges*. Compare Acts xxii. 24; Heb. xi. 36. Our word *plague* is from πληγή, Latin *plaga*, meaning a *blow*. Pestilence or disease is thus regarded as a *stroke* from a divine hand. *Πληγή* is used in classical Greek in this metaphorical sense. Thus Sophocles, "Ajax," 279: "I fear that a *calamity* (πληγή) is really come from heaven (θεοῦ, *god*)." So of *war*. Aeschylus, "Persae," 251: "O Persian land, how hath the abundant prosperity been destroyed by a single *blow* (ἐν μιᾷ πληγῇ). The word here, *scourges*, carries the same idea.

11. **The** unclean spirits (τὰ). The article indicating *those particular* spirits which took part in that scene. Mark's precision is shown in the use of the two articles and in the arrangement of the noun and adjective: *The spirits, the unclean ones.*

When they saw (ὅταν ἐθεώρουν). More accurately as Rev., *whenever they beheld.* The imperfect tense denotes a *repeated* act. The ἄν in ὅταν gives an indefinite force: *as often as they might see him.*

12. **He charged** (ἐπετίμα). The word is commonly rendered *rebuke* in the New Testament. In classical Greek its predominant sense is that of *severe*, strenuous reproach for unworthy deeds or acts. It is several times used in the New Testament, as here, in the sense of *charge*. In this sense the word carries, at bottom, a suggestion of a charge under *penalty* (τιμὴ).

That (ἵνα). According to the A. V. and Rev. the *that* indicates the *substance* of Christ's charge. Properly, however, it indicates the *intent* of his charge. He charged them *in order that* they should not make him known.

13. **Whom he would** (οὓς ἤθελεν αὐτός). Rev., more strictly, "whom *he himself* would;" not allowing any to offer themselves for special work. Out of the larger number thus called he selected twelve. See ver. 14.

14. **Ordained** (ἐποίησεν). Lit., *made.* Rev., *appointed.*

Might send them forth (ἀποστέλλῃ). As *apostles.* Compare the kindred noun ἀπόστολοι, *apostles.*

15. **To have power** (ἔχειν ἐξουσίαν). Note that he does not say *to preach and to cast out*, but *to preach and to have authority to cast out*. The power of preaching and the power of exorcising were so different that special mention is made of the divine authority with which they would need to be clothed. The power of driving out demons was given that they might apply it in confirmation of their teaching. Compare xvi. 20.

16. **And Simon he surnamed Peter.** Mark relates only his *naming* and not his *appointment*, leaving his appointment to be understood.

17. Although Mark mentions that the apostles were sent out in pairs (vi. 7), he does not classify them here in pairs. But he alone throws Peter and James and John, the three who shared the Lord's particular intimacy, into one group. Matthew and Luke both introduce Andrew between Peter and James.

He surnamed them Boanerges (*ἐπέθηκεν αὐτοῖς ὄνομα Βοανηργές*). Lit., *he put upon them the name*. Some uncertainty attaches to both the origin and the application of the name. Most of the best texts read *ὀνόματα*, *names*, instead of *name*. This would indicate that *each of the two* was surnamed a "son of thunder." Some, however, have claimed that it was a dual name given to them as a *pair*, as the name *Dioscuri* was given to Castor and Pollux. The reason of its bestowal we do not know. It seems to have been intended as a title of honor, though not perpetuated like the surname Peter, this being the only instance of its occurrence; possibly because the inconvenience of a common surname, which would not have sufficiently designated which of them was intended, may have hindered it from ever growing into an appellation. It is justified by the impetuosity and zeal which characterized both the brothers, which prompted them to suggest the calling of fire from heaven to consume the inhospitable Samaritan village (Luke ix. 54); which marked James as the victim of an early martyrdom (Acts xii. 2); and which sounds in the thunders of John's Apocalypse. The Greek Church calls John *Βροντόφωνος*, *the thunder-voiced.* The phrase, *sons of*, is a familiar Hebrew idiom, in which the distinguishing characteristic of the individual or thing named is regarded as his parent. Thus *sparks* are *sons of fire* (Job v. 7); *threshed corn* is *son of the floor* (Isa. xxi. 10). Compare *son of perdition* (John xvii. 12); *sons of disobedience* (Eph. ii. 2; v. 6).

18. **Andrew** (*'Ανδρέαν*). A name of Greek origin though in use among the Jews, from *ἀνήρ*, *man*, and signifying *manly*. He was one of the two who came earliest to Christ (Matt. iv. 18, 20; compare John i. 40, 41); and hence is always styled by the Greek fathers *πρωτόκλητος*, *first called.*

Philip (*Φίλιππον*). Another Greek name, meaning *fond of horses.* In ecclesiastical legend he is said to have been a chariot-driver.

Bartholomew. A Hebrew name—*Bar Tolmai, son of Tolmai.* Almost certainly identical with Nathanael. Philip and Nathanael are associated by John, as are Philip and Bartholomew in the parallel passages of the synoptics. Bartholomew is not mentioned in John's list of the twelve (xxi. 2), but Nathanael is; while the synoptists do not mention Nathanael in their lists, but do mention Bartholomew. Probably he had two names.

Matthew. See on the superscription of Matthew's Gospel.

Thomas. A Hebrew name, meaning *twin*, and translated by the Greek *Didymus* (John xi. 16).

Thaddaeus or Lebbaeus, as in Matt. x. 3. He is the Judas of John xiv. 22. Luther calls him *der fromme Judas* (*the good Judas*). The two surnames, Lebbaeus and Thaddaeus, mean the same thing—*beloved child.*

Simon the Canaanite. Properly, *Cananaean.* See on Matt. x. 4: "No name is more striking in the list than that of

Simon the Zealot, for to none of the twelve could the contrast be so vivid between their former and their new position. What revolution of thought and heart could be greater than that which had thus changed into a follower of Jesus one of the fierce war-party of the day, which looked on the presence of Rome in the Holy Land as treason against the majesty of Jehovah, a party who were fanatical in their Jewish strictures and exclusiveness?" (Geikie, "Life and Words of Christ").

19. **Judas Iscariot.** See on Matt. x. 4.

20. **Again.** Glancing back to the many notices of crowds in the preceding narrative. This reassembling of the multitudes, and its interference with the repast of Christ and the disciples, is peculiar to Mark.

21. **His friends** (*οἱ παρ' αὐτοῦ*). Lit., *they who were from beside him: i.e.*, by origin or birth. His mother and brethren. Compare vv. 31, 32. Wyc., *kinsmen.* Tynd., *they that belonged unto him.* Not his disciples, since they were in the house with him.

They said (*ἔλεγον*). Imperfect tense. Very graphic, *they kept saying.*

22. **Beelzebub.** See on Matt. x. 25.

And. Not connecting two parts of one accusation, but two accusations, as is evident from the two *ὅτις*, which are equivalent to quotation marks.

24. **And.** Note the way in which the sayings are linked by this conjunction; an impressive rhetorical progression.

26. **But hath an end.** Peculiar to Mark.

27. **Spoil** (*διαρπάσαι*). Mark uses the stronger and more vivid compound verb, where Matthew employs the simple *ἁρ-*

πάσαι. The verb means, primarily, *to tear in pieces; to carry away*, as the wind; *to efface*, as footsteps. So, generally, *to seize as plunder*, snatching right and left.

His goods (*τὰ σκεύη*). Lit., *his vessels*. So Wyc. Compare Mark xi. 16; Acts ix. 15; x. 11; 2 Tim. ii. 20. The special object of the robber may be precious vessels of gold or silver; but the word is probably used in its general sense of *household gear*.

28. Compare Matt. xii. 31; and note Mark's superior precision and fulness of detail.

29. **Guilty** (*ἔνοχος*). From *ἐν*, *in*, *ἔχω*, *to hold* or *have*. Lit., *is in the grasp of*, or *holden of*. Compare 1 Cor. xi. 27; James ii. 10.

Eternal damnation (*αἰωνίου ἁμαρτήματος*). An utterly false rendering. Rightly as Rev., *of an eternal sin*. So Wyc., *everlasting trespass*. The A. V. has gone wrong in following Tyndale, who, in turn, followed the erroneous text of Erasmus, *κρίσεως*, *judgment*, wrongly rendered *damnation*. See Matt. xxiii. 33, and compare Rev. there.

30. **They said** (*ἔλεγον*). Imperfect tense. *They kept saying*, or *persisted* in saying. An addition peculiar to Mark.

31, 32. **They sent unto him calling him, and a multitude was sitting about him.** Detail by Mark only; as also the words in ver. 34, **Looking round on them which sat round about him.**

CHAPTER IV.

1. **Again.** He had taught there before. See iii. 7–9.

In the sea. Mark only.

There was gathered (*συνάγεται*). The A. V. misses Mark's graphic use of the present, "There *is* gathered." So Rev.

7. **Choked** (συνέπνιξαν). The preposition, **συν** = *con* (*together*), carries the idea of *com*-pression.

It yielded no fruit. Added by Mark.

8. **That sprang up and increased** (ἀναβαίνοντα καὶ αὐξανόμενον). The Rev. literally renders the participles, *growing up* and *increasing*, thus describing the *process* more vividly. These two participles, moreover, explain the use of the imperfect tense ἐδίδου (*yielded*), denoting continuance. It began to yield and *kept yielding* as it increased.

Thirty (εἰς τριάκοντα). Lit., *up to thirty*.

10. **When he was alone.** Mark only.

They that were about him with the twelve. Mark only. Matthew and Luke, *the disciples*.

11. **Unto them that are without** (ἐκείνοις τοῖς ἔξω). The two latter words are peculiar to Mark. The phrase means *those outside of our circle*. Its sense is always determined by the contrast to it. Thus, 1 Cor. v. 12, 13, it is *non-Christians* in contrast with *me*. Col. iv. 5, *Christians* contrasted with *people of the world*. Compare 1 Thess. iv. 12; 1 Tim. iii. 7. Matthew (xiii. 11), with less precision, uses simply ἐκείνοις (*to them*), the pronoun of remote reference. Luke viii. 10, τοῖς λοιποῖς (*to the rest*).

13. Peculiar to Mark.

Parables (τὰς παραβολὰς). *The* parables, which I have spoken or may hereafter speak.

14. **The sower soweth the word.** More precise than either Matthew or Luke. Compare Matt. xiii. 19; Luke viii. 11.

19. **The lusts of other things entering in** (αἱ περὶ τὰ λοιπὰ ἐπιθυμίαι). *Lusts*, not in the limited sense of mere

sexual desire, but in the general sense of *longing*. The word is also used of desire for good and lawful things (Luke xxii. 15; Philip. i. 23).

20. **Such as.** A good rendering of the pronoun *οἵτινες*, which indicates *the class* of hearers.

21. **A candle** (*ὁ λύχνος*). Properly, *the lamp*, as Rev.

Brought (*ἔρχεται*). Lit., *cometh*. *Doth the lamp come?* This impersonation or investing the lamp with motion is according to Mark's lively mode of narrative, as is the throwing of the passage into the interrogative form. Compare Luke viii. 16. *The* lamp: the article indicating a *familiar* household implement. So also "*the* bed" and "*the* stand."

Bushel (*μόδιον*). The Latin *modius*. One of Mark's Latin words. See on Matt. v. 15. The *modius* was nearer a peck than a bushel.

Bed (*κλίνην*). A couch for reclining at table.

Candlestick (*λυχνίαν*). Rev., correctly, *stand*; i.e., *lamp-stand*. See on Matt. v. 15.

22. **Which shall not be manifested** (*ἐὰν μὴ ἵνα φανερωθῇ*). The A. V. makes Christ say that every hidden thing shall be revealed. This is wrong. He says that things are hidden *in order that they may be manifested*. Concealment is a means to revelation.

26–29. The parable of the seed growing secretly. Peculiar to Mark.

26. **Should cast** (*βάλῃ*). Lit., *should have cast*, the aorist tense, followed by the presents *sleep* and *rise* (*καθεύδῃ* and *ἐγείρηται*). The whole, literally, "As if a man *should have cast* seed into the ground, and *should be sleeping and rising* night

and day." The aorist tense indicates the single act of casting; the presents the repeated, continued sleeping and rising while the seed is growing.

Seed (τὸν σπόρον). *The* seed; that particular seed which he had to sow. Such is the force of the article.

27. **Grow** (μηκύνηται). Lit., *lengthen;* be extended by the seed lengthening out into blade and stalk.

He knoweth not how (ὡς οὐκ οἶδεν αὐτός). The Greek order is very lively: *how knoweth not he.*

28. **Of herself** (αὐτομάτη). Lit., *self-acting.* It occurs in only one other passage of the New Testament, Acts xii. 10; of the city gate which opened to Peter *of its own accord.*

29. **Is brought forth** (παραδοῖ). This rendering cannot be correct, for the verb is active, not passive, meaning to *deliver up.* Hence it is usually explained, *shall have delivered itself up to harvest;* which is stilted and artificial. Rev. *is ripe,* is a free rendering from the margin of A. V. It is, perhaps, better to explain, as Meyer does, whose rendering is adopted by Rev. in margin: *When the fruit shall have allowed,* i.e., shall have admitted of being harvested. Xenophon and Herodotus use the word in the sense of *permit* or *allow;* and an exact parallel to this occurs in the historian Polybius (xxii., 24, 9): "When the season *permitted*" (παραδιδούσης).

Putteth in (ἀποστέλλει). Lit., *sendeth forth.* So Rev. in margin. The rendering, *putteth in,* misses the figure. The verb is the same as that used of sending forth the apostles to reap the harvest of souls. See especially John iv. 38: "I sent (ἀπέστειλα) you to *reap.*"

30. Peculiar to Mark.

With what comparison shall we compare it? (ἐν τίνι αὐτὴν παραβολῇ θῶμεν;). Lit., *In what parable might we put* *it?* Rev., *In what parable shall we set it forth?* Note the *we*, taking the hearers, with a fine tact, into consultation.

31. **When it is sown** (ὅταν σπαρῇ). This phrase is repeated in ver. 32. Here the emphasis is on ὅταν, *when.* It is small at the time *when* it is sown. In ver. 32 the emphasis is on σπαρῇ, *it is sown.* It begins to grow great from the time when *it is sown.*

That are upon the earth. A little detail peculiar to Mark.

32. **Groweth up.** Mark only.

Herbs (τῶν λαχάνων). Rev., rightly, *the* herbs; those which people are wont to plant in their gardens. The word denotes garden—or pot-herbs, as distinguished from wild herbs.

Shooteth out great branches (ποιεῖ κλάδους μεγάλους). Lit., *maketh*, etc. Rev., *putteth out.* Peculiar to Mark. Matthew has *becometh a tree.* On *branches*, see note on Matt. xxiv. 32. One of the Talmudists describes the mustard-plant as a tree, of which the wood was sufficient to cover a potter's shed. Another says that he was wont to climb into it as men climb into a fig-tree. Professor Hackett says that on the plain of Akka, toward Carmel, he found a collection of mustard-plants from six to nine feet high, with branches from each side of a trunk an inch or more in thickness. Dr. Thomson relates that near the bank of the Jordan he found a mustard-tree more than twelve feet high.

Lodge (κατασκηνοῦν). See on Matt. viii. 20. Lit., *pitch their tents.*

33. **Such.** Implying that Mark knew yet more parables that were spoken at that time.

As they were able to hear it. Peculiar to Mark.

36. **Even as he was in the ship.** Rev., *boat.* Just as he was, in the boat in which he was then sitting. Mark adds the detail about the accompanying boats.

37. **Storm** (λαῖλαψ). So Luke. Distinctively a *furious* storm or *hurricane.* Compare Septuagint, Job xxxviii. 1, of the *whirlwind* out of which God answered Job. See, also, Job xxi. 18. Matthew uses σεισμὸς, *a shaking.* See on Matt. viii. 24. Mr. Macgregor ("Rob Roy on the Jordan") says that "on the sea of Galilee the wind has a singular force and suddenness; and this is no doubt because that sea is so deep in the world that the sun rarefies the air in it enormously, and the wind, speeding swiftly above a long and level plateau, gathers much force as it sweeps through flat deserts, until suddenly it meets this huge gap in the way, and it tumbles down here irresistible."

38. **A pillow** (τὸ προσκεφάλαιον). The definite article indicates a well-known part of the boat's equipment—the coarse leathern cushion at the stern for the steersman. The Anglo-Saxon version has *bolster.*

39. **Peace, be still** (σιώπα, πεφίμωσο). Lit., *be silent! be muzzled!* Wyc., rather tamely, *wax dumb!* How much more vivid than the narratives of either Matthew or Luke is this personification and rebuke of the sea as a raging monster.

Ceased (ἐκόπασεν). From κόπος, meaning, 1, *beating;* 2, *toil;* 3, *weariness.* A beautiful and picturesque word. The sea sank to rest as if exhausted by its own beating.

There was (ἐγένετο). More strictly, there *arose* or *ensued.* The aorist tense indicates something *immediate.* Tynd. has *followed.*

Calm. Wyc., *peaceableness.*

41. **They feared exceedingly** (ἐφοβήθησαν φόβον μέγαν). Lit., they *feared a great fear.*

What manner of man is this? (*τίς ἄρα οὗτός ἐστιν;*). The A. V. is rather a rendering of Matthew's *ποταπός*, *what manner of* (viii. 27), than of Mark's *τίς*, *who*. The Rev. gives it rightly: *Who then is this?* The *then* (*ἄρα*) is argumentative. Since these things are so, who then is this?

CHAPTER V.

3. The details of vv. 3–5 are peculiar to Mark. "The picture of the miserable man is fearful; and in drawing it, each evangelist has some touches which are peculiarly his own; but St. Mark's is the most eminently graphic of all, adding, as it does, many strokes which wonderfully heighten the terribleness of the man's condition, and also magnify the glory of his cure" (Trench, "Miracles").

Dwelling (*κατοίκησιν*). The *κατὰ*, *down*, gives the sense of a *settled* habitation. Compare our phrase *settled down*. So Tynd., *his abiding*.

The tombs (*τοῖς μνήμασιν*). "In unclean places, unclean because of the dead men's bones which were there. To those who did not on this account shun them, these tombs of the Jews would afford ample shelter, being either natural caves or recesses hewn by art out of the rock, often so large as to be supported with columns, and with cells upon their sides for the reception of the dead. Being, too, without the cities, and oftentimes in remote and solitary places, they would attract those who sought to flee from all fellowship of their kind" (Trench, "Miracles").

4. **With fetters and chains** (*πέδαις καὶ ἁλύσεσιν*). *πέδη*, *fetter*, is akin to *πέζα*, *the instep;* just as the Latin *pedica*, *a shackle*, is related to *pes*, a *foot*. The Anglo-Saxon plural of *fot* (*foot*) is *fet;* so that fetter is *feeter*. So Chaucer:

> "The pure *fetters* on his shinnes grete
> Were of his bitter salte teres wete."

Αλυσις (derivation uncertain) is *a chain*, a generic word, denoting a bond which might be on any part of the body.

Broken in pieces (*συντετρῖφθαι*). The verb *συντρίβω* means originally to *rub together*, to *grind* or *crush*. It has been suggested that the fetters might have been of cords which could be rubbed to pieces. Wyc. renders, *Had broken the stocks to small gobbets.*

5. **Crying** (*κράζων*). Rev., *crying out.* The verb denotes an *inarticulate* cry; a *shriek.* Aristophanes uses it of the frogs ("Ranae," 258), and of the bawling of a boor ("Equites," 285).

6. **Afar off** (*ἀπὸ μακρόθεν*). Peculiar to Mark, as is also *he ran.*

7. **Crying—he saith.** The inarticulate cry (ver. 5), and then the articulate speech.

What have I to do with thee? (*τί ἐμοὶ καὶ σοί;*). Lit., *what is there to me and thee?* What have we in common?

I adjure thee by God. Stronger than Luke's *I pray thee.* The verb *ὁρκίζω*, *I adjure*, is condemned by the grammarians as inelegant.

8. **For he said** (*ἔλεγεν*). Imperfect tense, *he was saying;* the force of which is lost both in the A. V. and Rev. The imperfect gives the reason for this strange entreaty of the demon. Jesus *was commanding*, was saying "*come out;*" and, as in the case of the epileptic child at the Transfiguration Mount, the baffled spirit wreaked his malice on the man. The literal rendering of the imperfect brings out the *simultaneousness* of Christ's exorcism, the outbreak of demoniac malice, and the cry *Torment me not.*

13. **Ran** (*ὥρμησεν*). The verb indicates *hasty*, *headlong* motion. Hence, as Rev., *rushed.*

Two Thousand. As usual, Mark alone gives the detail of number.

A steep place. But the noun has the definite article: τοῦ κρημνοῦ, *the steep*, as Rev.

15. **See** (θεωροῦσιν). Rev., rightly, *behold.* For it was more than simple *seeing.* The verb means looking *stedfastly*, as one who has an interest in the object, and with a view to search into and understand it: to look *inquiringly* and *intently.*

Clothed. Compare Luke viii. 27. *For a long time he had worn no clothes.*

18. **When he was come** (ἐμβαίνοντος αὐτοῦ). The participle is in the present tense. Not *after he had* embarked, but *while he was in the act.* Hence Rev., rightly, *as he was entering.* With this corresponds the graphic imperfect παρεκάλει: While he was stepping into the boat the restored man *was beseeching* him.

That (ἵνα). *In order that.* Not the *subject* but the *aim* of the entreaty.

23. **My little daughter** (τὸ θυγάτριον). This little endearing touch in the use of the diminutive is peculiar to Mark.

Lieth at the point of death (ἐσχάτως ἔχει). One of the uncouth phrases peculiar to Mark's style, and which are cited by some as evidence of the early composition of his gospel.

I pray thee come (ἵνα ἐλθὼν). The words *I pray thee* are not in the Greek. Literally the ruler's words run thus: *My little daughter lieth at the point of death—that thou come*, etc. In his anguish he speaks brokenly and incoherently.

He went (ἀπῆλθεν). Lit., *went away.* The aorist tense, denoting action once for all, is in contrast with the imperfects, ἠκολούθει, *kept following*, and συνέθλιβον, *kept thronging.* The multitude kept following and thronging as he went along. The preposition σύν, *together*, in the latter verb, indicates the *united* pressure of a crowd. Compare Tynd., ver. 31. *Thrusting thee on every side.*

26. Mark is much fuller and more vivid than Matthew or Luke.

Had suffered (παθοῦσα). To be taken, as everywhere in the New Testament, in the sense of *suffering pain*, not merely *subjected to treatment.* What she may have suffered will appear from the prescription for the medical treatment of such a complaint given in the Talmud. "Take of the gum of Alexandria the weight of a zuzee (a fractional silver coin); of alum the same; of crocus the same. Let them be bruised together, and given in wine to the woman that has an issue of blood. If this does not benefit, take of Persian onions three logs (pints); boil them in wine, and give her to drink, and say, 'Arise from thy flux.' If this does not cure her, set her in a place where two ways meet, and let her hold a cup of wine in her right hand, and let some one come behind and frighten her, and say, 'Arise from thy flux.' But if that do no good, take a handful of cummin (a kind of fennel), a handful of crocus, and a handful of fenugreek (another kind of fennel). Let these be boiled in wine and give them her to drink, and say, 'Arise from thy flux!'" If these do no good, other doses, over ten in number, are prescribed, among them this: "Let them dig seven ditches, in which let them burn some cuttings of vines, not yet four years old. Let her take in her hand a cup of wine, and let them lead her away from this ditch, and make her sit down over that. And let them remove her from that, and make her sit down over another, saying to her at each remove, 'Arise from thy flux!'" (Quoted from Lightfoot by Geikie, "Life and Words of Christ").

Of many physicians (ὑπὸ). Lit., *under;* i.e., under the hands of.

And was nothing bettered, but rather grew worse. Luke's professional pride as a physician kept him from such a statement. Compare Luke viii. 43.

28. **For she said** (ἔλεγεν). Imperfect tense. She *was* or *kept saying* as she pressed through the crowd, either to herself or to others.

29. **She knew—she was healed.** Note the graphic change in the tenses. ἔγνω, *she knew; ἴαται, she is healed.*

Plague. See on iii. 10.

30. **Knowing** (ἐπιγνοὺς). Rev., *perceiving.* Lit., having *fully* known.

That virtue had gone out of him (τὴν ἐξ αὐτοῦ δύναμιν ἐξελθοῦσαν). More correctly as Rev., *that the power proceeding from him had gone forth.* The object of the Saviour's knowledge was thus complex: 1st, *his power;* 2d, *that his power had gone forth.* This and the following sentence are peculiar to Mark.

32. **He looked round about** (περιεβλέπετο). Imperfect tense. He *kept looking* around for the woman, who had hidden herself in the crowd.

34. **In peace** (εἰς εἰρήνην). Lit., *into peace.* Contemplating the peace in store for her. Mark alone adds, *Be whole of thy plague.*

35. **From the ruler of the synagogue.** From his house; for the ruler himself is addressed.

Troublest (σκύλλεις). See on Matt. ix. 36. Compare Luke xi. 22, where occurs the cognate word σκῦλα, *spoils,* things *torn* or *stripped* from an enemy. Wyc., *travailest.* Tynd., *diseasest.*

36. **Heard.** This is from the reading ἀκούσας (Luke viii. 50). The correct reading is παρακούσας, which may be rendered either *not heeding,* as Rev. (compare Matt. xviii. 17), or *over-*

hearing, as Rev. in margin, which, on the whole, seems the more natural. *Disregarding* would be more appropriate if the message had been addressed to Jesus himself; but it was addressed to the ruler. Jesus *overheard* it. The present participle, λαλούμενον, *being spoken*, seems to fall in with this.

38. **Seeth** (θεωρεῖ). Rev., *beholdeth*. See on ver. 15.

Wailing (ἀλαλάζοντας). A descriptive word of the hired mourners crying *al-a-lai!*

40. **Put them out.** "Wonderful authority in the house of a stranger. He was really master of the house" (Bengel). Only Mark relates the taking of the parents with the three disciples into the chamber.

41. **Maid** (κοράσιον). Not a classical word, but used also by Matthew.

42. **Astonishment** (ἐκστάσει). Better Rev., *amazement*, which carries the sense of *bewilderment*. Ἔκστασις, of which the English *ecstasy* is a transcript, is from ἐκ, *out of*, and ἵστημι, *to place or put*. Its primitive sense, therefore, is that of *removal*; hence of a man removed *out of his senses*. In Biblical Greek it is used in a modified sense, as here, xvi. 8; Luke v. 26; Acts iii. 10, of *amazement*, often coupled with *fear*. In Acts x. 10; xi. 5; xxii. 17, it is used in the sense of our word *ecstasy*, and is rendered *trance*.

CHAPTER VI.

2. **Astonished.** See on Matt. viii. 28.

Mighty works (δυνάμεις). Lit., *powers*. See on Matt. xi. 20. Tynd., *virtues*. Outcomings of God's *power*: "powers of the world to come" (Heb. vi. 5), at work upon the earth.

3. **The carpenter.** This word "throws the only flash which falls on the continuous tenor of the first thirty years, from infancy to manhood, of the life of Christ" (Farrar, "Messages of the Books").

They were offended. See on Matt. v. 29. Tynd., *hurt.*

5. **Sick** (ἀῤῥώστοις). From ἀ, *not*, and ῥώννυμι, *to strengthen.* Sickness regarded as constitutional *weakness.*

7. **By two and two.** To help and encourage each other, and also for fulness of testimony.

8–12. See Matt. x.

14. **Was spread abroad.** "But for the rumor, Herod would not have known of him. A palace is late in hearing spiritual news" (Bengel).

Mighty works do show forth themselves in him (ἐνεργοῦσιν αἱ δυνάμεις ἐν αὐτῷ). Rev., *these powers work in him.* As Dr. Morison observes, "A snatch of Herod's theology and philosophy." He knew that John wrought no miracles when alive, but he thought that death had put him into connection with the unseen world, and enabled him to wield its powers.

16. **He is risen.** The *he*, οὗτος, is emphatic. This one. This very John.

17–29. On the peculiarities of Mark in this narrative, see Introduction.

19. **Had a quarrel against him** (ἐνεῖχεν αὐτῷ). There is some dispute about the rendering. The Rev. renders *Set herself against him,* with no alternative translation in the margin; and in Luke xi. 53, *Press upon him vehemently,* with *set themselves against him* in the margin. I see no objection to rendering *was angry at him,* taking ἐνεῖχεν αὐτῷ with an ellipsis

of χόλον, *anger*. Very literally, *had within herself* (ἐν) *anger against him*. So Herodotus, i., 118. *Astyages concealing the anger* (τόν χόλον) *which he felt toward him* (οἱ ἐνεῖχε). vi. 119, ἐνεῖχε σφῖ δεινὸν χόλον, *nourished a fierce anger against them*. So Moulton, Grimm, and De Wette.

Desired (ἤθελεν). Imperfect tense, *was desiring* all along. Her demand for John's murder was the result of a *long-cherished* wish.

20. **Observed him** (συνετήρει). A mistranslation. Rev., *kept him safe*. Peculiar to Mark. Compare Matt. ix. 17, *are preserved;* Luke ii. 19, *kept;* σύν, *closely;* τηρεῖν, to *preserve* or *keep*, as the result of guarding. See on John xvii. 12, and *reserved*, 1 Pet. i. 4.

Did many things (πολλὰ ἐποίει). The proper reading, however, is ἠπόρει; from ἀ, *not*, and πόρος, *a passage*. Hence, strictly, to be in circumstances where one cannot find a way out. So Rev., rightly, *he was much perplexed*. The other reading is meaningless.

21. **Convenient** (εὐκαίρου). Mark only. Convenient for Herodias' purpose. "Opportune for the insidious woman, who hoped, through wine, lust, and the concurrence of sycophants, to be able easily to overcome the wavering mind of her husband" (Grotius in Meyer).

Birthday. See on Matt. xiv. 6. The notice of the banquet and of the rank of the guests is peculiar to Mark.

Lords (μεγιστᾶσιν). Only here, and Apoc. vi. 15; xviii. 23. A late word, from μέγας, *great*.

High captains (χιλιάρχοις). Lit., *commanders of a thousand men*. Answering to a Roman military tribune. Both civil and military dignitaries were present, with other distinguished men of the district (*chief men*).

22. **The said Herodias** (*αὐτῆς τῆς Ἡρωδιάδος*). The A. V. misses the point of *αὐτῆς* by the translation *the said:* the object being not to particularize the Herodias just referred to, but to emphasize the fact that Herodias' *own daughter* was put forward instead of a professional dancer. Hence Rev., correctly, "the daughter of *Herodias herself*."

Damsel (*κορασίῳ*). See on Mark v. 41.

25. Mark's narrative emphasizes the eager haste with which the murder was pushed. She came in *straightway* and demanded the boon *forthwith.*

By and by (*ἐξαυτῆς*). Obsolete in the old sense of *immediately.* The A. V. translates **εὐθὺς**, *straightway*, in Matt. xiii. 21, *by and by:* **εὐθέως**, Mark iv. 17, *immediately:* and the same word in Luke xxi. 9, *by and by.* **Ἐξαυτῆς** is rendered *immediately*, Acts x. 33; xi. 11: *straightway*, Acts xxiii. 30: *presently*, Philip. ii. 23. Rev., *forthwith.* The expression *by and by* in older English was sometimes used of place. Thus Chaucer.

> "Right in the same chamber by and by" (close by).

and

> "Two young knights lying by and by" (near together).

Edward IV. is reported to have said on his death-bed: "I wote (know) not whether any preacher's words ought more to move you than I that is going by and by to the place that they all preach of."

Charger. See on Matt. xiv. 8.

26. **Exceeding sorry.** Where Matthew has *sorry.*

27. Mark's favorite *straightway.* The king is prompt in his response.

Executioner (*σπεκουλάτορα*). One of Mark's Latin words, *speculator.* A *speculator* was a guardsman, whose business it was to *watch* or *spy out* (*speculari*). It came gradually to denote one of the armed body-guard of the Roman emperor. Thus Suetonius says of Claudius that he did not dare to attend banquets unless his *speculatores* with their lances surrounded him. Seneca uses the word in the sense of *executioner*. "He met the executioners (*speculatoribus*), declared that he had nothing to say against the execution of the sentence, and then stretched out his neck." Herod imitated the manners of the Roman court, and was attended by a company of *speculatores*, though it was not their distinctive office to act as executioners. Wyc. renders *man-killer*, and Tynd. *hangman*.

29. **Corpse.** See on Matt. xxiv. 28.

Stier ("Words of Jesus") says of Herod: "This man, whose inner life was burnt out; who was made up of contradictions, speaking of his kingdom like Ahasuerus, and yet the slave of his Jezebel; willingly hearing the prophet, and unwillingly killing him; who will be a Sadducee, and yet thinks of a resurrection; who has a superstitious fear of the Lord Jesus, and yet a curiosity to see him."

31. **Come apart.** See on ch. iii. 7.

37. **Shall we go and buy,** etc. This question and Christ's answer are peculiar to Mark.

39. **By companies** (*συμπόσια συμπόσια*). Peculiar to Mark. The Jewish dining-room was arranged like the Roman: three tables forming three sides of a square, and with divans or couches following the outside line of the tables. The open end of the square admitted the servants who waited at table. This explains the arrangement of the multitude here described by Mark. The people sat down, literally, *in table-companies*, arranged like guests at table; some companies of a hundred and some of fifty, in squares or oblongs open at one end, so that the disciples could pass along the inside and distribute the loaves.

Green. Mark only.

40. **In ranks** (πρασιαὶ πρασιαὶ). Lit., *like beds in a garden.* The former adverb, *by companies*, describes the *arrangement*; this the *color.* The red, blue, and yellow clothing of the poorest orientals makes an Eastern crowd full of color; a fact which would appeal to Peter's eye, suggesting the appearance of flowerbeds in a garden.

41. **Brake and gave** (κατέκλασεν, ἐδίδου). The verbs are in different tenses; the former in the *aorist*, the latter in the imperfect. The aorist implies the *instantaneous*, the imperfect the *continuous* act. He *brake*, and *kept giving out.* Farrar remarks that the multiplication evidently took place in Christ's hands, between the acts of breaking and distributing.

All. Peculiar to Mark.

Were filled. See on Matt. v. 6.

43. **Baskets full** (κοφίνων πληρώματα). Lit., *fillings* of *baskets.* See on Matt. xiv. 20. Mark alone adds, *and of the fishes.*

44. **Men** (ἄνδρες). Not generic, including men and women, but literally *men.* Compare Matt. xiv. 21, *beside women and children;* a detail which we should have expected from Mark.

46. **When he had sent them away** (ἀποταξάμενος). Rev., more correctly, *after he had taken leave.* Unclassical, and used in this sense only in later Greek. So in Luke ix. 61; Acts xviii. 18; 2 Cor. ii. 13.

48. **He saw** (ἰδὼν). Participle. Rev., *seeing.* Better, however, the literal *having seen.* It was this which induced him to go to them.

Toiling (βασανιζομένους). Lit., *tormented.* Rev., *distressed.* See on Matt. iv. 24. Wyc., *travailing.* Tynd., *troubled.*

Fourth watch. Between 3 and 6 A.M.

Would have passed by them. Peculiar to Mark.

50. **They all saw him.** Peculiar to Mark.

Spake with them (ἐλάλησεν μετ' αὐτῶν). Both Matthew and John give the simple dative, αὐτοῖς, *to them*. Mark's *with them* is more familiar, and gives the idea of a more friendly and encouraging address. It is significant, in view of Peter's relation to this gospel, that Mark omits the incident of Peter's walk on the waves (Matt. xiv. 28–31).

51. **Ceased.** See on Mark iv. 38.

Sore amazed (λίαν ἐκ περισσοῦ ἐξίσταντο). Lit., *exceedingly beyond measure*. A strong expression peculiar to Mark. Ἐξίσταντο, *were amazed*. Compare the cognate noun ἔκστασις, and see on Mark v. 42.

52. Peculiar to Mark.

The miracle of the loaves (ἐπὶ τοῖς ἄρτοις). Rev., *concerning the loaves*. Lit., *upon; in the matter of*. They did not reason from the multiplying of the loaves to the stilling of the sea.

53. **Drew to the shore** (προσωρμίσθησαν). Peculiar to Mark. Rev., *moored to the shore*, though the meaning may be *near* the shore. Ἀνέβη, *he went up* (ver. 51), seems to indicate a vessel of considerable size, standing quite high out of the water. They may have anchored off shore.

55. **Ran round.** From place to place where the sick were, to bring them to Jesus. Matthew has *they sent*.

Carry about (περιφέρειν). περί, *about*; one hither and another thither, wherever Christ might be at the time.

Beds (κραβάττοις). Condemned as bad Greek, but used by both Luke and John. See on Mark ii. 4.

56. Peculiar to Mark.

In the streets (ἀγοραῖς). Rightly, Rev., *market-places.* See on Matt. xi. 16.

Border. See on Matt. ix. 20.

CHAPTER VII.

2. **Defiled** (κοιναῖς). Lit., *common;* and so Rev. in margin, Wyc., and Tynd.

That is. Added by way of explanation to Gentile readers.

Oft (πυγμῇ). Rev., *diligently.* A word which has given critics much difficulty, and on which it is impossible to speak decisively. The Rev. gives in the margin the simplest meaning, the literal one, *with the fist;* that is, rubbing the uncleansed hand with the other doubled. This would be satisfactory if there were any evidence that such was the custom in washing; but there is none. Edersheim ("Life and Times of Jesus," ii., 11, note) says "the custom is not in accordance with Jewish law." But he elsewhere says ("The Temple," 206, note), "For when water was poured upon the hands they had to be lifted, yet so that the water should neither run up above the wrist, nor back again upon the hand; best, therefore, by doubling the fingers into a fist. Hence (as Lightfoot rightly remarks) Mark vii. 3, should be translated *except they wash their hands with the fist.*" Tischendorf, in his eighth edition, retains an ancient reading, πυκνά, *frequently* or *diligently*, which may go to explain this translation in so many of the versions (Gothic, Vulgate, Syriac). Meyer, with his usual literalism gives *with the fist*, which I am inclined to adopt.

Holding (κρατοῦντες). Strictly, holding *firmly* or *fast.* So Heb. iv. 14; Apoc. ii. 25; denoting *obstinate adherence to the tradition.*

4. **Wash themselves** (βαπτίσωνται). Two of the most important manuscripts, however, read ῥαντίσωνται, *sprinkled themselves*. See Rev., in margin. This reading is adopted by Westcott and Hort. The American Revisers insist on *bathe*, instead of *wash*, already used as a translation of νίψωνται (ver. 3). The scope of this work does not admit of our going into the endless controversy to which this word has given rise. It will be sufficient to give the principal facts concerning its meaning and usage.

In classical Greek the primary meaning is *to merse*. Thus Polybius (i., 51, 6), describing a naval battle of the Romans and Carthaginians, says, "They *sank* (ἐβάπτιζον) many of the ships." Josephus ("Jewish War," iv., 3, 3), says of the crowds which flocked into Jerusalem at the time of the siege, "They *overwhelmed* (ἐβάπτισαν) the city." In a metaphorical sense Plato uses it of *drunkenness: drowned in drink* (βεβαπτισμένοι, "Symposium," 176); of a youth *overwhelmed* (βαπτιζόμενον) with the argument of his adversary ("Euthydemus," 277).

In the Septuagint the verb occurs four times: Isa. xxi, 4, *Terror hath frighted me*. Septuagint, *Iniquity baptizes me* (βαπτίζει); 2 Kings v. 15, of Naaman's *dipping* himself in Jordan (ἐβαπτίσατο); Judith xii. 7, Judith *washing* herself (ἐβαπτίζετο) at the fountain; Sirach xxxi. 25, being *baptized* (βαπτιζόμενος) from a dead body.

The New Testament use of the word to denote submersion for a religious purpose, may be traced back to the Levitical washings. See Levit. xi. 32 (of vessels); xi. 40 (of clothes); Num. viii. 6, 7 (sprinkling with purifying water); Exod. xxx. 19, 21 (of washing hands and feet). The word appears to have been at that time the technical term for such washings (compare Luke xi. 38; Heb. ix. 10; Mark vii. 4), and could not therefore have been limited to the meaning *immerse*. Thus the washing of pots and vessels for ceremonial purification could not have been by plunging them in water, which would have rendered impure the whole body of purifying water. The word may be taken in the sense of *washing* or *sprinkling*.

"The Teaching of the Apostles" (see on Matt. x. 10) throws light on the elastic interpretation of the term, in its directions for baptism. "Baptize—*in living* (i.e., running) water. But if thou hast not living water, baptize in other water; and if thou canst not in cold, then in warm. But if thou hast neither, *pour* water upon the head thrice into the name of the Father, and of the Son, and of the Holy Spirit" (Chap. VII.).

Pots (ξεστῶν). Another of Mark's Latin words, adapted from the Latin *sextarius*, a *pint measure*. Wyc., *cruets*. Tynd., *cruses*.

Brazen vessels (χαλκίων). More literally, *copper*.

Tables (κλινῶν). Omitted in some of the best manuscripts and texts, and by Rev. The A. V. is a mistranslation, the word meaning *couches*. If this belongs in the text, we certainly cannot explain βαπτισμοὺς as *immersion*.

6. **Well** (καλῶς). *Finely*, *beautifully*. Ironical.

10. **Honor.** Wyc. has *worship*. Compare his rendering of Matt. vi. 2, "That they be *worshipped* of men;" xiii. 57, "A prophet is not without *worship* but in his own country;" and especially John xii. 26, "If any man serve me, my Father shall *worship* him."

Die the death (θανάτῳ τελευτάτω). Lit., *come to an end by death*. See on Matt. xv. 4.

11. **Corban.** Mark only gives the original word, and then translates. See on Matt. xv. 5.

13. **Making of none effect.** Rev., *making void*. See on Matt. xv. 6.

Ye handed down. Note the past tense, identifying them for the moment with their forefathers. Compare Matt. xxiii. 35, *Ye slew*. Christ views the Jewish persecutors and bigots, ancient and modern, as a whole, actuated by one spirit, and ascribes to one section what was done by another.

17. **The disciples.** Matthew says *Peter.* There is no discrepancy. Peter spoke for the band.

18. **So.** So unintelligent as not to understand what I uttered to the crowd.

19. **Draught** (ἀφεδρῶνα). Liddell and Scott give only one definition—a *privy, cloaca;* and derive from ἕδρα, *seat, breech, fundament.* Compare English *stool.* The word does not refer to a part of the body.

Purging all meats (καθαρίζων πάντα τὰ βρώματα). According to the A. V. these words are in apposition with *draught:* the draught which makes pure the whole of the food, since it is the place designed for receiving the impure excrements.

Christ was enforcing the truth that all defilement comes from within. This was in the face of the Rabbinic distinctions between clean and unclean meats. Christ asserts that *Levitical* uncleanness, such as eating with unwashed hands, is of small importance compared with *moral* uncleanness. Peter, still under the influence of the old ideas, cannot understand the saying and asks an explanation (Matt. xv. 15), which Christ gives in vv. 18–23. The words *purging all meats* (Rev., *making all meats clean*) are not Christ's, but the Evangelist's, explaining the bearing of Christ's words; and therefore the Rev. properly renders, *this he said* (italics), *making all meats clean.* This was the interpretation of Chrysostom, who says in his homily on Matthew: "But Mark says that he said these things making all meats pure." Canon Farrar refers to a passage cited from Gregory Thaumaturgus: "And the Saviour, who purifies all meats, says." This rendering is significant in the light of Peter's vision of the great sheet, and of the words, "What God hath cleansed" (ἐκαθάρισε), in which Peter probably realized for the first time the import of the Lord's words on this occasion. Canon Farrar remarks: "It is doubtless due to the fact that St. Peter, the informant of St. Mark, in writing his Gospel, and as the sole ultimate authority for this vision in the Acts, is the source of both narratives,—that we owe the hitherto unnoticed circumstance that the two verbs, *cleanse* and *profane* (or *defile*), both in a peculiarly pregnant sense, are the two most prominent words in the narrative of both events" ("Life and Work of Paul," i., 276–7).

21. **Evil Thoughts** (διαλογισμοὶ οἱ κακοὶ). *Thoughts, those which are evil.* So Rev., in margin. *Thoughts that are evil.* The word διαλογισμοὶ, *thoughts*, does not in itself convey a bad sense; and hence the addition of adjectives denoting evil, as here and James ii. 4. Radically, it carries the idea of *discussion* or *debate*, with an under-thought of *suspicion* or *doubt*, either with one's own mind, as Luke v. 22; vi. 8; or with another, Luke ix. 46; Philip. ii. 14; Rom. xiv. 1.

22. **Wickedness** (πονηρίαι). Plural. Rev., *wickednesses.* From πονεῖν, *to toil.* The adjective πονηρός means, first, *oppressed by toils;* then *in bad case* or *plight*, from which it runs into the sense of *morally bad.* This conception seems to have been associated by the high-born with the life of the lower, laboring, slavish class; just as our word *knave* (like the German *knabe* from which it is derived) originally meant simply *a boy* or *a servant-lad.* As πόνος means *hard*, *vigorous* labor, battle for instance, so the adjective πονηρός, in a moral sense, indicates *active* wickedness. So Jeremy Taylor: "Aptness to do shrewd turns, to delight in mischiefs and tragedies; a loving to trouble one's neighbor and do him ill offices." Πονηρός, therefore, is *dangerous*, *destructive.* Satan is called ὁ πονηρός, *the wicked one.* Κακός, *evil* (see *evil thoughts*, ver. 21), characterizes evil rather as *defect:* "That which is not such as, according to its nature, destination, and idea it might be or ought to be" (Cremer). Hence of *incapacity in war;* of *cowardice* (κακία). Κακὸς δοῦλος, *the evil servant*, in Matt. xxiv. 48, is a servant *wanting* in proper fidelity and diligence. Thus the thoughts are styled *evil*, as being that which, in their nature and purpose, they ought not to be. Matthew, however (xv. 19), calls these thoughts πονηροί, the thoughts *in action*, taking shape in purpose. Both adjectives occur in Apoc. xvi. 2.

Lasciviousness (*ἀσέλγεια*). Derivation unknown. It includes lasciviousness, and may well mean that here; but is often used without this notion. In classical Greek it is defined as *violence, with spiteful treatment and audacity*. As in this passage its exact meaning is not implied by its being classed with other kindred terms, it would seem better to take it in as wide a sense as possible—that of *lawless insolence* and *wanton caprice*, and to render, with Trench, *wantonness*, since that word, as he remarks, "stands in remarkable ethical connection with *ἀσέλγεια*, and has the same duplicity of meaning" ("Synonyms of the New Testament"). At Rom. xiii. 13, where *lasciviousness* seems to be the probable meaning, from its association with *chambering* (*κοίταις*), it is rendered *wantonness* in A. V. and Rev., as also at 2 Pet. ii. 18.

Evil eye (*ὀφθαλμὸς πονηρὸς*). A *malicious, mischief-working* eye, with the meaning of *positive, injurious activity*. See on *wickednesses*.

Blasphemy (*βλασφημία*). The word does not necessarily imply blasphemy against God. It is used of *reviling, calumny, evil-speaking* in general. See Matt. xxvii. 39; Rom. iii. 8; xiv. 16; 1 Pet. iv. 4, etc. Hence Rev. renders *railing*.

Pride (*ὑπερηφανία*). From *ὑπέρ*, *above*, and *φαίνεσθαι*, *to show one's self*. The picture in the word is that of a man with his head held high above others. It is the sin of an uplifted heart against God and man. Compare Prov. xvi. 5; Rom. xii. 16 (mind not *high things*); 1 Tim. iii. 6.

24. **Went away.** See on ch. vi. 31. The entering into the house and the wish to be secluded are peculiar to Mark.

25. **Daughter** (*θυγάτριον*). Diminutive. Rev., *little daughter*. See on ch. v. 23.

26. **Syro-Phoenician.** Phoenician of *Syria*, as distinguished from a *Libyo-Phoenician* of North Africa, Libya being often used for Africa.

27. **Let the children first be filled.** Peculiar to Mark.

The dogs. Diminutive. See on Matt. xv. 26.

28. Mark adds *under the table.*

The children's crumbs. See on Matt. xv. 26. This would indicate that the little dogs were pet dogs of the children, their *masters.*

29, 30. Peculiar to Mark.

Laid (βεβλημένον). Lit., *thrown.* She had probably experienced some fearful convulsion when the demon departed. Compare Mark ix. 22, of the demon which possessed the boy: "It hath *cast* him, etc. (ἔβαλεν)." See also Mark i. 26; ix. 26.

32–37. A narrative peculiar to Mark.

32. **Deaf** (κωφὸν). See on Matt. ix. 32.

Had an impediment in his speech (μογιλάλον). Μόγις, *with difficulty;* λάλος, *speaking.* Not absolutely dumb. Compare *he spake plain*, ver. 35.

33. **Put** (ἔβαλεν). Lit., *threw: thrust.*

35. **Plain** (ὀρθῶς). Lit., *rightly.* So Wyc.

36. **Charged** (διεστείλατο). The verb means, first, to *separate;* then to *define* or *distinguish;* and as that which is separated and distinguished is *emphasized, to command* or *straitly charge.*

37. **Astonished.** See on Matt. vii. 28.

To speak (λαλεῖν). See on Matt. xxviii. 18. The emphasis is not on the *matter*, but on the *fact* of speech.

CHAPTER VIII.

2. **I have compassion** (σπλαγχνίζομαι). A peculiar verb, from σπλάγχνα, *the inward parts*, especially the nobler entrails —the heart, lungs, liver, and kidneys. These came gradually to denote the *seat of the affections*, like our word *heart*. This explains the frequent use of the word *bowels* in the A. V. in the sense of *tender mercy*, *affection*, *compassion*. See Luke i. 78; 2 Cor. vii. 15; Philip. i. 8; Philem. 7, 12, 20. The Rev. has properly rejected it in every such case, using it only in its literal sense in the single passage, Acts i. 18.

They have been with me (προσμένουσιν). Lit., *they continue*, as Rev.

3. **Faint.** See on Matt. xv. 32. Wyc., *fail.*

Some of them came from far. Peculiar to Mark.

6. **To sit down** (ἀναπεσεῖν). Lit., *to recline.*

Brake and gave. See on Mark vi. 41.

8. **Were filled.** See on Matt. v. 6. Wyc., *fulfilled.* Tynd., *sufficed.*

9. **Baskets.** See on Matt. xiv. 20.

Four thousand. Matthew (xv. 38) here adds a detail which we should rather expect in Mark: *beside women and children.*

10. **With his disciples.** Peculiar to Mark.

11. **Began.** The beginnings of things seem to have a peculiar interest for Mark. See i. 1, 45; iv. 1; v. 17, 20; vi. 2, 7, 34, 55.

Sign (σημεῖον). See on Matt. xi. 20. Wyc., *token.* As applied to the miracles of our Lord, this word emphasizes their ethical purport, as declaring that the miraculous act points back of itself to the grace and power or divine character or authority of the doer.

12. **Sighed deeply in his spirit.** Peculiar to Mark.

There shall no sign be given (εἰ δοθήσεται σημεῖον). Lit., *if a sign shall be given.* The expression is elliptical. It is a Hebrew idiom, and is really, at bottom, a form of imprecation. *If I do not thus or so, may some judgment overtake me.* Compare Heb. iii. 11.

14. The *one loaf* is a detail given by Mark only.

22–26. Peculiar to Mark.

23. **Took** (ἐπιλαβόμενος). Tynd., *caught.*

If he saw (εἴ τι βλέπεις). Rev., more accurately, renders the direct question: *Seest thou aught?* The change of tenses is graphic. *Asked* (imperfect). *Dost thou see* (present).

24. **I see men as trees walking** (following the reading, Βλέπω τοὺς ἀνθρώπους ὡς δένδρα περιπατοῦντας). The Rev. reads, following the amended text, *I see men, for* (ὅτι) *I behold* (ὁρῶ) *them as trees, walking.* He saw them *dimly.* They looked like trees, large and misshapen; but he knew they were men, for they were walking about.

25. **Made him look up.** The best texts omit, and substitute διέβλεψεν, *he looked stedfastly.* See on Matt. vii. 5. Instead of vaguely staring, he fixed his eyes on definite objects.

He saw (ἐνέβλεπεν). Imperfect tense. Continuous action. He saw and *continued* to see. Compare the aorist tense above: *He looked stedfastly*, fastened his eyes, denoting the single act, the first exercise of his restored sight.

Every man. Following the reading ἅπαντας. But the best texts read ἅπαντα, *all things*. So Rev.

Clearly (τηλαυγῶς). From τῆλε, *far*, αὐγή, *shining*. The farthest things were clearly seen.

29. **He saith** (ἐπηρώτα). More correctly, he *questioned* or *asked*. So Rev. Mark omits the commendation of Peter. See Introduction.

On vv. 31–33, compare notes on Matt. xvi. 21–28.

32. **He spake the saying openly.** Mark only. Not as a secret or mystery, as in his words about being *lifted up*, or *building the temple in three days*. Not ambiguously, but explicitly. Wyc., *plainly*.

34. Jesus now pauses; for what he has to say now is to be said to *all* who follow him. Hence he *calls the multitude* with his disciples. Peculiar to Mark.

Will (θέλει). Rev., *would*. See on Matt. i. 19. It is more than *is wishful*.

His cross. The pronoun αὐτοῦ, *his*, is in an emphatic position.

35. **And the gospel's.** Peculiar to Mark.

36. **Gain—lose.** See on Matt. xvi. 26.

38. **My words.** Bengel remarks that one may confess Christ in general and yet be ashamed of this or that saying.

In this adulterous and sinful generation. Peculiar to Mark.

CHAPTER IX.

Compare Matt. xvii. 1–13; Luke ix. 28–36.

2. **Transfigured.** See on Matt. xvii. 2.

3. **Shining** (*στίλβοντα*). Rev., *glistering.* The word is used of a gleam from polished surfaces—arms, sleek horses, water in motion, the twinkling of the stars, lightning.

As no fuller, etc. Peculiar to Mark.

5. **Answered.** Though no question had been asked him: but the Lord's transfiguration was an appeal to him and he desired to respond.

7. **Sore afraid.** Wyc., *aghast by dread.*

Beloved son. Wyc., *most dearworthy.*

8. **Suddenly** (*ἐξάπινα*). The Greek word only here in the New Testament.

9. **Tell** (*διηγήσωνται*). Mark's word is more graphic than Matthew's *εἴπητε*. The word is from *διά*, *through*, and *ἡγέομαι*, *to lead the way.* Hence to lead one through a series of events: to *narrate.*

Questioning. Wyc., *asking.* Tynd., *disputing.*

14. **The scribes.** The particularizing of the scribes as the questioners, and vv. 15, 16, are peculiar to Mark.

15. **Were greatly amazed** (*ἐξεθαμβήθησαν*). A word peculiar to Mark. See Introduction.

18. **It taketh him** (καταλάβῃ). Lit., *seizeth hold of him*. Our word *catalepsy* is derived from this.

Teareth (ῥήσσει). Rev., *dasheth down*, with *rendeth* in margin. The verb is a form of ῥήγνυμι, *to break*. The form ῥήσσω is used in classical Greek of dancers beating the ground, and of beating drums. Later, in the form ῥάσσειν, a term of fighters: *to fell*, or *knock down*, which is the sense adopted by Rev.

Gnasheth with his teeth. Rev., *grindeth*. This and the *pining away* are peculiar to Mark.

19. **Faithless** (ἄπιστος). *Faithless* has acquired the sense of *treacherous, not keeping faith*. But Christ means *without faith*, and such is Tyndale's translation. Wyc., *out of belief*. *Unbelieving* would be better here. The Rev. retains this rendering of the A. V. at 1 Cor. vii. 14, 15; Tit. i. 15; Apoc. xxi. 8, and elsewhere.

20. Mark is more specific in his detail of the convulsion which seized the lad as he was coming to Jesus. He notes the convulsion as coming on at the demoniac's sight of our Lord. "*When he saw him*, straightway the spirit," etc. Also his falling on the ground, wallowing and foaming. We might expect the detail of these symptoms in Luke, the physician.

21–27. Peculiar to Mark. He gives the dialogue between Jesus and the boy's father, and relates the process of the cure in graphic detail.

22. **Us.** Very touching. The father identifies himself with the son's misery. Compare the Syro-Phoenician, who makes her daughter's case entirely her own: "Have mercy *on me*" (Matt. xv. 22).

23. **If thou canst believe** (τὸ εἰ δύνῃ). Lit., *the if thou canst*. The word *believe* is wanting in the best texts. It is difficult to explain to an English reader the force of the definite article

here. "It takes up substantially the word spoken by the father, and puts it with lively emphasis, without connecting it with the further construction, in order to link its fulfilment to the petitioner's own faith" (Meyer). We might paraphrase thus. Jesus said: "that *if thou canst* of thine—as regards *that*, all things are possible," etc. There is a play upon the words *δύνῃ*, *canst*, and *δυνατὰ*, *possible*, which cannot be neatly rendered. "If thou *canst*—all things *can be*."

24. **Cried out and said** (*κράξας—ἔλεγεν*). The former denoting the *inarticulate* cry, the *ejaculation*, followed by the *words*, "Lord, I believe," etc.

30. **Passed through** (*παρεπορεύοντο*). Lit., *passed along* (*παρά*). Not tarrying. Bengel says, "not *through* the cities, but *past* them."

31. **He taught** (*ἐδίδασκεν*). The Rev. would have done better to give the force of the imperfect here: *He was teaching*. He sought seclusion because he was engaged for the time in instructing. The teaching was the continuation of the "*began* to teach" (viii. 31).

Is delivered. The present tense is graphic. The future is realized by the Lord as already present. See on Matt. xxvi. 2.

33–35. Peculiar to Mark.

35. **Servant** (*διάκονος*). Rev., *minister*. Probably from *διώκω*, *to pursue*; to be the *follower* of a person; to attach one's self to him. As distinguished from other words in the New Testament meaning *servant*, this represents the servant in his *activity*; while *δοῦλος*, *slave*, represents him in his *condition* or *relation* as a *bondman*. A *διάκονος* may be either a slave or a freeman. The word *deacon* is an almost literal transcription of the original. See Philip. i. 1; 1 Tim. iii. 8, 12. The word is often used in the New Testament to denote *ministers of the gospel*. See 1 Cor. iii. 5; Eph. iii. 7; 1 Thess. iii. 2, and elsewhere. Mark uses *δοῦλος* in x. 44.

36. **Let** (ἔστησεν). Wyc. renders *ordained.*

When he had taken him in his arms (ἐναγκαλισάμενος). The verb is found only in Mark, and only he records this detail.

37. **In my name.** Lit., "*upon* (ἐπὶ) my name." See on Matt. xviii. 5.

38. **In thy name.** John's conscience is awakened by the Lord's words. They had not received the man who cast out devils in Christ's name.

42. **Millstone.** Rev., *great millstone.* See on Matt. xviii. 6. Wyc., *millstone of asses.* Note the graphic present and perfect tenses; the millstone *is* hanged, and he *hath been cast.*

43. **Hell.** See on Matt. v. 22.

47. **With one eye** (μονόφθαλμον). Lit., *one-eyed.* One of Mark's words which is branded as slang. Wyc. oddly renders *goggle-eyed.*

50. **Have lost its saltness** (ἄναλον γένηται). Lit., *may have become saltless.* Compare on Matt. v. 13.

Will ye season (ἀρτύσετε). Lit., *will ye restore.* Compare Col. iv. 5.

CHAPTER X.

2. **Tempting.** See on Matt. vi. 13.

4. **Bill** (βιβλίον). See on Matt. xix. 7. Diminutive. Lit., *a little book;* Lat., *libellus,* from which comes our word *libel,* a written accusation. Accordingly Wyc. has *a libel of forsaking,* and Tynd. *a testimonial of her divorcement.*

7. **Shall cleave.** See on Matt. xix. 5. Tynd., *bide by.*

8. **Shall be one flesh** (*ἔσονται εἰς σάρκα μίαν*). Lit., "shall be *unto* one flesh." The preposition expresses more graphically than the A. V. the *becoming* of one from two. So Rev., *shall become.*

9. **What.** Regarding the two as one.

13. **They brought** (*προσέφερον*). Imperfect tense; *they were bringing*, as he went on his way. Similarly, *were rebuking*, as they were successively brought.

16. **Took them in his arms.** See on ix. 36.

Put his hands upon them and blessed them. The best texts read *κατευλόγει, τιθεὶς τὰς χεῖρας ἐπ' αὐτά*, *blessed them, laying his hands upon them;* including the laying on of hands in the blessing. The compound rendered *blessed* occurs only here in the New Testament. It is stronger than the simple form, and expresses the earnestness of Christ's interest. Alford renders *fervently blessed.*

17. **Running and kneeled.** Two details peculiar to Mark.

18. **Why callest thou,** etc. Compare Matt. xix. 17. The renderings of the A. V. and Rev. *here* are correct. There is no change of reading as in Matthew, where the text was altered to conform it to Mark and Luke.

22. **He was sad** (*στυγνάσας*). Applied to the sky in Matt. xvi. 3; *lowering*. The word paints forcibly the gloom which clouded his face.

25. **Needle** (*ῥαφίδος*). A word stigmatized by the grammarians as unclassical. One of them (Phrynichus) says, "As for *ῥαφίς*, nobody would know what it is." Matthew also uses it. See on Matt. xix. 24. Luke uses *βελόνης*, the *surgical* needle. See on Luke xviii. 25.

30. **Houses,** etc. These details are peculiar to Mark. Note especially *with persecutions*, and see Introduction. With beau-

tiful delicacy the Lord omits *wives;* so that Julian's scoff that the Christian has the promise of a hundred wives is without foundation.

32. **Were amazed.** The sudden awe which fell on the disciples is noted by Mark only.

42. **Which are accounted to rule.** Wyc., *that seem to have princehead on folks.*

43. **Minister.** See on ix. 35.

45. **For many** (ἀντὶ πολλῶν). *For*, in the sense of *over against, instead of;* not *on behalf of.*

46. **Son of Timaeus.** Mark, as usual, is particular about names.

Blind. Diseases of the eye are very common in the East. Thomson says of Ramleh, "The ash-heaps are extremely mischievous; on the occurrence of the slightest wind the air is filled with a fine, pungent dust, which is very injurious to the eyes. I once walked the streets counting all that were either blind or had defective eyes, and it amounted to about one-half the male population. The women I could not count, for they are rigidly veiled" ("Land and Book"). Palgrave says that ophthalmia is fearfully prevalent, especially among children. "It would be no exaggeration to say that one adult out of every five has his eyes more or less damaged by the consequences of this disease" ("Central and Eastern Arabia").

Beggar. See on Matt. v. 3.

49, 50. Peculiar to Mark, and adding greatly to the vividness of the narrative.

50. **Rose** (ἀναστὰς). The best texts read ἀναπήδησας, *leaped up*, or, as Rev., *sprang up.*

CHAPTER XI.

2. **Colt.** Only Matthew adds the *ass*. Mark and Luke have *colt* only.

4. **In a place where two ways met** (ἐπὶ τοῦ ἀμφόδου). Ἄμφοδον is literally any road which leads *round* (ἀμφί) a place or a block of buildings. Hence the *winding* way. The word occurs only here in the New Testament. Rev., *in the open street*, which in an Eastern town is usually crooked. Perhaps, by contrast with the usual crookedness, the street in Damascus where Paul lodged was called *Straight* (Acts ix. 11). "It is a topographical note," says Dr. Morison, "that could only be given by an eye-witness." The detail of ver. 4 is peculiar to Mark. According to Luke (xxii. 8), Peter was one of those sent, and his stamp is probably on the narrative.

8. **In the way.** Both Matthew and Luke have ἐν, *in;* but Mark, εἰς, *into*. They threw their garments *into* the way and spread them there.

Branches. Matthew, Mark, and John use each a different word for *branches*. Matt., κλάδους, from κλάω, *to break;* hence a *young slip* or *shoot*, such as is *broken off* for grafting—a *twig*, as related to a *branch*. Mark, στιβάδας, from στείβω, *to tread* or *beat down;* hence a mass of straw, rushes, or leaves *beaten together* or strewed loose, so as to form a bed or a carpeted way. A *litter* of branches and leaves cut *from the fields* (only Mark) near by. John, βαΐα, strictly *palm-branches*, the feathery fronds forming the tufted crown of the tree.

Hosanna. Meaning, *O save!*

11. **When he had looked round.** Peculiar to Mark. As the master of the house, *inspecting*. "A look serious, sorrowful, judicial" (Meyer). Compare iii. 5, 34.

13. **Afar off.** Peculiar to Mark.

Having leaves. An unusual thing at that early season.

If haply (εἰ ἄρα). If, *such being the case*, i.e., the tree having leaves—he might find fruit, which, in the fig, precedes the leaf. Mark alone adds, "for the time of figs was not yet."

14. **His disciples heard it.** Peculiar to Mark.

15. **Money-changers** (κολλυβιστῶν). Another unclassical word, but used also by Matthew. "Such words as these might naturally find their place in the mongrel Greek of the slaves and freedmen who formed the first congregations of the church in Rome" (Ezra Abbott, Art. "Gospels," in Encyc. Britannica). See on Matt. xxi. 12.

16. **Vessel** (σκεῦος). See on Matt. xii. 29; Mark iii. 27.

Temple (ἱεροῦ). See on Matt. iv. 5. The temple *enclosure*, not the *ναός*, or *sanctuary*. People would be tempted to carry vessels, etc., through this, in order to save a long circuit. The court of the Gentiles, moreover, was not regarded by the Jews as entitled to the respect due to the other part of the enclosure. This our Lord rebukes.

17. **Of all nations.** Which rendering implies, shall be called *by* all nations. But render with Rev., a house of prayer *for all the nations* (πᾶσιν τοῖς ἔθνεσιν).

Thieves (λῃστῶν). Rev., correctly, *robbers*. See on Matt. xxi. 13; xxvi. 55; John x. 1, 8. From ληΐς or λεία, *booty*. In classical usage mostly of cattle. The robber, conducting his operations on a large and systematic scale, and with the aid of bands, is thus to be distinguished from the *κλέπτης*, or *thief* who purloins or pilfers whatever comes to hand. A *den* would be appropriate to a band of *robbers*, not to thieves. Thus the traveller to Jericho, in Christ's parable (Luke x. 30), fell among *robbers*, not thieves.

19. **When** evening was come (ὅταν). Lit., *whenever* evening came on; not on the evening of the purging of the temple merely, but each day at evening.

20–24. All the details are peculiar to Mark. Compare Matt. xxi. 20–22.

23. **Shall come to pass** (γίνεται). Rather *cometh to pass*, as Rev.

24. **Receive** (ἐλάβετε). More lit., *received*. Rev., *have received*.

25. **Trespasses.** See on Matt. vi. 14.

27. **Walking.** An addition of Mark.

CHAPTER XII.

1–11. Compare Matt. xxi. 33–46.

1. **Wine-fat** (ὑπολήνιον). Rev., *wine-press*. Only here in New Testament. The wine-press was constructed in the side of a sloping rock, in which a trough was excavated, which was the wine-press proper. Underneath this was dug another trough, with openings communicating with the trough above, into which the juice ran from the press. This was called by the Romans *lacus*, or *the lake*. The word here used for the whole structure strictly means this trough *underneath* (ὑπό) *the press* (ληνός). This is the explanation of Wyc.'s translation, *dalf* (delved), *a lake*.

Went into a far country (ἀπεδήμησεν). But this is too strong. The word means simply *went abroad*. So Wyc., *went forth in pilgrimage;* and Tynd., *into a strange country*. Rev., *another country*. See on Matt. xxv. 14.

Of the fruits. Or, literally, *from* (ἀπὸ) the fruits, showing that the rent was to be paid in kind.

6. **Therefore.** The best texts omit.

Last. Mark only.

7. **Those husbandmen.** Lit., *they the husbandmen.* Wyc., *tenants.*

10. **Scripture** (γραφὴν). *A passage* of scripture: hence frequently *this* scripture; *another* scripture; the *same* scripture. Luke iv. 21; John xix. 37; Acts i. 16.

11. **The Lord's doing** (παρὰ κυρίου). Lit., *from the Lord.*

13–17. Compare Matt. xxii. 15–22.

13. **Catch** (ἀγρεύσωσιν). From ἄγρα, *hunting*, *the chase.* Hence the picture in the word is that of *hunting*, while that in Matthew's word, παγιδεύσωσιν, is that of *catching in a trap.* See on Matt. xxii. 15.

14. **Tribute.** See on Matt. xxii. 19.

Person (πρόσωπον). Lit., *face.*

Shall we give, etc. A touch peculiar to Mark.

15. **Penny.** See on Matt. xx. 2.

16. **Image and superscription.** See on Matt. xxii. 20.

17. **They marvelled** (ἐξεθαύμαζον). The preposition ἐξ, *out of*, indicates *great* astonishment. They marvelled *out of measure.* Hence Rev., *marvelled greatly*. The A. V. follows another reading, with the simple verb ἐθαύμαζον. The imperfect denotes *continuance: they stood wondering.*

18. **Who** (οἵτινες). This pronoun marks the Sadducees as a *class: of that party* characterized by their denial of the resurrection.

Asked (ἐπηρώτων). Stronger. They *questioned.*

24. **Therefore** (διὰ τοῦτο). A rendering which obscures the meaning. The words point forward to the next two clauses. The reason of your error is *your ignorance of the scriptures* and of *the power of God.* Hence Rev., correctly, *Is it not for this cause that ye err?*

Err (πλανᾶσθε). Lit., *wander out of the way.* Compare Latin *errare.* Of the wandering sheep, Matt. xviii. 12; 1 Pet. ii. 25. Of the martyrs wandering in the deserts, Heb. xi. 38. Often rendered in the New Testament *deceive.* See Mark xiii. 5, 6. Compare ἀστέρες πλανῆται, *wandering stars* (Jude 13), from which our word *planet.*

26. **How in the bush God spake.** An utterly wrong rendering. *In the bush* (ἐπὶ τοῦ βάτου), refers to a particular section in the Pentateuch, Exod. iii. 2–6. The Jews were accustomed to designate portions of scripture by the most noteworthy thing contained in them. Therefore Rev., rightly, *in the place concerning the bush.* Wyc., *in the book of Moses on the bush.* The article refers to it as something familiar. Compare Rom. xi. 2, ἐν Ἡλίᾳ; i.e., in the section of scripture which tells of Elijah. There, however, the Rev. retains the A. V. *of Elijah,* and puts *in* in the margin.

27. **Ye do greatly err.** An emphatic close, peculiar to Mark.

28. **Well** (καλῶς). Lit., *beautifully, finely, admirably.*

What (ποία). Rather, *of what nature.*

30. **With all thy heart** (ἐξ ὅλης τῆς καρδίας σου). Lit., *out of thy whole heart.* The *heart,* not only as the seat of the

affections, but as the centre of our complex being—physical, moral, spiritual, and intellectual.

Soul (ψυχῆς). The word is often used in the New Testament in its original meaning of *life*. See Matt. ii. 20; xx. 28; Acts xx. 10; Rom. xi. 3; John x. 11. Hence, as an emphatic designation of the man himself. See Matt. xii. 18; Heb. x. 38; Luke xxi. 19. So that the word denotes "life in the distinctness of individual existence" (Cremer). See farther on ψυχικός, *spiritual*, 1 Cor. xv. 44.

Mind (διανοίας). The faculty of thought: understanding, especially the *moral* understanding.

31. **Neighbor.** See on Matt. v. 43.

32–34. Peculiar to Mark.

32. **Well, Master, thou hast said the truth; for there is one God.** All the best texts omit *God*.

Well (καλῶς). Exclamatory, as one says *good!* on hearing something which he approves.

The truth (ἐπ' ἀληθείας). Incorrect. The phrase is adverbial; *of a truth*, *in truth*, *truthfully*, and qualifies the succeeding verb, *thou hast said*.

For (ὅτι). The A. V. begins a new and explanatory sentence with this word; but it is better with Rev. to translate *that*, and make the whole sentence continuous: *Thou hast truthfully said that he is one*.

33. **Understanding** (συνέσεως). A different word from that in ver. 30. From συνίημι, *to send* or *bring together*. Hence σύνεσις is a *union* or *bringing together* of the mind with an object, and so used to denote *the faculty of quick comprehension*, *intelligence*, *sagacity*. Compare on συνετῶν, *the prudent*, Matt. xi. 25.

34. **Discreetly** (νουνεχῶς). From νοῦς, *mind*, and ἔχω, *to have*. Having his mind in possession: "*having his wits about him*." The word occurs only here in the New Testament.

37. **The common people** (ὁ πολὺς ὄχλος). Not indicating a social distinction, but the *great mass of the people: the crowd at large*.

38. **Desire** (θέλοντων). See on Matt. i. 19.

39. **Uppermost rooms** (πρωτοκλισίας). More correctly, *the chief couches*. So Rev., *chief places*.

40. **Widows' houses.** People often left their whole fortune to the temple, and a good deal of the temple-money went, in the end, to the Scribes and Pharisees. The Scribes were universally employed in making wills and conveyances of property. They may have abused their influence with widows.

41. **The treasury.** In the Court of the Women, which covered a space of two hundred feet square. All round it ran a colonnade, and within it, against the wall, were the thirteen chests or "trumpets" for charitable contributions. These chests were narrow at the mouth and wide at the bottom, shaped like trumpets, whence their name. Their specific objects were carefully marked on them. Nine were for the receipt of what was legally due by worshippers, the other four for strictly voluntary gifts. See Edersheim, "The Temple."

Beheld (ἐθεώρει). Observed thoughtfully.

Cast. Note the graphic present tense: *are casting*.

Money (χαλκὸν). Lit., *copper*, which most of the people gave.

Cast in (ἔβαλλον). Imperfect tense: *were casting in as he looked*.

Much (πολλά). Lit., *many things;* possibly many pieces of current copper coin.

42. **A certain** (μία). Not a good translation. Lit., *one* as distinguished from the *many* rich. Better, simply the indefinite article, as Rev.

Poor (πτωχὴ). See on Matt. v. 3.

Mites (λεπτὰ). From λεπτός, *peeled, husked;* and thence *thin* or *fine.* Therefore of a very *small* or *thin* coin.

Farthing (κοδράντης). A Latin word, *quadrans*, or a quarter of a Roman *as;* quadrans meaning a *fourth*, as *farthing* is *fourthing.*

43. **This poor widow** (ἡ χήρα αὕτη ἡ πτωχὴ). The Greek order is very suggestive, forming a kind of climax: *this widow, the poor one*, or *and she poor.*

CHAPTER XIII.

1. **Stones.** The spring-stones of the arches of the bridge which spanned the valley of Tyropoeon (the cheese-makers), and connected the ancient city of David with the royal porch of the temple, measured twenty-four feet in length by six in thickness. Yet these were by no means the largest in the masonry of the temple. Both at the southeastern and southwestern angles stones have been found measuring from twenty to forty feet long, and weighing above one hundred tons (Edersheim, "Temple").

2. **Thrown down** (καταλυθῇ). Rather, *loosened down.* A very graphic word, implying gradual demolition.

3. Note the particularity of detail in Mark. He adds, *over against the temple*, and the names of the four who asked the question. With the following discourse compare Matt. xxiv.

6. **In** my name (ἐπί). Lit., *upon*. Basing their claims *on* the use of my name.

7. **Rumors of wars.** Wyc., *opinions of battles*. Such as would be a cause of terror to the Hebrew Christians; as the three threats of war against the Jews by Caligula, Claudius, and Nero. There were serious disturbances at Alexandria, A.D. 38, in which the Jews were the especial objects of persecution; at Seleucia about the same time, in which more than fifty thousand Jews were killed; and at Jamnia, near Joppa.

Troubled (θροεῖσθε). Θροέω is, literally, *to cry aloud*.

Earthquakes. Between the prophecy and the destruction of Jerusalem (A.D. 70) occurred: A great earthquake in Crete, A.D. 46 or 47: at Rome, on the day on which Nero entered his majority, A.D. 51: at Apameia, in Phrygia, A.D. 53; "on account of which," says Tacitus, "they were exempted from tribute for five years:" at Laodicea, in Phrygia, A.D. 60: in Campania, A.D. 63, by which, according to Tacitus, the city of Pompeii was largely destroyed.

Famines. During the reign of Claudius, A.D. 41–54, four famines are recorded: One at Rome, A.D. 41, 42; one in Judaea, A.D. 44; one in Greece, A.D. 50; and again at Rome, A.D. 52, when the people rose in rebellion and threatened the life of the emperor. Tacitus says that it was accompanied by frequent earthquakes, which levelled houses. The famine in Judaea was probably the one prophesied by Agabus, Acts xi. 28. Of the year 65 A.D., Tacitus says: "This year, disgraced by so many deeds of horror, was further distinguished by the gods with storms and sicknesses. Campania was devastated by a hurricane which overthrew buildings, trees, and the fruits of the soil in every direction, even to the gates of the city, within which a pestilence thinned all ranks of the population, with no atmospheric disturbance that the eye could trace. The houses were choked with dead, the roads with funerals: neither sex nor age escaped. Slaves and freemen perished equally amid the wailings of their wives and children, who were often hurried to the pyre by which they had sat in tears, and consumed together with them. The deaths of knights and senators, promiscuous as they were, deserved the less to be lamented, inasmuch as, falling by the common lot of mortality, they seemed to anticipate the prince's cruelty" ("Annals," xvi., 10–13).

9. **Sorrows** (ὠδίνων). Rev., rightly, *travail;* for the word is used especially of *birth-throes.*

Shall ye be beaten (δαρήσεσθε). The verb literally means *to skin* or *flay*, and by a slang usage, like our phrase *to tan* or *hide*, comes to mean *to cudgel* or *beat.*

11. **They lead** (ἄγωσιν). Present subjunctive; better perhaps, *may be leading.* While you are going along in custody to the judgment-seat, do not be worrying about your defences.

Take no thought beforehand (μὴ προμεριμνᾶτε). See on Matt. vi. 25.

14. **Abomination.** See on Matt. xxiv. 15.

15. **Housetop.** See on Matt. xxiv. 17.

19. **The creation which God created.** Note the peculiar amplification, and compare ver. 20, *the elect or chosen whom he chose.*

20. **Shortened.** See on Matt. xxiv. 22.

22. **Shall shew** (δώσουσιν). Lit., *shall give.* A few editors, however, read ποιήσουσιν, *shall make* or *do.*

24. **Light** (φέγγος). The word is used in the New Testament wherever the light of *the moon* is referred to. Compare Matt. xxiv. 29, the only other instance. It occurs also in Luke xi. 33. but meaning the light of a lamp.

25. **The stars of heaven shall fall.** A rendering which falls very far short of the graphic original: *οἱ ἀστέρες ἔσονται ἐκ τοῦ οὐρανοῦ πίπτοντες*: *the stars shall be falling from heaven.* So Rev., thus giving the sense of *continuousness*, as of a *shower* of falling stars.

27. **From the uttermost part of the earth to the uttermost part of heaven** (*ἀπ' ἄκρου γῆς ἕως ἄκρου οὐρανοῦ*). From the outermost border of the earth, conceived as a flat surface, to where the outermost border of the heaven sets a limit to the earth. Compare Matt. xxiv. 31. Mark's expression is more poetical.

28. **Parable.** See on Matt. xxiv. 32.

Branch. See on Mark xi. 8.

29. **Come to pass** (*γινόμενα*). The present participle, and therefore better as Rev., *coming to pass; in process of fulfilmetn.*

33. **Watch** (*ἀγρυπνεῖτε*). The word is derived from *ἀγρεύω*, *to hunt*, and *ὕπνος*, *sleep.* The picture is of one *in pursuit of sleep*, and therefore *wakeful, restless.* Wyc.'s rendering of the whole passage is striking: *See! wake ye and pray ye!*

34. **A man taking a far journey** (*ἄνθρωπος ἀπόδημος*). The A. V. is incorrect, since the idea is not that of a man *about to go*, as Matt. xxv. 14; but of one *already gone.* So Wyc., *gone far in pilgrimage;* and Tynd., *which is gone into a strange country.* The two words form one notion—*a man abroad.* Rev., *sojourning in another country.*

35. **Watch** (*γρηγορεῖτε*). A different word from that in ver. 33. See also ver. 34. The picture in this word is that of a sleeping man rousing himself. While the other word conveys the idea of simple *wakefulness*, this adds the idea of *alertness.* Compare Matt. xiv. 38; Luke xii. 37; 1 Pet. v. 8. The apos-

tles are thus compared with the *doorkeepers*, ver. 34; and the night season is in keeping with the figure. In the temple, during the night, the captain of the temple made his rounds, and the guards had to rise at his approach and salute him in a particular manner. Any guard found asleep on duty was beaten, or his garments were set on fire. Compare Apoc. xvi. 15: "Blessed is he that *watcheth and keepeth his garments*." The preparations for the morning service required all to be early astir. The superintending priest might knock at the door at any moment. The Rabbis use almost the very words in which scripture describes the unexpected coming of the Master. "Sometimes he came at the cockcrowing, sometimes a little earlier, sometimes a little later. He came and knocked and they opened to him" (Edersheim, "The Temple").

37. **Watch.** The closing and summary word is the stronger word of ver. 35: *Be awake and on guard.*

CHAPTER XIV.

1. **The feast of the passover and the unleavened bread** (*τὸ πάσχα καὶ τὰ ἄζυμα*). Lit., *the passover and the unleavened.* It was really one and the same festival.

Sought (*ἐζήτουν*). Imperfect tense: *were all this while seeking.*

3–9. Compare Matt. xxvi. 6–13.

3. **Alabaster box.** See on Matt. xxvi. 7.

Spikenard (*νάρδου πιστικῆς*). The meaning of *πιστικῆς* is greatly disputed. The best authorities define it *genuine* or *unadulterated: pure nard.*

Brake. Possibly by striking the brittle neck of the flask. This detail is peculiar to Mark.

4. **To what purpose,** etc. See on Matt. xxvi. 8.

5. **Murmured** (ἐνεβριμῶντο). See on Mark i. 43.

6. **Good.** See on Matt. xxvi. 10.

7. **And whensoever ye will,** etc. Note Mark's amplification.

8. **She hath done what she could** (ὃ ἔσχεν ἐποίησεν). Lit., *what she had she did.* Peculiar to Mark.

She is come aforehand to anoint (προέλαβεν μυρίσαι). Lit., *she anticipated to anoint.* Rev., *hath anointed beforehand.* The verb μυρίζω is found only here.

11. **Money.** See on Matt. xxvi. 15.

He sought (ἐζήτει). Imperfect tense. He *kept seeking: busied himself continuously* from that time.

Conveniently (εὐκαίρως). Might find a good opportunity (καιρός).

13. **A man.** A slave probably, whose business it was to draw water. See Deut. xix. 11.

Pitcher. Of *earthenware:* κεράμιον, from κέραμος, potter's clay.

14. **My guest-chamber** (κατάλυμά μου). Luke xxii. 11. The word is not classical, and as used by an oriental signifies a *khan* or *caravanserai.* Hence *inn* at Luke ii. 7. *My* chamber. It was a common practice that more than one company partook of the paschal supper in the same apartment; but Christ will have *his* chamber for himself and his disciples alone.

15. **And he** (αὐτὸς). The Greek is more emphatic. "He will *himself* show you." So Rev. Probably the owner of the house was a disciple.

Furnished (ἐστρωμένον). Lit., *strewed* with carpets, and with couches properly spread.

20. **Dish** (τρυβλίον). See on Matt. xxvi. 23.

23. **The cup.** The wine was the ordinary one of the country, only *red.* It was mixed with water, generally in the proportion of one part to two of water.

24. **Covenant.** See on Matt. xxvi. 28.

Is shed (τὸ ἐκχυννόμενον). Lit., *is being shed.* This present participle is significant. To the Lord's mind the sacrifice is *already being* offered.

25. **New.** See on Matt. xxvi. 29.

26. **Sung an hymn.** See on Matt. xxvi. 30.

28. **Go before.** See on Matt. xxvi. 32.

30. **Cock crow.** See on Matt. xxvi. 34. Mark alone adds *twice.*

Deny (ἀπαρνήσῃ). The compound verb signifies *utterly* deny.

31. **I will not deny** (οὐ μή σε ἀπαρνήσομαι). The double negative with the future forms the strongest possible assertion.

32. **Gethsemane.** See on Matt. xxvi. 36.

33. **To be sore amazed** (ἐκθαμβεῖσθαι). A word peculiar to Mark. Compare ix. 15; xvi. 5, 6.

35. **Prayed** (προσηύχετο). Imperfect tense: *began* to pray.

40. **Heavy** (καταβαρυνόμενοι). Lit., *weighed down: very* heavy.

41. **It is enough** (ἀπέχει). Peculiar to Mark. In this impersonal sense the word occurs nowhere else in the New Testament. Expositors are utterly at sea as to its meaning.

43. **One of the twelve.** See on Matt. xxvi. 47; as also on *multitude*.

44. **Token** (σύσσημον). A later Greek compound used only by Mark in this passage. Compare σημεῖον, Matt. xxvi. 48. The σύν, *with*, gives the force of a *mutual* token: a *concerted* signal.

45. **Kissed.** See on Matt. xxvi. 49.

47. **The servant.** See on Matt. xxvi. 51.

Ear (ὠτάριον). A word found only here and at John xviii. 10. See on Matt. xxvi. 51.

48. **A thief.** Rev., better, *robber*. See on Matt. xxvi. 55, and Mark xi. 17.

51, 52. The incident is related by Mark only. There is no means of knowing who the youth may have been. Conjecture has named Mark himself, John, James the Just, Lazarus, the brother of Martha and Mary, and St. Paul!

51. **Linen cloth** (σινδόνα). The probable derivation is from Ἰνδός, an *Indian:* India being the source from which came this fine fabric used for wrapping dead bodies, and in which Christ's body was enveloped. See Matt. xxvii. 59; Mark xv. 46; Luke xxiii. 53.

54. **Palace** (αὐλήν). Rather, *court*, as Rev., the quadrangle round which the chambers were built. See on Matt. xxvi. 3.

Sat with (ἦν συγκαθήμενος). The verb with the participle denoting *continuousness*. What occurred after occurred *while he was sitting*. So Rev.

Servants. Rev., *officers*. See on Matt. v. 25.

At the fire (πρὸς τὸ φῶς). Φῶς is never used of the *fire itself*, but of *the light* of the fire; and this is the point to which the evangelist directs attention: that the firelight, shining on Peter's face, called forth the challenge of the maid (ver. 66).

56. **Their witness agreed not.** Peculiar to Mark. Lit., *their testimonies were not equal.* Hence the difficulty of fulfilling the requirement of the law, which demanded *two* witnesses. See Deut. xvii. 6; and compare Matt. xviii. 16; 1 Tim. v. 19; Heb. x. 28.

58. **Made with hands.** Mark adds this detail; also *made without hands*, and the following sentence.

62. **I am.** See on Matt. xxvi. 64.

64. **Guilty of death.** See on Matt. xxvi. 66.

65. **Buffet.** See on Matt. xxvi. 67.

Palms of their hands (ῥαπίσμασιν). An unclassical word, but used also by John (xix. 3). The word means *blows*.

Did strike. Following the old reading, ἔβαλλον. The correct reading is ἔλαβον, *received.* So Rev. Received him into custody.

66. **Beneath.** In relation to the chambers round the court above.

68. **Porch** (προαύλιον). Only here in New Testament. The *vestibule*, extending from the outside gate to the court.

71. **Curse** (ἀναθεματίζειν). Compare on Matt. xxvi. 74; where the word is καταθεματίζειν, to call *down* (κατὰ) curses on

himself if he were not telling the truth. The words are synonymous.

72. **When he thought thereon** (ἐπιβαλὼν). From ἐπί, *upon*, and βάλλω, *to throw*. When he *threw his thought upon it*.

CHAPTER XV.

Compare vv. 1–5 with Matt. xxvii. 1, 2, 11–14.

7. **Them that had made insurrection with him** (συστασιαστῶν). *Fellow-rioters*. But the better texts read στασιαστῶν, *rioters*, omitting the σύν, *with* (*fellow*): and the Rev. accordingly omits *with him*.

Who (οἵτινες). Denoting a *class* of criminals.

The insurrection. Note the article: *the* insurrection for which Barabbas and his fellows had been imprisoned.

8. **Crying aloud** (ἀναβοήσας). But the best texts read ἀναβὰς, *having gone up*. So Rev., *went up*.

Ever (ἀεὶ). Omitted by the best texts.

11. **Moved** (ἀνέσεισαν). A feeble translation. Σείω is *to shake*. Hence σεισμός, *an earthquake*. See on Matt. xiii. 8. Better as Rev., *stirred up*. Wyc., *The bishops stirred the company of people*.

15. **To content** (τὸ ἱκανὸν ποιῆσαι). Lit., *to do the sufficient thing*. Compare the popular phrase, *Do the right thing*. A Latinism, and used by Mark only. Wyc., *to do enough to the people*.

16. **Into the hall called Pretorium.** Mark, as usual, amplifies. Matthew has simply *the Pretorium*. The *courtyard*, sur-

rounded by the buildings of the Pretorium, so that the people passing through the vestibule into this quadrangle found themselves in the Pretorium.

Band (σπεῖραν). Originally anything *wound* or *wrapped round;* as a ball, the coils of a snake, a knot or curl in wood. Hence a body of men-at-arms. The same idea is at the bottom of the Latin *manipulus*, which is sometimes (as by Josephus) used to translate σπεῖρα. *Manipulus* was originally a *bundle* or *handful*. The ancient Romans adopted a pole with a handful of hay or straw twisted about it as the standard of a company of soldiers; hence a certain number or body of soldiers under one standard was called *manipulus*.

17. **Purple.** See on Matt. xxvii. 28. Matthew adds the word for *soldier's cloak*. Mark has simply *purple*.

21. **Compel.** Better *impress*, as Rev. in margin. See on Matt. v. 41. Note the accuracy in designating Simon.

22. **Golgotha.** See on Matt. xxvii. 33.

23. **They gave** (ἐδίδουν). The imperfect tense is used in the same sense as in Matt. iii. 14 (Rev.), "John *would have hindered*." They were *for giving; attempted to give*. So Rev., excellently, *offered*.

Wine mingled with myrrh (ἐσμυρνισμένον οἶνον). Lit., *myrrhed wine*. See on Matt. xxvii. 34.

24. **What each should take** (τίς τί ἄρῃ). Lit., *who should take what*. An addition of Mark.

26. **The superscription of his accusation.** Matthew, simply *accusation;* Luke, *superscription;* John, *title*. See on Matt. xxvii. 37.

27. **Thieves.** Rev., *robbers*. See on Matt. xxvii. 38.

29. **Ah!** (οὐὰ). The Latin *vah!*

Destroyest. The same word as at xiii. 2.

32. **The Christ.** See on Matt. ii. 1. Referring to the confession before the high-priest (xiv. 62).

King of Israel. Referring to the confession before Pilate (xv. 2).

36. **Vinegar.** See on Matt. xxvii. 48.

38. **The veil.** See on Matt. xxvii. 51.

39. **Son of God.** Not *the* Son of God, which Rev. has retained, but *a* son of God. To the centurion Christ was a hero or demigod. See on Matt. xxvii. 54.

40. **Magdalene.** See on Matt. xxvii. 56.

41. **Followed—ministered** (ἠκολούθουν—διηκόνουν). Both imperfects: *were in the habit, accustomed to.*

42. **Even.** See on Matt. xxvii. 57.

The day before the Sabbath (προσάββατον). *The fore-Sabbath.* Peculiar to Mark, and only here.

43. **Joseph of Arimathaea** (Ἰωσὴφ ὁ ἀπὸ Ἀριμαθαίας). Lit., *Joseph, he from Arimathaea:* the article indicating a man well known.

Honorable (εὐσχήμων). Compounded of εὖ, *well,* and σχῆμα, *form, shape, figure.* On the latter word, see on Matt. xvii. 2. In its earlier use this adjective would, therefore, emphasize the dignified *external* appearance and deportment. So Plato, *noble bearing* ("Republic," 413). Later, it came to be used in the sense of *noble; honorable in rank.* See Acts xiii. 50; xvii. 12.

Counsellor. A member of the Sanhedrim, as appears from Luke xxiii. 51.

Went in boldly (τολμήσας εἰσῆλθεν). Lit., *having dared went in.* Daring all possible consequences.

44. **Wondered.** This query and the asking the centurion are peculiar to Mark.

45. **Body** (πτῶμα). Better, Rev., *corpse;* as the word is used only of a *dead* body. See on Matt. xxiv. 28.

46. **Stone.** See on Matt. xxvii. 60.

47. **Beheld** (ἐθεώρουν). Imperfect tense. *Were looking on meanwhile.* The verb also implies *steady* and *careful contemplation.* They took careful note.

CHAPTER XVI.

2. **At the rising of the sun** (ἀνατείλαντος τοῦ ἡλίου). More correctly, as Rev., *when the sun was risen.*

3. Peculiar to Mark.

5. **Affrighted.** See ix. 15, and Introduction. Rev., better, *amazed.* It was *wonder* rather than *fright.*

8. **Quickly.** Omitted by best texts.

Astonishment (ἔκστασις). See on Mark v. 42.

Afraid (ἐφοβοῦντο). The wonder merges into *fear.*

By a large number of the ablest modern critics the remainder of this chapter is held to be from some other hand than Mark's. It is omitted from the two oldest manuscripts.

9. **The first day of the week** (*πρώτῃ σαββάτου*). A phrase which Mark does not use. In ver. 2 of this chapter it is *μιᾶς σαββάτων*.

Out of whom he had cast seven devils. With Mark's well-known habit of particularizing, it is somewhat singular that this circumstance was not mentioned in either of the three previous allusions to Mary (xv. 40, 47; xvi. 1).

Out of whom (*ἀφ' ἧς*). An unusual expression. Mark habitually uses the preposition *ἐκ* in this connection (i. 25, 26; v. 8; vii. 26, 29; ix. 25). Moreover, *ἀπὸ*, *from*, is used with *ἐκβάλλειν*, *cast out*, nowhere else in the New Testament. The peculiarity is equally marked if we read with some, *παρ' ἧς*.

10. **She** (*ἐκείνη*). An absolute use of the pronoun unexampled in Mark. See also vv. 11, 13. It would imply an emphasis which is not intended. Compare iv. 11; xii. 4, 5, 7; xiv. 21.

Went (*πορευθεῖσα*). So in vv. 12, 15. *Went*, *go*. This verb for *to go* occurs nowhere else in this Gospel except in compounds.

Them that had been with him (*τοῖς μετ' αὐτοῦ γενομένοις*). A circumlocution foreign to the Gospels.

12. **After these things** (*μετά ταῦτα*). An expression never used by Mark.

Another form (*ἑτέρᾳ μορφῇ*). More correctly, a *different* form.

14. **Afterward** (*ὕστερον*). Not found elsewhere in Mark. Often in Matthew.

15. **To every creature** (*πάσῃ τῇ κτίσει*). Rightly, as Rev., *to the whole creation*.

16. **Shall be damned** (κατακριθήσεται). A most unfortunate rendering. The word is a judicial term, and, as Dr. Morison truthfully says, "determines, by itself, nothing at all concerning the nature, degree, or extent of the penalty to be endured." See on the kindred noun, κρῖμα, *judgment*, rendered by A. V. *damnation*, 1 Cor. xi. 29. Rev., rightly, *condemned*.

17. **Shall follow** (παρακολουθήσει). The preposition παρά, *alongside of*, gives the sense of *accompany*.

18. **The sick** (ἀρρώστους). See on Mark vi. 5.

20. **Following** (ἐπακολουθούντων). Following *closely:* force of ἐπί. Both this and the word for *follow*, in ver. 17, are foreign to Mark's diction, though he frequently uses the simple verb.

A manuscript of the eighth or ninth century, known as L, has, at the close of ver. 8, these words: "In some instances there is added as follows." Then we read: "But all the things enjoined they announced without delay to those who were around Peter (*i.e.*, to Peter and those who were with him). And afterward Jesus himself, from the east unto the west, sent forth through them the sacred and incorruptible message of eternal salvation."

The subject of the last twelve verses of this Gospel may be found critically discussed in the second volume of Westcott and Hort's Greek Testament; by Dean John W. Burgon in his monograph, "The Last Twelve Verses of the Gospel according to St. Mark Vindicated against Recent Objectors and Established;" Frederick Henry Scrivener, LL.D., "Introduction to the Criticism of the New Testament;" James Morison, D.D., "Practical Commentary on the Gospel according to St. Mark;" Samuel Davidson, D.D., "Introduction to the Study of the New Testament;" Philip Schaff, D.D., "History of the Christian Church;" Canon F. C. Cook in "Speaker's Commentary on Mark;" Samuel P. Tregelles, LL.D., "On the Printed Text of the Greek Testament;" also in the commentaries of Alford and Meyer.

LIST OF GREEK WORDS USED BY MARK ONLY.

ἀγρεύω, catch, xii., 13
ἅλς, salt, ix., 49
ἄλαλος, dumb, vii., 37 ; ix., 17, 25
ἀλεκτροφωνία, cockcrowing, xiii., 35
ἄμφοδον, a place where two ways meet, xi., 4
ἀμφιβάλλω, cast, i., 16
ἄναλος, saltless, ix., 50
ἀναπηδάω, leap up, x., 50
ἀναστενάζω, sigh deeply, viii., 12
ἀπέχει, it is enough, xiv., 41
ἀπόδημος, abroad, xiii., 34
ἀποστεγάζω, uncover, ii., 4
ἀφρίζω, foam, ix., 18, 20
Βοανεργές, sons of thunder, iii., 17
γαμίσκομαι, to be given in marriage, xii., 25
γναφεύς, fuller, ix., 3
δισχίλιοι, two thousand, v., 13
δύσκολος, hard, x., 24
εἰ, if (in swearing), viii., 12
ἐκθαμβέω, to be amazed, ix., 15 ; xiv., 33 ; xvi., 5, 6
ἐκθαυμάζω, to marvel, xii., 17
ἐκπερισσῶς, exceeding vehemently, xiv., 31
ἐναγκαλίζομαι, take in the arms, ix., 36 ; x., 16
ἐνειλέω, wrap, xv., 46
ἔννυχον, in the night, i., 35
ἐξάπινα, suddenly, ix., 8
ἐξουδενόω, set at naught, ix., 12
ἐπιβάλλω (neuter), beat, iv., 37
ἐπιῤῥάπτω, sew upon, ii., 21
ἐπισυντρέχω, come running together, ix., 25
ἐσχάτως, at the point of death, iv., 23
ἤφιεν, suffered (permitted), i., 34; xi., 16
θανάσιμος, deadly, xvi., 18
θαυμάζειν διὰ, to wonder because of, vi., 6
θυγάτριον, little daughter, v., 23, vii., 25
τὸ ἱκανὸν ποιεῖν, to content, xv., 15
κατάβα, come down, xv., 30
καταβαρύνω, weigh down, xiv., 40
καταδιώκω, follow after, i., 36
κατακόπτω, cut, v., 5
κατευλογέω, bless, x., 16
κατοίκησις, dwelling, v., 3
κεντυρίων, centurion, xv., 39, 44, 45
κεφαλαιόω, to wound in the head, xii., 4
κυλίομαι, wallow, ix., 20
κωμόπολις, village-town, i., 38
μεθόρια, borders, vii., 24
μηκύνομαι, grow, iv., 27
μογιλάλος, having an impediment in speech, vii., 32
μυρίζω, anoint, xiv., 8
νουνεχῶς, discreetly, xii., 34
ξέστης, pot, vii., 4
ὄμμα, eye, viii., 23
οὐά, ah! ha! xv., 29
παιδιόθεν, from a child, ix., 21
παρόμοιος, like, vii., 8, 13

περιτρέχω, run round about, vi., 55

πρασιά, a garden-plat, vi., 40

προαύλιον, porch or forecourt, xiv., 68

προμεριμνάω, take thought beforehand, xiii., 11

προσάββατον, day before the Sabbath, xv., 42

προσεγγίζω, come nigh unto, ii., 4

προσκεφάλαιον, cushion, iv., 38

προσορμίζομαι, moor to the shore, vi., 53

προσπορεύομαι, come unto, x., 35

πυγμῇ, with the fist, vii., 3

σκώληξ, worm, ix., 44, 46, 48

σπεκουλάτωρ, executioner, vi., 27

σμυρνίζω, mingle with myrrh, xv., 23

στασιαστής, insurrectionist, xv., 7

στίλβω, to be glistering, ix., 3

στίβας, branch, or layer of leaves, xi., 8

συμπόσιον, a table-party, vi., 39

συνθλίβω, to throng or crowd, v., 24, 31

συλλυπέομαι, to be grieved, iii., 5

Συραφοινίκισσα, a Syro-phoenician woman, vii., 26

σύσσημον, countersign, token, xiv., 44

τηλαυγῶς, clearly, viii., 25

τρίζω, gnash, ix., 18

ὑπερηφανία, pride, vii., 22

ὑπερπερισσῶς, beyond measure, vii., 37

ὑπολήνιον, wine-fat or wine-press, xii., 1

χαλκίον, brazen vessel, vii., 4

THE GOSPEL ACCORDING TO LUKE.

INTRODUCTION TO THE WRITINGS OF LUKE.

LEGEND has been busy with the name of Luke. The Greek Church, in which painting is regarded as a religious art, readily accepted the tradition which represented him as a painter, and the Greek painters carried it into Western Europe. A rude drawing of the Virgin, discovered in the Catacombs, with an inscription to the effect that it was one of seven painted by *Luca*, confirmed the popular belief that Luke the Evangelist was meant. According to the legend, he carried with him two portraits painted by himself—the one of the Saviour and the other of the Virgin—and by means of these he converted many of the heathen.

When we apply to historical sources, however, we find very little about this evangelist. He never mentions himself by name in the Gospel or in the Acts, and his name occurs in only three passages of the New Testament: Col. iv. 14; 2 Tim. iv. 11; Philem. 24.

That he was an Asiatic-Greek convert of Antioch, though resting upon no conclusive evidence, is supported by the fact that he gives much information about the church there (Acts xi. 19, 30; xiii. 1–3; xv. 1–3, 22, 35); that he traces the origin of the name "Christian" to that city, and that, in enumerating the seven deacons of Jerusalem, he informs us of the Antiochian origin of Nicholas (Acts vi. 5) without reference to the nationality of any of the others. That he was a physician and the companion of Paul are facts attested by Scripture, though his connection with Paul does not definitely appear before Acts xvi.

10, where he uses the first person plural. He accompanied Paul from Caesarea, through the shipwreck at Malta, to Rome, and remained there until his liberation. Tradition makes him to have died in Greece, and it was believed that his remains were transferred to Constantinople.

It has been assumed that he was a freedman, from the large number of physicians who belonged to that class, the Greeks and Romans being accustomed to educate some of their domestics in the science of medicine, and to grant them freedom in requital of services. Physicians often held no higher rank than slaves, and it has been noticed that contractions in *as*, like *Lucas* for *Lucanus*, were peculiarly common in the names of slaves.

His connection with Paul gave rise in the church, at a very early period, to the opinion that he wrote his Gospel under the superintendence of that apostle. While his preface says nothing about the Pauline sanction of his Gospel, the work, nevertheless, presents remarkable coincidences with Paul's epistles, both in language, ideas, and spirit. The Gospel itself sets forth that conception of Christ's life and work which was the basis of Paul's teaching. He represents the views of Paul, as Mark does of Peter. "There is a striking resemblance between the style of Luke and of Paul, which corresponds to their spiritual sympathy and long intimacy." Some two hundred expressions or phrases may be found which are common to Luke and Paul, and more or less foreign to other New Testament writers. Such, for instance, are:

Luke.	Paul.
ἀθετεῖν, *reject*, vii. 30; x. 16.	Gal. ii. 21; iii. 15; 1 Thess. iv. 8.
αἰχμαλωτίζειν, *lead captive*, xxi. 24.	Rom. vii. 23; 2 Cor. x. 5.
ἀνάγκη, xiv. 18; in the phrase ἔχω ἀνάγκην, *I must needs*.	1 Cor. vii. 37.
In the sense of *distress*, xxi. 23.	1 Cor. vii. 26; 2 Cor. vi. 4; xii. 10; 1 Thess. iii. 7, and not elsewhere.
ἀνακρίνειν, *to examine judicially*, xxiii. 14; Acts xii. 19; xxviii. 18.	1 Cor. ii. 15; iv. 3; ix. 3; ten times in all in that epistle.
ἀπὸ τοῦ νῦν, *from henceforth*, i. 48; v. 10; xii. 52; xxii. 69.	2 Cor. v. 16.

LUKE.	PAUL.
ἀπ' αἰῶνος, *since the world began*, i. 70; Acts iii. 21; xv. 18.	Col. i. 26; Eph. iii. 9.
ἐγκακεῖν, *to faint*, xviii. 1.	2 Cor. iv. 1, 16; Gal. vi. 9; Eph. iii. 13; 2 Thess. iii. 13.
διερμηνεύειν, *expound* or *interpret*, xxiv. 27; Acts ix. 36.	1 Cor. xii. 30; xiv. 5, 13, 27.
ἐνδύσασθαι, *endue*, *clothe*, xxiv. 49, in the moral sense.	Rom. xiii. 12, 14; 1 Cor. xv. 53; 2 Cor. v. 3, etc.
εἰ μήτι, *except*, ix. 13.	1 Cor. vii. 5; 2 Cor. xiii. 5.
ἐπιφαίνειν, *to give light*, *shine*, i. 79; Acts xxvii. 20.	Titus ii. 11; iii. 4.
καταργεῖν, *cumber*, xiii. 7.	Rom. iii. 3, *make without effect; make void; destroy; do away; bring to naught;* twenty-six times in Paul.
μεγαλύνειν, *exalt*, *magnify*, i. 46, 58; Acts v. 13; x. 46; xix. 17.	2 Cor. x. 15; Philip. i. 20.

Both are fond of words characterizing the freedom and universality of gospel salvation. For example, χάρις, *grace*, *favor*, occurs eight times in the Gospel, sixteen in the Acts, and ninety-five in Paul. Ἔλεος, *mercy*, six times in the Gospel and ten in Paul. Πίστις, *faith*, twenty-seven times in the Gospel and Acts, and everywhere in Paul. Compare, also, δικαιοσύνη, *righteousness*; δίκαιος, *righteous*; πνεῦμα ἅγιον, *Holy Spirit*; γνῶσις, *knowledge*.

They agree in their report of the institution of the Lord's Supper, both giving "This cup is the new covenant in my blood," for "This is my blood of the new covenant," and both adding, "in remembrance of me."

A few of the numerous instances of parallelism of thought and expression may also be cited:

LUKE.	PAUL.
iv. 22.	Col. iv. 6; Eph. iv. 29.
iv. 32.	1 Cor. ii. 4.
vi. 36.	2 Cor. i. 3; Rom. xii. 1.
vi. 39.	Rom. ii. 19.
vi. 48.	1 Cor. iii. 10.
viii. 15.	Col. i. 10, 11.

Luke.	Paul.
ix. 56.	2 Cor. x. 8.
x. 8.	1 Cor. x. 27.
x. 20.	Philip. iv. 3.
x. 21.	1 Cor. i. 19, 27.
xi. 41.	Tit. i. 15.
xii. 35.	Eph. vi. 14.
xx. 17, 18.	Rom. ix. 33.

Luke's long residence in Greece makes it probable that he had Greek readers especially in mind. The same humanitarian and Gentile character of his writings, as distinguished from Jewish writings, appears in the Acts as in the Gospel. Of the Acts, although attempts have been made to assign its composition to Timothy and to Silas, and to identify Silas with Luke, the universal testimony of the ancient church, no less than the identity of style, declare Luke to be the author. About fifty words not found elsewhere in the New Testament are common to both books.

From a purely literary point of view Luke's Gospel has been pronounced, even by Renan, to be the most beautiful book ever written. He says: "The Gospel of Luke is the most literary of the gospels. Everywhere there is revealed a spirit large and sweet; wise, temperate, sober, and reasonable in the irrational. Its exaggerations, its inconsistencies, its improbabilities, are true to the very nature of parable, and constitute its charm. Matthew rounds a little the rough outlines of Mark. Luke does better: he writes. He displays a genuine skill in composition. His book is a beautiful narrative, well contrived, at once Hebraic and Hellenic, uniting the emotion of the drama with the serenity of the idyl. . . . A spirit of holy infancy, of joy, of fervor, the gospel feeling in its primitive freshness, diffuse all over the legend an incomparably sweet coloring."

Luke is the best writer of Greek among the evangelists. His construction is rhythmical, his vocabulary rich and well selected, considerably exceeding that of the other evangelists. He uses over seven hundred words which occur nowhere else in the New Testament. He substitutes classical words for many which are used by Matthew and Mark, as *λίμνη*, *lake*, for *θάλασσα*, *sea*, when describing the lake of Galilee. He uses three distinct words for *bed* in the description of the healing of the paralytic (vv. 18–25), avoiding the vulgar κράββατος of Mark. The latter word, it is true, occurs in two passages in the Acts (v. 15; ix. 33), but both these passages are Petrine. So, too, we find ἐπιστάτης, *master*, instead of *Rabbi;* νομικοί, *lawyers*, for γραμματεῖς, *scribes;* ναὶ, ἀληθῶς, ἐπ' ἀληθείας, *yea, truly, of a truth*, for ἀμήν, *verily;* φόρος, *tribute*, for the Latin form, κῆνσος, *census*. He uses several Latin words, as δηνάριον, *denarius;* λεγεών, *legion;* σουδάριον, *napkin;* ἀσσάριον, *farthing*, though he avoids κοδράντης, *farthing*, in xxi. 2 (compare Mark xii. 42); μόδιος, *bushel*. He is less Hebraic than the other evangelists, except in the first two chapters—the history of the infancy—which he derived probably from Aramaic traditions or documents, and where his language has a stronger Hebrew coloring than any other portion of the New Testament. "The songs of Zacharias, Elizabeth, Mary, and Simeon, and the anthem of the angelic host, are the last of Hebrew psalms, as well as the first of Christian hymns. They can be literally translated back into the Hebrew without losing their beauty" (Schaff).

His style is clear, animated, picturesque, and unpretentious. Where he describes events on the authority of others, his manner is purely historical; events which have come under his own observation he treats in the minute and circumstantial style of an eye-witness. Compare, for instance, the detailed narrative of the events at Philippi with that of the occurrences at Thessalonica. The change of style at Acts xvi. 10, from the historical to the personal narrative, coincides with the time of his joining Paul at the first visit to Macedonia, and a similar change may be noted at Acts xx. 4–6.

But the style of Luke also acquires a peculiar flavor from his profession. His language, both in the Gospel and in the Acts, indicates a familiarity with the terms used by the Greek medical schools, and furnishes an incidental confirmation of the common authorship of the two books. As we have seen, Luke was probably a Greek of Asia Minor; and, with the exception of Hippocrates, all the extant Greek medical writers were Asiatic Greeks. Hippocrates, indeed, can hardly be called an exception, as he was born and lived in the island of Cos, off the coast of Caria. Galen was of Pergamus in Mysia; Dioscorides, of Anazarba in Cilicia; and Aretaeus, of Cappadocia.

The medical peculiarities of Luke's style appear, first, in words and phrases used in descriptions of diseases or of miracles of healing. His terms are of the technical character peculiar to a medical man. Thus, in the account of the healing of Simon's wife's mother (Luke iv. 38, 39), we read that she was *taken* (συνεχομένη) with a *great fever* (πυρετῷ μεγάλῳ). The word *taken* is used nine times by Luke, and only three times in the rest of the New Testament. It occurs frequently in this sense in the medical writers, as does also the simple verb ἔχω, *to have* or *hold*. Moreover, according to Galen, the ancient physicians were accustomed to distinguish between *great* and *little* fevers. In the parable of the rich man and Lazarus (Luke xvi. 19–26), we find εἱλκωμένος, *full of sores*, the regular medical term for *to be ulcerated:* ὀδυνῶμαι, *to be in pain*, occurs four times in Luke's writings, and nowhere else in the New Testament, but frequently in Galen, Aretaeus, and Hippocrates. Ἐξέψυξε, *gave up the ghost* (Acts v. 5, 10), is a rare word, used by Luke only, and occurring only three times in the New Testament. It seems to be almost confined to medical writers, and to be used rarely even by them. In the proverb of "the camel and the needle's eye," Matthew and Mark use for *needle* the vulgar word ῥαφίς, while Luke alone uses βελόνη, *the surgical needle.*

These terms will be pointed out in the notes as they occur.

Second, the ordinary diction of the evangelist, when dealing with unprofessional subjects, has often a medical flavor, which asserts itself in words peculiar to him, or more common in his writings than elsewhere in the New Testament, and all of which were in common use among the Greek physicians. Thus Matthew (xxiii. 4) says that the scribes and Pharisees will not *move* (κινῆσαι) the burdens they impose, with one of their fingers. Luke, recording a similar saying (xi. 46), says, "ye yourselves *touch* (προσψαύετε) not the burdens," using a technical term for gently feeling the pulse, or a sore or tender part of the body. The word occurs nowhere else in the New Testament. "No *mean* city" (ἄσημος, Acts xxi. 39). The word *mean*, peculiar to this passage, is the professional term for a disease without distinctive symptoms, and is applied by Hippocrates to a city. "*Delivered* the letter" (ἀναδόντες, Acts xxiii. 33). The verb occurs only here in the New Testament, and is a medical term for the *distribution* of blood through the veins, or of nourishment through the body. Hippocrates uses it of a messenger delivering a letter. In the parable of the sower, Matthew and Mark have ῥίζαν, "they have no *root*." Luke (viii. 6) has ἰκμάδα, *moisture*, the medical term for the *juices* of the body, of plants, and of the earth. In the same parable, for *sprung up* Matthew and Mark have ἐξανέτειλε, while Luke has **φυὲν—συμφυεῖσαι** (vv. 6, 7), *it grew—grew with it* (Rev.). These latter words are used by medical writers to describe the growth of parts of the body, of diseases, of vegetation, etc. Hippocrates uses together ἰκμάς, *moisture*, and φύεσθαι, *to grow*, comparing the juices of the body with those of the earth. **Συμφύεσθαι**, *to grow together*, was the professional word for the closing of wounds and ulcers, the uniting of nerves and of bones, and is used by Dioscorides precisely as here, of plants growing together in the same place.

Such peculiarities, so far from being strange or anomalous, are only what might naturally be expected. It is an every-day fact that the talk of specialists, whether in the professions or in mechanics, when it turns upon ordinary topics, unconsciously takes form and color from their familiar calling.

The attempt has been made to show that Paul's style was influenced by Luke in this same direction; so that his intercourse with his companion and physician showed itself in his use of certain words having a medical flavor. Dean Plumptre cites as illustrations of this, ὑγιαίνειν, *to be healthy*, in its figurative application to doctrine as *wholesome* or *sound* (1 Tim. i. 10; vi. 3; 2 Tim. i. 13): γάγγραινα, *canker* (2 Tim. ii. 17): τυφωθεὶς, *lifted up with pride;* Rev., *puffed up* (1 Tim. iii. 6; vi. 4): κεκαυτηριασμένων, *seared;* Rev., *branded* (1 Tim. iv. 2): κνηθόμενοι, *itching* (2 Tim. iv. 3): ἀποκόψονται, *cut themselves off* (Gal. v. 12).

Luke is also circumstantial, as well as technical, in his descriptions of diseases; noting their duration and symptoms, and the stages of the patient's recovery, etc. See Acts iii. 1–8; ix. 40, 41. The successive stages of Elymas' blindness are noted at Acts xiii. 11; and the process of Saul's restoration to sight at ix. 18. He also exhibits traces of professional sensitiveness, as in his omission of Mark's implied reflection upon the physicians who had treated the woman with the issue of blood (Luke viii. 43; Mark v. 26).

Luke's accurate observation and memory appear especially in the Acts, in his allusions, and in his descriptions of nautical and political matters. With nautical details, he exhibits the acquaintance often displayed by a landsman who has been much at sea and in frequent intercourse with seamen. It has been conjectured that at some period of his professional life he may have served as a surgeon on shipboard. In his political allusions he is precise in the use of terms. Thus, in Acts xiii. 7, his accuracy in naming the civil magistrates is noteworthy. He speaks of Sergius Paulus as the *proconsul* of Cyprus. Consuls were called by the Greeks ὕπατοι; and hence a *proconsul* was ἀνθύπατος, one who acts *instead of* (ἀντὶ) a consul. Roman provinces were of two classes, *senatorial* and *imperial;* and the proper title of the governor of a senatorial province was ἀνθύπατος. The governor of an imperial province was called ἀντιστράτηγος, or *propraetor*. Evidently, therefore, Luke regarded Cyprus as a senatorial province, governed by a proconsul; and we find that Augustus, though at first he reserved Cyprus for himself, and consequently governed it by a *propraetor*, afterward restored it to the senate and governed it by a proconsul—a fact confirmed by coins of the very time of Paul's visit to Cyprus, bearing the name of the emperor Claudius, and of the provincial governor, with the title ἀνθύπατος. So Luke speaks of Gallio (Acts xviii. 12) as proconsul (A. V., *deputy*) of Achaia, which was a senatorial province. When he comes to Felix or Festus, who were only deputy-governors of the propraetor of Syria, he calls them by the general term ἡγεμών, *governor* (Acts xxiii. 24; xxvi. 30). Similarly accurate is his designation of Philippi as a *colonia* (Acts xvi. 12), and his calling its magistrates στρατηγοί or *praetors*, a title which they were fond of giving themselves. So the city authorities of Thessalonica are styled *πολιτάρχαι*, *rulers of the city* (Acts xvii. 8); for Thessalonica was a free city, having the right of self-government, and where the local magistrates had the power of life and death over the citizens. Luke's accuracy on this point is borne out by an inscription on an archway in Thessalonica, which gives this title to the magistrates of the place, together with their number—seven—and the very names of some who held the office not long before Paul's time. This short inscription contains six names which are mentioned in the New Testament. We may also note the *Asiarchs*, *chiefs of Asia*, at Ephesus (Acts xix. 31), who, like the *aediles* at Rome, defrayed the charge of public amusements, and were, as presidents of the games, invested with the character of priests.

A similar accuracy appears in the Gospel in the dates of more important events, and in local descriptions, as of the Lord's coming to Jerusalem across the Mount of Olives (xix. 37–41). Here he brings out the two distinct views of Jerusalem on this route, an irregularity in the ground hiding it for a time after one has just caught sight of it. Verse 37 marks the first sight, and 41 the second.

In the narrative of the voyage and shipwreck, the precision of detail is remarkable. Thus there are fourteen verbs denoting the progression of a ship, with a distinction indicating the peculiar circumstances of the ship at the time. Seven of these are compounds of *πλέω*, *to sail.* Thus we have *ἀπέπλευσαν*, sailed *away* (xiii. 4); *Βραδυπλοοῦντες*, sailing *slowly* (xxvii. 7); *ὑπεπλεύσαμεν*, sailed *under* (the lee). So, also, *παραλεγόμενοι*, *hardly passing* (xxvii. 8); *εὐθυδρομήσαμεν*, *ran with a straight course* (xvi. 11), etc. Note also the technical terms for lightening the ship by throwing overboard the cargo: *ἐκβολὴν ἐποιοῦντο*; literally, *made a casting out* (xxvii. 18); *ἐκούφιζον*, *lightened* (xxvii. 38); and the names of various parts of the vessel.

Luke's Gospel is the gospel of *contrasts.* Thus Satan is constantly emphasized over against Jesus, as binding a daughter of Abraham; as cast down from heaven in Jesus' vision; as entering into Judas; as sifting Peter. The evangelist portrays the doubting Zacharias and the trusting Mary; the churlish

Simon and the loving sinner; the bustling Martha and the quiet, adoring Mary; the thankful and the thankless lepers; the woes added to the blessings in the Sermon on the Mount; the rich man and Lazarus; the Pharisee and the Publican; the good Samaritan and the priest and Levite; the prodigal and his elder brother; the penitent and impenitent thieves.

Luke's is the *universal* gospel. His frequent use of words expressing the freedom and universality of the Gospel has already been noted. His Gospel is for the Gentiles. The genealogy of Christ is traced back to the common father of the race, Adam, instead of to Abraham, the father of the Jewish nation, as by Matthew. He records the enrolment of Christ as a citizen of the Roman empire. Simeon greets him as a light for revelation to the Gentiles. The Baptist cites concerning him Isaiah's prophecy that *all flesh* shall see the salvation of God. Luke alone records the mission of the seventy, who represent the seventy Gentile nations, as the twelve represent the twelve tribes of Israel. He alone mentions the mission of Elijah to the heathen widow, and Naaman's cleansing by Elisha. He contrasts the gratitude of the one Samaritan leper with the thanklessness of the nine Jewish lepers. He alone records the refusal to call down fire on the inhospitable Samaritans, and the parable of the Good Samaritan is peculiar to him. He notes the commendation of the humble Publican in contrast with the self-righteous Pharisee, and relates how Jesus abode with Zacchaeus. He omits all reference to the law in the Sermon on the Mount.

Luke's is the gospel of the poor and outcast. As a phase of its universality, the humblest and most sinful are shown as not excluded from Jesus. The highest heavenly honor is conferred on the humble Mary of Nazareth. Only in Luke's story do we hear the angels' song of "Peace and good-will," and see the simple shepherds repairing to the manger at Bethlehem. It is Luke who gives the keynote of Keble's lovely strain:

"The pastoral spirits first
Approach thee, Babe divine,
For they in lowly thoughts are nurs'd,
Meet for thy lowly shrine:
Sooner than they should miss where thou dost dwell,
Angels from heaven will stoop to guide them to thy cell."

He pictures poor Lazarus in Abraham's bosom, and the calling of the poor and maimed and halt and blind to the great supper. It is the gospel of the publican, the harlot, the prodigal, the penitent thief.

Luke's is the gospel of womanhood. Woman comes prominently into view as discerning God's promises. The songs of Mary and Elizabeth, and the testimony of Anna, are full of a clear spiritual perception, no less than of a living and simple faith. She appears as ministering to the Lord and as the subject of his ministries. Mary of Magdala, Joanna, Susanna, Mary and Martha, with others, lavish upon him their tender care; while the daughter of Abraham whom Satan had bound, the sorrowful mother at Nain, she who touched the hem of his garment, and the weeping daughters of Jerusalem on the road to Calvary knew the comfort of his words and the healing and life-giving virtue of his touch. The word γυνὴ, *woman*, occurs in Matthew and Mark together forty-nine times, and in Luke alone forty-three. "He alone," says Canon Farrar, "preserves the narratives, treasured with delicate reserve and holy reticence in the hearts of the blessed Virgin and of the saintly Elizabeth—narratives which show in every line the pure and tender coloring of a woman's thoughts."

Luke's is the prayer-gospel. To him we are indebted for the record of our Lord's prayers at his baptism; after the cleansing of the leper; before the call of the twelve; at his transfiguration; and on the cross for his enemies. To him alone belong the prayer-parables of the Friend at Midnight, and the Unjust Judge.

Luke's is the gospel of song. He has been justly styled "the first Christian hymnologist." To him we owe the *Benedictus*, the song of Zacharias; the *Magnificat*, the song of Mary; the *Nunc Dimittis*, the song of Simeon; the *Ave Maria*, or the angel's salutation; and the *Gloria in Excelsis*, the song of the angels.

And, finally, Luke's is the gospel of infancy. He alone tells the story of the birth of John the Baptist; he gives the minuter details of the birth of Christ, and the accounts of his circumcision and presentation in the temple, his subjection to his parents and the questioning with the doctors. His Gospel "sheds a sacred halo and celestial charm over infancy, as perpetuating the paradise of innocence in a sinful world. The first two chapters will always be the favorite chapters for children, and all who delight to gather around the manger of Bethlehem, and to rejoice with shepherds in the field and angels in heaven" (Schaff).

THE GOSPEL ACCORDING TO LUKE.

CHAPTER I.

PROLOGUE.

1. **Forasmuch as** (ἐπειδήπερ). Only here in New Testament. A compound conjunction: ἐπεί, *since*, δή, *as is well known*, and περ, giving the sense of certainty.

Have taken in hand (ἐπεχείρησαν). Used by Luke only. A literal translation. The word carries the sense of a *difficult* undertaking (see Acts xix. 13), and implies that previous attempts have not been successful. It occurs frequently in medical language. Hippocrates begins one of his medical treatises very much as Luke begins his gospel. "As many as have *taken in hand* (ἐπεχείρησαν) to speak or to write concerning the healing art."

To set forth in order (ἀνατάξασθαι). Only here in New Testament. The A. V. is true to the core of the word, which is τάσσω, *to put in order*, or *arrange*. Rev. happily gives the force of the preposition ἀνὰ, *up*, by the rendering *draw up*.

A declaration (διήγησιν). Only here in New Testament. From διά, *through*, and ἡγέομαι, to *lead the way*. Hence something which leads the reader through the mass of facts: *a narrative*, as A. V., with the accompanying idea of *thoroughness*. Note the singular number. *Many* took in hand to draw up, not *narratives*, but *a narrative*, embracing the whole of the evangelic matter. The word was particularly applied to a medical treatise. Galen applies it at least seventy-three times to the writings of Hippocrates.

Which are most surely believed (τῶν πεπληροφορημένων). From πλήρης, *full*, and φορέω, the frequentative form of φέρω, *to bring*, meaning to bring *frequently* or *habitually*. Hence, *to bring full measure; to fulfil.* Compare 2 Tim. iv. 5, 17. Also of *full assurance.* Applied to persons. Rom. iv. 21; Heb. x. 22. As applied to *things*, therefore, the sense of the A. V. is inadmissible. Render as Rev., *have been fulfilled.* The word is chosen to indicate that these events happened in accordance with a preconceived design. Wyc., *been filled in us.*

Among us. Explained by the words in the next sentence, *who were eye-witnesses and ministers.*

2. **Even as.** Referring to the composition of the narrative.

Delivered (παρέδοσαν). Not necessarily excluding written traditions, but referring mainly to oral tradition. Note the distinction between the *many* who attempted to *draw up a narrative* and the *eye-witnesses* and *ministers* who *handed down* the facts.

From the beginning (ἀπ' ἀρχῆς). The *official* beginning, the commencement of Jesus' ministry. Compare Acts i. 1, 21, 22; John xv. 27.

Eye-witnesses and ministers. *Personal knowledge* and *practical experience* were necessary elements of an apostle. *Eye-witnesses* (αὐτόπται). Only here in New Testament. Peter uses another word, ἐπόπται (2 Pet. i. 16). Frequent in medical writers, of a personal examination of disease or of the parts of the body. Compare the modern medical term *autopsy. Ministers* (ὑπηρέται). See on Matt. v. 25. In medical language denoting the attendants or assistants of the principal physician.

3. **Having had perfect understanding** (παρηκολουθηκότι). Incorrect. The verb means *to follow closely*, and hence *to trace accurately*. See 2 Tim. iii. 10, where Rev. reads *thou didst follow* for *thou hast fully known*. Rev. renders here *having traced the course*. The word occurs frequently in medical writings, and sometimes, as here, with ἀκριβῶς, *accurately*. Tynd., *having searched out diligently*.

From the very first (ἄνωθεν). Lit., *from above;* the events being conceived in a descending series.

Accurately (ἀκριβῶς) From ἄκρον, *the highest* or *farthest point*. Hence to trace down to the last and minutest detail.

In order (καθεξῆς). Used by Luke only.

4. **Mightest know** (ἐπιγνῷς). See on Matt. vii. 16. With the idea of *full* knowledge; or, as regards Theophilus, of more accurate knowledge than is possible from the many who have undertaken the narration.

Certainty (ἀσφάλειαν). From ἀ, *not*, and σφάλλομαι, *to fall*. Hence *steadfastness*, *stability*, *security against* error.

Wast instructed (κατήχηθης). From κατηχέω, *to resound; to teach by word of mouth;* and so, in Christian writers, to instruct orally in the elements of religion. It would imply that Theophilus had, thus far, been orally instructed. See on *delivered*, ver. 2. The word *catechumen* is derived from it.

Things (λόγων). Properly *words* (so Wyc.), which Rev. gives in margin. If the word can mean *thing* at all, it is only in the sense of *the thing spoken of;* the *subject* or *matter* of discourse, in which sense it occurs often in classical Greek. Some render it *accounts*, *histories;* others, *doctrines of the faith*. Godet translates *instruction*, and claims that not only the *facts* of the gospel, but the *exposition* of the facts with a view to show their evangelical meaning and to their appropriation by faith, are included in the word. There is force in this idea; and if we hold to the meaning *histories*, or even *words*, this sense will be implied in the context. Luke has drawn up his account in order that Theophilus may have *fuller* knowledge concerning the accounts which he has heard by word of mouth. That his knowledge may go on from the facts, to embrace their doctrinal and evangelical import; that he may see the facts of Jesus' life and ministry as the true basis of the Gospel of salvation.

THE NARRATIVE.

5. **King.** A title decreed to Herod by the Roman Senate on the recommendation of Antony and Octavius. The Greek style now gives place to the Hebraized style. See Introduction.

Course (ἐφημερίας). Lit., *daily service.* The college of priests was divided into twenty-four courses. Each of these did duty for eight days, from one Sabbath to another, once every six months. The service of the week was subdivided among the various families which constituted a course. On Sabbaths the whole course was on duty. On feast-days any priest might come up and join in the ministrations of the sanctuary; and at the Feast of Tabernacles all the twenty-four courses were bound to be present and officiate. The course of Abijah was the eighth of the twenty-four. See 1 Chron. xxiv. 10.

6. **Before God.** A Hebrew expression. Compare Gen. vii. 1; Acts viii. 21.

7. **Well stricken** (προβεβηκότες). Lit., *advanced.* Wyc., *had gone far in their days.*

9. **His lot was** (ἔλαχε). Four lots were drawn to determine the order of the ministry of the day: the first, before daybreak, to designate the priests who were to cleanse the altar and prepare its fires; the second for the priest who was to offer the sacrifice and cleanse the candlestick and the altar of incense;

the third for the priest who should burn incense; and the fourth appointing those who were to lay the sacrifice and meat-offering on the altar, and pour out the drink-offering. There are said to have been twenty thousand priests in Christ's time, so that no priest would ever offer incense more than once.

Temple (ναὸν). The sanctuary. See on Matt. iv. 5.

Burn incense (θυμιᾶσαι). Only here in New Testament. The incensing priest and his assistants went first to the altar of burnt-offering, and filled a golden censer with incense, and placed burning coals from the altar in a golden bowl. As they passed into the court from the Holy Place they struck a large instrument called the *Magrephah*, which summoned all the ministers to their places. Ascending the steps to the holy place, the priests spread the coals on the golden altar, and arranged the incense, and the chief officiating priest was then left alone within the Holy Place to await the signal of the president to burn the incense. It was probably at this time that the angel appeared to Zacharias. When the signal was given, the whole multitude withdrew from the inner court, and fell down before the Lord. Silence pervaded the temple, while within, the clouds of incense rose up before Jehovah. (For a more detailed account see Edersheim, "The Temple, its Ministry," etc.).

13. **Is heard** (εἰσηκούσθη). If we render the aorist literally, *was heard*, we avoid the question as to what prayer is referred to. The reference is to the prayer *for offspring*, which, owing to his extreme years, Zacharias had probably ceased to offer, and which he certainly would not be preferring in that public and solemn service. Hence the aorist is appropriate, referring back to the past acts of prayer. "That prayer, which thou no longer offerest, *was heard*."

John. Meaning *God is favorable*, or *Jehovah showeth grace*.

14. **Joy and gladness** (χαρά καὶ ἀγαλλίασις). The latter word expresses *exultant* joy. See on 1 Pet. i. 6.

15. **Strong drink** (*σίκερα*). A Hebrew word, meaning any kind of intoxicating liquor not made from grapes. Wyc., *sydir*.

Even from his mother's womb. *Ἔτι*, *yet*, *still*, means *while yet unborn*. Tynd., *even in his mother's womb*. Compare ver. 41.

17. **Wisdom** (*φρονήσει*). Wyc., *prudence*. This is a lower word than *σοφία*, *wisdom* (see on Jas. iii. 13). It is an *attribute* or *result* of wisdom, and not necessarily in a good sense, though mostly so in the New Testament. Compare, however, the use of the kindred word *φρόνιμος* in Rom. xi. 25; xii. 16: *wise in your own conceits*; and the adverb *φρονίμως*, *wisely*, of the unjust steward, Luke xvi. 8. It is *practical* intelligence, which may or may not be applied to good ends. Appropriate here as a practical term corresponding to *disobedient*.

Prepared (*κατασκευασμένον*). *Adjusted, disposed, placed in the right moral state.*

18. **Whereby** (*κατὰ τί*). Lit., *according to what?* It demands a standard of knowledge, a sign.

For. I require a sign, *for* I am old.

19. **Gabriel.** Meaning *man of God*. In Jewish tradition the guardian of the sacred treasury. Michael (see on Jude 9) is the *destroyer*, the champion of God against evil, the minister of wrath. Gabriel is the messenger of peace and restoration. See Dan. viii. 16; ix. 21. "The former is the forerunner of Jehovah the Judge; the latter of Jehovah the Saviour" (Godet).

20. **Thou shalt be silent** (*ἔσῃ σιωπῶν*). Lit., *thou shalt be being silent*. The finite verb and participle denote continuance.

Not able to speak. Showing that the silence would not be voluntary.

My words **which** (οἵτινες). The pronoun is qualitative, denoting a class. "My words, which, incredible as they seem to you, *are of a kind which* shall be fulfilled.

In their season (εἰς τὸν καιρὸν). The preposition implies exactness: at the completion of the appointed time. The *process* of fulfilment, beginning *now*, will go on, εἰς, *up to*, the appointed time, and *at* the time will be consummated. **Καιρὸν**, *season*, is more specific than χρόνος, *time*. It is an *appointed*, *fitting* time: the right *point* of time when circumstances shall concur.

21. **Waited** (ἦν προσδοκῶν). The finite verb and participle, denoting *protracted* waiting. Hence, better as Rev., *were waiting*. Wyc., *was abiding*.

Marvelled. According to the Talmud, the priests, especially the chief priests, were accustomed to spend only a short time in the sanctuary, otherwise it was feared that they had been slain by God for unworthiness or transgression.

22. **They perceived** (ἐπέγνωσαν). *Clearly* perceived. See on Matt. vii. 16, and ver. 4.

He beckoned (ἦν διανεύων). Better Rev., *continued making signs*. Again the participle with the finite verb, denoting frequent repetition of the same signs. Wyc., *was beckoning*.

23. **Ministration** (λειτουργίας). From λεῖτος, *belonging to the people, public*, and ἔργον, *a work*. Hence *service of the state in a public office*. Trench observes that "when the Christian Church was forming its terminology, which it did partly by shaping new words, and partly by elevating old ones to higher than their previous uses, of the latter it more readily adopted those before employed in civil and political life, than such as had played their part in religious matters." Hence it adopted this word, already in use in the Septuagint, as the constant word for *performing priestly and ministerial functions;* and so in

the New Testament of *the ministry of the apostles, prophets, and teachers.*

24. **Conceived** (συνέλαβεν). Mr. Hobart ("Medical Language of Luke") says that the number of words referring to pregnancy, barrenness, etc., used by Luke, is almost as large as that used by Hippocrates. Compare i. 31; i. 24; ii. 5; i. 7; xx. 28. All of these, except i. 24, are peculiar to himself, and all, of course, in common use among medical writers.

Hid (περιέκρυβεν). Only here in New Testament. Περί signifies *completely;* entire seclusion.

25. Neither A. V. nor Rev. render ὅτι; taking it, as frequently, merely as recitative or equivalent to quotation marks. But it means *because.* Elizabeth assigns the reason for her peculiar seclusion. Her pregnancy was God's work, and she would leave it to him also to announce it and openly to take away her reproach. Hence the specification of *five months,* after which her condition would become apparent. Fully expressed, the sense would be: She hid herself, saying (I have hid myself) *because,* etc.

Looked upon (ἐπεῖδεν). Used by Luke only.

26. **Gabriel.** The annunciation and the angel Gabriel are favorite themes with Dante, and he pictures them with exquisite beauty. Thus both appear on the sculptured wall which flanks the inner side of the purgatorial ascent.

"The angel who came down to earth with tidings
Of peace that had been wept for many a year,
And opened heaven from its long interdict,
In front of us appeared so truthfully
There sculptured in a gracious attitude,
He did not seem an image that is silent.
One would have sworn that he was saying *Ave!*
For she was there in effigy portrayed
Who turned the key to ope the exalted love,
And in her mien this language had impressed,
Ecce ancilla Dei! as distinctly
As any figure stamps itself in wax."

Purgatory, x., 34–45.

In Paradise Gabriel appears as a light circling round the Virgin and singing:

> "I am angelic love, that circle round
> The joy sublime which breathes out from the womb
> That was the hostelry of our desire;
> And I shall circle, Lady of heaven, while
> Thou followest thy Son, and mak'st diviner
> The sphere supreme, because thou enterest there."
>
> *Paradise*, xxiii., 103–108.

And again:

> "And the same love that first descended then,
> *Ave Maria gratia plena* singing,
> In front of her his wings expanded wide."
>
> *Paradise*, xxxii., 94–96.

28. **Thou that art highly favored** (κεχαριτωμένη). Lit., as Rev. in margin, *endued with grace*. Only here and Eph. i. 6. The rendering *full of grace*, Vulgate, Wyc., and Tynd., is therefore wrong.

All the best texts omit *blessed art thou among women*.

Cast in her mind (διελογίζετο). See on Jas. ii. 4. The imperfect tense, "*began* to reason."

30. **Grace** (χάριν). From the same root as χαίρω, *to rejoice*. I. Primarily *that which gives joy or pleasure;* and hence *outward beauty, loveliness*, something which *delights* the beholder. Thus Homer, of Ulysses going to the assembly: "Athene shed down *manly grace* or *beauty* upon him" ("Odyssey," ii., 12); and Septuagint, Ps. xlv. 3, "*grace* is poured into thy lips." See also Prov. i. 9; iii. 22. Substantially the same idea, *agreeableness*, is conveyed in Luke iv. 22, respecting the *gracious words*, lit., *words of grace*, uttered by Christ. So Eph. iv. 29. II. *As a beautiful or agreeable sentiment felt and expressed toward another; kindness, favor, good-will*. 2 Cor. viii. 6, 7, 9; ix. 8; Luke i. 30; ii. 40; Acts ii. 47. So of the responsive sentiment of *thankfulness*. See Luke vi. 32, 33, 34; xvii. 9; but mostly in the formula *thanks to God;* Rom. vi. 17; 1 Cor. xv. 57; 2 Cor. ii. 14; 2 Tim. i. 3. III. The *substan-*

tial expression of good-will; a boon, a favor, a gift; but not in New Testament. See Rom. v. 15, where the distinction is made between χάρις, *grace*, and δωρεὰ ἐν χάριτι, *a gift in grace.* So a *gratification* or *delight*, in classical Greek only; as the delight in battle, in sleep, etc. IV. The higher Christian signification, based on the emphasis of *freeness* in the gift or favor, and, as commonly in New Testament, denoting the free, spontaneous, absolute loving-kindness of God toward men, and so contrasted with *debt, law, works, sin.* The word does not occur either in Matthew or Mark.

31. **Thou shalt conceive.** See on ver. 24.

Jesus. See on Matt. i. 21.

35. **Shall overshadow.** "Denoting the mildest and most gentle operation of divine power, that the divine fire should not consume Mary, but make her fruitful" (Bengel). Compare Exod. xxxiii. 22; Mark ix. 7. Compare the classical legend of Semele, who, being beloved of Jove, besought him to appear to her as he appeared in heaven, in all the terrors of the thunderer, and was consumed by his lightning. The metaphor in the word is taken from a cloud, in which God had appeared (Exod. xl. 34; 1 Kings viii. 10).

36. **Cousin** (συγγενής). The nature of the relationship, however, is unknown. The word is a general term, meaning *of the same family.* The best texts substitute for it a feminine form, συγγενίς, which is condemned by the grammarians as unclassical, but rightly rendered by Rev., *kinswoman.* Wyc., *cosyness*, i.e., *cousiness.*

37. **With God nothing shall be impossible** (οὐκ ἀδυνατήσει παρὰ τοῦ Θεοῦ πᾶν ῥῆμα). Ῥῆμα, *word*, as distinguished from λόγος, *word*, in classical Greek, signifies a constituent part of a speech or writing, as distinguished from the contents as a whole. Thus it may be either *a word* or *a saying.* Sometimes *a phrase*, as opposed to ὄνομα, *a single word.* The dis-

tinction in the New Testament is not sharp throughout. It is maintained that ῥῆμα in the New Testament, like the Hebrew *gabar*, stands sometimes for the *subject-matter* of the word; the *thing*, as in this passage. But there are only two other passages in the New Testament where this meaning is at all admissible, though the word occurs seventy times. These are Luke ii. 15; Acts v. 32. "Kept all these *things*" (Luke ii. 19), should clearly be *sayings*, as the A. V. itself has rendered it in the almost identical passage, ver. 51. In Acts v. 32, Rev. gives *sayings* in margin. In Luke ii. 15, though A. V. and Rev. render *thing*, the sense is evidently *saying*, as appears both from the connection with the angelic message and from the following words, *which has come to pass:* the saying which has become a fact. The Rev. rendering of this passage is, therefore, right, though a little stilted: *No word of God shall be void of power;* for the A. V. errs in joining οὐκ and πᾶν, *not every*, and translating *nothing*. The two do not belong together. The statement is, *Every* (πᾶν) *word of God shall not* (οὐκ) *be powerless*. The A. V. also follows the reading, παρὰ τῷ Θεῷ, *with God;* but all the later texts read παρὰ τοῦ Θεοῦ, *from God*, which fixes the meaning beyond question.

40. **Entered into the house.** "This detail," says Godet, "serves to put the reader in sympathy with the emotion of Mary at the moment of her arrival. With her first glance at Elizabeth she recognized the truth of the sign that had been given her by the angel, and at this sight the promise she had herself received acquired a startling reality."

41. **The babe** (τὸ βρέφος). See on 1 Pet. ii. 2.

42. **She spake out with a loud voice** (ἀνεφώνησε φωνῇ μεγάλῃ). For φωνῇ, voice, read κραυγῇ, *cry:* inarticulate, though φωνή may also be used of inarticulate utterance. Rev., rightly, *She lifted up her voice with a loud cry;* thus rendering in the verb the force of ἀνὰ, *up*, besides picturing the fact more naturally. Elizabeth's sudden and violent emotion at the appearance of Mary, and the movement of the child, prompted an exclama-

tion which was followed by words (εἶπεν, *said*). The verb ἀναφωνέω occurs only here in the New Testament. It was a medical term for a certain exercise of the voice.

44. **For joy** (ἐν ἀγαλλιάσει). Lit., *in joy*. See on ver. 14.

45. **For** (ὅτι). Many, however, prefer *that*, referring to the substance of her belief: "She believed *that* there shall be a fulfilment," etc. It is urged that the *conception*, which was the principal point of faith, had already taken place, so that the fulfilment was no longer future. On the other hand, the angel's announcement to Mary included more than the fact of conception; and Elizabeth, in the spirit of prophecy, may have alluded to what is predicted in vv. 32, 33.

46. **Said** (εἶπεν). Simply. Compare ver. 42. "Elizabeth's salutation was full of excitement, but Mary's hymn breathes a sentiment of deep inward repose" (Godet). Compare the song of Hannah (1 Sam. ii.). Hannah's song differs from Mary's in its sense of indignation and personal triumph compared with Mary's humility and calmness.

My soul—spirit (ψυχή—πνεῦμα). See on Mark xii. 30. The *soul* is the principle of individuality, the seat of personal impressions, having a side in contact with the material element of humanity, as well as with the spiritual element. It is thus the mediating organ between the spirit and the body, receiving impressions from without and from within, and transmitting them by word or sign. *Spirit* is the highest, deepest, noblest part of our humanity, the point of contact between God and man.

47. **God my Saviour** (τῷ θεῷ τῷ σωτῆρί μου). Note the two articles. "*The* God who is *the* or *my* Saviour." The title Saviour is often applied to God in the Old Testament. See Septuagint, Deut. xxxii. 15; Ps. xxiv. 5; xxv. 5; xcv. 1.

48. **Regarded** (ἐπέβλεψεν). See on Jas. ii. 3. Compare 1 Sam. i. 11; Ps. xxxi. 7; cxix. 132, Sept.

50. **Mercy** (ἔλεος). The word emphasizes the *misery* with which *grace* (see on ver. 30) deals; hence, peculiarly the sense of human wretchedness coupled with the impulse to relieve it, which issues in gracious ministry. Bengel remarks, "Grace takes away the *fault*, mercy the *misery*."

From generation to generation (εἰς γενεὰς καὶ γενεὰς). Lit., as Rev., *unto generations and generations*.

Fear (φοβουμένος). The word is used in both a good and a bad sense in the New Testament. For the latter, see Matt. xxi. 46; Mark vi. 20; xi. 32; Luke xii. 4. For the former, as here, in the sense of godly reverence, Acts x. 2, 22, 35; Col. iii. 22; Apoc. xiv. 7; xv. 4.

51. **Shewed strength** (ἐποίησεν κράτος). Lit., *made strength*. So Wyc., *made might*. A Hebrew form of expression. Compare Ps. cxviii. 15, Sept.: "The right hand of the Lord *doeth valiantly*" (ἐποίησε δύναμιν, *made strength*).

In the imagination (διανοίᾳ). The faculty of thought, understanding, especially *moral* understanding. Wyc. refers the word here to God: *with mind of his heart*. Some prefer to render "*by* the imagination," thus making the proud the instrument of their own destruction. Compare 2 Cor. x. 5.

54. **Hath holpen** (ἀντελαβέτο). The verb means to *lay hold on:* thence to *grasp helpfully* or *to help*. To lay hold in the sense of *partaking* (1 Tim. vi. 2), carries us back to the primitive meaning of the word according to its composition: to receive *instead of*, or *in return* (ἀντὶ), and suggests the old phrase *to take up for*, *espouse the cause of*. Wyc., has *took up*, but probably not in this sense.

Servant (παιδὸς). Often *child*, son or daughter, but here *servant*, in allusion to Isa. xli. 8. Meyer truthfully says that the *theocratic* notion of *sonship* is never expressed by παῖς. See Rev., Acts iii. 13, 26; iv. 27, 30.

58. **Had shewed great mercy upon her** (ἐμεγάλυνεν τὸ ἔλεος αὐτοῦ μετ' αὐτῆς). Lit., *magnified his mercy with her*. So Wyc. A Hebrew expression. See 1 Sam. xii. 24, Sept.

59. **They called** (ἐκάλουν). The imperfect tense signifies, as Rev., *they would have called:* they were about to call: or, as Bishop Lightfoot has happily suggested, *they were for calling*.

62. **They made signs** (ἐνένευον). Imperfect tense. While the colloquy between Elizabeth and her friends was going on, they *were consulting* Zacharias by signs.

63. **Writing-table** (πινακίδιον). *Table* was formerly used in the sense of *tablet*. Thus Shakspeare:

> "Yea, from the *table* of my memory,
> I'll wipe away all trivial fond records."
>
> *Hamlet*, i., 5.

Tynd., *writing-tables*. The meaning is a little writing-tablet, probably covered with wax. Only here in the New Testament. Used by medical writers of a physician's note-book. Wyc. has *a poyntel*, i.e., a *style* for writing.

Wrote, saying. A Hebrew form of expression. See 2 Kings x. 6.

64. **Immediately** (παραχρῆμα). Occurring nineteen times in the New Testament, and seventeen of these in Luke. Thirteen of the seventeen are in connection with miracles of healing, or the infliction of disease or death. Used in a similar way by medical writers.

65. **Were noised abroad** (διαλελεῖτο). Were *mutually* (διά) talked of.

69. **Horn.** Compare Ps. cxxxii. 17.

70. **That have been since the world began** (ἀπ' αἰῶνος). A needlessly verbose rendering, retained by Rev. The American Rev. insists on *of old.*

74. **Serve** (λατρεύειν). Originally to serve *for hire*, from λάτρον, *hire.* Plato uses it of the service of God.

75. **Holiness and righteousness** (ὁσιότητι καὶ δικαιοσύνῃ). The adjective ὅσιος, *holy*, is properly *what is confirmed by ancient sanction and precept.* Ὁσία is used in classical Greek to denote *the everlasting principles of right, not constituted by the laws or customs of men, but antedating them;* such as the paying of the proper rites of sepulture. Compare the fine passage in the "Antigone" of Sophocles (453–55):

> "Nor did I deem thy edicts strong enough,
> That thou, a mortal man, shouldst overpass
> The unwritten laws of God that know not change.
> They are not of to-day nor yesterday,
> But live forever, nor can man assign
> When first they sprang to being."

Hence ὁσιότης is concerned primarily with the eternal laws of God. It is "*the divine consecration and inner truth of righteousness*" (Meyer). Throughout the New Testament its look is godward. In no case is it used of moral excellence as related to men, though it is to be carefully noted that δικαιοσύνη, *righteousness*, is not restricted to *rightness toward men.* Compare Eph. iv. 24; *true holiness;* literally, *holiness of the truth.*

77. **Knowledge of salvation.** Wyc. has *the science of health.*

78. **Tender mercy** (σπλάγχνα ἐλέους). Lit., *bowels of mercy.* See on 1 Pet. iii. 8; Jas. v. 11. Rev. gives *heart of mercy* in margin. Wyc., frightfully, *entrails of mercy.*

The day-spring from on high (ἀνατολὴ ἐξ ὕψους). Lit., the *rising.* The word occurs in the Septuagint as a rendering of *branch*, as something *rising or springing up*, by which the Messiah is denoted (Jer. xxiii. 5; Zech. vi. 12). Also of the *rising of a heavenly body* (Isa. lx. 19, Sept.). Compare the kindred verb *arise* (ἀνατέλλω) in Isa. lx. 1; Mal. iv. 2. This latter is the sense here. See on Matt. ii. 2. Wyc. has *he springing up from on high.*

Hath visited (ἐπεσκέψατο). See on Matt. xxv. 36; 1 Pet. ii. 12. Some, however, read ἐπισκέψεται, *shall visit.* So Rev.

79. **To guide** (κατευθῦναι). From εὐθύς, *straight.* Wyc. has *dress*, which is formed through the old French *dresser*, to *arrange*, from the Latin *dirigere*, to *set in a straight line, draw up.* Hence the military term *dress* for arranging a line.

80. **The deserts** (ταῖς ἐρήμοις). The article indicating a well-known place.

Shewing (ἀναδείξεως). The word was used of the public announcement of an official nomination; hence of the public inauguration of John's ministry.

CHAPTER II.

1. **Decree** (δόγμα). Wyc., *mandment.* From δοκέω, *to think.* Hence, strictly, a *personal opinion;* and, as the opinion of one who can impose his opinion authoritatively on others, a *decree.*

The world (τὴν οἰκουμένην). Lit., *the inhabited (land).* The phrase was originally used by the Greeks to denote the land inhabited by themselves, in contrast with barbarian countries; afterward, when the Greeks became subject to the Romans, *the entire Roman world;* still later, for *the whole inhabited world.* In the New Testament this latter is the more common usage, though, in some cases, this is conceived in the mould of the Roman empire, as in this passage, Acts xi. 28; xix. 27. Christ uses it in the announcement that the Gospel shall be preached *in all the world* (Matt. xxiv. 14); and Paul in the prediction of a general judgment (Acts xvii. 31). Once it is used of *the world to come* (Heb. ii. 5).

Be taxed (*ἀπογράφεσθαι*). The word means properly *to register* or *enter in a list.* Commentators are divided as to whether it refers to an enrolment for taxation, or for ascertaining the population. Rev., *enrolled,* which may be taken in either sense.

2. **And this taxing was first made** (*αὕτη ἡ ἀπογραφὴ πρώτη ἐγένετο*). Rather, *this occurred as the first enrolment;* or, as Rev., *this was the first enrolment made;* with reference to a *second* enrolment which took place about eleven years later, and is referred to in Acts v. 37.

3. **Went** (*ἐπορεύοντο*). The A. V. and Rev. alike miss the graphic force of the imperfect tense, *were going.* The preparation and bustle and travel were in progress.

To his own city. The town to which the village or place of their birth belonged, and where the house and lineage of each were registered.

4. **House and lineage.** According to the Jewish mode of registration the people would be enrolled by *tribes, families* or *clans,* and *households.* Compare Josh. vii. 16–18. Rev., *house and family.*

5. **To be taxed with Mary.** We may read either, *went up with Mary,* denoting merely the fact of her accompanying him; or, *to enrol himself with Mary,* implying that both their names must be registered.

Espoused. Not merely *betrothed.* See Matt. i. 20, 24, 25; also on Matt. i. 18.

Great with child (*ἐγκύῳ*). See on Ch. i. 24. Only here in New Testament.

7. **Her first-born son.** The Greek reads literally, *her son, the first-born.*

Wrapped in swaddling-clothes (ἐσπαργάνωσεν). Only here and ver. 12. Naturally found often in medical writings. *Swaddle* is *swathel*, from the verb *to swathe.*

In a manger (ἐν φάτνῃ). Used by Luke only, here and xiii. 15. Wyc. has *a cracche,* spelt also *cratch.* Compare French *crèche,* a *manger.* Quite possibly a rock-cave. Dr. Thomson says: "I have seen many such, consisting of one or more rooms, in front of and including a cavern where the cattle were kept" ("Land and Book").

In the inn (ἐν τῷ καταλύματι). Only here, ch. xxiii. 11; Mark xiv. 14, on which see note. In both these passages it is rendered *guest-chamber,* which can hardly be the meaning here, as some have maintained. (See Geikie, "Life and Words of Christ," i., 121.) In that case the expression would be, they found no κατάλυμα, *guest-chamber.* The word refers to the ordinary *khan,* or *caravanserai.* Tynd., *hostrey.* "A Syrian *khan* is a fort and a mart; a refuge from thieves; a shelter from the heat and dust; a place where a man and his beast may lodge; where a trader may sell his wares, and a pilgrim may slake his thirst. . . . Where built by a great sheikh, it would have a high wall, an inner court, a range of arches or lewans, an open gallery round the four sides, and, in many cases, a tower from which the watcher might descry the approach of marauding bands. On one side of the square, but outside the wall, there is often a huddle of sheds, set apart from the main edifice, as stables for the asses and camels, the buffaloes and goats. In the centre of the khan springs a fountain of water, the first necessity of an Arab's life; and around the jets and troughs in which the limpid element streams, lies the gay and picturesque litter of the East. Camels wait to be unloaded; dogs quarrel for a bone; Bedaween from the desert, their red zannars choked with pistols, are at prayer. In the archways squat the merchants with their bales of goods. . . . Half-naked men are cleansing their hands ere sitting down to eat. Here a barber is at work upon a shaven crown; there a fellah lies asleep in the shade. . . . Each man has to carry his dinner and his bed; to litter his horse or camel; to dress his food; to draw his water; to light his fire, and to boil his mess of herbs" (Hepworth Dixon, "The Holy Land").

8. **Shepherds.** Luke's Gospel is the gospel of the poor and lowly. This revelation to the shepherds acquires additional meaning as we remember that shepherds, as a class, were under the Rabbinic ban, because of their necessary isolation from religious ordinances, and their manner of life, which rendered strict legal observance wellnigh impossible.

Keeping watch (*φυλάσσοντες φυλακὰς*). *Φυλακή* is sometimes used of a *watch* as *a measure of time*, as in Matt. xiv. 25; Mark vi. 48; Luke xii. 38. So possibly here. See Rev. in margin, *night-watches.* There is a play upon the words: *watching watches.* There was near Bethlehem, on the road to Jerusalem, a tower known as *Migdal Eder*, or *the watch-tower of the flock.* Here was the station where shepherds watched the flocks destined for sacrifice in the temple. Animals straying from Jerusalem on any side, as far as from Jerusalem to Migdal Eder, were offered in sacrifice. It was a settled conviction among the Jews that the Messiah was to be born in Bethlehem, and equally that he was to be revealed from Migdal Eder. The beautiful significance of the revelation of the infant Christ to shepherds watching the flocks destined for sacrifice needs no comment.

Their flock (*τὴν ποίμνην*). May not the singular number fall in with what has just been said?—*the flock*, the temple-flock, specially devoted to sacrifice. The pronoun *their* would furnish no objection, since it is common to speak of the flock as belonging to the shepherd. Compare John x. 3, 4.

9. **Behold.** Omitted by the best texts.

The angel. More correctly *an angel*, as Rev. The Greek has no article.

Came upon (ἐπέστη). The word is used in this sense in classical Greek, as well as in that of *to stand by*, which Rev. prefers here, as in Acts xii. 7. In ver. 38 of this chapter, Rev. renders *coming up*. The rendering *to come upon* has a hostile flavor, as properly in Acts xvii. 5, where the verb is rendered *assaulted;* so that the Rev. rendering here is preferable.

They were sore afraid. Lit., *feared with great fear*.

10. **I bring you good tidings of great joy** (εὐαγγελίζομαι ὑμῖν χαρὰν μεγάλην). Wyc. is strictly literal: *I evangelize to you a great joy*.

Which (ἥτις). Of a class or character which, etc.

People (τῷ λαῷ). Rev., rightly, "*the* people;" the article pointing specially to the people of Israel.

11. **Is born** (ἐτέχθη). It adds to the vividness of the narrative to keep to the strict rendering of the aorist, *was born*.

A Saviour. See on Matt. i. 21.

Christ. See on Matt. i. 1.

Lord. See on Matt. xxi. 3.

12. **Sign** (σημεῖον). See on Matt. xi. 20.

The babe (βρέφος). See on 1 Pet. ii. 2. Rev., properly, "*a* babe." No article

13. **A multitude of the heavenly host.** *Host* (στρατιᾶς) is literally *army*. "Here the army announces peace" (Bengel). Wyc., *heavenly knighthood*. Tynd., *heavenly soldiers*.

14. **Peace, good-will toward men** (εἰρήνη ἐν ἀνθρώποις εὐδοκία). Both Tischendorf and Westcott and Hort read εὐδοκίας, which the Rev. follows. According to this the rendering is, *unto men of good pleasure*, or as Rev., *among men in whom he is well pleased*. Wyc., *to men of good-will*. For a similar construction, see Acts ix. 15; Col. i. 13.

15. **The shepherds.** Some texts add οἱ ἄνθρωποι, *the men;* but the later texts omit.

Let us go (διέλθωμεν). The preposition διά, *through*, implies *through the intervening space*.

Thing (ῥῆμα). See on ch. i. 37. The utterance of the shepherds contains a climax: "Let us go and see *this saying*, which *has come to pass;* which *the Lord* made known."

16. **Found** (ἀνεῦραν). Only here and Acts xxi. 4. Ἀνά indicates the discovery of the facts *in succession*.

Mary and Joseph and the babe. Each has the article, pointing to the several parties already referred to.

17. **They made known.** See on ver. 8. These shepherds, having charge of flocks devoted to sacrifice, would presently be in the temple, and would meet those who came to worship and to sacrifice, and so proclaim the Messiah in the temple.

19. **Kept** (συνετήρει). See on the simple verb τηρέω, on 1 Pet. i. 4. The word signifies not merely *to guard*, but to *keep*, as the result of guarding. Hence the compound verb is very expressive: kept, σύν, *with* or *within herself:* closely. Note the imperfect tense: *was keeping* all the while.

Pondered (συμβάλλουσα). The present participle, *pondering*. Lit., *bringing together:* comparing and weighing facts. Wyc., *bearing together in her heart*. Vulg., *conferens*. Compare Sophocles, "Oedipus Coloneus," 1472–4.

"OEDIPUS. My children, the heaven-ordained end of life has come upon him who stands here, and there is no avoiding it.

"ANTIGONE. How dost thou know, and with what (fact) having *compared* (συμβαλὼν) thine opinion hast thou this?"

22. **The days of her purification** (*αἱ ἡμέραι τοῦ καθαρισμοῦ αὐτῆς*). The A. V. follows the reading *αὐτῆς, her:* but all the best texts read *αὐτῶν, their;* the plural including Joseph with Mary as partaking of the ceremonial defilement. The mother of a child was levitically unclean for forty days after the birth of a son, and for eighty days after the birth of a daughter. Women on this errand commonly rode to the temple on oxen; that the body of so large a beast between them and the ground might prevent any chance of defilement from passing over a sepulchre on the road. For details, see Edersheim, "Life and Times of Jesus," i., 195; "The Temple," p. 302; Geikie, "Life and Words of Christ," i., 127.

To present him to the Lord. The first-born son of every household must be redeemed of the priest at the price of five shekels of the sanctuary; about two dollars and fifty cents. Num. xviii. 15, 16; Exod. xiii. 2.

23. **The law of the Lord.** The word *law* occurs in this chapter five times; oftener than in all the rest of this Gospel put together. Luke emphasizes the fact that Jesus "was made under the law" (Gal. iv. 4), and accordingly elaborates the details of the fulfilment of the law by the parents of both John and Jesus.

24. **A pair of turtle-doves, or two young pigeons.** The offering of the poor. While the lamb would probably cost about one dollar and seventy-five cents, the doves would cost about sixteen cents. She would not bring the creatures themselves, but would drop the price into one of the thirteen trumpet-shaped chests in the Court of the Women. *Young pigeons:* lit., *young ones of pigeons* (νοσσοὺς περιστερῶν). Wyc. has *culver-birds; culver* being an old English term for *dove.* So Spenser:

"More light than *culver* in the falcon's fist."

25. **Devout** (εὐλαβής). Used by Luke only. The kindred word, εὐλάβεια, *godly-fear*, occurs twice: Heb. v. 7; xii. 28. From εὖ, *well*, and λαμβάνω, *to take hold of*. Hence of a circumspect or cautious person who takes hold of things carefully. As applied to morals and religion, it emphasizes the element of *circumspection*, a cautious, careful observance of divine law; and is thus peculiarly expressive of Old Testament piety, with its minute attention to precept and ceremony. Compare Acts ii. 5.

Consolation of Israel. Compare *hope of Israel*, Acts xxviii. 20, and Isa. xl. 1. The Messianic blessing of the nation. Of the Messiah himself, *Rest*. See Isa. xi. 10. A common form of adjuration among the Jews was, *So may I see the consolation*

26. **It was revealed** (ἦν κεχρηματισμένον). Lit., *it was having been revealed;* i.e., it *stood* revealed, while he waited for the fulfilment of the revelation. The verb means primarily *to have dealings with;* thence *to consult* or debate about business matters; and so of an oracle, to *give a response* to one consulting it. The word here implies that the revelation to Simeon had been given in answer to prayer. See on Matt. ii. 12.

27. **By the Spirit** (ἐν τῷ πνεύματι). Lit., as Rev., "*in* the Spirit:" the Holy Spirit prompting him. Indicating rather his spiritual *condition*, as one who walked with God, than a special divine impulse.

After the custom (κατὰ τὸ εἰθισμένον). Lit., *according to that which was wont to be done*. Only here in New Testament; and the kindred words, ἔθος, *custom*, and ἔθω, *to be accustomed*, occur more frequently in Luke than elsewhere. Very common in medical writings.

29. **Lettest thou thy servant depart** (ἀπολύεις τὸν δοῦλόν σου). Lit., *thou dost release*. The word is often used of manumitting or setting free on payment of ransom; and as Simeon uses the word for *bond-servant*, it is evident that his death is

conceived by him under the figure of enfranchisement from service. Godet's "release of a sentinel from duty" is fanciful.

O Lord (δέσποτα). See on 2 Pet. ii. 1.

In peace. Rev. properly puts this in its emphatic position at the end of the sentence.

31. **Of all people** (πάντων τῶν λαῶν). The noun is plural, *the peoples*, and refers equally to the Gentiles. See Introduction, on the universality of Luke's Gospel. Wyc., *all peoples;* and so Rev.

32. **A light** (φῶς). The light itself as distinguished from λύχνος, *a lamp*, which the A. V. often unfortunately renders *light.* See on Mark xiv. 54.

To lighten (εἰς ἀποκάλυψιν). Wrong. Rev., correctly, *for revelation.* Wyc., *to the shewing.* It may be rendered *the unveiling of the Gentiles.*

Gentiles (ἐθνῶν). Assigned to the same root as ἔθω, *to be accustomed*, and hence of a people bound together by like habits or customs. According to biblical usage the term is understood of people who are not of Israel, and who therefore occupy a different position with reference to the plan of salvation. Hence the extension of the gospel salvation to them is treated as a remarkable fact. See Matt. xii. 18, 21; xxiv. 14; xxviii. 19; Acts x. 45; xi. 18; xviii. 6. Paul is called distinctively an *apostle* and *teacher* of the Gentiles, and a *chosen vessel* to bear Christ's name among them. In Acts xv. 9; Eph. ii. 11, 18; iii. 6, we see this difference annihilated, and the expression at last is merely historical designation of the non-Israelitish nations which, as such, were formerly without God and salvation. See Acts xv. 23; Rom. xvi. 4; Eph. iii. 1. Sometimes the word is used in a purely moral sense, to denote *the heathen* in opposition to Christians. See 1 Cor. v. 1; x. 20; 1 Pet. ii. 12. *Light* is promised here to the *Gentiles* and *glory* to *Israel.*

The Gentiles are regarded as in darkness and ignorance. Some render the words εἰς ἀποκάλυψιν, above, *for the unveiling of the Gentiles*, instead of *for revelation*. Compare Isa. xxv. 7. Israel, however, has already received light by the revelation of God through the law and the prophets, and that light will expand into *glory* through Christ. Through the Messiah, Israel will attain its true and highest glory.

33. **And Joseph.** The best texts read ὁ πατὴρ αὐτοῦ, *his father*.

Marvelled (ἦν θαυμάζοντες). The Greek construction is peculiar. *His father was and his mother wondering;* the finite verb in the singular agreeing with the father, while the plural participle agrees with both. As usual, this combination of finite verb and participle denotes continuance or progression: *they were marvelling* while Simeon was speaking. So Rev.

34. **Them.** The parents; the child being separately and specially designated.

Is set (κεῖται). The verb means primarily *to be laid*, and so *to lie:* hence to be *set forth* or *promulgated*, as the law is said to be *laid down*, and so, *appointed* or *destined*, as here.

The fall and rising again (πτῶσιν καὶ ἀνάστασιν). For the *fall*, because he will be a stumbling-block to many (Isa. viii. 14; Matt. xxi. 42, 44; Acts iv. 11; Rom. ix. 33; 1 Cor. i. 23). For the *rising*, because many will be raised up through him to life and glory (Rom. vi. 4, 9; Eph. ii. 6). The A. V. predicates the falling and the rising of the same persons: *the fall and rising again of many*. The Rev., *the falling and rising up of many*, is ambiguous. The American Revisers give it correctly: *the falling and the rising*.

Which shall be spoken against (ἀντιλεγόμενον). The participle is the present; and the expression does not voice a prophecy, but describes an *inherent characteristic* of the sign:

a sign of which it is the character to experience contradiction from the world. In the beginning, as a babe, Jesus experienced this at the hands of Herod; so all through his earthly ministry and on the cross; and so it will be to the end, until he shall have put all enemies under his feet. Compare Heb. xii. 3. Wyc., a *token to whom it shall be gainsaid.*

35. **A sword** (*ῥομφαία*). Strictly, a large Thracian broadsword. Used in Septuagint of the sword of Goliath (1 Sam. xvii. 51). A figure of Mary's pang when her son should be nailed to the cross.

36. **A prophetess** (*προφῆτις*). Only here and Apoc. ii. 20.

Asher. That tribe was celebrated in tradition for the beauty of its women, and their fitness to be wedded to high-priests or kings.

Of great age (*προβεβηκυῖα ἐν ἡμέραις πολλαῖς*). Lit., *advanced in many days.*

37. **Of about fourscore and four years** (*ὡς ἐτῶν ὀγδοήκοντα τεσσάρων*). The A. V. might be supposed to be stating her *age;* but the best texts read *ἕως*, *until,* instead of *ὡς*, *about;* and the statement refers to the time of her widowhood; a *widow even for* (or *up to*) *fourscore and four years.* So Rev.

Served (*λατρεύουσα*). The present participle, *serving.* Rev., *worshipping.* See on ch. i. 74.

38. **Coming up** (*ἐπιστᾶσα*). See on ver. 9.

Gave thanks (*ἀνθωμολογεῖτο*). The verb originally means *to make a mutual agreement;* and the idea of reciprocity is retained in the expression "to *return* thanks" for something received. Compare Sept., Ps. lxxix. 13.

Spake. Not a public utterance, for which the words, *those that waited,* etc., would be inappropriate. It was to the pious ones who were with her in the temple, waiting for the Messiah.

In Jerusalem (ἐν Ἱερουσαλήμ). All the best texts omit ἐν, *in*. Render, as Rev., *the redemption of Jerusalem*. Nearly equivalent to *the consolation of Israel*, ver. 25. Compare ch. i. 68, and see Isa. xl. 2.

39. **Nazareth.** See on Matt. ii. 23.

40. **The child grew,** etc. The Jews marked the stages of a child's development by nine different terms: the new-born babe (Isa. ix. 6); the suckling (Isa. xi. 8); the suckling beginning to ask for food (Lam. iv. 4); the weaned child (Isa. xxviii. 9); the child clinging to its mother (Jer. xl. 7); the child becoming firm and strong (Isa. vii. 14, of the virgin-mother); the youth, literally, he that shakes himself free; the ripened one, or warrior (Isa. xxxi. 8).

41. **His parents.** Though women were not bound to present themselves in person.

42. **Twelve years old.** At which age he was known as a *son of the law*, and came under obligation to observe the ordinances personally.

43. **Had fulfilled the days.** Not necessarily the whole seven days of the festival. With the third day commenced the so-called *half-holidays*, when it was lawful to return home.

44. **The company** (συνοδίᾳ). From σύν, *with*, and ὁδός, *the way*. The company that shared the journey.

Went a day's journey. Before they missed him.

They sought (ἀνεζήτουν). From ἀνὰ, *from the bottom up*, and ζητέω, *to seek*. Thus implying a *thorough* search: they looked for him *up and down*.

45. **Seeking him** (ἀναζητοῦντες). All the way as they went. Force of ἀνὰ, as above.

46. **After three days.** From the time of separation.

In the temple. "We read in the Talmud that the members of the Temple-Sanhedrin, who, on ordinary days, sat as a court of appeal from the close of the morning to the time of the evening sacrifice, were wont, upon Sabbaths and feast-days, to come out upon the terrace of the temple, and there to teach. In such popular instruction the utmost latitude of questioning would be given. It is in this audience, which sat upon the ground, surrounding and mingling with the doctors, and hence *during*, not *after*, the feast, that we must seek the child Jesus" (Edersheim, "Life and Times," etc., i. 247). From this, Edersheim argues that the parents set out for home before the close of the feast.

Sitting. Not occupying a teacher's place, but sitting in the circle among the doctors and their hearers. See above. Compare Acts xxii. 3.

47. **Understanding** (συνέσει). From *συνίημι*, *to bring together*. Hence that quality of mind which *combines:* understanding not only of facts, but of facts in their mutual relations. See on Mark xii. 33; where there is meant "the love of a well-pondered and duly considered resolution which determines the whole person; the love which clearly understands itself" (Cremer).

48. **They were amazed** (ἐξεπλάγησαν). A very strong word; the verb meaning, literally, *to strike out* or *drive away from;* and so *to drive out of one's senses*. Hence in the general sense of great amazement. *Amaze* is to throw into a *maze* or labyrinth; and so is closely akin to the Greek word here, and is a faithful rendering.

Son (τέκνον). Lit., *child*. See on Matt. i. 1.

Thy father. "Up to this time Joseph had been so called by the holy child himself; but from this time never" (Alford).

Have sought (ἐζητοῦμεν). Imperfect tense: *were seeking;* Mary is going over in mind the process of the search.

49. **And he said.** The first saying of Jesus which is preserved to us.

Must (δεῖ). Lit., *it is necessary*, or *it behoves.* A word often used by Jesus concerning his own appointed work, and expressing both the inevitable fulfilment of the divine counsels and the absolute constraint of the principle of duty upon himself. See Matt. xvi. 21; xxvi. 54; Mark viii. 31; Luke iv. 43; ix. 22; xiii. 33; xxiv. 7, 26, 46; John iii. 14; iv. 4; xii. 34.

About my Father's business (ἐν τοῖς τοῦ πατρός). Lit., *in the things of my Father.* The words will bear this rendering; but the Rev. is better, *in my Father's house.* Mary's question was not as to what her son had been doing, but as to where he had been. Jesus, in effect, answers, "Where is a child to be found but in his Father's house?"

50. **The saying** (τὸ ῥῆμα). See on ch. i. 37.

51. **Was subject** (ἦν ὑποτασσόμενος). The participle and finite verb, denoting *habitual, continuous* subjection. "Even before, he had been subject to them; but this is mentioned now, when it might seem that he could by this time have exempted himself. Not even to the angels fell such an honor as to the parents of Jesus" (Bengel). Compare Heb. i. 4–8.

Kept (διετήρει). Only here and Acts xv. 29. The preposition διά, *through*, indicates *close, faithful, persistent* keeping, through all the circumstances which might have weakened the impression of the events. Compare Gen. xxxvii. 11.

52. **Stature** (ἡλικίᾳ). Which Rev. rightly retains. The word may be rendered *age*, which would be superfluous here.

CHAPTER III.

1–18. Compare Matt. iii. 1–12; Mark i. 1–8.

1. **Pontius Pilate.** Wyc., *Pilat of Pounce.*

Tetrarch. See on Matt. xiv. 1.

2. **Came** (ἐγένετο). Lit., *arose,* or *came to pass.*

John. The Synoptists introduce him under different titles. Here, *the son of Zacharias;* Matthew, *the Baptist;* Mark, *the Baptizer.*

3. **The country about Jordan.** Which both Matthew and Mark call *the wilderness.* See on Matt. iii. 1.

Baptism of repentance. Wyc., *penaunce.*

For (εἰς). Better as Rev., *unto,* denoting the *destination* of the rite.

Remission (ἄφεσιν). See on Jas. v. 15. The word occurs in Luke more frequently than in all the other New Testament writers combined. Used in medical language of the relaxation of disease. Both Luke and John use the kindred verb ἀφίημι, in the same sense. Luke iv. 39; John iv. 52.

4. **Isaiah.** In this prophetic citation Mark adds to Isaiah Malachi iii. 1, which does not appear in either Matthew or Luke. Luke adds vv. 4, 5 of Isa. xl., which do not appear in the others.

Paths (τρίβους). From τρίβω, *to rub* or *wear.* Hence *beaten* tracks.

5. **Valley** (φάραγξ). Strictly, of a chasm or ravine in a mountain-side.

Shall be filled—brought low. In allusion to the practice of Eastern monarchs. On occasions of their progress, heralds were sent out to call on the people to clear and improve the old roads or to make new ones. "When Ibrahim Pacha proposed to visit certain places in Lebanon, the emirs and sheiks sent forth a general proclamation, somewhat in the style of Isaiah's exhortation, to all the inhabitants to assemble along the proposed route and prepare the way before him. The same was done in 1845, on a grand scale, when the Sultan visited Brusa. The stones were gathered out, the crooked places straightened, and rough ones made level and smooth. I had the benefit of these labors a few days after his majesty's visit. The exhortation 'to gather out the stones' (Isa. lxii. 10) is peculiarly appropriate. These farmers do the exact reverse—gather up the stones from their fields and cast them into the highway; and it is this barbarous custom which, in many places, renders the paths uncomfortable and even dangerous" (Thomson, "Land and Book").

7. **He said** (ἔλεγεν) **to the multitudes that came forth** (ἐκπορευομένοις). The use of the tenses is graphic. *He said*, the imperfect, and *came forth*, the present participle; both denoting action in progress, or customary action; so that the sense is, he *kept saying*, or he *used to say* to those who *were coming out*, to the crowds of people which kept pouring out successively. Compare ἐξεπορεύετο, *went out*, also imperfect, Matt. iii. 5. Luke gives the substance of the Baptist's preaching summarily.

Generation (γεννήματα). Lit., *births*. Rev., better, *offspring*. It has been observed that John's figurative language is altogether the language of the desert. Notice the succession of images: *Brood of vipers; fruits* (of repentance); *the axe at the root of the tree; the slave-boy loosing or bearing the sandals; the baptism of fire; the winnowing-fan, the threshing-floor, the garner, and the burning of the chaff.*

Warned (ὑπέδειξεν). From ὕπο, *under*, and δείκνυμι, *to shew*. Hence, literally, to *shew secretly*. The word implies a private or confidential hint or reminder. Compare ch. xii. 5; Acts ix. 16; xx. 35.

8. **Fruits** (καρποὺς). Matthew has the singular number, καρπὸν, *fruit*.

Repentance (τῆς μετανοίας). Note the article: *the* repentance which you profess in coming to my baptism. Rev., in margin, "*your* repentance." See on Matt. iii. 2.

Begin. With the first accusing of your conscience. "He anticipates even *attempt* at excuse" (Bengel). Matthew has *think not*, indicating a delusive fancy.

Father. The word stands first in the sentence, "We have Abraham to our father," and is therefore emphatic, and with reason; for it was on their *descent* that the answer of these Jews to John's rebuke turned: "Our *father* is Abraham."

These stones. See on Matt. iii. 9.

9. See on Matt. iii. 10.

10. **Asked** (ἐπηρώτων). Imperfect tense, indicating the frequent repetition of these questions.

11. **Coats** (χιτῶνας). See on Matt. v. 40.

11. **Publicans** (τελῶναι). From τέλος, *a tax*, and ὠνέομαι, *to buy*. The collectors of Roman imposts. The Romans farmed out the direct taxes and customs-duties to capitalists, on their payment of a certain sum *in publicum*, *into the public treasury*, whence they were called *publicani*, *publicans*. Sometimes this sum, being greater than any one person could pay, was paid by a company. Under these were the *submagistri*, living in the provinces; and under these again the *portitores*, or actual cus-

tom-house officers, who are referred to by the term τελῶναι in the New Testament. They were often chosen from the dregs of the people, and were so notorious for their extortions that they were habitually included in the same category with harlots and sinners. "If a Jew could scarcely persuade himself that it was right to *pay* taxes, how much more heinous a crime must it have been in his eyes to become the questionably honest instrument for *collecting* them. If a publican was hated, how still more intense must have been the disgust entertained against a publican who was also a Jew" (Farrar, "Life of Christ"). The word "publican," as a popular term of reproach, was used even by our Lord (Matt. xviii. 17). Even the Gentiles despised them. Farrar cites a Greek saying, "All publicans are robbers."

13. **Exact** (πράσσετε). The change of the Rev. to *extort* is unfortunate. The word is used of the exaction of legal tribute, and *excessive* exaction is expressed by the following words: John would hardly have commanded them to *extort* in *any* case.

14. **Soldiers** (στρατευόμενοι). Strictly, soldiers *on service:* hence the participle, *serving as soldiers*, instead of the more comprehensive term στρατιῶται, *soldiers by profession.* Some explain it of soldiers engaged in police inspection in connection with the customs, and hence naturally associated with the publicans.

What shall we do? The *we* in the Greek is emphatic, closing the question. Hence Rev., very aptly, *and we, what must we do?*

Do violence (διασείσητε). Only here in New Testament. Lit., *to shake violently;* hence to *agitate* or *terrify;* and so to extort money from one by terrifying him. The corresponding Latin word *concutere* is used by later writers in the same sense. Xenophon says of Socrates: "I know of his once having heard from Crito that life at Athens was a hard thing for a man who desired to mind his own business. 'For,' said he, 'they bring actions against me, not because they are wronged by me, but because they think I would rather pay money than have any trouble'" ("Memorabilia," ii., 9, 1). For this process of blackmail, σείω, to *shake*, was used. Thus Aristophanes ("Knights," 840):

"Thou shalt make much money by *falsely accusing and frightening*" (σείων τε καὶ ταράττων).

And again ("Peace," 639):

"And of their allies they falsely accused (ἔσειον) the substantial and rich."

The word in this passage of Luke has the later, secondary meaning, *to extort;* and therefore the American Revisers rightly insist on, *extort from no man by violence.* It is used by medical writers, as, for instance, by Hippocrates, of shaking the palsied or benumbed limbs of a patient; or of a shaking by which the liver was relieved of an obstruction. Luke also uses two other compounds of the verb σείω: κατασείω, *to beckon*, Acts xii. 17 (peculiar to Luke); and ἀνασείω, to *stir up*, which occurs also in Mark xv. 11. Both these are also used by medical writers.

Accuse any falsely (συκοφαντήσητε). The common explanation of this word is based on the derivation from σῦκον, *a fig*, and φαίνω, *to make known;* hence of informing against persons who exported figs from Attica, contrary to the law, or who plundered sacred fig-trees. As informers were tempted to accuse innocent persons by the reward paid for pointing out violators of the law, the verb acquired the meaning *to accuse falsely.* Such is the old explanation, which is now rejected by scholars, though the real explanation is merely conjectural. The fig-tree was the pride of Attica, ranking with honey and olives as one of the principal products, and there is no authority for the statement that there was a time when figs were scarce, and required legal protection against export. Neither is it proven that there was a *sacred* kind of fig. Rettig, in an interesting paper in the "Studien und Kritiken" (1838), explains that, as tribute in Attica was paid *in kind* as well as in money, and as figs represented a great deal of property, there was a temptation to make false returns of the amount of figs to the assessors; and that thus a class of informers arose who detected and reported these false returns, and received a percentage of the fine which was imposed. These were known as *fig-shewers*. Another writer has suggested that the reference is to one who brings figs to light by shaking the tree; and so, metaphorically, to one who makes rich men yield up the fruits of their labor or rascality by false accusation. Whatever explanation we may accept, it is evident that the word had some original connection with *figs*, and that it came to mean to *slander* or *accuse falsely*. From it comes our word *sycophant*. The sycophants as a class were encouraged at Athens, and their services were rewarded. Socrates is said by Xenophon to have advised Crito to take a sycophant into his pay, in order to thwart another who was annoying him; and this person, says Xenophon, "quickly discovered on the part of Crito's accusers many illegal acts, and many persons who were enemies to those accusers; one of whom he summoned to a public trial, in which it would be settled what he should suffer or pay, and he would not let him off until he ceased to molest Crito and paid a sum of money besides." Demosthenes thus describes one: "He glides about the market like a scorpion, with his venomous sting all ready, spying out whom he may surprise with misfortune and ruin, and from whom he can most easily extort money, by threatening him with an action dangerous in its consequences. . . . It is the bane of our city that it protects and cherishes this poisonous brood, and uses them as informers, so that even the honest man must flatter and court them, in order to be safe from their machinations." The word occurs only here and ch. xix. 8, of Zacchaeus, the publican. The American Revisers hold to the A. V., and render *neither accuse any one wrongfully*, extortion being described by the previous word. Wyc., *neither make ye false challenge*. In the Sept. it is used in the sense of *to oppress* or *deceive*.

Wages (ὀψωνίοις). From ὄψον, *cooked meat*, and later, generally, *provisions*. At Athens, especially, *fish*. Compare ὀψάριον, *fish*, John xxi. 9, 10, 13. Hence ὀψώνιον is primarily *provision-*

money, and so used of supplies and pay for an army. With this understanding the use of the word at Rom. vi. 23, "*the wages* of sin," becomes highly suggestive.

15. **Mused** (διαλογιζομένων). Better as Rev., *reasoned*. Compare ch. i. 29; and see on Jas. ii. 4.

16. **One mightier** (ὁ ἰσχυρότερος). The definite article points to an expected personage. Hence better as Rev., *he that is mightier*.

Unloose (λῦσαι). So also Mark; but Matthew βαστάσαι, *to bear*. See on Matt. iii. 11.

17. **Fan—floor—purge.** See on Matt. iii. 12.

18. **Other** (ἕτερα). Rather, *various, different*.

Preached (εὐηγγελίζετο). Rev. preserves the fuller meaning of the word according to its etymology: *preached good tidings*. See on *Gospel*, Superscription of Matthew.

19, 20. Compare Matt. xiv. 3–5; Mark vi. 17–20.

19. **Being reproved** (ἐλεγχόμενος). See on Jas. ii. 9.

Evils (πονηρῶν). Of several words in the New Testament denoting evil, this emphasizes evil in its activity. Hence Satan is ὁ πονηρός, *the evil one*. An *evil eye* (Mark vii. 22) is a *mischief-working* eye. See on Mark vii. 22.

Added (προσέθηκεν). Used by Luke twice as often as in all the rest of the New Testament. A very common medical word, used of the application of remedies to the body, as our *apply, administer*. So Hippocrates, "*apply* wet sponges to the head;" and Galen, "*apply* a decoction of acorns," etc.

In prison. See on Matt. xiv. 3.

21–23. Compare Matt. iii. 13–17; Mark i. 9–11.

21. **Was opened** (ἀνεωχθῆναι). So Matthew, but Mark σχιζομένους, *rent.*

22. **The Holy Ghost.** Better, *Spirit.* Matthew has *the Spirit of God:* Mark, *the Spirit.*

In a bodily shape. Peculiar to Luke.

Thou art my beloved son. Lit., *Thou art my son, the beloved.* So Mark. But Matthew, *This is my son, the beloved.*

23. **Began to be about thirty years of age** (ἦν ἀρχόμενος ὡσεὶ ἐτῶν τριάκοντα). Peculiar to Luke. A. V. is wrong. It should be as Rev., *when he began* (to teach) *was about thirty years of age.*

CHAPTER IV.

1–13. Compare Matt. iv. 1–11; Mark i. 12–13.

1. **Was led.** So Matthew. Mark says, "The Spirit *driveth,* (ἐκβάλλει) or *thrusteth him forth.*

By the Spirit (ἐν τῷ πνεύματι). The American Revisers render *in* the spirit, indicating the *sphere* rather than the *impulse* of his action.

Into the wilderness. The A. V. has followed the reading εἰς, *into.* The proper reading is ἐν, *in.* He was not only impelled *into* the wilderness, but guided *in* the wilderness by the Spirit.

2. **Forty days.** This should be joined with the preceding words, indicating the duration of his *stay* in the wilderness, not of his *temptation,* as A. V., *being forty days tempted.* Read as Rev., *in the wilderness during forty days.*

The devil. See on Matt. iv. 1.

He did eat nothing. Mark does not mention the fast. Matthew uses the word νηστεύσας, *having fasted*, which, throughout the New Testament, is used of abstinence for religious purposes; a ritual act accompanying seasons of prayer.

3. **This stone.** Matthew, *these stones*.

Bread (ἄρτος). Lit., *a loaf*. See on Matt. iv. 3. Matthew has the plural *loaves*.

4. **It is written.** See on Matt. iv. 4.

By bread (ἐπ' ἄρτῳ). Lit., "*on* bread," implying dependence. Compare, *by every word* (ἐπὶ παντὶ ῥήματι, Matt. iv. 4).

5. **The world.** See on ch. ii. 1.

In a moment of time (ἐν στιγμῇ χρόνου). Peculiar to Luke. Στιγμή is literally *a mark made by a pointed instrument, a dot:* hence a point of time. Only here in New Testament. Compare στίγματα, *brand-marks*, Gal. vi. 17. Tynd., *in the twinkling of an eye*.

6. Note the emphatic position of the pronouns: "To *thee* will I give—for to *me* it hath been delivered: *thou*, therefore, if thou wilt worship," etc. Luke, in his narrative, enlarges upon Matthew. Compare Matt. iv. 9.

8. **Serve.** See on ch. i. 74.

9. **He brought** (ἤγαγεν). Rev., *led*. See on παραλαμβάνει, *taketh*, Matt. iv. 5.

Pinnacle of the temple. See on Matt. iv. 5.

Down from hence. Matthew has *down* only.

10. **To keep** (*διαφυλάξαι*). Only here in New Testament. Better as Rev., *guard*. See on 1 Pet. i. 4. The preposition implies *close, careful* guarding. The phrase, *to guard thee*, is wanting in Matthew.

11. **In their hands** (*ἐπὶ χειρῶν*). Rev., correctly, *on*. See on Matt. iv. 6.

12. **It is said.** For Matthew's *it is written*, Matt. iv. 7. Luke omits Matthew's *again*. See Matt. iv. 7.

13. **Had ended all the temptation.** Peculiar to Luke. The verb *συντελέσας*, from *σύν*, *together*, and *τελέω*, to *accomplish*, means *to bring to one end together;* hence to bring to an end *utterly*. Better therefore as Rev., *completed*. The temptations formed a complete cycle, so that it could afterward be said of Jesus that "he was *in all points* tried like as we are" (Heb. iv. 15).

All the temptation (*πάντα πειρασμὸν*). Incorrect. Rev., rightly, *every temptation*. So Wyc., *Every temptation ended.*

For a season (*ἄχρι καιροῦ*). Peculiar to Luke. More strictly, *until a convenient time;* since Satan meant to assail him again, as he did in the person of Peter (Mark viii. 33); by the Pharisees (John viii. 40 sq.); and at Gethsemane. See ch. xxii. 53.

15. **He taught** (*αὐτὸς ἐδίδασκεν*). Lit., "*he himself* taught," verifying the favorable reports about himself in person. The imperfect tense denotes a *course* of teaching.

16–31. Peculiar to Luke.

16. **Nazareth.** With the article; *that* Nazareth where he had been brought up.

Stood up. Not as a sign that he wished to expound, but being summoned by the superintendent of the synagogue.

To read (ἀναγνῶναι). Usually in New Testament of *public* reading.* After the liturgical services which introduced the worship of the synagogue, the "minister" took a roll of the law from the ark, removed its case and wrappings, and then called upon some one to read. On the Sabbaths, at least seven persons were called on successively to read portions of the law, none of them consisting of less than three verses. After the law followed a section from the prophets, which was succeeded immediately by a discourse. It was this section which Jesus read and expounded. See Acts xiii. 15; Neh. viii. 5, 8. For a detailed account of the synagogue-worship, see Edersheim, "Life and Times of Jesus," i., 430 sq.

17. **The book** (βιβλίον). A diminutive of βίβλος, *the inner bark of the papyrus*, used for writing. Hence *a roll.* The word is also used to denote a division of a work, and is therefore appropriate here to mark the writings of a single prophet as related to the whole body of the prophetic writings.

Opened (ἀναπτύξας). Lit., *unrolled.* Both this and the simple verb πτύσσω, *to close* (ver. 30), occur only once in the New Testament. The former word was used in medical language of the opening out of various parts of the body, and the latter of the rolling up of bandages. The use of these terms by Luke the physician is the more significant from the fact that elsewhere in the New Testament ἀνοίγω is used for the *opening of a book* (Apoc. v. 2–5; x. 2, 8; xx. 12); and εἱλίσσω, for *rolling it up* (Apoc. vi. 14).

Found. As if by chance: reading at the place where the roll opened of itself, and trusting to divine guidance.

Was written (ἦν γεγραμμένον). Lit., *was having been written;* i.e., *stood written.*

18. **Anointed.** See on *Christ*, Matt. i. 1.

To preach good tidings. See on *Gospel*, Superscription of Matthew.

---

* In post-classical Greek, sometimes of reading aloud with comments. This may explain the parenthesis in Matt. xxiv. 15.

To the poor (πτωχοῖς). See on Matt. v. 3.

To heal the broken-hearted. The best texts omit. So Rev.

To preach (κηρύξαι). Better as Rev., *proclaim*, as a herald. See on 2 Pet. ii. 5.

To the captives (αἰχμαλώτοις). From αἰχμή, a *spear-point*, and ἁλίσκομαι, *to be taken* or *conquered*. Hence, properly, of prisoners of war. Compare Isa. xlii. 7: "To bring out captives from the prison, and those who sit in darkness from the house of restraint." The allusion is to Israel, both as captive exiles and as prisoners of Satan in spiritual bondage. Wyc. has *caytifs*, which formerly signified *captives*.

To set at liberty (ἀποστεῖλαι) Lit., *to send away in discharge*. Inserted from the Sept. of Isa. lviii. 6. See on ch. iii. 3, and Jas. v. 15.

Them that are bruised (τεθραυσμένους). Lit., *broken in pieces*. Only here in New Testament. Wyc., *to deliver broken men into remission*. The same Hebrew word is used in Isa. xlii. 3: "a *crushed* reed shall he not break," which the Septuagint translates by τεθλασμένον, a word which does not occur in the New Testament. In the citation of this latter passage (Matt. xii. 20, on which see) the word for *bruised* is συντρίβω, which the Septuagint uses for *break*.

19. **To preach** (Rev., *proclaim*) **the acceptable year of the Lord.** As on the first day of the year of Jubilee, when the priests went through the land proclaiming, with sound of trumpet, the blessings of the opening year (Lev. xxv. 8–17). Note ver. 10, where liberty is to be proclaimed to all in that year. Wyc., *the year of the Lord pleasant*. A literal interpretation of the word *year* gave rise among some of the Christian fathers to the theory that our Lord's ministry lasted but a single year.

20. **He closed** (πτύξας). See on ver. 17.

Minister (ὑπηρέτῃ). See on Matt. v. 25. Lit., as Rev., *attendant*. *Minister* is likely to be misunderstood as referring to the president of the congregation, who, as the teaching elder, would have addressed the people if Jesus had not done so. It means the attendant who had charge of the sacred rolls. He was a salaried officer, a kind of chapel-clerk.

Sat down. As about to teach; that being the habitual position of a Jewish teacher.

Were fastened (ἦσαν ἀτενίζοντες). The participle and finite verb denoting continuous, steadfast attention. The verb, from τείνω, *to stretch*, denotes fixed attention. Indeed, the word *attention* itself, etymologically considered, conveys the same idea.

21. **He began.** Not necessarily denoting his first words, but indicating a solemn and weighty opening.

22. **Bare him witness.** Compare ver. 14. They confirmed the reports which had been circulated about him. Note the imperfect tense. There was a continuous stream of admiring comment. Similarly, *were wondering*.

At the gracious words (λόγοις τῆς χάριτος). Literally and correctly, as Rev., *words of grace*. See on ch. i. 30.

Is not (οὐχὶ). Expecting an affirmative answer.

23. **Surely** (πάντως). Lit., *by all means*. Rev., *doubtless*.

Proverb (παραβολὴν). Rev., *parable*. See on Matt. xiii. 3. Wyc., *likeness*.

Physician, heal thyself. A saying which Luke alone records, and which would forcibly appeal to him as a physician.

Galen speaks of a physician who should have cured himself before he attempted to attend patients. The same appeal was addressed to Christ on the cross (Matt. xxvii. 40, 42).

25. **A great famine was throughout all the land** (ἐγένετο λιμὸς μέγας ἐπὶ πᾶσαν τὴν γῆν). More literally and correctly, as Rev., *there came* (*or arose*) *a great famine over all the land.*

27. **Lepers.** Wyc. renders *meselis*, the middle-English word for a leper, and derived from *misellus*, a diminutive of the Latin *miser*, *wretched.*

29. **The brow** (ὀφρύος). Only here in New Testament. Wyc., *cope*, which is originally *cap* or *hood.* The word is used in medical language both of the eyebrows and of other projections of the body. It would naturally occur to a physician, especially since the same epithets were applied to the appearance of the eyebrows in certain diseases as were applied to *hills.* Thus Hippocrates, describing a deadly fever, says, "The eyebrows seem to *hang over*," the same word which Homer uses of a rock. So Aretaeus, describing the appearance of the eyebrows in elephantiasis, depicts them as προβλῆτες, *projecting*, and ὀχθώδεις, *like mounds.* Stanley says: "Most readers probably from these words imagine a town built on the summit of a mountain, from which summit the intended precipitation was to take place. This is not the situation of Nazareth; yet its position is still in accordance with the narrative. It is built *upon*, that is, *on the side of* a mountain, but the brow is not beneath, but *over* the town, and such a cliff as is here implied is found in the abrupt face of a limestone rock about thirty or forty feet high, overhanging the Maronite convent at the south-west corner of the town" ("Sinai and Palestine").

Cast him down headlong (κατακρημνίσαι). Only here in New Testament, and in the Septuagint only in 2 Chron. xxv. 12.

31-37. Compare Mark i. 21-28.

31. **Taught** (ἦν διδάσκων). Correctly, as Rev., *was teaching.* The finite verb and participle denoting continuance.

On the Sabbath-days (τοῖς σάββασιν). Rev., *day.* The word is often used in the plural form for the single day, as in ver. 16; probably after the analogy of plural names of festivals, as τὰ ἄζυμα, *the feast of unleavened bread;* τὰ γενέσια, *the birth-day;* or perhaps following the Aramaic plural.

32. **They were astonished** (ἐξεπλήσσοντο). See on Matt. vii. 28.

33. **A spirit of an unclean devil.** Where the rendering should be *demon.* This is the only case in which Luke adds to that word the epithet *unclean.*

34. **What have we to do with thee** (τί ἡμῖν καὶ σοί)? Lit., *what is there to us and to thee? i.e.*, what have we in common? So Wyc.

35. **Hold thy peace** (φιμώθητι). Lit., *be muzzled* or *gagged.* See on Matt. xxii. 12.

Had thrown (ῥῖψαν). Used in connection with disease by Luke only, and only here. In medical language, of convulsions, fits, etc.

Hurt him not (μηδὲν βλάψαν αὐτόν). Lit., *in no possible way.* Mark omits this detail, which a physician would be careful to note. Βλάπτειν, to *injure*, occurs but twice in New Testament—here and Mark xvi. 18. It is common in medical language, opposed to ὠφελεῖν, *to benefit*, as of medicines or diet hurting or benefiting.

36. **They were all amazed** (ἐγένετο θάμβος ἐπὶ πάντας). Lit., as Rev., *amazement came upon all.* Θάμβος, *amazement*, is used by Luke only. The kindred verb, θαμβέομαι, *to be amazed*, occurs only once in Luke (Acts ix. 6), and three times in Mark; while Mark alone has the strong compound ἐκθαμβέω, *to be greatly amazed* (Mark ix. 15).

37. **The fame** (ἦχος). Lit., *noise.* Rev., *rumor.* Only here, ch. xxi. 25, where the correct reading is ἤχους, *the roaring*, and Acts ii. 2. Heb. xii. 19 is a quotation from the Septuagint. It is the word used in Acts ii. 2 of the mighty rushing wind at Pentecost. Mark uses ἀκοή, in its earlier sense of *a report.* The same word occurs in Luke, but always in the sense in which medical writers employed it—*hearing* or the *ears.* See ch. vii. 1; Acts xvii. 20; xxviii. 26. *Ἦχος* was the medical term for sound in the ears or head. Hippocrates uses both words together: "the *ears* (ἀκοαὶ) are full of *sound* (ἤχου);" and Aretaeus of the noise of the sea, as Luke xxi. 25.

38–41. Compare Matt. viii. 14–17; Mark i. 29–34.

38. **Taken** (συνεχομένη). Rev., *holden.* So Wyc. See on Matt. iv. 24. The word is used nine times by Luke, and only three times elsewhere. Paul uses it of the *constraining* of Christ's love (2 Cor. v. 14), and of being *in a strait* (Philip. i. 23). In Acts xxviii. 8, it is joined with fever, as here, and is a common medical term in the same sense.

A great fever (πυρετῷ μεγάλῳ). Another mark of the physician. The epithet *great* is peculiar to Luke. The ancient physicians distinguished fevers into *great* and *small.*

39. **He stood over her.** As a physician might do. Peculiar to Luke.

Rebuked. Peculiar to Luke.

40. **When the sun was setting.** The people brought their sick at that hour, not only because of the coolness, but because it was the end of the Sabbath, and carrying a sick person was regarded as work. See John v. 10.

Diseases (νόσοις). See on Matt. iv. 23. Wyc., *Sick men with divers languishings.*

Laid his hands on. Peculiar to Luke.

Every one. "Implying the solicitude and indefatigableness of this miraculous ministry of love" (Meyer).

41. **Crying out** (*κραυγάζοντα*). The inarticulate demoniac scream.

Saying. The articulate utterance.

Mr. Hobart ("Medical Language of St. Luke") remarks that the medical bias of Luke may be seen from the words he abstains from using as well as from those he does use in respect of disease. Thus he never uses *μαλακία* for *sickness*, as Matthew does (iv. 23; ix. 35; x. 1), since this word is never so used in medical language, but is confined to the meaning of *delicacy*, *effeminacy*. So, too, he never uses *βασανίζειν*, *to torment*, of sickness, as Matthew does (viii. 6), as it is never so used in medical language, the word there meaning to examine some part of the body or some medical question.

42–44. Compare Mark i. 35–39.

42. **Sought after** (*ἐπεζήτουν*). Imperfect tense: *were seeking*.

Came unto him (*ἦλθον ἕως αὐτοῦ*). Stronger than *came to*; for *ἕως* is *even up to*, showing that they did not discontinue their search until they found him. Mark's narrative here is fuller and more graphic.

CHAPTER V.

1–11. Compare Matt. iv. 18–22; Mark i. 16–20.

1. **Pressed** (*ἐπικεῖσθαι*). Lit., *were laid upon*.

To hear. The A. V. is correct according to the reading *τοῦ ἀκούειν*, which it follows. The true reading is *καὶ ἀκούειν*, *and heard*. So Rev.

He stood (αὐτὸς ἦν ἑστὼς). The pronoun distinguishes him from the crowd which pressed upon him: *he on his part stood.* Render the participle and finite verb as Rev., *was standing.*

Lake (λίμνην). An illustration of the more classical style of Luke as compared with Matthew and Mark. They and John also use θάλασσα, *sea.* See on Matt. iv. 18.

2. **Ships** (πλοῖα). Used of vessels in general. Some texts read πλοιάρια, a diminutive form, meaning *little boats.*

Were washing. From the sand and pebbles accumulated during the night's work. Luke uses four different words for washing or cleansing: πλύνω, here, see also Apoc. vii. 14; ἀπομάσσω, of wiping the dust from the feet, only at ch. x. 11; ἐκμάσσω, of the woman wiping Christ's feet with her hair, ch. vii. 38, 44; ἀπολούω, of washing away sins, Acts xxii. 16; λούω, of washing the prisoners' stripes and the body of Dorcas, Acts xvi. 33; ix. 37. The reading ἀποπλύνω is rejected by the best texts, so that ἀπομάσσω is the only one peculiar to Luke. All the words were common in medical language.

3. **Thrust out** (ἐπαναγαγεῖν). Rev., *put out.* The special nautical word for putting out to sea.

Taught (ἐδίδασκεν). The imperfect. He *continued* the teaching he had begun on the shore.

4. **Launch out.** Rev., *put out.* The singular number, addressed to Peter as master of the craft.

Let down (χαλάσατε). The plural, addressed to the whole of the boat's crew. Originally, *to slacken* or *loosen,* as a bowstring or the reins of horses; hence *to let sink* as a net. Also of unbarring a door. Metaphorically, *to be indulgent, to pardon.* The word occurs in the New Testament seven times, and five of these in Luke. He uses it of letting down Paul in a basket at

Damascus (Acts ix. 25); of striking a ship's sails, and of letting down a boat into the sea (Acts xxvii. 17, 30). Matthew, Mark, and John use *βάλλω* or *ἀμφιβάλλω*, for casting a net (Matt. iv. 18; xiii. 47; Mark i. 16; John xxi. 6), which appears also in the compound noun for a *casting-net* (*ἀμφίβληστρον*, see on Matt. iv. 18). The word used by Luke was in common use in medical writings, to denote relaxation of the limbs; loosening of bandages; abatement of sickness; letting herbs down into a vessel to be steeped.

5. **Master** (*ἐπιστάτα*). Used by Luke only, and always with reference to Jesus. He never uses *Rabbi*, as John especially. Wyc., *commander*.

Toiled (*κοπιάσαντες*). From *κόπος*, *suffering*, *weariness*; and therefore indicating *exhausting* toil.

At thy word (*ἐπί*). Relying *on*: *on the ground of*.

The net (*δίκτυον*). A general term for a net, whether for fish or fowl. See on Matt. iv. 18. Some, as Rev., read *τὰ δίκτυα*, *the nets*.

Brake (*διεῤῥήγνυτο*). Some texts read *διερήσσετο*, from the later form of the verb. The difference is unimportant. The A. V. fails to give the force of the imperfect, *were breaking*, as Rev.; or even better, possibly, *began to break*. Trench suggests *were at the point to break*. The word occurs also at ch. viii. 29; Acts xiv. 14, and only twice beside in the New Testament. Luke alone uses the two compounds *περιῤῥήγνυμι*, of *rending off clothes* (Acts xvi. 22), and *προσρήγνυμι*, *to beat violently* (ch. vi. 48, 49). See on those passages. All the words occur in medical writings.

7. **They beckoned** (*κατένευσαν*). The word originally means *to nod assent*, and so, generally, *to make a sign*. They made signs because of the distance of the other boat; hardly, as has been suggested, because they were too much amazed to speak.

Help (συλλαβέσθαι). Lit., *take hold with.* Compare Philip. iv. 3.

Began to sink (βυθίζεσθαι). Only here and 1 Tim. vi. 9, of *drowning* men in destruction. From βυθός, *the depth.* Wyc., *they were almost drenched.*

8. **Fell down at Jesus' knees.** Compare Sophocles, "Oedipus at Colonus," 1605:

> "Zeus from the dark depths thundered, and the girls
> Heard it, and shuddering, at their father's knees
> Falling, they wept."

9. **He was astonished** (θάμβος περιέσχεν αὐτὸν). Lit., *amazement encompassed him.* See on 1 Pet. ii. 6.

The draught (τῇ ἄγρᾳ). The word is used both of the *act* of catching and of *that which is caught.* In ver. 4 it has the former sense: "let down your net *for catching:*" here, the latter, *the catch* or *haul.*

10. **Partners** (κοινωνοὶ). In ver. 7 the word rendered *partners* is μέτοχοι; from μετά, *with,* and ἔχω, *to have.* The word here denotes a closer association, a common interest. The kindred noun, κοινωνία, *fellowship,* is used of the fellowship of believers with Christ (1 Cor. i. 9); the *communion* of the body and blood of Christ (1 Cor. x. 16); the *communion* of the Holy Ghost (2 Cor. xiii. 14). The persons referred to in ver. 7 might have been only hired workmen (Mark i. 20), temporarily associated with the principals.

Thou shalt catch (ἔσῃ ζωγρῶν). Lit., *thou shalt be catching,* the participle and finite verb denoting that this is to be his habitual calling. Both Matthew and Mark make the promise to be addressed to Peter and his companions; Luke to Peter alone. The verb ζωγρέω, *to catch,* is compounded of ζωός, *living,* and ἀγρεύω, *to catch* or *take.* Hence, lit., *to take alive:* in war, *to* *take captive*, instead of killing. Thus Homer, when Menelaus threatens the prostrate Adrastus:

> "Adrastus clasped the warrior's knees and said,
> O son of Atreus, *take me prisoner*" (ζώγρει).
>
> *Iliad*, vi., 45, 6; compare *Iliad*, x., 378.

So Herodotus: "The Persians took Sardis, and captured Croesus himself alive" (ἐζώγρησαν).—I., 86.

There is certainly a reason for the use of this term, as indicating that Christ's ministers are called to win men *to life*. Compare 2 Tim. ii. 26, where, according to the best supported rendering, the servant of God is represented as taking men alive out of the power of Satan, to be preserved unto the will of God; *i.e.*, as instruments of his will (compare A. V. and Rev.). The word thus contains in itself an answer to the sneering remark of the Apostate Julian, that Christ aptly termed his apostles *fishers*; "for, as the fisherman draws out the fish from waters where they were free and happy, to an element in which they cannot breathe, but must presently perish, so did these."

12–16. Compare Matt. viii. 2–4; Mark i. 40–45.

12. **Full of leprosy.** Matthew and Mark have simply *a leper*. The expression, *full* of leprosy, seems to be used here with professional accuracy. Leprosy was known among physicians under three forms: the *dull white*, the *clear white*, and the *black*. Luke means to describe an aggravated case. The word *full* in this connection is often used by medical writers, as, *full of disease*; the veins *full of blood*; the ears *full of roaring*.

Make me clean (καθαρίσαι). All three evangelists say *cleanse* instead of *heal*, because of the notion of uncleanness which specially attached to this malady.

13. **I will** (θέλω). See on Matt. i. 19.

Be thou clean (καθαρίσθητι). Rev., more accurately, gives the force of the passive voice, *be thou made clean*.

14. **He charged** (παρήγγειλεν). A strong word, often of military orders. Aristotle uses it of a physician: *to prescribe.* Mark has ἐμβριμησάμενος, *strictly* or *sternly charged.* See on Mark i. 43.

No one (μηδενὶ). The conditional negative: no one *that he might chance to meet.*

Go, shew thyself. A lively change from the narrative to direct address.

15. **Went abroad** (διήρχετο). *Διά, throughout* the region. Wyc., *the word walked about.*

Came together (συνήρχοντο). Imperfect. *Kept coming together*, or *were coming.*

To be healed (θεραπεύεσθαι). Originally, *to be an attendant, to do service;* and therefore of a physician, *to attend upon*, or *treat* medically. In classical writers it has also the meaning *to heal*, as undoubtedly in the New Testament, and in Luke (xiii. 14; Acts iv. 14, etc.). See on Matt. viii. 7, and compare ἰάομαι, *to heal*, in ver. 17.

Infirmities (ἀσθενειῶν). A strictly literal rendering; ἀ, *not*, and σθένος, *strength*, exactly answering to the Latin *in, not*, and *firmus, strong.*

16. **Withdrew** (ἦν ὑποχωρῶν). The participle with the imperfect of the finite verb denoting something in progress, and thus corresponding to the imperfect in ver. 15. The multitudes *were coming* together, but he *was engaged in* retirement and prayer, so that he was inaccessible. The word occurs only in Luke, the usual New Testament word for *withdraw* being **ἀναχωρέω.** See Matt. ii. 12; xii. 15; Mark iii. 7.

17–26. Compare Mark ii. 1–12.

17. **He was teaching.** The pronoun has a slightly emphatic force: *he* as distinguished from the Pharisees and teachers of the law.

Doctors of the law (*νομοδιδάσκαλοι*). Only in Luke and 1 Tim. i. 7. Luke often uses *νομικὸς*, *conversant with the law*, but in the other word the element of *teaching* is emphasized, probably in intentional contrast with Christ's teaching.

Judaea and Jerusalem. The Rabbinical writers divided Judaea proper into three parts—*mountain*, *sea-shore*, and *valley*—Jerusalem being regarded as a separate district. "Only one intimately acquainted with the state of matters at the time, would, with the Rabbis, have distinguished Jerusalem as a district separate from all the rest of Judaea, as Luke markedly does on several occasions (Acts i. 8; x. 39)" (Edersheim, "Jewish Social Life").

Was present to heal them. The A. V. follows the reading, *αὐτούς*, *them;* i.e., the sufferers who were present, referring back to ver. 15. The best texts, however, read *αὐτόν*, *him*, referring to Christ, and meaning *was present that he should heal;* i.e., in aid of his healing. So Rev.

18. **Taken with a palsy** (*παραλελυμένος*). Rev., more neatly, *palsied*. Whenever Luke mentions this disease, he uses the verb and not the adjective *παραλυτικός*, *paralytic* (as Matt. iv. 24; viii. 6; Mark ii. 3–10; compare Acts viii. 7; ix. 33); his usage in this respect being in strict accord with that of medical writers.

19. **Tiles.** Wyc. has *sclattis, slates.*

Couch (*κλινιδίῳ*). Luke uses four words for the beds of the sick: *κλίνη*, as ver. 18, the general word for a bed or couch; *κράββατος* (Acts v. 15; ix. 33), a rude pallet (see on Mark ii. 4); *κλινίδιον*, a small couch or litter, as here, a couch so light that a woman could lift and carry it away. Thus, in the

"Lysistrata" of Aristophanes, 916, Myrrine says: "Come now, let me carry our couch" (κλινίδιον). The fourth term, κλινάριον (Acts v. 15), cannot be accurately distinguished from the last. The last two are peculiar to Luke.

Into the midst before Jesus. See on Mark ii. 4.

21. **To reason.** See on Mark ii. 6. The words *who is this that speaketh blasphemy*, form an iambic verse in the Greek.

22. **Perceived.** See on Mark ii. 8.

23. **Walk** (περιπάτει). Lit., *walk about.*

24. **Unto thee** (σοὶ). Standing first for emphasis. Luke emphasizes the direct address to the *man: unto thee* I say, in contrast with the apparently less direct, *thy sins be forgiven thee.* In Jesus' mind the connection between the sins and the man's personal condition was assumed; now he brings out the personal side of the connection. In forgiving the man's sins he had healed him radically. The command to rise and walk was of the same piece.

26. **They were all amazed** (ἔκστασις ἔλαβεν ἅπαντας). Lit., *amazement took hold on all*, as Rev. On ἔκστασις, *amazement*, see on Mark v. 42.

Strange things (παράδοξα). From παρά, *contrary to*, and δόξα, *opinion.* Something contrary to received opinion, and hence *strange.* Compare the English *paradox.* Only here in New Testament.

27, 28. Compare Matt. ix. 9; Mark ii. 13, 14.

27. **He saw** (ἐθεάσατο). Better, as Rev., *beheld*, since the verb denotes looking *attentively*. See on Matt. xi. 7.

A publican. See on ch. iii. 12.

Receipt of custom. See on Matt. ix. 9.

28. **He followed** (ἠκολούθει). Imperfect. He *began* to follow, and *continued* following.

29–39. Compare Matt. ix. 10–17; Mark ii. 15–22.

29. **Feast** (δοχὴν). Only here and ch. xiv. 13. From the same root as δέχομαι, *to receive*. A *reception*.

31. **They that are whole** (οἱ ὑγιαίνοντες). Both Matthew and Mark use ἰσχύοντες, *the strong*. This use of the verb in its primary sense, *to be in sound health*, is found in Luke vii. 10; xv. 27; and once in John, 3 Ep. ver. 2. For this meaning it is the regular word in medical writings. Paul uses it only in the metaphorical sense: *sound* doctrine, *sound* words, *sound* in faith, etc. See 1 Tim. i. 10; vi. 3; Tit. i. 13, etc.

33. **Often** (πυκνὰ). Only here, Acts xxiv. 26; 1 Tim. v. 23. The word literally means *close-packed*, as a thicket, or the plumage of a bird.

Prayers (δεήσεις). Used by no other evangelist. From δέομαι, *to want*, and hence distinctively of *petitionary* prayer. In classical Greek the word is not restricted to sacred uses, but is employed of requests preferred to men. Rev., more correctly, *supplications*.

34. **Children of the bride-chamber.** Better, as Rev., *sons* (υἱοὺς). See on Mark ii. 19.

35. **But the days will come when,** etc. (ἐλεύσονται δὲ ἡμέραι καὶ ὅταν). The A. V. follows a reading which omits καὶ, *and*, which is inserted in all the best texts. The thought is broken off. "The days shall come—*and* when the bridegroom shall be taken away, then shall they fast." So Rev.

36. **A parable.** "From a garment and from wine, especially appropriate at a banquet" (Bengel).

Putteth a piece of a new garment upon an old (*ἐπίβλημα ἱματίου καινοῦ ἐπιβάλλει ἐπὶ ἱμάτιον παλαιόν*). The best texts, however, insert *σχίσας*, *having rent*, which directly governs *ἐπίβλημα*, *piece;* so that the rendering is, *No man having rent a piece from a new garment, putteth it*, etc. So Rev., *No man rendeth a piece and putteth.* Both Matthew and Mark have *cloth* instead of *garment*, by the use of which latter term "the incongruity of the proceeding comes more strongly into prominence" (Meyer). *Ἐπίβλημα*, *a piece*, is, literally, *a patch*, from *ἐπί*, *upon*, and *βάλλω*, *to throw:* something *clapped on.* Compare the kindred verb here, *ἐπιβάλλει*, *putteth upon.*

The new maketh a rent (*τὸ καινὸν σχίζει*). The best texts read *σχίσει*, *will rend*, governing *the new*, instead of being used intransitively. Render, as Rev., *He will rend the new.*

Agreeth not (*οὐ συμφωνεῖ*). The best texts read *συμφωνήσει*, the future; *will not agree.* So Rev.

In Matthew and Mark there is only a single damage, that, namely, to the old garment, the rent in which is enlarged. In Luke the damage is twofold; first, in injuring the new garment by cutting out a piece; and second, in making the old garment appear patched, instead of widening the rent, as in Matthew and Mark.

37. **Bottles** (*ἀσκοὺς*). Rev., *wine-skins.* See on Matt. ix. 17.

39. **Better** (*χρηστότερος*). The best texts read *χρηστός*, *good.* See on Matt. xi. 30.

CHAPTER VI.

1–5. Compare Matt. xii. 1–8; Mark ii. 23–28.

1. **The second after the first** (*δευτεροπρώτῳ*). Only here in New Testament. Many high authorities omit it, and its exact meaning cannot be determined. Rev. omits.

Went through (*διαπορεύεσθαι*). Rev., *was going*. Compare *παραπορεύεσθαι*, *went along beside*—Mark ii. 23.

Cornfields. See on Matt. xii. 1.

Plucked (*ἔτιλλον*). Imperfect; *were plucking*, as they walked. In classical Greek the word is used mostly of pulling out hair or feathers. See on Mark ii. 23.

Did eat (*ἤσθιον*). Imperfect, *were eating*.

Rubbing (*ψώχοντες*). The verb means to *rub small*.

2. **Not lawful.** See on Matt. xii. 2.

3. **Have ye not read** (*οὐδὲ ἀνέγνωτε*)? The A. V. misses the force of *οὐδὲ*: "have ye not *so much as* read?" Rev., "have ye not read *even* this?"

4. **Did take.** Peculiar to Luke.

The shew-bread. See on Mark ii. 26.

5. **Lord of the Sabbath.** See on Matt. xii. 6.

6-11. Compare Matt. xii. 9-14; Mark iii. 1-6.

6. **His right hand** (*ἡ χεὶρ αὐτοῦ ἡ δεξιὰ*). A very precise mode of statement. Lit., *his hand the right one*. Luke only specifies which hand was withered. This accuracy is professional. Ancient medical writers always state whether the right or the left member is affected.

Withered. See on Mark iii. 1.

7. **They watched** (*παρετηροῦντο*). Imperfect. They *kept watching*. See on Mark iii. 2.

He would heal (θεραπεύσει). So Rev. Some authorities, however, read θεραπεύει, "whether he *is healing*." This may mean either "whether *it is his habit* to heal," which is far-fetched, or "*whether he is actually healing.*"

Find. Peculiar to Luke, and emphasizing the eagerness of the Pharisees to discover a ground of accusation.

8. **He knew** (ᾔδει). Imperfect. He was *all along* aware.

Thoughts (διαλογισμοὺς) See on Jas. ii. 4; Matt. xv. 19.

9. **I will ask** (ἐπερωτήσω). Peculiar to Luke's narrative. The best texts read ἐπερωτῶ, the present tense, *I ask*. So Rev.

Life (ψυχὴν). Better as Rev., *a life*. Though the question is a general one, it carries a hint of an *individual* life thrown into it by the special case at hand. See on Mark xii. 30. Wyc., *to make a soul safe*.

10. **Thy hand.** The *arm* was not withered.

11. **They were filled with madness.** Peculiar to Luke. *Ἄνοια*, *madness*, is, properly, *want of understanding*. The word thus implies *senseless* rage, as distinguished from intelligent indignation.

12–16. Compare Matt. x. 2–4; Mark iii. 13–19.

12. **A mountain** (τὸ ὄρος). The article denotes a familiar place. Rev., rightly, *the mountain*.

Continued all night (ἦν διανυκτερεύων). Only here in New Testament. Used in medical language. The all-night prayer is peculiar to Luke's narrative.

13. **Chose** (ἐκλεξάμενος). Mark has ἐποίησεν, *he made* or *constituted*.

He named apostles. Peculiar to Luke.

14. On the order of the names, see on Mark iii. 17.

Andrew. See on Mark iii. 18.

James and John. See on Mark iii. 17.

Philip and Bartholomew. See on Mark iii. 18.

15. **Matthew.** See on Superscription of Matthew.

Thomas. See on Mark iii. 18.

Simon. Distinguished by Matthew and Mark as *the Cananaean.* See on Matt. x. 4; Mark iii. 18.

16. **Judas.** See on *Thaddaeus,* Mark iii. 18.

Judas Iscariot. See on Matt. x. 4.

17. **In the plain** (ἐπὶ τόπου πεδινοῦ). There is no article. More literally, and better, as Rev., *in a plain or level place.* There is a discrepancy in the two narratives. Matthew says *he went up into the mountain and sat down.* Vv. 17–19 are peculiar to Luke.

Judaea and Jerusalem. See on ch. v. 17.

18. **Vexed** (ὀχλούμενοι). The best texts read ἐνοχλούμενοι, occurring only here and Heb. xii. 15. From ὄχλος, *a crowd* or *mob,* with the idea of *want of arrangement and discipline,* and therefore of *confusion* and *tumult.* Hence it is applied to the *noise* and *tumult* of a crowd, and so passes into the sense of the *trouble* and *annoyance* caused by these, and of trouble generally, like the Latin *turbae.* Thus Herodotus says of Croesus, when on the funeral-pile he uttered the name of Solon, and the interpreters begged him to explain what he meant, " and as they

pressed for an answer and *grew troublesome* (καὶ ὄχλον παρεχόντων)"—I., 86. Frequent in medical language. Thus Hippocrates, "*troubled* (ἐνοχλουμένῳ) with a spasm or tetanus."

19. **Sought—went out** (ἐζήτουν—ἐξήρχετο). Both imperfects. The A. V. and Rev. lose in vividness by not rendering them accordingly. The multitudes *were all the while seeking* to touch him, for virtue *was going* out of him.

Healed (ἰᾶτο). Compare Matt. xiv. 36; Mark vi. 56, where διεσώθησαν, *were thoroughly saved*, and ἐσώζοντο, *were saved*, are used. Luke is more technical, using the strictly medical term, which occurs twenty-eight times in the New Testament, seventeen of these in Luke. Luke also uses the two words employed by Matthew and Mark, but always with some addition showing the nature of the saving. Thus Luke vii. 3, where διασώσῃ (A. V., *heal*) is explained by ver. 7, ἰαθήσεται, the technical word, *shall be healed*, and by ver. 10, "found the servant *whole* (ὑγιαίνοντα, another professional word—see on ch. v. 31) that had been *sick*." Compare, also, Luke viii. 35, 36, 44, 47, 48. Medical writers do not use σώζειν or διασώζειν, *to save*, as equivalent to ἰᾶσθαι, *to heal*, but in the sense of escaping from a severe illness or from some calamity. Luke employs it in this sense—Acts xxvii. 44; xxviii. 1.

The Sermon on the Mount.

20–49. Compare Matt. v. 1 to viii. 1.

20. **Lifted up his eyes.** Peculiar to Luke. Compare *he opened his mouth* (Matt. v. 1). Both indicate a solemn and impressive opening of a discourse.

Blessed. See on Matt. v. 3.

Ye poor. See on Matt. v. 3. Luke adopts the style of direct address; Matthew of abstract statement.

Kingdom of God (ἡ βασιλεία τοῦ θεοῦ). Matthew has *kingdom of heaven*, or *of the heavens* (τῶν οὐρανῶν), a phrase used by him only, and most frequently employed by Christ himself to describe the kingdom; though Matthew also uses, less frequently, *kingdom of God*. The two are substantially equivalent terms, though the *pre-eminent* title was *kingdom of God*, since it was expected to be fully realized in the Messianic era, when God should take upon himself the kingdom by a visible representative. Compare Isa. xl. 9, "Behold *your God*." The phrase *kingdom of Heaven* was common in the Rabbinical writings, and had a double signification: the *historical* kingdom and the *spiritual and moral* kingdom. They very often understood by it *divine worship; adoration of God; the sum of religious duties;* but also the Messianic kingdom.

The kingdom of God is, essentially, the absolute dominion of God in the universe, both in a physical and a spiritual sense. It is "an organic commonwealth which has the principle of its existence in the will of God" (Tholuck). It was foreshadowed in the Jewish theocracy. The idea of the kingdom advanced toward clearer definition from Jacob's prophecy of the Prince out of Judah (Gen. xlix. 10), through David's prophecy of the everlasting kingdom and the king of righteousness and peace (Ps. xxii., lxxii.), through Isaiah, until, in Daniel, its eternity and superiority over the kingdoms of the world are brought strongly out. For this kingdom Israel looked with longing, expecting its realization in the Messiah; and while the common idea of the people was narrow, sectarian, Jewish, and political, yet "there was among the people a certain consciousness that the principle itself was of universal application" (Tholuck). In Daniel this conception is distinctly expressed (vii. 14–27; iv. 25; ii. 44). In this sense it was apprehended by John the Baptist.

The ideal kingdom is to be realized in the absolute rule of the eternal Son, Jesus Christ, by whom all things are made and consist (John i. 3; Col. i. 16–20), whose life of perfect obedience to God and whose sacrificial offering of love upon the cross reveal to men their true relation to God, and whose spirit works to bring them into this relation. The ultimate idea of the kingdom is that of "a redeemed humanity, with its divinely revealed destiny manifesting itself in a *religious* communion, or *the Church;* a *social* communion, or the *state;* and an *aesthetic* communion, expressing itself in forms of knowledge and art."

This kingdom is both *present* (Matt. xi. 12; xii. 28; xvi. 19; Luke xi. 20; xvi. 16; xvii. 21; see, also, the parables of the Sower, the Tares, the Leaven, and the Drag-net; and compare the expression "theirs, or yours, *is* the kingdom," Matt. v. 3; Luke vi. 20) and *future* (Dan. vii. 27; Matt. xiii. 43; xix. 28; xxv. 34; xxvi. 29; Mark ix. 47; 2 Pet. i. 11; 1 Cor. vi. 9; Apoc. xx. sq.). As a present kingdom it is incomplete and in process of development. It is expanding in society like the grain of mustard seed (Matt. xiii. 31, 32); working toward the pervasion of society like the leaven in the lump (Matt. xiii. 33). God *is* in Christ reconciling the world unto himself, and the Gospel of Christ is the great instrument in that process (2 Cor. v. 19, 20). The kingdom develops from within outward under the power of its essential divine energy and law of growth, which insures its progress and final triumph against all obstacles. Similarly, its work in reconciling and subjecting the world to God begins at the fountain-head of man's life, by implanting in his heart its own divine potency, and thus giving a divine impulse and direction to the whole man, rather than by moulding him from without by a moral code. The law is written in his heart. In like manner the State and the Church are shaped, not by external pressure, like the Roman empire and the Romish hierarchy, but by the evolution of holy character in men. The kingdom of God in its present development is not identical with the Church. It is a larger movement which includes the Church. The Church is identified with the kingdom to the degree in which it is under the power of the spirit of Christ. "As the Old Testament kingdom of God was perfected and completed when it ceased to be external, and became internal by being enthroned in the heart, so, on the other hand, the perfection of the New Testament kingdom will consist in its complete incarnation and externalization; that is, when it shall attain an outward manifestation, adequately expressing, exactly corresponding to its internal principle" (Tholuck). The consummation is described in Apoc. xxi., xxii.

21. **Now.** Peculiar to Luke.

Shall be filled. See on Matt. v. 6.

Weep (*κλαίοντες*). Strictly, to weep *audibly*. See on *πενθοῦντες*, *mourn*, Matt. v. 4.

Laugh (*γελάσετε*). Matthew, *shall be comforted.*

22. Compare Matt. v. 11.

Son of Man. The phrase is employed in the Old Testament as a circumlocution for *man*, with special reference to his frailty as contrasted with God (Num. xxiii. 19; Ps. viii. 4; Job xxv. 6; xxxv. 8; and eighty-nine times in Ezekiel). It had also a Messianic meaning (Dan. vii. 13 sq.), to which our Lord referred in Matt. xxiv. 30; xxvi. 64. It was the title which Christ most frequently applied to himself; and there are but two instances in which it is applied to him by another, viz., by Stephen (Acts vii. 56) and by John (Apoc. i. 13; xiv. 14); and when acquiescing in the title "Son of God," addressed to himself, he sometimes immediately after substitutes "Son of Man" (John i. 50, 52; Matt. xxvi. 63, 64).

The title asserts Christ's humanity—his absolute identification with our race: "his having a genuine humanity which could deem nothing human strange, and could be touched with a feeling of the infirmities of the race which he was to judge" (Liddon, "Our Lord's Divinity"). It also exalts him as the representative ideal man. "All human history tends to him and radiates from him; he is the point in which humanity finds its unity; as St. Irenaeus says, 'He recapitulates it.' He closes the earlier history of our race; he inaugurates its future. Nothing local, transient, individualizing, national, sectarian dwarfs the proportions of his world-embracing character. He rises above the parentage, the blood, the narrow horizon which bounded, as it seemed, his human life. He is the archetypal man, in whose presence distinction of race, intervals of ages, types of civilization, degrees of mental culture are as nothing" (Liddon).

But the title means more. As Son of Man he asserts the authority of judgment over all flesh. By virtue of what he is as Son of Man, he must be more. "The absolute relation to the world which he attributes to himself demands an absolute relation to God. . . . He is the Son of Man, the Lord of the world, the Judge, only because he is the Son of God" (Luthardt). Christ's humanity can be explained only by his divinity. A humanity so unique demands a solution. Divested of all that is popularly called miraculous, viewed simply as a man, under the historical conditions of his life, he is a greater miracle than all his miracles combined. The solution is expressed in Heb. i.

23. **Leap for joy** (σκιρτήσατε). See ch. i. 41, 44. Compare Matthew, *be exceeding glad* (ἀγαλλιᾶσθε: see on 1 Pet. i. 6).

Their fathers. Peculiar to Luke.

24. **Woe.** These woes are not noted by Matthew.

Have received (ἀπέχετε). In Matt. vi. 5, 16, the Rev. has properly changed "*they have* their reward" to "*they have received.*" The verb, compounded of ἀπό, *off* or *from*, and ἔχω, *to have*, literally means *to have nothing left to desire.* Thus in Philip. iv. 18, when Paul says, "*I have all things* (ἀπέχω πάντα)," he does not mean merely an acknowledgment of the receipt of the Church's gift, but that he is *fully* furnished. "I have all things to the full."

Consolation (παράκλησις). From παρά, *to the side of*, and καλέω, *to call* or *summon.* Literally, *a calling to one's side to help;* and therefore *entreaty*, passing on into the sense of *exhortation*, and thence into that of *consolatory* exhortation; and so coming round to mean *that which one is summoned to give to a suppliant—consolation.* Thus it embodies the *call* for help, and the *response* to the call. Its use corresponds with that of the kindred verb παρακαλέω, *to exhort* or *console.* In its original sense of *calling for aid* the noun appears in the New

Testament only in 2 Cor. viii. 4: *with much entreaty*. The verb appears frequently in this sense, rendered *beseech, pray* (Matt. viii. 34; xiv. 36; Mark i. 40; v. 12, etc.). In the sense of *consolation* or *comfort* the noun occurs in Luke ii. 25; vi. 24; 2 Cor. i. 3; vii. 4; Philem. 7. The verb, in Matt. ii. 18; v. 4; Luke xvi. 25; 2 Cor. i. 4. In some instances, however, the meaning wavers between *console* and *exhort*. In the sense of *exhortation* or *counsel*, the noun may be found in Acts xiii. 15; Rom. xii. 8; Heb. xiii. 22. The verb, in Acts ii. 40; xi. 23; xiv. 22; Rom. xii. 8; Tit. ii. 15. Neither the noun nor the verb appear in the writings of John, but the kindred word παράκλητος, the *Paraclete*, *Comforter*, or *Advocate*, is peculiar to him. On this word, see on John xiv. 16. It should be noted, however, that the word *comfort* goes deeper than its popular conception of *soothing*. It is from the later Latin *confortare*, to *make strong*. Thus Wycliffe renders Luke i. 80, "the child waxed, and *was comforted* in spirit" (A. V., *waxed strong*); and Tyndale, Luke xxii. 43, "there appeared an angel from heaven *comforting* him" (A. V., *strengthening*). The *comfort* which Christ gives is not always soothing. The Holy Spirit, the Comforter, is to convince of *sin* and of *judgment*. Underlying the word is the sense of a wise counsel or admonition which rouses and braces the moral nature and encourages and strengthens it to do and to endure. When, therefore, Christ says "they that mourn shall be comforted," he speaks in recognition of the fact that all sorrow is the outcome of sin, and that true comfort is given, not only in pardon for the past, but in strength to fight and resist and overcome sin. The atmosphere of the word, in short, is not the atmosphere of the sick-chamber, but the tonic breath of the open world, of moral struggle and victory; the atmosphere for him that climbs and toils and fights.

25. **Mourn and weep** (πενθήσετε καὶ κλαύσετε). See on Matt. v. 4.

26. **Well** (καλῶς). Handsomely, fairly.

27. **Which hear.** With the sense of hearing *in order to heed: giving heed*. Compare Matt. xi. 15.

29. **Cheek** (σιαγόνα). Lit., *the jaw*. The cheek is παρειά. The blow intended is not, therefore, a mere *slap*, but a heavy blow; an act of *violence* rather than of *contempt*.

Taketh away (αἴροντος). Lit., *taketh up, lifteth*.

Cloke—coat. See on Matt. v. 40.

30. **Every one.** Peculiar to Luke. Augustine remarks, "*omni* petenti, non *omnia* petenti; give to *every one* that asks, but not *everything* he asks."

Asketh (αἰτοῦντι). See on Matt. xv. 23. Compare Matt. v. 42.

Ask again (ἀπαίτει). Only here and ch. xii. 20. Used in medical language of diseases *demanding* or *requiring* certain treatment.

32. **What** thank (ποία)? What *kind* of thanks? Not *what* is your reward, but what is its *quality?* On *thank* (χάρις), see on ch. i. 30.

34. **Lend** (δανείζετε). Properly, at interest.

Sinners (οἱ ἁμαρτωλοὶ). The article marks them as a class. So, often in New Testament, as when classed with publicans.

Love. Not φιλοῦσι, which implies an *instinctive, affectionate* attachment, but ἀγαπῶσιν, of a sentiment based on judgment and calculation, which selects its object for a reason. See, farther, on John xxi. 15–17. Tynd., *the very sinners love their lovers*.

35. **Hoping for nothing again** (μηδὲν ἀπελπίζοντες). A later Greek word, only here in New Testament, and meaning originally *to give up in despair*, a sense which is adopted by some high authorities, and by Rev., *never despairing*. Luke

was familiar with this sense in the Septuagint. Thus Isa. xxix. 19, "The poor among men (οἱ ἀπηλπισμένοι τῶν ἀνθρώπων) shall rejoice." So in Apocrypha, 2 Mac. ix. 18, "*despairing* of his health;" Judith ix. 11, "A saviour of them that are *without hope* (ἀπηλπισμένων)." According to this, the sense here is, "do good as those who consider nothing as lost." The verb and its kindred adjective are used by medical writers to describe desperate cases of disease.

Children of the Highest (υἱοὶ ὑψίστου). Rev., rightly, *sons*. Compare Matt. v. 45, 48.

Kind (χρηστός). See on Matt. xi. 30.

36. **Merciful** (οἰκτίρμονες). See on Jas. v. 11.

37. **Forgive** (ἀπολύετε). Lit., *release*. So Rev., Christ exhorts to the opposite of what he has just forbidden: "do not *condemn*, but *release*." Compare ch. xxii. 68; xxiii. 16, 17.

38. **Pressed down** (πεπιεσμένον). Only here in New Testament. A common medical term for pressing strongly on a part of the body, and opposed to ψαύειν, *to touch gently*.

Shaken together, running over. Bengel says, "*Pressed down*, as *dry* articles; *shaken together*, as *soft goods; running over*, as *liquids*." But this is fanciful and incorrect. The allusion in every case is to a dry measure; and the climax in the three participles would be destroyed by Bengel's interpretation.

Bosom (τὸν κόλπον). The gathered fold of the wide upper garment, bound together with the girdle, and thus forming a pouch. In the Eastern markets at this day vendors may be seen pouring the contents of a measure into the bosom of a purchaser. In Ruth iii. 15, Boaz says to Ruth, "Bring the *vail* (*the mantle*, so Rev., Old Testament), that thou hast upon thee, and *hold* it (hold it open): and he measured six measures of barley into it." Compare Isa. lxv. 7, "I will *measure* their former work *into their bosom;* also Jer. xxxii. 18. In Acts xxvii. 39, the word is used of a *bay* in a beach, forming a bend in the land like the hollow of a robe. Similarly, the Latin *sinus* means both the hanging, baggy bosom of a robe and a bay.

39. **Can the blind** (*μήτι δυναται τυφλὸς*)? The interrogative particle expects a negative reply. *Surely the blind cannot,* etc.

Lead (ὁδηγεῖν). Better, *guide,* as Rev., since the word combines the ideas of *leading* and *instructing.*

Shall they not (*οὐχὶ*)? Another interrogative particle, this time expecting an affirmative answer.

40. **Perfect** (*κατηρτισμένος*). Rev., rendering the participle more literally, *perfected.* See on Matt. iv. 21. The word signifies to *readjust, restore, set to rights,* whether in a physical or a moral sense. See 1 Cor. i. 10, where Paul exhorts to be *perfectly joined together* (*κατηρτισμένοι*) in opposition to *being divided.* In Gal. vi. 1, it is used of *restoring* a brother taken in a fault. Hence the meaning to *perfect,* as Eph. iv. 12. Used in medical language of setting a bone or joint.

41. **Beholdest** (*βλέπεις*)—**considerest** (*κατανοεῖς*)—**mote** (*κάρφος*)—**beam** (*δοκὸν*). See on Matt. vii. 3.

42. **Brother.** "Expressing the pretence of fraternal duty. To this is opposed 'Thou hypocrite!'" (Bengel).

Let me cast out (*ἄφες ἐκβάλω*) with a studied courtesy: *allow me to cast out.*

See clearly to cast out. See on Matt. vii. 5.

43. **A good tree bringeth not forth corrupt fruit** (*οὐ ἔστιν δένδρον καλὸν, ποιοῦν καρπὸν σαπρόν*). Rev., more correctly, *there is no good tree that bringeth,* etc. *Σαπρόν, corrupt,* is ety-

mologically akin to σήπω, in Jas. v. 2: "Your riches *are corrupted*." The word means *rotten, stale.*

Neither. Rev., *nor again.* The A. V. omits *again* (πάλιν, *on the other hand*).

44. **Bramble-bush** (βάτου.) Matthew has τριβολῶν, *thistles.* The word occurs only once outside of Luke's writings, in Mark xii. 26, where it is used as the familiar title of a section of the Pentateuch. Luke also uses it in the same way (xx. 37). He was doubtless acquainted with it medicinally, as it was extensively used by ancient physicians. Galen has a chapter on its medicinal uses, and the medical writings abound in prescriptions of which it is an ingredient. Galen also has a saying similar to our Lord's: "A farmer could never make a bramble bear grapes." It is the word employed by the Septuagint for the bush out of which God spoke to Moses.

Grapes (σταφυλὴν). Lit., *a cluster of grapes.*

45. **Evil.** See on Luke iii. 19.

47. **I will shew you to whom he is like.** Peculiar to Luke. See on Matt. vii. 24.

48. **Digged deep** (ἔσκαψεν καὶ ἐβάθυνεν). The A. V. regards the two words as a strong expression of a single idea; but the idea is twofold: he *dug* (through the sand), and *deepened* down into the solid rock. So Rev., rightly, *he digged and went deep.*

The flood (πλημμύρας). There is no article: *a flood.* The word occurs in Luke only, and only in this passage. As a medical term it is used of excess of fluids in the body: *flooding.*

Beat vehemently (προσέῤῥηξεν). Rev., more literally, *brake.* Used by physicians of a rupture of the veins. It occurs only here and ver. 49. Matthew has προσέκοψαν, *beat.*

49. **Upon the earth without a foundation.** Matthew, upon *the sand.* The two men are conceived as alike selecting a spot where the sand overlies the rock. The one builds directly upon the sand, the other digs through and down into the rock.

It fell (ἔπεσεν). But the best texts read συνέπεσεν, *fell together, collapsed.* Rev., *fell in.* Only here in New Testament. In medical language used of the falling-in of parts of the body. Thus Hippocrates, "the temples *fallen in:* the limb quickly *collapses* or *shrivels.*" Matthew uses the simple verb ἔπεσεν, *fell.*

Ruin (ῥῆγμα). Lit., *breaking.* Only here in New Testament. A medical term for a laceration or rupture. Matthew has πτῶσις, *the fall.*

CHAPTER VII.

1–10. Compare Matt. viii. 5–13.

1. **Sayings** (ῥήματα). See on ch. i. 37.

In the ears (εἰς τὰς ἀκοὰς). Lit., *into the ears.* See on *ears*, Luke iv. 37.

2. **Centurion** (ἑκατοντάρχου). From ἑκατον, *a hundred*, and ἄρχω, *to command.* Commander of a hundred men. Mark uses κεντυρίων, a Graecized form of the Latin word *centurio.* A *centuria* was originally a division consisting of a hundred things of a kind; and thence came to mean any division, whether consisting of a hundred or not. In military language it meant a division of troops, *a company*, not necessarily of a hundred, the captain of which was called *centurio.* The numbers of a century varied from about fifty to a hundred. The Roman legion consisted of ten *cohorts* or σπεῖραι, *bands*, as "the Italian band," of which Cornelius was a centurion (Acts x. 1). The commanders of these cohorts were called *chiliarchs*, or *chief captains*

(John xviii. 12, Rev.). Each cohort contained six *centuries*, or companies, of which the commanders were called *centurions*. The duty of the centurion was chiefly confined to the regulation of his own corps, and the care of the watch. The badge of his office was the *vitis*, or *vine-stock*. He wore a short tunic, and was also known by letters on the crest of his helmet. Dean Howson ("Companions of St. Paul") remarks on the favorable impression left upon the mind by the officers of the Roman army mentioned in the New Testament, and cites, besides the centurion in this passage, the one at the cross, and Julius, who escorted Paul to Rome. See, further, on Acts x. 1.

Servant (δοῦλος). A bond-servant. Matthew has **παῖς**, a *servant*, which occurs also at ver. 7.

Dear (ἔντιμος). Lit., *held in honor* or *value*. It does not necessarily imply an affectionate relation between the master and the servant, though such may well have existed. It may mean only that he was a valuable servant. See on 1 Pet. ii. 4. In this case Luke omits the mention of the disease, which is given by Matthew.

Beseeching (ἐρωτῶν). Too strong. Better *asking*, as Rev. The word to *beseech* (**παρακαλέω**) occurs in the next verse. See on Matt. xv. 23.

Heal (διασώσῃ). Better as Rev., *save*. See on ch. vi. 19.

4. **They besought him instantly** (παρεκάλουν σπουδαίως). On *besought*, see on ch. vi. 24. *Instantly*, which commonly means *at once*, is used in its older meaning, *pressingly*, from the Latin *instare*, to *urge* or *press upon*. So Rom. xii. 12, "*instant* in prayer." Wyc., *prayed busily*.

That he was worthy (ὅτι ἄξιός ἐστιν). The A. V. renders ὅτι as a conjunction, *that*. The Rev., more correctly, takes it as a mark of quotation, besides properly rendering ἐστιν *is*, instead of *was*. Render as Rev., *He is worthy that thou shouldst* *do this;* for the best texts read παρέξῃ, the second person, *thou shouldst do*, instead of the third person, παρέξει, *he shall do.*

5. **He hath built** (αὐτὸς ᾠκοδόμησεν). *He* is emphatic; *himself, at his own expense.*

A synagogue (τὴν συναγωγὴν). The article, "*the* synagogue," marks the particular synagogue which these elders represented. Hence Rev., rightly, "*our* synagogue." "He did not merely avoid profaning the synagogue" (Bengel).

6. **Went** (ἐπορεύετο). The imperfect tense is explained by what follows. He *was going*, was on the way, when he was met by the second messenger from the centurion.

Friends. Possibly kinsmen, not *elders* now.

Trouble (σκύλλου). Lit., *worry.* See on Matt. ix. 36; Mark v. 35.

Worthy (ἱκανός). Lit., *sufficient.* Compare Matt. iii. 11, "*worthy* to bear;" and 2 Cor. iii. 5, "not that we are *sufficient* (ἱκανοί), but our *sufficiency* (ἱκανότης) is of God." It is also used in the sense of *much, many, long.* See ch. vii. 12; viii. 27, 32; xx. 9; Acts ix. 23.

7. **Say in a word.** Lit., "say *with* a word."

My servant shall be healed (ἰαθήτω ὁ παῖς μοῦ). It is strange that the Rev. should have omitted to note the imperative mood here, at least in the margin. The literal rendering is the more graphic: *Let my servant be healed.* Note the professional word for *heal.* See on ch. vi. 19.

8. **Also.** See on Matt. viii. 9.

Set under authority (ὑπὸ ἐξουσίαν τασσόμενος). It is not easy to render the exact force of these words. The sense of the present participle with the verb εἰμί, *I am*, is very subtle. The words *set under* are commonly understood to mean *placed in a subordinate position;* but this would be more accurately expressed by the perfect participle, τεταγμένος. The present participle indicates something *operating daily*, and the centurion is describing not his *appointed position* so much as his *daily course* of life. The word *set* originally means *arranged, drawn up in order;* so that the words might be paraphrased thus: "I am a man whose daily course of life and duty is appointed and arranged by superior authority." The centurion speaks in a figure which is well explained by Alford: "I know how to obey, being myself under authority; and I know how others obey, having soldiers under me. If then I, in my subordinate station of command, am obeyed, how much more thou, who art over all, and whom diseases serve as their Master." Just what estimate of Jesus these words imply we cannot say. It seems evident, at least, that the centurion regarded him as more than man. If that be so, it is a question whether the word *man* (ἄνθρωπός) may not imply more than is commonly assigned to it. Taking the Greek words in their order they may read, "For I also, *a man* (as compared with thee), am set under authority, having soldiers under *myself*. See on Matt. viii. 9.

10. **Whole** (ὑγιαίνοντα). See on ch. v. 31. The best texts omit *that had been sick*.

11–17. Peculiar to Luke.

11. **The day after** (ἐν τῇ ἑξῆς). Others read ἐν τῷ ἑξῆς, *soon after*. So Rev. Luke's usage favors the latter.

Nain. Mentioned nowhere else in the Bible. "On the northern slope of the rugged and barren ridge of Little Hermon, immediately west of Endor, which lies in a further recess of the same range, is the ruined village of Nain. No convent, no tradition marks the spot. But, under these circumstances, the name alone is sufficient to guarantee its authenticity. One entrance alone it could have had—that which opens on the rough hillside in its downward slope to the plain. It must have been in this steep descent, as, according to Eastern custom, they 'carried out the dead man,' that, 'nigh to the gate' of the village, the bier was stopped, and the long procession of mourners stayed, and 'the young man delivered back to his mother'" (Stanley, "Sinai and Palestine"). "It is in striking accord with the one biblical incident in the history of Nain that renders it dear to the Christian heart, that about the only remains of antiquity are tombs. These are cut in the rock, and are situated on the hillside to the east of the village" (Thomson, "Land and Book").

12. **Carried out.** The tombs were outside of the city.

13. **The Lord.** See on Matt. xxi. 3.

Saw her. Edersheim says, "Had it been in Judaea, the hired mourners and musicians would have *preceded* the bier; in Galilee they followed. First came the women; for, as an ancient Jewish commentary explains, woman, who brought death into our world, ought to lead the way in the funeral procession" ("Jewish Social Life").

Had compassion (ἐσπλαγχνίσθη). From σπλάγχνα, *the nobler entrails*, regarded as the seat of the affections. See on *pitiful*, 1 Pet. iii. 8.

14. **Touched.** Not fearing the ceremonial defilement of contact with the dead.

The bier (σορός). In classical Greek, originally, of a vessel for holding anything: sometimes of a cinerary urn. Here the *open* bier. Edersheim says "of *wicker-work.*"

15. **Sat up** (ἀνεκάθισεν). Compare Acts ix. 40. In this intransitive sense the word is used mostly by medical writers.

Delivered (ἔδωκεν). Rev., *gave.* "For he had already ceased to belong to his mother" (Bengel). Compare ch. ix. 42.

16. **There came a fear on all** (ἔλαβεν δὲ φόβος ἅπαντας). Lit., as Rev., *fear took hold on all.*

17. **This rumor.** Rev., *report:* viz., of a great prophet who had vindicated his claims by raising the dead.

18–35. Compare Matt. xi. 2–19.

19. **Two** (δύο τινὰς). Lit., *two certain ones.* Rev., in margin, *certain two.*

Art thou. The *thou* is emphatic. See on Matt. xi. 3.

21. **Diseases—plagues** (νόσων—μαστίγων). See on Matt. iv. 23; Mark iii. 10. Marking the two classes of disease recognized in medical writings, *chronic* and *acute.*

Evil spirits (πνευμάτων πονηρῶν). On πονηρός, *evil,* see ch. iii. 19. It is applied to evil spirits by Luke only, with the single exception of Matt. xii. 45. In accordance with its signification of evil *on its active side,* it is applied in medicine to that which spreads destruction or corruption; as the poison of serpents. Note, moreover, that Luke distinguishes here between *disease* and *demoniac possession,* as often. See ch. vi. 17, 18; viii. 2; xiii. 32.

He gave (ἐχαρίσατο). More is expressed by this verb than simple *giving.* He gave as a *free, gracious, joy-giving* gift. See on χάρις, *favor,* ch. i. 30; and compare *freely give,* Rom. viii. 32. Also, 1 Cor. ii. 12.

22. **The blind receive,** etc. Better, *are receiving, are walking,* even while Jesus is speaking and John is in doubt.

23. **Shall not be offended** (μὴ σκανδαλισθῇ). Rev., *shall find none occasion of stumbling.* See on Matt. v. 29. Note also the conditional *not* (μὴ): "shall not find, *whatever may occur.*"

24. **To see** (θεάσασθαι). Rev. is correct but awkward, *to behold.* The verb implies *steadfast, intent gazing.* See on Matt. xi. 7.

25. **Gorgeously apparelled** (ἐν ἱματισμῷ ἐνδόξῳ). Lit., *in splendid clothing.*

Live delicately (τρυφῇ ὑπάρχοντες). Lit., *are in luxury.* On ὑπάρχοντες, *are*, see on Jas. ii. 15. On τρυφῇ, *luxury*, see on 2 Pet. ii. 13, the only other place where it occurs. Compare the kindred verb τρυφάω, *to live in luxury,* Jas. v. 5.

Kings' courts (βασιλείοις). Only here in New Testament. Often rendered *palaces.* Sometimes, in later Greek, applied to a capital or royal city, a royal treasury, and a royal diadem.

26. **A prophet** (προφήτην). The popular conception of a prophet is limited to his foretelling future events. This is indeed included in the term, but does not cover its meaning entirely. The word is from φημί, *to speak,* and πρό, *before, in front of.* This meaning of the preposition may have reference to *time,* viz., *before, beforehand;* or *to place,* viz., *in front of,* and so, *publicly;* and this latter meaning, in turn, easily runs into that of *in behalf of; for.* The prophet is, therefore, primarily, one who speaks standing *before* another, and thus forming a medium between him and the hearer. This sense runs naturally into that of *instead of.* Hence it is the technical term for *the interpreter of a divine message.* So Plato: "For this reason it is customary to appoint diviners or interpreters to be judges of the true inspiration. Some persons call them *diviners, seers* (μάντεις); they do not know that they are only repeaters of dark sayings and visions, and are not to be called *diviners* at all, but *interpreters* (προφῆται) of things divine" ("Timaeus," 72). Similarly of an *advocate* to speak *for,* or *instead of* one. The central idea of the word is, one to whom God reveals himself and through whom he speaks. The revelation may or may not relate to the future. The prophet is a *forth-teller,* not necessarily a *foreteller.* The essence of the prophetic character

is immediate intercourse with God. One of the Hebrew names for "prophet," and, as some maintain, the earlier name, signified a *shewer* or *seer*. See 1 Sam. ix. 10; and in 1 Cor. xiv. 26-30, Paul shows that revelation stands in necessary connection with prophesying.

27. **Prepare** (*κατασκευάσει*). See on ch. i. 17.

Least (*μικρότερος*). Lit., *less*. Rev., *but little*; or, as we might say, "*comparatively* little."

29. **Justified God.** Declaring, by being baptized, that God's will concerning John's baptism was right.

30. **Lawyers** (*νομικοὶ*). Not *legal practitioners*, but interpreters and doctors of the Mosaic law.

Rejected (*ἠθέτησαν*). *Set aside*, or *annulled*; made it vain through their disobedience.

Against themselves (*εἰς ἑαυτούς*). More strictly, *with reference to* themselves.

32. **Children** (*παιδίοις*). Diminutive; *little* children. See on Matt. xi. 16.

Market-place. See on Matt. xi. 16.

We piped. Playing at wedding.

Mourned (*ἐθρηνήσαμεν*). Rev., much better, *wailed*: playing at funeral.

Weep (*ἐκλαύσατε*). Of *audible* weeping. See on Matt. v. 4. Matthew has *ἐκόψασθε*, *beaten your breasts*. See on Matt. xi. 17.

33. **Bread and wine.** Peculiar to Luke.

37. A woman **who** (ἥτις). Of that class which was, etc.

A sinner. Wyc., a *sinneress*. Her presence there is explained by the Oriental custom of strangers passing in and out of a house during a meal to see and converse with the guests. Trench cites a description of a dinner at a consul's house in Damietta. "Many came in and took their places on the side-seats, uninvited and yet unchallenged. They spoke to those at table on business or the news of the day, and our host spoke freely to them" ("Parables"). Bernard beautifully says: "Thanks to thee, most blessed sinner: thou hast shown the world a safe enough place for sinners—the feet of Jesus, which spurn none, reject none, repel none, and receive and admit all. Where alone the Pharisee vents not his haughtiness, there surely the Ethiopian changes his skin, and the leopard his spots" (cit. by Trench, "Parables").

Sat (κατάκειται). Lit., *is reclining at meat:* a lively change to the present tense.

Alabaster. See on Matt. xxvi. 7.

38. **At his feet behind.** The body of the guest rested on the couch; the feet were turned from the table toward the walls, and the left elbow rested on the table.

Wash (βρέχειν). More literally and better, as Rev., *wet*, as with rain.

Wiped (ἐξέμασσεν). See on ch. v. 2.

41. **Creditor** (δανειστῇ). From δάνειον, *a loan*. Properly a lender of money *at interest*. Rev., *lender*. See on ch. vi. 34.

Pence (δηνάρια). See on Matt. xx. 2.

42. **Frankly forgave** (ἐχαρίσατο). Rev. omits *frankly*, which is implied in the verb. See on ver. 21.

43. **I suppose** (ὑπολαμβάνω). The verb literally means *to take up by getting under*. It might be rendered, accordingly, *I take it*.

45. **Ceased** (διέλιπεν). Only here in New Testament. Common in medical language, meaning *to be intermittent*, and to discontinue giving remedies for a time.

To kiss (καταφιλοῦσα). The compound verb has the force of kissing *tenderly*, *caressing*.

46. **Oil** (ἐλαίῳ). In vv. 37, 38, the word μύρον, *liquid ointment*, is used. This was the finer and costlier of the two. Christ means to say to Simon, "thou didst not anoint my *head*, the nobler part, with *ordinary* oil. She hath anointed my *feet* with *costly* ointment.

49. **They began.** Luke notes the first uprising of the thought.

Within themselves (ἐν ἑαυτοῖς). Better, *among* themselves, as Rev., in margin.

Also (καὶ). Much better as Rev., "who *even* forgiveth sins."

50. **In peace** (εἰς εἰρήνην). Lit., *into* peace. See on Mark v. 34.

CHAPTER VIII.

1–3. Peculiar to Luke.

1. **Afterward** (ἐν τῷ καθεξῆς). Rev., *soon afterward*. See on ch. vii. 11.

Throughout every city and village (κατὰ πόλιν καὶ κώμην). Lit., *by city and village*. See on ver. 4.

Preaching (κηρύσσων). Or *proclaiming*, as a *herald*. Compare ch. iv. 18, and see on 1 Pet. ii. 5.

And the twelve were with him. The *were* is supplied by the translators. Better, "he *himself* went about," etc., "and the twelve (went) with him;" or, as Rev., *and with him the twelve.*

3. **Steward** (ἐπιτρόπου). From ἐπιτρέπω, *to turn toward;* thence to *turn over to*, *transfer*, and so *commit* or *intrust to.* The word thus literally means, one to whom the management of affairs is *turned over.*

4–18. Compare Matt. xiii. 1–23; Mark iv. 1–25.

4. **Out of every city** (κατὰ πολίν). City by city.

Were come (ἐπιπορευομένων). The present participle denoting something in progress. They *kept coming.* Rev., *resorted.*

5. **To sow.** See on Matt. xiii. 3.

His seed. Peculiar to Luke.

By the way-side. See on Matt. xiii. 4.

Was trodden down. A rendering which would apply better to standing grain. Render, as Rev., *trodden under foot.* Peculiar to Luke.

6. **The rock** (τὴν πέτραν). Matthew has *the rocky places*, and Mark *the rocky ground.*

Sprung up (φυὲν). Lit., *having sprung up.* Rev., better, *grew. Sprung up* is Matthew's ἐξανέτειλεν. Only here and Heb. xii. 15, where it is a quotation from the Septuagint. See on Matt. xiii. 7.

Moisture (*ἰκμάδα*). Only here in New Testament. Matthew and Mark have *depth of earth*. The word is the medical expression for juices of the body, of plants, and of the earth. Aristophanes, metaphorically, *the juice of thought* ("Clouds," 233). Hippocrates uses this and the preceding word together, comparing the juices of the body with those of the earth.

7. **Among** (*ἐν μέσῳ*). In the midst. Stronger than the simple *ἐν*, *in*, as giving more prominence to the danger.

Sprung up with it (*συμφυεῖσαι*). Only here in New Testament. See on ver. 6, and Matt. xiii. 7. The technical word among physicians for *closing* of wounds or ulcers, and the *uniting* of nerves or bones. Dioscorides uses it, as here, of plants growing in the same place: "The hellebore *grows together with* the vines."

Choked (*ἀπέπνιξαν*). Lit., choked *off*. Matthew has the simple *ἔπνιξαν*, *choked*; and Mark *συνέπνιξαν*; the *σύν*, *together*, emphasizing the idea of *compression*. Luke is very fond of compounds and sonorous words. See on ch. xxiii. 51.

8. **A hundred-fold.** Omitting the *thirty* and *sixty* of Matthew and Mark. See on Matt. xiii. 8.

10. **Mysteries.** See on Matt. xiii. 11.

Understand (*συνιῶσιν*). See on *understanding*, the kindred noun, Mark xii. 33.

11. **The parable is this.** According to its interpretation.

13. **For awhile believe.** See on Matt. xiii. 21. Matthew and Mark have *endureth*, or *endure for a while*.

In time of temptation. Matthew and Mark have, *when tribulation or persecution cometh*.

Fall away. Lit., *withdraw* or *stand aloof.* Matthew and Mark have *stumble.*

14. **Go forth** (πορευόμενοι). The present participle. Much better Rev., "they that have heard, and *as they go on their way* are choked," etc.

Choked **with** (ὕπο, *under*). Implying the impulse *under which* they pursue their course.

Bring (no fruit) **to perfection** (τελεσφοροῦσιν). Only here in New Testament. Matthew and Mark have, *it becometh unfruitful.* The verb literally means *to bring to an end* or *accomplishment.*

15. **These are they which** (οὗτοί εἰσιν οἵτινες). *Which* denotes them as belonging to a class. Hence Rev., rightly, *such as.*

Honest and good heart. Peculiar to Luke. *Honest;* lit., *fair, noble.* Honest, not in the popular sense, but in the sense of the Latin *honestus; noble, virtuous, worthy.*

Keep (κατέχουσιν). Much better Rev., *hold it fast,* giving the force of the compound verb.

With patience. Or *in* patience. Peculiar to Luke. In contrast with *fall away,* ver. 13.

16. **Candle** (λύχνον). Rev., properly, *lamp.* See on Mark iv. 21.

Candlestick (λυχνίας). Correctly, as Rev., *a stand.* See on Matt. v. 15.

17. **Nothing is secret—manifest.** Correctly rendered in A. V., but not so the parallel passage, Mark iv. 22, on which see note.

18. **How** ye hear (πῶς). The manner of hearing. Mark has τί, *what* ye hear; the matter.

Seemeth (δοκεῖ). Peculiar to Luke. Rev. renders "*thinketh* he hath," as Jas. i. 26, on which see note. Wyc., *guesseth;* Tynd., *supposeth.*

19–21. Compare Matt. xii. 46–50; Mark iii. 31–35.

Come at him (συντυχεῖν). Only here in New Testament. The word properly carries the idea of an *accidental* meeting, and slightly so here. Jesus was lost in the crowd, and his friends could not *fall in with* him.

22–25; ix. 57–62. Compare Matt. viii. 18–27; Mark iv. 35–41.

22. **Let us go over unto the other side of the lake.** Wyc. has, *pass we over the standing water.* On *lake,* see on ch. v. 1.

Launched forth (ἀνήχθησαν). See on ch. v. 3. The verb literally means to *lead up;* hence to lead up to the high sea, or *take to sea; put to sea.* It is the word used of Jesus' being *led up* into the wilderness and the mount of temptation (Matt. iv. 1; Luke ii. 22); also of *bringing up* a sacrifice to an idol-altar (Acts vii. 41). Often in Acts in the accounts of Paul's voyages.

23. **He fell asleep** (ἀφύπνωσεν). Very graphic. He fell *off* (ἀπό) into sleep.

Came down (κατέβη). More vivid than either Matthew or Mark, who have *there arose.* The word describes the action of the sudden storms which literally *come down* from the heights surrounding the lake. See on Matt. viii. 24.

Storm (λαῖλαψ). See on Mark iv. 37. Matthew has σεισμὸς, *a shaking.* See on Matt. viii. 24.

They were filling with water (συνεπληροῦντο). Used by Luke only. Mark, as usual, goes into minuter detail, and describes how the waves beat into the boat. Note the imperfects: *they were filling;* they *were beginning to be* in danger, contrasted with the instantaneous descent of the storm expressed by the aorist *came down.*

24. **Master.** See on ch. v. 5.

Rebuked. Compare the more detailed narrative of Mark, iv. 39, and see notes there. Wyc., *blamed.*

The raging (κλύδωνι). See on Jas. i. 6.

Arose (διεγερθεὶς). Wrong. It is the word used just before, *awoke.* Lit., *having been thoroughly awakened.* Rev., correctly, *he awoke.* Luke is especially fond of compounds with διά.

A calm. Matthew and Mark have "a *great* calm."

25. **He commandeth.** Peculiar to Luke.

26. **They arrived** (κατέπλευσαν). The verb means literally to sail *down* from the sea to the shore. Compare *launched forth,* ver. 22. Only here in New Testament. The two prepositions, *up* and *down,* are used in our nautical terms *bear up* and *bear down.* See Introduction, on Luke's variety of words for *sailing.* Matthew and Mark have *came* (ἐλθόντος, ἦλθον).

Gerasenes. The texts vary, some reading *Gadarenes,* as A. V., others *Gergesenes.*

Over against (ἀντιπέρα). Only here in New Testament.

27. **There met him out of the city.** The words *out of the city* belong rather with *a certain man.* So Rev.

Which had devils long time. The best texts insert καὶ, *and*, after *devils* (demons), and read "who had demons, *and* for a long time he had worn," etc. *Long* (ἱκανῷ). See on ch. vii. 16.

Tombs. See on Matt. viii. 28. Compare Mark v. 4–6.

28. **Fell down** (προσέπεσεν). Mark has προσεκύνησεν, which often implies religious or superstitious feeling, as Matt. iv. 9, 10. This is the prostration of abject terror.

Cried out (ἀνακράξας). The compound verb with ἀνά, *up*, implies what is conveyed by our phrase, lifting *up* the voice. See on Mark v. 5.

What have I to do with thee? See on Mark v. 7.

Torment (βασανίσῃς). See on Matt. iv. 24. Luke never uses the word of *sickness*, as Matt. viii. 6. See on ch. iv. 41.

29. **He had commanded** (παρήγγελλεν). Imperfect tense. Rev. does not improve by reading *he commanded.* The imperfect expresses the simultaneousness of the exorcism and the cry *torment me not.* Better, *for he was commanding*. So the Am. Rev.

It had seized (συνηρπάκει). Used by Luke only. See Acts vi. 12; xxvii. 15. The verb literally means to *snatch and carry away with* (σύν).

He was kept bound (ἐδεσμεύετο φυλασσόμενος). Lit., *he was bound, being guarded.* Rev., *was kept under guard and bound.* The A. V. does not sufficiently bring out the vigilance with which he was attended.

Chains and fetters. See on Mark v. 4.

Breaking (διαρρήσσων). Compare Mark iv. 4, and see note there.

Was driven, etc. Peculiar to Luke.

30. **Many devils were,** etc. Compare Mark v. 9.

31. **Command them.** The plural, referring to the *legion.*

The deep (ἄβυσσον). Lit., *the bottomless.* Transcribed into our *abyss,* as Rev. Mark has a quite different request, that he would not send them out of the country (v. 10). In Rom. x. 7, used of *Hades,* to which Christ descended; and in Apoc. always of *the bottomless pit.* The demons refer to their place of abode and torment.

33. **Ran violently** (ὥρμησεν). Rev., more neatly, *rushed.* Only Mark gives the number of the swine, *two thousand.*

A steep place. See on Matt. ix. 32.

36. **He that was possessed with devils.** Expressed in the Greek by two words, ὁ δαιμονισθείς, *the demonized.*

Was healed (ἐσώθη). See on ch. vi. 19.

37. **They were taken** (συνείχοντο). See on ch. iv. 38. The same word as of the *fever.*

38. **Besought** (ἐδέετο). Imperfect: *was beseeching.* See on *prayers,* ch. v. 33. Rev., *prayed. Beseech* is used to render παρακαλέω (Mark v. 10). See on *consolation,* ch. vi. 24. Παρακαλέω, *beseech,* is used of prayer *to God* in only one instance, 2 Cor. xii. 8, where Paul *besought* the Lord to remove the thorn in the flesh. Frequently of requests to Christ while on earth. Δέομαι, *to pray,* often of prayer to God (Matt. ix. 38; Luke x. 2; Acts viii. 22). It is noticeable that in ver. 28, where the demons address Christ as the Son of the highest God, they say δέομαι, *I pray.* In vv. 31, 32, where they ask not to be sent away, and to be allowed to enter into the swine, they say παρακαλέω, *I beseech.* The restored man, recognizing

Jesus' divine power, *prayed* (ἐδεῖτο) to be with him. The distinction, however, must not be closely pressed. The two words seem to be often used interchangeably in the New Testament.

39. **Shew** (διηγοῦ). Rather *relate*, *recount*, with the idea of telling the story *throughout* (διά). See on *declaration*, ch. i. 1.

Throughout the whole city. Mark says *in Decapolis.*

How great things (ὅσα). Lit., *how many* things, and thus according with *recount.* Declared all things *throughout, as many as* Jesus had done.

41–56. Compare Matt. ix. 18–26; Mark v. 22–43.

41. **Jairus.** The name of one of the Israelite chiefs, *Jair*, who conquered and settled Bashan (Num. xxxii. 41; Josh. xiii. 30). "His name lingered down to the time of the Christian era, when, in the same region as that which he conquered, we find a ruler of the synagogue named Jair" (Stanley, "Jewish Church").

42. **Thronged** (συνέπνιγον). With the idea of pressing *together* (σύν) upon him: *stifling.* The simple verb is that rendered *choke*, as in vv. 8, 33.

43. **Had spent** (προσαναλώσασα). Only here in New Testament. Some texts omit *who had spent all her living upon physicians.* Luke, with professional sensitiveness, omits Mark's statement that she had suffered many things from many physicians, and was not bettered but made worse.

44. **Hem.** See on Matt. ix. 20.

Stanched (ἔστη). A common medical term.

45. **Who touched** (τίς ὁ ἁψαμενός). Lit., *who is he that touched?* Rev., *who is it that.*

Throng and press (*συνέχουσιν—ἀποθλίβουσιν*). On the former word, see ver. 37, and ch. iv. 38. Rev. renders the latter, which occurs here only, more literally, *crush*. It means to *squeeze out*, as wine from grapes. See on *tribulation*, Matt. xiii. 21.

46. **Hath touched** (*ἥψατο*)—**I perceive** (*ἔγνων*). Rev. renders the two aorists strictly: *did touch*, and *I perceived*, with reference to Jesus' knowledge of the touch at the moment it was applied.

Virtue (*δύναμιν*). Rev., *power*. The evangelists use the word frequently of *miracles—mighty works*. It is used here in the sense of *virtue*, according to its use by naturalists and physicians. Still, too much stress must not be laid upon it as a mark of Luke's professional accuracy, as Dean Plumptre in "The Expositor," iv., 139; since Mark uses it in his narrative of the same incident, and in the same sense (Mark v. 30).

47. **Falling down.** Not in worship, but in terror. See on *fell down*, v. 28.

48. **In peace.** See on ch. vii. 50.

49. **From the ruler of the synagogue's house.** A. V. and Rev. properly supply *house*, as the ruler himself is present with Jesus.

Dead. Placed first in the Greek order, for emphasis. "*Dead* is thy daughter."

Trouble. See on Matt. ix. 36; Mark v. 35. Tyndale renders *dis-ease*, in the old verbal sense of *disturb*.

52. **Wept and bewailed.** Both imperfects, *were weeping and bewailing*. So, rightly, Rev. Compare on *bewailing*, Mark v. 38.

54. **Maid** (ἡ παῖς). Instead of the unclassical κορασίον, *damsel*, of Matthew and Mark.

CHAPTER IX.

1–6. Compare Matt. x. 1, 7, 9–11, 14; Mark vi. 7–13.

1. **Called together.** Matthew and Mark have *called to.*

3. **Take**(αἴρετε). Lit., *lift*, with a view of carrying away.

Staves. Following the reading ῥάβδους, for which read ῥάβδον, *staff.*

Two coats (ἀνὰ δύο χιτῶνας). Lit., *two apiece:* the force of ἀνά, as in John ii. 6.

4. **There abide.** See on Matt. x. 10.

5. **Shake off.** See on Matt. x. 14.

6. **Throughout the towns** (κατὰ τὰς κώμας). Rev., rightly, *villages.* The preposition is distributive, *village by village.*

7–9. Compare Matt. xiv. 1–2; 6–12. Mark vi., 14–16, 21–29.

7. **The tetrarch.** See on Matt. xiv. 1.

That was done (τὰ γινόμενα). The present participle. Lit., *all that is being done.*

Was perplexed (διηπόρει). Used by Luke only. From διά, *through*, and ἀπορέω, *to be without a way out.* The radical idea of the compound verb seems to be of one who goes *through* the whole list of possible ways, and finds no way out. Hence, *to be in perplexity.*

9. **He desired** (ἐζήτει). Rev., *he sought*. He did more than desire.

10–17. Compare Mark vi. 30–44.

10. **Declared** (διηγήσαντο). Related everything *throughout* (διά). See on ver. 39; ch. i. 1.

Bethsaida. Peculiar to Luke. It means *Fishing-place.*

Healed (ἰᾶτο) **them that had need of healing** (θεραπείας). See on ch. v. 15.

12. **And when the day began to wear away.** Omit *when.* Render, *and the day began*, etc. *To wear away* (κλίνειν). Lit., *to decline.* Wyc., very literally, *to bow down.*

Lodge (καταλύσωσιν). Peculiar to Luke. Primarily the verb means to *break up* or *dissolve.* Hence often in New Testament to *destroy* (Matt. v. 17; Mark xiii. 2). Intransitively, *to take up one's quarters; lodge;* either because the harness of the travellers' horses is loosed, or because the fastenings of their garments are untied. The kindred word κατάλυμα, a *guest-chamber*, occurs, Mark xiv. 14; or *inn*, Luke ii. 7.

Victuals (ἐπισιτισμόν). Only here in New Testament. Properly *a stock of provisions.* Thus Xenophon. "Cyrus hastened the whole journey, except when he halted in order to furnish himself with *supplies*" (ἐπισιτισμοῦ ἕνεκα).

Desert (ἐρήμῳ). See on Matt. xiv. 15.

13. **Give ye.** The *ye* emphatic, closing the sentence in the Greek order. See on Matt. xiv. 15.

Buy food. Compare Mark vi. 37.

14. **In a company** (κλισίας). The plural, *in companies.* Lit., *table-companies.* The word is also used in classical Greek

of a *couch* for reclining at table. Only here in New Testament. See on Mark vi. 39.

16. **Brake and gave** (κατέκλασεν—ἐδίδου). Note the two tenses, as in Mark vi. 41, and see note there.

To set before (παραθεῖναι). Lit., *to set beside*, since the table was at the side of the guest. A common word for serving up a meal. Compare Luke x. 8; Acts xvi. 34. From the sense of *placing beside*, comes that of *putting in charge*, *committing* (Luke xii. 48; xxiii. 46; 1 Tim. i. 18). Hence the kindred noun παραθήκη (2 Tim. i. 12), *a deposit:* that *which I have committed.*

17. **Were filled.** See on Matt. v. 6.

There were taken up of fragments that remained to them twelve baskets (καὶ ἤρθη τὸ περισσεῦσαν αὐτοῖς κλασμάτων κόφινοι δώδεκα). The Rev. is more accurate, putting the comma after αὐτοῖς, *to them*, instead of after κλασμάτων, *fragments;* and making the latter word depend on κόφινοι, *baskets.* Render, therefore, *And there was taken up that which remained over to them, of broken pieces, twelve baskets.*

Baskets. See on Matt. xiv. 20.

18–21. Compare Matt. xvi. 13–20. Mark viii. 27–30.

18. **As he was praying.** Peculiar to Luke.

20. **Ye.** Emphatic: "but *ye*, whom do ye say that I am?"

The Christ of God. Each evangelist gives Peter's confession differently. Matthew, *The Christ, the Son of the living God.* Mark, *The Christ.* See on Matt. xvi. 15. On *Christ*, see on Matt. i. 1.

21. **He straitly charged** (ἐπιτιμήσας). The word implies

an *emphatic, solemn* charge; its meaning being, strictly, *to lay a penalty upon one*, and thence, *to charge under penalty*.

No man (μηδενὶ). The conditional negative: no man, whoever he might be.

22–27. Compare Matt. xvi. 21–28; Mark viii. 31–38; ix. 1.

22. **Be rejected** (ἀποδοκιμασθῆναι). The verb means to reject *on scrutiny* or *trial*, and therefore implies *deliberate* rejection.

Of the elders (ἀπό). Lit., *from the side of;* on the part of.

23. **Will** come after (θέλει). Not the future tense of the verb *come*, but the present of the verb *to will: wills to come*. See on Matt. i. 19; and Mark viii. 34. Rev., properly, *would come*.

Daily. Peculiar to Luke.

24. **Will** save (θέλῃ σῶσαι). The same construction as *will come after* (ver. 23). Rev., *would save*.

Life (ψυχὴν). See on *soul*, Mark xii. 30.

25. **Gain** (κερδήσας). A merchant's word. Jesus is putting the case as a common-sense question of profit and loss.

Lose (ἀπολέσας). "When he might have been saved" (Bengel). This word, in classical Greek, is used: 1. Of *death* in battle or elsewhere. 2. Of *laying waste*, as a city or heritage. 3. Of *losing* of life, property, or other objects. As an active verb, to *kill* or *demolish*. 4. Of *being demoralized*, morally abandoned or ruined, as children under bad influences. In New Testament of *killing* (Matt. ii. 13; xii. 14). Of *destroying* and *perishing*, not only of human life, but of material and intellectual things (1 Cor. i. 19; John vi. 27; Mark ii. 22; 1 Pet. i. 7; Jas. i. 11; Heb. i. 11). Of *losing* (Matt. x. 6, 42; Luke xv. 4, 6, 8). Of *moral abandonment* (Luke xv. 24, 32). Of *the doom* *of the impenitent* (Matt. x. 28; Luke xiii. 3; John iii. 15; John x. 28; 2 Pet. iii. 9; Rom. ii. 12.

Cast away (ζημιωθείς). Another business term. The word means *to fine, amerce, mulct;* to punish by exacting forfeit. Hence Rev., correctly, *forfeit his own self.* See on *win your souls,* Luke xxi. 19. Also on Matt. xvi. 26.

26. **Shall be ashamed** (ἐπαισχυνθῇ). The feeling expressed by this word has reference to incurring dishonor or shame in the eyes of men. It is "the grief a man conceives from his own imperfections considered with relation to the world taking notice of them; grief upon the sense of disesteem" ("South," cit. by Trench). Hence it does not spring out of a reverence for right in itself, but from fear of the knowledge and opinion of men. Thus in the use of the kindred noun αἰσχύνη, *shame,* in the New Testament. In Luke xiv. 9, the man who impudently puts himself in the highest place at the feast, and is bidden by his host to go lower down, begins *with shame* to take the lowest place; not from a right sense of his folly and conceit, but from being humiliated in the eyes of the guests. Thus, Heb. xii. 2, Christ is said to have "endured the *shame,*" *i.e.,* the public disgrace attaching to crucifixion. So, too, in the use of the verb, Rom. i. 16: "I am not *ashamed* of the gospel," though espousing its cause subjects me to the contempt of the Jew and of the Greek, to whom it is a stumbling-block and foolishness. Onesiphorus was not ashamed to be known as the friend of a prisoner (2 Tim. i. 16). Compare Heb. ii. 11; xi. 16. It is used of the Son of Man here by a strong metaphor. *Literally,* of course, the glorified Christ cannot experience the sense of shame, but the idea at the root is the same. It will be as if he should feel himself disgraced before the Father and the holy angels in owning any fellowship with those who have been ashamed of him.

His glory, etc. Threefold glory. His own, as the exalted Messiah; the glory of God, who owns him as his dearly beloved son, and commits to him the judgment; and the glory of the angels who attend him.

27. **Taste of death.** The word *taste*, in the sense of *experience*, is often used in classical Greek; as, to taste of *toils*, of *sorrow*, of *freedom*, but never of *death*. The phrase, *taste of death*, is common in Rabbinical writings. In the New Testament only here and Heb. ii. 9, used of Christ. Chrysostom (cited by Alford) compares Christ to a physician who first tastes his medicines to encourage the sick to take them.

The kingdom of God. See on ch. vi. 20.

28–36. Compare Matt. xvii. 1-13; Mark ix. 2–13.

28. **A mountain.** Rev., *the mountain*. The tradition that this mountain was Tabor is generally abandoned, and Mount Hermon is commonly supposed to have been the scene of the transfiguration. "Hermon, which is indeed the centre of all the Promised Land, from the entering in of Hamath unto the river of Egypt; the mount of fruitfulness, from which the springs of Jordan descended to the valleys of Israel. Along its mighty forest-avenues, until the grass grew fair with the mountain lilies, his feet dashed in the dew of Hermon, he must have gone to pray his first recorded prayer about death, and from the steep of it, before he knelt, could see to the south all the dwelling-place of the people that had sat in darkness, and seen the great light—the land of Zabulon and of Naphtali, Galilee of the nations; could see, even with his human sight, the gleam of that lake by Capernaum and Chorazin, and many a place loved by him and vainly ministered to, whose house was now left unto them desolate; and, chief of all, far in the utmost blue, the hills above Nazareth, sloping down to his old home: hills on which the stones yet lay loose that had been taken up to cast at him, when he left them forever" (Ruskin, "Modern Painters," iv., 374).

To pray. Peculiar to Luke.

29. **Was altered** (ἐγένετο ἕτερον). Lit., *became different*. Luke avoids Matthew's word, μεταμορφώθη, *was metamorphosed*.

He was writing for Greek readers, to whom that word represented the transformations of heathen deities into other forms. See, for instance, the story of the capture of Proteus by Menelaus, in the fourth book of Homer's "Odyssey." See on Matt. xvii. 2.

White (λευκὸς). In classical Greek very indefinite as an expression of color; being used, not only of the whiteness of the snow, but of gray dust. Its original sense is *clear*. All three evangelists use the word, but combined with different terms. Thus, Matthew, *as the light*. Mark, στίλβοντα, *glistering* (see on Mark ix. 3). Luke, ἐξαστράπτων (only here in New Testament), *flashing as with the brilliance of lightning*. Rev., *dazzling*.

30. **There talked** (συνελάλουν). The imperfect is graphic; as the vision revealed itself, the two *were in the act of* talking.

31. This verse is peculiar to Luke. **Spake** (ἔλεγον). Imperfect, *were speaking*.

Decease (ἔξοδον). The Rev. retains the word of the A. V., though it has, to modern ears, a somewhat formal sound. No word, however, could more accurately represent the original, which is compounded of ἐξ, *out of*, and ὁδός, *a journeying*; and thus corresponds to the Latin *decessus*, *a going away*, whence the word *decease*. The Greek word is familiar to us as *exodus*, applied principally to the migration of the Hebrews from Egypt, and thus used at Heb. xi. 22, *departing*. In the mouth of Christ it covers the ideas both of death and ascension. Peter uses it of his own death (2 Pet. i. 15, where see note).

He should accomplish (ἔμελλεν πληροῦν). Better, as Rev., *he was about to accomplish*. "Accomplish," or "fulfil," is very significant with reference to Christ's death. Moses and Joshua had *begun* an *exodus* from *Egypt*, but had not *accomplished* the going out of God's people from this present world. See Heb. iii. 18; iv. 8.

32. **Heavy** (βεβαρημένοι). The perfect participle. Lit., *burdened* or *oppressed*. "It was but natural for these men of simple habits, at night, and after the long ascent, and in the strong mountain air, to be heavy with sleep; and we also know it as a psychological fact, that, in quick reaction, after the overpowering influence of the strongest emotions, drowsiness would creep over their limbs and senses" (Edersheim).

33. **As they were departing** (ἐν τῷ διαχωρίζεσθαι αὐτοὺς). Lit., *in their departing*. The verb only here in New Testament. The whole sentence is peculiar to Luke's narrative.

Master. See on ch. v. 5.

Let us make. See on Matt. xvii. 4.

Tabernacles. See on Matt. xvii. 4. "Jesus might have smiled at the naive proposal of the eager apostle that they six should dwell forever in the little *succôth* of wattled boughs on the slopes of Hermon" (Farrar).

Not knowing what he said. Not implying any reproach to Peter, but merely as a mark of his bewilderment in his state of ecstasy.

34. **A cloud.** "A strange peculiarity has been noticed about Hermon, in the extreme rapidity of the formation of cloud on the summit. In a few minutes a thick cap forms over the top of the mountain, and as quickly disperses and entirely disappears" (Edersheim).

Overshadowed them (ἐπεσκίαζεν). A beautiful imperfect: "*began* to overshadow them;" thus harmonizing with the words, "as they entered into." *Them* (αὐτοὺς) must, I think, be confined to Moses, Elias, and Jesus. Grammatically, it might include all the six; but the disciples hear the voice *out of* the cloud, and the cloud, as a symbol of the divine presence, rests on these three as a sign to the disciples. See Exod. xiv. 19; xix. 16; 1 Kings viii. 10; Ps. civ. 3.

36. **When the voice was past** (ἐν τῷ γενέσθαι τὴν φωνὴν). Lit., *in the coming to pass of the voice.* Rev., *when the voice came*, with A. V. in margin.

37–43. Compare Matt. xvii. 14–21; Mark ix. 14–29.

37. **Come down** (κατελθόντων). Very frequent in Luke, and only once elsewhere: Jas. iii. 15.

38. **Master** (διδάσκαλε). Teacher.

Look upon (ἐπίβλεψαι). Only here and Jas. ii. 3. To look with pitying regard; and by medical writers of examining the condition of a patient.

39. **Taketh** (λαμβάνει). See on Mark ix. 18.

Suddenly (ἐξαίφνης). Used only once outside of the writings of Luke: Mark xiii. 36. Naturally, frequent in medical writers, of sudden attacks of disease. Luke has more medical details in his account than the other evangelists. He mentions the sudden coming on of the fits, and their lasting a long time. Mr. Hobart remarks that Aretaeus, a physician of Luke's time, in treating of epilepsy, admits the possibility of its being produced by demoniacal agency. Epilepsy was called by physicians "the sacred disease."

Bruising (συντρῖβον). See on *bruised*, ch. iv. 18. The word literally means *crushing together*. Rev. expresses the *σύν*, *together*, by *sorely*. Compare the details in Mark, *gnashing the teeth* and *pining away* (ix. 18). The details in Mark ix. 21, 22, we might rather expect to find in Luke; especially Christ's question, how long he had been subject to these attacks. See note on Mark ix. 20.

41. **Faithless.** See on Mark ix. 19.

Perverse. See on Matt. xvii. 17.

How long (ἕως πότε). Lit., *until when.*

Suffer (ἀνέξομαι). Better as Rev., *bear with.* See Acts xviii. 14; 2 Cor. xi. 1. The literal meaning is to "bear *up* (ἀνά) under."

42. **Threw him down** (ἔῤῥηξεν). See on *teareth,* Mark ix. 18.

Tare (συνεσπάραξεν). Only here in New Testament. *Convulse,* which is the exact Latin equivalent, would, perhaps, be the nearest rendering. Σπαραγμός, a kindred noun, is the word for a *cramp.*

43–45. Compare Matt. xvii. 22, 23; Mark ix. 30–32.

43. **Astonished** (ἐξεπλήσσοντο). See on Matt. vii. 28.

Mighty power (μεγαλειότητι). Used only by Luke and at 2 Pet. i. 16, on which see note.

He did (ἐποίει). Imperfect. Better, *was doing.*

44. **Let these sayings sink down into your ears.** Lit., *put these sayings into your ears.*

Shall be delivered (μέλλει παραδίδοσθαι). Rather, *is about to be delivered.*

46–50. Compare Matt. xviii. 1–35; Mark ix. 33–50.

46. **A reasoning** (διαλογισμὸς). A debate or discussion. See on ch. xxiv. 38, and Jas. i. 22; ii. 4.

47. **He took a little child** (ἐπιλαβόμενος παιδίου). Strictly, *having laid hold of.*

By him (παρ' ἑαυτῷ). Lit., *by himself.* Mark alone records the taking him in his arms.

48. **In my name.** See on Matt. xviii. 5.

51–56. Peculiar to Luke.

51. **When the time was come** (ἐν τῷ συμπληροῦσθαι τὰς ἡμέρας). Lit., *in the fulfilling of the days.* This means when the days *were being* fulfilled; not when they *were* fulfilled: when the time was drawing near. Rev., *were well-nigh come.* Luke is speaking of a *period* beginning with the first announcement of his sufferings, and extending to the time of his being received up.

That he should be received up (τῆς ἀναλήμψεως αὐτοῦ). Lit., *the days of his being taken up:* his ascension into heaven. Ἀνάλημψις occurs nowhere else in the New Testament; but the kindred verb, ἀναλαμβάνω, is the usual word for being received into heaven. See Acts i. 2, 11, 22; 1 Tim. iii. 16.

57–62. Compare Matt. viii. 19–27; Mark iv. 35–41.

57. **A certain man.** Matthew, *a scribe.*

Thou goest (ἀπέρχῃ). Lit., "goest *away*" (ἀπό). I will follow thee whithersoever-away thou goest.

58. **Holes.** See on Matt. viii. 20.

Birds (πετεινὰ). Strictly, *flying fowl.* The common word for *bird* in the New Testament. Ὄρνις occurs Matt. xxiii. 37; Luke xiii. 34; but both times in the sense of *hen.* See on Matt. xxiii. 37. Ὄρνεον is found in Apoc. xviii. 2; xix. 17, 21; and πτηνόν, another form for the word in this passage, occurs 1 Cor. xv. 30.

Nests. See on Matt. viii. 20.

60. **Their dead** (τοὺς ἑαυτῶν νεκρούς). As Rev., *their own* dead.

Preach (διάγγελλε). *Publish abroad,* as Rev. διά, *throughout* all regions.

61, 62. Peculiar to Luke.

61. **To bid farewell** (ἀποτάξασθαι). In this sense the word is used only in later Greek. In classical Greek it signifies to *set apart* or *assign*, as a soldier to his post or an official to his office, and later to *detach* soldiers. Hence to dismiss one with orders. This latter sense may, as Kypke suggests, be included in the meaning of the word in this passage; the man desiring to return home, not merely to take formal leave, but also to give his final instructions to his friends and servants. Similarly, Acts xviii. 18, of Paul *taking leave* of the brethren at Corinth, and, presumably, giving them instructions at parting. In the New Testament the word is used invariably in the sense of bidding farewell. Mark vi. 46 is rendered by Rev. *after he had taken leave of them.* See note there, and compare Luke xiv. 33; 2 Cor. ii. 13.

62. **Put his hand to** (ἐπιβαλὼν ἐπί). Lit., *having laid his hand upon.*

Back (εἰς τὰ ὀπίσω). Lit., *to things behind.* "The figure is that of a man who, while engaged in labor, instead of keeping his eye on the furrow which he is drawing, looks behind at some object which attracts his interest. He is only half at work, and half-work only will be the result" (Godet).

Fit (εὔθετος). Lit., *well-placed:* adjusted.

CHAPTER X.

1–16. Peculiar to Luke.

1. **Appointed** (ἀνέδειξεν). Used by Luke only. Lit., *to lift up and shew*, as Acts i. 24: "*Shew* which one thou hast chosen." Hence to *proclaim any one elected* to an office. See on the kindred noun, *shewing*, ch. i. 80.

Other seventy. Wrong; for he had not appointed seventy previously. Rev., rightly, *seventy others*, with reference to the twelve.

2. **The harvest** (θερισμὸς). From θέρος, *summer* (compare θέρομαι, *to become warm*). Harvest, that which is gathered in summer. Wyc., *much ripe corn is, but few workmen.*

Pray. See on ch. viii. 38.

Send forth (ἐκβάλῃ). Lit., *drive* or *thrust* forth, implying the urgency of the mission. See on Mark i. 12.

3. **I send forth** (ἀποστέλλω). See on Matt. x. 2.

4. **Purse** (βαλλάντιον). Used by Luke only. For money.

Scrip (πήραν). For victuals. Rev., *wallet.*

Shoes. Not that they were to go unshod, but that they were not to carry a change of sandals. See Deut. xxix. 5; xxxiii. 25.

Salute no man. Oriental salutations are tedious and complicated. The command is suited to a rapid and temporary mission. Compare 2 Kings iv. 29. "These instructions were also intended to reprove another propensity which an Oriental can hardly resist, no matter how urgent his business. If he meets an acquaintance, he must stop and make an endless number of inquiries, and answer as many. If they come upon men making a bargain, or discussing any other matter, they must pause and intrude their own ideas, and enter keenly into the business, though it in nowise concerns them; and, more especially, an Oriental can never resist the temptation to assist when accounts are being settled or money counted out. The clink of coin has a positive fascination to them" (Thomson, "Land and Book").

5. **Peace to this house.** The usual oriental salutation. See Judg. xix. 20.

6. **If a son of peace be there.** So Rev. A Hebraism, referring to the character of the head of the house, and the tone of the household. Compare Job xxi. 9.

7. **The workman is worthy**, etc. See on Matt. x. 10.

11. **Dust** (κονιορτὸν). From κόνις, *dust*, and ὄρνυμι, *to stir up*. Strictly, dust that is *raised* by walking.

Cleaveth. See on Matt. xix. 5. Frequent in medical language of the uniting of wounds.

Wipe off (ἀπομάσσομεθα). See on Luke v. 2. Only here in New Testament.

13. **Mighty works.** See on Matt. xi. 20.

Sackcloth (σάκκῳ). From the Hebrew *sak:* what is *knotted* together; *net-shaped; coarsely woven.* It was made of goats' or camels' hair (Apoc. vi. 12), and was a material similar to that upon which Paul wrought in tent-making. The same word in Hebrew is used to describe a grain-sack, and this coarse material of which it is made (Gen. xlii. 25; Josh. ix. 4). So the Greek σαγή means a *pack* or *baggage.* The same root, according to some etymologists, appears in σαγήνη, *a drag-net* (see Matt. xiii. 47), and σάγος, Latin *sagum*, a *coarse, soldier's cloak.* It was employed for the rough garments for mourners (Esth. iv. 1; 1 Kings xxi. 27), in which latter passage the sackcloth is put next the flesh in token of extreme sorrow. Compare 2 Kings vi. 30; Job xvi. 15.

Ashes (σποδῷ). As a sign of mourning. Defiling one's self with dead things, as ashes or dirt, as a sign of sorrow, was common among the Orientals and Greeks. Thus Homer describes Achilles on hearing of the death of Patroclus:

> "Grasping in both hands
> The ashes of the hearth, he showered them o'er
> His head, and soiled with them his noble face."
>
> *Iliad*, xviii., 23.

And Priam, mourning for Hector:

> "In the midst the aged man
> Sat with a cloak wrapped round him, and much dust
> Strewn on his head and neck, which, when he rolled
> Upon the earth, he gathered with his hands."
>
> *Iliad*, xxiv., 162-5.

See 1 Sam. iv. 12; 2 Sam. i. 2; xiii. 19; Job ii. 12; Ezek. xvii. 30; Apoc. xviii. 19. In Judith iv. 14, 15, in the mourning over the ravages of the Assyrians, the priests minister at the altar, girded with sackcloth, and with ashes on their mitres. Sir Gardner Wilkinson, describing a funeral at Thebes, says: "Men, women, and children, with the body exposed above the waist, throw dust on their heads, or cover their faces with mud" ("Modern Egypt and Thebes"). Stifling with ashes was a Persian mode of punishment. Compare Apocrypha, 2 Macc. xiii. 5-7. Herodotus relates that Nitocris, an Egyptian queen, after having drowned the murderers of her brother, threw herself into an apartment full of ashes, in order to escape the vengeance of their friends.

14. **But** (πλὴν). Rev., *howbeit*. See on Matt. xi. 22.

15. **Which art exalted to heaven.** For ἡ, the article, rendered *which*, the best texts give μὴ, the interrogative particle; and for the participle *having been exalted*, the future *shalt be exalted*. Render, as Rev., *Shalt thou be exalted*, etc.?

Hell. Rev., *Hades*. See on Matt. xvi. 18.

16. **Despiseth** (ἀθετεῖ). See on Luke vii. 30, and compare Gal. ii. 21; iii. 15.

17. **The seventy.** "The fuller development of the new dispensation begins with the mission of the seventy, and not with the mission of the apostles. Its ground-work, from Luke's point of sight, is the symbolic evangelization of every nation upon earth, and not the restoration of the twelve tribes of Israel. According to Jewish tradition, there were seventy or seventy-two

different nations and tongues in the world. In ch. x. 1, some read *seventy-two* instead of *seventy*" (Westcott, "Int. to the Study of the Gospels").

18. **I beheld** (ἐθεώρουν). The verb denotes calm, intent, continuous contemplation of an object which remains before the spectator. So John i. 14, *we beheld*, implying that Jesus' stay upon earth, though brief, was such that his followers could calmly and leisurely contemplate his glory. Compare John ii. 23: "they *beheld* his miracles," *thoughtfully* and *attentively*. Here it denotes the rapt contemplation of a vision. The imperfect, *was beholding*, refers either to the time when the seventy were sent forth, or to the time of the triumphs which they are here relating. "While you were expelling the *subordinates*, I *was beholding* the *Master* fall" (Godet). The Revisers do not seem to have had any settled principle in their rendering of this word throughout the New Testament. See my article on the Revised New Testament, *Presbyterian Review*, October, 1881, p. 646 sq.

Satan. A transcription of the Hebrew word, derived from a verb *to lie in wait* or *oppose*. Hence *an adversary*. In this sense, of David, 1 Sam. xxix. 4, and of the angel who met Balaam, Num. xxii. 22. Compare Zech. iii. 1, 2; Job i., ii. *Διάβολος*, *devil*, is the more common term in the New Testament. In Apoc. xii. 9, both terms are applied to him.

As lightning. Describing vividly a dazzling brilliance suddenly quenched.

Fall (πεσόντα). Lit., *having fallen*. The aorist marks the *instantaneous* fall, like lightning.

21. The best texts omit *Jesus*.

Rejoiced. See on 1 Pet. i. 6.

In spirit. The best texts add τῷ ἁγίῳ, *the holy*, and render *in the Holy Spirit*.

I thank. See on Matt. xi. 25. From this point to ver. 25, compare Matt. xi. 25–27, and xiii. 16, 17.

Prudent. See on Matt. xi. 25.

22. **Are delivered** (παρεδόθη). See on Matt. xi. 27.

25. **Lawyer.** See on ch. vii. 30.

Tempted. See on *temptation*, Matt. vi. 13.

To inherit. See on *inheritance*, 1 Pet. i. 4.

Eternal (αἰώνιον). The word will be fully discussed in the second volume.

26. **Read.** See on ch. iv. 16.

27. **Thou shalt love,** etc. See on Mark xii. 30. Luke adds *strength.*

THE PARABLE OF THE GOOD SAMARITAN, 29–37. Peculiar to Luke.

29. **Willing** (θέλων). Rev., *desiring.* See on Matt. i. 19. I think this is stronger than *desiring;* rather, *determined.*

Neighbor (πλησίον). See on Matt. v. 43.

30. **Answering** (ὑπολαβὼν). Used by Luke only, and in this sense only here. See on ch. vii. 43. It means, strictly, *to take up;* and hence, of conversation, to take up another's discourse and reply.

Fell among. See on Jas. i. 2.

Thieves (λῃσταῖς). See on Matt. xxvi. 55; and Luke xxiii. 39–43. These were not petty *stealers*, but men of violence, as was shown by their treatment of the traveller. The road from Jerusalem to Jericho passed through a wilderness (Josh. xvi. 1), which was so notorious for robberies and murders that a portion of it was called "the red or bloody way," and was protected by a fort and a Roman garrison.

Stripped. Not of his clothing only, but of all that he had.

Wounded (*πληγὰς ἐπιθέντες*). Lit., *having laid on blows*. *Blows* or *stripes* is the usual sense of the word in the New Testament. See ch. xii. 48; Acts xvi. 23. It has the metaphorical sense of *plagues* in Apoc. xv. 1, 6, 8, etc.

Half dead (*ἡμιθανῆ τυγχάνοντα*). The full force of the expression cannot be rendered into English. The word *τυγχάνοντα* throws an element of *chance* into the case. Lit., *happening to be half dead;* or "leaving him half dead, *as it chanced;*" his condition being a matter of unconcern to these robbers. The word *ἡμιθανῆ*, *half dead*, occurs nowhere else in the New Testament. The best texts, however, omit *τυγχάνοντα*.

31. **By chance** (*κατὰ συγκυρίαν*). Only here in New Testament. The word means, literally, a *coincidence*. By coincidence of circumstances.

There came down. Imperfect, *was going down*, as Rev.

Priest. The Talmudists said that there were almost as many priests at Jericho as at Jerusalem.

Passed by on the other side (*ἀντιπαρῆλθεν*). The verb occurs only here and ver. 32.

32. **Came and looked.** Rev., *saw*. Seeming to imply that the Levite went farther than the priest in coming near to the wounded man, and, having observed his condition, passed on.

33. **Came where he was.** There is a strong contrast with the other cases, and a downright heartiness in the words, κατ' αὐτὸν, *down to him.* The Levite had come κατὰ τόπον, "down to the *place.*"

34. **Bound up** (κατέδησεν). Only here in New Testament.

Wounds (τραύματα). Only here in New Testament.

Pouring in (ἐπιχέων). Rather *upon* (ἐπί), as Rev. Wine to cleanse, and oil to soothe. See Isa. i. 6.

Oil and wine. Usual remedies for sores, wounds, etc. Hippocrates prescribes for ulcers, "Bind with soft wool, and sprinkle with wine and oil."

Beast (κτῆνος). Perhaps akin to κτῆμα, a *possession;* since animals anciently constituted wealth, so that a piece of property and a beast were synonymous terms.

Inn (πανδοχεῖον). Only here in New Testament. From πᾶν, *all,* and δέχομαι, *to receive:* a place of common reception. See on *inn,* ch. ii. 7. Remains of two *khans,* or inns, on the road between Jericho and Jerusalem are mentioned by modern travellers. Porter ("Handbook of Syria and Palestine") speaks of one about a mile from Bethany, and another farther on, at the most dangerous part of the road, an extensive, ruined caravanserai, called *Khan el Almah,* situated on the top of a bleak ridge. Concerning the former, Hepworth Dixon ("Holy Land") says: "About midway in the descent from Bethany to Jericho, in a position commanding a view of the road above and below, . . . on the very spot where search would be made for them, if no such ruins were suspected of existing, stands a pile of stones, archways, lengths of wall, which the wandering Arabs call *Khan Houdjar,* and still make use of as their own resting-place for the night. These ruins are those of a noble inn; the lewan, the fountain, and the court, being plainly traceable in the ruins."

35. **Two pence.** About thirty-five cents. See on Matt. xx. 2.

I will repay. The *I* is expressed (ἐγὼ), and is emphatic. Trouble *him* not for the reckoning; *I* will repay.

36. **Was neighbor** (πλησίον γεγονέναι). More correctly, *has become neighbor*. Jesus throws himself back to the time of the story. So Rev., *proved* neighbor. "The neighbor Jews *became* strangers. The stranger Samaritan *became* neighbor to the wounded traveller" (Alford).

37. **He that shewed mercy on him.** Rather *with* him (μετά): dealt *with* him as with a brother. The lawyer avoids the hated word *Samaritan*.

THE VISIT AT THE HOUSE IN BETHANY, 38–42. Peculiar to Luke.

38. **Received** (ὑπεδέξατο). From ὑπο, *under*, and δέχομαι, to *receive*. Received him *under* her roof. Martha is marked as the head of the household. It was *her* house. She received the guest, and was chiefly busy with the preparations for his entertainment (ver. 40).

39. **Sat** (παρακαθέσθεισα). Only here in New Testament. Lit., *sat beside* (παρά).

40. **Was cumbered** (περιεσπᾶτο). Only here in New Testament. The Rev. might better have inserted in the text the marginal rendering, *was distracted*. The verb means, literally, *to draw from around* (περί). Martha's attention, instead of centring *round* Jesus, was drawn hither and thither. The περί, *around*, in composition with the verb, is followed immediately by another περί, "*about* much serving."

Came to him (ἐπιστᾶσα). Came *up* to him, as Rev., suddenly stopping in her hurry.

Hath left (κατέλιπεν). The aorist, as Rev., *did leave*, indicating that she had been assisting before she was drawn off by Jesus' presence. Some read κατέλειπεν, the imperfect, *was leaving*.

Help (συναντιλάβηται). The verb consists of three elements: λαμβάνω, *to take hold*; σύν, *together with*; ἀντί, *reciprocally*—doing her part as Martha does hers. It might be paraphrased, therefore, *take hold and do her part along with me*. It occurs only here and Rom. viii. 26, of the Spirit *helping* our infirmities, where all the elements of the verb are strikingly exemplified.

41. **Thou art anxious** (μεριμνᾷς). See on Matt. vi. 25.

Troubled (θορυβάζῃ). From θόρυβος, *tumult*. *Anxious* denotes the *inward* uneasiness: *troubled*, the *outward* confusion and bustle.

CHAPTER XI.

2–4. Compare Matt. vi. 9–13.

3. **Daily bread** (τὸν ἄρτον τὸν ἐπιούσιον). Great differences of opinion exist among commentators as to the strict meaning of the word rendered *daily*. The principal explanations are the following:

1. From ἐπιέναι, *to come on*. Hence,
   - *a.* The *coming*, or to-morrow's bread.
   - *b.* *Daily*: regarding the days in their future succession.
   - *c.* *Continual*.
   - *d.* *Yet to come*, applied to Christ, the Bread of life, who is to come hereafter.
2. From ἐπί and οὐσία, *being*. Hence,
   - *a.* *For our sustenance* (physical), and so *necessary*.
   - *b.* *For our essential life* (spiritual).
   - *c.* *Above all being*, hence *pre-eminent*, *excellent*.
   - *d.* *Abundant*.

It would be profitless to the English reader to go into the discussion. A scholar is quoted as saying that the term is "the rack of theologians and grammarians." A satisfactory discussion must assume the reader's knowledge of Greek. Those who are interested in the question will find it treated by Tholuck ("Sermon on the Mount"), and also very exhaustively by Bishop Lightfoot ("On a Fresh Revision of the New Testament"). The latter adopts the derivation from ἐπιέναι, *to come on*, and concludes by saying, "the familiar rendering, *daily*, which has prevailed uninterruptedly in the Western Church from the beginning, is a fairly adequate representation of the original; nor, indeed, does the English language furnish any one word which would answer the purpose so well." The rendering in the margin of Rev. is, *our bread for the coming day*. It is objected to this that it contradicts the Lord's precept in Matt. vi. 34, not to be anxious for the morrow. But the word does not necessarily mean the *morrow*. "If the prayer were said in the evening, no doubt it would mean *the following day*; but supposing it to be used before dawn, it would designate the day then breaking" (the *coming* day). "And further, if the command not to be anxious is tantamount to a prohibition against prayer for the object about which we are forbidden to be anxious, then not only must we not pray for to-morrow's food, but we must not pray for food at all; since the Lord bids us (Matt. vi. 25) not to be anxious for our *life*" (Lightfoot, condensed).

4. **Forgive.** See on ch. iii. 3; Jas. v. 15.

Sins (ἁμαρτίας). See on Matt. i. 21. Compare *debts*, Matt. vi. 12.

That is indebted. Matthew's *debts* appears here.

Lead (εἰσενέγκῃς). Rev. gives "*bring* us not," which, besides being a more accurate rendering of the word (εἰς, *into*, φέρω, *to bear* or *bring*), avoids the invidious hint of *seducing* or *enticing* which attaches to *lead*. James tells us that God does not tempt any man (i. 13); but the circumstances of a man's life often, indeed *always*, involve possibilities of temptation. A caution is written even over the door of God's own house (Eccl. v. 1). God also sends trials to prove and chasten us; but something may change the salutary power of trial into the corrupting power of evil solicitation; and that something, as James tells us (i. 14), is our own evil desire. *God* tempteth no man; but "every man is tempted when he is drawn away of his own lust and enticed." We pray, therefore, "suffer us not to be drawn away by our own lusts: keep us out of the power of our own evil hearts. Thou knowest our frame, and rememberest that we are dust. Remember our weakness. What thou imposest we would not shun. What thou dost not impose, keep us from seeking. Forbid that our evil desire should convert our temptable condition into actual temptation. Keep us out of situations in which, so far as we can judge, it would be beyond our present strength to keep from sinning." It is not a coward's prayer. No man is a coward for being afraid of his own heart. It marks the highest quality of courage to know what to be afraid of and to fear it. To pray that God will not bring us within the *possibility* of temptation, would be to ignore our manhood, or to pray to be taken out of the world. But we *may* pray, and *will surely* pray, the more keenly conscious we become of the weakness of our nature, that God will not suffer the trials of life to become temptations to evil.

Temptation. See on Matt. vi. 13.

THE PARABLE OF THE FRIEND AT MIDNIGHT, 5–9. Peculiar to Luke.

5. **Set before.** See on ch. ix. 16.

7. **My children are with me in bed.** "A whole family—parents, children, and servants—sleep in the same room" (Thomson, "Land and Book"). Tynd., *my servants are with me in the chamber*.

8. **Importunity** (ἀναίδειαν). Only here in New Testament. A very striking word to describe persistence. Lit., *shamelessness.* As related to prayer, it is illustrated in the case of Abraham's intercession for Sodom (Gen. xviii. 23–33); and of the Syro-Phoenician woman (Matt. xv. 22–28).

9. **Ask** (αἰτεῖτε). The word for the asking of an inferior (Acts xii. 20; iii. 2); and hence of man from God (Matt. vii. 7; Jas i. 5). Christ never uses the word of his own asking from the Father, but always ἐρωτῶ, as asking on equal terms. Martha shows her low conception of his person when she uses the term of his asking God (John xi. 22).*

Ask, seek, knock. "The three repetitions of the command are more than mere repetitions; since to seek is more than to ask, and to knock than to seek" (Trench, "Parables").

11. **Of any of you** (τίνα). The A. V. renders as though the pronoun were indefinite; but it is interrogative and commences the sentence. Rev., therefore, rightly, *of which of you that is a father*, etc.

13. **Being** (ὑπάρχοντες). See on Jas. ii. 15.

Heavenly Father. Lit., *the Father, he who is from Heaven.*

14, 15, 17–23. Compare Matt. xii. 22–37.

14. **Dumb** (κωφόν). See on Matt. ix. 32.

15. **Beelzebub.** See on Matt. x. 25.

16. **Tempting.** See on *temptation*, Matt. vi. 13.

Sign. See on Matt. xi. 20.

17. **Thoughts** (διανοήματα). Only here in New Testament. Primarily with a sense of *intent, purpose.*

---

* Further examination has convinced me that this distinction is unfounded. See Prof. Ezra Abbot's "Critical Essays."

A house divided against itself falleth (οἶκος ἐπὶ οἶκον πίπτει). Some make this an enlargement on the previous sentence—a more detailed description of the general *is brought to desolation*, and render *house falleth upon house.* So Rev., margin. It might be taken metaphorically: the divided kingdom is brought to desolation, and its families and households in their party strifes are brought to ruin. Wyc., *and an house shall fall on an house.* Tynd., *one house shall fall upon another.*

18. **Satan.** See on ch. x. 18.

Be divided. See on Matt. xii. 26.

20. **Is come upon you.** See on Matt. xii. 28.

21. **A strong man** (ὁ ἰσχυρὸς). It has the article: *the* strong man. So Rev. See on Matt. xii. 29.

Armed (καθωπλισμένος). *Fully* armed: *down* (κατά) from head to heel.

His palace (ἑαυτοῦ αὐλήν). Lit., his *own.* 'Αυλή is strictly the open *court* in front of a house: later, the court round which the house is built, and so applied to the house generally, as our *door* or *roof.* Rev., *court;* for there, in the open space, commanding the doors, he would mount guard.

22. **A stronger.** Also with the article: *the* stronger.

All his armor (τὴν πανοπλίαν). Wrong; for the armor is regarded as a whole—*the panoply*—which is a transcript of this word. Rightly, Rev., *his whole armor.* Tynd., *his harness.*

Spoils (τὰ σκῦλα). See on Mark v. 35. Compare on *goods*, Matt. xii. 29.

24. **Dry places** (ἀνύδρων τόπων). Rev., more literally, *waterless.* The haunts of evil spirits (Isa. xiii. 21, 22; xxxiv. 14).

By *satyrs* in these two passages are meant goblins shaped like goats, which were sacrificed to by some of the Israelites (Lev. xvii. 7; 2 Chron. xi. 15); a remnant of the Egyptian worship of Mendes or Pan, who, under the figure of a goat, was worshipped by the Egyptians as the fertilizing principle in nature. In Isa. xxxiv. 14, it is said "the *screech-owl* shall rest there." This is rendered in margin of A. V. and in the Rev., Old Testament, the *night-monster* (Hebrew, *Lilith*); and by Cheyne (Isaiah) *night-fairy*. The reference is to a popular superstition that Lilith, Adam's first wife, forsook him and became a demon which murdered young children and haunted desert places.

Rest. See on Matt. xi. 28.

26. **Taketh to him** (*παραλαμβάνει*). See on Matt. iv. 5.

Seven. Emphatic: "taketh spirits, *seven* of them."

More wicked. See on ch. iii. 19; Mark vii. 21.

Dwell (*κατοικεῖ*). Settle *down* (*κατά*) to make their *dwelling* (*οἶκος*) there.

27. **Blessed,** etc. "She speaks well, but womanly" (Bengel).

29–36. Compare Matt. xii. 38–45.

29. **Were gathered thick together** (*ἐπαθροιζομένων*). The present participle; and therefore, as Rev., *were gathering together unto him*, or *upon* him (*ἐπί*). Only here in New Testament.

Evil. See on *adulterous*. Matt. xii. 39.

30. **A sign to the Ninevites.** Compare Matt. xii. 40.

31. **Shall rise up** (*ἐγερθήσεται*). From the dead.

A greater (πλεῖον). Lit., *something more.* See on Matt. xii. 6. Wyc., *here is more than Solomon.*

32. **Shall rise up** (ἀναστήσονται). This verb is also used of rising from the dead, and that is implied here; but the meaning is, *shall appear as witness.* Hence Rev., *stand up.* See on Matt. xii. 41.

Preaching (κήρυγμα). The proclamation. See on 2 Pet. ii. 5.

33. **Candle.** Properly, *lamp.*

Secret place (κρυπτὴν). Rather, a *cellar* or *crypt,* which latter is the Greek word transcribed.

The bushel. See on Matt. v. 15.

Candlestick. Properly *stand.* See on Matt. v. 15.

Which enter in (εἰσπορευόμενοι). Better with the continuous force of the present participle, *are entering in* from time to time.

Light (φέγγος). The word occurs in only two other places: Matt. xxiv. 29; Mark xiii. 24, on which see notes.

34. **Single—full of light.** See on Matt. vi. 22.

35. **The light that is in thee.** Lit., *the light, that, namely, which is in thee;* thus emphasizing the inward light. See on Matt. vi. 23.

36. **The bright shining of a candle** (ὁ λύχνος τῇ ἀστραπῇ). More correctly, as Rev., *the lamp with its bright shining.* Ἀστραπή means *lightning:* see ch. x. 18; and that is the usual meaning in classical Greek, though it occurs, rarely, of the light of a lamp. It is used here to emphasize the idea of moral illumination.

37. **Besought** (ἐρωτᾷ). Too strong. Better, as Rev., *asketh*. The present tense.

Dine (ἀριστήσῃ). See on *dinner*, Matt. xxii. 4. The morning meal, immediately after the return from morning prayers in the synagogue.

38. **Washed** (ἐβαπτίσθη). See on Mark vii. 4.

39. **Platter** (πίνακος). The word rendered *charger* in Matt. xiv. 8, on which see note. Compare, also, παροψίς, *platter*, Matt. xxiii. 25.

41. **Such things as ye have** (τὰ ἐνόντα). Only here in New Testament. Commentators differ as to the meaning, but generally reject that of the A. V. Rev., *those things which are within*. The meaning is, give alms of the *contents* of the cups and platters. Jesus is insisting upon *inward* righteousness as against pharisaic externalism, and says: "Your virtue consists in washing the *outside*, and making a respectable appearance. Cultivate rather the loving, brotherly spirit of *inward* righteousness, which will prompt you to give of the food which the vessels contain (that which is within) to your suffering brother." "Do you think it is enough to wash your hands before eating? There is a surer means. Let some poor man partake of your meats and wines" (Godet). So Bengel, Meyer, Alford. Compare Matt. ix. 13; Hos. vi. 6. Wyc., *That thing that is over* (i.e., remaining in the dishes) *give ye alms*.*

42. **Ye tithe** (ἀποδεκατοῦτε). *Tithe* is *tenth*. See on Matt. xxiii. 23.

Rue (πήγανον). Probably from πήγνυμι, *to make fast*; because of its thick, fleshy leaves. Matthew has *anise*. See on xxiii. 23.

---

* The Rev. is not open to the charge of Mr. Yonge (Expositor, 2d Series, v., 318) of "construing through a brick wall." The rendering is quite "intelligible;" quite as much so as Mr. Y.'s "cleanse the within by alms."

Herb (λάχανον). See on Mark iv. 32. Wyc. has *wort*, originally the general term for a plant. Hence *colewort*, *liverwort*, and similar words. Compare the German *wurz*, *root* or *herb*.

43. **Pharisees** (τοῖς Φαρισαίοις). Luke's form of expression differs from that of Matthew, who says, "*ye Pharisees;* while Luke has "woe unto you, *the* Pharisees," marking them by the article as a well-known religious body.

44. **Tombs which appear not** (τὰ μνημεῖα τὰ ἄδηλα). Lit., *the tombs, the unseen ones*. The word ἄδηλος, *unapparent*, occurs only here and 1 Cor. xiv. 8, of the trumpet giving an *uncertain* sound.

That walk over (περιπατοῦντες). The participle, and without the article; and therefore better, *as they walk;* walk *about* (περί) on their daily business. In Matthew the sepulchres are whitened, that men may see them and avoid ceremonial defilement. Here they are not seen, and men walking on them are unconsciously defiled. See on Matt. xxiii. 27.

45. **Reproachest** (ὑβρίζεις). The lawyer converts Jesus' *reproach* (see Mark xvi. 14, *upbraided*) into an *insult;* the word meaning to *outrage* or *affront*.

Us also (καὶ ἡμᾶς). Or perhaps better, *even us*, the learned.

46. **Also** (καὶ). Emphatic. "*Even* or *also* unto you lawyers, woe." Note the article as in the address to the Pharisees (ver. 43): You, *the* lawyers.

Ye lade. Compare *heavy laden*, Matt. xi. 28.

Grievous to be borne (δυσβάστακτα). Only here and Matt. xxiii. 4.

Touch (προσψαύετε). Only here in New Testament. A technical term in medicine for feeling gently a sore part of the body, or the pulse. Matt. xxiii. 4, has κινῆσαι, *move*.

47. **Ye build.** Or *are building*, carrying on the work now. See on Matt. xxiii. 29.

Tombs of the prophets. See on Matt. xxiii. 29.

48. **Ye bear witness that ye allow** (μάρτυρές ἐστε καὶ συνευδοκεῖτε). Rev., more correctly, *ye are witnesses and consent.* The compound verb means "give your *full* approval." Ye *think* (δοκεῖτε); *favorably* (εὖ); *along with them* (σύν).

51. **The altar and the temple.** Οἴκου, *temple*, lit., *house*, is equivalent to ναοῦ, *sanctuary* (Rev.), in Matt. xxiii. 35. The altar is the altar of burnt-offering. See on Matt. iv. 5; and compare 2 Chron. xxiv. 18–21.

53. **To urge him vehemently** (δεινῶς ἐνέχειν). See on Mark vi. 19.

Provoke to speak (ἀποστοματίζειν). Only here in New Testament. From ἀπό, *from*, and στόμα, *the mouth*. Originally to dictate to a pupil what he is to learn by heart. Thus Plato: "When the grammar-master dictated (ἀποστοματίζοι) to you" ("Euthydemus," 276). Hence to catechize, with the idea of putting words into Christ's mouth, and making him say what they wanted him to say.

54. **Lying in wait—to catch** (ἐνεδρεύοντες—θηρεῦσαι). Metaphors from hunting.

CHAPTER XII.

1. **An innumerable multitude** (τῶν μυριάδων τοῦ ὄχλου). The word μυριάς strictly means *a number of ten thousand.* It is our word *myriad.* Hence, generally, of any countless number.

First of all. Many connect this with what follows: "first of all beware," etc.

Leaven. See on Matthew xiii. 33.

Which (ἥτις). Classifying the leaven: which belongs to the category of hypocrisy.

Hypocrisy. See on *hypocrites*, Matt. xxiii. 13.

2. **Covered up** (συγκεκαλυμμένον). Only here in New Testament: implying *close* concealment.

3. **Closets** (ταμείοις). The word has the same root as τέμνω, to *cut* or *divide*, and means an apartment where supplies are divided and apportioned: a *treasury*, *magazine*, and therefore a secret and well-guarded place. There the *steward* (ταμίας), the *distributor*, has his seat.

House-tops. See on Matt. xxiv. 17.

4. **Unto you, my friends** (ὑμῖν τοῖς φίλοις μου). See on *Pharisees* and *lawyers*, ch. xi. 43, 46. Not an *address*, "O my friends," but, "unto you, *the* friends of me."

Be not afraid of (μὴ φοβηθῆτε ἀπὸ). Lit., "fear not *from*;" i.e., from the hands of.

5. **I will forewarn** (ὑποδείξω). Rev., *warn*. See on *warned*, ch. iii. 7.

Hell. See on Matt. v. 22.

6. **Sparrows.** See on Matt. x. 29.

Fall. See on Matt. x. 29.

7. **Confess me.** Lit., "confess *in* me." See on Matt. x. 32.

10. **A word** (λόγον). Distinguished from *blaspheme*, which follows. A word against the poor and humble Son of Man might, as Godet observes, have proceeded from a sincerely pious Jew, under the influence of his early education, which taught him to regard Jesus as an enthusiast or even as an im-

postor. The sin of the Jews was in rejecting and resisting the power of the Spirit of Pentecost. Pardon was offered them there for the sin of crucifying the Lord (see Acts ii. 38–40, and compare Acts iii. 17–19).

11. **Answer** (*ἀπολογήσησθε*). See on 1 Pet. iii. 15.

14. **Made** (*κατέστησεν*). Appointed or constituted.

15. **Beware of** (*φυλάσσεσθε ἀπὸ*). Lit., *guard yourselves from.*

17. **Bestow** (*συνάξω*). Lit., *gather together.*

18. **Fruits** (*γενήματα*). Some texts, however, read **τὸν σῖτον**, *my corn.* So Rev.

19. **Soul** (*ψυχή*). See on Mark xii. 30.

Take thine ease. See on Matt. xi. 28.

20. **Fool** (*ἄφρων*). Senseless. In Xenophon's "Memorabilia," Socrates, addressing Aristodemus, says, "Which do you take to be the more worthy of admiration, those who make images *without sense* (*ἀφρονά*) or motion, or those who make *intelligent* and active creations?" (1, iv., 4). Sometimes, also, in the sense of *crazed, frantic*, but never in New Testament.

Is required (*ἀπαιτοῦσιν*). Lit., *they require;* i.e., the messengers of God. The indefiniteness is impressive.

Whose shall those things be which thou hast provided? The Greek order puts that first which was uppermost in the rich man's thought—*his accumulations:* "and *the things which thou hast provided* (Rev., *prepared*), whose shall they be?" God does not say, "the things which thou *hast* or *possessest.*" The whole question of the tenure of his property is opened for the rich man. He had said *my* fruits and *my* goods. Now his proprietorship is ignored. They are not his. Whose shall they be? He is to be dispossessed at once. Plato relates how Pluto complained to Zeus that the souls of the dead found their way to the wrong places, because the judged have their clothes on, and evil souls are clothed in fair bodies, so that the judges, who also have their clothes on and their souls veiled by their mortal part, are deceived. Zeus replies: "In the first place, I will deprive men of the foreknowledge of death which they now have. In the second place, they shall be entirely stripped before they are judged, for they shall be judged when they are dead; and the judge, too, shall be naked; that is to say, dead. He, with his naked soul, shall pierce into the other naked soul, and they shall die suddenly and be deprived of all their kindred, and leave their brave attire strewn upon the earth" ("Gorgias," 523).

22. **Take no thought.** See on Matt. vi. 25.

24. **Consider.** See on Matt. vii. 3.

Storehouse (*ταμεῖον*). See on ver. 3.

25. **Stature** (*ἡλικίαν*). The original meaning of the word is *time of life, age.* So, commonly, in classical Greek. See, also, John ix. 21, 23; Heb. xi. 11. The other meaning, *stature,* also occurs. Herodotus speaks of one who was of the same *height* (*ἡλικιήν*) with another (iii. 16). But both the usage and the connection are in favor of the meaning *age.* A measure of time is sometimes represented by a measure of length, as in Ps. xxxix. 5; but, most of all, the addition of a cubit (a foot and a half) to one's *stature* would not be a *small* one, as the text implies (*that which is least*), but a very large one. Moreover, Christ is speaking of food and clothing, the object of which is to foster and prolong *life.* Rev., *age,* in margin.

27. **How they grow.** Some texts omit *they grow,* and read *how they toil not,* etc.

Toil—spin (κοπιᾷ—νήθει). Some read, instead of *toil*, ὑφαίνει, *weave.*

28. **Which is to-day in the field.** Construe *in the field* with *the grass;* and render *is* absolutely: *exists, lives.* So Rev., *the grass in the field which to-day is.*

Oven (κλίβανον). Strictly, a covered earthen vessel, wider at bottom than at top, in which bread was baked by putting hot embers round it. The regular oven or furnace is ἰπνός. Herodotus, speaking of the papyrus-plant (*byblus*), the lower portion of which is used for food, says, "Such as wish to enjoy the byblus in full perfection, bake it first in a *closed vessel* (ἐν κλιβάνῳ), heated to a glow" (ii., 92).

And seek not what ye, etc. *Ye* is emphatic: "and *ye*, seek not what," etc.

29. **Be ye of doubtful mind** (μετεωρίζεσθε). Only here in New Testament. The verb primarily means to *raise to a height; buoy up,* as with false hopes; and so to *unsettle,* or *excite,* or keep in fluctuation. Thus Thucydides says of the war between Athens and Sparta: "All Hellas was *excited* (μετέωρος) by the coming conflict between the two chief cities" (ii., 8).

33. **Bags** (βαλλάντια). From βάλλω, *to throw.* Something into which money and other things are *cast.* Rev., *purses.* See on ch. x. 4. Wyc., *satchels.*

Moth. Compare Jas. v. 2.

36. **Shall return** (ἀναλύσῃ). The verb means, originally, to *unloose:* so of vessels, to unloose their moorings and go to sea. Of *departing* generally. This is its sense in the only other passage where it occurs, Philip. i. 23, "having a desire to *depart,* or *break up;* the metaphor being drawn from breaking up an encampment." Compare *departure* (ἀναλύσεως), 2 Tim. iv. 6. The rendering *return* is a kind of inference from this: when he shall *leave the wedding* and return.

Wedding (τῶν γάμων). Properly, the marriage-*feast.* See on Matt. xxii. 2.

37. **Watching.** See on Mark xiii. 35.

Gird himself. As a servant girding up his loose garments to wait on the table.

Serve. See on *minister*, Matt. xx. 26.

38. **Second watch.** See on Mark xiii. 35.

39. **What hour** (ποίᾳ ὥρᾳ). See on Matt. xxiv. 42.

Would come. Lit., *cometh.* See on Matt. xxiv. 43.

Broken through. See on Matt. vi. 19.

42. **That faithful and wise steward.** Lit., *that faithful steward, the wise man.*

Household (θεραπείας). From its original meaning of *waiting on*, *attendance* (Luke ix. 11), it comes to mean *the retinue* of attendants; the body of household servants.

Portion of meat (σιτομέτριον). Lit., *measure of food.*

In due season. At the appointed time for distributing rations. See on Matt. xxiv. 45.

45. **Delayeth.** The emphatic word, since the thought of the lord's *delay* and of the *postponement* of the reckoning is uppermost in the servant's thought.

46. **Unbelievers** (ἀπίστων). Much better as Rev., *the unfaithful;* for it is of *fidelity*, not of *faith*, that Christ is speaking. Wyc., *unfaithful men.*

48. **Stripes.** See on ch. x. 30.

Commit. See on *set before*, ch. ix. 16.

49. **Fire.** A spiritual impulse which shall result in the divisions described in the following verses.

50. **Am I straitened.** See on ch. iv. 38, and compare 2 Cor. v. 14; Philip. i. 23. Wyc., *constrained.*

53. **The father shall be divided,** etc. But the verb is in the plural. Rightly, as Rev., "*They* shall be divided, the father against the son," etc.

Daughter-in-law. See on Matt. x. 35.

54. **A cloud.** With the definite article, *the* cloud, which you so often see.

There cometh a shower. Or, *a shower is coming.* See on Jas. v. 7.

It is (γίνεται). Better, as Rev., *it cometh to pass.*

55. **Heat** (καύσων). See on Jas. i. 10; Matt. xx. 12.

Discern (δοκιμάζειν). See on *trial* and *tried*, 1 Pet. i. 7. It means here *test* or *prove.* You can test and prove the weather by your signs; but you cannot apply the proof which lies in the signs of the times. Rev., *interpret*, gives the idea. Wyc., *prove.*

57. **Of yourselves.** In the exercise of your ordinary habits of observation which you apply to the heavens.

58. **When thou goest** (ὡς γὰρ ὑπάγεις). The A. V. does not translate γὰρ, *for.* Rev., correctly, *for as thou art going.* Their own judgment should show them the necessity of repentance toward God; and this duty is urged under the figure of a debtor who meets his creditor in the way, and whose best policy it is to make terms on the spot.

As thou art in the way. Emphatic, standing first in the Greek order: "*On the way* give diligence."

Hale (κατασύρῃ). Drag. Compare *haul.* Only here in New Testament.

Officer (πράκτορι). From πράσσω, *to effect* or *accomplish;* to bring things to an issue, and hence to *exact.* The name *praktor* was given at Athens to an officer charged with the collection of taxes; hence an *exactor*, as Rev., in margin. Only here in New Testament.

Mite (λεπτὸν). See on Mark xii. 42.

CHAPTER XIII.

4. **Sinners** (ὀφειλέται). Lit., *debtors.* Possibly with reference to the figure at the close of the last chapter. Compare Matt. v. 25; vi. 12; xviii. 24; Luke xi. 4.

7. **These three years I come.** The best texts insert ἀφ' οὗ, *from which,* or *since.* "It is three years *from the time at which* I came."

Cut it down (ἔκκοψον). Rather, "cut it *out*" (ἐκ) from among the other trees and the vines.

Why cumbereth it. The A. V. omits the very important καὶ, *also* (Rev.), which, as Trench observes, is the key-word of the sentence. Besides being barren in itself, it *also* injures the soil. "Not only is it unfruitful, but it draws away the juices which the vines would extract from the earth, intercepts the sun, and occupies room" (Bengel). The verb *cumbereth* (καταργεῖ) means to *make of no effect.* So Rom. iii. 3, 31; Gal. iii. 17. *Cumbereth* expresses the meaning in a very general and comprehensive way. The specific elements included in it are expressed by Bengel above. De Wette, *makes the land unfruitful.* See on *barren and unfruitful*, 2 Pet. i. 8.

9. **And if it bear fruit, well; and if not, then after that.** Join *after that* with *bear fruit.* "If it bear fruit *for the future* (εἰς τὸ μέλλον, Rev., *thenceforth*), well; but if not, thou shalt cut it down." Trench ("Parables") cites an Arabian writer's receipt for curing a palm-tree of barrenness. "Thou must take a hatchet, and go to the tree with a friend, unto whom thou sayest, 'I will cut down this tree, for it is unfruitful.' He answers, 'Do not so, this year it will certainly bear fruit.' But the other says, 'It must needs be—it must be hewn down;' and gives the stem of the tree three blows with the back of the hatchet. But the other restrains him, crying, 'Nay, do it not, thou wilt certainly have fruit from it this year, only have patience with it, and be not overhasty in cutting it down; if it still refuses to bear fruit, then cut it down.' Then will the tree that year be certainly fruitful and bear abundantly." Trench adds that this story appears to be widely spread in the East.

Thou shalt cut it down. The vine-dresser does not say, "*I* will cut," but refers that to the master.

11. **Spirit of infirmity.** A spirit which caused infirmity. An evil demon, see ver. 16, though it is not certain that it was a case of possession. The details of the disease, and the noting of the time of its continuance, are characteristic of a physician's narrative.

Bowed together (*συγκύπτουσα*). Only here in New Testament.

Lift herself up (*ἀνακύψαι*). Only here in New Testament, unless John viii. 7–10 be accepted as genuine. Used by Galen of strengthening the vertebrae of the spine.

12. **Thou art loosed** (*ἀπολέλυσαι*). The only passage in the New Testament where the word is used of disease. Medical writers use it of releasing from disease, relaxing tendons, and taking off bandages.

13. **She was made straight** (ἀνορθώθη). The verb occurs, Acts xv. 16, of *setting up* the tabernacle of David, and Heb. xii. 12, of *lifting up* the hands which hang down.

15. **Loose** (λύει). Compare *thou art loosed*, ver. 12.

Stall. See on ch. ii. 7.

16. **Satan.** "True to its principle of contrast, this book gives Satan a prominent position" (Abbot). See ch. iv. 13; x. 18; xxii. 3, 31. See Introduction.

17. **Were ashamed.** Rev., more correctly, *were put to shame.*

Glorious things. See on Matt. xi. 10.

Were done (γινομένοις). Lit., *are being done*, denoting their being then in progress.

19. **His garden.** Properly, as Rev., *his own* (ἑαυτοῦ) where he could personally observe and tend it.

Great tree. The best texts omit *great.*

Birds. See on ch. ix. 58.

Branches (κλάδοις). See on Mark xi. 8.

21. **Leaven.** See on Matt. xii. 33.

24. **Strive.** Used only by Luke and Paul, except John xviii. 36. Originally to contend for a prize in the public games; and thus conveying a sense of *struggle.* The kindred noun, ἀγωνία, *agony*, is used of Christ's struggle in Gethsemane (ch. xxii. 44). Compare 1 Tim. vi. 12; 2 Tim. iv. 7.

Strait gate (στενῆς θύρας). Rev., *narrow door.* See on Matt. vii. 13. The *door of a house*, and not a *gate*, is meant (ver. 25). In Matt. vii. 13, where the image is of a *gate* opening into a *way*, πύλη, *gate*, is used.

25. **When once** (ἀφ' οὗ). Lit., *from the time that.* Compare ver. 7. Some editors connect this with the previous sentence: "Shall not be able *when once*," etc.

Whence (πόθεν). Of what family. Ye do not belong to *my* household. See John vii. 27: "We know *whence* he (Jesus) is;" *i.e.*, we know his birthplace and family.

26. **In thy presence** (ἐνώπιον σοῦ). Not as beloved and familiar guests. Compare *with you* (μεθ' ὑμῶν), Matt. xxvi. 29.

27. **I know not whence.** "The sentence is fixed, but it is repeated with emphasis" (Bengel).

Shall sit down (ἀνακλιθήσονται). Sit down *at table.* Jesus casts his thought into a familiar Jewish image. According to the Jewish idea, one of the main elements of the happiness of the Messianic kingdom was the privilege of participating in splendid festive entertainments along with the patriarchs of the nation. With this accords ver. 30, in allusion to places at the banquet. Compare ch. xiv. 7–9; Matt. xxiii. 6.

31. **Day.** The best texts read *hour.*

Will kill (θέλει ἀποκτεῖναι). As in so many cases the A. V. renders as the future of the verb *to kill;* whereas there are two distinct verbs; to *will* or *determine*, and *to kill.* The meaning is, Herod *willeth* or *is determined* to kill thee. Rev., *would fain*, seems rather feeble.

32. **That fox.** Herod. Describing his cunning and cowardice.

Cures (ἰάσεις). Used by Luke only.

I shall be perfected (τελειοῦμαι). The present tense: "the present of the certain future" (Meyer). The meaning is, *I come to an end: I have done.* Expositors differ greatly. Some interpret, "I end *my career of healing*," etc.; others, *my life.*

33. **It cannot be** (οὐκ ἐνδέχεται). The verb means to *accept* or *admit;* so that the sense is, "it is not *admissible* that." The expression is ironical and hyperbolical, with reference to Jerusalem as having a monopoly of such martyrdoms. "It would be contrary to use and wont, and, in a manner, to theocratic decorum, if such a prophet as I should perish elsewhere than in Jerusalem" (Godet).

34. **Would I have gathered** (ἠθέλησα ἐπισυνάξαι). Lit., "I *desired* to gather." See on *will kill*, ver. 31.

Hen. See on Matt. xxiii. 37.

CHAPTER XIV.

1. **Watched** (ἦσαν παρατηρούμενοι). The participle and finite verb, *were engaged in watching.* Closely (παρά). See on Mark iii. 2.

2. **Which had the dropsy** (ὑδρωπικὸς). Lit., *a dropsical man.* The usual way of marking a dropsical patient in medical language.

4. **Took.** Took hold of him. Luke xx. 20; 1 Tim. vi. 12.

5. **Pit** (φρέαρ). The primary meaning is a *well*, as distinguished from a *fountain.*

Pull out. More correctly *up* (ἀνά).

7. **They chose.** Imperfect: *were choosing.* Something going on before his eyes.

The chief seats. Or *couches.* The Greek writers refer to the absurd contentions which sometimes arose for the chief seats at table. Theophrastus designates one who thrusts himself into the place next the host as μικροφιλότιμος, *one who seeks petty distinctions.*

8. **Wedding.** More properly, *marriage-feast.*

9. **Begin.** Emphasizing the shame of the reluctant movement toward the lower place.

The lowest. Since the other, intervening places are all assigned.

10. **Sit down** (ἀνάπεσε). Lit., *lay yourself back.*

11. **Humbled.** See on *lowly,* Matt. vii. 29.

12. **Dinner—supper.** See on Matt. xxii. 4. *Supper* (δεῖπνον) is the principal meal at evening, and corresponding to the modern late dinner.

Call not thy friends, etc. A striking parallel occurs in Plato's "Phaedrus," 233. "And, in general, when you make a feast, invite not your friend, but the beggar and the empty soul, for they will love you, and attend you, and come about your doors, and will be the best pleased, and the most grateful, and will invoke blessings on your head."

13. **Feast** (δοχήν). Or *reception.* Used by Luke only. See on ch. v. 29.

15. **Blessed.** See on Matt. v. 3.

16. **Made** (ἐποίει). Imperfect, *was making.* His preparations were in progress. A definite act among these preparations is described by the aorist, *he bade* (ἐκάλεσεν), the technical word for inviting to a festival. See Matt. xxii. 3; John ii. 2.

Sent his servant. "If a sheikh, bey, or emeer invites, he always sends a servant to call you at the proper time. This servant often repeats the very formula mentioned in Luke xiv. 17: *Come, for the supper is ready.* The fact that this custom is confined to the wealthy and to the nobility is in strict agreement with the parable, where the man who made the supper is supposed to be of this class. It is true now, as then, that to refuse is a high insult to the maker of the feast (Thomson, "Land and Book"). Palgrave mentions a similar formula of invitation among the Bedouins of Arabia. "The chief, or some unbreeched youngster of his family, comes up to us with the customary *tefaddaloo*, or *do us the favor*" ("Central and Eastern Arabia").

18. **Make excuse** (παραιτεῖσθαι). Also rendered in New Testament *refuse*, Heb. xii. 19, 25, where both meanings occur. See also 2 Tim. ii. 23, Rev. Our phrase, *beg off*, expresses the idea here.

I must needs (ἔχω ἀνάγκην). Lit., *I have necessity:* a strong expression.

Go (ἐξελθεῖν). Go *out* (ἐξ) from the city.

20. **I cannot.** A newly married man had special indulgence allowed him. See Deut. xxiv. 5. Herodotus relates how Croesus refused for his son an invitation to a hunt on this ground. "But Croesus answered, 'Say no more of my son going with you; that may not be in anywise. He is but just joined in wedlock, and is busy enough with that'" (i., 36). The man who had the most plausible excuse returned the surliest and most peremptory answer. Compare 1 Cor. vii. 33.

21. **Streets** (πλατείας)—**lanes** (ῥύμας). The former word from πλατύς, *broad;* the broad streets contrasted with the narrow *lanes.* Wyc., *great streets and small streets.*

22. **As thou hast commanded.** Following the reading ὡς, *as.* The best texts substitute ὃ, *what.* Render as Rev., "*What* thou didst command is done."

23. **Hedges** (φραγμοὺς). See on Matt. xxi. 33. It may mean either a *hedge*, or a *place enclosed with a hedge*. Here the hedges beside which vagrants rest.

Compel. Compare *constrained*, Matt. xiv. 22; Acts xxvi. 11; Gal. vi. 12. Not to use force, but to constrain them against the reluctance which such poor creatures would feel at accepting the invitation of a great lord.

May be filled (γεμισθῇ). A very strong word; properly of loading a ship. "Nature and grace alike abhor a vacuum" (Bengel).

27. **His cross.** More correctly, *his own*. An important charge. All must bear the cross, but not all *the same* cross: each one *his own*.

28. **A tower.** The subject of the parable is the life of Christian discipleship, which is figured by a tower, a lofty structure, as something distinguished from the world and attracting attention.

Counteth (ψηφίζει). Only here and Apoc. xiii. 18. From ψῆφος, a *pebble* (see Apoc. ii. 17), used as a counter. Thus Herodotus says that the Egyptians, when they calculate (λογίζονται ψήφοις, *reckon with pebbles*), move their hand from right to left (ii., 36). So Aristophanes, "Reckon roughly, not with pebbles (ψήφοις), but on the hand" ("Wasps," 656). Similarly *calculate*, from Latin *calculus, a pebble*. Used also of *voting*. Thus Herodotus: "The Greeks met at the altar of Neptune, and took *the ballots* (τὰς ψήφους) wherewith they were to give their votes." Plato: "And you, would you *vote* (ἂν ψῆφον θεῖο, *cast your pebble*) with me or against me?" ("Protagoras," 330). See Acts xxvi. 10.

Cost (τὴν δαπάνην). Allied to δάπτω, *to devour*. Hence *expense*, as something which *eats up* resources.

Sufficient (εἰς ἀπαρτισμόν). Lit., *unto completion.* The kindred verb ἀπαρτίζω, not used in New Testament, means to *make even* or *square*, and hence to *complete.*

29. **To finish** (ἐκτελέσαι). Lit., "to finish *out*" (ἐκ).

Behold (θεωροῦντες). Attentively watching the progress of the building. See on ch. x. 18.

Begin to mock. As his resources come to an end.

30. **This man** (οὗτος ὁ ἄνθρωπος). With sarcastic emphasis.

Was not able (οὐκ ἴσχυσεν). From ἰσχύς, *strength.* See on *power*, 2 Pet. ii. 11. To be strong in body or in resources, and so *to be worth*, as Lat., *valere.* "This man was not *worth* enough, or was not *good* for the completion." In this latter sense, Matt. v. 13, "*good* for nothing."

31. **To make war against another king** (ἑτέρῳ βασιλεῖ συμβαλεῖν εἰς πόλεμον). Lit., *to come together with another king for war.* So Rev., *to encounter another king in war.*

> "Out he flashed,
> And into such a song, such fire for fame,
> Such trumpet-blowings in it, coming down
> To such a stern and iron-clashing close,
> That when he stopped we longed *to hurl together.*"
>
> TENNYSON, *Idyls of the King.*

With ten thousand (ἐν δέκα χιλιάσιν). Lit., *in* ten thousands: i.e., *in the midst* of; *surrounded by.* Compare Jude 14.

32. **Asketh** (ἐρωτᾷ). On a footing of equality: king treating with king. See on ch. xi. 9.

Conditions of peace (τὰ πρὸς εἰρήνην). Lit., *things looking toward peace: preliminaries.* Compare Rom. xiv. 19, *things which make for peace* (τὰ τῆς εἰρήνης, *the things of peace*).

33. **Forsaketh** (ἀποτάσσεται). *Bids good-by to.* Rev., *renounceth.* See on ch. ix. 61. "In that *forsaketh* lies the key to the whole passage" (Trench). Christian discipleship is founded in self-renunciation.

34. **Have lost its savor.** See on Matt. v. 34.

Shall it be seasoned. See on Mark ix. 50.

CHAPTER XV.

4. **In the wilderness.** Not a desert place, but uncultivated plains; pasturage. Note that the sheep are being *pastured* in the wilderness. A traveller, cited anonymously by Trench, says: "There are, indeed, some accursed patches, where scores of miles lie before you like a tawny Atlantic, one yellow wave rising before another. But far from infrequently there are regions of wild fertility where the earth shoots forth a jungle of aromatic shrubs" ("Parables").

5. **When he hath found it.** Matthew, *If so be that he find it.*

On his shoulders. Lit., his *own* shoulders. "He might have employed a servant's aid, but love and joy make the labor sweet to himself" (Bengel). The "Good Shepherd" is a favorite subject in early Christian art. "We cannot go through any part of the catacombs, or turn over the pages of any collection of ancient Christian monuments, without coming across it again and again. We know from Tertullian that it was often designed upon chalices. We find it ourselves painted in fresco upon the roofs and walls of the sepulchral chambers; rudely scratched upon gravestones, or more carefully sculptured on sarcophagi; traced in gold upon glass, moulded on lamps, engraved on rings; and, in a word, represented on every species of Christian monument that has come down to us. . . . It was selected because it expressed the whole sum and substance of the Christian dispensation. . . . He is sometimes represented alone with his flock; at other times accompanied by his apostles, each attended by one or more sheep. Sometimes he stands amidst many sheep; sometimes he caresses one only; but most commonly—so commonly as almost to form a rule to which other scenes might be considered the exceptions —he bears a lost sheep, or even a goat, upon his shoulders" (Northcote and Brownlow, "Roma Sotteranea"). A beautiful specimen is found in the mausoleum of Galla Placidia, at Ravenna, erected about 450 A.D. It is a mosaic in green and gold. The figure is a beautiful one, youthful in face and form, as is usual in the early mosaics, and surrounded by his sheep. Facing this appears, over the altar, the form of Christ seated beside a kind of furnace, on the other side of which stands a little open bookcase. He is engaged in casting heretical books into the fire. Are they, indeed, the same—the Shepherd Christ of the Gospels, and the polemic Christ of the ecclesiastics?

6. **With me.** "Not with the sheep. Our life is *his* joy" (Gregory, cited by Trench).

7. **Repenteth.** See on Matt. iii. 2.

8–32. THE PARABLES OF THE LOST COIN AND OF THE PRODIGAL SON. Peculiar to Luke.

8. **Pieces of silver** (δραχμὰς). Used by Luke only. A coin worth about eighteen cents, commonly with the image of an owl, a tortoise, or a head of Pallas. As a weight, 65.5 grains. A common weight in dispensing medicines and writing prescriptions. Wyc., transcribing the Greek word, *dragmes*. Tynd., *grotes*.

9. **Her friends.** Female friends, for the noun is used in the feminine form.

I lost. Through her own carelessness. Of the sheep, Jesus says "*was* lost." "A sheep strays of itself, but a piece of money could only be lost by a certain negligence on the part of such as should have kept it" (Trench). In the one case, the attention is fastened on the condition of the thing lost; in the other, upon the sorrow of the one who has lost.

12. **The portion.** According to the Jewish law of inheritance, if there were but two sons, the elder would receive two portions, the younger the third of all movable property. A man might, during his lifetime, dispose of all his property by gift as he chose. If the share of younger children was to be diminished by gift or taken away, the disposition must be made by a person presumably near death. No one in good health could diminish, except by gift, the legal portion of a younger son. The younger son thus was entitled by law to his share, though he had no right to claim it during his father's lifetime. The request must be regarded as asking a favor (Edersheim).

Unto them. Even to the elder, who did not ask it.

13. **All.** Everything was taken out of the father's hands.

Took his journey (ἀπεδήμησεν). Answering to our phrase *went abroad.*

Wasted (διεσκόρπισεν). The word used of winnowing grain. See on Matt. xxv. 24.

With riotous living (ζῶν ἀσώτως). Lit., *living unsavingly.* Only here in New Testament. The kindred noun, ἀσωτία, is rendered by the Rev., in all the three passages where it occurs, *riot* (Eph. v. 18; Tit. i. 6; 1 Pet. iv. 4). See note on the last passage.

14. **Spent.** See on *cost,* ch. xiv. 28.

In that land. Want is characteristic of the "far country." The prodigal feels the evil of his environment. "*He* (with a shade of emphasis) began to be in want."

To be in want (ὑστερεῖσθαι). From ὕστερος, *behind.* Compare our phrase of one in straitened circumstances, *to fall behind.*

15. **Joined himself** (ἐκολλήθη). The verb means to *glue* or *cement.* Very expressive here, implying that he *forced himself* upon the citizen, who was unwilling to engage him, and who took him into service only upon persistent entreaty. "The unhappy wretch is a sort of appendage to a strange personality" (Godet). Compare Acts ix. 26. Wyc., *cleaved.* See, also, on Acts v. 13.

To feed swine. As he had received him reluctantly, so he gave him the meanest possible employment. An ignominious occupation, especially in Jewish eyes. The keeping of swine was prohibited to Israelites under a curse.

16. **He would fain** (ἐπεθύμει). *Longing* desire. Imperfect tense, *he was longing,* all the while he was tending the swine.

Filled his belly (γεμίσαι τὴν κοιλίαν). The texts vary. The Rev. follows the reading χορτασθῆναι, "He would fain *have been filled,*" using the same word which is employed of *filling* those who hunger and thirst after righteousness (Matt. v. 6, see note), and of the five thousand (Matt. xiv. 20). He had wanted the wrong thing all along, and it was no better now. All he wanted was to fill his belly.

Husks (κερατίων). Carob-pods. The word is a diminutive of κέρας, *a horn,* and means, literally, *a little horn,* from the shape of the pod. The tree is sometimes called in German *Bockshornbaum, Goat's-horn-tree.* "The fleshy pods are from six to ten inches long, and one broad, lined inside with a gelatinous substance, not wholly unpleasant to the taste when thoroughly ripe" (Thomson, "Land and Book"). The shell or pod alone is eaten. It grows in Southern Italy and Spain, and it is said that during the Peninsular War the horses of the British cavalry were often fed upon the pods. It is also called

Saint John's bread, from a tradition that the Baptist fed upon its fruit in the wilderness. Edersheim quotes a Jewish saying, "When Israel is reduced to the carob-tree, they become repentant."

17. **Came to himself.** A striking expression, putting the state of rebellion against God as a kind of *madness*. It is a wonderful stroke of art, to represent the beginning of repentance as the return of a sound consciousness. Ackermann ("Christian Element in Plato") observes that Plato thinks of redemption as *a coming to one's self*; an apprehending of one's self as existent; as a severing of the inmost being from the surrounding element. Several passages of Plato are very suggestive on this point. "He who bids a man know himself, would have him know his soul" ("Alcibiades," i., 130). "'To see her (the soul) as she really is, not as we now behold her, marred by communion with the body and other miseries, you should look upon her with the eye of reason, in her original purity, and then her beauty would be discovered, and in her image justice would be more clearly seen, and injustice, and all the things which we have described. Thus far we have spoken the truth concerning her as she appears at present; but we must remember also that we have seen her only in a condition which may be compared to that of the sea-god Glaucus, whose original image can hardly be discerned, because his natural members are broken off and crushed, and in many ways damaged by the waves; and incrustations have grown over them of sea-weed and shells and stones, so that he is liker to some sea-monster than to his natural form. And the soul is in a similar condition, disfigured by ten thousand ills: but not there, Glaucon, not there must we look.'

"'Where, then?'

"'At her love of wisdom. Let us see whom she affects, and what converse she seeks, in virtue of her near kindred with the immortal and eternal and divine; also, how different she would become, if wholly following this superior principle, and borne by a divine impulse out of the ocean in which she now is, and disengaged from the stones and shells and things of earth and rock, which, in wild variety, grow around her, because she feeds upon earth, and is crusted over by the good things of this life as they are termed. Then would you see her as she is'" ("Republic," 611).

Have bread enough and to spare (περισσεύονται ἄρτων). Lit., *abound in loaves.* Wyc., *plenty of loaves.*

Perish. Better, *I am perishing.* The best texts insert ὧδε, *here*, in contrast with the father's *house*, suggested by the father's *servants.*

20. **His father.** An affecting touch in the Greek: *his own* father.

Ran. Trench cites an Eastern proverb: "Who draws near to me (God) an *inch*, I will draw near to him an *ell;* and whoso *walks* to meet me, I will *leap* to meet him."

Kissed. See on Matt. xxvi. 49.

21. **To be called thy son.** He omits *make me a servant.* The slavish spirit vanishes in the clasp of the father's arms. Bengel suggests that the father would not suffer him to utter the news. I once heard Norman McLeod say in a sermon, "Before the prodigal son reached his home he thought over what he should do to merit restoration. He would be a hired servant. But when his father came out and met him, and put his arms round him, and the poor boy was beginning to say this and that, *he just shut his mouth*, and said, 'I take you to my heart, and that's enough.'"

22. **To his servants.** Bond-servants. There is a fine touch in throwing in the *bond-servants* immediately after *thy son* (ver. 21).

Bring forth. Some texts add *quickly* (ταχὺ). So Rev.

The best robe (*στολὴν τὴν πρώτην*). Lit., *a robe, the first.* Properly of a long, flowing robe, a *festive* garment. See Mark xvi. 5; Luke xx. 46.

Ring. See on Jas. ii. 2. Compare Gen. xli. 42.

Shoes. Both the ring and the shoes are marks of a free man. Slaves went barefoot.

23. **The fatted calf.** The article denoting one set apart for a festive occasion. Tynd., "*that* fatted calf."

24. **Is alive—is found** (*ἀνέζησεν—εὑρέθη*). Both aorists, and pointing back to a definite time in the past; doubtless the moment when he "came to himself." Wyc., *hath lived.*

The Prodigal Son is a favorite subject in Christian art. The return of the penitent is the point most frequently chosen, but the dissipation in the far country and the degradation among the swine are also treated. The dissipation is the subject of an interesting picture by the younger Teniers in the gallery of the Louvre. The prodigal is feasting at a table with two courtesans, in front of an inn, on the open shutter of which a tavern-score is chalked. An old woman leaning on a stick begs alms, possibly foreshadowing the fate of the females at the table. The youth holds out his glass, which a servant fills with wine. In the right-hand corner appears a pigsty where a stable-boy is feeding the swine, but with his face turned toward the table, as if in envy of the gay revellers there. All the costumes and other details of the picture are Dutch. Holbein also represents him feasting with his mistress, and gambling with a sharper who is sweeping the money off the table. The other points of the story are introduced into the background. Jan Steen paints him at table in a garden before an inn. A man plays the guitar, and two children are blowing bubbles—"an allegory of the transient pleasures of the spendthrift." Mrs. Jameson remarks that the riotous living is treated principally by the Dutch painters. The life among the swine is treated by Jordaens in the Dresden Gallery. The youth, with only a cloth about his loins, approaches the trough where the swine are feeding, extends his hand, and seems to ask food of a surly swineherd, who points him to the trough. In the left-hand corner a young boor is playing on a pipe, a sorrowful contrast to the delicious music of the halls of pleasure. Salvator Rosa pictures him in a landscape, kneeling with clasped hands amid a herd of sheep, oxen, goats, and swine. Rubens, in a farm-stable, on his knees near a trough, where a woman is feeding some swine. He looks imploringly at the woman. One of the finest examples of the treatment of the return is by Murillo, in the splendid picture in the gallery of the Duke of Sutherland. It is thus described by Stirling ("Annals of the Artists of Spain"): "The repentant youth, locked in the embrace of his father, is, of course, the principal figure; his pale, emaciated countenance bespeaks the hardships of his husk-coveting time, and the embroidery on his tattered robe the splendor of his riotous living. A little white dog, leaping up to caress him, aids in telling the story. On one side of this group a man and a boy lead in the fatted calf; on the other appear three servants bearing a light-blue silk dress of Spanish fashion, and the gold ring; and one of them seems to be murmuring at the honors in preparation for the lost one."

25. **Music** (συμφωνίας). A symphony: concerted music.

26. **Inquired** (ἐπυνθάνετο). Imperfect. *Began to inquire.*

27. **Is come—safe and sound.** Compare *is alive—is found.* "How nice is the observance of all the lesser proprieties of the narration. The father, in the midst of all his natural affection, is yet full of the moral significance of his son's return—that he has come back another person from what he was when he went, or while he tarried in that far land; he sees into the deep of his joy, that he is receiving him now indeed a son, once dead but now alive; once lost to him and to God, but now found alike by both. But the servant confines himself to the more external features of the case, to the fact that, after all he has gone through of excess and hardship, his father has yet received him *safe and sound*" (Trench).

28. **He was angry** (ὠργίσθη). Not with a mere temporary fit of passion, but, as the word imports, with a deep-seated wrath.

29. **Kid** (ἔριφον). Some read the diminutive, ἐρίφιον, "a *little* kid." In any event a contrast is intended between the kid and the fatted calf.

30. **This thy son.** Not *my brother*, but with the bitterest sarcasm.

Was come (ἦλθεν). He says *came*, as of a stranger. Not *returned.*

Devoured (καταφαγών). We say "eat *up;*" the Greek said "eat *down*" (κατά). The word is suggested, no doubt, by the mention of the calf, the kid, and the feasting.

CHAPTER XVI.

1–8. THE PARABLE OF THE UNJUST STEWARD. Peculiar to Luke.

1. **Steward** (οἰκονόμον). From οἶκος, *a house*, and νέμω, *to distribute* or *dispense.* Hence, one who assigns to the members of the household their several duties, and pays to each his wages. The paymaster. He kept the household stores under lock and seal, giving out what was required; and for this purpose received a signet-ring from his master. Wyc., *fermour*, or *farmer*. Here probably the *land*-steward.

Was accused (διεβλήθη). Only here in New Testament. From διά, *over*, *across*, and βάλλω, *to throw*. *To carry across*, and hence to carry reports, etc., from one to another; to carry *false* reports, and so to *calumniate* or *slander*. See on *devil*, Matt. iv. 1. The word implies *malice*, but not necessarily *falsehood.* Compare Latin *traducere* (*trans*, *over*, *ducere*, *to lead*), whence *traduce.*

Had wasted (ὡς διασκορπίζων). Lit., *as wasting.* Rev., *was wasting;* not merely a past offence, but something going on at the time of the accusation. See ch. xv. 13.

2. **How is it that I hear this** (τί τοῦτο ἀκούω)? Better as Rev., *What is this that I hear?*

Give an account (ἀπόδος τὸν λόγον). Lit., "give *back*" (ἀπό). Rev., *render. The* (τὸν) account which is due. Aristophanes has a striking parallel: "And now give back my signet; for thou shalt no longer be my steward" ("Knights," 947).

Thou mayest (δυνήσῃ). More strictly, as Rev., *thou canst.*

3. **Taketh away.** Or *is taking away.* He was not yet dispossessed, as is shown by what follows.

I cannot (οὐκ ἰσχύω). See on ch. xiv. 30. "I have not strength." His luxurious life had unfitted him for hard labor. In Aristophanes ("Birds," 1431), a sycophant is asked: "Tell me, being a young man, do you lodge informations against strangers?" He replies: "Yes; why should I suffer, for I know not how to dig?"

To beg (ἐπαιτεῖν). See on *besought,* Matt. xv. 23.

4. **They may receive.** The debtors of his master (ver. 5).

5. **He called.** Alford and Trench think that the debtors were together; but the words seem to me to indicate that he dealt with them separately. He called to him *each* one, and said unto the *first; after that* (ἔπειτα) another.

6. **Measures** (βάτους). Lit., *baths.* The *bath* was a Hebrew measure, but the amount is uncertain, since, according to Edersheim, there were three kinds of measurement in use in Palestine: the original Mosaic, corresponding with the Roman; that of Jerusalem, which was a fifth larger; and the common

Galilaean measurement, which was more than a fifth larger than the Jerusalem. Assuming the first standard, the bath would be about fifty-six pints, and the debt, therefore, a large one.

Take thy bill (δέξαι σου τὰ γράμματα). Lit., *take back thy writings*. Rev., *bond*. Wyc., *obligation;* and in ver. 7, *letters*. The plural is used for a single document. The *bill* is the *bond* which the buyer has given, and which is in the steward's keeping. He gives it *back* to the debtor for him to alter the figures.

Sit down quickly. It was a secret transaction, to be hurried through.

7. **To another** (ἑτέρῳ). A *different* one with a different debt, and his circumstances demanding a different rate of discount.

Measures (κόρους). *Cors*. A *cor* was ten *baths;* the dry and the fluid measures being the same.

8. **The lord.** Of the steward. Rev., properly, "*his* lord."

Commended. Admiring his shrewdness, though he himself was defrauded.

Unjust steward. Lit., *steward of injustice*. See on *forgetful hearer*, Jas. i. 25; and compare *words of grace*, Luke iv. 22; *unjust judge*, Luke xviii. 6; *son of his love*, Col. i. 13; *lust of uncleanness*, 2 Pet. ii. 10. The idiom is a Hebrew one. The phrase expresses Jesus' judgment on what the steward's master praised.

Wisely (φρονίμως). See on Matt. x. 16. Wyc., *prudently*. I would suggest *shrewdly*, though in the modern sense of *sagaciously*, since the earlier sense of *shrewd* was *malicious*, or *wicked*. Plato says: "All knowledge separated from righteousness and other virtue appears to be *cunning* and not *wisdom*." In Matt. vii. 24–26, it is applied to the sagacious man who built his house on the rock, opposed to the *foolish* (μωρός) man who built on the sand. "It is a middle term, not bringing out prominently the moral characteristics, either good or evil, of the action to which it is applied, but recognizing in it a skilful adaptation of the means to the end—affirming nothing in the way of moral approbation or disapprobation, either of means or end, but leaving their worth to be determined by other considerations" (Trench, "Parables").

In their generation (εἰς τὴν γενεὰν τὴν ἑαυτῶν). The A. V. misses the point, following Wyc. Lit., *in reference to their own generation;* i.e., the body of the children of this world to which they belong, and are kindred. They are shrewd in dealing with *their own kind;* since, as is shown in the parable, where the debtors were accomplices of the steward they are all alike unscrupulous. Tynd., *in their kind.*

Than the children of light. Lit., *sons of the light.* The men of the world make their intercourse with one another more profitable than the sons of light do *their* intercourse with their own kind. The latter "forget to use God's goods to form bonds of love to the contemporaries who share their character" (Godet); forget to "*make* friends of the mammon," etc.

9. **Make to yourselves friends.** Compare Virgil, "Aeneid," vi., 664. Among the tenants of Elysium he sees "those who, by good desert, made others mindful of them."

Of the mammon of unrighteousness (ἐκ τοῦ μαμωνᾶ τῆς ἀδικίας). The same idiom as in ver. 8, *steward of injustice.* Compare *unrighteous mammon,* ver. 11. *Mammon* should be spelt with one *m.* It is a Chaldee word, meaning *riches.* It occurs only in this chapter and at Matt. vi. 24. "*Of* the mammon" is, literally, *by means of.* In the phrase *of unrighteousness,* there is implied no condemnation of property as such; but it is styled *unrighteous,* or *belonging to unrighteousness,* because it is the characteristic and representative object and delight and desire of the selfish and unrighteous world:

their love of it being a root of all evil (1 Tim. vi. 10). Wyc., *the riches of wickedness.*

Ye fail (ἐκλίπητε). But all the best texts read *ἐκλίπῃ*, "when *it* (the mammon) fails."

They may receive. The friends.

Habitations (σκηνάς). Lit., *tents* or *tabernacles.*

10. **That which is least.** A general proposition, yet with a reference to mammon as the *least* of things. See next verse.

11. **Faithful.** Fidelity is, therefore, possible toward the unrighteous mammon.

12. **That which is another's.** God's. Riches are not *ours*, but given us in trust.

Your own. Equivalent *to the true riches.* That which forms part of our eternal being—the redeemed self. Compare the parable of the Rich Fool (ch. xii. 20), where the *life* or *soul* is distinguished from the *possessions.* "Thy *soul* shall be required; whose shall the *wealth* be?" Compare, also, *rich toward God* (ch. xii. 21). Chrysostom, cited by Trench, says of Abraham and Job, "They did not serve mammon, but *possessed and ruled themselves,* and were masters, and not servants."

13. **Servant** (οἰκέτης). Properly, *household* servant.

Serve. See on *minister*, Matt. xx. 26.

The other. See on Matt. vi. 24.

Hold to. See on Matt. vi. 24.

14. **Covetous** (φιλάργυροι). Rev. renders literally, according to the composition of the word, *lovers of money.* Only here

and 2 Tim. iii. 2. Compare the kindred noun, 1 Tim. vi. 10. The usual word for covetous is πλεονέκτης (1 Cor. v. 10, 11; vi. 10).

Derided (ἐξεμυκτήριζον). Only here and ch. xxiii. 35. Lit., *to turn up the nose at.* The Romans had a corresponding phrase, *naso adunco suspendere, to hang on the hooked nose:* i.e., to turn up the nose and make a hook of it, on which (figuratively) to hang the subject of ridicule. Thus Horace, in one of his satires, giving an account of a pretentious banquet at the house of a rich miser, describes one of the guests as *hanging everything to his nose;* i.e., making a joke of everything that occurred. The simple verb occurs at Gal. vi. 7, of mocking God.

15. **Abomination.** See on Matt. xxiv. 15.

16. **Presseth.** Rev., *entereth violently.* See on Matt. xi. 12. Wyc., *maketh violence into it.* Tynd., *striveth to go in.*

17. **Tittle.** See on Matt. v. 18.

19–31. THE PARABLE OF DIVES AND LAZARUS. Peculiar to Luke.

19. **Was clothed.** Imperfect, and frequentative; denoting his *habitual* attire.

Purple (πορφύραν). Originally the purple *fish* from which the color was obtained, and thence applied to the color itself. Several kinds of these were found in the Mediterranean. The color was contained in a vein about the neck. Under the term *purple* the ancients included three distinct colors: 1. A deep violet, with a black or dusky tinge; the color meant by Homer in describing an ocean wave: "As when the great sea grows *purple* with dumb swell" ("Iliad," xiv., 16). 2. Deep scarlet or crimson—the Tyrian purple. 3. The deep blue of the Mediterranean. The dye was permanent. Alexander is said by Plutarch to have found in the royal palace at Susa garments which preserved their freshness of color though they had been laid up for nearly two hundred years; and Mr. St. John ("Manners and Customs of Ancient Greece") relates that a small pot of the dye was discovered at Pompeii which had preserved the tone and richness attributed to the Tyrian purple. This fixedness of color is alluded to in Isa. i. 18—*though your sins were as scarlet*, the term being rendered in the Septuagint φοινικοῦν, which, with its kindred words, denoted darker shades of red. A full and interesting description of the purple may be found in J. A. St. John's "Manners and Customs of Ancient Greece," iii., 224 sq.

Fine linen (*βύσσον*). *Byssus.* A yellowish flax, and the linen made from it. Herodotus says it was used for enveloping mummies (ii., 86), a statement confirmed by microscopic examinations. He also speaks of it as a bandage for a wound (vii., 181). It is the word used by the Septuagint for linen (Exod. xxv. 4; xxviii. 5; xxxv. 6, etc.). Some of the Egyptian linen was so fine that it was called *woven air*. Sir Gardner Wilkinson says that some in his possession was, to the touch, comparable to silk, and not inferior in texture to the finest cambric. It was often as transparent as lawn, a fact illustrated by the painted sculptures, where the entire form is often made distinctly visible through the outer garment. Later Greek writers used the word for *cotton* and for *silk*. See Wilkinson's "Ancient Egyptians," first series, iii., 114 sq., and Rawlinson's "History of Ancient Egypt," i., 487, 512. A yellow byssus was used by the Greeks, the material for which grew around Elis, and which was enormously costly. See Aeschylus, "Persae," 127.

Fared sumptuously (*εὐφραινόμενος λαμπρῶς*). Lit., *making merry in splendor*. Compare ch. xv. 23, 24, 29, 32. Wyc., *he ate, each day, shiningly*.

20. **Beggar.** See on *poor*, Matt. v. 3.

Lazarus. Abbreviated from *'Ελεάζαρος*, *Eleazar*, and meaning *God a help*. "It is a striking evidence of the deep impression which this parable has made on the mind of Christendom, that the term *lazar* should have passed into so many languages as it has, losing altogether its signification as a proper name" (Trench).

Was laid (ἐβέβλητο). Lit., *was thrown:* cast carelessly down by his bearers and left there.

Gate (πυλῶνα). The *gateway*, often separated from the house or temple. In Matt. xxvi. 71, it is rendered *porch*.

Full of sores (εἱλκωμένος). Only here in New Testament. The regular medical term for *to be ulcerated*. John uses the kindred noun ἕλκος, *an ulcer* (Apoc. xvi. 2). See next verse.

21. **Desiring** (ἐπιθυμῶν). Eagerly, and not receiving what he desired. The same thing is implied in the story of the prodigal, where the same word is used, "*he would fain* have been filled" (ch. xv. 16), but the pods did not satisfy his hunger.

The crumbs that fell (τῶν πιπτόντων). Lit., *the things falling*. The best texts omit ψιχίων, *crumbs*.

Moreover (ἀλλὰ καὶ). Lit., *but even*. "*But* (instead of finding compassion), *even* the dogs," etc.

Licked (ἐπέλειχον). Only here in New Testament. Cyril, cited by Hobart, says: "The only attention, and, so to speak, medical dressing, which his sores received, was from the dogs who came and licked them."

22. **Abraham's bosom.** A Rabbinical phrase, equivalent to being with Abraham in Paradise. "To the Israelite Abraham seems the personal centre and meeting-point of Paradise" (Goebel).

23. **Hell.** Rev., *Hades*. Where Lazarus also was, but in a different region. See on Matt. xvi. 18.

24. **Cool** (καταψύχειν). Only here in New Testament. Common in medical language. See on ch. xxi. 26. Compare the exquisite passage in Dante, where Messer Adamo, the false coiner, horribly mutilated, and in the lowest circle of Malebolge, says:

> "I had, while living, much of what I wished;
> And now, alas! a drop of water crave.
> The rivulets that from the verdant hills
> Of Cassentin descend down into Arno,
> *Making their channels to be soft and cold,*
> Ever before me stand, and not in vain:
> For far more doth their image dry me up
> Than the disease which strips my face of flesh."
>
> *Inferno*, xxx., 65 sq.

Tormented (ὀδυνῶμαι). Used by Luke only. *Tormented* is too strong. The word is used of the sorrow of Joseph and Mary when the child Jesus was missing (ch. ii. 48); and of the grief of the Ephesian elders on parting with Paul (Acts xx. 38). Rev., *I am in anguish.*

25. **Son** (τέκνον). Lit., *child.*

Receivedst (ἀπέλαβες). Received *back* (ἀπό) as a reward or quittance. Compare ch. vi. 34; xviii. 30; xxiii. 41.

Gulf (χάσμα). From χάσκω, *to yawn.* Transcribed into the English *chasm.* In medical language, of the cavities in a wound or ulcer.

Is fixed (ἐστήρικται). Compare ch. xxii. 32; and see on 1 Pet. v. 10.

27. **Send him to my father's house.** Compare Dante, where Ciacco, the glutton, says to Dante:

> "But when thou art again in the sweet world,
> I pray thee to the mind of others bring me."
>
> *Inferno*, vi., 88.

31. **Be persuaded.** Dives had said, "they will repent." Abraham replies, "they will not be even *persuaded.*"

Though one rose. Dives had said, "if one *went.*"

From the dead (ἐκ νεκρῶν). Dives had said *from* the dead, but using a different preposition (ἀπό). It is wellnigh impossible to give the English reader this nice play of prepositions. The general distinction is ἀπό, *from the outside;* ἐκ, *from within.* Thus Luke ii. 4, Joseph went up *from* (ἀπό) Galilee, the *province, out of* (ἐκ) the *city* of Nazareth. Abraham's preposition (ἐκ, *out of*) implies a more complete identification with the dead than Dives' ἀπό, *from.* A rising *from among* the dead was more than a messenger going *from* the dead. "We can hardly pass over the identity of the name Lazarus with that of him who actually was recalled from the dead; but whose return, far from persuading the Pharisees, was the immediate exciting cause of their crowning act of unbelief" (Alford).

CHAPTER XVII.

1. **Impossible** (ἀνένδεκτον). *Inadmissible.* Only here in New Testament. See on *it cannot be*, ch. xiii. 33.

Offences. See on *offend*, Matt. v. 29; and compare on Matt. xvi. 23.

2. **It were better** (λυσιτελεῖ). Only here in New Testament. The verb means *to pay what is due*, and is equivalent to our phrase, *it pays.*

Millstone. Compare Matt. xviii. 6. The correct reading here is λίθος μυλικὸς, *a millstone;* not *a great millstone* as Matt.

Thrown (ἔῤῥιπται). *Hurled:* with an underlying sense of violence, called out by so great an outrage.

3. **Rebuke.** See on *straitly charged*, ch. ix. 21.

6. **Sycamine.** Or *mulberry*. Luke distinguishes between this and συκομορέα, *the fig-mulberry* (ch. xix. 4). The names were sometimes confused, but a physician would readily make the distinction, as both were used medicinally.

9. **I trow not.** Omitted by the best texts.

10. **Unprofitable** (ἀχρεῖοι). From χρεία, *requirement;* something which the master *must* pay. Not *useless*, but having rendered no service beyond what was *due*. "The *profit* does not begin until the servant goes beyond his obligation" (Meyer). "A *servant* owes *all things*" (Bengel).

11. **Through the midst of.** It may also mean *between* or *on the borders of*. The Am. Rev. insists on the latter.

12. **Lepers.** See on ch. v. 12.

20. **With observation** (μετὰ παρατηρήσεως). Only here in New Testament. The progress of the kingdom cannot be defined by visible marks like that of an earthly kingdom. Its growth in the world is a process of *pervasion*, like the working of the leaven through the lump.

21. **Within.** Better, *in the midst of*. Meyer acutely remarks that "*you* refers to the Pharisees, in whose hearts nothing certainly found a place less than did the ethical kingdom of God." Moreover, Jesus is not speaking of the *inwardness* of the kingdom, but of its *presence*. "The whole language of the kingdom of heaven being within men, rather than men being within the kingdom, is modern" (Trench, after Meyer).

24. **Lighteneth** (ἀστράπτουσα). Only here and ch. xxiv. 4.

25. **Rejected.** See on *disallowed*, 1 Pet. ii. 4; and *tried*, 1 Pet. i. 7.

31. **Goods.** See on Matt. xii. 29.

On the house-top. See on Matt. xxiv. 17.

33. **Shall preserve** (ζωογονήσει). Only here and Acts vii. 19. Originally to *engender*; thence to *produce alive* or *endue with life*, and so to *preserve alive*. Wyc., *shall quicken it*.

37. **Eagles.** See on Matt. xxiv. 28.

CHAPTER XVIII.

1–14. The Parables of the Unjust Judge and the Pharisee and Publican. Peculiar to Luke.

1. **To the end that men ought** (πρὸς τὸ δεῖν). Lit., *with reference to its being necessary* always to pray, etc.

Faint (ἐγκακεῖν). To turn coward or lose heart.

2. **Regarded** (ἐντρεπόμενος). See on Matt. xxi. 37.

3. **Avenge** (ἐκδίκησον). The word is too strong. It means *do me justice*. See on Rom. xii. 19.

5. **Lest by her continual coming she weary me** (ἵνα μὴ εἰς τέλος ἐρχομένη ὑπωπιάζῃ με). *Εἰς τέλος*, lit., *unto the end*, may mean *continually*; but *weary* or *wear out* for ὑπωπιάζῃ is more than doubtful. That word is from ὑπώπιον, *the part of the face under the eyes*, and means *to strike under the eye*; to give one a black eye. It is used only once again, by Paul, 1 Cor. ix. 27, and in its literal sense: "I *buffet* my body;" treat it as the boxer does his adversary. The more literal sense of this word, and of εἰς τέλος, *in the end*, or *finally*, give a sound and much livelier meaning here. "Lest *at last* she come and *assault* me." So Goebel and Meyer, and so Wyc., "Lest *at the last* she, coming, *strangle* me;" and Tynd., "Lest at the last she come and *rail on me*." The judge fears lest importunity

may culminate in personal violence. Perhaps, also, as Goebel suggests, he intentionally exaggerates his fear.

6. **The unjust judge.** Lit., *the judge of injustice*. See on ch. xvi. 8.

7. **And shall not God.** The emphasis is on God. In the Greek order, "and *God*, shall he not," etc.

Though he bear long with them. A very difficult passage, and interpretations vary greatly.

(1.) The verb μακροθυμέω means *to be long-suffering*, or to *endure patiently*. Such is its usual rendering in the New Testament.

(2.) *Them* (αὐτοῖς) refers not to the *persecutors* of God's elect, but to the *elect themselves*. The Rev. cuts the knot by the most literal of renderings: "and he is long-suffering over (ἐπι) them."

(3.) The secondary meaning of *restraining* or *delaying* may fairly be deduced from the verb, and explained either (*a*) of *delaying punishment*, or (*b*) of delaying *sympathy* or *help*.

The Am. Rev. adopts the former, and throws the sentence into the form of a question: "And is he slow to punish on their behalf" (ἐπ' αὐτοῖς)? I venture to suggest the following: ***Καὶ*** not infrequently has the sense of *yet*, or *and yet*. So Euripides: "Thou art Jove-born, and yet (καὶ) thy utterance is unjust" ("Helena," 1147). Aristophanes: "O crown, depart, and joy go with thee: *yet* (καὶ) I part from thee unwillingly" ("Knights," 1249). So John ix. 30: "Ye know not from whence he is, *and yet* (καὶ) he hath opened my eyes." John xvi. 32: "Ye shall leave me alone, and *yet* (καὶ) I am not alone," etc. Render, then, "Shall not God avenge his own elect, which cry unto him day and night; yet he delayeth help on their behalf," even as the unjust judge delayed to avenge the widow? Surely he will, and that ere long. This rendering, instead of *contrasting* God with the judge, carries out the parallel. The judge delays through *indifference*. God delays also, or seems to delay, in order to try his children's faith, or because his purpose is not ripe; but he, too, will do justice to the suppliant. Tynd., *Yea, though he defer them.*

"He hides himself so wondrously,
As though there were no God;
He is least seen when all the powers
Of ill are most abroad.

O there is less to try our faith,
In our mysterious creed,
Than in the godless look of earth
In these our hours of need.

It is not so, but so it looks;
And we lose courage then;
And doubts will come if God hath kept
His promises to men."

FABER.

8. **Nevertheless.** Notwithstanding God is certain to vindicate, will the Son of man find on earth a persistence in faith answering to the widow's?

9. **Despised** (ἐξουθενοῦντας). Lit., *made nothing of.* Rev., *set at nought.*

Others (τοὺς λοιποὺς). The expression is stronger. Lit., *the rest.* They threw all others beside themselves into one class. Rev., correctly, *all others.*

10. **The other** (ἕτερος). With an implication of his being a *different* man. See on Matt. vi. 24.

Publican. See on ch. iii. 12.

11. **Stood** (σταθεὶς). Lit., *having been placed.* Took his stand. It implies taking up his position *ostentatiously;* striking an attitude. But not necessarily in a bad sense. See on ch. xix. 8; and compare Acts v. 20. Standing was the ordinary posture of the Jews in prayer. Compare Matt. vi. 5; Mark xi. 25.

Prayed (προσηύχετο). Imperfect: *began* to pray, or *proceeded* to pray.

Other men (οἱ λοιποὶ τῶν ἀνθρώπων). Lit., *the rest of men*. See on ver. 9. A Jewish saying is quoted that a true Rabbin ought to thank God every day of his life; 1, that he was not created a Gentile; 2, that he was not a plebeian; 3, that he was not born a woman.

Extortioners. As the publicans.

This publican. Lit., *this* (*one*), *the publican*. This publican here. "He lets us see, even in the general enumeration, that he is thinking of the publican, so, afterward, he does not omit directly to mention him" (Goebel).

12. **Twice in the week.** The law required only one fast in the year, that on the great day of Atonement (Lev. xvi. 29; Num. xxix. 7); though public memorial fasts were added, during the Captivity, on the anniversaries of national calamities. The Pharisees fasted every Monday and Thursday during the weeks between the Passover and Pentecost, and again between the Feast of Tabernacles and that of the Dedication of the Temple.

I give tithes (ἀποδεκατῶ). See on Matt. xxiii. 23.

Possess (κτῶμαι). Wrong. The Israelite did not pay tithes of his *possessions*, but only of his *gains*—his annual increase. See Gen. xxviii. 22; Deut. xiv. 22. Besides, the verb, in the present tense, does not mean to *possess*, but *to acquire;* the meaning *possess* being confined to the perfect and pluperfect. Rev., *get*. Compare Matt. x. 9 (Rev.); Acts xxii. 28; Luke xxi. 19 (on which see note); 1 Thess. iv. 4 (Rev.).

13. **Standing** (ἑστὼς). In a timid attitude: *merely* standing, not *posturing* as the Pharisee. See on ver. 11.

Afar off. Some explain, from *the sanctuary;* others, from the *Pharisee.*

Lift up his eyes. As worshippers ordinarily.

Be merciful (ἱλάσθητι). Lit., *be propitiated.*

A sinner (τῷ ἁμαρτωλῷ). With the definite article, "*the* sinner." "He thinks about no other man" (Bengel).

15–17. Compare Matt. xix. 13–15; Mark x. 13–16.

15. **Infants** (τὰ βρέφη). See on 1 Pet. ii. 2.

Touch. So Mark. Matthew has *lay his hands on them and pray.*

16. **Suffer.** See on Matt. xix. 14. Only Mark notes the taking in his arms.

18–30. Compare Matt. xix. 16–30; xx. 1–16; Mark x. 17–31.

18. **Ruler.** Peculiar to Luke.

20. **Why callest thou me good?** See on Matt. xix. 17.

Do not commit adultery, etc. Compare the different arrangement of the commandments by the three synoptists.

22. **Yet lackest thou one thing** (ἔτι ἕν σοι λείπει). Lit., *still one thing is lacking to thee.* Mark alone adds that Jesus, looking upon him, loved him.

Come (δεῦρο). Lit., *hither.*

23. **He was very sorrowful.** Rev., more correctly renders ἐγενήθη, *he became.* See on Mark x. 22.

Very rich. The Greek order forms a climax: "rich *exceedingly*."

25. **Camel.** See on Matt. xix. 24.

To go through the eye of a needle (διὰ τρήματος βελόνης εἰσελθεῖν). Rev., more literally, *to enter in through a needle's eye.* Both Matthew and Mark use another word for needle (ῥαφίς); see on Mark x. 25. Luke alone has βελόνη, which, besides being an older term, is the peculiar word for the *surgical* needle. The other word is condemned by the Greek grammarians as barbarous.

28. **All** (πάντα). The best texts read τὰ ἴδια, *our own.* So Rev.

31–34. Compare Matt. xx. 17–19. Mark x. 32–34.

31. **By** the prophets (διά). Lit., *through;* the preposition expressing secondary agency.

34. **Saying** (ῥῆμα). See on ch. i. 37.

Were said (λεγόμενα). Or, more correctly, which *were being said* to them at the moment.

35–43; xix. 1. Compare Matt. xx. 29–34. Mark x. 46–52.

39. **Cried** (ἔκραζεν). A stronger word than ἐβόησεν, *cried,* in the previous verse, which is merely to *cry* or *shout,* while this is to cry *clamorously; to scream* or *shriek.* Compare Matt. xv. 23; Mark v. 5; Acts xix. 28–34.

To be brought unto (ἀχθῆναι πρὸς). Used by Luke alone in the sense of bringing the sick to Christ. He also uses the compound verb προσάγω, which was a common medical term for bringing the sick to a physician, both in that and in other senses. See ch. ix. 41; Acts xvi. 20; xxvii. 27.

CHAPTER XIX.

1–10. The Story of Zacchaeus. Peculiar to Luke.

1. **Jericho.** The city was close to the fords of the Jordan, on the frontier of Peraea, and on the richest plain of Palestine, abounding most in the choicest productions, especially balsam; and was, therefore, an appropriate seat for an officer of superior rank to preside over the collection of revenues. See on Matt. ix. 9; Luke iii. 12.

2. **Named** (ὀνόματι καλούμενος). Lit., *called by name.* Compare ch. i. 61.

Zacchaeus. *Saccai*, "the just."

3. **He sought** (ἐζήτει). Imperfect. He was busy seeking as Jesus passed.

Who he was. Lit., *is.* Not to see *what kind of a person*, but *which one of the crowd* he was.

Stature (ἡλικίᾳ). See on ch. xii. 25.

4. **Sycamore** (συκομορέαν). From συκῆ, *fig-tree*, and μόρον, the *mulberry*. The fig-mulberry, resembling the fig in its fruit, and the mulberry in its leaves. Some old writers derived it from μωρὸς, *foolish*, because it produced worthless figs. Dr. Thomson says that it bears several crops yearly, which grow on short stems along the trunk and the large branches. They are very insipid, and none but the poorer classes eat them. Hence Amos expresses the fact that he belongs to the humblest class of the community, by calling himself a gatherer of sycamore fruit (Amos vii. 14). It grows with its large branches low down and wide open, so that Zacchaeus could easily have climbed into it. It is a favorite and pleasant conceit with old

commentators that Zacchaeus' sycamore that day bore precious fruit.

5. **I must abide.** "Adopting the royal style which was familiar to him, and which commends the loyalty of a vassal in the most delicate manner by freely exacting his services" ("Ecce Homo").

7. **To be guest** (καταλῦσαι). More correctly, Rev., *lodge*. See on ch. ix. 12.

A sinner. See on ch. iii. 12.

8. **Stood** (σταθεὶς). See on ch. xviii. 11. Describing a formal act, as of one who is about to make a solemn declaration. He was like the Pharisee in attitude, but not in spirit. The more formal word for standing, applied to the *Pharisee* in the temple, is here used of *the publican*.

I give. Not, It is my practice to give. Zacchaeus' statement is not a *vindication*, but a *vow*. "I now give by way of restoration."

If I have taken anything by false accusation (εἴ τι ἐσυκοφάντησα). *If—anything* does not state a merely possible case, as if Zacchaeus were unconscious of any such extortion; but is a milder way of saying "*Whatever* I have taken." See on ch. iii. 14. It is an odd coincidence, nothing more, that the *fig*-mulberry (sycamore) should occur in connection with the *fig*-shewer (sycophant). It was common for the publicans to put a fictitious value on property or income, or to advance the tax to those unable to pay, and then to charge usurious interest on the private debt. On the harsh exaction of such debts, see Matt. xviii. 28; Luke xii. 58.

Fourfold. The restoration required of a *thief* (Exod. xxii. 1).

11. **Appear** (ἀναφαίνεσθαι). Only here and Acts xxi. 3. It means *to be brought to light; shown forth*. The common phrase *show up* (ἀνά) represents it.

13. **His ten servants** (δέκα δούλους ἑαυτοῦ). Rev., rightly, changes to *ten servants of his*, since the *his* is emphatic; lit., *his own*. Moreover, it would be absurd to suppose that this nobleman, of consequence enough to be raised to a royal dignity, had but ten servants. The number of slaves in a Roman household was enormous, sometimes reaching hundreds. Toward the end of the Republic, it was considered reprehensible not to have a slave for every sort of work.

Pounds (μνᾶς.) *Minas*. Between sixteen and eighteen dollars apiece. Meyer very aptly remarks: "The small sum astonishes us. Compare, on the other hand, the talents (Matt. xxv.). But in Matthew, the Lord transfers to his servant his *whole property;* here he has only devoted a definite sum of money to the purpose of putting his servants to the proof therewith; and the smallness of the amount corresponds to what is so carefully emphasized in our parable, viz., the relation of faithfulness *in the least* to its great recompense (ver. 17); which relation is less regarded in the parable in Matthew" ("Commentary on Luke").

Occupy (πραγματεύσασθε). The word *occupy* has lost the sense which it conveyed to the makers of the A. V.—that of *using* or *laying out what is possessed*. An *occupier* formerly meant *a trader*. *Occupy*, in the sense of *to use*, occurs Judges xvi. 11: "new ropes that never were *occupied;*" which Rev. changes to *wherewith no work hath been done*. Compare the Prayer-Book version of the Psalter, Ps. cvii. 23: "*occupy* their business in great waters." So Latimer, "Sermons," "He that *occupieth* usury." Rev., *trade ye*. Wyc., *merchandise ye*. Tynd., *buy and sell*. See on *traded*, Matt. xxv. 16.

Till I come (ἕως ἔρχομαι). It is strange that the Rev. follows this reading without comment, while the Revisers' text takes no notice whatever of the reading of four of the leading manuscripts, which is adopted by both Tischendorf and Westcott and Hort; ἐν ᾧ ἔρχομαι, "*while* I come," a condensed form of expression for *while I go and return*.

15. **Had gained by trading** (διεπραγματεύσατο). Only here in New Testament. See on ver. 13.

16. **Hath gained** (προσηργάσατο). Only here in New Testament. Lit., *hath worked besides* (πρὸς) the original sum. Rev., *made*.

Have thou authority (ἴσθι ἐξουσίαν ἔχων). Lit., *Be thou having authority*.

Cities. "A city for a pound, yet not even a cottage could be bought for a pound" (Bengel).

18. **Made** (ἐποίησεν). See on Matt. xxv. 16.

20. **I kept** (εἶχον). The imperfect. I was keeping while thou wert absent.

Napkin (σουδαρίῳ). The Latin *sudarium*, from *sudor*, *perspiration:* a cloth for wiping off the sweat. Trench notes that the napkin which the idle servant does not need for its proper use (Gen. iii. 19) he uses for the wrapping up of his pound.

21. **Austere** (αὐστηρὸς). From αὔω, *to dry*. *Dry*, and thence *hard*. See on *hard*, Matt. xxv. 24.

Sow (ἔσπειρας). See on *strawed*, Matt. xxv. 24.

22. **Thou knewest.** To be read interrogatively. "Didst thou know that? Then, for that reason, thou shouldst have been the more faithful."

23. **Bank** (τράπεζαν). Lit., the *table* of the money-changer. Wyc., *board*. See on *exchangers*, Matt. xxv. 27.

Usury (τόκῳ). Better *interest*, as Rev. See on *usury*, Matt. xxv. 27.

27. **But** (πλὴν). Rev., *howbeit*. However it may be with the unfaithful servant.

Slay (κατασφάξατε). Only here in New Testament. A strong word: *slaughter;* cut them *down* (κατά).

29–44. Compare Matt. xxi. 1–11; Mark xi. 1–11.

29. **Bethphage.** See on Matt. xxi. 1.

31. **The Lord.** See on Matt. xxi. 3.

35. **Their garments.** More strictly, *their own* garments (ἑαυτῶν), in their reverence and love for their Lord. See on Matt. xxv. 7.

36. **Spread** (ὑπεστρώννυον). Only here in New Testament.

37. **The descent.** Two distinct sights of Jerusalem are caught on this route, an inequality of ground hiding it for a time after one has first seen it. Verse 37 marks the *first* sight, verse 41 the *second* and nearer view (see Introduction, on Luke's topographical accuracy). "At this point (the former) the first view is caught of the southeastern corner of the city. The temple and the more northern portions are hid by the slope of Olivet on the right: what is seen is only Mount Zion, now, for the most part, a rough field, crowned with the mosque of David, and the angle of the western walls, but then covered with houses to its base, and surmounted by the castle of Herod, on the supposed site of the palace of David. . . . It was at this point that the shout of triumph burst forth from the multitude" (Stanley, "Sinai and Palestine").

41. **He drew nigh.** "Again the procession advanced. The road descends a slight declivity, and the glimpse of the city is again withdrawn behind the intervening ridge of Olivet. A few moments, and the path mounts again; it climbs a rugged ascent, it reaches a ledge of smooth rock, and in an instant the

whole city bursts into view. . . . It is hardly possible to doubt that this rise and turn of the road was the exact point where the multitude paused again, and He, when he beheld the city, wept over it" (Stanley).

42. **Wept** (*ἔκλαυσεν*). With audible weeping.

43. **A trench** (*χάρακα*). Rev., correctly, as Tynd., *a bank*. Only here in New Testament. The word literally means *a pointed stake*, used in fortifying the intrenchments of a camp, and thence the palisade itself. In fortifying a camp or besieging a city, a ditch was dug round the entire circuit, and the earth from it thrown up into a wall, upon which sharp stakes were fixed. Every Roman soldier carried three or four of these stakes on the march. Wyc., *with pale*.

Keep thee in (*συνέξουσιν*). See on ch. iv. 38.

44. **Lay thee even with the ground** (*ἐδαφιοῦσιν*). Only here in New Testament. Primarily, to *beat level*, like a threshing-floor or pavement. The Septuagint uses it in the sense of *dashing down to the ground* (Ps. cxxxvii. 9, and elsewhere). So Rev., from the succeeding reference to the children, and in allusion to the Psalm.

Visitation. See on 1 Pet. ii. 12.

45–48. Compare Matt. xxi. 12–19; Mark xi. 12–19.

46. **Thieves** (*λῃστῶν*). See on Matt. xxvi. 55; Luke x. 30; Mark xi. 17.

48. **Were very attentive** (*ἐξεκρέματο*). Only here in New Testament. Lit., as Rev., *hung upon him*. Tynd., *stuck by him*.

CHAPTER XX.

1–8. Compare Matt. xxi. 23–32; Mark xi. 27–33.

5. **They reasoned** (*συνελογίσαντο*). Only here in New Testament. The preposition, *σύν*, *together*, and the additional *with themselves*, denote a very close conference.

6. **Will stone** (*καταλιθάσει*). Only here in New Testament. "Stone us *down*" (*κατά*); *i.e.*, stone us to death.

They be persuaded (*πεπεισμένος ἐστιν*). Lit., *It* (the people collectively) *is having been persuaded.* Denoting a long-standing and settled persuasion.

9–19. Compare Matt. xxi. 33–46; Mark xii. 1–12.

9. **Let it out.** See on Matt. xxi. 33.

Went into a far country. Not necessarily *far*, but as Rev., *another* country. See on Mark xiii. 34.

A long time (*ἱκανούς*). See on ch. vii. 6.

10. **Of the fruit.** See on Mark xii. 2.

11. **He sent yet** (*προσέθετο πέμψαι*). Lit., *he added to send.* A Hebrew form of expression.

12. **Wounded** (*τραυματίσαντες*). Only here and Acts xix. 16.

13. **It may be** (*ἴσως*). Only here in New Testament. The adverb of *ἴσος*, *equal.* It expresses more than *perhaps*, implying rather a strong probability. Compare the phrase, *it is an even chance that.*

Reverence. See on Matt. xxi. 37.

16. **Destroy.** See on Matt. 21. 41.

God forbid (μὴ γένοιτο). Lit., *may it not be.*

17. **The stone,** etc. See on 1 Pet. ii. 4–7.

18. **Shall be broken** (συνθλασθήσεται). Rev., rightly, *broken to pieces.* See on Matt. xxi. 44.

Grind him to powder (λικμήσει). See on Matt. xxi. 44.

20–26. Compare Matt. xxii. 15–22; Mark xii. 13–17.

20. **Watched.** See on Mark iii. 2.

Spies (ἐγκαθέτους). Only here in New Testament. From ἐγκαθίημι, *to send in, as a garrison into a city.* Hence of persons sent in for the purpose of *espionage.*

Which should feign (ὑποκρινομένους). Lit., *feigning.* Rev., *which feigned.* Only here in New Testament. See on *hypocrites,* Matt. xxiii. 13.

The power and authority (τῇ ἀρχῇ καὶ τῇ ἐξουσίᾳ). The former, the Roman power in general; the latter, the specific authority of the official.

21. **Acceptest not the person.** See on Jas. ii. 1.

22. **Tribute** (φόρον). From φέρω, *to bring.* Something, therefore, which is *brought in* by way of payment. Luke uses the Greek word instead of the Latin κῆνσον, *census,* in Matthew and Mark.

23. **Perceived.** See on *considerest,* Matt. vii. 3.

Craftiness (πανουργίαν). From πᾶν, *every,* and ἔργον, *deed.* Readiness for every and any deed. Hence *unscrupulousness,* and so, generally, *knavery.*

24. **Penny.** See on Matt. xx. 2.

Image and superscription. See on Matt. xxii. 20.

26. **His words** (ῥήματος). Singular number. Rev., properly, *saying*. See on ch. i. 37.

27–40. Compare Matt. xxii. 23–33; Mark xii. 18–27.

27, **Asked.** See on Mark xii. 18.

36. **Equal unto the angels** (ἰσάγγελοι). Only here in New Testament.

37. **Shewed** (ἐμήνυσεν). Originally *to disclose something secret*. Hence, generally, to *make known*.

At the bush (ἐπὶ τῆς βάτου). Wrong. Render as Rev., *in the place concerning the bush*. See on Mark xii. 26.

41–44. Compare Matt. xxii. 41–46; Mark xii. 35–37.

43. **Of thy feet** (τῶν ποδῶν σου). A. V. omits.

46. **Chief rooms.** Rev., correctly, *chief places*. See on Mark xii. 39.

47. **Widows' houses.** See on Mark xii. 40.

CHAPTER XXI.

1–4. Compare Mark xii. 41–44.

1. **Treasury.** See on Mark xii. 41.

Rich. Standing last and emphatically in the sentence, "Saw them that were casting, etc.—*rich men*." Not the rich only were casting in. Compare Mark xii. 41.

2. **Poor.** See on Matt. v. 3.

Mites. See on Mark xii. 42.

3. **This poor widow.** See on Mark xii. 43.

4. **Offerings of God.** The best texts omit *of God*. Rev., more simply, *unto the gifts*.

Penury (ὑστερήματος). Lit., *lack*. Rev., neatly, *of her want*.

5–19. Compare Matt. xxiv. 1–14; Mark xiii. 1–13.

5. **Stones.** See on Mark xiii. 1.

Offerings (ἀναθήμασιν). Only here in New Testament. From ἀνατίθημι, *to set up*. Hence of something *set up* in the temple as a votive offering. Such were the golden vines presented by Herod the Great, with bunches of grapes as large as a man, and mounted above the entrance to the holy place. The magnificent porch of the temple was adorned with many such dedicated gifts, such as a golden wreath which Sosius offered after he had taken Jerusalem in conjunction with Herod; and rich flagons which Augustus and his wife had given to the sanctuary. Gifts were bestowed by princes friendly to Israel, both on the temple and on provincial synagogues. The word ἀνάθεμα (Gal. i. 8, Rev.), is the same word, something *devoted*, and so devoted to *evil* and *accursed*. Luke uses the classical form. The other is the common or Hellenistic form. The two forms develop gradually a divergence in meaning; the one signifying *devoted* in a *good*, the other in a *bad* sense. The same process may be observed in other languages. Thus *knave*, *lad*, becomes a *rascal*: *villain*, a *farmer*, becomes a *scoundrel*: *cunning*, *skilful*, becomes *crafty*.

6. **Behold** (θεωρεῖτε). See on ch. x. 18.

Thrown down. See on Mark xiii. 2.

8. **Deceived.** Rev., rightly, *led astray.* See on Matt. xxiv. 4.

In my name. See on Matt. xviii. 5.

9. **Commotions** (ἀκαταστασίας). From ἀ, *not*, and καθίστημι, *to establish.* Hence *disestablishments; unsettlements.* Rev., *tumults.*

Be not terrified (μὴ πτοηθῆτε). Only here and ch. xxiv. 37.

By and by (εὐθέως). Better as Rev., *immediately.*

11. **Earthquakes.** See on Matt. xiii. 8.

Famines and pestilences (λιμοὶ καὶ λοιμοὶ). Some texts reverse the order of the words. A *paronomasia* or combination of like-sounding words: *limoi, loimoi.* Especially common in Paul's epistles.

Fearful sights (φοβητρά). Only here in New Testament, and rare in classical Greek. In Septuagint, Isa. xix. 17. Not confined to *sights*, but fearful *things.* Rev., better, *terrors.* Used in medical language by Hippocrates, of fearful objects imagined by the sick.

13. **It shall turn** (ἀποβήσεται). Lit., *turn out; issue.*

14. **To answer.** See on *answer*, 1 Pet. iii. 15.

19. **Possess ye** (κτήσεσθε). Wrong. See on ch. xviii. 12. Rev. rightly, *ye shall win.*

20–36. Compare Matt. xxiv. 15–42. Mark xiii. 14–37.

22. **Vengeance** (ἐκδικήσεως). Of rendering *full* justice, or satisfaction. See on *avenge*, ch. xviii. 3.

23. **Distress** (ἀνάγκη). Originally *constraint, necessity;* thence *force* or *violence*, and in the classical poets, *distress, anguish.*

24. **Edge** (στόματι). Lit., *the mouth*. So Wyc. Either in the sense of the *foremost* part, or picturing the sword as a devouring monster. In Heb. xi. 33, 34, the word is used in both senses: "the *mouths* of lions;" "the *edge* of the sword."

Led away captive. See on *captives*, ch. iv. 18.

Trodden down. Denoting the oppression and contempt which shall follow conquest.

25. **Signs** (σημεῖα). See on Matt. xxiv. 24.

Distress (συνοχὴ). Only here and 2 Cor. ii. 4. Kindred with συνεχομένη, *taken* (ch. iv. 38), on which see note. The original idea of the word is *being held in a tight grasp*.

With perplexity, the sea and the waves roaring. The A. V. follows the reading ἠχούσης, the participle, *roaring*. The proper reading is ἠχοῦς, the noun, *the roaring*. Render *perplexity for the roaring of the sea*, etc. *'Ηχώ*, *roaring*, is properly a *returned* sound, an *echo*. Generally a *ringing* sound, as of the blows on an anvil.

Waves (σάλου). Only here in New Testament. The radical notion of the word is *unsteady motion*, especially the rolling swell of the sea. Rev., better, *billows*.

26. **Failing** (ἀποψυχόντων). Only here in New Testament. The word originally means to *leave off breathing;* to *swoon*. Thus Homer, when Laertes recognizes Ulysses:

> "He threw
> Round his dear son his arms. The hardy chief,
> Ulysses, drew him *fainting* (ἀποψύχοντα) to his heart."
>
> *Odyssey*, xxiv., 346.

So also Sophocles, of Hector dragged behind Achilles' chariot:

> "He *breathed out his life* (ἀπέψυξεν βίον).
>
> *Ajax*, 1031.

Matthew alone uses the simple verb, ψύχω, to *breathe* or *blow*. See on *wax cold*, Matt. xxiv. 12. Luke uses four compounds of this simple verb, all of which are peculiar to him. Compare *cool*, ch. xvi. 24; *refreshing*, Acts iii. 19; *gave up the ghost*, Acts v. 5, 10.

Expectation (προσδοκίας). Only here and Acts xii. 11.

The world. See on ch. ii. 1.

Shall be shaken (σαλευθήσονται). Compare Matt. xi. 7; Luke vi. 38; Acts iv. 31; Heb. xii. 26, 27. The root of the verb is the same as that of *billows*, ver. 25.

28. **Look up.** See on ch. xiii. 11. Graphic, as implying being previously *bowed down* with sorrow.

Redemption (ἀπολύτρωσις). See on *lettest depart*, ch. ii. 29.

29. **Parable.** See on Matt. xxiv. 32.

30. **Ye see** (βλέποντες). Lit., "*looking*, ye know," etc. Implying careful *observation*, with a view to determine the progress of the season.

Know (γινώσκετε). *Perceive* would be better.

31. **Come to pass** (γινόμενα). The present participle. Rev., more correctly, "*coming* to pass:" in process of fulfilment. Compare Mark xiii. 29.

34. **Overcharged** (βαρηθῶσιν). Weighed down. Compare ch. ix. 32; 2 Cor. v. 4.

Surfeiting (κραιπάλῃ). Only here in New Testament. Derivation uncertain: akin to the Latin *crapula*, *intoxication*. Trench finds an equivalent in *fulsomeness*, in its original sense of *fulness*. In the medical writings it is used of *drunken nausea* or *headache*.

Drunkenness (μέθη). Compare *are well drunk*, John ii.10. This and kindred words in the New Testament always refer to intoxication, or that which intoxicates. See note on John ii. 10.

Cares (μερίμναις). See on Matt. vi. 25.

Of this life (βιωτικαῖς). The rendering is too general; though it might be difficult to give a better. *Βίος, life*, means life considered either as to its *duration* (1 Pet. iv. 3); the *means of support* (Mark xii. 44; Luke viii. 43; xxi. 4; 1 John iii. 17); or *the manner of leading it* (1 Tim. ii. 2). The meaning here is *pertaining to the support* or *luxury of life;* and so in the only other passages where it occurs, 1 Cor. vi. 3, 4. The parallel is Matt. vi. 31. Wyc., *business of this life.*

Suddenly (αἰφνίδιος). Only here and 1 Thess. v. 3.

35. **As a snare.** Join with the previous sentence: "come suddenly as a snare." Compare *entangle*, Matt. xxii. 15.

36. **Watch.** See on Mark xiii. 33.

37. **Abode** (ηὐλίζετο). Only here and Matt. xxi. 17.

38. **Came early in the morning** (ὤρθριζεν). Only here in New Testament.

CHAPTER XXII.

1–6. Compare Matt. xxvi. 17–19. Mark xiv. 12–16.

1. **Feast** (ἑορτὴ). Properly *festival.* See on Mark xiv. 1.

Drew nigh. Imperfect: "*was drawing* nigh."

2. **Sought.** Imperfect, *were seeking*, contemporaneously with the approach of the feast.

Kill (ἀνέλωσιν). Lit., *to take up and carry off*, and so *to make way with.*

3. **Satan.** See on ch. xiii. 16.

Iscariot. See on Matt. x. 5.

4. **Captains** (στρατηγοῖς). The leaders of the temple-guards Compare Acts iv. 1.

6. **Promised** (ἐξωμολόγησεν). See on Matt. iii. 6; xi. 25. The idea is that of an *open* and *fair* consent or pledge.

10. **A man—pitcher.** See on Mark xiv. 13.

11. **Guest-chamber.** See on Mark xiv. 14.

12. **And he** (κἀκεῖνος). See on Mark xiv. 15.

Furnished. See on Mark xiv. 15. Wyc., *strewed.*

14–18; 24–30. Compare Matt. xxvi. 20; Mark xiv. 17.

14. **The apostles.** Both Matthew and Mark have *the twelve.*

15. **With desire I have desired.** Expressing *intense* desire. Compare John iii. 29, *rejoiceth with joy;* Acts iv. 17, *threaten with threatening.*

19–20. Compare Matt. xxvi. 26–29. Mark xiv. 22–25. 1 Cor. xi. 23–25.

19. **Bread** (ἄρτον). Better, *a loaf.*

20. **The cup.** See on Mark xiv. 23.

Testament (διαθήκη)—**shed.** See on Matt. xxvi. 28.

21. **Betrayeth** (παραδιδόντος). The present participle: *is now engaged in betraying.*

With me. "He does not say *with you:* thus separating the traitor from the rest of the disciples, and showing that now he alone has to do with that wretch, as with an enemy" (Bengel).

24. **A strife** (*φιλονεικία*). Properly, "an *eager* contention." Only here in New Testament.

Greatest. Strictly, *greater.*

26. **Doth serve.** See on *minister*, Matt. xx. 26.

28. **Continued** (*διαμεμενηκότες*). Lit., "have remained *through*" (*διά*).

29. **I appoint** (*διατίθεμαι*). Implying *allotment:* assigning in the course of *distribution* (*διά*). Wyc., *dispose.* Luke is especially fond of compounds with *διά*.

31. **Hath desired** (*ἐξητήσατο*). Only here in New Testament. It sometimes means *to obtain* by asking, or *to beg off.* So Xenophon, "Anabasis," i., 1, 3. The mother of Cyrus, who is charged with an attempt to kill his brother, *begged him off* (*ἐξαιτησαμένη*). Rev., in margin, *obtained you by asking.* The result proved that Satan had obtained him for the time.

Sift (*σινιάσαι*). Only here in New Testament.

Wheat (*σῖτον*). A general term, *grain.*

32. **Prayed** (*ἐδεήθην*). See on *prayers*, ch. v. 33.

Art converted (*ἐπιστρέψας*). Converted is simply the Latinized rendering of the word *to turn round* (*convertere*). Rev. renders the aorist participle, denoting a definite act, by *once:* "when *once* thou *hast turned again.*"

Strengthen (*στήριξον*). See on ch. xvi. 25, and 1 Pet. v.

10. Rev., *stablish*, which is much better. *Strengthen* may denote only a *temporary* effect. The word implies *fixedness*.

34. **Peter.** The only instance of Christ's directly addressing him as Peter. He refers to him by that name, Mark xvi. 7.

The cock. See on Matt. xxvi. 34

Deny. See on Mark xiv. 30.

36. **He that hath no sword,** etc. But *sword* is not governed by *hath*. It is too far off in the sentence. The meaning is, he that hath not a *purse* or *scrip* (and is therefore penniless), let him sell his garment and buy a sword. So Wyc.

37. **Have an end** (τέλος ἔχει). The phrase is synonymous with *be accomplished* (τελεσθῆναι, Rev., *fulfilled*). In classical Greek this latter word is often used of the fulfilment of an oracle: also of things which are settled beyond controversy. The two expressions here give the two meanings. The prophecy is *fulfilled;* the things concerning me are *finally settled*.

39–46. Compare Matt. xxvi. 30, 36–46; Mark xiv. 26, 32–42.

40. **The place.** See on *Gethsemane*, Matt. xxvi. 36.

41. **Was withdrawn** (ἀπεσπάσθη). The Vulgate has *avulsus est*, "he was *torn* away," as by an inward urgency. Godet adopts this view, and so, apparently, Wyc., *he was taken away*. Meyer inclines to it; De Wette decidedly rejects it. Compare Acts xxi. 1.

Prayed. Imperfect, *began to pray*.

43. **There appeared** (ὤφθη). The word most commonly used in the New Testament of seeing visions. See Matt. xvii. 3; Mark ix. 4; Luke i. 11; xxii. 43; Acts ii. 17; vii. 35. The

kindred noun ὀπτασία, wherever it occurs in the New Testament, means *a vision*. See Luke i. 22; xxiv. 23, etc.

Strengthening (ἐνισχύων). Only here and Acts ix. 19. See on *was not able*, ch. xiv. 30; and *cannot*, ch. xvi. 3. Commonly intransitive; *to prevail in or among*. Used transitively only by Hippocrates and Luke.

44. **Being in an agony** (γενόμενος ἐν ἀγωνίᾳ). There is in the aorist participle a suggestion of a *growing intensity* in the struggle, which is not conveyed by the simple *being*. Literally, though very awkwardly, it is, *having become in an agony:* having progressed from the first prayer (*began to pray*, ver. 41) into an intense struggle of prayer and sorrow. Wycliffe's rendering hints at this: *and he, made in agony, prayed*. *Agony* occurs only here. It is used by medical writers, and the fact of a *sweat* accompanying an agony is also mentioned by them.

More earnestly (ἐκτενέστερον). See on *fervently*, 1 Pet. i. 22.

Was (ἐγένετο). More correctly, as Rev., *became*. See on γενόμενος, *being*, above.

Great drops (θρόμβοι). Only here in New Testament: *gouts* or *clots*. Very common in medical language. Aristotle mentions a bloody sweat arising from the blood being in poor condition; and Theophrastus mentions a physician who compared a species of sweat to blood.

45. **For sorrow.** The mention of the cause of the drowsiness is characteristic.

47–53. Compare Matt. xxvii. 47–56; Mark xiv. 43–52.

47. **Multitude—one of the twelve.** See on Matt. xxvi. 47

To kiss. See on Matt. xxvi. 47.

50. **The servant.** See on Matt. xxvi. 51.

His right ear. Lit., *his ear, the right one.* See on Matt. xxvi. 51; and compare Mark xiv. 47. Both Matthew and Mark use diminutives.

51. **Suffer ye thus far.** This is variously interpreted. I think the text requires that the words should be addressed to the disciples, and taken as the answer to the question, *shall we smite*, etc. The meaning then is, *permit them to go so far as to seize me.* The expression thus corresponds with Matt. xxvi. 52,

Ear (ὠτίου). This time Luke uses the diminutive. Wyc., *little ear.*

Healed. Only Luke records the healing.

52. **Thief** (λῃστὴν). See on Matt. xxvi. 55; Luke x. 30; Mark xi. 17.

54–62. Compare Matt. xxvi. 57, 58, 69–75; Mark xiv. 53, 54, 66–72.

55. **Kindled** (περιαψάντων). Lit., *kindled all round* (περί): set in full blaze.

Hall. Or *court.* See on Mark xiv. 54.

56. **By the fire** (πρὸς τὸ φῶς). See on Mark xiv. 54.

63. **Smote** (δέροντες). Originally to *flay;* thence to *cudgel.* Compare our vulgarism, to *tan* or *hide.*

66. **The elders** (πρεσβυτέριον). More correctly, the *assembly of the elders.* So Rev.

CHAPTER XXIII.

1–5. Compare Matt. xxvii. 1, 2; 11, 14; Mark xv. 1–5.

2. **We found.** In a judicial sense: as the result of their examination before the council.

5. **Were the more fierce** (ἐπίσχυον). Only here in New Testament. The verb means, literally, *to grow strong*. See on ch. xiv. 30; xvi. 3. Here the sense is, they were *more energetic and emphatic*. Rev., *urgent*. Wyc., *waxed stronger*.

Stirreth up (ἀνασείει). See on Mark xv. 11. The increased urgency is shown by the use of a stronger word than *perverteth* (ver. 2).

6. **Of Galilee.** The best texts omit.

7. **Sent** (ἀνέπεμψεν). Lit., sent him *up* (ἀνα). Used of sending up to a higher court. Compare Acts xxv. 21, of sending Paul to Caesar. It also means to *send back*, as in ver. 11, and Philem. 11.

8. **Of a long time** (ἐξ ἱκανοῦ). See on ch. vii. 6.

Hoped (ἤλπιζεν). Imperfect; *was hoping*—all this long time.

Miracle (σημεῖον). See on Matt. xi. 20; and compare Acts ii. 22, Rev.

9. **Many** (ἱκανοῖς). Compare *long*, ver. 8.

10. **Vehemently** (εὐτόνως). Only here and Acts xviii. 28, of the preaching of Apollos. Originally the word means *well-strung;* hence, in medical language, of a well-toned body.

11. **Gorgeous** (λαμπρὰν). Lit., *bright* or *brilliant*. Compare Acts x. 30; Apoc. xv. 6. Wyc. and Tynd., *white*. Mark has *purple* (πορφύραν), and Matthew *scarlet* (κοκκίνην).

Apparel (ἐσθῆτα). The general term for raiment. Matthew specifies the garment (xxvii. 28). Mark has simply *purple* (xv. 17).

13–25. Compare Matt. xxvii. 15–26; Mark xv. 6–15.

14. **Perverteth** (ἀποστρέφοντα). Another compound of στρέφω, *to turn*; διαστρέφοντα is rendered by the same word in ver. 2. Probably the words are used without any intentional distinction of meaning. Διαστρέφοντα implies more of the idea of *distraction* (compare Wyc., *turning upside down*); turning different ways; while ἀποστρέφοντα emphasizes the turning *away* (ἀπό) of the people from their civil and religious allegiance. So Wyc., *turning away*.

Examined (ἀνακρίνας). Originally implying a *thorough* examination; ἀνά, *up*, from bottom to top. Technically, of a legal examination.

16. **Chastise** (παιδεύσας). Originally to *bring up a child* (παῖς). Hence, *to instruct*; so Acts vii. 22, of Moses *instructed* in the wisdom of the Egyptians; and Acts xxii. 3, of Paul *instructed* in the law. To *discipline* or *correct*, as Heb. xii. 6, 7. The word is not synonymous with *punish*, since it always implies an infliction which contemplates the subject's amendment; and hence answers to *chastise* or *chasten*. So Heb. xii. 10; Apoc. iii. 19. In popular speech *chastise* and *punish* are often confounded. *Chasten* is from the Latin *castus*, "pure," "chaste;" and to *chasten* is, properly, to *purify*. This meaning underlies even the use of the word by Pilate, who was not likely to be nice in his choice of words. Instead of *punishing* him with death, he will *chastise* him, in order to teach him better. So Wyc., *I shall deliver him amended.*

18. **All together** (παμπληθεὶ). The whole multitude (πλῆθος) of them. Only here in New Testament.

Away (αἶρε). Lit., *take away*. Compare Acts xxi. 36; xxii. 22.

19. **Who** (ὅστις). Classifying him. One of such a kind as that he had been imprisoned, etc.

20. **Spake** (προσεφώνησεν). Addressed. Compare Acts xxi. 40; xxii. 2. Always in the New Testament in the sense of *to accost*, whether an individual or a crowd.

21. **Shouted** (ἐπεφώνουν). Imperfect. *Kept shouting*. Used by Luke only. Compare Acts xii. 22; xxii. 24.

22. **Said** (εἶπεν). Dropping the speech-making tone, and simply asking a question.

23. **They were instant** (ἐπέκειντο). *Instant*, in the sense of *urgent, pressing*. See on ch. vii. 4. Compare Rom. xii. 12; 2 Tim. iv. 2; Luke vii. 4; Acts xxvi. 7. The verb means *to lie upon*, and answers to our vulgarism, *to lay one's self down to work*. Compare Aristophanes, "Knights," 253: κἀπικείμενος βόα, *roar with all your might*. Lit., *roar, lying down to it*.

Their voices. Omit *of the chief priests*.

Prevailed (κατίσχυον). Had *power* (ἰσχύς) to bear *down* (κατά) the remonstrances of Pilate. Only here and Matt. xvi. 18.

24. **Gave sentence** (ἐπέκρινεν). Pronounced the final sentence. Only here in New Testament.

26–33. Compare Matt. xxvii. 31–34; Mark xv. 20–23.

26. **Laid hold on** (ἐπιλαβόμενοι). Compare the peculiar word used by Matthew and Mark. See on Matt. v. 41.

27–32. Peculiar to Luke. See Introduction, on the gospel of womanhood.

30. **Hills** (βουνοῖς). Only here and ch. iii. 5.

31. **Tree** (ξύλῳ). Originally *wood, timber*. In later Greek, *a tree*. Used of the *cross* by Peter, Acts v. 30; x. 39; and 1 Pet. ii. 24. Compare Gal. iii. 13.

32. **Two other.** The possible omission of a comma before *malefactors* in the A. V. might make a very awkward and unpleasant statement. Better Rev., *two others, malefactors*.

Put to death (ἀναιρεθῆναι). Lit., *to take up and carry away*; so that the Greek idiom answers to our *taken off*. So Shakspeare:

> "The deep damnation of his *taking off*."
>
> *Macbeth*, i., 7.

> "Let her who would be rid of him, devise
> His speedy *taking off*."
>
> *Lear*, v., 1.

33. **Calvary** (Κρανίον). The Greek word is the translation of the Hebrew *Golgotha*. See on Matt. xxvii. 33.

35–43. Compare Matt. xxvii. 39–44; Mark xv. 29–32.

35. **Beholding.** See on ch. x. 18.

Scoffed. See on ch. xvi. 14.

If he. The A. V. does not give the contemptuous emphasis on οὗτος, *this fellow*.

36. **Coming to him.** Coming up close to the cross.

Vinegar. See on Matt. xxvii. 34.

38. **Superscription.** See on Mark xv. 26.

39. **Railed** (ἐβλασφήμει). Imperfect: *kept up a railing.*

41. **Receive.** *Are receiving* would be better.

Amiss (ἄτοπον). Lit., *out of place,* and so *strange, eccentric, perverse;* as in 2 Thess. iii. 2, where it is rendered *unreasonable.* The expression here answers nearly to our familiar phrase, "has done nothing *out of the way.*" Compare Acts xxviii. 6; *no harm.*

42. **Into thy kingdom.** Some texts read for εἰς, *into,* ἐν, *in.* So Rev. In that case we must understand, "in thy kingly glory."

43. **In Paradise** (παραδείσῳ). Originally *an enclosed park,* or *pleasure-ground.* Xenophon uses it of the parks of the Persian kings and nobles. "There (at Celaenae) Cyrus had a palace and a great park (παράδεισος), full of wild animals, which he hunted on horseback. . . . Through the midst of the park flows the river Maeander ("Anabasis," i., 2, 7). And again: "The Greeks encamped near a great and beautiful *park,* thickly grown with all kinds of trees" (ii., 4, 14.) In the Septuagint, Gen. ii. 8, of the garden of Eden. In the Jewish theology, the department of Hades where the blessed souls await the resurrection; and therefore equivalent to *Abraham's bosom* (ch. xvi. 22, 23). It occurs three times in the New Testament: here; 2 Cor. xii. 4; Apoc. ii. 7; and always of the abode of the blessed.

> "Where'er thou roam'st, one happy soul, we know,
> Seen at thy side in woe,
> Waits on thy triumph—even as all the blest
> With him and Thee shall rest.
> Each on his cross, by Thee we hang awhile,
> Watching thy patient smile,
> Till we have learn'd to say, ''Tis justly done,
> Only in glory, Lord, thy sinful servant own.'"
>
> KEBLE, *Christian Year.*

44–46. Compare Matt. xxvii. 45–50; Mark xv. 33–37.

44. **Sixth hour.** Midday.

Ninth hour. See on Matt. xxvii. 46.

45. **Veil.** See on Matt. xxvii. 51.

46. **I commend** (παρατίθεμαι). See on ch. ix. 16.

Gave up the ghost (ἐξέπνευσεν). Lit., *breathed out* (*his life*). Wyc., *sent out the spirit.* See on Matt. xxvii. 50.

47–49. Compare Matt. xxvii. 51–56; Mark xv. 38–41.

49. **That followed** (συνακολουθοῦσαι). Lit., followed *with* (σύν). So Rev. See on Matt. xxvii. 55.

50. **Councillor.** See on Mark xv. 43. Matthew calls him *rich;* Mark, *honorable;* Luke, *good and just.*

51. **Consented** (συγκατατεθειμένος). Only here in New Testament. Another of Luke's numerous compounds. The Greek student will be struck with the array of compounds, from ver. 49 to 56, inclusive. The verb means *to put* (τίθημι), *down* (κατά), *along with* (σύν). Hence to put down the same *vote* or *opinion* with another: to agree with or assent to.

53. **Linen** (σινδόνι). See on Mark xiv. 51; and compare Luke xvi. 19.

Hewn in stone (λαξευτῷ). Only here in New Testament, and not at all in classical Greek.

56. **Returned** (ὑποστρέψασαι). This word occurs thirty-two times in Luke, and only three times in the rest of the New Testament. It is a significant fact that, reckoning the aggregate space occupied by the four Gospels, nearly one-sixth of the whole amount is occupied with the account of the twenty-four hours beginning with the last supper and ending with the

burial of Jesus. There is no day in all Bible history narrated with the fulness of that day. If we possessed the whole life of Christ, written with the same detail, the record would occupy *one hundred and eighty* volumes as large as the *whole Bible.*

CHAPTER XXIV.

1–3. Compare Matt. xxviii. 1; Mark xvi. 2–4.

1. **Very early in the morning** (*ὄρθρου βαθέως*). Lit., *at deep dawn*, or *the dawn being deep.* It is not uncommon in Greek to find *βαθύς*, *deep*, used of *time;* as *deep* or *late* evening. Plutarch says of Alexander, that he supped "at *deep evening;*" i.e., late at night. Philo says that the Hebrews crossed the Red Sea "*about deep dawn* (as here), while others were yet in bed." So Socrates, in prison, asks Crito the time of day. He replies, *ὄρθρος βαθύς*, *the dawn is deep*, i.e. *breaking* (Plato, "Crito," 43).

4–8. Compare Matt. xxviii. 5–7; Mark xvi. 5–7.

4. **Shining** (*ἀστραπτούσαις*). Only here and ch. xvii. 24. Akin to *ἀστράπη*, *lightning.* See on *bright shining*, ch. xi. 36; and compare ch. xvii. 24.

11. **To them** (*ἐνώπιον αὐτῶν*). Rev., literally, *in their sight.*

Idle tales (λῆρος). Lit., *silly talk; nonsense.* Only here in New Testament. Used in medical language of the wild talk of delirium. Wyc., *madness.* Tynd., *feigned things.*

12. **Stooping down.** See on *looketh*, Jas. i. 25. The best texts omit this verse.

Clothes. Not *garments*, but the linen *bandages* in which the body had been rolled. So Rev., *cloths.*

13. **Threescore furlongs.** Seven miles.

15. **Went with** (συνεπορεύετο). The use of the imperfect here is very beautiful. Jesus drew near while they were absorbed in their talk, and *was already walking* with them when they observed him.

17. **Ye have** (ἀντιβάλλετε). Lit., *throw back and forth; exchange.*

> "Discussed a doubt and tossed it to and fro" (Tennyson).

And are sad (σκυθρωποί). Only here and Matt. vi. 16, on which see note. The best texts put the interrogation point after *walk*, add καὶ ἐστάθησαν, and render, *and they stood still, looking sad.* So Rev.

18. **Art thou only a stranger in Jerusalem** (σὺ μόνος παροικεῖς Ἰερουσαλὴμ). *Παροικεῖν, to dwell as a stranger*, is used in later Greek of strangers who have no rights of citizenship, and no settled home. Compare Heb. xi. 9. See on *strangers*, 1 Pet. i. 1; and compare *sojourning*, 1 Pet. i. 17. The *only* of the A. V. is commonly understood adverbially: "Are you *nothing but* a stranger?" But the emphasis of the question falls there, and the word is an adjective. Render "Dost thou *alone* dwell as a stranger in Jerusalem?" Are you the *only* one who sojourns as a stranger in Jerusalem, and who does not know, etc. So, nearly, Wyc., *Thou alone art* a pilgrim in Jerusalem.

18. **What things** (ποῖα). Lit., "*what kind* of things."

21. **Trusted** (ἠλπίζομεν). More correctly, *hoped.* Imperfect: *were hoping* all the while.

Should have redeemed. Rev., more correctly, *should redeem* (λυτροῦσθαι). See on 1 Pet. i. 18.

Beside all this (σὺν πᾶσιν τούτοις). Lit., *with all these things:* his betrayal and crucifixion, etc.

To-day is the third day (τρίτην ταύτην ἡμέραν ἄγει σήμερον). The best texts omit *to-day*. The phrase forms an idiom which cannot be neatly rendered. Literally it is, "He (Christ) is *passing* (ἄγει) this day as the third." Rev., *It is now the third day since*, etc.

22. **Made us astonished** (ἐξέστησαν). Literally the verb means to *put out of place;* and so, to *drive one out of his senses*. Hence the A. V. is feeble. Rev., better, *amazed us*.

Early (ὀρθριναὶ). Lit., *early ones*. Only here and Apoc. xxii. 16. Compare ὄρθρος, *dawn*, ver. 1.

23. **That they had seen—which said.** Cleopas, absorbed in his story, throws himself back to the time of his interview with the women. Lit., "They came saying that *they have seen* a vision of angels which *say*" (λέγουσιν).

25. **Fools and slow of heart** (ἀνόητοι καὶ βραδεῖς τῇ καρδίᾳ). This is an unfortunate translation, in the light of the ordinary, popular use of the word *fool*. Jesus would never have called those sorrowful disciples *fools* in that sense. The word is compounded of ἀ, *not*, and νοέω, which implies, besides *seeing*, perception *of the mind* as consequent upon sight. It is therefore equivalent to *dull of perception*. They had read what the prophets had spoken, but had failed to *perceive* its application to Christ. While this rebuke relates to the *understanding*, the following one, *slow of heart*, goes deeper, and contemplates the region of *feeling* and *moral susceptibility*. Your heart is dull and slow to respond to these testimonies of your own prophets. Compare *hardness of heart*, Mark xvi. 14.

All (ἐπὶ πᾶσιν). Rev., rightly, *in all; relying upon* (ἐπί) all the utterances of the prophets.

26. **Ought not** (οὐχὶ ἔδει). The A. V. does not convey the precise meaning, which is, that, in the eternal order of things, and in fulfilment of the eternal counsel of God as expressed in

the prophecies, it was *essentially fitting* that Christ should suffer. Rev. is clumsy but correct: *behoved it not the Christ to suffer?*

27. **He expounded** (διερμήνυεν). Or *interpreted: throughout* (διά). Imperfect, he *went on* interpreting from passage to passage.

28. **They went** (ἐπορεύοντο). Imperfect, *were going*. So Rev.

Made as though (προσεποιήσατο). The verb means originally *to add or attach to;* hence to take to one's self what does not belong to him; and so, *to pretend;* though *pretending* as implying anything false, does not attach to this act of Jesus. He *was* going on, and would have gone on but for their invitation. Only here in New Testament.

29. **They constrained** (παρεβιάσαντο). *Contrary to* (παρά) his apparent intention of going on. Only here and Acts xvi. 15.

Is far spent (κέκλικεν). Lit., *has declined.* Wyc., *is now bowed down.*

30. **And gave** (ἐπεδίδου). A very beautiful use of the imperfect, indicating that while he was *in the act of distributing* they recognized him. He blessed, and having broken, *was giving* it to them, when, in an instant, their eyes *were opened* (aorist tense).

31. **They knew** (ἐπέγνωσαν). *Clearly* recognized.

And he vanished out of their sight (αὐτὸς ἄφαντος ἐγένετο ἀπ' αὐτῶν). Lit., *he, invisible, became away from them.* It is not simply, he suddenly departed from them, but he passed away from them invisibly. The ἐγένετο, *became,* is construed with ἀπ' αὐτῶν, *from them.**

---

* Not ἄφαντος αὐτοῖς, *became invisible to them,* which would imply that his body remained, but invisibly; but ἀπ' αὐτῶν, *away from them,* implying a real removal (Beza, cited by Alford and Meyer).

32. **Did not our heart burn—while he talked—opened.** (οὐχὶ ἡ καρδία ἡμῶν καιομένη ἦν—ὡς ἐλάλει—διήνοιγεν). The A. V., as usual, pays no attention to the graphic imperfects here. They are speaking of something which was in progress: "*was* not our heart *burning* (finite verb and participle) while he *was speaking*, and *was opening* the scriptures?"

34. **Is risen** (ἠγέρθη)—**appeared** (ὤφθη). Both aorists. The Lord *rose* and *appeared*. So Wyc. See on *appeared*, ch. xxii. 43.

35. **They told** (ἐξηγοῦντο). Rev., *rehearsed* is better, because the verb means to *tell at length* or *relate in full*.

36. **Jesus himself.** The best texts omit *Jesus*. Render as Rev., "*he himself* stood."

And saith unto them, Peace be unto you. The best texts omit.

38. **Thoughts** (διαλογισμοί). See on Jas. ii. 4, and *deceiving*, Jas. i. 22. Rev., *reasonings*. As if he had said, "Why do you reason about a matter which your spiritual perception ought to discern at once." Compare note on *fools*, ver. 25.*

39. **Handle** (ψηλαφήσατε). Compare 1 John i. 1. The word occurs also Acts xvii. 27; Heb. xii. 18. "It never expresses the so handling an object as to exercise a moulding, modifying influence upon it, but at most a feeling of its surface; this, it may be, with the intention of learning its composition (Gen. xxvii. 12, 21, 22); while, not seldom, it signifies

* *Reasonings*, *doubtings*, *scruples*, are more or less distinctly implied in every occurrence of the word in the New Testament. In Phil. ii. 14, *disputings* (Rev.) is, as Meyer observes, unsuitable to the reference of *murmurings* to God, and means rather *scrupulous considering* or *hesitations*, indicating uncertainty in the consciousness of duty. So in 1 Tim. ii. 8, the A. V. *doubting* is better. Rom. xiv. 1, is *decisions of doubts* (Rev., margin) or *scruples*. So Meyer, Godet, Lange, Beet, Shedd, Hodge, Tholuck, Alford, De Wette.

no more than a feeling *for* or *after* an object, without any actual coming in contact with it at all" (Trench, "Synonyms"). Compare Acts xvii. 27. Used of groping in the dark, Job v. 14; of the blind, Isa. lix. 10; Deut. xxviii. 29; Judges, xvi. 26. See on Heb. xii. 18.

41. **Meat** (*βρώσιμον*). Only here in New Testament. Lit., *anything eatable.* Wyc., *anything that shall be eaten.* Rev., better, *anything to eat*, as the word *meat* has largely lost, in popular usage, its old sense of *food* in general.

42. **Broiled.** Only here in New Testament.

Of an honey-comb. The best texts omit.

44. **The words.** The best texts insert *my.*

Must (*δεῖ*). See on *ought not*, ver. 26.

45. **Understanding** (*νοῦν*). Which had been closed. See on *fools*, ver. 25.

46. **Thus it behoved.** The best texts omit. Render, as Rev., *thus it is written that the Christ should suffer.*

Christ (*τὸν Χριστὸν*). Note the article, *the* Christ, and see on Matt. i. 1.

47. **Should be preached.** See on *preacher*, 2 Pet. ii. 5.

In his name. On the foundation of (*ἐπί*). See on Matt. xxiv. 5.

Remission. See on ch. iii. 3; and on *forgiven*, Jas. v. 15.

Beginning from Jerusalem. Some editors place a period

after *nations*, and join these words with the next sentence, omitting *and*: "beginning from Jerusalem ye are witnesses." *

49. **I send** (ἐγὼ ἐξαποστέλλω). Rev., better, send *forth*, giving the force of ἐξ. *I* emphatic.

Endued with power. The Rev. has properly substituted the simpler *clothed*, which, to the English reader, conveys the exact figure in the word. This metaphorical sense of *clothed* is found in classical Greek. Aristophanes has *clothed with audacity*; Homer, *clothed with strength*; Plutarch, *clothed with nobility and wealth*.

51. **And was carried up into heaven.** Some texts omit.

---

* Tischendorf (8th ed.), Westcott and Hort, and Rev. text read ἀρξάμενοι, referring to the disciples. The old reading, ἀρξάμενον, is explained as the impersonal accusative neuter, referring to κηρυχθῆναι.

THE ACTS OF THE APOSTLES.

CHAPTER I.

1. **The former** (τὸν πρῶτον). Lit., *the first.* Luke refers to his Gospel.

Treatise (λόγον). Or narrative.

Began (ἤρξατο). This is interpreted in two ways. Either, (1), as a simple historical statement equivalent to "all that Jesus did and taught." In favor of this is the fact that the synoptists often record that which is done or said *according to its moment of commencement*, thus giving vividness to the account. See Matt. xi. 20; xxvi. 22, 37; Mark vi. 7; xiv. 19; Luke vii. 38, etc. According to this explanation the word serves "to recall to the recollection from the Gospel all the several incidents and events, up to the ascension, in which Jesus had *appeared* as doer and teacher" (Meyer). Or, (2), as indicating that the Gospel contains the *beginning*, and the Acts of the Apostles the *continuation*, of the doings and teachings of Jesus. "The earthly life of Jesus, concluded with the ascension, has its fruit and continued efficacy; and his heavenly life, commencing with the ascension, has its manifestation and proof in the acts and experiences of the apostles and first churches. The history of the Church was under the immediate control of the exalted Redeemer, and may justly be considered as the continuation in heaven of the work which he had begun on earth" (Baumgarten and Gloag). While the truth and importance of this statement are admitted, it is objected that such an intention on

Luke's part would have been more clearly intimated, and not left to be inferred from a single doubtful phrase. As regards Luke's *intention*, I think the first explanation is more likely to be correct. The second, however, states a truth, the value and importance of which cannot be overestimated, and which should be kept in mind constantly in the study of the book of Acts. This is well put by Bernard (" Progress of Doctrine in the New Testament," Lect. IV.): " Thus the history which follows is *linked* to, or (may I not rather say) *welded* with, the past; and the founding of the Church in the earth is presented as one continuous work, begun by the Lord in person, and perfected by the same Lord through the ministry of men. . . . 'The former treatise' delivered to us, not all that Jesus did and taught, but 'all that Jesus *began* to do and teach *until* the day when he was taken up.' The following writings appear intended to give us, and do, in fact, profess to give us, that which Jesus *continued* to do and teach *after* the day in which he was taken up."

2. **Had given commandment** (ἐντειλάμενος). Special injunctions or charges. Compare Matt. iv. 6; Mark xiii. 34; Heb. xi. 22.

Through the Holy Ghost. Construe with *had given commandment:* by means of the Holy Spirit, which inspired him. Not, as some interpreters, with *whom he had chosen.*

3. **Shewed himself** (παρέστησεν). This verb is rendered in a variety of ways in the New Testament, as *give* or *furnish*, *present*, *provide*, *assist*, *commend.* The original meaning is *to place beside*, and so *commend to the attention.* Hence, to *set before the mind; present*, *shew.*

Infallible proofs (τεκμηρίοις). The word is akin to **τέκμαρ**, a *fixed boundary*, *goal*, *end;* and hence a *fixed* or *sure sign* or *token.* The Rev. omits *infallible*, probably assuming that a *proof* implies certainty.

Being seen (ὀπτανόμενος). Only here in New Testament. Rev., *appearing*.

Forty days (δι' ἡμερῶν τεσσεράκοντα). Lit., "*through* forty days." Rev., by *the space of*. The only passage where the interval between the resurrection and the ascension is given.

4. **Being assembled together** (συναλιζόμενος). From σύν, *together*, and ἁλής, *thronged* or *crowded*. Both the A. V. and Rev. give *eating together* in margin, following the derivation from σύν, *together*, and ἅλς, *salt:* eating salt together, and hence generally of association at table.

Commanded (παρήγγειλεν). Originally to *pass on* or *transmit;* hence, as a military term, of *passing a watchword* or *command;* and so generally to *command*.

To wait for (περιμένειν). Only here in New Testament.

The promise (ἐπαγγελίαν). Signifying a *free* promise, given without solicitation. This is the invariable sense of the word throughout the New Testament, and this and its kindred and compound words are the only words for *promise* in the New Testament. Ὑπισχνέομαι, meaning to promise *in response to a request*, does not occur; and ὁμολογέω, Matt. xiv. 7, of Herod promising Salome, really means to *acknowledge* his obligation for her lascivious performance. See note there.

Not many days hence (οὐ μετὰ πολλὰς ταύτας ἡμέρας). Lit., *not after many of these days*. Not after *many*, but after a *few*.

6. **Asked** (ἐπηρώτων). The imperfect, denoting the *repetition* and urging of the question.

7. **The times—the seasons** (χρόνους—καιροὺς). Rev. properly omits the article. The former of these words, *time abso-*

lutely, without regard to circumstances; the latter, *definite periods, with the idea of fitness.*

His own (τῇ ἰδίᾳ). Stronger than the simple possessive pronoun. The adjective means *private, personal.* Often used adverbially in the phrase κατ' ἰδίαν, *apart, privately.* See Matt. xvii. 1; xxiv. 3.

8. **Unto me** (μοι). The best texts read μου, *of me;* or, as Rev., *my witnesses.*

Samaria. Formerly they had been commanded not to enter the cities of the Samaritans (Matt. x. 5).

10. **Looked steadfastly** (ἀτενίζοντες ἦσαν). See on Luke iv. 20.

12. **A Sabbath-day's journey** (σαββάτου ἔχον ὁδόν). Lit., *having a Sabbath's way.* The way conceived as belonging to the mountain; connected with it in reference to the neighborhood of Jerusalem. A Sabbath-day's journey, according to Jewish tradition, was about three-quarters of a mile. It was the supposed distance between the camp and the tabernacle in the wilderness (Josh. iii. 4).

13. **An upper room** (τὸ ὑπερῷον). With the article, denoting some well-known place of resort. It was the name given to the room directly under the flat roof. Such rooms were often set apart as halls for meetings. In such an apartment Paul delivered his farewell address at Troas (Acts xx. 8), and the body of Dorcas was laid (Acts ix. 37). Used by Luke only.

Abode (ἦσαν καταμένοντες). The participle and finite verb, denoting *continuance* or *habitual residence.* Hence more correctly, as Rev., "where *they were abiding.*"

14. **Continued** (ἦσαν προσκαρτεροῦντες). Participle and finite verb, as above. The verb is from καρτερὸς, *strong, stanch,* and means originally to *persist obstinately in.* In this

sense here, and in Rom. xii. 12 ; xiii. 6. Hence to *adhere firmly to.* So in Mark iii. 9, "that a small ship should *wait on him;*" i.e., keep near at hand. The idea of *steady persistence* is supplied by the Rev., *steadfastly.*

With one accord (ὁμοθυμαδὸν). See on *agree,* Matt. xviii. 19.

In prayer. The best texts omit *and supplication.*

Mary. Mentioned here for the last time in the New Testament.

15. **Of the disciples** (τῶν μαθητῶν). The best texts read ἀδελφῶν, *brethren.*

The number of the names together were about, etc. (ἦν τε ὄχλος ὀνομάτων ἐπὶ τὸ αὐτὸ). Much better as Rev., *and there was a multitude of persons gathered together, about,* etc. Ὄχλος, *multitude,* would not be used of a *number* about to be stated.

16. **Men and brethren** (ἄνδρες ἀδελφοὶ). Lit., *men, brothers.* Brother-men. More dignified and solemn than the simple *brethren.*

This scripture. The best texts substitute *the.* See on Mark xii. 10.

The Holy Ghost (τὸ Πνεῦμα τὸ Ἅγιον). Lit., *The Spirit, the Holy.*

Guide. See on *lead,* Luke vi. 39.

17. **Numbered** (κατηριθμημένος). Only here in New Testament.

With (σύν). The best texts read ἐν, *among.* So Rev.

Obtained (ἔλαχε). Strictly, "received *by lot*." Rev., better, *received*. Compare Luke i. 9. In classical Greek, of receiving public magistracies.

Part (τὸν κλῆρον). The A. V. does not give the force of the article, *the* lot which was his. So Rev., "*his* portion:" lit., *lot*.

Ministry. See on *minister*, Matt. xx. 26. Compare *bishopric*, ver. 20.

18. **Purchased** (ἐκτήσατο). See on *possess*, Luke xviii. 12. Better, as Rev., *obtained*. Judas did not purchase the field, but the priests did with the money which he returned to them (Matt. xxvii. 7). The expression means merely that the field was purchased with the money of Judas.

Falling headlong (πρηνὴς γενόμενος). Lit., *having become headlong*.

He burst asunder (ἐλάκησε). Only here in New Testament. Lit., *to crack*, to burst with a noise. So Homer, of the bones cracking beneath a blow ("Iliad," xiii., 616). Compare Aristophanes, "Clouds," 410.

19. **Aceldama.** Or, more properly, *Akeldamach*. The word is Aramaic, the language then spoken in Palestine.

20. **Habitation** (ἔπαυλις). Only here in New Testament. The word is used in classical Greek of a place for cattle. So Herodotus (i., 111): "The herdsman took the child in his arms, and went back the way he had come, till he reached the *fold*" (ἔπαυλιν). Also of a *farm-building*, a *country-house*.

Bishopric (ἐπισκοπὴν). See on 1 Pet. ii. 12. Rev., better, *office*, with *overseership* in margin. Compare Luke xix. 44.

Another (ἕτερος). And *different* person. See on ch. ii. 4

21. **Went in and went out.** An expression for constant intercourse. Compare Deut. xviii. 19; Ps. cxxi. 8; John x. 9; Acts ix. 28.

Among us (ἐφ' ἡμᾶς). The margin of Rev., *over us*, i.e., *as our head*, is a sound rendering, and supported by Matt. xxv. 21, 23; Luke ix. 1. The rendering *before*, *in the presence of*, occurs Matt. x. 18; Luke xxi. 12.

22. **Witness** (μάρτυρα). One who shall bear testimony: not a *spectator*, a mistake often made on Heb. xii. 1. Compare Acts ii. 32.

23. **Barsabas.** A patronymic, *son of Saba:* like Bar Jona, Matt. xvi. 17.

24. **Which knowest the hearts** (καρδιογνῶστα). Only here and ch. xv. 8. Lit., *heart-knower*.

25. **That he may take part** (λαβεῖν τὸν κλῆρον). Lit., *to take the lot*. But the best texts read τὸν τόπον, *the place*. Rev., *to take the place*.

By transgression fell (παρέβη). See on *trespasses*, Matt. vi. 14. The rendering of the A. V. is explanatory. Rev., better, *fell away*.

His own place. Compare "*the place* in this ministry." *Τὸν ἴδιον*, *his own*, is stronger than the simple possessive pronoun. It is the place which was *peculiarly* his, as befitting his awful sin —Gehenna.

26. **He was numbered** (συγκατεψηφίσθη). Only here in New Testament. See on *counteth*, Luke xiv. 28.

CHAPTER II.

1. **Was fully come** (συμπληροῦσθαι). Used by Luke only. See on Luke ix. 51. Lit., as Rev., margin, *was being fulfilled.* The day, according to the Hebrew mode, is conceived as a *measure* to be filled up. So long as the day had not yet arrived, the measure was not full. The words denote *in process of fulfilment.*

Pentecost. Meaning *fiftieth;* because occurring on the fiftieth day, calculated from the second day of unleavened bread. In the Old Testament it is called *the feast of weeks,* and *the feast of harvest.* Its primary object was to thank God for the blessings of harvest. See Deut. xvi. 10, 11.

With one accord (ὁμοθυμαδὸν). The best texts substitute ὁμοῦ, *together.* So Rev.

2. **A sound** (ἦχος). See on Luke iv. 37.

Of a rushing mighty wind (φερομένης πνοῆς βιαίας). Lit., of *a mighty wind borne along.* Πνοή is a *blowing,* a *blast.* Only here and ch. xvii. 25. Rev., *as of the rushing of a mighty wind.*

The house. Not merely the *room.* Compare ch. i. 13.

Were sitting. Awaiting the hour of prayer. See ver. 15.

3. **There appeared.** See on Luke xxii. 43.

Cloven tongues (διαμεριζόμεναι γλῶσσαι). Many prefer to render *tongues distributing themselves,* or *being distributed* among the disciples, instead of referring it to the cloven appearance of each tongue. Rev., *tongues parting asunder.*

Like as of fire. Not *consisting of fire*, but *resembliny* (ὡσεὶ).

It sat. Note the singular. *One* of these luminous appearances sat upon each.

4. **Began.** Bringing into prominence the *first impulse* of the act. See on *began*, ch. i. 1.

With other tongues (ἑτέραις γλώσσαις). Strictly *different*, from their native tongues, and also different tongues spoken by the different apostles. See on Matt. vi. 24.

Gave (ἐδίδου). A graphic imperfect; *kept giving* them the language and the appropriate words as the case required from time to time. It would seem that each apostle was speaking to a group, or to individuals. The *general* address to the multitude followed from the lips of Peter.

Utterance (ἀποφθέγγεσθαι). Used only by Luke and in the Acts. Lit., *to utter*. A peculiar word, and purposely chosen to denote the *clear*, *loud* utterance under the miraculous impulse. It is used by later Greek writers of the utterances of oracles or seers. So in the Septuagint, of prophesying. See 1 Chron. xxv. 1; Deut. xxxii. 2; Zech. x. 2; Ezek. xiii. 19.

5. **Dwelling** (κατοικοῦντες). Denoting an *abiding*; but here it must be taken in a wide sense, since among these are mentioned those whose permanent residence was in Mesopotamia, etc. See ver. 9.

Devout. See on Luke ii. 25.

6. **When this was noised abroad** (γενομένης δὲ τῆς φωνῆς ταύτης). Wrong. Lit., *And this sound having taken place*. Rev., correctly, *when this sound was heard*. The sound of the rushing wind.

Were confounded (συνεχύθη). Lit., *was poured together*; so that *confound* (Latin, *confundere*) is the most literal rendering possible. Used only by Luke and in the Acts. Compare xix. 32; xxi. 31.

Heard (ἤκουον). Imperfect, *were hearing.*

Language (διαλέκτῳ). Rather, *dialect;* since the foreigners present spoke, not only different languages, but different *dialects* of the same language. The Phrygians and Pamphylians, for instance, both spoke Greek, but in different idioms; the Parthians, Medes, and Elamites all spoke Persian, but in different provincial forms.

7. **Amazed** and **marvelled** (ἐξίσταντο καὶ ἐθαύμαζον). The former word denotes the first overwhelming surprise. The verb is literally *to put out of place;* hence, out of *one's senses.* Compare Mark iii. 21: "*He is beside himself.*" The latter word, *marvelled*, denotes the continuing wonder; meaning to *regard* with amazement, and with a suggestion of beginning to speculate on the matter.

Galilaeans. Not regarded as a *sect*, for the name was not given to Christians until afterward; but with reference to their *nationality.* They used a peculiar dialect, which distinguished them from the inhabitants of Judaea. Compare Mark xiv. 70. They were blamed for neglecting the study of their language, and charged with errors in grammar and ridiculous mispronunciations.

9. **Parthians, Medes, and Elamites.** Representing portions of the Persian empire.

Judaea. The dialect of Galilee being different from that of Judaea.

Asia. Not the Asiatic continent nor Asia Minor. In the time of the apostles the term was commonly understood of the proconsular province of Asia, principally of the kingdom of Pergamus left by Attalus III. to the Romans, and including

Lydia, Mysia, Caria, and at times parts of Phrygia. The name Asia Minor did not come into use until the fourth century of our era.

10. **Egypt.** Where the Jews were numerous. Two-fifths of the population of Alexandria were said to have been Jews.

Cyrene. In Libya, west of Egypt.

Strangers (ἐπιδημοῦντες). See on 1 Pet. i. 1. Rev., rightly, *sojourners.*

11. **Arabians.** Whose country bordered on Judaea, and must have contained many Jews.

Speak (λαλούντων). Rev., rightly, gives the force of the participle, *speaking.*

Wonderful works (μεγαλεῖα). See on *majesty*, 2 Pet. i. 16. From μέγας, *great.* Rev., *mighty works.* Used by Luke only.

12. **Were in doubt** (διηπόρουν). Used by Luke only. See on Luke ix. 7. Better, as Rev., *perplexed.*

13. **Others** (ἕτεροι). Of a *different* class. The first who commented on the wonder did so *curiously*, but with no prejudice. Those who now spoke did so in a hostile spirit. See on ver. 4.

Mocking (διαχλευάζοντες; so the best texts). From χλεύη, *a joke.* Only here in New Testament.

New wine (γλεύκους). Lit., "*sweet* swine." Of course intoxicating.

14. **Standing up** (σταθεὶς). See on Luke xviii. 11; xix. 8.

Said (ἀπεφθέγξατο). See on ver. 4. Better, Rev., *spake forth.* "This most solemn, earnest, yet sober speech" (Bengel).

Hearken (*ἐνωτίσασθε*). Only here in New Testament. From *ἐν*, *in;* and *οὖς*, the ear. Rev., *give ear.*

Words (*ῥήματα*). See on Luke i. 37.

15. **Third hour.** Nine in the morning: the hour of morning prayer. Compare 1 Thess. v. 7.

17. **All flesh.** Without distinction of age, sex, or condition.

Visions (*ὁράσεις*). Waking visions.

Dream dreams (*ἐνύπνια ἐνυπνιασθήσονται*). The best texts read *ἐνυπνίοις*, *with dreams.* The verb occurs only here and Jude 8. The reference is to visions in *sleep.*

19. **I will shew** (*δώσω*). Lit., *I will give.*

Wonders (*τέρατα*). Or *portents.* See on Matt. xi. 20.

Signs. See on Matt. xi. 20.

20. **That great and notable day of the Lord come.** The Rev. heightens the emphasis by following the Greek order, *the day of the Lord, that great and notable day. Notable* (*ἐπιφανῆ*) only here in New Testament. The kindred noun *ἐπιφάνεια*, *appearing* (compare our word *Epiphany*), is often used of the second coming of the Lord. See 1 Tim. vi. 14; 2 Tim. iv. 1; Tit. ii. 13.

22. **Approved** (*ἀποδεδειγμένον*). The verb means to *point out* or *shew forth. Shewn* to be that which he claimed to be.

Miracles (*δυνάμεσι*). Better, Rev., *mighty works.* Lit., *powers.* See on Matt. xi. 20.

23. **Being delivered** (*ἔκδοτον*). An adjective: *given forth, betrayed.*

Ye have taken. The best texts omit.

Wicked hands. The best texts read by *the hand of lawless men.*

Crucified (προσπήξαντες). Only here in New Testament. The verb simply means to *affix* to or on anything. The idea of the cross is left to be supplied.

Have slain (ἀνείλετε). See on Luke xxiii. 32. Rev., rendering the aorist more closely, *did slay.*

24. **Pains** (ὠδῖνας). The meaning is disputed. Some claim that Peter followed the Septuagint mistranslation of Ps. xviii. 5, where the Hebrew word for *snares* is rendered by the word used here, *pains;* and that, therefore, it should be rendered *snares* of death; the figure being that of escape from the snare of a huntsman. Others suppose that death is represented *in travail*, the birth-pangs ceasing with the delivery; *i.e.*, the resurrection. This seems to be far-fetched, though it is true that in classical Greek the word is used commonly of birth-throes. It is better, perhaps, on the whole, to take the expression in the sense of the A. V., and to make the *pains of death* stand for death generally.

25. **I foresaw** (προωρώμην). Not to *see beforehand*, but to *see before one's self*, as in Ps. xvi. 8.

I should not be moved (μὴ σαλευθῶ). Or be *shaken.* Generally so rendered in the New Testament. See Matt. xi. 7; xxiv. 29; Heb. xii. 26, etc.

26. **Rejoiced** (ἠγαλλιάσατο). Rev., *was glad.* See on 1 Pet. i. 6.

Shall rest (κατασκηνώσει). See on *nests*, Matt. viii. 20. Better, as Rev., *dwell.* Lit., *dwell in a tent* or *tabernacle.* Rendered *lodge*, Matt. xiii. 32; Mark iv. 32; Luke xiii. 19. It is a beautiful metaphor. My flesh shall *encamp on hope;* pitch its tent there to rest through the night of death, until the morning of resurrection.

In hope (ἐπ' ἐλπίδι). Lit., *on* hope: resting on the hope of resurrection; his body being poetically conceived as hoping.

27. **Leave** (ἐγκαταλείψεις). Lit., leave *behind*.

Suffer (δώσεις). Lit., *give*.

29. **Let me speak** (ἐξὸν εἰπεῖν). Lit., *it is permitted me*. Rev., *I may*. It is allowable for him to speak, because the facts are notorious.

Freely (μετὰ παῤῥησίας). Lit., *with freedom*. The latter word from πᾶν, *all*, and ῥῆσις, *speech; speaking everything*, and therefore without reserve.

The patriarch (πατριάρχου). From ἄρχω, *to begin*, and πατριά, *a pedigree*. Applied to David as the father of the royal family from which the Messiah sprang. It is used in the New Testament of Abraham (Heb. vii. 4), and of the sons of Jacob (Acts vii. 8).

He is dead and buried (ἐτελεύτησε καὶ ἐτάφη). Aorists, denoting what occurred at a definite past time. Rev., rightly, *he both died and was buried*.

His sepulchre is with us. Or *among* us (ἐν ἡμῖν). On Mount Zion, where most of the Jewish kings were interred in the same tomb.

30. **According to the flesh, he would raise up Christ.** The best texts omit. Render as Rev., *he would set one upon his throne*.

34. **Is not ascended** (οὐ ἀνέβη). Aorist, *did not ascend*.

35. **Thy footstool.** A. V. omits *of thy feet.*

36. **Assuredly** (ἀσφαλῶς). From ἀ, *not*, and **σφάλλω**, *to cause to fall.* Hence, *firmly*, *steadfastly.*

37. **They were pricked** (*κατενύγησαν*). Only here in New Testament. The word does not occur in profane Greek. It is found in the Septuagint, as Gen. xxxiv. 7, of the grief of the sons of Jacob at the dishonor of Dinah. See, also, Ps. cix. (Sept. cviii.) 16: "*broken* in heart." The kindred noun *κατάνυξις* occurs Rom. xi. 8, in the sense of *slumber* (Rev., *stupor*). Compare Isa. xxix. 10. See, also, Ps. lx. (Sept. lix.) 3: *οἶνον κατανύξεως*, *the wine of astonishment* (Rev., *wine of staggering*). The radical idea of the word is given in the simple verb *νύσσω*, *to prick with a sharp point.* So Homer, of the puncture of a spear; of horses *dinting* the earth with their hoofs, etc. Here, therefore, of the sharp, painful emotion, the *sting* produced by Peter's words. Cicero, speaking of the oratory of Pericles, says that his speech left *stings* in the minds of his hearers ("De Oratore," iii., 34.

38. **Repent.** See on Matt. iii. 2.

In the name (*ἐπὶ τῷ ὀνόματι*). Lit., *upon* the name. See on Matt. xxviii. 19.

Remission. See on Luke iii. 3; Jas. v. 15.

39. **Afar off** (*εἰς μακρὰν*). Lit., *unto a long way.* Referring probably to the Gentiles, who are described by this phrase both in the Old and New Testaments. See Zech. vi. 15; Eph. ii. 11–13. Peter knew the *fact* that the Gentiles were to be received into the Church, but not the *mode.* He expected they would become Christians through the medium of the Jewish religion. It was already revealed in the Old Testament that they should be received, and Christ himself had commanded the apostles to preach *to all nations.*

Shall call (προσκαλέσηται). Rev. gives the force of πρός, *to:* "shall call *unto him.*"

40. **Other** (ἑτέροις). And various.

Did he testify (διεμαρτύρετο). The preposition διά gives the force of *solemnly, earnestly.*

Save yourselves (σώθητε). More strictly, *be ye saved.*

Untoward (σκολιᾶς). Lit., *crooked. Toward* in earlier English meant *docile, apt.* The opposite is *froward* (*fromward*). So Shakespeare:

> "'Tis a good hearing when children are *toward,*
> But a harsh hearing when women are *froward.*"
> *Taming of the Shrew,* v., 2.

> "Spoken like a *toward* prince."
> 3 *Henry VI.*, ii., 2.

Untoward, therefore, meant *intractable, perverse.* So Shakespeare:

> "What means this scorn, thou most *untoward* knave?"
> *K. John,* i., 1.

> "And if she be froward,
> Then hast thou taught Hortensio to be *untoward.*"
> *Taming of the Shrew,* iv., 5.

Compare Deut. xxxii. 5.

42. **Continued steadfastly.** See on ch. i. 14.

Doctrine (διδαχῇ). Better, *teaching.*

Fellowship (κοινωνίᾳ). From κοινός, *common.* A relation between individuals which involves a common interest and a mutual, active participation in that interest and in each other. The word answers to the Latin *communio,* from *communis,* *common.* Hence, sometimes rendered *communion,* as 1 Cor. x. 16; 2 Cor. xiii. 14. *Fellowship* is the most common rendering. Thus Philip. i. 5: "your *fellowship* in the gospel," signifying *co-operation* in the widest sense; *participation* in sympathy, suffering, and labor. Compare 1 John i. 3, 6, 7. Occasionally it is used to express the particular form which the spirit of fellowship assumes; as in Rom. xv. 26; Heb. xiii. 16, where it signifies the giving of alms, but always with an emphasis upon the principle of Christian fellowship which underlies the gift.

Breaking (κλάσει). Used by Luke only, and only in the phrase *breaking of bread.* The kindred verb κλάζω or κλάω, *to break,* occurs often, but, like the noun, only of breaking bread. Hence used to designate the celebration of the Lord's Supper.

Prayers (προσευχαῖς). Always of prayer to God. Compare on δεήσεις, *prayers,* Luke v. 33; and *besought,* Luke viii. 38.

43. **Fear** (φόβος). Not *terror,* but reverential *awe:* as Mark iv. 41; Luke vii. 16; 1 Pet. i. 17, etc.

44. **Common** (κοινὰ). Compare *fellowship,* ver. 42.

45. **Possessions** (κτήματα). Landed property.

Goods (ὑπάρξεις). Possessions in general; movables.

46. **With one accord** (ὁμοθυμαδὸν). See on Matt. xviii. 19.

From house to house (κατ' οἶκον). Better, as Rev., *at home,* contrasted with *in the temple.* Compare Philem. 2; Col. iv. 15; 1 Cor. xvi. 19.

Did eat their meat (μετελάμβανον τροφῆς). Rev., *take their food. Partake* would be better, giving the force of μετά, *with.* Note the imperfect: "*continued* to partake."

Singleness (ἀφελότητι). Only here in New Testament. Derived from ἀ, *not*, and φελλεύς, *stony ground*. Hence of something *simple* or *plain*.

47. **Added** (προσετίθει). Imperfect: *kept adding*.

Such as should be saved (τοὺς σωζομένους). Lit., as Rev., those *that were being saved*. The rendering of the A. V. would require the verb to be in the future, whereas it is the present participle. Compare 1 Cor. i. 18. Salvation is a thing of the *present*, as well as of the *past* and *future*. The verb is used in all these senses in the New Testament. Thus, *we were saved* (not *are*, as A. V.), Rom. viii. 24; *shall* or *shalt* be saved, Rom. x. 9, 13; *ye are being saved*, 1 Cor. xv. 2. "Godliness, righteousness, is life, is salvation. And it is hardly necessary to say that the divorce of morality and religion must be fostered and encouraged by failing to note this, and so laying the whole stress either on the past or on the future—on the first call, or on the final change. It is, therefore, important that the idea of salvation as a rescue from sin, through the knowledge of God in Christ, and therefore a *progressive condition*, a present state, should not be obscured, and we can but regret such a translation as Acts ii. 47, 'The Lord added to the church daily such *as should be saved*,' where the Greek implies a different idea" (Lightfoot, "On a Fresh Revision of the New Testament").

To the church. See on Matt. xvi. 18.

CHAPTER III.

1. **Went up** (ἀνέβαινον). The imperfect: *were going up*. So Rev., ascending the terraces, on the highest of which the temple stood.

Ninth hour. The time of the evening sacrifice; or, as the words *of prayer* indicate, half an hour later, for the prayer which accompanied the offering of incense.

2. **That was** (ὑπάρχων). Lit., *being*. See on Jas. ii. 15.

Was carried (ἐβαστάζετο). Imperfect: "was *being* carried as they *were going up* (ver. 1).

They laid (ἐτίθουν). Imperfect: "they were *wont* to lay."

4. **Fastening his eyes** (ἀτενίσας). See on Luke iv. 20; and compare Acts i. 10.

Look (βλέψον). Attentively. See on Matt. vii. 3.

6. **Silver and gold** (ἀργύριον καὶ χρυσίον). Properly, silver and gold *money*. See on 1 Pet. i. 18.

7. **He took** (πιάσας). The verb means originally to *press* or *squeeze;* and hence implies taking hold with a *firm* grasp.

Feet (βάσεις). A peculiar, technical word, used by Luke only, and described by Galen as the part of the foot lying beneath the leg, upon which the leg directly rests, as distinguished from the ταρσὸς, *the flat of* the foot between the toes and heel, and πεδίον, *the part next the toes.*

Ankle-bones (σφυρά). Only here in New Testament. Also technical. Some of the best texts read σφυδρά, but the meaning is the same.

Received strength (ἐστερεώθησαν). Used by Luke only. Compare "the churches were *established* (ch. xvi. 5), and the kindred noun στερέωμα, *steadfastness* (Col. ii. 5). In medical language applied to the bones in particular.

8. **Leaping up** (ἐξαλλόμενος). Strictly, *leaping forth.* Only here in New Testament. Used in medical language of the sudden starting of a bone from the socket, of starting from sleep, or of the sudden bound of the pulse.

Walked (περιεπάτει). The imperfect. Correctly, as Rev., *began to walk;* or, perhaps, *continued* walking about, testing his newly acquired power.

The medical notes of the case are, that the disease was congenital, had lasted over forty years (ch. iv. 22), and the progressive steps of the recovery—leaped up, stood, walked.

10. **They knew** (ἐπεγίνωσκον). Or *recognized.* Rev., *took knowledge.*

Wonder (θάμβους). Used by Luke only. See on Luke iv. 36.

Amazement (ἐκστάσεως). See on Mark v. 42; and compare Luke v. 26.

11. **The lame man which was healed.** The best texts omit. Render *as he held.*

Held (κρατοῦντος). Held them *firmly*, took *fast* hold. The verb from κράτος, *strength.*

Greatly wondering (ἔκθαμβοι). Wondering *out of* measure (ἐκ). Compare *wonder* (ver. 10).

12. **He answered.** The question expressed in the people's explanations of surprise.

Men of Israel. Lit., *men, Israelites.* An honorable and conciliatory form of address. The term Israelite gradually gave place to that of *Jew;* but Israel was the sacred name for the Jews, as the nation of the theocracy, the people under God's covenant, and hence was for the Jew his especial badge and title of honor. "To be descendants of Abraham, this honor they must share with the Ishmaelites; of Abraham and Isaac, with the Edomites; but none except themselves were the seed of Jacob, such as in this name of Israelite they were declared to be. Nor was this all, but more gloriously still, their descent was herein traced up to him, not as he was Jacob, but as he was

Israel, who, as a prince, had power with God and with men, and had prevailed" (Trench, "Synonyms"). So Paul, in enumerating to the Philippians his claims to have confidence in the flesh, says he was "of the stock of *Israel*." It is said that the modern Jews in the East still delight in this title.

Our own (ἰδίᾳ). See on ch. i. 7.

13. **His son** (παῖδα). Rightly, *servant*, as Rev. See on Luke i. 54. The A. V. renders, in Matt. xii. 18, *servant*, quoting from Isa. xlii. 1; but elsewhere, where applied to Jesus, *son* or *child*, which Rev. in every case has changed to *servant*. The word is continually used, like the Latin *puer*, in the sense of *servant*, and in the Septuagint as the *servant of God*. See 2 Sam. vii. 5, 8, 19, 20, 21, 25, 26. Compare Luke i. 69. The term *servant of Jehovah*, or *servant of the Lord*, is applied in the Old Testament (1) to a worshipper of God, Neh. i. 10; Dan. vi. 21; so to Abraham, Ps. cv. 6, 42; to Joshua, Josh. xxiv. 29; to Job, Job i. 8. (2) To a minister or ambassador of God called to any service, Isa. xlix. 6; of Nebuchadnezzar, Jer. xxvii. 6; of the prophets, Amos iii. 7; of Moses, Deut. xxxiv. 5. (3) Peculiarly of the Messiah, Isa. xlii. 1; lii. 13; as God's chosen servant for accomplishing the work of redemption. "Unless we render *servant* in the passages where the phrase παῖς Θεοῦ occurs in the New Testament, there will be no allusion throughout it all to that group of prophecies which designate the Messiah as the servant of Jehovah, who learned obedience by the things which he suffered" (Trench, "On the Authorized Version of the New Testament").

When he. *He* is ἐκείνου, the pronoun of more definite and emphatic reference, *the latter*, *Pilate*, "in order to make the contrast felt between what *Pilate* judged and what *they* did." This is further emphasized in the next verse.

14. **Desired** (ᾐτήσασθε). Or *demanded*. See on Luke xi. 9.

A murderer (ἄνδρα φονέα). Lit., *a man who was a murderer*.

To be granted (χαρισθῆναι). By way of favor (χάρις).

15. **The Prince of life** (ἀρχηγὸν τῆς ζωῆς). The Greek brings out by the position of these words what Bengel calls "the magnificent antithesis" between a *murderer* and the *Prince of life*. "Ye demanded a *murderer*, but the *Prince of life* ye killed." This is the only place where the phrase occurs. Ἀρχηγός, though sometimes rendered *prince*, means, primarily, *beginning*, and thence *originator, author*. Better here as Rev., in margin, *author*, and so by Rev. at Heb. ii. 10; xii. 2.

16. **Through faith** (ἐπὶ τῇ πίστει). Note the article: *the* faith which *we* had; not the cripple's faith, which was not demanded as a condition of his cure. *Through* faith (ἐπί) is rather *on account of*, or *on the basis of*. Rev., *by*. Compare ch. ii. 38; and see on Matt. xxviii. 19.

Made strong (ἐστερέωσε). See on ver. 7.

Ye see (θεωρεῖτε). See on Luke x. 18.

Perfect soundness (ὁλοκληρίαν). Only here in New Testament. From ὅλος, *entire*, and κλῆρος, *a lot*. Denoting, therefore, the condition of one who has his *entire allotment*.

19. **Be converted** (ἐπιστρέψατε). Not a good rendering, because the verb is in the active voice. Better as Rev., *turn again*. See on Luke xxii. 32.

Blotted out (ἐξαλειφθῆναι). Forgiveness of sins under the figure of the erasure of hand-writing. The word is used thus in Ps. li. (Sept. l.), 1; Isa. xliii. 25. Also at Col. ii. 14. In classical Greek the verb is opposed to ἐγγράφειν, *to enter a name*. So Aristophanes: "They do things not to be borne, *entering* (ἐγγράφοντες) some of us, and others, *erasing* (ἐξαλείφοντες) up and down, twice or thrice" ("Peace," 1180). More especially with reference to an item in an account.

When (ὅπως ἂν). Wrong. Render *in order that*, or *that* (so there may come), as Rev.

Times (καιροὶ). Better, *seasons*. See on ch. i. 7.

Of refreshing (ἀναψύξεως). Only here in New Testament. The word means *cooling*, or *reviving with fresh air*. Compare the kindred verb, *to wax cold*, Matt. xxiv. 12, and see note.

Presence (προσώπου). Lit., *the face*.

20. **Which before was preached** (τὸν προκεκηρυγμένον). But the best texts read προκεχειρισμένον, *appointed*. Compare ch. xxii. 14. Used by Luke only, ch. xxii. 14; xxvi. 16. The verb originally means *to take in hand*.

21. **Of restitution** (ἀποκαταστάσεως). Only here in New Testament. The kindred verb, *to restore*, occurs Matt. xvii. 11; Acts i. 6, etc. As a technical medical term, it denotes *complete restoration of health; the restoring to its place of a dislocated joint*, etc.

Since the world began (ἀπ' αἰῶνος). The American Revisers insist on *from of old*.

23. **Shall be destroyed** (ἐξολοθρευθήσεται). Only here in New Testament. Rev., "*utterly* destroyed," giving the force of ἐξ, *out*.

25. **Covenant** (διαθήκης). See on Matt. xxvi. 28.

Made (διέθετο). The Rev. gives *covenanted* in margin. The noun *covenant* is derived from the verb διατίθημι, originally to *distribute* or *arrange*. Hence to arrange or settle *mutually; to make a covenant with*.

26. **His Son Jesus.** The best texts omit *Jesus*. Render *servant* for *son*, and see on ver. 13.

CHAPTER IV.

1. **Captain of the temple.** It was the duty of the Levites to keep guard at the gates of the temple, in order to prevent the unclean from entering. To them the duties of the temple-police were entrusted, under the command of an official known in the New Testament as "the captain of the temple," but in Jewish writings chiefly as "the man of the temple mount." Josephus speaks of him as a person of such consequence as to be sent, along with the high-priest, prisoner to Rome.

Came upon (ἐπέστησαν). Or *stood by them*, suddenly. Compare Luke xxiv. 4; Acts xxii. 20; xxiii. 11. Of *dreams* or *visions, to appear to.*

2. **Being grieved** (διαπονούμενοι). Only here and ch. xvi. 18. The Rev. renders the force of διά by "*sore* troubled;" vexed *through and through.*

The resurrection. The Sadducees denied both the resurrection and a future state. "In the Gospels the Pharisees are represented as the great opponents of Christ; in the Acts it is the Sadducees who are the most violent opponents of the apostles. The reason of this seems to be, that in the Gospels Jesus Christ came in direct collision with the Pharisees, by unmasking their hypocrisies and endangering their influence among the people; whereas the apostles, in testifying to the resurrection of Christ, opposed the creed of the Sadducees. Perhaps, also, in attacking the apostles, who taught the resurrection of that Jesus whom the Pharisees had persecuted and crucified, the Sadducees aimed an indirect blow at the favorite dogma of their rival sect" (Gloag, "Commentary on Acts").

3. **In hold** (εἰς τήρησιν). A somewhat antiquated rendering. Better, as Rev., *in ward.* See on 1 Pet. i. 4.

4. **The number was about five thousand.** Translate ἐγενήθη as Rev., *came to be;* indicating the addition to the original number of *the many that believed.*

7. **What power—what name.** Lit., what *sort* of power; what *kind* of name.

Have ye done. The *ye* closes the sentence in the Greek with a contemptuous emphasis: *you people.*

12. **Salvation** (*ἡ σωτηρία*). Note the article: *the* salvation; the Messianic deliverance.

13. **Boldness.** See on *freely*, ch. ii. 29.

Perceived (*καταλαβόμενοι*). The word, meaning originally to *seize upon* or *lay hold of*, occurs frequently in the New Testament in different phases of this original sense. Thus, to *apprehend* or *grasp*, Eph. iii. 18; Philip. iii. 12, 13; Rom. ix. 30: of *seizure* by a demon, Mark ix. 18: of something *coming upon* or *overtaking*, John xii. 35; 1 Thess. v. 4: of *comprehending*, grasping *mentally*, as here, Acts x. 34; xxv. 25.

Unlearned (*ἀγράμματοι*). Or, very literally, *unlettered.* With special reference to Rabbinic culture, the absence of which was conspicuous in Peter's address.

Ignorant (*ἰδιῶται*). Originally, one in a *private* station, as opposed to one in office or in public affairs. Therefore one without professional knowledge, a layman; thence, generally, *ignorant, ill-informed;* sometimes *plebeian, common.* In the absence of certainty it is as well to retain the meaning given by the A. V., perhaps with a slight emphasis on the want of *professional* knowledge. Compare 1 Cor. xiv. 16, 23, 24; 2 Cor. xi. 6.

Took knowledge (*ἐπεγίνωσκον*). Or *recognized.* See on ch. iii. 10.

15. **Conferred** (*συνέβαλον*). See on *pondered*, Luke ii. 19.

17. **It spread** (*διανεμηθῇ*). Only here in New Testament. Lit., *be distributed.* In 2 Tim. ii. 17, "their word will *eat* as a

canker," is, literally, *will have distribution or spreading* (νομὴν ἕξει). Bengel, however, goes too far when he represents the members of the council as speaking in the figure of a canker. "They regard the whole as a canker."

18. **To speak** (φθέγγεσθαι). See on 2 Pet. ii. 16.

21. **Punish** (κολάσωνται). Originally, to *curtail* or *dock*; to *prune* as trees: thence to *check, keep in bounds, punish*.

24. **Lord** (δέσποτα). See on 2 Pet. ii. 1.

25. **Servant** (παιδός). See on ch. iii. 13.

Rage (ἐφρύαξαν). Only here in New Testament. Originally, to *neigh* or *snort* like a horse. Of men, to give one's self haughty airs, and to act and speak insolently. Philo describes a proud man as "walking on tiptoe, and *bridling* (φρυαττόμενος), with neck erect like a horse."

27. **Didst anoint** (ἔχρισας). See on *Christ*, Matt. i. 1.

28. **Thy hand.** Thy disposing power.

32. **Heart and soul.** See on Mark xii. 30.

33. **Gave** (ἀπεδίδουν). Lit., *gave back* (ἀπό); as something which they were in duty bound to give.

37. **The money** (τὸ χρῆμα). The *sum* of money.

CHAPTER V.

2. **Kept back** (ἐνοσφίσατο). Only here, ver. 3, and Tit. ii. 10, where it is rendered *purloining*. From νόσφι, *aloof, apart*. The verb means to *set apart for one's self*; hence to *appropriate wrongfully*.

3. **To lie to** (ψεύσασθαι). Rather, *to deceive*. The design of Satan was to *deceive* the Holy Ghost. *To lie to* would require a different case in the noun, which occurs in ver. 4, where the same verb is properly rendered *lie* (unto God). Satan fills the heart to *deceive*. The result of the attempt is merely to *lie*.

4. **Whiles it remained, was it not thine own** (οὐχὶ μένον ? σοὶ ἔμενε). A play on the words. Lit., *remaining, did it not remain to thee?* Rev., very happily, *whiles it remained, did it not remain thine own?*

Conceived (ἔθου). Lit., *put* or *fixed*. *Wherefore didst thou fix this deed in thy heart?*—i.e., *resolve upon it*.

5. **Gave up the ghost** (ἐξέψυξε). Used by Luke only. A rare word, occurring in the Septuagint, and in medical writers. See Ezek. xxi. 7, "Every spirit *shall faint*." See, also, on *failing*, Luke xxi. 26.

6. **Wound him up** (συνέστειλαν). Better, as Rev., *wrapped him round*. The verb means to *draw together*, or *draw in;* hence used for *shortening sail*, *reducing expenses*, *lowering* or *humbling* a person. In 1 Cor. vii. 29, it occurs in the phrase, "the time is *short* (συνεσταλμένος, Rev., properly, *shortened*);" i.e., *drawn together*, *contracted*. In the sense of *wrapping up* it is found in Aristophanes, of *wrapping cloaks or garments about one;* also of *tucking up* the garments about the loins, as a preparation for service. In the sense of *shrouding for burial*, it occurs in Euripides ("Troades," 382): "They were not *shrouded* (συνεπεστάλησαν) by the hands of a wife." In medical language, of *bandaging* a limb; of the *contraction* of tumors, and of organs of the body, etc. Some, however, as Meyer, refer the word here to the *pressing together* of the dead man's limbs.

8. **Answered.** "The woman, whose entrance into the assembly of the saints was like a speech" (Bengel).

For so much (τοσούτου). Perhaps pointing to the money still lying at his feet.

9. **Ye have agreed together** (συνεφωνήθη ὑμῖν). The verb is passive. Lit., *was it agreed by you.* The figure in the word is that of *concord of sounds.* Your souls were *attuned* to each other respecting this deceit. See on *music*, Luke xv. 25.

To tempt (πειράσαι). To put it to the proof whether the Holy Spirit, ruling in the apostles, could be deceived. See on ver. 3.

The feet. Graphic. The steps of the young men returning from the burial are heard at the door.

12. **Were wrought** (ἐγένετο). The best texts read ἐγίνετο, the imperfect, *were being wrought* from time to time.

All. The whole body of believers.

13. **The rest.** Unbelievers, deterred by the fate of Ananias from uniting themselves to the church under false pretences.

Join himself (κολλᾶσθαι). See on Luke xv. 15; x. 11. In all but two instances (Rom. xii. 9; 1 Cor. vi. 17), the word implies a forced, unnatural, or unexpected union. Thus Philip would not, without a special command, have "joined himself" to the chariot of the Ethiopian prince (Acts viii. 29). Saul's attempt to join himself to the apostles was regarded by them with suspicion (Acts ix. 26); and the fact that certain persons "clave to" Paul in Athens is expressly contrasted with the attitude of the citizens at large. The sense of an *unnatural* union comes out clearly in 1 Cor. vi. 16.

14. **Were added** (προσετίθεντο). Imperfect: *kept being added.*

15. **Couches** (κραββάτων). See on Mark ii. 4.

The shadow of Peter passing by. But the proper rendering is, *as Peter passed by, his shadow might*, etc.*

18. **In the common prison** (ἐν τηρήσει δημοσίᾳ). Incorrect. *Τήρησις* is not used in the sense of *prison*, but is an abstract term meaning *ward* or *keeping*, as in ch. iv. 3. There is no article, moreover. Note, too, that another word is used for *the prison* in the next verse (τῆς φυλακῆς). Rev., therefore, correctly, *in public ward.*

19. **By night** (διὰ τῆς νυκτὸς). More correctly, *during the night: διά, in the course of.* Compare ch. xvi. 9.

20. **Stand.** Compare ch. ii. 14; and see on Luke xviii. 11; xix. 8.

Of this life. The eternal life which Christ revealed. It is a peculiar use of the phrase, which is commonly employed in contrast with *the life to come*, as 1 Cor. xv. 19. Compare John vi. 63, 68. Not equivalent *to these words of life.*

21. **Early in the morning** (ὑπὸ τὸν ὄρθρον). *Ὑπό, beneath*, is often used in the sense of *just about*, or *near*. *Ὄρθρον* is from ὄρνυμι, *to cause to arise: the dawn.* See on Luke xxiv. 1. Render as Rev., *about daybreak.*

Taught (ἐδίδασκον). Imperfect: *began teaching.*

The council (συνέδριον). The Sanhedrim.

The senate (γερουσίαν). From γέρων, *an old man*, like the Latin *senatus*, from *senex, old.* Taking on very early an official sense, the notion of *age* being merged in that of *dignity.* Thus in Homer γέροντες are the chiefs who form the king's council. Compare the Latin *patres, fathers,* the title used

---

* The construction is plainly the genitive absolute, ἐρχομένου Πέτρου, *Peter passing by.*

in addressing the Roman senate. The word in this passage is the name of the Spartan assembly, *Gerousia*, the *assembly of elders*, consisting of thirty members, with the two kings. "The well-known term," as Meyer remarks, "is fittingly transferred from the college of the Greek *gerontes* to that of the Jewish presbyters." They summoned, not only those elders of the people who were likewise members of the Sanhedrim, but the whole council (*all the senate*) of the representatives of the people.

Prison (δεσμωτήριον). Still another word for prison. Compare vv. 18, 19. Rev., *prison-house*. The different words emphasize different aspects of confinement. Τήρησις is *keeping*, as the result of guarding. See on ver. 18. Φυλακή emphasizes the being put under *guard*, and δεσμωτήριον the being put in *bonds*.

22. **Officers** (ὑπηρέται). See on Matt. v. 25.

24. **They doubted** (διηπόρουν). See on Luke ix. 5. Rev., *were much perplexed*, giving the force of διά, *thoroughly* at a loss. Compare Luke xxiv. 4.*

28. **Did not.** The best texts omit οὐ, *not*, and the question.

We straitly charged. So Rev. (παραγγελίᾳ παρηγγείλαμεν). Lit., *we charged you with a charge*. See on Luke xxii. 15, *with desire I have desired*.

Intend (βούλεσθε). Or *ye want*. See on *willing*, Matt. i. 19.

This man's. The phrase is remarkable as furnishing the first instance of that avoidance of the name of Christ which makes the Talmud, in the very same terms, refer to him most frequently as *Pelonî*, "so and so."

---

* Where, however, the best texts read the simple verb ἀπορεῖσθαι, *were perplexed*, for διαπορεῖσθαι, "were *greatly* perplexed."

29. **We ought** (δεῖ). Stronger, *we must.*

To obey (πειθαρχεῖν). Not often used in the New Testament to express obedience, the most common word being ὑπακούω. Sometimes πείθω is used. But this word, in itself, is the only one of the several in use which expresses the conception of *obedience* exclusively. Ὑπακούειν is to obey as the result of *listening* to another: πείθεσθαι is to obey as the result of *persuasion.* This is the special term for the obedience which one owes to authority (ἀρχή). It occurs four times in the New Testament: Acts v. 29, 32; xxvii. 21; Tit. iii. 1; and in every case, of obedience to established authority, either of God or of magistrates. In Acts xxvii. 21, where it is used of the ship's officers *hearkening* to Paul's admonition not to loose from Crete, Paul speaks of his admonition as divinely inspired; compare xxvii. 10. In ch. iv. 19, Peter and John say *hearken* (ἀκούειν). That is a mere *listening to* or *considering* the proposition made to them. This is a deliberate course of action.

30. **Ye slew** (διεχειρίσασθε). Only here and ch. xxvi. 21. To slay with one's own hands.

Tree. See on Luke xxiii. 31.

31. **Prince.** See on ch. iii. 15.

Repentance—remission. See on Matt. iii. 2; Jas. v. 15; Luke iii. 3.

32. **Witnesses.** See on Acts i. 22.

Obey. See on ver. 29.

33. **They were cut to the heart** (διεπρίοντο). Only here and ch. vii. 54. The verb means, originally, *to saw asunder.* A strong figure for exasperation.

To slay. See on Luke xxiii. 32.

34. **The apostles.** The best texts substitute τοὺς ἀνθρώπους, *the men.*

A little space (βραχύ). Better as Rev., *a little while.*

36. **Joined themselves** (προσεκολλήθη). The best texts read προσεκλίθη, *were inclined;* i.e., *leaned to,* or *took sides with.*

37. **Obeyed.** Note the word for *obeyed* (ἐπείθοντο), implying the *persuasive* power of Theudas' boasting. See on ver. 29.

Taxing (ἀπογραφῆς). See on Luke ii. 1, 2.

Much people. The best texts omit *much.*

Were dispersed (διεσκορπίσθησαν). See on Matt. xxv. 24.

38. **Refrain** (ἀπόστητε). Lit., *stand off.*

Of men (ἐξ ἀνθρώπων). *Out of* men, proceeding out of their devices.

It will come to naught (καταλυθήσεται). Lit., be *loosened down.* Used of the dilapidation of the temple (Luke xxi. 6), and of the dissolution of the body under the figure of striking a tent (2 Cor. v. 1). See on Mark xiii. 2.

39. **To fight against God** (θεομάχοι). Lit., to be *God-fighters.*

41. **They were counted worthy to suffer shame** (κατηξιώθησαν ἀτιμασθῆναι). This is an instance of what rhetoricians style an *oxymoron,* from ὀξύς, *sharp,* and μωρός, foolish; a *pointedly foolish* saying, which is witty or impressive through sheer contradiction or paradox, as *laborious idleness, sublime indifference.* In this case the apostles are described as *dignified by indignity.*

CHAPTER VI.

1. **And** (δὲ). Better *but*, as a contrast is now introduced with the prosperous condition of the Church indicated at the close of the last chapter.

Was multiplied (πληθυνόντων). Lit., "when the disciples *were* multiplying;" the present participle indicating something in progress.

A murmuring (γογγυσμὸς). See on the kindred word *murmurers*, Jude 16.

Grecians (Ἑλληνιστῶν). Rev., much better, *Grecian Jews*, with *Hellenists* in *margin*. "Grecians" might easily be understood of Greeks in general. The word *Hellenists* denotes *Jews*, not *Greeks*, but Jews *who spoke Greek*. The contact of Jews with Greeks was first effected by the conquests of Alexander. He settled eight thousand Jews in the Thebais, and the Jews formed a third of the population of his new city of Alexandria. From Egypt they gradually spread along the whole Mediterranean coast of Africa. They were removed by Seleucus Nicator from Babylonia, by thousands, to Antioch and Seleucia, and under the persecutions of Antiochus Epiphanes scattered themselves through Asia Minor, Greece, Macedonia, and the Ægean islands. The vast majority of them adopted the Greek language, and forgot the Aramaic dialect which had been their language since the Captivity. The word is used but twice in the New Testament—here and ch. ix. 29—and, in both cases, of Jews who had embraced Christianity, but who spoke Greek and used the Septuagint version of the Bible instead of the original Hebrew or the Chaldaic *targum* or paraphrase. The word Ἕλλην, *Greek*, which is very common in the New Testament, is used in antithesis, either to "Barbarians" or to "Jews." In the former case it means all nations which spoke the Greek language (see Acts xviii. 17; Rom. i. 14; 1 Cor. i. 22, 23). In the latter it is equivalent to *Gentiles* (see Rom. i. 16; ii. 9; 1 Cor. x. 32; Gal. ii. 3). Hence, in either case, it is wholly different from *Hellenist.*

Hebrews. *Hebrew* is the proper antithesis to *Hellenist.* A man was *Ἰουδαῖος*, a *Jew*, who traced his descent from Jacob, and conformed to the religion of his fathers. He might speak Greek and be a Hellenist. He was *Ἑβραῖος, a Hebrew,* only as he spoke Hebrew and retained Hebrew customs. The distinction between Hebrew and Hellenist was a distinction within the Jewish nation, and not between it and other nations. Thus Paul calls himself a *Hebrew of Hebrews;* i.e., a Hebrew and of Hebrew parents (Philip. iii. 5; compare 2 Cor. xi. 22).

Were neglected (παρεθεωροῦντο). Only here in New Testament. Lit., *were overlooked.* The imperfect denoting something habitual.

Daily (καθημερινῇ). Only here in New Testament.

Ministration (διακονίᾳ). Or *service.* See on *minister,* Matt. xx. 26. The reference is to the distribution of provision.

2. **Reason** (ἀρεστόν). Lit., *pleasing* or *agreeable.*

Leave (καταλείψαντας). Rather *forsake* or *abandon: leave in the lurch.*

Serve tables. Superintend the distribution of food.

3. **Of good report** (μαρτυρουμένους). Lit., *attested, having witness borne them.*

4. **We will give ourselves continually** (προσκαρτερήσομεν). See on ch. i. 14. Rev., *continue steadfastly.*

5. **Stephen,** etc. The names are all Greek. There is no reason to infer from this that they were all Hellenists. It was

customary among the Jews to have two names, the one Hebrew and the other Greek. They were probably partly Hebrews and partly Hellenists.

7. **To the faith** (τῇ πίστει). Opinions differ greatly as to whether this is to be taken as meaning *faith in Jesus Christ*, or *faith* considered as *Christian doctrine—the Gospel; the faith* in the ecclesiastical sense. This passage and Gal. i. 23 are the strong passages in favor of the latter view; but the general usage of the New Testament, added to the fact that in both these passages the former meaning gives a good, intelligible, and perfectly consistent sense, go to confirm the former interpretation.

1. In the great majority of New Testament passages *faith* is clearly used in the sense of *faith in Jesus Christ:* "the conviction and confidence regarding Jesus Christ as the only and perfect mediator of the divine grace and of eternal life, through his work of atonement" (Meyer).

2. This interpretation is according to the analogy of such expressions as *obedience of Christ* (2 Cor. x. 5), where the meaning is, clearly, obedience *to* Christ: *obedience of the truth* (1 Pet. i. 22). Accordingly, faith, though it becomes in man the *subjective* moral power of the new life, regenerated through the power of the Spirit, is regarded *objectively* as a *power*—the authority which commands submission.

3. This interpretation is according to the analogy of the expression *hearing of faith* (Gal. iii. 2), which is to be rendered, not as equivalent to *the reception of the Gospel*, but as the *report* or *message* of faith; i.e., *which treats of* faith, ἀκοή, *hearing* being always used in the New Testament in a passive sense, and often rendered *fame*, *rumor*, *report* (see Matt. iv. 24; xiv. 1; Mark i. 28; John xii. 38; Rom. x. 16). Compare, also, *obedience of faith* (Rom. i. 5; xvi. 26), where faith is to be taken as the *object*, and not as the *source*, of the obedience; and hence is not to be explained as the obedience which *springs from faith*, but as the obedience *rendered to faith* as the authoritative impulse of the new life in Christ.

The great majority of the best modern commentators hold

that faith is to be taken as the *subjective principle* of Christian life (though often regarded objectively as a spiritual power), and not as *Christian doctrine.*

8. **Did** (ἐποίει). Imperfect: *was working wonders* during the progress of the events described in the previous verse.

9. **Synagogue.** See on *Church*, Matt. xvi. 18.

Of the libertines. In Jerusalem, and probably in other large cities, the several synagogues were arranged according to nationalities, and even crafts. Thus we have in this verse mention of the synagogues of the Cyrenians, Alexandrians, Cilicians, and Asiatics. *Libertines* is a Latin word (*libertini, freedmen*), and means here Jews or their descendants who had been taken as slaves to Rome, and had there received their liberty; and who, in consequence of the decree of Tiberius, about 19 A.D., expelling them from Rome, had returned in great numbers to Jerusalem. They were likely to be the chief opponents of Stephen, because they supposed that by his preaching, their religion, for which they had suffered at Rome, was endangered in Jerusalem.

10. **They were not able** (οὐκ ἴσχυον). See on Luke xiv. 30; xvi. 3.

11. **Suborned** (ὑπέβαλον). Only here in New Testament. The verb originally means to *put under*, as carpets under one's feet; hence, to *put one person in place of another;* to *substitute*, as another's child for one's own; to *employ a secret agent in one's place*, and to *instigate* or *secretly instruct* him.

12. **They stirred up the people** (συνεκίνησαν τὸν λαὸν). The verb occurs only here in the New Testament. It implies to stir up as *a mass*, to move them *together* (σύν). This is the first record of the hostility of *the people* toward the disciples. See ch. ii. 47.

Caught (συνήρπασαν). Used by Luke only. Better as Rev., *seized.* See on Luke viii. 29.

14. **This Jesus of Nazareth.** Contemptuous.

CHAPTER VII.

1. **Then said the high-priest.** "The glorified countenance of Stephen has caused a pause of surprise and admiration, which the high-priest interrupts by calling upon the accused for his defence" (Gloag).

2. **Brethren.** Addressing the audience generally.

Fathers. Addressing the members of the Sanhedrim.

Of glory. *Outward, visible* glory, as in the shekinah and the pillar of fire.

Appeared (ὤφθη). See on Luke xxii. 43.

5. **Inheritance** (κληρονομίαν). See on 1 Pet. i. 4.

Not so much as to set his foot on (οὐδὲ βῆμα ποδός). Lit., *not even the stepping of a foot.* From the original meaning, a *pace* or *step*, which occurs only here in the New Testament, comes the sense of a *step* considered as a *raised place* or *seat*, and hence a *tribune* or *judgment-seat*, which is its meaning in every other passage of the New Testament.

Possession (κατάσχεσιν). Only here and ver. 45. See on *keep*, Luke viii. 15. It denotes a *permanent* possession.

8. **The covenant of circumcision.** There is no article, and it is better omitted in rendering. He gave him *a covenant*, the peculiar character of which is defined by the next word—

of circumcision; i.e., of which circumcision was the completion and seal.

9. **Moved with envy** (ζηλώσαντες). Compare Jas. iv. 1; and see on *envying*, Jas. iii. 14.

10. **Afflictions** (θλίψεων). See on Matt. xiii. 21.

11. **Sustenance** (χορτάσματα). For their cattle: *fodder*. See on *shall be filled*, Matt. v. 6.

12. **In Egypt** (ἐν Αἰγύπτῳ). But the best texts read εἰς Αἴγυπτον, *into Egypt*, and construe with *sent forth:* "he sent forth our fathers *into Egypt*."

13. **Joseph's race.** Note the repetition of the name. "A certain sense of patriotic pride is implied in it."

14. **Threescore and fifteen.** Lit., "*in* (ἐν) threescore and fifteen;" the idiom expressing the sum *in which* all the individuals were included.

17. **When** (καθὼς). Rev., more correctly, *as;* the word being not a particle of *time*, but meaning *in proportion as*.

18. **Another** (ἕτερος). Not merely a *successor*, but a monarch of a *different* character.

Knew not. As sixty years had elapsed since Joseph's death, and a new dynasty was coming to the throne, this may be taken literally: did not know his history and services. Some explain, *did not recognize his merits*.

19. **Dealt subtilely** (κατασοφισάμενος). Only here in New Testament. Lit., to *employ cunning against*. See on σοφὸς, *wise*, Jas. iii. 13.

So that they cast out (τοῦ ποιεῖν ἔκθετα). Lit., *make exposed*. The verb ἐκτίθημι, to *set out*, or *place outside*, is not uncommon in classical Greek for the *exposure* of a new-born child. Thus Herodotus, of Cyrus, exposed in infancy: "The herdsman's wife entreated him not to *expose* (ἐκθεῖναι) the babe" (i., 112). The rendering of the A. V., "*so that* they cast out," is correct, expressing the *result*, and not Pharaoh's design.

Young children (βρέφη). Incorrect. See on 1 Pet. ii. 2. Rev., rightly, *babes.*

Live (ζωογονεῖσθαι). Or, *be preserved alive.* See on Luke xvii. 33.

20. **Time** (καιρῷ). Better, *season* or *juncture.* "Sad, seasonable" (Bengel). See on Acts i. 7.

Exceeding fair (ἀστεῖος τῷ θεῷ). Lit., *fair unto God:* a Hebrew superlative. Compare Jon. iii. 3: *great unto God;* A. V., *exceeding great.* Gen. x. 9, of Nimrod: *a mighty hunter before the Lord.* 2 Cor. x. 4: *mighty unto God;* i.e., *in God's sight.* 'Αστεῖος, *fair* (only here and Heb. xi. 23), is from ἄστυ, *a town,* and means originally *town-bred;* hence *refined, elegant, comely.* The word is used in the Septuagint of Moses (Exod. ii. 2), and rendered *goodly.* The Jewish traditions extol Moses' beauty. Josephus says that those who met him, as he was carried along the streets, forgot their business and stood still to gaze at him.

21. **Took up** (ἀνείλετο). Used among Greek writers of taking up exposed children; also of *owning* new-born children. So Aristophanes: "I exposed (the child) and some other woman, having taken it, *adopted* (ανείλετο) it" ("Clouds," 531). There is no reason why the meaning should be limited to *took him up from the water* (as Gloag).

23. **It came into his heart** (ἀνέβη ἐπὶ τὴν καρδίαν). Lit., "*it arose* into his heart." "There may be something in the depth of the soul which afterward emerges and ascends from that sea into the heart as into an island" (Bengel). The ex-

pression is imitated from the Hebrew, and occurs in the Septuagint: "The ark shall not *come to mind;*" lit., *go up into the heart* (Jer. iii. 16). See, also, Jer. xxxii. 35; Isa. lxv. 17.

24. **Defended** (ἠμύνατο). Only here in New Testament. The word means originally to ward off from one's self, with a collateral notion of *requital* or *revenge*.

25. **Understood** (συνιέναι). See on *understanding*, Mark xii. 33.

26. **Appeared** (ὤφθη). With the suggestion of a *sudden* appearance as in a vision; possibly with the underlying notion of a messenger of God. See on Luke xxii. 43.

Would have set them at one (συνήλασεν αὐτοὺς εἰς εἰρήνην). Lit., *drove them together to peace; urged* them.

31. **The sight** (τὸ ὅραμα). Always in the New Testament of a *vision*. See on Matt. xvii. 9.

To behold (κατανοῆσαι). See on Matt. vii. 3. Compare Luke xii. 24, 27.

32. **Trembled** (ἔντρομος γενόμενος). Lit., *having become trembling;* having fallen into a tremor.

34. **I have seen, I have seen** (ἰδὼν εἶδον). Lit., *having seen I saw*. A Hebraism. See Exod. iii. 7 (Sept.). Compare Judg. i. 28: *utterly drive them out;* lit., *removing did not utterly remove*. Judg. iv. 9: *going I will go;* i.e., *I will surely go*. Gen. xxxvii. 8: *reigning shalt thou reign;* i.e., *shalt thou indeed reign*. So Rev. here, "I have *surely* seen."

35. **Deliverer** (λυτρωτὴν). Strictly, a *ransomer* or *redeemer*. Only here in New Testament. See on *ransom*, Matt. xx. 28; and *redeemed*, 1 Pet. i. 18.

By the hand (ἐν χειρὶ). The best texts read *σύν χειρὶ*, "*with* the hand;" i.e., *in association with* the protecting and helping power of the angel.

38. **Lively.** Better, *living*, as Rev. Compare 1 Pet. ii. 4, 5.

39. **Turned back in their hearts.** Not desiring to go back, but longing for the idolatries of Egypt.

40. **Shall go before us.** As symbols to be borne before them on the march. Compare Neh. ix. 18.

41. **They made a calf** (ἐμοσχοποίησαν). Only here in New Testament, and not in Septuagint. Bengel says, "A very notorious crime is denoted by an extraordinary and newly-coined word." This was in imitation of the Egyptian bull-worship. Several of these animals were worshipped at different places in Egypt. *Apis* was worshipped at Memphis. Herodotus says: "Now this Apis, or Epaphus, is the calf of a cow which is never afterward able to bear young. The Egyptians say that fire comes down from heaven upon the cow, which thereupon conceives Apis. The calf which is so called has the following marks: He is black, with a square spot of white upon his forehead, and on his back the figure of an eagle. The hairs in his tail are double, and there is a beetle upon his tongue" (iii., 28). He was regarded by the Egyptians, not merely as an emblem, but as a god. He was lodged in a magnificent court, ornamented with figures twelve cubits high, which he never quitted except on fixed days, when he was led in procession through the streets. His festival lasted seven days, and all came forward from their houses to welcome him as he passed. He was not allowed to reach the natural term of his life. If a natural death did not remove him earlier, he was drowned when he reached the age of twenty-five, and was then embalmed and entombed in one of the sepulchral chambers of the Serapeum, a temple devoted expressly to the burial of these animals.

Another sacred bull was maintained at Heliopolis, in the great Temple of the Sun, under the name of *Mnevis*, and was honored with a reverence next to Apis. Wilkinson thinks that it was from this, and not from Apis, that the Israelites borrowed their notions of the golden calf. "The offerings, dancing, and rejoicings practised on the occasion, were doubtless in imitation of a ceremony they had witnessed in honor of Mnevis during their sojourn in Egypt" ("Ancient Egyptians," 2 ser., vol. ii., p. 197). A third sacred bull, called *Bacis*, was maintained at Hermonthis, near Thebes. It was a huge, black animal, and its hairs were said to grow the wrong way. Other bulls and cows did not hold the rank of gods, but were only sacred.

Offered (ἀνήγαγον). Lit., *led up*. See on Jas. ii. 21.

42. **To worship** (λατρεύειν). Rev., more correctly, *serve*. See on Luke i. 74.

The host of heaven. Star-worship, or Sabaeanism, the remnant of the ancient heathenism of Western Asia, which consisted in the worship of the stars, and spread into Syria, though the Chaldaean religion was far from being the simple worship of the host of heaven; the heavenly bodies being regarded as real persons, and not mere metaphorical representations of astronomical phenomena. It is to the Sabaean worship that Job alludes when, in asserting the purity of his life (xxxi. 26, 27), he says: "If I beheld the sun when it shined, or the moon walking in brightness, and my heart hath been secretly enticed, or my mouth hath kissed my hands: this also were an iniquity to be punished by the judge: for I should have denied the God that is above." Though not a part of the religion of the Egyptians, Rawlinson thinks it may have been connected with their earlier belief, since prayer is represented in hieroglyphics by a man holding up his hands, accompanied by a star (Herodotus, vol. ii., p. 291).

43. **Tabernacle of Moloch.** The portable tent-temple of the god, to be carried in procession. Moloch was an Ammonite idol to whom children were sacrificed. According to Rabbinical tradition, his image was hollow, heated from below, with the

head of an ox and outstretched arms, into which children were laid, their cries being stifled by the beating of drums.

Remphan. The texts vary between *Remphan*, *Rephan*, and *Romphan*. It is supposed to be the Coptic name for *Saturn*, to which the Arabs, Egyptians, and Phoenicians paid divine honors.

45. **That came after** (διαδεξάμενοι). Only here in New Testament. The verb originally means to *receive from one another, in succession;* and that appears to be the more simple and natural rendering here: *having received it* (from Moses). Rev., very neatly, *in their turn.*

Jesus. Joshua. The names are the same, both signifying *Saviour*. See on Matt. i. 21.

Into the possession (ἐν τῇ κατασχέσει). Rev., *when they entered on the possession.**

Before the face (ἀπὸ προσώπου). More strictly, "*away from* the face." The same expression occurs in the Septuagint, Deut. xi. 23.

46. **Desired** (ᾐτήσατο). More correctly, *asked:* through Nathan. See 2 Sam. vii. 2.

Tabernacle (σκήνωμα). It was not a *tabernacle* or *tent* which David proposed to build, but a *house*. See 2 Sam. vii.

---

* The A. V. apparently assumes that ἐν, *in*, stands for εἰς, *into*, which is inadmissible. The preposition may be explained as combining the ideas of *entrance into* and *subsequent rest;* and this seems to be the explanation adopted by the Rev. Alford's rendering, *at their taking possession of the Gentiles*, is condemned by the fact that κατάσχεσις does not mean *taking* possession, but *holding* possession, which is clearly the meaning in ver. 5, the only other New Testament passage where it occurs. Meyer, in his anxiety to preserve the strict force of ἐν, renders *during the possession of the Gentiles*, or *while the Gentiles were in the state of possession*, which, though grammatically defensible, I cannot help thinking forced and unnatural. On the whole, it seems best to hold by the rendering of the Rev.

2. Rev., rightly, *habitation*. Compare *οἶκον*, a *house*, ver. 47, and 2 Chron. vi. 18.

48. **The Most High.** In contrast with heathen gods, who were confined to their temples.

Temples made with hands (*χειροποιήτοις ναοῖς*). The best texts omit *ναοῖς*, *temples*. The meaning is more general: *in things made with hands*. The expression is, however, used of a sanctuary in Isa. xvi. 12: "Moab shall come to his *sanctuary* (*τὰ χειροποίητα*)." The phrase *work*, or *works of men's hands*, is common in the Old Testament of *idols*. See Deut. iv. 28; 2 Kings xix. 18; 2 Chron. xxxii. 19; Ps. cxv. 4. Compare Mark xiv. 58; Eph. ii. 11; Heb. ix. 11, 24; 2 Cor. v. 1.

49. **What house.** Rev., more correctly, "*what manner* of house" (*ποῖον*).

51. **Stiff-necked and uncircumcised** (*σκληροτράχηλοι καὶ ἀπερίτμητοι*). Both only here in New Testament.

Resist (*ἀντιπίπτετε*). It is a very strong expression, implying *active* resistance. Lit., *to fall against* or *upon*. Used of *falling upon* an enemy. Only here in New Testament.

Ye have been (*γεγένησθε*). More correctly, as Rev., *ye have become*.

53. **Who** (*οἵτινες*). Stronger than the simple relative *who*, and emphasizing their sin by contrast with their privileges: *inasmuch as ye were those who received*, etc.

By the disposition of angels (*εἰς διαταγὰς ἀγγέλων*). Lit., *unto ordinances of angels*. *Εἰς* means *with reference to*. *Disposition* (*διαταγή*) is used by A. V. in the sense of *arrangement*, as we say a general *disposed* his troops. The word occurs only here and Rom. xiii. 2, where it is rendered *ordinance*. The kindred verb *διατάσσω* occurs often, and mostly in the sense of *command* or *appoint*. See Matt. xi. 1; Luke iii. 13. In 1 Cor. xi. 34, it is translated *set in order*. The reference is most probably to the Jewish tradition that the law was given through the agency of angels. See Deut. xxxiii. 2. Compare Ps. lxviii. 17. Paul expressly says that the law was *administered by the medium of angels* (Gal. iii. 19). Compare *the word spoken by angels* (Heb. ii. 2). Render, therefore, as Rev., *as it was ordained by angels*.

54. **They were cut.** See on ch. v. 33. In both instances, of *anger*. A different word is used to express *remorse*, ch. ii. 37.

Gnashed (ἔβρυχον). Originally to *eat greedily*, with a noise, as wild beasts: hence *to gnash* or grind the teeth.

55. **Being** (ὑπάρχων). See on Jas. ii. 15.

Looked up steadfastly. Compare ch. i. 10; iii. 4, 12; vi. 15; and see on Luke iv. 20.

Standing. Rising from the throne to protect and receive his servant. Usually Jesus is represented in the New Testament as *seated* at the Father's right hand. See Eph. i. 20; Col. iii. 1; Heb. i. 3.

56. **I see** (θεωρῶ). See on Luke x. 18.

The Son of man. A title never applied to Christ by any of the apostles or evangelists, except here by Stephen. See on Luke vi. 22.

57. **Stopped** (συνέσχον). Lit., *held together*.

58. **Stoned.** According to the Rabbis, the scaffold to which the criminal was to be led, with his hands bound, was to be twice the size of a man. One of the witnesses was to smite him with a stone upon the breast, so as to throw him down. If he were not killed, the second witness was to throw another stone at

him. Then, if he were yet alive, all the people were to stone him until he was dead. The body was then to be suspended till sunset.

A young man (νεανίου). Which, however, gives no indication of his age, since it is applied up to the age of forty-five. Thirty years after Stephen's martyrdom, Paul speaks of himself as *the aged* (Philem. 9).

Saul. The first mention of the apostle to the Gentiles.

59. **Calling upon God.** *God* is not in the Greek. From the vision just described, and from the prayer which follows, it is evident that *Jesus* is meant. So Rev., *the Lord.*

Jesus. An unquestionable prayer to *Christ.*

60. **Lay not this sin to their charge** (*μὴ στήσῃς αὐτοῖς τὴν ἁμαρτίαν ταύτην*). Lit., *fix not this sin upon them.*

He fell asleep (ἐκοιμήθη). Marking his calm and peaceful death. Though the pagan authors sometimes used *sleep* to signify *death*, it was only as a poetic figure. When Christ, on the other hand, said, "Our friend Lazarus *sleepeth* (κεκοίμηται)," he used the word, not as a figure, but as the expression of a *fact.* In that mystery of death, in which the pagan saw only nothingness, Jesus saw continued life, rest, waking—the elements which enter into sleep. And thus, in Christian speech and thought, as the doctrine of the resurrection struck its roots deeper, the word *dead*, with its hopeless finality, gave place to the more gracious and hopeful word *sleep.* The pagan burying-place carried in its name no suggestion of hope or comfort. It was a *burying-place*, a *hiding-place*, a *monumentum*, a mere *memorial* of something gone; a *columbarium*, or dove-cot, with its little pigeon-holes for cinerary urns; but the Christian thought of death as sleep, brought with it into Christian speech the kindred thought of a chamber of rest, and embodied it in the word *cemetery* (κοιμητήριον)—*the place to lie down to sleep.*

CHAPTER VIII.

1. **Death** (*ἀναιρέσει*). Lit., *taking off.* See on Luke xxiii. 32.

2. **Devout.** See on Luke ii. 25.

Carried to his burial (*συνεκόμισαν*). Only here in New Testament. Lit., *to carry together;* hence, either to *assist in burying* or, better, to bring the dead to *the company* (*σύν*) of the other dead. The word is used of bringing in harvest.

Stephen (*Στέφανον*). Meaning *crown.* He was the first who received the martyr's crown.

Lamentation (*κοπετὸν*). Lit., *beating* (of the breast). Only here in New Testament.

3. **Made havoc** (*ἐλυμαίνετο*). Only here in New Testament. In Septuagint, Ps. lxxix. 13, it is used of the *laying waste* of a vineyard by the wild boar. Compare Acts ix. 21, where the A. V. has *destroyed,* but where the Greek is *πορθήσας, devastated.* Canon Farrar observes: "The part which he played at this time in the horrid work of persecution has, I fear, been always underrated. It is only when we collect the separate passages—they are no less than eight in number—in which allusion is made to this sad period,* it is only when we weigh the terrible significance of the expressions used that we feel the load of remorse which must have lain upon him, and the taunts to which he was liable from malignant enemies" ("Life and Work of St. Paul"). Note the imperfect, of *continued* action.

5. **Philip.** The *deacon* (Acts vi. 5). Not the *apostle.* On the name, see on Mark iii. 18.

---

* See Acts viii. 3; ix. 2; xxii. 3, 4; xxvi. 9, 10.

Christ (τὸν Χριστόν). Note the article, "*the* Christ," and see on Matt. i. 1.

He did (ἐποίει). Imperfect. *Kept doing* from time to time, as is described in the next verse.

7. **Taken with palsies** (παραλελυμένοι). Rev., more neatly, *palsied*. See on Luke v. 18.

Were healed. See on Luke v. 15.

9. **Used sorcery** (μαγεύων). Only here in New Testament. One of the wizards so numerous throughout the East at that time, and multiplied by the general expectation of a great deliverer and the spread of the Messianic notions of the Jews, who practised upon the credulity of the people by conjuring and juggling and soothsaying.

Bewitched (ἐξιστῶν). Better as Rev., *amazed*. See on ch. ii. 7.

10. **The great power of God.** The best texts add ἡ καλουμένη, *which is called*, and render *that power of God which is called great*. They believed that Simon was an *impersonated* power of God, which, as the highest of powers, they designated as *the great*.

11. **Bewitched.** *Amazed*, as ver. 9.

13. **Continued with.** See on ch. i. 14.

Miracles and signs (σημεῖα καὶ δυνάμεις). Lit., *signs* and *powers*. See on Matt. xi. 20; Acts ii. 22.

Which were done (γινομένας). The present participle. Lit., *are coming to pass*.

He was amazed. After having *amazed* the people by his tricks. See ver. 9. The same word is employed.

14. **Samaria.** The *country*, not the city. See vv. 5, 9.

16. **They were** (ὑπῆρχον). See on Jas. ii. 15. Rev., more literally, *had been.*

In the name (εἰς τὸ ὄνομα). Lit., "*into* the name." See on Matt. xxviii. 19.

20. **Perish with thee** (σὺν σοὶ εἴη εἰς ἀπώλειαν). Lit., *be along with thee unto destruction.* Destruction overtake thy money and thyself.

21. **Part nor lot.** *Lot* expresses the same idea as *part,* but figuratively.

Matter (λόγῳ). The matter of which we are talking: the subject of discourse, as Luke i. 4; Acts xv. 6.

Right (εὐθεῖα). Lit., *straight.*

22. **If perhaps.** The doubt suggested by the heinousness of the offence.

Thought (ἐπίνοια). Only here in New Testament. Lit., *a thinking on* or *contriving;* and hence implying a *plan* or *design.*

23. **In the gall** (εἰς χολὴν). Lit., *into.* Thou hast fallen *into* and continuest in. *Gall,* only here and Matt. xxvii. 34. *Gall of bitterness* is bitter enmity against the Gospel.

Bond of iniquity (σύνδεσμον ἀδικίας). Thou hast fallen into iniquity as into fetters. The word σύνδεσμον denotes a *close, firm* bond (σύν, *together*). It is used of the bond of Christian peace (Eph. iv. 3); of the close compacting of the church represented as a body (Col. ii. 19); and of love as the *bond* of perfectness (Col. iii. 14). See Isa. lviii. 6.

26. **The south** (μεσημβρίαν). A contracted form of μεσημερία, *midday, noon,* which is the rendering at Acts xxii. 6,

the only other passage where it occurs. Rev. gives *at noon* in margin.

Desert. Referring to the *route*. *On desert*, see on Luke xv. 4. There were several roads from Jerusalem to Gaza. One is mentioned by the way of Bethlehem to Hebron, and thence through a region actually called a desert.

27. **Of Ethiopia.** The name for the lands lying south of Egypt, including the modern Nubia, Cordofan, and Northern Abyssinia. Rawlinson speaks of subjects of the Ethiopian queens living in an island near Meroë, in the northern part of this district. He further remarks: "The monuments prove beyond all question that the Ethiopians borrowed from Egypt their religion and their habits of civilization. They even adopted the Egyptian as the language of religion and of the court, which it continued to be till the power of the Pharaohs had fallen, and their dominion was again confined to the frontier of Ethiopia. It was through Egypt, too, that Christianity passed into Ethiopia, even in the age of the apostles, as is shown by the eunuch of Queen Candace."

Of great authority (δυνάστης). A general term for a potentate.

Candace. The common name of the queens of Meroë: a titular distinction, like Pharaoh in Egypt, or Caesar at Rome.

Treasure (γάζης). Only here in New Testament. A Persian word.

29. **Join thyself** (κολλήθητι). See on Luke xv. 15; x. 11; Acts v. 12.

30. **Understandest thou what thou readest** (ἆρά γε γινώσκεις ἃ ἀναγινώσκεις); The play upon the words cannot be translated. The interrogative particles which begin the question indicate a doubt on Philip's part.

31. **How can I** (πῶς γὰρ ἂν δυναίμην)? Lit., *for how should I be able?* the *for* connecting the question with an implied negative: "No; for how could I understand except," etc.

32. **The place of the scripture** (ἡ περιοχὴ τῆς γραφῆς). Strictly, *the contents of the passage.* See on Mark xii. 10; 1 Pet. ii. 6.

He read. Rev., correctly, *was reading;* imperfect.

33. **Humiliation.** See on Matt. xi. 29.

Generation. His contemporaries. Who shall declare their wickedness?

35. **Opened his mouth.** Indicating a solemn announcement. Compare Matt. v. 2.

37. The best texts omit this verse.

39. **Caught away.** Suddenly and miraculously.

And he went, etc. (ἐπορεύετο γὰρ). A mistranslation. Rev., rightly, "*for* he went." A reason is given for the eunuch's seeing Philip no more. He did not stop nor take another road to seek him, but went on his way.

CHAPTER IX.

1. **Breathing out** (ἐμπνέων). Lit., *breathing upon* or *at,* and so corresponding to *against the disciples.*

Threatenings and slaughter (ἀπειλῆς καὶ φόνου). Lit., *threatening;* so Rev. In the Greek construction, the case in which these words are marks them as the *cause* or *source* of the "breathing;" breathing hard *out of* threatening, and murderous desire.

2. **Of this way** (τῆς ὁδοῦ). Rev., more correctly, "*the* way." A common expression in the Acts for the Christian religion: "the characteristic direction of life as determined by faith on Jesus Christ" (Meyer). See ch. xix. 9; xxii. 4; xxiv. 22. For the fuller expression of the idea, see ch. xvi. 17; xviii. 25.

Women. Paul three times alludes to his persecution of women as an aggravation of his cruelty (ch. viii. 3; ix. 2; xxii. 4).

3. **There shined round about** (περιήστραψεν). Only here and ch. xxii. 6. *Flashed.* See on Luke xi. 36; xxiv. 4.

A light. Compare ch. xxii. 6; xxvi. 13.

4. **Saying.** In Paul's own account he says that the words were spoken in Hebrew (ch. xxvi. 14).

5. **It is hard for thee,** etc. Transferred from ch. xxvi. 14, and omitted by the best texts.

6. **Trembling and astonished.** The best texts omit.

7. **Speechless** (ἐνεοί). Only here in New Testament.

11. **Street** (ῥύμην). See on Luke xiv. 21. A *narrow* street or *lane.*

Straight. So called from its running in a direct line from the eastern to the western gate of the city.

15. **Chosen vessel** (σκεῦος ἐκλογῆς). Lit., *an instrument of choice.* On *vessel,* see on Matt. xii. 29; and on the figure, compare 2 Cor. iv. 7.

16. **How great things** (ὅσα). Rev., more correctly, *how many.*

17. **Brother.** In Christ.

18. **There fell—scales** (ἀπέπεσον—λεπίδες). Both words occur only here in the New Testament. In Paul's own account of his conversion in ch. xxvi. he does not mention his blindness: in ch. xxii. he mentions both the blindness and the recovery of sight, but not the particular circumstances which Luke records. The mention of the *scales*, or incrustations, such as are incidental to ophthalmia, is characteristic of the physician, and ἀποπίπτειν, *to fall off*, was used technically by medical writers of the falling of scales from the skin, and of particles from diseased parts of the body. "We may suppose that Luke had often heard Paul relate how he felt at that moment" (Hackett).

20. **Christ.** The correct reading is *Jesus*, the individual or personal name of the Lord. *Christ* was not yet current as his personal name. Paul's object was to establish the identity of Jesus the Nazarene with the Messiah.

21. **Destroyed** (πορθήσας). Rather, *laid waste, made havoc of*, as Rev. Compare ch. viii. 3. Paul uses the same word in Gal. i. 13.

22. **Confounded.** See on ch. ii. 6.

Proving (συμβιβάζων). The verb means *to bring* or *put together:* hence to *compare* and *examine*, as *evidence*, and so to *prove*. Used in the literal and physical sense in Eph. iv. 16. In Col. ii. 2, of being *knit together* in love. In 1 Cor. ii. 16, of *instructing*, *building up*, by *putting* together. In this sense the word occurs in the Septuagint. See Levit. x. 11; Judg. xiii. 8.

The Christ. Note the article. Not a *proper name*, but an *appellative*. See on ver. 20.

23. **To kill.** See on Luke xxiii. 32.

24. **Laying await** (ἐπιβουλή). So rendered by A. V. wherever it occurs, viz., ch. xx. 3, 19; xxiii. 30; but properly

changed by Rev., in every case, to *plot*. "Laying await" refers rather to the *execution* of the plot than to the plot itself.

Watched. See on Mark iii. 2. Imperfect: *they were* or *kept watching*, day and night.

25. **By the wall** (διὰ τοῦ τείχους). Rev., more accurately, *through* the wall, as is explained by 2 Cor. xi. 33. Either through the window of a house overhanging the wall, or through a window in the wall itself opening to houses on its inner side. Hackett says that he observed such windows in the wall at Damascus. On the mode of escape, compare Josh. ii. 15; 1 Sam. xix. 12.

Basket (σπυρίδι). See on Matt. xiv. 20. In Paul's account of this adventure he uses σαργάνη, a *plaited* or *braided* basket of wicker-work; or, as some think, of *ropes*.

26. **Join himself.** See on ch. v. 13; Luke xv. 15; x. 11.

27. **Declared** (διηγήσατο). Related throughout. See on Luke viii. 39; and compare on *declaration*, Luke i. 1.

Had preached boldly (ἐπαῤῥησιάσατο). See on *freely*, ch. ii. 29.

29. **Grecians.** Rev., correctly, *Grecian Jews*. See on ch. vi. 1.

Went about (ἐπεχείρουν). Better, *attempted:* lit., *took in hand*.

31. **The churches.** The best texts read *the church;* embracing all the different churches throughout the three provinces of Palestine.

Edified. Or *built up*.

Comfort (παρακλήσει). From παρακαλέω, *to call toward* or *to one's side* for help. The word is rendered in the New Testament both *exhortation* and *consolation*. Compare Acts xiii. 15; Rom. xii. 8; 2 Cor. viii. 17; Heb. xii. 5; and Luke ii. 25 (see note); 2 Thess. ii. 16; Matt. v. 4. In some passages the meaning is disputed, as Philip. ii. 1, where, as in 1 Cor. xiv. 3, it is joined with παραμύθιον or παραμυθία, the meaning of which also varies between *incentive* and *consolation* or *assuagement*. Here *exhortation* is the rendering approved by the best authorities, to be construed with *was multiplied: was multiplied by the exhortation of the Holy Ghost;* i.e., by the Holy Spirit inspiring the preachers, and moving the hearts of the hearers.

32. **Lydda.** The *Lod* of the Old Testament (Ezra ii. 33); about a day's journey from Jerusalem.

33. **Eight years.** The duration of the malady, and the fact of his having been bedridden for the whole time, are characteristic of the physician's narrative.

Bed. See on Mark ii. 14.

Sick of the palsy. Better, as Rev., *palsied.* See on Luke v. 18.

34. **Jesus Christ.** But note the article: Jesus *the* Christ; *the Anointed; Messiah.*

Maketh thee whole (ἰᾶταί σε). Rev., *healeth thee.* See on Luke vi. 19.

Make thy bed (στρῶσον σεαυτῷ). Lit., *strew for thyself.* Not, *henceforth*, but *on the spot*, as an evidence of restoration.

35. **Saron.** Rev., properly, *Sharon.* Always with the definite article: *the plain;* extending thirty miles along the sea from Joppa to Caesarea.

36. **Disciple** (μαθήτρια). A feminine form, only here in New Testament.

Tabitha—Dorcas. The latter word being the Greek equivalent of the former, which is Aramaic, and meaning *gazelle*, which in the East was a favorite type of beauty. See Song of Solomon ii. 9, 17; iv. 5; vii. 3. It was customary at this time for the Jews to have two names, one Hebrew and the other Greek or Latin; and this would especially be the case in a seaport like Joppa, which was both a Gentile and a Jewish town. She may have been known by both names.

37. **Upper chamber.** See on ch. i. 13.

38. **That he would not delay** (μὴ ὀκνῆσαι). The best texts read ὀκνήσῃς, putting the request in the form of a direct address, *Delay not.*

To come (διελθεῖν). Lit., to *come through.* Rev., *come on.*

39. **Coats and garments.** See on Matt. v. 40.

Which (ὅσα). Lit., *as many as.*

Made (ἐποίει). The imperfect: *was accustomed to make.*

CHAPTER X.

1. **Centurion.** See on Luke vii. 2.

Band (σπείρης). See on Mark xv. 16.

Italian. Probably because consisting of Roman soldiers, and not of natives of the country.

2. **Devout** (εὐσεβὴς). See on *godliness*, 2 Pet. i. 3.

Prayed (δεόμενος). See on *prayers*, Luke v. 33.

"Unheard by all but angel ears
The good Cornelius knelt alone,
Nor dream'd his prayers and tears
Would help a world undone.

"The while upon his terrac'd roof
The lov'd apostle to his Lord,
In silent thought aloof
For heavenly vision soared."

KEBLE, *Christian Year.*

3. **A vision.** See on ch. vii. 31.

Evidently (φανερῶς). Better, *clearly* or *distinctly*, as opposed to a *fancy*.

4. **When he looked** (ἀτενίσας). Rev., more accurately, *fastening his eyes*. Compare ch. vii. 55; and see on Luke iv. 20.

6. **A tanner.** Showing that the strictness of the Jewish law was losing its hold on Peter; since the tanner's occupation was regarded as unclean by strict Jews, and the tanners were commanded to dwell apart. "If a tanner married without mentioning his trade, his wife was permitted to get a divorce. The law of levirate marriage might be set aside if the brother-in-law of the childless widow was a tanner. A tanner's yard must be at least fifty cubits from any town" (Farrar, "Life and Work of St. Paul").

By the seaside. Outside the walls, both for proximity to the business, and because of the ceremonial requirement referred to above. Mr. William C. Prime, describing a visit to Joppa, says: "I was walking along the sea-beach, looking for shells, and at about a fourth of a mile from the city, to the southward, I found two tanneries directly on the seaside. I observed that the rocks in front of them were covered with the water a few inches deep, and that they soaked their hides on these rocks, and also submitted them to some process in the water which I did not stop to understand" ("Tent-life in the Holy Land").

Of them that waited on him continually (προσκαρτερούντων αὐτῷ). See on ch. i. 14.

8. **Declared** (ἐξηγησάμενος). Better, as Rev., *rehearsed.* See on Luke xxiv. 35.

9. **They** (ἐκείνων). *Those* messengers, the servants and the soldier. The pronoun has a more specific reference than the English *they.*

10. **Very hungry** (πρόσπεινος). Only here in New Testament.

Would have eaten (ἤθελε γεύσασθαι). Rev., correctly, *desired to eat.* Γεύεσθαι is rendered both to *eat* and to *taste,* more frequently the latter. See Matt. xxvii. 34; John ii. 9; 1 Pet. ii. 3; and compare Acts xx. 11.

He fell into a trance (ἐπέπεσεν ἐπ' αὐτὸν ἔκστασις). Lit., *an ecstasy fell upon him.* The best texts, however, read ἐγένετο, *came upon him,* or *happened to him.* See on *astonishment,* Mark v. 42. Luke alone employs the word in this sense of *ecstasy* or *trance.*

11. **Saw** (θεωρεῖ). Rev., better, and more literally, *beholdeth.* See on Luke x. 18. The present tense is graphically introduced into the narrative.

Unto him. The best texts omit.

Sheet (ὀθόνην). Only here and ch. xi. 5. Originally *fine linen;* later, *sail-cloth* or a *sail.* Dr. J. Rawson Lumby suggests that the word, "applied to loose, bellying sails of ships," may indicate that the form of vessel which appeared to Peter "recalled an image most familiar to his previous life—the wind-stretched canvas of the craft on the Lake of Galilee" ("Expositor," iii., 272).

Knit (δεδεμένον). If this is retained, we must render *bound*, or *attached;* but the best texts omit, together with the following *and*. Render, as Rev., *let down by four corners*. Compare ch. xi. 5.

Corners (ἀρχαῖς). Lit., *beginnings;* the *extremity* or *corner*, marking a *beginning* of the sheet. "We are to imagine the vessel, looking like a colossal four-cornered linen cloth, letting itself down, while the corners attached to heaven to support the whole." The word is used in this sense by Herodotus, describing the sacrifices of the Scythians. The victim's forefeet are bound with a cord, "and the person who is about to offer, taking his station behind the victim, pulls *the end* (ἀρχὴν) of the rope, and thereby throws the animal down" (iv., 60). The suggestion of *ropes* holding the corners of the sheet (Alford, and, cautiously, Farrar) is unwarranted by the usage of the word. It was the technical expression in medical language for the *ends of bandages*. The word for *sheet* in this passage was also the technical term for a *bandage*, as was the kindred word ὀθόνιον, used of the *linen bandages* in which the Lord's body was swathed. See Luke xxiv. 12; John xix. 40; xx. 5, 6, 7. Mr. Hobart says: "We have thus in this passage a technical medical phrase—the ends of a bandage—used for the ends of a sheet, which hardly any one except a medical man would think of employing" ("Medical Language of St. Luke").

12. **All manner of four-footed beasts** (πάντα τὰ τετράποδα). Lit., *all the four-footed beasts*. Without exception, clean and unclean. Not, *of very many kinds*.

Wild beasts. The best texts omit.

14. **Not so** (μηδαμῶς). Stronger: *by no means*. "With that simple and audacious self-confidence which in his (Peter's) character was so singularly mingled with fits of timidity and

depression, he boldly corrects the voice which orders him, and reminds the divine Interlocutor that he must, so to speak, have made an oversight" (Farrar, "Life and Works of Paul"). Compare Matt. xvi. 22.

Common (κοινὸν). *Unholy.*

15. **Call not thou common** (σὺ μὴ κοίνου). The thought goes deeper than merely *styling* "common." Lit., *do not thou defile.* Do not *profane* it by *regarding* and calling it common. Rev., "*make not thou common.*"

17. **Doubted** (διηπόρει). See on Luke ix. 7.

In himself. On reflection, as compared with his ecstatic state.

Had made inquiry (διερωτήσαντες). "Having inquired *out;*" having asked their way *through* (διά) streets and houses, until they found the dwelling of the tanner, who was an obscure man, and not easily found.

18. **Called.** A general summons to any one within, in order to make inquiries.

19. **Thought on** (διενθυμουμένου). Was *earnestly* (διά) pondering.

22. **Was warned** (ἐχρηματίσθη). See on Matt. ii. 12.

24. **Near** (ἀναγκαίους). The word originally means *necessary;* hence of those who are bound by *necessary* or *natural* ties; *blood-relations.* But as *relatives* or *kinsmen* is expressed by συγγενεῖς, this must be taken in the sense of *intimate friends*, a meaning which it has in later Greek writers.

25. **Worshipped** (προσεκύνησεν). An unfortunate translation, according to modern English usage, but justified by the

usage of earlier English, according to which to *worship* meant simply to *honor*. *Worship* is *worthship*, or honor paid to *dignity* or *worth*. This usage survives in the expressions *worshipful* and *your worship*. In the marriage-service of the English Church occurs the phrase, "With my body I thee *worship*." So Wycliffe renders Matt. xix. 19, "*Worship* thy father and thy mother;" and John xii. 26, "If any man serve me, my Father shall *worship* him." Here the meaning is that Cornelius paid reverence by prostrating himself after the usual oriental manner.

28. **An unlawful thing** (ἀθέμιτον). The word is peculiar to Peter, being used only here and 1 Pet. iv. 3. See note there. It emphasizes the violation of *established order*, being from the same root as τίθημι, to *lay down* or *establish*. The Jews professed to ground this prohibition on the law of Moses; but there is no direct command in the Mosaic law forbidding Jews to associate with those of other nations. But Peter's statement is general, referring to the general practice of the Jews to separate themselves in common life from uncircumcised persons. Juvenal says that the Jews were taught by Moses "not to show the way except to one who practises the same rites, and to guide the circumcised alone to the well which they seek" (Sat., xiv., 104, 105). Tacitus also says of the Jews that "among themselves they are inflexibly faithful, and ready with charitable aid, but hate all others as enemies. They keep separate from all strangers in eating, sleeping, and matrimonial connections" ("Histories," v., 5).

Of another nation (ἀλλοφύλῳ). Only here in New Testament. Used of the Philistines, 1 Sam. xiii. 3–5 (Sept.).

Me. Emphatic, by contrast with *ye*. "*Ye* know," etc., "but God hath showed *me*."

29. **With what intent** (τίνι λόγῳ). More strictly, *for what reason*.

30. **Four days ago** (ἀπὸ τετάρτης ἡμέρας). Lit., *from the fourth day;* reckoning backward from the day on which he was speaking.

I was fasting, and. The best texts omit.

At the ninth hour I prayed (τὴν ἐννάτην προσευχόμενος). Lit., *praying during the ninth hour.* With the omission of *I was fasting, and,* the rendering is as Rev., *Four days ago, until this hour, I was keeping the ninth hour of prayer.**

31. **Said** (φησι). Rev., *saith.* The historical present, giving vividness to the narrative.

33. **Well** (καλῶς). You have done a courteous and handsome thing in coming. Compare 3 John 5, 6.

34. **I perceive.** See on ch. iv. 13.

Respecter of persons (προσωπολήμπτης). See on *respect of persons,* Jas. ii. 1. Only here in New Testament.

36. **The word** (τὸν λόγον). The message.

37. **That word** (ῥῆμα). The contents of the message: the *report* or *history* which it proclaimed.

38. **Anointed** (ἔχρισεν). See on *Christ,* Matt. i. 1.

Went about (διῆλθεν). Lit., went *through* (the country). Compare ch. viii. 4.

And healing. The *and* (καὶ) has a particularizing force: doing good, *and in particular,* healing.

---

* It must be confessed that this statement, as thus amended, is obscure, and that the rendering would be greatly simplified by retaining the omitted words, as is done by several high authorities, as Meyer, Alford, Hackett, Gloag, De Wette, though against strong MS. evidence. They explain the omission in these MSS. by the fact that no mention of fasting is made in ver. 3.

Oppressed (καταδυναστευομένους). Only here and Jas. ii. 6, on which see note.

39. **They slew.** The best texts insert καὶ, *also:* "whom *also* they slew;" *also* having an *incressive* force. They added this crowning atrocity to other persecutions.

Tree. See on Luke xxiii. 31.

40. **Shewed him openly** (ἔδωκεν αὐτὸν ἐμφανῆ γενέσθαι). Lit., *gave him to become manifest.* Compare, for the construction, ch. ii. 27.

41. **Chosen before** (προκεχειροτονημένοις). Only here in New Testament. The simple verb χειροτονέω, *to appoint*, occurs Acts xiv. 23; 2 Cor. viii. 19; and originally means to *stretch out the hand* for the purpose of giving a vote. Hence to *elect* by show of hands, and generally *to appoint.* Plato uses the word of the election of leaders of choruses ("Laws," 765). In later ecclesiastical usage it signified *ordain*, as bishops or deacons.

Who (οἵτινες). The compound pronoun marks them more strongly as belonging to the *class* of eye-witnesses.

42. **Testify** (διαμαρτύρασθαι). See on ch. ii. 40.

Remission. See on Luke iii. 3; Jas. v. 15.

43. **His name.** As in the Lord's prayer: not simply the *title*, but all that is embraced and expressed by the name: Christ's "entire perfection, as the object revealed to the believer for his apprehension, confession, and worship" (Meyer).

44. **The Holy Ghost fell.** The only example of the bestowment of the Spirit before baptism.

45. **They of the circumcision.** From this point Luke distinguishes Christians into two classes—those of the circumcision

and those of the uncircumcision; calling the former *Jews*, and the latter *Gentiles* or *Greeks*.

Were amazed. See on ch. ii. 7.

47. **Water** (τὸ ὕδωρ). Note the article: *the* water; co-ordinating the water with the Spirit (see 1 John v. 8), and designating water as the recognized and customary element of baptism.

CHAPTER XI.

1. **In Judaea** (κατὰ τὴν Ἰουδαίαν). More correctly, "*throughout* Judaea."

2. **They of the circumcision.** See on ch. x. 45.

3. **Men uncircumcised** (ἄνδρας ἀκροβυστίαν ἔχοντας). An indignant expression. See Eph. ii. 11.

4. **Began.** Graphically indicating the solemn purport of the speech (compare Luke xii. 1), or perhaps, in connection with *expounded*, his beginning with the first circumstances and going through the whole list of incidents.

6. **I considered.** See on Matt. vii. 3; Luke xxii. 24, 27.

12. **Nothing doubting** (μηδὲν διακρινόμενον). The Rev. renders *making no distinction*, taking the verb in its original sense, which is *to separate* or *distinguish*. The rendering seems rather strained, *doubting* being a common rendering in the New Testament and giving a perfectly good sense here. See Matt. xxi. 21; Mark xi. 23, and note on Jas. i. 6. It was natural that Peter should hesitate.

The six brethren. The men of Joppa who had gone with Peter to Cornelius, and had accompanied him also to Jerusalem, either as witnesses for him or for their own vindication, since they had committed the same offence.

13. **An angel.** It has the definite article: "*the* angel," mentioned in ch. x.

17. **Forasmuch as** (εἰ). Better, as Rev., *if.*

The like (ἴσην). Lit., *equal;* making them, *equally* with us, recipients of the Holy Spirit.

19. **They which were scattered abroad** (οἱ διασπαρέντες). On the technical expression, *the dispersion*, see on 1 Pet. i. 1. Not so used here.

20. **The Greeks** (Ἕλληνας). Some, however, read Ἑλληνιστὰς, *the Grecian Jews.* See on ch. vi. 1. The express object of the narrative has been to describe the admission of *Gentiles* into the church. There would have been nothing remarkable in these men preaching to Hellenists who had long before been received into the church, and formed a large part of the church at Jerusalem. It is better to follow the rendering of A. V. and Rev., though the other reading has the stronger MS. evidence. Note, also, the contrast with the statement in ver. 19, *to the Jews only.* There is no contrast between Jews and Hellenists, since Hellenists are included in the general term *Jews.*

23. **Purpose** (προθέσει). Originally, *placing in public; setting before.* Hence of the *shew-bread*, the loaves *set forth* before the Lord (see on Mark ii. 26). Something *set before* one as an object of attainment: a *purpose.*

24. **Good** (ἀγαθὸς). More than strictly *upright.* Compare Rom. v. 7, where it is distinguished from δίκαιος, *just* or *righteous.* "His benevolence effectually prevented him censuring anything that might be new or strange in these preachers to the Gentiles, and caused him to rejoice in their success" (Gloag).

25. **To seek** (ἀναζητῆσαι). Strictly, like our "hunt *up*" (ἀνά).

26. **Were called Christians** (χρηματίσαι Χριστιανούς). The former of these two words, rendered *were called*, meant, originally, to *transact business*, to *have dealings with*; thence, in the course of business, to *give audience to*, to *answer*, from which comes its use to denote *the responses of an oracle*; a divine *advice* or *warning*. See Acts x. 22; and compare Matt. ii. 12; Heb. xi. 7. Later, it acquires the meaning to *bear a name*; to *be called*, with the implication of a name used in the ordinary *transactions* and *intercourse* of men; the name under which one passes.* This process of transition appears in the practice of naming men according to their occupations, as, in English, "John the Smith," "Philip the Armorer;" a practice which is the origin of many familiar family names, such as *Butler*, *Carpenter*, *Smith*, *Cooper*. Compare in New Testament *Alexander the coppersmith* (2 Tim. iv. 14); *Matthew the publican* (Matt. x. 3); *Luke the physician* (Col. iv. 14); *Erastus the chamberlain* (Rom. xvi. 23); *Rahab the harlot* (Heb. xi. 31). In the same line is the use of the word *calling*, to denote one's business. The meaning of the word in this passage is illustrated by Rom. vii. 3.

The disciples *were called*. They did not assume the name themselves. It occurs in only three passages in the New Testament: here; ch. xxvi. 28; and 1 Pet. iv. 16; and only in the last-named passage is used by a Christian of a Christian. The name was evidently not given by the Jews of Antioch, to whom *Christ* was the interpretation of *Messiah*, and who would not have bestowed that name on those whom they despised as apostates. The Jews designated the Christians as *Nazarenes* (Acts xxiv. 5), a term of contempt, because it was a proverb that nothing good could come out of Nazareth (John i. 47). The name was probably not assumed by the disciples themselves; for they were in the habit of styling each other *believers*, *disciples*, *saints*, *brethren*, *those of the way*. It, doubtless, was bestowed by the Gentiles. Some suppose that it was

---

* The Rev. Samuel Cox's application of the word to Christians, as making Christianity *the daily business of their lives*, is forced (Biblical Expositions, p. 341).

applied as a term of ridicule, and cite the witty and sarcastic character of the people of Antioch, and their notoriety for inventing names of derision; but this is doubtful. The name may have been given simply as a distinctive title, naturally chosen from the recognized and avowed devotion of the disciples to Christ as their leader. The Antiochenes mistook the nature of the name, not understanding its use among the disciples as an *official* title—*the Anointed*—but using it as a *personal* name, which they converted into a *party* name.

27. **Prophets.** See on Luke vii. 26.

28. **The world.** See on Luke ii. 1.

29. **According to his ability** (καθὼς ηὐπορεῖτό τις). Lit., *according as any one of them was prospered.* The verb is from εὔπορος, *easy to pass or travel through;* and the idea of prosperity is therefore conveyed under the figure of an easy and favorable journey. The same idea appears in our *farewell; fare* meaning originally to *travel.* Hence, to bid one *farewell* is to wish him a *prosperous journey.* Compare *God-speed.* So the idea here might be rendered, *as each one fared well.*

To send relief (εἰς διακονίαν πέμψαι). Lit., *to send for ministry.*

CHAPTER XII.

1. **That time** (ἐκεῖνον τὸν καιρὸν). More correctly, that *juncture.* See on ch. i. 7. The date is A.D. 44.

Herod the king. Called also Agrippa, and commonly known as Herod Agrippa I., the grandson of Herod the Great.

Stretched forth his hands (ἐπέβαλεν τὰς χεῖρας). Lit., *laid on his hands.* The A. V. is wrong, and so is the Rev. Render, *laid hands on certain of the church to afflict them.*

Vex (κακῶσαι). *Vex* is used in the older and stronger sense of *torment* or *oppress.* See Exod. xxii. 21; Num. xxv. 17; Matt. xv. 22. Its modern usage relates rather to petty annoyances. Rev., better, *afflict.*

2. **Killed—with the sword.** While the martyrdom of Stephen is described at length, that of James, the first martyr among the apostles, is related in two words.

3. **He proceeded to take** (προσέθετο συλλαβεῖν). Rev., *seize.* Lit., *he added to take.* A Hebrew form of expression. Compare Luke xix. 11, *he added and spake;* Luke xx. 12, *again he sent a third;* lit., *he added to send.*

4. **Quaternions.** A quaternion was a body of four soldiers; so that there were sixteen guards, four for each of the four night-watches.

The passover. The whole seven days of the feast.

Bring him forth (ἀναγαγεῖν αὐτὸν). Lit., *lead him up;* i.e., to the elevated place where the tribunal stood, to pronounce sentence of death before the people. See John xix. 13.

5. **Without ceasing** (ἐκτενὴς). Wrong. The word means *earnest.* See on *fervently,* 1 Pet. i. 22; and compare *instantly,* Acts xxvi. 7; *more earnestly,* Luke xxii. 44; *fervent,* 1 Pet. iv. 8. The idea of *continuance* is, however, expressed here by the finite verb with the participle. Very literally, *prayer was arising earnest.*

6. **Would have brought.** Rev., correctly, *was about to bring.*

Kept (ἐτήρουν). See on *reserved,* 1 Pet. i. 4. The imperfect, *were keeping.*

7. **Came upon** (ἐπέστη). Better, as Rev., *stood by.* See on ch. iv. i.; and compare Luke ii. 9.

Prison (*οἰκήματι*). Not the prison, but the *cell* where Peter was confined. So, rightly, Rev.

8. **Garment** (*ἱμάτιον*). The *outer* garment, or mantle. See on Matt. v. 40.

10. **Ward** (*φυλακὴν*). Better, *watch:* the soldiers on guard. Explanations of the *first* and *second* watch differ, some assuming that the first was the single soldier on guard at the door of Peter's cell, and the second, another soldier at the gate leading into the street. Others, that *two* soldiers were at each of these posts, the two in Peter's cell not being included in the four who made up the watch.

12. **When he had considered** (*συνιδὼν*). The verb strictly means to *see together*, or at the same time. Hence, to *see in one view*, to *take in at a glance.* Peter's mental condition is described by two expressions: First, he *came to himself* (ver. 12), or, lit., *when he had become present in himself;* denoting his awaking from the dazed condition produced by his being suddenly roused from sleep and confronted with a supernatural appearance (see ver. 9). Secondly, *when he had become aware* (*συνιδὼν*); denoting his *taking in the situation*, according to the popular phrase. I do not think that any of the commentators have sufficiently emphasized the force of *σύν*, *together*, as indicating his *comprehensive perception* of all the elements of the case. They all refer the word to his recognition of his deliverance from prison, which, however, has already been noted in ver. 11. While it may include this, it refers also to all the circumstances of the case present at that moment. He had been freed; he was there in the street alone; he must go somewhere; there was the house of Mary, where he was sure to find friends. Having *taken in* all this, *perceived* it all, he went to the house of Mary.*

---

* This force of the verb is illustrated by Xenophon (Anabasis, i., 5, 9). "For one who directed his attention to it (*i.e.*, the numerous evidences of power furnished by a great empire) might *see* (*συνιδεῖν*, in a comprehensive glance) that the king was powerful." So Plato (Laws, 904), speaking of God,

13. **Door of the gate.** The small outside door, forming the entrance from the street, and opening into the πυλών, or *door-way*, the passage from the street into the court. Others explain it as the *wicket*, a small door in the larger one, which is less probable.

A damsel (παιδίσκη). Or *maid*. The word was used of a young female slave, as well as of a young girl or maiden generally. The narrative implies that she was more than a mere menial, if a servant at all. Her prompt recognition of Peter's voice, and her joyful haste, as well as the record of her name, indicate that she was one of the disciples gathered for prayer.

Rhoda. *Rose.* The Jews frequently gave their female children the names of plants and flowers: as *Susannah* (lily); *Esther* (myrtle); *Tamar* (palm-tree). "God, who leaves in oblivion names of mighty conquerors, treasures up that of a poor girl, for his church in all ages" (Quesnel).

14. **She knew.** Or *recognized.*

15. **Constantly affirmed** (διϊσχυρίζετο). Better, *confidently* affirmed; *constant* is used in its older sense of *consistent*. The verb contains two ideas: *strong* assertion (ἰσχύς), and *holding to* the assertion *through* all contradiction (διά); hence, she *strongly* and *consistently* asserted.

Angel. Guardian angel, according to the popular belief among the Jews that every individual has his guardian angel, who may, on occasion, assume a visible appearance resembling that of the person whose destiny is committed to him.

17. **Beckoning** (κατασείσας). Lit., *having shaken downward* with his hand, in order to bespeak silence and attention. It was a familiar gesture of Paul. See ch. xxi. 40; xxvi. 1.

---

says, "When he saw that our actions had life," etc., going on to enumerate various details, "He, *seeing all this* (ταῦτα πάντα συνιδών)." Compare, also, Acts xiv. 6.

19. **Examined** (ἀνακρίνας). See on Luke xxiii. 14; and compare ch. iv. 9.

Put to death (ἀπαχθῆναι). Lit., *led away;* i.e., to execution. A technical phrase like the Latin *ducere.* Compare Matt. xxvii. 31.

Abode (διέτριβεν). Originally, to *rub away,* or *consume;* hence, of *time,* to *spend.*

20. **Highly displeased** (θυμομαχῶν). Originally, *to fight desperately:* but as there is no record of any war of Herod with the Tyrians and Sidonians, the word is to be taken in the sense of the A. V. Only here in New Testament.

Chamberlain (τὸν ἐπὶ τοῦ κοιτῶνος). Lit., *the one over the bedchamber.*

21. **Set** (τακτῇ). Appointed. Only here in New Testament. What the festival was, is uncertain. According to some, it was in honor of the emperor's safe return from Britain. Others think it was to celebrate the birthday of Claudius; others that it was the festival of the Quinquennalia, observed in honor of Augustus, and dating from the taking of Alexandria, when the month *Sextilis* received the name of the Emperor—*August.*

Arrayed (ἐνδυσάμενος). More literally, *having arrayed himself.*

Royal apparel. Josephus says he was clothed in a robe entirely made of silver.

Throne. See on ch. vii. 5. The elevated seat or throne-like box in the theatre, set apart for the king, from which he might look at the games or address the assembly.

Made an oration (ἐδημηγόρει). Only here in New Testament. The word is used especially of a *popular harangue* (δῆμος, *the commons*). "At Jerusalem Agrippa enacted the Jew, with solemn gait and tragic countenance, amidst general acclamation; but at Caesarea he allowed the more genial part of a Greek to be imposed on him. It was at a festival in this Hellenic capital, after an harangue he had addressed to the populace, that they shouted, "It is the voice of a god and not of a man" (Merivale, "History of the Romans under the Empire").

22. **The people** (δῆμος). The *assembled* people.

A god. As most of the assembly were heathen, the word does not refer to the Supreme Being, but is to be taken in the pagan sense—*a god*.

23. **An angel of the Lord smote him.** An interesting parallel is furnished by the story of Alp Arslan, a Turkish prince of the eleventh century. "The Turkish prince bequeathed a dying admonition to the pride of kings. 'In my youth,' said Alp Arslan, 'I was advised by a sage to humble myself before God; to distrust my own strength; and never to despise the most contemptible foe. I have neglected these lessons, and my neglect has been deservedly punished. Yesterday, as from an eminence, I beheld the numbers, the discipline, and the spirit of my armies; the earth seemed to tremble under my feet, and I said in my heart, surely thou art the king of the world, the greatest and most invincible of warriors. These armies are no longer mine; and, in the confidence of my personal strength, I now fall by the hand of an assassin'" (Gibbon, "Decline and Fall").

Eaten of worms (σκωληκόβρωτος). Only here in New Testament. Of Pheretima, queen of Cyrene, distinguished for her cruelties, Herodotus says: "Nor did Pheretima herself end her days happily. For on her return to Egypt from Libya, directly after taking vengeance on the people of Barca, she was overtaken by a most horrid death. Her body swarmed with worms, which ate her flesh while she was still alive" (iv., 205). The term, as applied to disease in the human body, does not occur in any of the medical writers extant. Theophrastus, however, uses it of a disease in plants. The word σκώληξ is used by medical writers of intestinal worms. Compare the account of the death of Antiochus Epiphanes, the great persecutor of the Jews. "So that the worms rose up out of the body of this wicked man, and whiles he lived in sorrow and pain, his flesh fell away, and the filthiness of his smell was noisome to all his army" (2 Macc. ix. 9). Sylla, the Roman dictator, is also said to have suffered from a similar disease.

Gave up the ghost. See on ch. v. 5.

CHAPTER XIII.

1. **Prophets.** See on Luke vii. 26.

Lucius of Cyrene. Attempts have been made to identify him with Luke the evangelist; but the name *Lucas* is an abbreviation of *Lucanus*, and not of *Lucius*. It is worth noting, however, that, according to Herodotus (iii., 131), the physicians of Cyrene had the reputation of being the second best in Greece, those of Crotona being the best; and that Galen the physician says that Lucius was before him a distinguished physician in Tarsus of Cilicia. From this it has been conjectured that Luke was born and instructed in medicine in Cyrene, and left that place for Tarsus, where he made Paul's acquaintance, and was, perhaps, converted by him (Dr. Howard Crosby, "The New Testament, Old and New Version"). But, apart from the form of the name (see above), the mention of the evangelist's name here is not in accord with his usual practice, since he nowhere mentions his own name, either in the Gospel or in the Acts; and if the present passage were an exception, we should have expected to find his name last in the list of the worthies of Antioch. Of the five here named, four are known to be Jews; and therefore, probably, Lucius was also a Jew from Cyrene, where Jews are known to have abounded. Luke the evangelist, on the contrary, was a Gentile. Nothing certain can be inferred from Rom. xvi. 21, where Lucius is enumerated by Paul among his *kinsmen.* If συγγενεῖς, *kinsmen,* means here, as is claimed by some, *countrymen,* it would prove Lucius to be a Jew; but the word is commonly used of relatives in the New Testament. In Rom. ix. 3, Paul applies the term to his fellow-countrymen, "my brethren, my *kinsmen* according to the flesh, *who are Israelites.*"

Which had been brought up with (σύντροφος). Some render *foster-brother,* as Rev.; others, *comrade.* The word has both meanings.

2. **Ministered** (λειτουργούντων). See on the kindred noun *ministration,* Luke i. 23. This noun has passed through the following meanings: 1. A *civil service,* especially in the technical language of Athenian law. 2. A *function or office* of any kind, as of the bodily organs. 3. *Sacerdotal ministration,* both among the Jews and the heathen (see Heb. viii. 6; ix. 21). 4. The *eucharistic services.* 5. *Set forms of divine worship* (Lightfoot, "On Philippians," ii., 17). Here, of the performance of Christian worship. Our word *liturgy* is derived from it.

Separate. The Greek adds δή, *now,* which is not rendered by A. V. or Rev. It gives precision and emphasis to the command, implying that it is for a special purpose, and to be obeyed at the time. Compare Luke ii. 15; Acts xv. 36; 1 Cor. vi. 20.

4. **Sailed.** On Luke's use of words for *sailing,* see Introduction.

5. **Synagogues.** The plural implies that the Jews were numerous in Salamis. Augustus, according to Josephus, made Herod the Great a present of half the revenue of the copper-mines of Cyprus, so that numerous Jewish families would be settled in the island. In the reign of Trajan, upon the breaking out of a Jewish insurrection, the whole island fell into the hands of the Jews, and became a rallying-point for the revolt.

It is said that two hundred and forty thousand of the native population were sacrificed to the fury of the insurgents. When the rebellion was extinguished, the Jews were forbidden thenceforth, on pain of death, to set foot on the island.

Minister (ὑπηρέτην). Better, as Rev., *attendant*. See on Matt. v. 25.

6. **Sorcerer** (μάγον). That the man was an impostor is told us in the next word, but not in this term. It is the word used of the *wise men* who came to the Saviour's cradle. See Matt. ii. 1, 7, 16. Elymas was a *magian;* of what kind is shown by *false prophet*. See on Matt. ii. 1.

Bar-Jesus. Son of Jesus or Joshua.

7. **The deputy** (ἀνθυπάτῳ). Better, Rev., *proconsul*. See Introduction to Luke, on Luke's accuracy in designating public officers.

Sergius Paulus. Di Cesnola relates the discovery at Soli, which, next to Salamis, was the most important city in the island, of a slab with a Greek inscription containing the name of Paulus, proconsul.

Prudent (συνετῷ). Better, as Rev., *a man of understanding*. See on Matt. xi. 25.

8. **Elymas.** An Arabic word, meaning *the wise*, and equivalent to *Magus*. See on ver. 6.

Withstood. "The position of soothsayer to a Roman proconsul, even though it could only last a year, was too distinguished and too lucrative to abandon without a struggle" (Farrar, "Life and Work of Paul").

9. **Saul—Paul.** The first occurrence of the name of Paul in the Acts. Hereafter he is constantly so called, except when

there is a reference to the earlier period of his life. Various explanations are given of the change of name. The most satisfactory seems to be that it was customary for Hellenistic Jews to have two names, the one Hebrew and the other Greek or Latin. Thus John was also called *Marcus;* Symeon, *Niger;* Barsabas, *Justus.* As Paul now comes prominently forward as the apostle to the Gentiles, Luke now retains his Gentile name, as he did his Jewish name during his ministry among the Jews. The connection of the name Paul with that of the deputy seems to me purely accidental. It was most unlike Paul to assume the name of another man, converted by his instrumentality, out of respect to him or as a memorial of his conversion. Farrar justly observes that there would have been in this "an element of vulgarity impossible to St. Paul."

Set his eyes on him. See on Luke iv. 20.

10. **Mischief** (ῥᾳδιουργίας). Only here in New Testament. Originally, *ease* or *facility in doing;* hence readiness in turning the hand to anything, bad or good; and so *recklessness, unscrupulousness, wickedness.* A kindred word (ῥᾳδιούργημα, *lewdness,* Rev., *villany*) occurs at ch. xviii. 14.

Right ways. Or *straight,* possibly with an allusion to Elymas' *crooked* ways.

11. **Mist** (ἀχλὺς). Only here in New Testament. The word is used by medical writers as a name for a disease of the eyes. The mention of the successive stages, first *dimness,* then *total darkness,* are characteristic of the physician. "The first miracle which Paul performed was the infliction of a judgment; and that judgment the same which befell himself when arrested on his way to Damascus" (Gloag).

12. **Astonished** (ἐκπλησσόμενος). See on Matt. vii. 28.

13. **Loosed** (ἀναχθέντες). See on Luke viii. 22.

Paul and his company (*οἱ περὶ τὸν Παῦλον*). Lit., *those around Paul.* In later writers, used to denote the principal person alone, as John xi. 19, *came to Mary and Martha;* where the Greek literally reads, *came to the women around Mary and Martha.* Paul, and not Barnabas, now appears as the principal person.

15. **Exhortation.** See on ch. ix. 31.

16. **Beckoning.** See on ch. xii. 17.

Men of Israel. See on ch. iii. 12.

17. **People** (*λαοῦ*). Restricted in the Acts to the people of Israel.

18. **Suffered he their manners** (*ἐτροποφόρησεν*). From *τρόπος*, *fashion* or *manner*, and *φορέω*, *to bear* or *suffer.* The preferable reading, however, is *ἐτροφοφόρησεν*; from *τροφός*, *a nurse;* and the figure is explained by, and probably was drawn from, Deut. i. 31. The American revisers properly insist on the rendering, *as a nursing-father bare he them.*

19. **Divided by lot** (*κατεκληρονόμησεν*). The A. V. gives the literal rendering. The Rev., *gave them their land for an inheritance*, is correct, so far as the meaning *inheritance* is concerned (see on 1 Pet. i. 4), but does not give the sense of *distribution* which is contained in the word.

24. **Before his coming** (*πρὸ προσώπου τῆς εἰσόδου αὐτοῦ*). Lit., *before the face of his entrance.* A Hebrew form of expression.

25. **Think ye** (*ὑπονοεῖτε*). Originally, *to think secretly:* hence *to suspect, conjecture.*

26. **To you.** The best texts read *to us.*

33. **Hath fulfilled** (*ἐκπεπλήρωκε*). *Completely* fulfilled; force of *ἐκ*, *out and out.*

34. **The sure mercies** (τὰ ὅσια τὰ πιστά). Lit., *the holy things, the sure.* Rev., *the holy and sure blessings.*

35. **Suffer** (δώσεις). Lit., *give.*

36. **Was laid unto** (προσετέθη). Lit., was *added unto.* Compare ch. ii. 47; v. 14.

41. **Perish** (ἀφανίσθητε). Lit., *vanish.*

Declare (ἐκδιηγῆται). Only here and ch. xv. 3. See on *shew,* Luke viii. 39. The word is a very strong expression for the fullest and clearest declaration: *declare throughout.*

42. **Next** (μεταξὺ). The word commonly means *intermediate,* and hence is explained by some as referring to the intermediate week. But the meaning is fixed by ver. 44; and though the word does not occur in the New Testament elsewhere in the sense of *next,* it has that meaning sometimes in later Greek.

43. **Religious** (σεβομένων). Lit., *worshipping.* Compare ver. 50 and ch. xvi. 14.

Proselytes (προσηλύτων). Originally, one who *arrives at* a place; *a stranger;* thence of one who *comes over* to another faith.

45. **Envy** (ζήλου). Rev., *jealousy.* See on Jas. iii. 14.

46. **Put** (ἀπωθεῖσθε). Not strong enough. Better, as Rev., *thrust,* denoting *violent* rejection.

Lo (ἰδοὺ). Marking a *crisis.*

50. **Honorable** (εὐσχήμονας). See on Mark xv. 43. Women of *rank,* or, as Rev., of *honorable estate.*

Coasts (ὁρίων). Not a good rendering, because it implies merely a *sea-coast;* whereas the word is a general one for *boundaries.*

51. **Shook off.** See on Matt. x. 14.

Dust. See on Luke x. 11.

CHAPTER XIV.

3. **Long** (ἱκανὸν). See on Luke vii. 6.

Abode. See on ch. xii. 19.

In the Lord. Lit., *upon* (ἐπί) the Lord: *in reliance on* him.

5. **Assault** (ὁρμὴ). Too strong, as is also the Rev., *onset.* In case an actual assault had been made, it would have been absurd for Luke to tell us that "they were ware of it." It is rather the *purpose* and *intention* of assault beginning to assume the character of a *movement.* See on Jas. iii. 4.

To stone. Paul says he was stoned *once* (2 Cor. xi. 25). This took place at Lystra (see ver. 19).

6. **Were ware** (συνιδόντες). Rev., *became aware.* See on *considered,* ch. xii. 12.

7. **They preached the gospel** (ἦσαν εὐαγγελιζόμενοι). The finite verb with the participle, denoting *continuance.* They prolonged their preaching for some time.

8. **Impotent** (ἀδύνατος). The almost universal meaning of the word in the New Testament is *impossible* (see Matt. xix. 26; Heb. vi. 4, etc.). The sense of *weak* or *impotent* occurs only here and Rom. xv. 1.

9. **Heard** (ἤκουε). The force of the imperfect should be given here. He *was hearing* while Paul preached.

10. **Upright** (ὀρθός). Only here and Heb. xii. 13. Compare *made straight*, Luke xiii. 13, and see note there.

Leaped (ἥλατο). Better, as Rev., *leaped up*. Note the aorist tense, indicating a *single* act, while the imperfect, *walked*, denotes *continuous* action.

11. **In the speech of Lycaonia.** The apostles had been conversing with them in Greek. The fact that the people now spoke in their native tongue explains why Paul and Barnabas did not interfere until they saw the preparations for sacrifice. They did not understand what was being said by the people about their divine character. It was natural that the surprise of the Lystrans should express itself in their own language rather than in a foreign tongue.

In the likeness of men (ὁμοιωθέντες ἀνθρώποις). Lit., *having become like to men*. A remnant of the earlier pagan belief that the gods visited the earth in human form. Homer, for example, is full of such incidents. Thus, when Ulysses lands upon his native shore, Pallas meets him

> "in the shape
> Of a young shepherd delicately formed,
> As are the sons of kings. A mantle lay
> Upon her shoulder in rich folds; her feet
> Shone in their sandals; in her hands she bore
> A javelin."
>
> *Odyssey*, xiii., 221–225.

Again, one rebukes a suitor for maltreating Ulysses:

> "Madman! what if he
> Came down from heaven and were a god! The gods
> Put on the form of strangers from afar,
> And walk our towns in many different shapes,
> To mark the good and evil deeds of men."
>
> *Odyssey*, xvii., 485 sq.

12. **Barnabas Jupiter, and Paul Mercury.** The Greek names of these deities were *Zeus* and *Hermes*. As the herald of the gods, Mercury is the god of skill in the use of speech and

of eloquence in general, for the heralds are the public speakers in the assemblies and on other occasions. Hence he is sent on messages where persuasion or argument are required, as to Calypso to secure the release of Ulysses from Ogygia ("Odyssey," i., 84); and to Priam to warn him of danger and to escort him to the Grecian fleet ("Iliad," xxiv., 390). Horace addresses him as the "eloquent" grandson of Atlas, who artfully formed by oratory the savage manners of a primitive race ("Odes," i., 10). Hence the tongues of sacrificial animals were offered to him. As the god of ready and artful speech, his office naturally extended to business negotiations. He was the god of prudence and skill in all the relations of social intercourse, and the patron of business and gain. A merchant-guild at Rome was established under his protection. And as, from its nature, commerce is prone to degenerate into fraud, so he appears as the god of thievery, exhibiting cunning, fraud, and perjury.* "He represents, so to speak, the utilitarian side of the human mind. . . . In the limitation of his faculties and powers, in the low standard of his moral habits, in the abundant activity of his appetites, in his indifference, his ease, his good-nature, in the full-blown exhibition of what Christian theology would call conformity to the world, he is, as strictly as the nature of the case admits, a product of the invention of man. He is the god of intercourse on earth" (Gladstone, "Homer and the Homeric Age").

The chief speaker (ὁ ἡγούμενος τοῦ λόγου). Lit., *the leader in discourse.* Barnabas was called *Jupiter*, possibly because his personal appearance was more imposing than Paul's (see 2 Cor. x. 1, 10), and also because Jupiter and Mercury were commonly represented as companions in their visits to earth.†

13. **Of Jupiter** (τοῦ Διὸς). Properly, *the* Jupiter, the tute-

---

* See the Homeric Hymn to Hermes, and Horace, Odes, B. i., Ode x.; Iliad, v., 390; xxiv., 24.

† As, for instance, in the beautiful story of Baucis and Philemon, as related by Ovid (Metamorphoses, viii., 626–724).

lary deity of Lystra. It is unnecessary to supply *temple*, as Rev. The god himself was regarded as present in his temple.

The gates (πυλῶνας). What gates are intended is uncertain. Some say, the *city gates;* others, the *temple gates;* and others, the *doors of the house* in which Paul and Barnabas were residing. See on ch. xii. 13.

14. **Ran in** (εἰσεπήδησαν). A feeble translation, even if this reading is retained. The verb means *to leap* or *spring*. The best texts read ἐξεπήδησαν, *sprang forth*, probably from the gate of their house, or from the city gate, if the sacrifice was prepared in front of it.

Crying out (κράζοντες). Inarticulate shouts to attract attention.

15. **Of like passions** (ὁμοιοπαθεῖς). Only here and Jas. v. 17, on which see note. Better, *of like nature.*

Turn (ἐπιστρέφειν). Compare 1 Thess. i. 9, where the same verb is used.

16. **Times** (γενεαῖς). More correctly, *generations*, as Rev.

17. **Rains.** Jupiter was lord of the air. He dispensed the thunder and lightning, the rain and the hail, the rivers and tempests. "All signs and portents whatever, that appear in the air, belong primarily to him, as does the genial sign of the rainbow" (Gladstone, "Homer and the Homeric Age"). The mention of rain is appropriate, as there was a scarcity of water in Lycaonia.

Food. Mercury, as the god of merchandise, was also the dispenser of food.

"No one can read the speech without once more perceiving its subtle and inimitable coincidence with his (Paul's) thoughts and expressions. The rhythmic conclusion is not unaccordant with the style of his most elevated moods; and besides the appropriate appeal to God's natural gifts in a town not in itself unhappily situated, but surrounded by a waterless and treeless plain, we may naturally suppose that the 'filling our hearts with food and gladness' was suggested by the garlands and festive pomp which accompanied the bulls on which the people would afterward have made their common banquet" (Farrar, "Life and Work of Paul"). For the coincidences between this discourse and other utterances of Paul, compare ver. 15, and 1 Thess. i. 9; ver. 16, and Rom. iii. 25; Acts xvii. 30; ver. 17, and Rom. i. 19, 20.

19. **Stoned.** See on ver. 5.

20. **To Derbe.** A journey of only a few hours.

21. **Taught** (μαθητεύσαντες). More correctly, *made disciples of*, as Rev. See on Matt. xiii. 52.

Many. See on Luke vii. 6.

22. **Confirming.** See on *stablish*, 1 Pet. v. 10.

23. **Ordained** (χειροτονήσαντες). Only here and 2 Cor. viii. 19. Rev., more correctly, *appointed*. The meaning *ordain* is later. See on ch. x. 41.

Elders (πρεσβυτέρους). For the general superintendence of the church. The word is synonymous with ἐπίσκοποι, *overseers* or *bishops* (see on *visitation*, 1 Pet. ii. 12). Those who are called *elders*, in speaking of Jewish communities, are called *bishops*, in speaking of Gentile communities. Hence the latter term prevails in Paul's epistles.

Commended (παρέθεντο). See on *set before*, Luke ix. 16; and *commit*, 1 Pet. iv. 19.

27. **With them** (μετ' αὐτῶν). In connection with them; assisting them.

And how (καὶ ὅτι). Better, *that.* The *and* has an incressive and particularizing force: "and *in particular*, *above all.*"

CHAPTER XV.

1. **Taught.** Rather the imperfect, *were teaching.* They had not merely broached the error, but were inculcating it.

Manner (ἔθει). Better, *custom*, as Rev.

2. **Question** (ζητήματος). Found only in the Acts, and always of a question *in dispute.*

3. **Being brought on their way** (προπεμφθέντες). Lit., *having been sent forth;* under escort as a mark of honor.

Declaring. See on ch. xiii. 41. In the various towns along their route.

4. **Were received** (ἀπεδέχθησαν). The word implies a *cordial welcome*, which they were not altogether sure of receiving.

5. **Arose.** In the assembly.

Sect. See on *heresies*, 2 Pet. ii. 1.

7. **The word of the gospel** (τὸν λόγον τοῦ εὐαγγελίου). This phrase occurs nowhere else; and εὐαγγέλιον, *gospel*, is found only once more in Acts (ch. xx. 24).

8. **Which knoweth the heart** (καρδιογνώστης). Only here and ch. i. 24.

10. **Were able** (ἰσχύσαμεν). See on Luke xiv. 30; xvi. 3.

12. **Hearkened.** The imperfect (ἤκουον) denotes attention to a continued narrative.

Declaring (ἐξηγουμένων). Better, as Rev., *rehearsing*. See on Luke xxiv. 35.

What miracles, etc. Lit., *how many* (ὅσα).

13. **James.** See Introduction to Catholic Epistles.

18. **Known unto God,** etc. The best texts join these words with the preceding verse, from which they omit *all;* rendering, *The Lord, who maketh these things known from the beginning of the world.*

19. **Trouble** (παρενοχλεῖν). Only here in New Testament. See on *vexed*, Luke vi. 18.

20. **Write** (ἐπιστεῖλαι). Originally, to *send to*, as a message; hence, by *letter*. The kindred noun ἐπιστολή, whence our *epistle*, means, originally, *anything sent by a messenger*. *Letter* is a secondary meaning.

Pollutions (ἀλισγημάτων). A word not found in classical Greek, and only here in the New Testament. The kindred verb ἀλισγεῖν, *to pollute*, occurs in the Septuagint, Dan. i. 8; Mal. i. 7, and both times in the sense of defiling by food. Here the word is defined by *things sacrificed to idols* (ver. 29); the flesh of idol sacrifices, of which whatever was not eaten by the worshippers at the feasts in the temples, or given to the priests, was sold in the markets and eaten at home. See 1 Cor. x. 25–28; and Exod. xxxiv. 15.

Fornication. In its literal sense. "The association of *fornication* with three things in themselves indifferent is to be explained from the then moral corruption of heathenism, by which fornication, regarded from of old with indulgence, and even with favor, nay, practised without shame even by philosophers, and surrounded by poets with all the tinsel of lasciviousness, had become in public opinion a thing really indifferent" (Meyer). See Döllinger, "The Gentile and the Jew," ii., 237 sq.

Strangled. The flesh of animals killed in snares, and whose blood was not poured forth, was forbidden to the Israelites.

23. **Greeting** (*χαίρειν*). The usual Greek form of salutation. It occurs nowhere else in the salutation of a New Testament epistle save in the Epistle of James (i. 1). See note there. It appears in the letter of Claudius Lysias (ch. xxiii. 26).

24. **Subverting** (*ἀνασκευάζοντες*). Only here in New Testament, and not found either in the Septuagint or in the Apocrypha. Originally, it means to *pack up baggage*, and so to *carry away;* hence, to *dismantle* or *disfurnish*. So Thucydides (iv., 116) relates that Brasidas captured Lecythus, and then pulled it down and *dismantled* it (*ἀνασκευάσας*). From this comes the more general meaning to *lay waste*, or *ravage*. The idea here is that of turning the minds of the Gentile converts upside down; throwing them into confusion like a dismantled house.

We gave no commandment (*οὐ διεστειλάμεθα*). The word originally means to *put asunder;* hence, to *distinguish*, and so of a commandment or injunction, to *distinguish* and *emphasize* it. Therefore implying *express orders*, and so always in the New Testament, where it is almost uniformly rendered *charge*. The idea here is, then, "we gave no *express injunction* on the points which these Judaizers have raised."

25. **Barnabas and Paul.** Here, as in ver. 12, Barnabas is named first, contrary to the practice of Luke since Acts xiii. 9. Barnabas was the elder and better known, and in the church at Jerusalem his name would naturally precede Paul's. The use of the Greek salutation, and this order of the names, are two undesigned coincidences going to attest the genuineness of this

first document preserved to us from the Acts of the primitive church.

29. **Blood.** Because in the blood was the animal's life, and it was the blood that was consecrated to make atonement. See Gen. ix. 6; Lev. xvii. 10–14; Deut. xii. 23, 24. The Gentiles had no scruples about eating blood; on the contrary, it was a special delicacy. Thus Homer:

> "At the fire
> Already lie the paunches of two goats,
> Preparing for our evening meal, and both
> Are filled with fat and blood. Whoever shows
> Himself the better man in this affray,
> And conquers, he shall take the one of these
> He chooses."
>
> *Odyssey*, xviii., 44 sq.

The heathen were accustomed to drink blood mingled with wine at their sacrifices.

Farewell (ἔῤῥωσθε). Lit., *be strong*, like the Latin *valete*. Compare the close of Claudius Lysias' letter to Festus (ch. xxiii. 30).

31. **Consolation.** See on Acts ix. 31.

32. **Many words.** Or, lit., *much discourse;* adding the *spoken* to the *written* consolation.

Exhorted. Or *comforted.* See on ver. 31. The latter agrees better with *consolation* there.

Confirmed. See on ch. xiv. 22.

36. **Let us go again and visit** (ἐπιστρέψαντες δὴ ἐπισκεψώμεθα). Lit., *Having returned, let us now visit.* The A. V. omits *now.* See on ch. xiii. 2.

In every city (κατὰ πᾶσαν πόλιν). *Κατά* has the force of *city by city.*

38. **Him** (τοῦτον). Lit., *that one.* It marks him very strongly, and is an emphatic position at the end of the sentence.

Departed (ἀποστάντα). Rev., *withdrew.* It furnishes the derivation of our word *apostatize.*

39. **The contention was so sharp** (ἐγένετο παροξυσμὸς). More correctly, *there arose a sharp contention.* Only here and Heb. x. 24. Our word *paroxysm* is a transcription of παροξυσμὸς. An angry dispute is indicated.

Barnabas. The last mention of him in the Acts.

40. **Recommended.** Which was not the case with Barnabas, leading to the inference that the church at Antioch took Paul's side in the dispute.

CHAPTER XVI.

3. **To go forth** (ἐξελθεῖν). The word is used of going forth *as a missionary* in Luke ix. 6; 3 John 7.

5. **Were established** (ἐστερεοῦντο). Rather, were *strengthened.* Another word is used for *established.* See ch. xiv. 22; xv. 32, 41; xviii. 23. There is a difference, moreover, between being *strengthened* and *established.* See 1 Pet. v. 10.

6. **Asia.** See on ch. ii. 9.

8. **Passing by Mysia.** Not *avoiding,* since they could not reach Troas without traversing it; but *omitting* it as a preaching-place.

Came down. From the highlands to the coast.

10. **We sought.** Note the introduction, for the first time here, of the first person, intimating the presence of the author with Paul.

Assuredly gathering (συμβιβάζοντες). See on *proving*, ch. ix. 22.

11. **Came with a straight course** (εὐθυδρομήσαμεν). Lit., *we ran a straight course.* A nautical term for *sailing before the wind.*

12. **Chief** (πρώτη). Some explain, the *first city* to which they came in Macedonia.

A colony (κολωνία). Roman towns were of two classes: *municipia*, or *free towns*, and *colonies.* The distinction, however, was not sharply maintained, so that, in some cases, we find the same town bearing both names. The two names involved no difference of right or of privilege. The historical difference between a colony and a free town is, that the free towns were taken into the state from without, while the colonies were offshoots from within. "The municipal cities insensibly equalled the rank and splendor of the colonies; and in the reign of Hadrian it was disputed which was the preferable condition, of those societies which had issued from, or those which had been received into, the bosom of Rome" (Gibbon, "Decline and Fall").

The colony was used for three different purposes in the course of Roman history: as a fortified outpost in a conquered country; as a means of providing for the poor of Rome; and as a settlement for veterans who had served their time. It is with the third class, established by Augustus, that we have to do here. The Romans divided mankind into *citizens* and *strangers.* An inhabitant of Italy was a citizen; an inhabitant of any other part of the empire was a *peregrinus*, or *stranger.* The colonial policy abolished this distinction so far as privileges were concerned. The idea of a colony was, that it was another Rome transferred to the soil of another country. In his establishment of colonies, Augustus, in some instances, expelled the existing inhabitants and founded entirely new towns with his colonists; in others, he merely added his settlers to the existing population of the town then receiving the rank and title of a colony. In some instances a place received these without receiving any new citizens at all. Both classes of citizens were in possession of the same privileges, the principal of which were, exemption from scourging, freedom from arrest, except in extreme cases, and, in all cases, the right of appeal from the magistrate to the emperor. The names of the colonists were still enrolled in one of the Roman tribes. The traveller heard the Latin language and was amenable to the Roman law. The coinage of the city had Latin inscriptions. The affairs of the colony were regulated by their own magistrates, named *Duumviri*, who took pride in calling themselves by the Roman title of *praetors* (see on ver. 20).

13. **Out of the city** (ἔξω τῆς πόλεως). The best texts read πύλης, *the gate.*

River. Probably the *Gangas* or *Gangites.*

Where prayer was wont to be made (οὗ ἐνομίζετο προσευχὴ εἶναι). The best texts read ἐνομίζομεν προσευχὴν, *where we supposed there was a place of prayer.* The number of Jews in Philippi was small, since it was a military and not a mercantile city; consequently there was no synagogue, but only a *proseucha*, or *praying-place*, a slight structure, and often open to the sky. It was outside the gate, for the sake of retirement, and near a stream, because of the ablutions connected with the worship.

14. **Lydia.** An adjective: *the Lydian;* but as Lydia was a common name among the Greeks and Romans, it does not follow that she was named from her native country.

A seller of purple. On *purple*, see note on Luke xvi. 19.

Thyatira. The district of Lydia, and the city of Thyatira in particular, were famous for purple dyes. So Homer:

> "As when some Carian or Maeonian * dame
> Tinges with purple the white ivory,
> To form a trapping for the cheeks of steeds."
>
> *Iliad*, iv., 141.

An inscription found in the ruins of Thyatira relates to the guild of dyers.

Heard (ἤκουεν). Imperfect, *was hearing* while we preached.

15. **Constrained** (παρεβιάσατο). Only here and Luke xxiv. 29, on which see note. The constraint was from ardent gratitude.

16. **Damsel.** See on ch. xii. 13.

Spirit of divination (πνεῦμα Πύθωνα). Lit., *a spirit, a Python*. Python, in the Greek mythology, was the serpent which guarded Delphi. According to the legend, as related in the Homeric hymn, Apollo descended from Olympus in order to select a site for his shrine and oracle. Having fixed upon a spot on the southern side of Mount Parnassus, he found it guarded by a vast and terrific serpent, which he slew with an arrow, and suffered its body to *rot* (πυθεῖν) in the sun. Hence the name of the serpent *Python* (rotting); *Pytho*, the name of the place, and the epithet *Pythian*, applied to Apollo. The name *Python* was subsequently used to denote a prophetic *demon*, and was also used of *soothsayers* who practised *ventriloquism*, or speaking from the belly. The word ἐγγαστρίμυθος, *ventriloquist*, occurs in the Septuagint, and is rendered *having a familiar spirit* (see Levit. xix. 31; xx. 6, 27; 1 Sam. xxviii. 7, 8). The heathen inhabitants of Philippi regarded the woman as inspired by Apollo; and Luke, in recording this case, which came under his own observation, uses the term which would naturally suggest itself to a Greek physician, a *Python-spirit*, presenting phenomena identical with the convulsive movements and wild cries of the Pythian priestess at Delphi.

---

* Caria, the province adjoining Lydia on the south; Maeonia, the ancient name of Lydia.

Soothsaying (*μαντευομένη*). Akin to *μαίνομαι*, *to rave*, in allusion to the temporary madness which possessed the priestess or sibyl while under the influence of the god. Compare Virgil's description of the Cumaean Sibyl:

> "And as the word she spake
> Within the door, all suddenly her visage and her hue
> Were changed, and all her sleekèd hair and gasping breath she drew,
> And with the rage her wild heart swelled, and greater was she grown,
> Nor mortal-voiced; for breath of god upon her heart was blown
> As he drew nigher."
>
> *Aeneid*, vi., 45 sq.

18. **Grieved** (*διαπονηθεὶς*). Not strong enough. Rather, *worn out*. Both grieved at the sad condition of the woman, and thoroughly annoyed and indignant at the continued demonstrations of the evil spirit which possessed her. Compare ch. iv. 2.

19. **Was gone** (*ἐξῆλθεν*). Went *out* with the evil spirit.

20. **Magistrates** (*στρατηγοῖς*). Their usual name was *duumviri*, answering to the consuls of Rome; but they took pride in calling themselves *στρατηγοί*, or *praetors*, as being a more honorable title. This is the only place in the Acts where Luke applies the term to the rulers of a city. See Introduction to Luke.

Jews. Who at this time were in special disgrace, having been lately banished from Rome by Claudius (see Acts xviii. 2). The Philippians do not appear to have recognized the distinction between Christians and Jews.

21. **Being Romans.** The Romans granted absolute toleration to conquered nations to follow their own religious customs, and took the gods of these countries under their protection. Otho, Domitian, Commodus, and Caracalla were zealous partisans of the worship of Isis; Serapis and Cybele were patronized at Rome; and in the reign of Nero the religious dilettanti at Rome affected Judaism, and professed to honor the name of Moses and the sacred books. Poppaea, Nero's consort, was

their patroness, and Seneca said, "the Jewish faith is now received on every hand. The conquered have given laws to the conquerors." On the other hand, there were laws which forbade the introduction of strange deities among the Romans themselves. In 186 B.C., when stringent measures were taken by the government for the repression of Bacchanalian orgies in Rome, one of the consuls, addressing an assembly of the people, said: "How often in the ages of our fathers was it given in charge to the magistrates to prohibit the performance of any foreign religious rites; to banish strolling sacrificers and soothsayers from the forum, the circus, and the city; to search for and burn books of divination; and to abolish every mode of sacrificing that was not conformable to the Roman practice" (Livy, xxxix., 16). It was contrary to strict Roman law for the Jews to propagate their opinions among the Romans, though they might make proselytes of other nations.

22. **Rent off their clothes** (περιῤῥήξαντες). Only here in New Testament. By the usual formula of command to the lictors: *Go, lictors; strip off their garments; let them be scourged!*

To beat (ῥαβδίζειν). From ῥάβδος, *a rod.* Rev. properly adds, *with rods.*

23. **Prison.** See on ch. v. 21.

24. **The inner prison.** Some have supposed this to be the *lower* prison, being misled by the remains of the Mamertine prison at Rome, on the declivity of the Capitoline, and near the Arch of Septimius Severus. This consists of two chambers, one above the other, excavated in the solid rock. In the centre of the vault of the lower chamber is a circular opening, through which it is supposed that prisoners were let down into the dungeon. Modern excavations, however, have shown that these two chambers were connected with a series of large chambers, now separated by an alley from the prison of St. Peter. The opening into the passage leading to these was discovered in the lower dungeon. Under this passage ran a drain, which formed

a branch of the Cloaca Maxima, or main sewer. Six of these chambers have been brought to light, evidently apartments of a large prison in the time of the Roman kings. Mr. John Henry Parker, from whose elaborate work on the primitive fortifications of Rome these details are drawn, believes that the prison of St. Peter now shown to tourists formed the vestibule and guard-room of the great prison. It was customary to have a vestibule, or house for the warder, at a short distance from the main prison. Thus he distinguishes the *inner* prison from this vestibule. With this agrees the description in the Rev. John Henry Newman's "Callista:" "The state prison was arranged on pretty much one and the same plan through the Roman empire, nay, we may say throughout the ancient world. It was commonly attached to the government buildings, and consisted of two parts. The first was the *vestibule*, or *outward* prison, approached from the praetorium, and surrounded by cells opening into it. The prisoners who were confined in these cells had the benefit of the air and light which the hall admitted. From the vestibule there was a passage into the *interior* prison, called *Robur* or *Lignum*, from the beams of wood which were the instruments of confinement, or from the character of its floor. It had no window or outlet except this door, which, when closed, absolutely shut out light and air. This apartment was the place into which Paul and Silas were cast at Philippi. The utter darkness, the heat, and the stench of this miserable place, in which the inmates were confined day and night, is often dwelt upon by the martyrs and their biographers."

Stocks (*ξύλον*). Lit., *the timber*. An instrument of torture having five holes, four for the wrists and ankles and one for the neck. The same word is used for *the cross*, ch. v. 30; x. 39; Gal. iii. 13; 1 Pet. ii. 24.

25. **Prayed and sang praises** (*προσευχόμενοι ὕμνουν*). Lit., *praying, they sang hymns*. The praying and the praise are not described as distinct acts. Their singing of hymns was their prayer, probably Psalms.

27. **Would have killed** (ἔμελλεν ἀναιρεῖν). Rev., more correctly, *was about to kill*. Knowing that he must suffer death for the escape of his prisoners.

29. **A light** (φῶτα). Rev., more correctly, *lights*. Several lamps, in order to search everywhere.

Sprang in. See on *ran in*, ch. xiv. 14.

33. **He took** (παραλαβὼν). Strictly, "took them *along with* (παρά) *him*:" to some other part of the prison.

Washed their stripes (ἔλουσεν ἀπὸ τῶν πληγῶν). Properly, "washed them *from* (ἀπό) their stripes." The verb λούειν expresses the *bathing* of the *entire* body (Heb. x. 23; Acts ix. 37; 2 Pet. ii. 22); while νίπτειν commonly means the *washing* of a *part* of the body (Matt. vi. 17; Mark vii. 3; John xiii. 5). The jailer *bathed* them; cleansing them from the blood with which they were besprinkled from the stripes.

34. **Brought** (ἀναγαγών). Lit., "brought up (ἀνά)." His house would seem to have been above the court of the prison where they were. See on *took*, ver. 33.

Believing (πεπιστευκὼς). More correctly, *having believed*; assigning the reason for his joy: "in that he had believed."

35. **Serjeants** (ῥαβδούχους). Lit., *those who hold the rod*. The Roman *lictors*. They were the attendants of the chief Roman magistrates.

> "Ho, trumpets, sound a war-note!
> Ho, lictors, clear the way!
> The knights will ride, in all their pride,
> Along the streets to-day."
>
> MACAULAY, *Lays of Ancient Rome*.

They preceded the magistrates one by one in a line. They had to inflict punishment on the condemned, especially on Roman citizens. They also commanded the people to pay proper respect to a passing magistrate, by uncovering, dismounting from horseback, and standing out of the way. The badge of their office was the *fasces*, an axe bound up in a bundle of rods; but in the colonies they carried staves.

Those men. Contemptuous.

37. **They have beaten us publicly, uncondemned, men that are Romans.** Hackett remarks that "almost every word in this reply contains a distinct allegation. It would be difficult to find or frame a sentence superior to it in point of energetic brevity." Cicero in his oration against Verres relates that there was a Roman citizen scourged at Messina; and that in the midst of the noise of the rods, nothing was heard from him but the words, "I am a Roman citizen." He says: "It is a *dreadful deed* to *bind* a Roman citizen; it is a *crime* to *scourge* him; it is almost *parricide* to *put him to death*."

40. **They went out.** Note that Luke here resumes the third person, implying that he did not accompany them.

CHAPTER XVII.

3. **Opening and alleging.** The latter word is rather *propounding*, or *setting forth* (παρατιθέμενος). See on *set before*, Luke ix. 16; and *commit*, 1 Pet. iv. 19. Bengel remarks, "Two steps, as if one, having broken the rind, were to disclose and exhibit the kernel."

4. **Consorted with** (προσεκληρώθησαν). Only here in New Testament. More strictly, "were *added* or *allotted* to."

Chief women. The position of women in Macedonia seems to have been exceptional. Popular prejudice, and the verdict of Grecian wisdom in its best age, asserted her natural inferiority. The Athenian law provided that everything which a man might do by the counsel or request of a woman should be null in law. She was little better than a slave. To educate her was to advertise her as a harlot. Her companions were principally children and slaves. In Macedonia, however, monuments were erected to women by public bodies; and records of male proper names are found, in Macedonian inscriptions, formed on the mother's name instead of on the father's. Macedonian women were permitted to hold property, and were treated as mistresses of the house. These facts are borne out by the account of Paul's labors in Macedonia. In Thessalonica, Beroea, and Philippi we note additions of women of rank to the church; and their prominence in church affairs is indicated by Paul's special appeal to two ladies in the church at Philippi to reconcile their differences, which had caused disturbance in the church, and by his commending them to his colleagues as women who had labored with him in the Lord (Philip. iv. 2, 3).

5. **Of the baser sort** (ἀγοραίων). From ἀγορά, the *market-place;* hence *loungers in the market-place; the rabble.* Cicero calls them *subrostrani*, those who hung round the *rostra*, or platform for speakers in the forum; and Plautus, *subbasilicani*, the loungers round the *court-house* or *exchange.* The word occurs only here and ch. xix. 38, on which see note.

Gathered a company (ὀχλοποιήσαντες). Rev., better, *a crowd.* Only here in New Testament.

6. **Rulers of the city** (πολιτάρχας). Another illustration of Luke's accuracy. Note that the magistrates are called by a different name from those at Philippi. Thessalonica was not a *colony*, but a *free city* (see on *colony*, ch. xvi. 12), and was governed by its own rulers, whose titles accordingly did not follow those of Roman magistrates. The word occurs only here and ver. 8, and has been found in an inscription on an arch at Thessalonica, where the names of the seven *politarchs* are mentioned. The arch is thought by antiquarians to have been standing in Paul's time.

7. **Contrary to the decrees of Caesar.** The charge at Philippi was that of introducing new customs; but as Thessalonica was not a colony, that charge could have no force there. The accusation substituted is that of treason against the emperor; that of which Jesus was accused before Pilate. "The law of treason, by which the ancient legislators of the republic had sought to protect popular liberty from the encroachments of tyranny, . . . was gradually concentrated upon the emperor alone, the sole impersonation of the sovereign people. The definition of the crime itself was loose and elastic, such as equally became the jealousy of a licentious republic or of a despotic usurper" (Merivale, "History of the Romans under the Empire").

9. **Security** (τὸ ἱκανὸν). See on Luke vii. 6. *Bail*, either personal or by a deposit of money. A law term. They engaged that the public peace should not be violated, and that the authors of the disturbance should leave the city.

11. **Searched.** Or *examined.* See on Luke xxiii. 14.

12. **Honorable women.** See on ver. 4, and Mark xv. 43.

15. **They that conducted** (καθιστῶντες). Lit., *brought to the spot.* Note the different word employed, ch. xv. 3 (see note there).

16. **Was stirred** (παρωξύνετο). Better, as Rev., was *provoked.* See on the kindred word *contention* (παροξυσμὸς), ch. xv. 39.

Saw (θεωροῦντι). Better, *beheld.* See on Luke x. 18.

Wholly given to idolatry (κατείδωλον). Incorrect. The word, which occurs only here in the New Testament, and nowhere in classical Greek, means *full of idols.* It applies to the *city,* not to the *inhabitants.* "We learn from Pliny that at the time of Nero, Athens contained over three thousand public statues, besides a countless number of lesser images within the walls of private houses. Of this number the great majority were statues of gods, demi-gods, or heroes. In one street there stood before every house a square pillar carrying upon it a bust of the god Hermes. Another street, named the Street of the Tripods, was lined with tripods, dedicated by winners in the Greek national games, and carrying each one an inscription to a deity. Every gateway and porch carried its protecting god. Every street, every square, nay, every purlieu, had its sanctuaries, and a Roman poet bitterly remarked that it was easier in Athens to find gods than men" (G. S. Davies, "St. Paul in Greece").

18. **Epicureans.** Disciples of Epicurus, and atheists. They acknowledged God in words, but denied his providence and superintendence over the world. According to them, the soul was material and annihilated at death. Pleasure was their chief good; and whatever higher sense their founder might have attached to this doctrine, his followers, in the apostle's day, were given to gross sensualism.

Stoics. Pantheists. God was the soul of the world, or the world was God. Everything was governed by fate, to which God himself was subject. They denied the universal and perpetual immortality of the soul; some supposing that it was swallowed up in deity; others, that it survived only till the final conflagration; others, that immortality was restricted to the wise and good. Virtue was its own reward, and vice its own punishment. Pleasure was no good, and pain no evil. The name *Stoic* was derived from *stoa*, a *porch*. Zeno, the founder of the Stoic sect, held his school in the *Stoa Pœcile*, or *painted* portico, so called because adorned with pictures by the best masters.

Babbler (σπερμολόγος). Lit., *seed-picker:* a bird which picks up seeds in the streets and markets; hence one who picks up and retails scraps of news. Trench ("Authorized Version of the New Testament") cites a parallel from Shakespeare:

> "This fellow picks up wit as pigeons peas,
> And utters it again when Jove doth please.
> He is wit's pedler, and retails his wares
> At wakes, and wassails, meetings, markets, fairs."
> *Love's Labor's Lost*, v., 2.

Setter-forth (*καταγγελεὺς*). See on *declare*, ver. 23. Compare 1 Pet. iv. 4, 12.

Strange. Foreign.

19. **Areopagus.** The Hill of Mars: the seat of the ancient and venerable Athenian court which decided the most solemn questions connected with religion. Socrates was arraigned and condemned here on the charge of innovating on the state religion. It received its name from the legend of the trial of Mars for the murder of the son of Neptune. The judges sat in the open air upon seats hewn out in the rock, on a platform ascended by a flight of stone steps immediately from the market-place. A temple of Mars was on the brow of the edifice, and the sanctuary of the Furies was in a broken cleft of the rock immediately below the judges' seats. The Acropolis rose above it, with the Parthenon and the colossal statue of Athene. "It was a scene with which the dread recollections of centuries were associated. Those who withdrew to the Areopagus from the Agora, came, as it were, into the presence of a higher power. No place in Athens was so suitable for a discourse upon the mysteries of religion" (Conybeare and Howson).*

20. **Strange** (*ξενίζοντα*). A participle: *surprising*. Compare 1 Pet. iv. 4, 12.

21. **All the Athenians.** No article. Lit., "Athenians, all of them." The Athenian people collectively.

---

* For fuller descriptions, see Lewin, Life and Epistles of St. Paul; Davies, St. Paul in Greece; Smith, Dictionary of Greek and Roman Geography, Art., *Athens*.

Strangers which were there (οἱ ἐπιδημοῦντες ξένοι). Rev., more correctly, *the strangers sojourning there*. See on 1 Pet. i. 1.

Spent their time (εὐκαίρουν). The word means *to have good opportunity; to have leisure:* also, *to devote one's leisure to something; to spend the time.* Compare Mark vi. 31; 1 Cor. xvi. 12.

Something new (τι καινότερον). Lit., *newer:* newer than that which was then passing current as new. The comparative was regularly used by the Greeks in the question *what news?* They contrasted what was new with what had been new up to the time of asking. The idiom vividly characterizes the state of the Athenian mind. Bengel aptly says, "New things at once became of no account; newer things were being sought for." Their own orators and poets lashed them for this peculiarity. Aristophanes styles Athens *the city of the gapers* ("Knights," 1262). Demades said that the crest of Athens ought to be a great tongue. Demosthenes asks them, "Is it all your care to go about up and down the market, asking each other, 'Is there any news?'" In the speech of Cleon to the Athenians, given by Thucydides (iii., 38), he says: "No men are better dupes, sooner deceived by novel notions, or slower to follow approved advice. You despise what is familiar, while you are worshippers of every new extravagance. You are always hankering after an ideal state, but you do not give your minds even to what is straight before you. In a word, you are at the mercy of your own ears."

22. **I perceive** (θεωρῶ). I *regard* you, in my careful observation of you. See on Luke x. 18.

Too superstitious (δεισιδαιμονεστέρους). This rendering and that of the Rev., *somewhat superstitious*, are both unfortunate. The word is compounded of δείδω, *to fear*, and δαίμων, *a deity*. It signifies either a *religious* or a *superstitious* sentiment, according to the context. Paul would have been unlikely to begin his address with a charge which would have awakened the anger of his audience. What he means to say is, *You are more divinity-fearing than the rest of the Greeks.* This propensity to reverence the higher powers is a good thing in itself, only, as he shows them, it is misdirected, not rightly conscious of its object and aim. Paul proposes to guide the sentiment rightly by revealing him whom they ignorantly worship. The American revisers insist on *very religious.* The kindred word δεισιδαιμονία occurs ch. xxv. 19, and in the sense of *religion,* though rendered in A. V. *superstition.* Festus would not call the Jewish religion a superstition before Agrippa, who was himself a Jew. There is the testimony of the Ephesian town-clerk, that Paul, during his three years' residence at Ephesus, did not rudely and coarsely attack the worship of the Ephesian Diana. "Nor yet blasphemers of your goddess" (Acts xix. 37).

23. **As I passed by** (διερχόμενος). More strictly, "passing *through* (διά)" your city, or your streets.

Beheld (ἀναθεωρῶν). Only here and Heb. xiii. 7. Rev., much better, *observed.* The compound verb denotes a very attentive consideration (ἀνά, *up and down, throughout*).

Devotions (σεβάσματα). Wrong. It means *the objects of their worship*—temples, altars, statues, etc.

An altar (βωμὸν). Only here in New Testament, and the only case in which a *heathen* altar is alluded to. In all other cases θυσιαστήριον is used, signifying an altar *of the true God.* The Septuagint translators commonly observe this distinction, being, in this respect, more particular than the Hebrew scriptures themselves, which sometimes interchange the word for the heathen altar and that for God's altar. See, especially, Josh. xxii., where the altar reared by the Transjordanic tribes is called βωμὸς, as being no true altar of God (vv. 10, 11, 16, 19, 23, 26, 34); and the legitimate altar, θυσιαστήριον (vv. 19, 28, 29).

To the unknown God (ἀγνώστῳ Θεῷ). The article is wanting. Render, as Rev., *to an unknown God.* The origin of these altars, of which there were several in Athens, is a matter of conjecture. Hackett's remarks on this point are sensible, and are borne out by the following words: "whom therefore," etc. "The most rational explanation is unquestionably that of those who suppose these altars to have had their origin in the feeling of uncertainty, inherent, after all, in the minds of the heathen, whether their acknowledgment of the superior powers was sufficiently full and comprehensive; in their distinct consciousness of the limitation and imperfection of their religious views, and their consequent desire to avoid the anger of any still unacknowledged god who might be unknown to them. That no deity might punish them for neglecting his worship, or remain uninvoked in asking for blessings, they not only erected altars to all the gods named or known among them, but, distrustful still lest they might not comprehend fully the extent of their subjection and dependence, they erected them also to any other god or power that might exist, although as yet unrevealed to them. . . . Under these circumstances an allusion to one of these altars by the apostle would be equivalent to his saying to the Athenians thus: 'You are correct in acknowledging a divine existence beyond any which the ordinary rites of your worship recognize; there is such an existence. You are correct in confessing that this Being is unknown to you; you have no just conceptions of his nature and perfections.'"

Ignorantly (*ἀγνοοῦντες*). Rather, *unconsciously: not knowing*. There is a kind of play on the words *unknown, knowing* not. *Ignorantly* conveys more rebuke than Paul intended.

Declare I (*καταγγέλλω*). Compare *καταγγελεὺς*, *setter-forth*, in ver. 18. Here, again, there is a play upon the words. Paul takes up their noun, *setter-forth*, and gives it back to them as a verb. "You say I am a *setter-forth* of strange gods: I now *set forth* unto you (Rev.) the true God."

24. **God.** With the article: "*the* God."

The world (*τὸν κόσμον*). Originally, *order*, and hence *the order of the world; the ordered universe.* So in classical Greek.

In the Septuagint, never *the world*, but *the ordered total of the heavenly bodies; the host of heaven* (Deut. iv. 19; xvii. 3; Isa. xxiv. 21; xl. 26). Compare, also, Prov. xvii. 6, and see note on Jas. iii. 6. In the apocryphal books, of the universe, and mainly in the relation between God and it arising out of the creation. Thus, *the king of the world* (2 Macc. vii. 9); *the creator or founder of the world* (2 Macc. vii. 23); *the great potentate of the world* (2 Macc. xii. 15). In the New Testament: 1. In the classical and physical sense, *the universe* (John xvii. 5; xxi. 25; Rom. i. 20; Eph. i. 4, etc.). 2. As *the order of things of which man is the centre* (Matt. xiii. 38; Mark xvi. 15; Luke ix. 25; John xvi. 21; Eph. ii. 12; 1 Tim. vi. 7). 3. *Humanity as it manifests itself in and through this order* (Matt. xviii. 7; 2 Pet. ii. 5; iii. 6; Rom. iii. 19). Then, as sin has entered and disturbed the order of things, and made a breach between the heavenly and the earthly order, which are one in the divine ideal—4. *The order of things which is alienated from God, as manifested in and by the human race:* humanity as alienated from God, and acting in opposition to him (John i. 10; xii. 31; xv. 18, 19; 1 Cor. i. 21; 1 John ii. 15, etc.). The word is used here in the classical sense of the visible creation, which would appeal to the Athenians. Stanley, speaking of the name by which the Deity is known in the patriarchal age, the plural *Elohim*, notes that Abraham, in perceiving that all the *Elohim* worshipped by the numerous clans of his race meant *one God*, anticipated the declaration of Paul in this passage ("Jewish Church," i., 25). Paul's statement strikes at the belief of the Epicureans, that the world was made by "a fortuitous concourse of atoms," and of the Stoics, who denied the creation of the world by God, holding either that God animated the world, or that the world itself was God.

Made with hands (χειροποιήτοις). Probably pointing to the magnificent temples above and around him. Paul's epistles abound in architectural metaphors. He here employs the very words of Stephen, in his address to the Sanhedrim, which he very probably heard. See ch. vii. 48.

25. **Is worshipped** (θεραπεύεται). Incorrect. Render, as Rev., *served*. Luke often uses the word in the sense of to *heal* or *cure*; but this is its primary sense. See on Luke v. 15. It refers to the clothing of the images of the gods in splendid garments, and bringing them costly gifts and offerings of food and drink.

As though he needed (προσδεόμενος). Properly, "needed anything *in addition* (πρός) to what he already has."

26. **Before appointed** (προτεταγμένους). The Rev., properly, omits *before*, following the reading of the best texts, προστεταγμένους, *assigned*.

Bounds (ὁροθεσίας). Only here in New Testament. The word, in the singular, means the *fixing* of boundaries, and so is transferred to the fixed boundaries themselves.

27. **Might feel after.** See on *handle*, Luke xxiv. 39. Compare Tennyson:

> "I stretch lame hands of faith, and *grope*
> And gather dust and chaff, and call
> To what I feel is Lord of all."
>
> *In Memoriam*, lv.

28. **We are also his offspring.** A line from Aratus, a poet of Paul's own province of Cilicia. The same sentiment, in almost the same words, occurs in the fine hymn of Cleanthes to Jove. Hence the words, "Some of your own poets."

29. **The Godhead** (τὸ θεῖον). Lit., *that which is divine*.

Like to gold, etc. These words must have impressed his hearers profoundly, as they looked at the multitude of statues of divinities which surrounded them.

Graven (χαράγματι). Not a participle, as A. V., but a noun, in apposition with *gold*, *silver*, and *stone*: "a *graving* or *carved-work of art*," etc.

30. **Winked at** (ὑπεριδὼν). Only here in New Testament. Originally, to *overlook*; to *suffer to pass unnoticed*. So Rev., *overlooked*.

32. **Resurrection.** This word was the signal for a derisive outburst from the crowd.

Mocked (ἐχλεύαζον). From χλεύη, *a jest*. Only here in New Testament, though a compound, διαχλευάζω, *mock*, occurs, according to the best texts, at ch. ii. 13. The force of the imperfect, *began to mock*, should be given here in the translation, as marking the outbreak of derision.

In this remarkable speech of Paul are to be noted: his prudence and tact in not needlessly offending his hearers; his courtesy and spirit of conciliation in recognizing their piety toward their gods; his wisdom and readiness in the use of the inscription "to the unknown God," and in citing their own poets; his meeting the radical errors of every class of his hearers, while seeming to dwell only on points of agreement; his lofty views of the nature of God and the great principle of the unity of the human race; his boldness in proclaiming Jesus and the resurrection among those to whom these truths were foolishness; the wonderful terseness and condensation of the whole, and the rapid but powerful and assured movement of the thought.

34. **Clave.** See on Luke x. 11; xv. 15; Acts v. 13.

The Areopagite. One of the judges of the court of Areopagus. Of this court Curtius remarks: "Here, instead of a single judge, a college of twelve men of proved integrity conducted the trial. If the accused had an equal number of votes for and against him, he was acquitted. The Court on the hill of Ares is one of the most ancient institutions of Athens, and none achieved for the city an earlier or more widely spread recognition. The Areopagitic penal code was adopted as a norm by all subsequent legislators" ("History of Greece," i., 307).

CHAPTER XVIII.

1. **Found.** "A Jewish guild always keeps together, whether in street or synagogue. In Alexandria the different trades sat in the synagogue arranged into guilds; and St. Paul could have no difficulty in meeting, in the bazaar of his trade, with the like-minded Aquila and Priscilla" (Edersheim, "Jewish Social Life").

2. **Lately** (προσφάτως). Only here in New Testament, though the kindred adjective, rendered *new*, is found in Heb. x. 20. It is derived from φένω, *to slay*, and the adjective means, originally, *lately slain*; thence, *fresh*, *new*, *recent*. It is quite common in medical writings in this sense.

3. **Of the same craft** (ὁμότεχνον). It was a Rabbinical principle that whoever does not teach his son a trade is as if he brought him up to be a robber. All the Rabbinical authorities in Christ's time, and later, were working at some trade. Hillel, Paul's teacher, was a wood-cutter, and his rival, Shammai, a carpenter. It is recorded of one of the celebrated Rabbis that he was in the habit of discoursing to his students from the top of a cask of his own making, which he carried every day to the academy.

Tent-makers (σκηνοποιοὶ). Not weavers of the goat's-hair cloth of which tents were made, which could easily be procured at every large town in the Levant, but makers of *tents* used by shepherds and travellers. It was a trade lightly esteemed and poorly paid.

5. **Was pressed in the spirit** (συνείχετο τῷ πνεύματι). Instead of *spirit* the best texts read λόγῳ, *by the word.* On *pressed* or *constrained*, see note on *taken*, Luke iv. 38. The meaning is, *Paul was engrossed by the word.* He was relieved of anxiety by the arrival of his friends, and stimulated to greater activity in the work of preaching the word.

6. **Opposed themselves** (*ἀντιτασσομένων*). Implying an *organized* or *concerted* resistance. See on *resisteth*, 1 Pet. v. 5.

12. **Gallio.** Brother of the philosopher Seneca (Nero's tutor), and uncle of the poet Lucan, the author of the "Pharsalia." Seneca speaks of him as amiable and greatly beloved.

Deputy. See on ch. xiii. 7. The verb, *to be deputy*, occurs only here.

Judgment-seat. See on ch. vii. 5.

14. **Lewdness** (*ῥᾳδιούργημα*). See on *mischief*, ch. xiii. 10. Rev., *villany*.

15. **Question.** The best texts read the plural, *questions*. See on ch. xv. 2.

Judge. In the Greek the position of the word is emphatic, at the beginning of the sentence: "*Judge* of these matters I am not minded to be."

17. **Cared for none of these things.** Not said to indicate his indifference to religion, but simply that he did not choose to interfere in this case.

18. **Took his leave** (*ἀποταξάμενος*). See on Luke ix. 61; Mark vi. 46.

Priscilla and Aquila. They are named in the same order, Rom. xvi. 3; 2 Tim. iv. 19.

Having shorn his head. Referring to Paul, and not to Aquila.

He had a vow. A private vow, such as was often assumed by the Jews in consequence of some mercy received or of some deliverance from danger. Not the Nazarite vow, though similar in its obligations; for, in the case of that vow, the cutting of the hair, which marked the close of the period of obligation, could take place only in Jerusalem.

21. **I must by all means keep this feast that cometh in Jerusalem.** The best texts omit.

24. **Eloquent** (λόγιος). Only here in New Testament. The word is used in Greek literature in several senses. As λόγος means either *reason* or *speech*, so this derivative may signify either one who has thought much, and has much to say, or one who can say it well. Hence it is used: 1. Of one *skilled in history*. Herodotus, for example, says that the Heliopolitans are the *most learned in history* (λογιώτατοι) of all the Egyptians. 2. Of an *eloquent* person. An epithet of Hermes or Mercury, as the god of speech and eloquence. 3. Of a *learned* person generally. There seems hardly sufficient reason for changing the rendering of the A. V. (Rev., *learned*), especially as the scripture-learning of Apollos is specified in the words *mighty in the scriptures*, and his superior eloquence appears to have been the reason why some of the Corinthians preferred him to Paul. See 1 Cor. i. 12; ii. 4; 2 Cor. x. 10.

25. **Instructed.** See on Luke i. 4.

Fervent (ζέων). *Fervent*, which is formed from the participle of the Latin *ferveo*, *to boil* or *ferment*, is an exact translation of this word, which means *to seethe* or *bubble*, and is therefore used figuratively of mental states and emotions. See on *leaven*, Matt. xiii. 33.

Diligently (ἀκριβῶς). Rather, *accurately;* so far as his knowledge went. The limitation is given by the words following: *knowing only the baptism of John*. See on Luke i. 3; and compare the kindred verb, *inquired diligently*, Matt. ii. 7, where Rev. renders *learned carefully*.

26. **More perfectly** (ἀκριβέστερον). The comparative of the same word. *More accurately*.

27. **Exhorting** (προτρεψάμενοι). Originally, *to turn forward*, as in flight. Hence, *to impel* or *urge*. The word may apply either to the disciples at Corinth, in which case we must render as A. V., or to Apollos himself, as Rev., *encouraged him*. I prefer the former. Hackett very sensibly remarks that Apollos did not need encouragement, as he *was disposed* to go.

Helped (συνεβάλετο). The radical sense of the word is to *throw together:* hence, to *contribute;* to *help;* to *be useful to*. He threw himself into the work along with them. On different senses of the word, see notes on Luke ii. 19; xiv. 31; and compare Acts iv. 15; xvii. 18; xviii. 27; xx. 14.

Through grace. *Grace* has the article, *the* special grace of God imparted. Expositors differ as to the connection; some joining *through grace* with *them which had believed*, insisting on the Greek order of the words; and others with *helped*, referring to grace conferred on Apollos. I prefer the latter, principally for the reason urged by Meyer, that "the design of the text is to characterize Apollos and his work, and not those who believed."

28. **Mightily** (εὐτόνως). See on Luke xxiii. 10.

Convinced (διακατηλέγχετο). Only here in New Testament. See on *tell him his fault*, Matt. xviii. 15. The compound here is a very strong expression for *thorough* confutation. *Confute* (Rev.) is better than *convince*. Note the prepositions. He confuted them *thoroughly* (διά), *against* (κατά) all their arguments.

CHAPTER XIX.

1. **Upper coasts** (τὰ ἀνωτερικὰ μέρη). *Coasts* is a bad rendering. Better, as Rev., "the upper *country;*" lit., *parts* or *districts*. The reference is to districts like Galatia and Phrygia, lying *up* from the sea-coast and farther inland than Ephesus. Hence the expedition of Cyrus from the sea-coast toward Central Asia was called *Anabasis*, a *going-up*.

Certain disciples. Disciples of John the Baptist, who, like Apollos, had been instructed and baptized by the followers of the Baptist, and had joined the fellowship of the Christians. Some have thought that they had been instructed by Apollos himself; but there is no sufficient evidence of this. "There they were, a small and distinct community about twelve in number, still preparing, after the manner of the Baptist, for the coming of the Lord. Something there was which drew the attention of the apostle immediately on his arrival. They lacked, apparently, some of the tokens of the higher life that pervaded the nascent church; they were devout, rigorous, austere, but were wanting in the joy, the radiancy, the enthusiasm which were conspicuous in others" (Plumptre, "St. Paul in Asia Minor").

2. **Have ye received the Holy Ghost since ye believed?** The two verbs are in the aorist tense, and therefore denote instantaneous acts. The A. V. therefore gives an entirely wrong idea, as there is no question about what happened *after* believing; but the question relates to what occurred *when* they believed. Hence Rev., rightly, *Did ye receive the Holy Ghost when ye believed?*

We have not heard. Also the aorist. *We did not hear;* referring back to the time of their beginning.

Whether there be any Holy Ghost. But, as Bengel observes, "They could not have followed either Moses or John the Baptist without having heard of the Holy Ghost." The words, therefore, are to be explained, not of their being unaware of the *existence* of the Holy Ghost, but of his presence and baptism on earth. The word ἔστιν, *there be*, is to be taken in the sense of *be present*, or *be given*, as in John vii. 39, where it is said, "The Holy Ghost *was not* yet (οὔπω ἦν)," and where the translators rightly render, "was not yet *given*."

3. **Unto what** (εἰς τί). Rev., more correctly, *into*. See on Matt. xxviii. 19.

John. The last mention of John the Baptist in the New Testament. "Here, at last, he wholly gives place to Christ" (Bengel).

10. **Asia.** See on ch. ii. 9.

11. **Special** (οὐ τὰς τυχούσας). A peculiar expression. Lit., *not usual* or *common*, such as one might *fall in with* frequently.

12. **Body** (χρωτὸς). Properly, the *surface* of the body, the *skin;* but, in medical language, of the *body*.

Handkerchiefs (σουδάρια). See on Luke xix. 20.

Aprons (σιμικίνθια). Only here in New Testament. A Latin word, *semicinctia*. Lit., something passing *half-way round* the body: an *apron* or *waistband*. Perhaps garments worn by Paul when engaged at his trade.

13. **Vagabond** (περιερχομένων). Lit., *going about*. Rev., *strolling*.

Exorcists (ἐξορκιστῶν). Only here in New Testament. The kindred verb, *adjure*, occurs Matt. xxvi. 63, and means, originally, *to administer an oath*. These Jewish exorcists pretended to the power of casting out evil spirits by magical arts derived from Solomon.

14. **Did** (ποιοῦντες). The participle denotes a *practice*.

15. **I know—I know** (γινώσκω—ἐπίσταμαι). There is a purpose in using two different words to denote the demon's recognition of the Divine Master and of the human agent, though it is not easy to convey the difference in a translation. It is the difference between an instinctive *perception* or *recognition* of a supreme power and the more intimate *knowledge* of a human agent. A divine mystery would invest Jesus, which the demon would feel, though he could not penetrate it. His

knowledge of a *man* would be greater, in his own estimation at least. The difference may be given roughly, thus: "Jesus I *recognize*, and Paul *I am acquainted with*."

Overcame them (*κατακυριεύσας*). The best texts read *both of them*, which would imply that only two of the seven were concerned in the exorcism. Rev., better, *mastered*, thus giving the force of *κύριος*, *master*, in the composition of the verb.

16. **Prevailed against** (*ἴσχυσε*). See on Luke xiv. 30; xvi. 3.

17. **Was known** (*ἐγένετο γνωστὸν*). More correctly, *became known*.

18. **Confessed and shewed** (*ἐξομολογούμενοι καὶ ἀναγγέλλοντες*). The two words denote the fullest and most open confession. They *openly* (*ἐξ*) confessed, and declared *thoroughly* (*ἀνά*, *from top to bottom*) their deeds. See on Matt. iii. 6.

19. **Curious arts** (*τὰ περίεργα*). The word means, literally, *overwrought*, *elaborate*, and hence *recondite* or *curious*, as magical practices. Only here and 1 Tim. v. 13, in its original sense of those who busy themselves *excessively* (*περί*): *busybodies*. The article indicates the practices referred to in the context.

Books. Containing magical formulas. Heathen writers often allude to the *Ephesian letters*. These were symbols, or magical sentences written on slips of parchment, and carried about as amulets. Sometimes they were engraved on seals.

Burned (*κατέκαιον*). Burned them *up* (*κατά*). The imperfect is graphic, describing them as throwing book after book on the pile.

Counted (*συνεψήφισαν*). Only here in New Testament. See on Luke xiv. 28. The preposition *σύν*, *together*, in the compound verb, indicates the reckoning up of the sum-total.

Fifty thousand pieces of silver. If reckoned in Jewish money, about thirty-five thousand dollars; if in Greek drachmæ, as is more probable, about nine thousand three hundred dollars.

23. **The way.** See on ch. ix. 2.

24. **Silversmith** (ἀργυροκόπος). Lit., *a silver-beater*.

Shrines. Small models of the temple of Diana, containing an image of the goddess. They were purchased by pilgrims to the temple, just as rosaries and images of the Virgin are bought by pilgrims to Lourdes, or bronze models of Trajan's column or of the Colonne Vendôme by tourists to Rome or Paris.*

Craftsmen (τεχνίταις). In the next verse he mentions *the workmen* (ἐργάτας), the two words denoting, respectively, the *artisans*, who performed the more delicate work, and the *laborers*, who did the rougher work.

25. **Wealth** (εὐπορία). See on *ability*, ch. xi. 29. Lit., *welfare*. *Wealth* is used by the A. V. in the older and more general sense of *weal*, or *well-being* generally. Compare the Litany of the English Church: "In all time of our tribulation, in all time of our *wealth*."

27. **Craft** (μέρος). Lit., *part* or department of trade.

To be set at nought (εἰς ἀπελεγμὸν ἐλθεῖν). Lit., *to come into refutation* or *exposure;* hence, *disrepute*, as Rev. Compare ch. xviii. 28, and see note there. Ἀπελεγμός, *refutation*, occurs only here in New Testament.

Diana. Or *Artemis*. We must distinguish between the Greek Artemis, known to the Romans as Diana, and the Ephesian goddess. The former, according to the legend, was the daughter of Zeus (Jove), and the sister of Apollo. She was

* For descriptions of the temple, see Conybeare and Howson; and Lewin, Life and Epistles of St. Paul; Farrar, Life and Work of St. Paul; and Wood's Ephesus.

the patroness of the chase, the huntress among the immortals, represented with bow, quiver, and spear, clad in hunting-habit, and attended by dogs and stags. She was both a destroyer and a preserver, sending forth her arrows of death, especially against women, but also acting as a healer, and as the special protectress of women in childbirth. She was also the goddess of the moon. She was a maiden divinity, whose ministers were vowed to chastity.

The Ephesian Artemis is totally distinct from the Greek, partaking of the Asiatic character, and of the attributes of the Lydian Cybele, the great mother of the gods. Her worship near Ephesus appears to have existed among the native Asiatic population before the foundation of the city, and to have been adopted by the Greek immigrants, who gradually transferred to her features peculiar to the Grecian goddess. She was the personification of the fructifying and nourishing powers of nature, and her image, as represented on current coins of the time, is that of a swathed figure, covered with breasts, and holding in one hand a trident, and in the other a club. This uncouth figure, clad in a robe covered with mystic devices, stood in the shrine of the great temple, hidden by a purple curtain, and was believed to have fallen down from heaven (ver. 35). In her worship the oriental influence was predominant. The priests were eunuchs, and with them was associated a body of virgin priestesses and a number of slaves, the lowest of whom were known as *neocori*, or temple-sweepers (ver. 35). "Many a time must Paul have heard from the Jewish quarter the piercing shrillness of their flutes, and the harsh jangling of their timbrels; many a time have caught glimpses of their detestable dances and Corybantic processions, as, with streaming hair, and wild cries, and shaken torches of pine, they strove to madden the multitudes into sympathy with that orgiastic worship which was but too closely connected with the vilest debaucheries" (Farrar, "Life and Work of Paul").

Magnificence. See on 2 Pet. i. 16.

28. **Cried out** (*ἔκραζον*). The imperfect is graphic; they

continued crying. This reiteration was a characteristic of the oriental orgiastic rites.

29. **The theatre.** The site of which can still be traced. It is said to have been capable of seating fifty-six thousand persons.

Having seized (συναρπάσαντες). Lit., "having seized *along with* (σύν):" carried them along with the rush.

Companions in travel (συνεκδήμους). Only here and 2 Cor. viii. 19. The word is compounded of σύν, *along with*, ἐκ, *forth*, and δῆμος, *country* or *land*, and means, therefore, one who has gone *forth with* another from his *country*.

31. **Of the chief officers of Asia** (τῶν Ἀσιαρχῶν). *The Asiarchs.* These were persons chosen from the province of Asia, on account of their influence and wealth, to preside at the public games and to defray their expenses.

33. **They drew** (προεβίβασαν). More correctly, *urged forward.* See on *before instructed*, Matt. xiv. 8.

34. **With one voice cried out.** The reverberations of their voices from the steep rock which formed one side of the theatre must have rendered their frenzied cries still more terrific.

35. **The town-clerk.** Or *recorder*, who had charge of the city-archives, and whose duty it was to draw up official decrees and present them to assemblies of the people. Next to the commander, he was the most important personage in the Greek free cities.

Worshipper (νεωκόρον). Lit., a *temple-sweeper*. See on ver. 27. This title, originally applied to the lowest menials of the temple, became a title of honor, and was eagerly appropriated by the most famous cities. Alexander says, "The city of Ephesus is the *sacristan* of the great goddess Artemis."*

---

* See Bp. Lightfoot's "Essays on Supernatural Religion," p. 297, and Euripides, "Iphigenia in Tauris," 87.

36. **Quiet** (κατεσταλμένους). Compare *quieted* (ver. 35). The verb means to *let down* or *lower;* and so is applied, metaphorically, to *keeping one's self in check; repressing.*

Rash (προπετὲς). Lit., *headlong.*

37. **Robbers of churches** (ἱεροσύλους). The A. V. puts a droll anachronism into the mouth of the town-clerk of a Greek city. Render, rather, as Rev., robbers of *temples.*

38. **The law is open** (ἀγοραῖοι ἄγονται). Lit., *the court-days are being kept.* Rev., *the courts are open.* Compare ch. xvii. 5.

Deputies (ἀνθύπατοι). Proconsuls, by whom Asia, as a senatorial province, was governed. See Introduction to Luke.

40. **Concourse** (συστροφῆς). Lit., a *twisting together:* hence of anything which is rolled or twisted into a mass; and so of a mass of people, with an underlying idea of *confusion:* a mob. Compare ch. xxiii. 12.

CHAPTER XX.

1. **Embraced** (ἀσπασάμενος). Better, as Rev., *took leave.* The word is used for a salutation either at meeting or parting. See ch. xxi. 6, 7.

2. **Greece.** The Roman province of Achaia, comprehending Greece proper and the Peloponnesus. Luke uses *Achaia* (ch. xix. 21) and *Greece* synonymously, as distinguished from Macedonia.

3. **Sail** (ἀνάγεσθαι). Better, as Rev., *set sail.* See on Luke viii. 22; and compare Luke v. 3.

4. **Sopater.** The best texts add, *the son of Pyrrhus.* Compare Rom. xvi. 21.

Aristarchus. Compare Acts xix. 29.

Gaius. Not the one mentioned in ch. xix. 29, who was a Macedonian.

Tychicus and Trophimus. See Col. iv. 7, 8; Eph. vi. 21, 22; 2 Tim. iv. 12; Titus iii. 12; Acts xxi. 29; 2 Tim. iv. 20.

5. **Us.** The first person resumed, indicating that Luke had joined Paul.

6. **In five days** (ἄχρις ἡμερῶν πέντε). Lit., "*up to* five days," indicating the duration of the voyage from Philippi.

7. **First** (τῇ μιᾷ). Lit., "the *one* day." The cardinal numeral here used for the ordinal.

Week (σαββάτων). The plural used for the singular, in imitation of the Hebrew form. The noun *Sabbath* is often used after numerals in the signification of *a week*. See Matt. xxviii. 1; Mark xvi. 2; John xx. 19.

To break bread. The celebration of the eucharist, coupled with the *Agape*, or love-feast.

Preached (διελέγετο). Better, as Rev., *discoursed with them*. It was a mingling of preaching and conference. Our word *dialogue* is derived from the verb.

8. **Many lights.** A detail showing the vivid impression of the scene upon an eye-witness. It has been remarked that the abundance of lights shows how little of secrecy or disorder attached to these meetings.

The upper chamber. See on ch. i. 13.

9. **The window.** See on ch. ix. 25. The windows of an Eastern house are closed with lattice-work, and usually reach down to the floor, resembling a door rather than a window. They open, for the most part, to the court, and not to the street, and are usually kept open on account of the heat.

Fallen into a deep sleep (καταφερόμενος ὕπνῳ βαθεῖ). Lit., *borne down by*, etc. A common Greek phrase for being overcome by sleep. In medical language the verb was more frequently used in this sense, absolutely, than with the addition of *sleep*. In this verse the word is used twice: in the first instance, in the present participle, denoting the coming on of drowsiness —*falling* asleep; and the second time, in the aorist participle, denoting his being *completely overpowered* by sleep. Mr. Hobart thinks that the mention of the causes of Eutychus' drowsiness—the heat and smell arising from the numerous lamps, the length of the discourse, and the lateness of the hour—are characteristic of a physician's narrative. Compare Luke xxii. 45.

Dead (νεκρός). Actually dead. Not *as* dead, or *for* dead.

10. **Fell on him.** Compare 1 Kings xvii. 21; 2 Kings iv. 34.

Trouble not yourselves (μὴ θορυβεῖσθε). Rev., more correctly, *make ye no ado*. They were beginning to utter passionate outcries. See Matt. ix. 23; Mark v. 39.

His life is in him. In the same sense in which Christ said, "The damsel is not dead, but sleepeth" (Luke viii. 52).

11. **Having gone up.** From the court to the chamber above.

Talked (ὁμιλήσας). Rather, *communed*. It denotes a more familiar and confidential intercourse than *discoursed*, in ver. 7.

13. **To go afoot** (πεζεύειν). Only here in New Testament. There is no good reason for changing this to *by land*, as Rev. The A. V. preserves the etymology of the Greek verb. The distance was twenty miles; less than half the distance by sea.

15. **Arrived** (παρεβάλομεν). Only here and Mark iv. 30, where it is used more nearly according to its original sense, *to*

throw beside; to bring one thing beside another in comparison. Here, of bringing the vessel alongside the island. The *narrative* implies that they only *touched* (Rev.) there, but not necessarily the *word.*

16. **To spend time** (*χρονοτριβῆσαι*). Only here in New Testament. The word carries the suggestion of a *waste* of time, being compounded with *τρίβω*, *to rub; to wear out by rubbing.* The sense is nearly equivalent to our expression, *fritter away time.*

17. **Having sent to Ephesus.** About thirty miles.

Elders. Called *overseers* or *bishops* in ver. 28.

20. **Kept back** (*ὑπεστειλάμην*). A picturesque word. Originally, *to draw in* or *contract.* Used of furling sails, and of closing the fingers; of drawing back for shelter; of keeping back one's real thoughts; by physicians, of withholding food from patients. It is rather straining a point to say, as Canon Farrar, that Paul is using a nautical metaphor suggested by his constantly hearing the word for furling sail used during his voyage. Paul's metaphors lie mainly on the lines of military life, architecture, agriculture, and the Grecian games. The statement of Canon Farrar, that he "constantly draws his metaphors from the sights and circumstances immediately around him," is rather at variance with his remark that, with one exception, he "cannot find a single word which shows that Paul had even the smallest susceptibility for the works of nature" ("Paul," i., 19). Nautical metaphors are, to say the least, not common in Paul's writings. I believe there are but three instances: Eph. iv. 14; 1 Tim. i. 19; vi. 9. Paul means here that he suppressed nothing of the truth through fear of giving offence. Compare Gal. ii. 12; Heb. x. 38.

21. **Repentance toward God.** *Repentance* has the article: *the* repentance which is due to God. So, also, *faith: the* faith which is due toward Christ, as the advocate and mediator.

22. **Bound in the spirit.** In *his own* spirit. Constrained by an invincible sense of duty. Not *by the Holy Spirit*, which is mentioned in the next verse and distinguished by the epithet *the Holy*.

23. **Testifieth** (διαμαρτύρεται). The compound verb signifies *full*, *clear* testimony. Not by internal intimations of the Spirit, but by prophetic declarations "in every city." Two of these are mentioned subsequently, at Tyre and Caesarea (ch. xxi. 4, 11).

24. **But none of these things move me, neither count I,** etc. The best texts omit *neither count I*, and render, *I esteem my life of no account, as if it were precious to myself.*

Dear (τιμίαν). Of value; precious.

Course (δρόμον). A favorite metaphor of Paul, from the race-course. See 1 Cor. ix. 24–27; Philip. iii. 14; 2 Tim. iv. 7.

25. **I know.** The *I* is emphatic: *I* know through these special revelations to myself (ver. 23).

26. **This day** (τῇ σήμερον ἡμέρᾳ). Very forcible. Lit., *on to-day's day;* this, our parting day.

27. **Shunned.** The same word as in ver. 20: *kept back.*

28. **To yourselves and to all the flock.** To *yourselves* first, that you may duly care for the *flock*. Compare 1 Tim. iv. 16.

Overseers (ἐπισκόπους). Denoting the official function of the elders, but not in the later ecclesiastical sense of *bishops*, as implying an order distinct from *presbyters* or elders. The two terms are synonymous. The *elders*, by virtue of their office, were *overseers*.*

* See Bishop Lightfoot's Commentary on Philippians, p. 93; and the Essay on the Christian Ministry, in the same volume, p. 179 sq.; also, Conybeare and Howson, vol. i., ch. xiii.

To feed (ποιμαίνειν). See on Matt. ii. 6. The word embraces more than *feeding*; signifying all that is included in the office of a shepherd: *tending*, or *shepherding*.

Purchased (περιεποιήσατο). Only here and 1 Tim. iii. 13. See on *peculiar people*, 1 Pet. ii. 9. The verb means, originally, *to make* (ποιέω) *to remain over and above* (περί): hence *to keep* or *save for one's self*; *to compass* or *acquire*.

29. **Grievous** (βαρεῖς). Lit., *heavy*: violent, rapacious.

31. **Watch** (γρηγορεῖτε). See on Mark xiii. 35.

To warn (νουθετῶν). From νοῦς, *the mind*, and τίθημι, *to put*. Lit., *to put in mind*; *admonish* (so Rev., better than *warn*). "It's fundamental idea is the well-intentioned seriousness with which one would influence the mind and disposition of another by advice, admonition, warning, putting right, according to circumstances" (Cremer).

32. **I commend.** See on 1 Pet. iv. 19.

Build you up. A metaphor in constant use by Paul, and preserved in the words *edify*, *edification* (Latin, *aedes*, "a house," and *facere*, "to make") by which οἰκοδομέω and its kindred words are frequently rendered. In old English the word *edify* was used in its original sense of *build*. Thus Wycliffe renders Gen. ii. 22, "The Lord God *edified* the rib which he took of Adam, into a woman."

So, too, Spenser:

> "a little wide
> There was a holy temple edified."
> *Faerie Queene*, i., 1, 34.

33. **Raiment.** Mentioned along with gold and silver because it formed a large part of the wealth of orientals. They traded in costly garments, or kept them stored up for future use. See on *purple*, Luke xvi. 19; and compare Ezra ii. 69; Neh. vii. 70; Job xxvii. 16. This fact accounts for the allusions to the destructive power of the moth (Matt. vi. 19; Jas. v. 2).

35. **I have shewed you all things** (πάντα ὑπέδειξα ὑμῖν). The verb means *to shew by example*. Thus, Luke vi. 47, "I will *shew* you to whom he is like," is followed by the illustration of the man who built upon the rock. So Acts ix. 16. God will shew Paul by practical experience how great things he must suffer. The kindred noun ὑπόδειγμα is always rendered *example* or *pattern*. See John xiii. 15; Jas. v. 10, etc.; and note on 2 Pet. ii. 6. Rev., correctly, *In all things I gave you an example.*

So. As I have done.

To help (ἀντιλαμβάνεσθαι). See on Luke i. 54.

He said (αὐτὸς εἶπε). Rev., more strictly, "*he himself* said." This saying of Jesus is not recorded by the Evangelists, and was received by Paul from oral tradition.

The speech of Paul to the Ephesian elders "bears impressed on it the mark of Paul's mind: its ideas, its idioms, and even its very words are Pauline; so much so as to lead Alford to observe that we have probably the literal report of the words spoken by Paul. 'It is,' he remarks, 'a treasure-house of words, idioms, and sentences peculiar to the apostle himself'" (Gloag).

37. **Kissed** (κατεφίλουν). See on Matt. xxvi. 49.

38. **See** (θεωρεῖν). See on Luke x. 18. The word for *steadfast, earnest* contemplation suggests the interest and affection with which they looked upon his countenance for the last time.

CHAPTER XXI.

1. **Gotten from** (ἀποσπασθέντας). Withdrawn. Some see in the word an expression of the grief and reluctance with which they parted, and render *having torn ourselves away*. See on Luke xxii. 41.

With a straight course. See on ch. xvi. 11.

2. **Set forth** (ἀνήχθημεν). Or *set sail.* See on Luke viii. 22; v. 3.

3. **Discovered** (ἀναφάναντες). Better, *sighted.* A nautical phrase. The verb literally means *to bring to light:* and its use here is analogous to the English marine phrase, *to raise the land.*

4. **Finding disciples** (ἀνευρόντες τοὺς μαθητὰς). The verb means to discover *after search;* and the article, *the* disciples, refers to the disciples who lived and were recognized members of the church there. The A. V. overlooks both the preposition and the article. The verb might be rendered strictly by our common phrase, "having *looked up* the disciples." See on Luke ii. 16. A small number of disciples is implied in ver. 5.

5. **Accomplished** (ἐξαρτίσαι). Only here and 2 Tim. iii. 17, where it is used in the sense of *equip* or *furnish.*

Children. The first time that children are mentioned in the notice of a Christian church.

Shore (αἰγιαλὸν). Rev., *beach.* See on Matt. xiii. 2.

6. **Taken leave.** See on ch. xx. 1.

7. **Finished** (διανύσαντες). Only here in New Testament.

Saluted. The word rendered *take leave* in ver. 6. See on ch. xx. 1.

8. **We that were of Paul's company.** The best texts omit.

Philip. See ch. viii.

The seven. The first deacons. See ch. vi. 5.

11. **Bound his own feet and hands.** Imitating the symbolical acts of the Old Testament prophets. See 1 Kings xxii. 11; Isa. xx. 1–3; Jer. xiii. 1–7; Ezek. iv. 1–6. Compare John xxi. 18.

12. **Besought him not to go up.** This suggests the case of Luther when on his journey to the Diet of Worms, and the story of Regulus the Roman, who, being permitted to return to Rome with an embassy from the Carthaginians, urged his countrymen to reject the terms of peace, and to continue the war, and then, against the remonstrances of his friends, insisted on fulfilling his promise to the Carthaginians to return in the event of the failure of negotiations, and went back to certain torture and death.

13. **I am ready** (ἑτοίμως ἔχω). Lit., *I hold myself in readiness.*

15. **Took up our carriages** (ἀποσκευασάμενοι). The verb means *to pack up and carry off*, or simply *to pack* or *store away*. Hence, some explain that Paul packed and stored the greater part of his luggage in Caesarea. The best texts, however, read ἐπισκευασάμενοι, *having equipped ourselves. Carriages* is used in the old English sense, now obsolete, of *that which is carried, baggage.* See 1 Sam. xvii. 22, A. V.

16. **Bringing with them,** etc. This would imply that Mnason was at Caesarea, and accompanied Paul and his companions to Jerusalem. It seems better to suppose that the disciples accompanied the apostle in order to introduce him to Mnason, whom they knew. Render, *conducting us to Mnason, with whom we should lodge.*

Old (ἀρχαίῳ). Better, as Rev., *early*. The rendering *old* might be taken to mean *aged;* whereas the word means *of long standing.*

21. **They are informed** (κατηχήθησαν). More than *in-*

formed. They had been *carefully instructed*, probably by the Judaizing teachers. See on *instructed*, Luke i. 4.

To forsake Moses (ἀποστασίαν ἀπὸ Μωσέως). Lit., *apostasy from Moses*. Compare 2 Thess. ii. 3.

22. **What is it therefore?** How does the matter lie? What is to be done?

The multitude must needs come together. Some texts omit. So Rev. If retained, we should read *a* multitude.

23. **A vow.** The Nazarite vow. See Num. vi. 1–21.

24. **Be at charges with them** (δαπάνησον ἐπ' αὐτοῖς). Lit., *spend upon them*. Pay the necessary charges on their account. Hence Rev., rightly, "*for* them." The person who thus paid the expenses of poor devotees who could not afford the necessary charges shared the vow so far that he was required to stay with the Nazarites until the time of the vow had expired. "For a week, then, St. Paul, if he accepted the advice of James and the presbyters, would have to live with four paupers in the chamber of the temple which was set apart for this purpose; and then to pay for sixteen sacrificial animals and the accompanying meat-offerings" (Farrar, "Life and Work of Paul"). He must also stand among the Nazarites during the offering of the sacrifices, and look on while their heads were shaved, and while they took their hair to burn it under the caldron of the peace-offerings, "and while the priest took four sodden shoulders of rams, and four unleavened cakes out of the four baskets, and four unleavened wafers anointed with oil, and put them on the hands of the Nazarites, and waved them for a wave-offering before the Lord" (Farrar).

Walkest orderly (στοιχεῖς). See on *elements*, 2 Pet. iii. 10.

25. **Blood.** See on ch. xv. 29.

26. **Purifying himself** (*ἁγνισθεὶς*). See on 1 Pet. i. 22; Jas. iv. 8.

Declaring (*διαγγέλλων*). To the priests who directed the sacrifices and pronounced release from the vow.

Fulfilment—until, etc. There is some dispute and confusion here as to the precise meaning. The general sense is that, having entered the temple toward the close of the period required for the fulfilment of these men's vow, he gave notice that the vowed number of Nazarite days had expired, after which only the concluding offering was required

27. **Asia.** See on ch. ii. 9.

Stirred up (*συνέχεον*). Only here in New Testament. Lit., *poured together*, *threw into confusion*. See on *confounded*, ch. ii. 6; and *confusion*, ch. xix. 29.

28. **This place.** The temple. Compare the charge against Stephen, ch. vi. 13.

Greeks. See on ch. vi. 1.

Temple (*ἱερὸν*). See on Matt. iv. 5. The Jews evidently meant to create the impression that Paul had introduced Gentiles into the inner court, which was restricted to the Jews. The temple proper was on the highest of a series of terraces which rose from the outer court, or Court of the Gentiles. In this outer court any stranger might worship. Between this and the terraces was a balustrade of stone, with columns at intervals, on which Greek and Latin inscriptions warned all Gentiles against advancing farther on pain of death. Beyond this balustrade rose a flight of fourteen steps to the first platform, on which was the Court of the Women, surrounded by a wall. In this court were the treasury, and various chambers, in one of which the Nazarites performed their vows. It was here that the Asiatic Jews discovered Paul.

29. **Trophimus.** See on ch. xx. 4. As an Ephesian he would be known to the Asiatic Jews.

30. **Drew him out of the temple.** Better, as Rev., *dragged* (εἷλκον). Out of the sacred enclosure and down the steps to the outer court, as they would not defile the temple proper with blood.

The doors were shut. Between the inner and outer courts.

31. **Chief captain** (χιλιάρχῳ). A commander of a thousand men. See on Mark vi. 21; and on *centurion*, Luke vii. 2.

Band (σπείρης). Or *cohort.* See on Mark xv. 16. These troops were quartered in the tower of Antonia, which was at the northwestern corner of the temple-area, and communicated with the temple-cloisters by staircases.

32. **Centurions.** See on Luke vii. 2.

Unto them (ἐπ' αὐτούς). Better, *upon* them.

33. **Chains** (ἁλύσεσι). See on Mark v. 4.

34. **Castle** (παρεμβολήν). Better, *barracks.* The main tower had a smaller tower at each corner, the one at the south-eastern corner being the largest and overlooking the temple. In this tower were the quarters of the soldiers. The word is derived from the verb παρεμβάλλω, *to put in beside*, used in military language of distributing auxiliaries among regular troops and, generally, of drawing up in battle-order. Hence the noun means, *a body drawn up in battle-array*, and passes thence into the meaning of an *encampment, soldiers' quarters, barracks.* In Heb. xi. 34, it occurs in the earlier sense of *an army;* and in Heb. xiii. 11, 13; Apoc. xx. 9, in the sense of *an encampment.* In grammatical phraseology it signifies a *parenthesis*, according to its original sense of *insertion* or *interpolation.*

35. **Stairs.** Leading from the temple-court to the tower. There were two flights, one to the northern and the other to the western cloister, so that the guard could go different ways among the cloisters in order to watch the people at the Jewish festivals.

So it was (συνέβη). Lit., *it happened.* The verb means, literally, to *come together;* hence, of a *coincidence of events.* It is designedly introduced here to express more vividly the fact of the peculiar emergency and the peril of Paul's situation. Things *came to such a pass* that he had to be carried up the stairs.

37. **Canst thou speak** (γινώσκεις). Lit., *dost thou know?* So Rev.

38. **Art thou not** (οὐκ ἄρα σὺ εἶ). Indicating the officer's surprised recognition of his own mistake. "Thou art not, then, as I supposed." Rev. properly adds *then* (ἄρα).

The Egyptian. A false prophet, who, in the reign of Nero, when Felix was governor of Judaea, collected a multitude of thirty thousand, whom he led from the wilderness to the Mount of Olives, saying that the walls of Jerusalem would fall down at his command and give them free entrance to the city. Felix with an army dispersed the multitude, and the Egyptian himself escaped. There is a discrepancy in the number of followers as stated by Josephus (30,000) and as stated by the commandant here (4,000). It is quite possible, however, that Josephus alludes to the whole rabble, while Lysias is referring only to the armed followers.

Madest an uproar. Better, as Rev., *stirred up to sedition.* The rendering of the A. V. is too vague. The verb means to *unsettle* or *upset,* and the true idea is given in the A. V. of Acts xvii. 6, *have turned the world upside down.* Compare Gal. v. 12, and kindred words in Mark xv. 7; Luke xxiii. 19.

That were murderers (τῶν σικαρίων). The A. V. is too

general, and overlooks the force of the article, which shows that the word refers to a class. Rev., rightly, *the assassins*. The word, which occurs only here, and notably on the lips of a Roman officer, is one of those Latin words which "followed the Roman domination even into those Eastern provinces of the empire which, unlike those of the West, had refused to be Latinized, but still retained their own language" (Trench, "Synonyms"). The Sicarii were so called from the weapon which they used—the *sica*, or short, curved dagger. Josephus says: "There sprang up in Jerusalem another description of robbers called *Sikars*, who, under the broad light of day, and in the very heart of the city, assassinated men; chiefly at the festivals, however, when, mixing among the crowd, with daggers concealed under their cloaks, they stabbed those with whom they were at variance. When they fell, the murderers joined in the general expressions of indignation, and by this plausible proceeding remained undetected" ("Jewish War," c. xiii.). The general New Testament term for *murderer* is φονεύς (see Matt. xxii. 7; Acts iii. 14; xxviii. 4, etc.).

39. **Mean** (ἀσήμου). Lit., *without a mark* or *token* (σῆμα). Hence used of uncoined gold or silver: of oracles which give no intelligible response: of inarticulate voices: of disease without distinctive symptoms. Generally, as here, *undistinguished*, *mean*. There is a conscious feeling of patriotism in Paul's expression.

40. **Beckoned with the hand.** Compare ch. xxvi. 1.

Tongue (διαλέκτῳ). Lit., *dialect:* the language spoken by the Palestinian Jews—a mixture of Syriac and Chaldaic.

CHAPTER XXII.

1. **Defence** (ἀπολογίας). See on *answer*, 1 Pet. iii. 15.

2. **Kept—silence** (παρέσχον ἡσυχίαν). Lit., *gave quiet.*

3. **At the feet.** Referring to the Jewish custom of the pupils sitting on benches or on the floor, while the teacher occupied an elevated platform.

Gamaliel. One of the seven Rabbis to whom the Jews gave the title *Rabban*. *Rab*, "teacher," was the lowest degree; *Rabbi*, "my teacher," the next higher; and *Rabban*, "our teacher," the highest. Gamaliel was a liberal Pharisee. "As Aquinas among the schoolmen was called *Doctor Angelicus*, and Bonaventura *Doctor Seraphicus*, so Gamaliel was called *the Beauty of the Law*. He had no antipathy to the Greek learning. Candor and wisdom seem to have been features of his character" (Conybeare and Howson). See ch. v. 34 sq.

Instructed (*πεπαιδευμένος*). See on *chastise*, Luke xxiii. 16.

According to the perfect manner (*κατὰ ἀκρίβειαν*). Lit., *according to the strictness*. See on *perfect understanding*, Luke i. 3; and *diligently*, Acts xviii. 25. Compare, also, Acts xviii. 26; xxvi. 5.

Zealous (*ζηλωτὴς*). Or *a zealot*. On the word as a title, see on Mark iii. 18.

4. **Way.** See on ch. ix. 2.

5. **Estate of the elders** (*πρεσβυτέριον*). The eldership or Sanhedrim.

Went. The imperfect: *was journeying*.

6. **About noon.** Not mentioned in ch. ix.

8. **Of Nazareth** (*ὁ Ναζωραῖος*). Lit., *the Nazarene*. Not mentioned in ch. ix.

9. **Heard not** (*οὐκ ἤκουσαν*). The verb is to be taken in the sense of *understood*, as Mark iv. 33; 1 Cor. xiv. 2, which explains the apparent discrepancy with ch. ix. 7.

11. **For the glory of that light.** The cause of his blindness is not stated in ch. ix.

12. **A devout man,** etc. In ch. ix. 10, he is called a *disciple*. Paul here "affirms that he was not introduced to Christianity by an opponent of Judaism, but by a strict Jew" (Gloag).

13. **Stood** (ἐπιστὰς). More correctly, as Rev., "standing *by* (ἐπί)."

Receive thy sight (ἀνάβλεψον). Better, *look up*. See the following words: *I looked up upon him*. The word admits of both translations, *to look up* and *to recover sight*.

I looked up upon him. Some unite both meanings here: *I looked up with recovered sight*. So Rev., in margin.

14. **The God of our fathers—Just One.** A conciliatory touch in Paul's speech, mentioning both God and Christ by their Jewish names. Compare ch. iii. 14; vii. 52.

Hath chosen (προεχειρίσατο). See on ch. iii. 20. Better, as Rev., *appointed*.

15. **All men.** He keeps back the offensive word *Gentiles* (ch. ix. 15).

16. **Wash away** (ἀπόλουσαι). See on ch. xvi. 33.

17. **I was in a trance** (γενέσθαι με ἐν ἐκστάσει). Rev., more correctly, *I fell into a trance;* the verb meaning *to become*, rather than the simple *to be*. On *trance*, see note on *astonishment*, Mark v. 42; and compare note on Acts x. 10.

20. **Martyr.** Better, as Rev., *witness*. The special sense of the word was probably not in use at this time. See on ch. i. 22. It occurs, however, in Apoc. ii. 13; xvii. 6.

Standing by. See on ver. 13.

Consenting (συνευδοκῶν). See on *allow*, Luke xi. 48; and compare Acts viii. 1.

Slew. See on Luke xxiii. 32.

21. **Gentiles.** "The fatal word, which hitherto he had carefully avoided, but which it was impossible for him to avoid any longer, was enough. . . . The word 'Gentiles,' confirming all their worst suspicions, fell like a spark on the inflammable mass of their fanaticism" (Farrar, "Life and Work of Paul").

22. **They gave him audience** (ἤκουον). The imperfect. Up to this word *they were listening.*

Lifted up their voice, etc. "Then began one of the most odious and despicable spectacles which the world can witness, the spectacle of an oriental mob, hideous with impotent rage, howling, yelling, cursing, gnashing their teeth, flinging about their arms, waving and tossing their blue and red robes, casting dust into the air by handfuls, with all the furious gesticulations of an uncontrolled fanaticism" (Farrar). Hackett cites Sir John Chardin ("Travels into Persia and the East Indies") as saying that it is common for the peasants in Persia, when they have a complaint to lay before their governors, to repair to them by hundreds or a thousand at once. They place themselves near the gate of the palace, where they suppose they are most likely to be seen and heard, and there set up a horrid outcry, rend their garments, and throw dust into the air, at the same time demanding justice. Compare 2 Sam. xvi. 13.

24. **Examined** (ἀνετάζεσθαι). Only here and ver. 29. Not found in classical Greek. Apocrypha, *Susanna*, ver. 14.

By scourging (μάστιξιν). Lit., *with scourges.*

25. **Bound him with thongs** (*προέτειναν αὐτὸν τοῖς ἱμᾶσιν*). Against the rendering of the A. V. is the word *προέτειναν*, *they stretched forward*, in allusion to the position of the victim for scourging, and the article with *thongs*; "*the* thongs," with reference to some well-known instrument. If the words referred simply to binding him, *with thongs* would be superfluous. It is better, therefore, to take *thongs* as referring to the scourge, consisting of one or more lashes or cords, a sense in which it occurs in classical Greek, and to render *stretched him out for* (*or before*) *the thongs*. The word is used elsewhere in the New Testament of *a shoe-latchet* (Mark i. 7; Luke iii. 16; John i. 27).

Roman. See on ch. xvi. 37.

28. **Sum** (*κεφαλαίου*). Lit., *capital*. The purchase of Roman citizenship was an investment. Under the first Roman emperors it was obtained only at large cost and with great difficulty; later, it was sold for a trifle.

I was free-born (*ἐγὼ καὶ γεγέννημαι*). Lit., *I am even so born*, leaving the mind to supply *free* or *a Roman*. Better, as Rev., *I am a Roman born*.

30. **Brought Paul down.** To the meeting-place of the Sanhedrim: probably not their usual place of assembly, which lay within the wall of partition, which Lysias and his soldiers would not have been allowed to pass.

CHAPTER XXIII.

1. **Earnestly beholding.** See on Luke iv. 20. Some, who hold that Paul's eyesight was defective, explain this steadfast look in connection with his imperfect vision.

Men and brethren. He addresses the Sanhedrim as an equal.

I have lived (*πεπολίτευμαι*). Lit., *have lived as a citizen*, with special reference to the charge against him that he taught men against the law and the temple. He means that he had lived as a true and loyal Jew.

Conscience (συνειδήσει). See on 1 Pet. iii. 16.

2. **Ananias.** He is described as a revengeful and rapacious tyrant. We are told that he reduced the inferior priests almost to starvation by defrauding them of their tithes, and sent his creatures to the threshing-floors with bludgeons to seize the tithes by force.

3. **Shall smite thee** (τύπτειν σε μέλλει). More strictly, *is about to smite.* The words are not an imprecation, but a prophecy of punishment for his violent dealing. According to Josephus, in the attack of the Sicarii upon Jerusalem, he was dragged from his hiding-place, in a sewer of the palace, and murdered by assassins.

Thou whited wall. Compare Matt. xxiii. 27.

Contrary to the law (παρανομῶν). A verb. Lit., *transgressing the law.*

4. **Revilest** (λοιδορεῖς). The word signifies *vehement abuse, scolding, berating.*

6. **The one part were Sadducees,** etc. Perceiving the impossibility of getting a fair hearing, Paul, with great tact, seeks to bring the two parties of the council into collision with each other.

The resurrection. A main point of contention between the Pharisees and Sadducees, the latter of whom denied the doctrine of the resurrection, of a future state, and of any spiritual existence apart from the body.

8. **Both.** Showing that *two* classes of doctrines peculiar to

the Sadducees, and not *three*, are meant: 1. The resurrection. 2. The existence of spirits, whether angels or souls of men; "neither angel nor spirit."

9. **Strove.** The diversion was successful. The Pharisees' hatred of the Sadducees was greater than their hatred of Christianity.

What if a spirit, etc. Neither the A. V. nor Rev. give the precise form of this expression. The words form a broken sentence, followed by a significant silence, which leaves the hearers to supply the omission for themselves: "But if a spirit or angel has spoken to him——" The words which the A. V. supplies to complete the sentence, *let us not fight against God*, are spurious, borrowed from ch. v. 39.

12. **Banded together** (ποιήσαντες συστροφὴν). Lit., *having made a conspiracy*. See on *concourse*, ch. xix. 40.

Bound themselves under a curse (ἀνεθεμάτισαν ἑαυτοὺς). Lit., *anathematized* or *cursed themselves;* invoked God's curse on themselves if they should violate their vow. On the kindred noun ἀνάθεμα, *a curse*, see note on *offerings*, Luke xxi. 5. In case of failure, they could procure absolution from their oath by the Rabbis.

13. **Conspiracy** (συνωμοσίαν). Lit., *swearing together; conjuration.* According to its etymology, *conspiracy* is a *breathing* or *blowing together* (Latin, *conspirare*). Hence, of concerted thought and action.

14. **We have bound ourselves under a great curse** (ἀναθέματι ἀνεθεματίσαμεν ἑαυτοὺς). Lit., *we have anathematized ourselves with an anathema.* A very strong expression. For similar expressions, see Luke xxii. 15; John iii. 29; Acts iv. 17.

15. **Enquire** (διαγινώσκειν). Only here and ch. xxiv. 22. Originally, *to distinguish* or *discern;* hence, *to decide*, as a suit. Rev., more correctly, therefore, *judge*.

More perfectly (ἀκριβέστερον). Rev., better, *more exactly.* See on Luke i. 3; Acts xviii. 25, 26.

Concerning him (τὰ περὶ αὐτοῦ). Lit., *the things about him.* Rev., better, *his case.*

18. **The prisoner** (ὁ δέσμιος). From δέω, *to bind.* Paul, as a Roman citizen, was held in *custodia militaris,* "military custody." Three kinds of custody were recognized by the Roman law: 1. *Custodia publica* (public custody); confinement in the public jail. This was the worst kind, the common jails being wretched dungeons. Such was the confinement of Paul and Silas at Philippi. 2. *Custodia libera* (free custody), confined to men of high rank. The accused was committed to the charge of a magistrate or senator, who became responsible for his appearance on the day of trial. 3. *Custodia militaris* (military custody). The accused was placed in charge of a soldier, who was responsible with his life for the prisoner's safe-keeping, and whose left hand was secured by a chain to the prisoner's right. The prisoner was usually kept in the barracks, but was sometimes allowed to reside in a private house under charge of his guard.

21. **Have bound themselves.** "If we should wonder how, so early in the morning, after the long discussion in the Sanhedrim, which must have occupied a considerable part of the day, more than forty men should have been found banded together, under an anathema, neither to eat nor to drink till they had killed Paul; and, still more, how such a conspiracy, or, rather, conjuration, which, in the nature of it, would be kept a profound secret, should have become known to Paul's sister's son—the circumstances of the case furnish a sufficient explanation. The Pharisees were avowedly a *fraternity* or *guild;* and they, or some of their kindred fraternities, would furnish the ready material for such a band, to whom this additional vow would be nothing new or strange, and, murderous though it sounded, only seem a further carrying out of the principles of their order. Again, since the wife and all the children of a member were

ipso facto members of the guild, and Paul's father had been a Pharisee (ver. 6), Paul's sister also would, by virtue of her birth, belong to the fraternity, even irrespective of the probability that, in accordance with the principles of the party, she would have married into a Pharisaical family" (Edersheim, "Jewish Social Life").

23. **Soldiers** (στρατιώτας). Heavy-armed footmen: legionaries.

Spearmen (δεξιολάβους). Only here in New Testament, and not in classical Greek. From δεξιός, *right*, and λαμβάνω, *to take*. The exact meaning is uncertain. Some explain it as *those who take the right side* of the prisoners whom they have in charge; others, those who *grasp* (*their weapon*) *with the right hand;* others, again, *those who hold* (*a second horse*) *by the right hand.* They are here distinguished from the heavy-armed legionaries and the cavalry. They were probably light-armed troops, javelin-throwers or slingers. One of the principal manuscripts reads δεξιοβόλους, "those who *throw* with the right hand."

24. **Beasts** (κτήνη). See on Luke x. 34.

25. **After this manner** (περιέχουσαν τὸν τύπον τοῦτον). Lit., *containing this form or type.* See on *it is contained,* 1 Pet. ii. 6.

26. **To the most excellent** (τῷ κρατίστῳ). "His excellency:" an official title. Compare ch. xxiv. 3; xxvi. 25.

Greeting (χαίρειν). See on ch. xv. 23.

27. **Rescued.** Bengel says, "a lie." Lysias wishes to make the impression that Paul's citizenship was the cause of his rescuing him; whereas he did not know of this until afterward. He says nothing about the proposed scourging.

29. **Questions.** See on ch. xv. 2.

Nothing—worthy of death or of bonds. Every Roman magistrate before whom the apostle is brought declares him innocent.

30. **When it was told** (μηνυθείσης). Lit., *pointed out*, or *shown*, as Rev. See on Luke xx. 37.

Farewell. The best texts omit. See on ch. xv. 29.

31. **Took** (ἀναλαβόντες). Lit., "having taken *up*." Compare *set Paul on*, ver. 24.

To Antipatris. A hard night's ride: forty miles.

32. **On the morrow.** After arriving at Antipatris.

33. **Caesarea.** Twenty-six miles from Antipatris.

34. **Of what province** (ἐκ ποίας ἐπαρχίας). Rather, "*from what kind* of a province;" whether senatorial or imperial. See Introduction to Luke. Cilicia was an imperial province.

35. **I will hear thee** (διακούσομαι). Better, as Rev., *will hear thy cause;* the word meaning "to hear *fully* (διά) in a judicial sense." The present questioning was merely preliminary.

Herod's palace. Built by Herod the Great. Judaea being now a Roman province, the palace of its former kings had become the governor's official residence. It thus appears that Paul was leniently dealt with, and not cast into the common prison.

CHAPTER XXIV.

1. **An orator** (ῥήτορος). An advocate. The Jews, being little acquainted with Roman forms and laws, had to employ Roman advocates.

3. **Very worthy deeds** (κατορθωμάτων). From κατορθόω, *to set upright.* Hence, *a success consequent on right judgment; a right action.* The best texts, however, read διορθωμάτων, *settings right; amendments.* Thus the sentence reads, literally, *obtaining much peace through thee, and amendments taking place for this nation through thy providence, we accept,* etc.

Providence (προνοίας). Forethought. *Providentia Augusti* (*the providence of the emperor*) was a common title on the coins of the emperors.

4. **Be tedious** (ἐγκόπτω). See on *hindered,* 1 Pet. iii. 7. The meaning is, rather, "that I may not further *hinder* thee, or *detain* thee.

Clemency (ἐπιεικείᾳ). See on *gentle,* 1 Pet. ii. 18.

A few words (συντόμως). Lit., *concisely.* From συντέμνω, *to cut down* or *cut short.*

5. **Pestilent fellow** (λοιμὸν). Lit., a *plague* or *pest.*

Ringleader (πρωτοστάτην). Originally, *one who stands first on the right of a line; a file-leader.* Thus Thucydides says that all armies when engaging are apt to thrust outward their right wing; and adds, "*The first man in the front rank* (ὁ πρωτοστάτης) of the right wing is originally responsible for the deflection" (v., 71). Here, of course, metaphorically, as A. V. and Rev. Only here in New Testament.

Sect (αἱρέσεως). See on *heresies,* 2 Pet. ii. 1.

Nazarenes. The only passage in scripture where this term is used to denote the Christians. See on Matt. ii. 23.

6. **To profane** (βεβηλῶσαι). The word is akin to βηλός, *threshold,* and βαίνω, *to step;* and its fundamental idea, therefore, is that of overstepping the threshold of sacred places. The

word *profane* is the Latin *pro fanum*, *in front of the sanctuary*; that which is kept outside the *fane* because unholy.

We laid hold. The best texts omit all after these words as far as *by examining*.

8. **From whom.** Paul. It would refer to Lysias if the omitted passage above were retained.

9. **Assented** (συνέθεντο). But the best texts read συνεπέθεντο, *jointly set upon or assailed*. So Rev., *joined in the charge*.

10. **The more cheerfully** (εὐθυμότερον). The best texts read the positive of the adverb, εὐθύμως, *cheerfully*.

14. **The way.** See on ch. ix. 2.

A sect. See on ver. 5. The word is commonly used in an indifferent sense, as signifying merely a *school* or *party*. So ch. xv. 5; xxviii. 22. Here, however, in a bad sense—a *schismatic* sect, as in 1 Cor. xi. 19.

Worship (λατρεύω). Better, as Rev., *serve*. See on Luke i. 74.

God of my fathers (τῷ πατρῴῳ Θεῷ). A familiar classical phrase, and therefore well known to Felix. Thus Demosthenes calls Apollo the πατρῷος (ancestral god) of Athens. Socrates is asked (Plato, "Euthydemus," 302), "Have you an *ancestral* Zeus (Ζεὺς πατρῷος)?" So, frequently, in the classics. Similarly, the Roman phrase, *Di patrii*, "the gods of *the forefathers*." On the Roman reverence for the ancestral religion, see note on ch. xvi. 21. The Roman's own sentiment would prepare him to respect Paul's.

15. **Allow** (προσδέχονται). Or, as Rev., *look for*. The word admits of either sense.

16. **Exercise myself** (ἀσκῶ). Originally, *to work raw material*, *to form:* hence, to *practise*, *exercise*, *discipline;* and so, in ecclesiastical language, *to mortify the body.* Of the kindred adjective ἀσκητικός, our word *ascetic* is a transcript.

Void of offence (ἀπρόσκοπον). Lit., *without stumbling; unshaken.* The word is used thus in a *passive* sense here, as in Philip. i. 10. In 1 Cor. x. 32, it occurs in the *active* sense of *giving offence* to others, or causing them to stumble.

18. **Whereupon** (ἐν οἷς). More correctly, *in which* (occupation); *while so engaged.* The best texts, however, read ἐν αἷς, *in which*, the pronoun agreeing in gender with *offerings.* The sense, according to this, is, as Rev., margin, *in presenting which* (*offerings*).

22. **Deferred** (ἀνεβάλετο). Adjourned the case. Only here in New Testament.

I will know the uttermost (διαγνώσομαι). Better, as Rev., *I will determine.* See on ch. xxiii. 15.

23. **Liberty** (ἄνεσιν). From ἀνίημι, to *send up;* thence, *to loosen*, *release.* It is almost exactly expressed by our vulgarism, *to let up.* The noun here is more correctly rendered by Rev., *indulgence.* In all the other New Testament passages it is rendered *rest*, *ease*, or *relief.* See 2 Cor. ii. 13; vii. 5; viii. 13; 2 Thess. i. 7.

To minister (ὑπηρετεῖν). See on *officer*, Matt. v. 25.

25. **Righteousness, temperance, the judgment to come.** Three topics which bore directly upon the character of Felix. Tacitus says of him that he "exercised the authority of a king with the spirit of a slave;" and that, by reason of the powerful influence at his command, "he supposed he might perpetrate with impunity every kind of villany." He had persuaded his wife Drusilla to forsake her husband and marry him. He had

employed assassins to murder the high-priest Jonathan, and might well tremble at the preaching of the judgment to come. *Temperance* (ἐγκράτεια) is, properly, *self-control;* holding the passions in hand.

Trembled (ἔμφοβος γενόμενος). Lit., *having become in fear.* Rev., better, *was terrified.*

For this time (τὸ νῦν ἔχον). Or, *for the present.* Very literally, *as to what has itself now.*

26. **He hoped also** (ἅμα δὲ καὶ ἐλπίζων). A comma should be placed after *thee* (ver. 25), and the participle ἐλπίζων, *hoping,* joined with *answered:* "Felix answered, 'Go thy way, etc.,' hoping withal that money would be given him."

Communed (ὡμίλει). See on *talked,* ch. xx. 11.

27. **Porcius Festus came into Felix's room** (ἔλαβε διάδοχον ὁ Φῆλιξ Πόρκιον Φῆστον). Rev., better, *Felix was succeeded by Porcius Festus.* The Greek idiom is, *Felix received Porcius Festus as a successor.*

To shew the Jews a pleasure (χάριτας καταθέσθαι τοῖς Ἰουδαίοις). Lit., *to lay up thanks for himself with the Jews.* Rev., correctly, *to gain favor with the Jews.*

CHAPTER XXV.

1. **Was come into the province** (ἐπιβὰς τῇ ἐπαρχίᾳ). Lit., *having entered upon the province.*

2. **Besought.** The imperfect denotes their persistence: *kept beseeching.*

3. **Laying wait** (ἐνέδραν ποιοῦντες). Lit., *making* or *arranging an ambush.*

4. **Should be kept** (τηρεῖσθαι). This puts it as a peremptory denial of the Jews' request by Festus; whereas it is only his statement of a fact. Render, as Rev., *that Paul was kept in charge*. Festus' reply is conciliatory, and is put on the ground of convenience.

6. **Judgment-seat.** See on ch. vii. 5.

8. **Have I offended** (ἥμαρτον). See on the kindred noun ἁμαρτία, *sin*, Matt. i. 21.

9. **Do a pleasure.** See on ch. xxiv. 27. Rev., better, *to gain favor*.

Before me (ἐπ' ἐμοῦ). Not with him as judge, but by the Sanhedrim in his presence.

10. **Very well** (κάλλιον). The force of the comparative should be preserved: "thou knowest *better* than thy question implies."

11. **Deliver** (χαρίσασθαι). With an underlying sense of giving him up as *a favor* to the Jews.

I appeal (ἐπικαλοῦμαι). The technical phrase for lodging an appeal. The Greek rendering of the Latin formula *appello*.

12. **The council.** A body of men chosen by the governor himself from the principal Romans of the province. These were called *assessors*, sometimes *friends*, sometimes *captains*. Though a Roman citizen had the right of appeal to the emperor, a certain discretion was allowed the governors of provinces as to admitting the appeal. It might be disallowed if the affair did not admit of delay, or if the appellant were a known robber or pirate. In doubtful cases the governor was bound to consult with his council, and his failure to do so exposed him to censure. Cicero, in his impeachment of Verres, the brutal governor of Sicily, says: "Will you deny that you dismissed your council,

the men of rank with whom your predecessor and yourself had been wont to consult, and decided the case yourself?" (ii., 33). That Festus exercised this discretion in Paul's case is shown by his conferring with the council.

13. **Agrippa the king.** Herod Agrippa II., son of the Herod whose death is recorded in Acts xii. 20–23.

Bernice. Sister of Drusilla, the wife of Felix. She is said to have lived in incestuous relations with her brother. Juvenal, in his sixth satire, alludes to this: "A most notable diamond, made more precious by having been worn on the finger of Bernice. This a barbarian king once gave to his incestuous love. This Agrippa gave to his sister."

16. **Opportunity** (τόπου). Lit., *place.* An unclassical use of the word.

18. **Stood up** (σταθέντες). See on Luke xviii. 11; xix. 8.

19. **Superstition** (δεισιδαιμονίας). See on ch. xvii. 22. Better, *religion*, as Rev. As Agrippa was a Jew by religion, Festus would not have insulted him by applying the word *superstition* to his faith. Note, however, that he speaks of it as *their own* religion, not identifying Agrippa with them. It was a non-committal expression, since the word meant either *religion* or *superstition* according to circumstances. He left Agrippa "to take the word in a good sense, but reserved his own view, which was certainly the Roman one" (Meyer). There is, indeed, a similar tact in Paul's use of the word to the Athenians. He selected "a word which almost imperceptibly shaded off from praise to blame" (Trench).*

---

* "Bernhardy very aptly remarks that the entrance of the word δεισιδαιμονία marks a critical point in the history of the life of the Greek people. It marks the wavering between scepticism and despondency. It leaves the conception of the object of religious reverence wavering between God and demon, and thus *fearing* becomes the dominant notion. Hence the word carries more reproach than credit" (Zeschwitz, Profangräcität und Biblischer Sprachgeist).

Affirmed (ἔφασκεν). The imperfect implies something habitual. "Paul *kept asserting*."

21. **Of the Emperor** (τοῦ Σεβαστοῦ). Lit., the *august one;* hence a translation of *Augustus*, which was not a proper name, but a title of the Roman emperors.

26. **Lord** (κυρίῳ). An instance of Luke's accuracy. The title "lord" was refused by the first two emperors, Augustus and Tiberius. The emperors who followed accepted it. In the time of Domitian it was a recognized title. Antoninus Pius was the first who put it on his coins.

27. **Crimes** (αἰτίας). Rev., more correctly, *charges.*

CHAPTER XXVI.

2. **Happy** (μακάριον). See on *blessed*, Matt. v. 3.

Answer (ἀπολογεῖσθαι). See on 1 Pet. iii. 15.

3. **Expert** (γνώστην). Lit., *a knower.*

Questions (ζητημάτων). See on ch. xv. 2.

4. **My manner of life,** etc. The repeated articles give additional precision to the statement: "*the* manner of life, *that* which was from my youth; *that* which was from the beginning."

6. **For the hope** (ἐπ' ἐλπίδι). Lit., "*on the ground of* the hope."

Made of God. The article clearly defines what promise, "*the one, namely, made of God.*"

7. **Twelve tribes** (δωδεκάφυλον). Only here in New Testament. A collective term, embracing the tribes as a whole. Meyer renders *our twelve-tribe-stock.*

Instantly (ἐν ἐκτενείᾳ). Only here in New Testament. Lit., *in intensity*. See on *fervently*, 1 Pet. i. 22. Compare *more earnestly*, Luke xxii. 44; *without ceasing*, Acts xii. 5; *fervent*, 1 Pet. iv. 8. See, also, on *instantly* and *instant*, Luke vii. 4; xxiii. 23.

Serving. Compare ch. xxiv. 14; and see on Luke i. 74.

Come (καταντῆσαι). Lit., *to arrive at*, as if at a goal. Compare ch. xvi. 1; xviii. 19; xxv. 13, etc. Rev. *attain*.

8. **That God should raise the dead** (εἰ ὁ Θεὸς νεκροὺς ἐγείρει). Much better, as Rev., *if God raises the dead*. He does not put it as a supposition, but as a fact: *if God raises the dead*, as you admit that he has the power to do, and as your own writings tell you that he has done.

10. **Saints** (τῶν ἁγίων). Lit., *the holy ones*. Paul did not call the Christians by this name when addressing the Jews, for this would have enraged them; but before Agrippa he uses the word without fear of giving offence. On this word ἅγιος, *holy*, which occurs over two hundred times in the New Testament, it is to be noted how the writers of the Greek scriptures, both in the New Testament and, what is more remarkable, in the Septuagint, bring it out from the background in which it was left by classical writers, and give preference to it over words which, in pagan usage, represented conceptions of mere externality in religion. Even in the Old Testament, where externality is emphasized, ἅγιος is the standard word for holy.*

---

* Thus, though the priest is ἱερεύς, the holy place is τὸ ἅγιον, and the most holy place, τὰ ἅγια τῶν ἁγίων: ἱερόν is never used in the Septuagint for the temple, except in 1 Chron. xxix. 4; Ezek. xlv. 19; and in both cases the temple is referred to in its outward aspect. In Ezek. xxvii. 6; xxviii. 18, τὰ ἱερά is used of the heathen sanctuaries of Tyre. In the New Testament ἱερός never implies moral excellence. Excepting in the neuter form, τὸ ἱερόν, *the temple*, it occurs but twice (1 Cor. ix. 13; 2 Tim. iii. 15), and is never used of a person. Σεμνός is *reverend; ἁγνός*, *pure*, in the sense of *chastity*, *freedom from admixture of evil;* and is applied once to God himself (1 John iii. 3). Ὅσιος is holy *by sanction*. Trench remarks the sharp distinction maintained

Gave my voice (κατήνεγκα ψῆφον). Lit., *laid down my vote.* See on *counteth,* Luke xiv. 28. Some suppose that Paul here refers to casting his vote as a member of the Sanhedrim; in which case he must have been married and the father of a family. But this there is no reason for believing (compare 1 Cor. vii. 7, 8); and the phrase may be taken as expressing merely moral assent and approval.

12. **Whereupon** (ἐν οἷς). See on ch. xxiv. 18. Better, *on which errand;* in which affairs of persecution.

13. **Above the brightness of the sun.** Peculiar to this third account of Paul's conversion. The other peculiarities are: the falling of his companions to the ground along with himself; the voice addressing him in Hebrew; and the words, "It is hard for thee to kick against the pricks."

14. **It is hard for thee to kick against the pricks.** Or, *goads.* The sharp goad carried in the ploughman's hand, against which the oxen kick on being pricked. The metaphor, though not found in Jewish writings, was common in Greek and Roman writings. Thus, Euripides ("Bacchae," 791): "Being enraged, I would kick against the goads, a mortal against a god." Plautus ("Truculentus, 4, 2, 55): "If you strike the goads with your fists, you hurt your hands more than the goads." "Who knows whether at that moment the operation of ploughing might not be going on within sight of the road along which the persecutor was travelling? (Howson, "Metaphors of St. Paul").

16. **Have I appeared** (ὤφθην). See on Luke xxii. 43.

To make (προχειρίσασθαι). Better, as Rev., *appoint.* See on ch. iii. 20.

---

by the Septuagint translators between it and ἅγιος; the two words being used to render two different Hebrew words, and never interchanged. The Greek student will find an interesting discussion of this subject in Zeschwitz, Profangräcität und Biblischer Sprachgeist.

A minister and a witness. See on Matt. v. 25; Acts i. 22.

17. **The people.** The Jews.

22. **Help of God** (ἐπικουρίας τῆς παρὰ τοῦ Θεοῦ). Lit., "help *that is* from God." The article defines the nature of the help more sharply than A. V. The word for *help* originally meant *alliance*.

23. **That Christ should suffer** (εἰ παθητὸς ὁ Χριστὸς). Rather, *if* or *whether the Messiah is liable to suffering*. He expresses himself in a problematic form, because it was the point of debate among the Jews whether a suffering Messiah was to be believed in. They believed in a triumphant Messiah, and the doctrine of his sufferings was an obstacle to their receiving him as Messiah. Note the article, "*the* Christ," and see on Matt. i. 1.

24. **Much learning doth make thee mad** (τὰ πολλά σε γράμματα εἰς μανίαν περιτρέπει). The A. V. omits the article with *much learning:* "*the* much knowledge" with which thou art busied. Rev., "*thy* much learning." *Doth make thee mad:* literally, *is turning thee to madness.*

25. **Speak forth** (ἀποφθέγγομαι). See on ch. ii. 4.

28. **Almost thou persuadest** (ἐν ὀλίγῳ με πείθεις). Lit., *in a little thou persuadest.* The rendering *almost* must be rejected, being without sufficient authority. The phrase, *in a little*, is adverbial, and means *in brief; summarily.* We may supply *pains* or *talk.* "With little pains, or with a few words." The words are ironical, and the sense is, "*You are trying to persuade me off hand to be a Christian.*" *Thou persuadest* (πείθεις) is, rather, *thou art for persuading; thou attemptest to persuade;* a force which both the present and the imperfect sometimes have.*

* As in John x. 32: "For which of these works *are you for* stoning me (λιθάζετε)?" John xiii. 6: "Dost thou *mean to wash* (νίπτεις) my feet?" Luke i. 59: "They *were for calling* (ἐκάλουν) him Zacharias." Matt. iii. 14: "John *tried to prevent* (διεκώλυεν)."

29. **Almost and altogether** (ἐν ὀλίγῳ καὶ ἐν μεγάλῳ).* Lit., *in little and in great;* i.e., with little or with great pains.

Were (γενέσθαι). Better, as Rev., *might become.* Agrippa's word, "*to become* a Christian," is repeated.

Except these bonds. An exquisite touch of Christian courtesy.

30. **The king, the governor, Bernice.** Mentioned in the order of their rank.

31. **Doeth.** Referring, not to Paul's past conduct, but to the general character of his life.

CHAPTER XXVII.

1. **Sail** (ἀποπλεῖν). Lit., *sail away.*

Band. See on Mark xv. 16.

2. **Meaning to sail** (μέλλοντες πλεῖν). This refers the intention to the voyagers; but the best texts read μέλλοντι, agreeing with πλοίῳ, *ship;* so that the correct rendering is, as Rev., *a ship—which was about to sail.*

3. **Touched** (κατήχθημεν). From κατά, *down,* and ἄγω, *to lead* or *bring.* To bring the ship *down* from deep water to the land. Opposed to ἀνήχθημεν, *put to sea* (ver. 2); which is to bring the vessel *up* (ἀνά) from the land to deep water. See on Luke viii. 22. *Touched* is an inferential rendering. *Landed* would be quite as good. From Caesarea to Sidon, the distance was about seventy miles.

Courteously (φιλανθρώπως). Only here in New Testament. Lit., *in a man-loving way; humanely; kindly.* Rev., *kindly,*

---

* So the best texts, instead of πολλῷ, *much.*

better than *courteously*. *Courteous*, from *court*, expresses rather polish of *manners* than real kindness.

To refresh himself (ἐπιμελείας τυχεῖν). Lit., *to receive care* or *attention*.

4. **We sailed under** (ὑπεπλεύσαμεν). Rev., correctly, *under the lee of:* under the protection of the land.

6. **A ship of Alexandria.** Employed in the immense corn trade between Italy and Egypt. See ver. 38. The size of the vessel may be inferred from ver. 37.

7. **Many** (ἱκαναῖς). See on Luke vii. 6.

Scarce (μόλις). Incorrect. Render, as Rev., *with difficulty*. So, also, *hardly*, in ver. 8. The meaning is not that they had scarcely reached Cnidus when the wind became contrary, nor that they had come only as far as Cnidus in many days; but that they were retarded by contrary winds between Myra and Cnidus, a distance of about one hundred and thirty miles, which, with a favorable wind, they might have accomplished in a day. Such a contrary wind would have been the northwesterly, which prevails during the summer months in that part of the Archipelago.

9. **The Fast.** The great day of atonement, called "the Fast" by way of eminence. It occurred about the end of September. Navigation was considered unsafe from the beginning of November until the middle of March.

10. **I perceive** (θεωρῶ). As the result of careful observation. See on Luke x. 18.

Hurt (ὕβρεως). The word literally means *insolence*, *injury*, and is used here metaphorically: *insolence of the winds and waves*, "like our 'sport' or 'riot' of the elements" (Hackett). Some take it literally, *with presumption*, as indicating the folly of undertaking a voyage at that season; but the use of the word in ver. 21 is decisive against this.

Damage (ζημίας). Better, as Rev., *loss*. *Hurt and damage* (A. V.) is tautological. See on the kindred verb, notes on *lose*, Matt. xvi. 26, and *cast away*, Luke ix. 25.

11. **Master** (κυβερνήτῃ). Only here and Apoc. xviii. 17. Lit., *the steersman*.

12. **Not commodious** (ἀνευθέτου). Lit., *not well situated*.

Lieth toward the southwest and northwest (βλέποντα κατὰ Λίβα καὶ κατὰ Χῶρον). Instead of *lieth*, Rev., literally and correctly, renders *looking*. The difference between the Rev. and A. V., as to the points of the compass, turns on the rendering of the preposition κατά. The words *southwest* and *northwest* mean, literally, the southwest and northwest *winds*. According to the A. V., κατά means *toward*, and has reference to the quarter *from which* these winds blow. According to the Rev., κατά means *down:* "looking *down* the southwest and northwest winds," *i.e.*, in the direction *toward* which they blow, viz., northeast and southeast. This latter view assumes that Phenice and Lutro are the same, which is uncertain. For full discussion of the point, see Smith, "Voyage and Shipwreck of St. Paul;" Hackett, "Commentary on Acts;" Conybeare and Howson, "Life and Epistles of St. Paul."

13. **Loosing thence** (ἄραντες). Lit., *having taken up*. It is the nautical phrase for *weighing anchor*. So Rev.

14. **There arose against it** (ἔβαλε κατ' αὐτῆς). Against what? Some say, *the island of Crete;* in which case they would have been driven against the island, whereas we are told that they were driven away from it. Others, *the ship*. It is objected that the pronoun αὐτῆς, *it*, is feminine, while the feminine noun for *ship* (ναῦς) is not commonly used by Luke, but rather the neuter, πλοῖον. I do not think this objection

entitled to much weight. Luke is the only New Testament writer who uses ναῦς (see ver. 41), though he uses it but once; and, as Hackett remarks, "it would be quite accidental which of the terms would shape the pronoun at this moment, as they were both so familiar." A third explanation refers the pronoun to the island of Crete, and renders, "there beat down *from it.*" This is grammatical, and according to a well-known usage of the preposition. The verb βάλλω is also used intransitively in the sense of to *fall;* thus Homer ("Iliad," xi., 722), of a river *falling* into the sea. Compare Mark iv. 37: "the waves *beat* (ἐπέβαλλεν) into the ship;" and Luke xv. 12: "the portion of goods that *falleth* (ἐπιβάλλον) to me." The rendering of the Rev. is, therefore, well supported, and, on the whole, preferable: *there beat down from it.* It is also according to the analogy of the expression in Luke viii. 23, *there came down a storm.* See note there, and on Matt. viii. 24.

A tempestuous wind (ἄνεμος τυφωνικὸς). Lit., *a typhonic wind.* The word τυφῶν means *a typhoon,* and the adjective formed from it means *of the character of a typhoon.*

Euroclydon (Εὐροκλύδων). The best texts read Εὐρακύλων, *Euraquilo:* i.e., between *Eurus,* "the E.S.E. wind," and *Aquilo,* "the north-wind, or, strictly, N. ⅓ E." Hence, E. N. E.

15. **Bear up** (ἀντοφθαλμεῖν). Only here in New Testament. From ἀντί, *opposite,* and ὀφθαλμός, *the eye.* Lit., *to look the wind in the eye.* The ancient ships often had an eye painted on each side of the bow. To sail "into the eye of the wind" is a modern nautical phrase.

We let her drive (ἐπιδόντες ἐφερόμεθα). Lit., *having given up to it, we were borne along.*

16. **We had much work to come by the boat** (μόλις ἰσχύσαμεν περικρατεῖς γενέσθαι τῆς σκάφης). Lit., *we were with difficulty able to become masters of the boat:* i.e., to secure on deck the small boat which, in calm weather, was attached by a

rope to the vessel's stern. Rev., *we were able with difficulty to secure the boat.* On *with difficulty*, see note on *scarce*, ver. 7.

17. **Helps** (βοηθείαις). Any apparatus on hand for the purpose: ropes, chains, etc.

Undergirding (ὑποζωννύντες). In modern nautical language, *frapping:* passing cables or chains round the ship's hull in order to support her in a storm. Mr. Smith ("Voyage and Shipwreck of St. Paul") cites the following from the account of the voyage of Captain George Back from the arctic regions in 1837: "A length of the stream chain-cable was passed under the bottom of the ship four feet before the mizzen-mast, hove tight by the capstan, and finally immovably fixed to six ring-bolts on the quarter-deck. The effect was at once manifest by a great diminution in the working of the parts already mentioned; and, in a less agreeable way, by impeding her rate of sailing."

Quicksands (τὴν σύρτιν). The rendering of the A. V. is too general. The word is a proper name, and has the article. There were two shoals of this name—the "Greater Syrtis" (*Syrtis Major*), and the "Smaller Syrtis" (*Syrtis Minor*). It was the former upon which they were in danger of being driven; a shallow on the African coast, between Tripoli and Barca, southwest of the island of Crete.

Strake sail (χαλάσαντες τὸ σκεῦος). Lit., as Rev., *lowered the gear.* See on *goods*, Matt. xii. 29. It is uncertain what is referred to here. To strike sail, it is urged, would be a sure way of running upon the Syrtis, which they were trying to avoid. It is probably better to understand it generally of the gear connected with the fair-weather sails. "Every ship situated as this one was, when preparing for a storm, sends down upon deck the 'top-hamper,' or gear connected with the fair-weather sails, such as the topsails. A modern ship sends down top-gallant masts and yards; a cutter strikes her topmast when preparing for a gale" (Smith, "Voyage," etc.). The storm sails were probably set.

18. **Lightened** (*ἐκβολὴν ἐποιοῦντο*). Lit., *made a casting out.* Rev., *began to throw the freight overboard.* Note the imperfect, *began* to throw. The whole cargo was not cast overboard: the wheat was reserved to the last extremity (ver. 38).

19. **Tackling** (*σκευὴν*). The word means *equipment, furniture.* The exact meaning here is uncertain. Some suppose it to refer to the main-yard; an immense spar which would require the united efforts of passengers and crew to throw overboard. It seems improbable, however, that they would have sacrificed so large a spar, which, in case of shipwreck, would support thirty or forty men in the water. The most generally received opinion is that it refers to the furniture of the ship—beds, tables, chests, etc.

21. **Hearkened** (*πειθαρχήσαντας*). See on *obey*, ch. v. 29.

Loosed (*ἀνάγεσθαι*). Rev., *set sail.* See on Luke viii. 22.

Harm (*ὕβριν*). See on ver. 10.

23. **The angel.** Rev., correctly, *an angel.* There is no article.

Of God (*τοῦ Θεοῦ*). Rev., correctly, supplies the article: "*the* God," added because Paul was addressing heathen, who would have understood by *angel* a messenger of the gods.

27. **Adria.** The Adriatic Sea: embracing all that part of the Mediterranean lying south of Italy, east of Sicily, and west of Greece.

Deemed (*ὑπενόουν*). Better, as Rev., *suspected* or *surmised.*

That they drew near to some country. Lit., *that some land is drawing near to them.*

30. **Under color** (*προφάσει*). Lit., *on pretence.*

Cast (ἐκτείνειν). Lit., *to stretch out.* The meaning is, *to carry out* an anchor to a distance from the prow by means of the small boat. Rev., *lay out.*

33. **While the day was coming on** (ἄχρι δὲ οὗ ἔμελλεν ἡμέρα γίνεσθαι). Lit., *until it should become day:* in the interval between midnight and morning.

39. **Bay** (κόλπον). See on *bosom*, Luke vi. 38.

Shore (αἰγιαλὸν). See on Matt. xiii. 2. Better, as Rev., *beach.*

They were minded (ἐβουλεύσαντο). Better, as Rev., *took counsel.* See on Matt. i. 19.

40. **Taken up** (περιελόντες). Wrong. The word means *to remove*, and refers here to cutting the anchor-cables, or *casting off*, as Rev.

Committed themselves (εἴων). Wrong. The reference is to the anchors. Rev., correctly, *left them in the sea.*

Rudder-bands (ζευκτηρίας τῶν πηδαλίων). Lit., *the bands of the rudders.* The larger ships had two rudders, like broad oars or paddles, joined together by a pole, and managed by one steersman. They could be pulled up and fastened with *bands* to the ship; as was done in this case, probably to avoid fouling the anchors when they were cast out of the stern. The bands were now loosened, in order that the ship might be driven forward.

Mainsail (ἀρτέμωνα). Only here in New Testament. Probably the *foresail.* So Rev.

Made toward (κατεῖχον). Lit., *held; bore down for.*

CHAPTER XXVIII.

1. **They knew.** The best texts read *we knew: ascertained* or *recognized:* with a reference to ver. 39.

2. **Barbarous people.** From the Roman point of view, regarding all as barbarians who spoke neither Greek nor Latin. Not necessarily *uncivilized.* It is equivalent to *foreigners.* Compare Rom. i. 14; 1 Cor. xiv. 11. The inhabitants of Malta were of Carthaginian descent. "Even in the present day the natives of Malta have a peculiar language, termed the Maltese, which has been proved to be essentially an Arabic dialect, with an admixture of Italian" (Gloag).

No little (*οὐ τυχοῦσαν*). See on *special,* ch. xix. 11. Rev., much better, "*no common* kindness."

Kindness (*φιλανθρωπίαν*). See on the kindred adverb *courteously,* ch. xxvii. 3.

Present rain (*ὑετὸν τὸν ἐφεστῶτα*). Lit., *which was upon us,* or *had set in.* No mention of rain occurs up to this point in the narrative of the shipwreck. The tempest may thus far have been unattended with rain, but it is hardly probable.

3. **Of sticks** (*φρυγάνων*). Only here in New Testament. From *φρύγω,* to *roast* or *parch.* Hence, *dry* sticks.

Out of (*ἐκ*). The best texts read *ἀπό, by reason of.*

4. **Justice** (*Δίκη*). Personified.

Suffereth not (*οὐκ εἴασεν*). The aorist tense: *did not suffer.* His death is regarded as fixed by the divine decree.

5. **The beast** (*τὸ θηρίον*). Luke uses the word in the same way as the medical writers, who employed it to denote venom-

ous serpents, and particularly the viper; so much so that an antidote, made chiefly from the flesh of vipers, was termed *θηριακή*. A curious bit of etymological history attaches to this latter word. From it came the Latin *theriaca*, of which our *treacle* (molasses) is a corruption. Treacle, therefore, is originally a preparation of viper's flesh, and was used later of any antidote. Thus Coverdale's translation of Jer. viii. 22 has, "There is no more *treacle* in Gilead." Gurnall ("Christian in Complete Armor") says: "The saints' experiences help them to a sovereign *treacle* made of the scorpion's own flesh (which they through Christ have slain), and that hath a virtue above all other to expel the venom of Satan's temptations from the heart." So Jeremy Taylor: "We kill the viper and make *treacle* of him."

6. **Swollen** (*πίμπρασθαι*). Only here in New Testament. The usual medical word for inflammation.

Looked (*προσδοκώντων*). Occurring eleven times in Luke, and only five times in the rest of the New Testament. Frequent in medical writers, to denote expectation of the fatal result of illness.

No harm (*μηδὲν ἄτοπον*). Lit., *nothing out of place*. The word *ἄτοπος* occurs three times in Luke, and only once elsewhere in the New Testament (2 Thess. iii. 2). Used by physicians to denote something *unusual* in the symptoms of disease, and also something *fatal* or *deadly* as here. Rev., *nothing amiss*. Compare Luke xxiii. 41; and Acts xxv. 5, where the best texts insert the word.

Said (*ἔλεγον*). The imperfect, denoting current talk.

A god. "Observe," says Bengel, "the fickleness of human reasoning. He is either an *assassin*, say they, or a *god*. So, at one time *bulls*, at another *stones*" (Acts xiv. 13, 19).

7. **The chief man** (*τῷ πρώτῳ*). Official title, without refer-

ence to his rank and possessions. Though not occurring as the official designation of the governor of Malta in any ancient author, it has been found in two inscriptions discovered in the island.

8. **Sick** (συνεχόμενον). Lit., *taken* or *holden*. See on *taken*, Luke iv. 38.

Fever (πυρετοῖς). Lit., *fevers*. This peculiarly medical use of the plural is confined to Luke in the New Testament. It denotes successive and varying attacks of fever.

Bloody flux (δυσεντερίᾳ). Only here in New Testament. Our word *dysentery* is nearly a transcript of it. Hippocrates often speaks of the two complaints in combination.

Healed (ἰάσατο). See on Luke vi. 19.

10. **Honors** (τιμαῖς). The word was applied to payments for professional services, and that fact may have influenced Luke in selecting it; but it is evidently not used in that sense here.

11. **Sign.** Answering to the ship's *name* in modern times. It was the image of a god, a man, a beast, or of some other object, sculptured or painted on the prow. The figure of the guardian deity was affixed to the stern.

Castor and Pollux. Known as the *twin brothers* and the *Dioscuri*, or sons of Jove. They were regarded as tutelary deities of sailors.

16. **The centurion delivered the prisoners to the captain of the guard.** The best texts omit.

20. **I am bound** (περίκειμαι). Lit., *compassed*.

22. **We desire** (ἀξιοῦμεν). Rather, *we think it fitting*. Compare ch. xv. 38.

Sect. See on *heresies*, 2 Pet. ii. 1.

25. **Agreed not.** See on *agreed together*, ch. v. 9.

27. **Waxed gross.** See on Matt. xiii. 15.

Their ears are dull of hearing. Lit., *with their ears they heard heavily.*

Closed. See on Matt. xiii. 15.

30. **Hired house** (*μισθώματι*). Probably different from the *ξενία*, or *lodging-place*, where he resided for the first few days, perhaps as the guest of friends, though under custody, and where he received the Jews (ver. 23).

LIST OF GREEK WORDS USED BY LUKE ONLY.

(A. *Acts.*)

ἀγκάλη, arm, ii., 28
ἁγνισμός, purification, A. xxi., 26
ἄγνωστος, unknown, A. xvii., 23
ἀγοραῖος, pertaining to the market-place, base, A. xvii., 5
ἀγοραῖοι, court-days, A. xix., 38
ἄγρα, draught, v., 4, 9
ἀγράμματος, unlearned, A. iv., 13
ἀγραυλέω, abide in the field, ii., 8
ἀγωνία, agony, xxii., 44
αἰσθάνομαι, perceive, ix., 45
αἰτίαμα, complaint, A. xxv., 7
αἴτιον, fault, xxiii., 4, 14, 22; A. xix., 40
αἰχμάλωτος, captive, iv., 18, 19
ἀκατάκριτος, uncondemned, A. xvi., 37; xxii., 25
ἀκρίβεια, exactness, perfect manner, A. xxii., 3
ἀκριβέστατος, most strict, A. xxvi., 5
ἀκριβέστερον, more perfect, A. xviii., 26; xxiii., 15, 20; xxiv., 22
ἀκροατήριον, place of hearing, A. xxv., 23
ἀκωλύτως, without hindrance, A. xxviii., 31
ἀλίσγημα, pollution, A. xv., 20
ἀλλογενής, stranger, xvii., 18
ἀλλόφυλος, of another nation, A. x., 28
ἀμάρτυρος, without witness, A. xiv., 17
ἀμπελουργός, dresser of the vineyard, xiii., 7
ἀμύνομαι, defend, A. vii., 24
ἀναβαθμός, stair, A. xxi., 35, 40
ἀναβάλλομαι, put off, defer, A. xxiv., 22
ἀνάβλεψις, recovering of sight, iv., 18
ἀναβολή, delay, A. xxv., 17
ἀναγνωρίζομαι, to be made known, A. vii., 13
ἀναδείκνυμι, appoint, shew, x., 1; A. i., 24
ἀνάδειξις, shewing, i., 80
ἀναδίδωμι, deliver, A. xxiii., 33
ἀναζητέω, seek, ii., 44; A. xi., 25
ἀνάθημα, gift, offering, xxi., 5
ἀναίδεια, importunity, xi., 8
ἀναίρεσις, death, A. viii., 1; xxii., 20
ἀνακαθίζω, set up, vii., 15; A. ix., 40
ἀνάκρισις, examination, A. xxv., 26
ἀνάληψις, taking up, ix., 51
ἀναντίῤῥητος, not to be spoken against, A. xix., 36
ἀναντιῤῥήτως, without gainsaying, A. x., 29
ἀναπείθω, persuade, A. xviii., 13
ἀναπτύσσω, open, unroll, iv., 17
ἀνασκευάζω, subvert, A. xv., 24
ἀνασπάω, pull or draw up, xiv., 5; A. xi., 10
ἀνατάσσομαι, set forth in order, i., 1

ἀνατρέφω, nourish up, A. vii., 20, 21; xxii., 3

ἀναφαίνω, bring to light, appear, to sight, xix., 11; A. xxi., 3

ἀναφωνέω, speak out, i., 42

ἀνάψυξις, refreshing, A. iii., 19

ἀνέκλειπτος, that faileth not, xii., 33

ἀνένδεκτον, impossible, xvii., 1

ἀνετάζω, examine, A. xxii., 24, 29

ἀνεύθετος, not commodious, A. xxvii., 12

ἀνευρίσκω, find, ii., 16; A. xxi., 4

ἀνθομολογέομαι, give thanks, ii., 38

ἀνθυπατεύω, to be deputy or proconsul, A. xviii., 12

ἀνθύπατος, deputy, proconsul, A. xiii., 7, 8, 12; xix., 38

ἀνοικοδομέω, build again, A. xv., 16

ἀντεῖπον, gainsay, xxi., 15; A. iv., 14

ἀντιβάλλω, exchange, have one to another, xxiv., 17

ἀντικαλέω, bid again in return, xiv., 12

ἀντικρύ, over against, A. xx., 15

ἀντιπαρέρχομαι, pass by on the other side, x., 31, 32

ἀντιπέραν, over against, viii., 26

ἀντιπίπτω, resist, A. vii., 51

ἀντοφθαλμέω, bear up into (into the eye of), A. xxvii., 15

ἀνωτερικός, upper, A. xix., 1

ἀπαιτέω, ask again, require, vi., 30; xii., 20

ἀπαρτισμός, finishing, xiv., 28

ἄπειμι, go (away), A. xvii., 10

ἀπελαύνω, drive away, A. xviii., 16

ἀπελεγμός, refutation, contempt, A. xix., 27

ἀπελπίζω, hope for in return, vi., 35

ἀπερίτμητος, uncircumcised, A. vii., 51

ἀπογραφή, taxing (enrolment), ii., 2; A. v., 37

ἀποδέχομαι, receive, viii., 40; A. ii., 41; xv., 4; xviii., 27; xxiv., 3; xxviii., 30

ἀποθλίβω, press, viii., 45

ἀποκατάστασις, restitution, A. iii., 21

ἀποκλείω, shut to, xiii., 25

ἀπομάσσομαι, wipe off, x., 11

ἀποπίπτω, fall from, A., ix., 18

ἀποπλέω, sail away, A. xiii., 4; xiv., 26; xx., 15; xxvii., 1

ἀπορία, perplexity, xxi., 25

ἀποῤῥίπτω, cast, A. xxvii., 43

ἀποστοματίζω, provoke to speak, xi., 53

ἀποτινάσσω, shake off, ix., 5; A. xxviii., 5

ἀποφθέγγομαι, speak forth, A. ii., 4, 14; xxvi., 25

ἀποφορτίζομαι, unlade, A. xxi., 3

ἀποψύχω, fail at heart, xxi., 26

ἅπτω, to light, viii., 16; xi., 33; xv., 8; xxii., 55

ἀπωθέομαι, put away from, A. xiii., 46

ἀργυροκόπος, silversmith, A. xix., 24

ἀρήν (ἀρνός, ἀμνός), lamb, x., 3

ἄροτρον, plough, ix., 62

ἀρτέμων, mainsail, A. xxvii., 40

ἀρχιερατικός, of the high-priest, A. iv., 6

ἀρχιτελώνης, chief among the publicans, xix., 2

ἄσημος, mean, undistinguished, A. xxi., 39

ἀσιτία, abstinence, A. xxvii., 21

ἄσιτος, fasting, A. xxvii., 33

ἀσκέω, to exercise, A. xxiv., 16

ἀσμένως, gladly, A. ii., 41; xxi., 17

ἆσσον, close by, nearer, A. xxvii., 13

ἀστράπτω, to lighten (of lightning), xvii., 24; xxiv., 4

ἀσύμφωνος, not agreeing, A. xxviii., 25

ἀσώτως, wastefully, unsavingly, xv., 13
ἄτεκνος, without children, xx., 28, 29, 30
ἄτερ, in the absence of, without, xxii., 6, 35
αὐγή, break of day, A. xx., 11
αὐστηρός, austere, xix., 21, 22
αὐτόπτης, eye-witness, i., 2
αὐτόχειρ, with one's own hands, A. xxvii., 19
ἄφαντος, vanished out of sight, xxiv., 31
ἀφελότης, singleness, A. ii., 46
ἄφιξις, departure, A. xx., 29
ἄφνω, suddenly, A. ii., 2; xvi., 26; xxviii., 6
ἀφρός, foaming, ix., 39
ἀφυπνόω, fall asleep, viii., 23
ἀχλύς, mist, A. xiii., 11

βαθύνω, deepen, make deep, vi., 48
βαλάντιον, purse, x., 4; xii., 33; xxii., 35, 36
βασίλεια, royal mansion, king's court, vii., 25
βάσις, foot, A. iii., 7
βάτος, measure, xvi., 6
βελόνη, needle, xviii., 25
βία, violence, A. v., 26; xxi., 35; xxiv., 7; xxvii., 41
βίαιος, mighty, A. ii., 2
βίωσις, manner of life, A. xxvi., 4
βολή, a throw, cast, xxii., 41
βολίζω, to sound (with a lead), A. xxvii., 28
βουνός, hill, iii., 5; xxiii., 30
βραδυπλοέω, sail slowly, A. xxvii., 7
βρύχω, gnash, A. vii., 54
βρώσιμος, meat, xxiv., 41
βυρσεύς, tanner, A. ix., 43; x., 6, 32
βωμός, altar, A. xvii., 23

γάζα, treasure, A. viii., 27
γελάω, laugh, vi., 21, 25
γερουσία, senate, A. v., 21
γῆρας, old age, i., 36
γλεῦκος, new or sweet wine, A. ii., 13
γνώστης, expert, A. xxvi., 3

δακτύλιος, ring, xv., 22
δανειστής, creditor, vii., 41
δαπάνη, cost, xiv., 28
δεισιδαιμονέστερος, very religious, A. xvii., 22
δεισιδαιμονία, religiousness, A. xxv., 19
δεξιολάβος, spearman, A. xxiii., 23
δεσμέω, to bind, viii., 29
δεσμοφύλαξ, jailer, A. xvi., 23, 27, 36
δεσμώτης, prisoner, A. xxvii., 1, 42
δευτεραῖος, on the second day, A. xxviii., 13
δευτερόπρωτος, second after the first, vi., 1
δημηγορέω, make an oration, A. xii., 21
δῆμος, people, A. xii., 22; xvii., 5; xix., 30, 33
δημόσιος, public, open, A. v., 18; xvi., 37; xviii., 28; xx., 20
διαβάλλομαι, to be accused, xvi., 1
διαγινώσκω, judge, determine, A. xxiii., 15; xxiv., 22
διάγνωσις, decision, A. xxv., 21
διαγογγύζω, murmur, xv., 2; xix., 7
διαγρηγορέω, to keep awake, or be fully awake, ix., 32
διαδέχομαι, receive by succession, A. vii., 45
διάδοχος, successor, A. xxiv., 27
διακατελέγχομαι, convince, A. xviii., 28
διακούομαι, hear (a cause), A. xxiii., 35

διαλαλέω, noise abroad, converse, i., 65; vi., 11

διαλείπω, cease, vii., 45

διάλεκτος, tongue, dialect, A. i., 19; ii., 6, 8; xxi., 40; xxii., 2; xxvi., 14

διαλύομαι, to be scattered, A. v., 36

διαμάχομαι, strive, A. xxiii., 9

διαμερισμός, division, xii., 51

διανέμομαι, to be spread abroad, A. iv., 17

διανεύω, to beckon, i., 21

διανόημα, thought, xi., 17

διανυκτερεύω, continue all night, vi., 12

διανύω, finish, A. xxi., 7

διαπλέω, sail over, A. xxvii., 5

διαπονέομαι, to be grieved, A. iv., 2; xvi., 18

διαπορέω, to be perplexed, ix., 7; xxiv., 4; A. ii., 12; v., 24; x., 17

διαπραγματεύομαι, gain by trading, xix., 15

διαπρίομαι, to be cut to the heart; lit., *sawn*, A. v., 33; vii., 54

διασείω, do violence, iii., 14

διασπείρω, scatter abroad, A. viii., 1, 4; xi., 19

διάστημα, space, A. v., 7

διαταράττω, to trouble, i., 29

διατελέω, to continue, A. xxvii., 33

διατηρέω, to keep, ii., 51; A. xv., 29

διαφεύγω, to escape, A. xxvii., 42

διαφθορά, corruption, A. ii., 27, 31; xiii., 34, 35, 36, 37

διαφυλάττω, keep, iv., 10

διαχειρίζομαι, slay, A. v., 30; xxvi., 21

διαχλευάζω, mock, A. ii., 13

διαχωρίζομαι, depart, ix., 33

διερωτάω, make inquiry, A. x., 17

διετία, two years, A. xxiv., 27; xxviii., 30

διήγησις, declaration, i., 1

διθάλασσος, where two seas meet, A. xxvii., 41

διΐστημι, separate, intervene, put a space between, xxii., 59; xxiv., 51; A. xxvii., 28

διϊσχυρίζομαι, confidently affirm, xxii., 59; A. xii., 15

δικαστής, judge, xii., 14; A. vii., 27, 35

διοδεύω, go throughout, viii., 1; A. xvii., 1

διοπετής, fallen from Jupiter, A. xix., 35

διόρθωμα, a setting right, A. xxiv., 3

δούλη, handmaid, i., 38, 48; A. ii., 18

δοχή, feast, reception, v., 29; xiv., 13

δραχμή, drachma, xv., 8, 9

δυσεντερία, dysentery, A. xxviii., 8

δωδεκάφυλον, the twelve tribes (collective), A. xxvi., 7

ἑβδομήκοντα, seventy, x., 1, 17; A. vii., 14; xxiii., 23; xxvii., 37

ἑβραϊκός, Hebraic, xxiii., 38

ἑβραΐς, Hebrew, A. xxi., 40; xxii., 2; xxvi., 14

ἐγκάθετος, spy, xx. 20

ἔγκλημα, charge, A. xxiii., 29; xxv., 16

ἔγκυος, great with child, ii., 5

ἐδαφίζω, lay even with the ground, xix., 44

ἔδαφος, ground, A. xxii., 7

ἐθίζω, to accustom, ii., 27

εἰσκαλέω, call in, A. x., 23

εἰσπηδάω, spring in, A. xiv., 14; xvi., 29

εἰστρέχω, run in, A. xii., 14

ἑκατοντάρχης, centurion, A. x., 1, 22; xxiv., 23; xxvii., 1, 31
ἐκβολή, casting out, A. xxvii., 18
ἐκγαμίσκομαι, to be given in marriage, xx., 34, 35
ἐκδιηγέομαι, declare, A. xiii., 41; xv., 3
ἔκδοτος, delivered, A. ii., 23
ἐκεῖσε, thither, A. xxi., 3; xxii., 5
ἔκθαμβος, greatly wondering, A. iii., 11
ἔκθετος, exposed, A. vii., 19
ἐκκολυμβάω, swim out, A. xxvii., 42
ἐκκομίζομαι, to be carried out, vii., 12
ἐκκρέμαμαι, to hang upon, be attentive, xix., 48
ἐκλαλέω, tell, A. xxiii., 22
ἐκμυκτηρίζω, deride, xvi., 14; xxiii. 35
ἐκπέμπω, send forth, A. xiii., 4; xvii., 10
ἐκπλέω, sail forth, A. xv., 39; xviii., 18; xx., 6
ἐκπληρόω, fulfil, A. xiii., 33
ἐκπλήρωσις, accomplishment, A. xxi., 26
ἐκταράσσω, exceedingly trouble, A. xvi., 20
ἐκτελέω, finish, xiv., 29, 30
ἐκτένεια, intensity, A. xxvi., 7
ἐκτενέστερον, more earnestly, xxii., 44
ἐκτίθημι, cast out, set forth, expound, A. vii., 21; xi., 4; xviii., 26; xxviii., 23
ἐκχωρέω, depart out, xxi., 21
ἐκψύχω, give up the ghost, A. v., 5, 10; xii., 23
ἐλαίων, of olives, Olivet, A. i., 12
ἔλευσις, coming, A. vii., 52
ἑλκόομαι, to be ulcerated, xvi., 20
ἐμβάλλω, cast into, xii., 5
ἐμβιβάζω, cause to enter, A. xxvii., 6
ἐμμαίνομαι, to be mad, A. xxvi., 11
ἐμπιπλάω, fill, A. xiv., 17
ἐμπνέω, breathe, A. ix., 1
ἔναντι, before, i., 8
ἐνδεής, needy, A. iv., 34
ἐνδέχεται, it is admissible or possible, xiii., 33
ἐνδιδύσκομαι, to be clothed, viii., 27; xvi., 19
ἐνέδρα, a lying in wait, A. xxiii., 16; xxv., 3
ἐνεδρεύω, to lie in wait, xi., 54; xxiii., 21
ἔνειμι, to be in (ye have), xi., 41
ἐνισχύω, to strengthen, xxii., 43; A. ix., 19
ἐννέα, nine, xvii., 17
ἐνεός, speechless, A. ix., 7
ἐννεύω, make signs, i., 62
ἐντόπιος, belonging to a place, A. xxi., 12
ἐνύπνιον, dream, A. ii., 17
ἐνωτίζομαι, hearken, A. ii., 14
ἐξαιτέομαι, to desire, xxii., 31
ἐξάλλομαι, leap up, A. iii., 8
ἐξαστράπτω, to be glistering, ix., 29
ἔξειμι, depart, A. xiii., 42; xvii., 15; xx., 7; xxvii., 43
ἑξῆς, next (day), vii., 11; ix., 37; A. xxi., 1; xxv., 17; xxvii., 18
ἐξολοθρεύομαι, to be destroyed, A. iii., 23
ἐξορκιστής, exorcist, A. xix., 13
ἐξοχή, eminence, A. xxv., 23
ἔξυπνος, out of sleep, awakened, A. xvi., 27
ἐξώθω, drive out, A. vii., 45; xxvii., 39
ἐπαθροίζομαι, to be gathered thickly together, xi., 29
ἐπαιτέω, to beg, xvi., 3
ἐπακροάομαι, to listen, A. xvi., 25
ἐπάναγκες, necessary, A. xv., 28

ἐπανέρχομαι, to return, x., 35; xix., 15
ἐπαρχία, province, A. xxiii., 34; xxv., 1
ἔπαυλις, habitation, A. i., 20
ἐπεγείρω, stir up, A. xiii., 50; xiv., 2
ἐπειδήπερ, forasmuch, i., 1
ἐπέκεινα, beyond, A. vii., 43
ἐπιβιβάζω, to set upon, x., 34; xix., 35; A. xxiii., 24
ἐπιβοάω, to cry out upon, A. xxv., 24
ἐπιβουλή, plot, A. ix., 24; xx., 3, 19; xxiii., 30
ἐπιγίνομαι, spring up, arise, A. xxviii., 13
ἐπιδημέω, to dwell as a stranger, A. ii., 10; xvii., 21
ἐπικουρία, help, A. xxvi., 22
ἐπικρίνω, give sentence, xxiii., 24
ἐπιλείχω, lick, xvi., 21
ἐπιμέλεια, care, A. xxvii., 3
ἐπιμελῶς, diligently, xv., 8
ἐπινεύω, to consent, A. xviii., 20
ἐπίνοια, thought, A. viii., 22
ἐπιοῦσα, next (day), A. vii., 26; xvi., 11; xx., 15; xxi., 18; xxiii., 11
ἐπιπορεύομαι, to come to, viii., 4
ἐπισιτισμός, victuals, ix., 12
ἐπισκευάζω, to prepare baggage, A. xxi., 15
ἐπίστασις, a stirring up, A. xxiv., 12
ἐπιστάτης, master, v., 5; viii., 24, 45; ix., 33, 49; xvii., 13
ἐπιστηρίζω, confirm, A. xiv., 22; xv., 32, 41; xviii., 23
ἐπιστροφή, conversion, A. xv., 3
ἐπισφαλής, dangerous, A. xxvii., 9
ἐπισχύω, to grow stronger, become more vehement, xxiii., 5
ἐπιτροπή, commission, A. xxvi., 12
ἐπιφανής, notable, A. ii., 20
ἐπιφωνέω, cry upon or against, xxiii., 21; A. xii., 22; xxii., 24

ἐπιχειρέω, take in hand, i., 1; A. ix., 29; xix., 13
ἐπιχέω, pour upon, x., 34
ἐποκέλλω, run aground, A. xxvii., 41
ἐρείδω, stick fast, A. xxvii., 41
ἔσθησις, raiment, xxiv., 4
ἑσπέρα, evening, xxiv., 29; A. iv., 3; xxviii., 23
εὐεργετέω, do good, A. x., 38
εὐεργέτης, benefactor, xxii., 25
εὐθυδρομέω, run straight, A. xvi., 11; xxi., 1
εὔθυμος, of good cheer, A. xxvii., 36
εὐθυμότερον, more cheerfully, A. xxiv., 10
εὐλαβής, devout, ii., 25; A. ii., 5; viii., 2
εὐπορέομαι, to prosper, A. xi., 29
εὐπορία, prosperity, A. xix., 25
εὐτόνως, vehemently, strongly, xxiii., 10; A. xviii., 28
εὐφορέω, bring forth plentifully, xii., 16
ἐφάλλομαι, leap upon, A. xix., 16
ἐφημερία, course (of priests), i., 5, 8
ἐφοράω, look upon, i., 25; A. iv., 29

ζεῦγος, pair, yoke, ii., 24; xiv., 19
ζευκτηρία, rudder-bands, A. xxvii., 40
ζήτημα, question, A. xv., 2; xviii., 15; xxiii., 29; xxv., 19; xxvi., 3
ζωογονέω, to preserve alive, xvii., 33; A. vii., 19

ἡγεμονία, reign, iii., 1
ἡγεμονεύω, to be governor, ii., 2; iii., 1

θάμβος, amazement, iv., 36; v., 9; A. iii., 10
θάρσος, courage, A. xxviii., 15

θεά, goddess, A. xix., 27, 35, 37
θεομαχέω, to fight against God, A. xxiii., 9
θεομάχος, a fighting against God, A. v., 39
θέρμη, heat, A. xxviii., 3
θεωρία, a sight, xxiii., 48
θηρεύω, to catch (as a hunter), xi., 54
θορυβάζομαι, to be troubled, x., 41
θραύω, bruise, iv., 18
θρόμβος, great drop, xxii., 44
θυμιάω, to burn incense, i., 9
θυμομαχέω, to be highly displeased, A. xii., 20

ἴασις, cure, healing, xiii., 32; A. iv., 22, 30
ἱδρώς, sweat, xxii., 44
ἱερατεύω, to perform the priest's duty, i., 8
ἱερόσυλος, robber of temples, A. xix., 37
ἰκμάς, moisture, viii., 6
ἱππεύς, horseman, A. xxiii., 23, 32
ἰσάγγελος, equal to the angels, xx., 36
ἴσως, perhaps, xx., 13

καθάπτω, fasten, seize upon, A. xxviii., 3
καθεξῆς, in order or succession, i., 3; viii., 1; A. iii., 24; xi., 4; xviii., 23
καθημερινός, daily, A. vi., 1
καθίημι, let down, v., 19; A. ix., 25; x., 11; xi., 5
καθόλου, at all, A. iv., 18
καθοπλίζομαι, to be fully armed, xi., 21
καθότι, because, according as, i., 7; xix., 9; A. ii., 24, 45; iv., 35
κάκωσις, affliction, A. vii., 34
καρδιογνώστης, knower of the heart, A. i., 24; xv., 8
καρποφόρος, fruitful, A. xiv., 17
κατάβασις, descent, xix., 37
καταγγελεύς, setter forth, A. xvii., 18
καταδέω, bind up, x., 34
κατακλείω, shut up, iii., 20; A. xxvi., 10
κατακληροδοτέω, divide by lot, A. xiii., 19
κατακλίνω, to make recline, ix., 14; xiv., 8; xxiv., 30
κατακολουθέω, follow after, xxiii., 55; A. xvi., 17
κατακρημνίζω, to cast down headlong, iv., 29
καταλιθάζω, to stone, xx., 6
κατάλοιπος, residue, A. xv., 17
καταμένω, abide, i., 13
κατανεύω, beckon, v., 7
κατανύσσω, to prick or pierce, A. ii., 37
καταπίπτω, to fall down, A. xxvi., 14; xxviii., 6
καταπλέω, arrive at (by sea), viii., 26
καταριθμέομαι, to be numbered with, A. i., 17
κατασείω, to move (the hand), as a signal of silence, A. xii., 17; xiii., 16; xix., 33; xxi., 40
κατασοφίζομαι, deal subtly with, A. vii., 19
καταστέλλω, to appease, quiet, A. xix., 35, 36
κατασύρω, to drag along, xii., 58
κατασφάττω, slay, xix., 27
κατάσχεσις, possession, A. vii., 5, 45
κατατρέχω, run down, A. xxi., 32
καταφέρω, bear down; oppress, A. xx., 9; xxvi., 10
καταφρονητής, despiser, A. xiii., 41
καταψύχω, to cool, xvi., 24
κατείδωλος, full of idols, A. xvii., 16

κατοικία, habitation, A. xvii., 26
κέραμος, tiling, v., 19
κεράτιον, husk, xv., 16
κηρίον, comb (honey), xxiv., 42
κλάσις, breaking, xxiv., 35; A. ii., 42
κλινίδιον, couch, v., 19, 24
κλισία, company (at table), ix., 14
κοιτών, bedchamber, A. xii., 20
κολυμβάω, swim, A. xxvii., 43
κολωνία, colony, A. xvi., 12
κοπετός, lamentation, A. viii., 2
κοπρία, dung, xiii., 8; xiv., 35
κόραξ, raven, xii., 24
κόρος, measure, xvi., 7
κουφίζω, lighten (as a ship), A. xxvii., 38
κραιπάλη, surfeiting, xxi., 34
κράτιστος, most excellent, i., 3; A. xxiii., 26; xxiv., 3; xxvi., 25
κτήτωρ, possessor, A. iv., 34

λακέω, burst asunder, A. i., 18
λακτίζω, to kick, A. xxvi., 14
λαξευτός, rock-hewn, xxiii., 53
λεῖος, smooth, iii., 5
λεπίς, a scale, A. ix., 18
λῆρος, tattle, idle talk, xxiv., 11
λιμήν, a haven, A. xxvii., 8, 12
λίψ, the southwest wind, A. xxvii., 12
λόγιος, eloquent, A. xviii., 24
λυμαίνομαι, to make havoc, A. viii., 3
λυσιτελεῖ, it is better, xvii., 2
λυτρωτής, deliverer, A. vii., 35

μαγεία, sorcery, A. viii., 11
μαγεύω, to use sorcery, A. viii., 9
μαθήτρια, female disciple, A. ix., 36
μακροθύμως, patiently, A. xxvi., 3
μανία, madness, A. xxvi., 24
μαντεύομαι, to divine, practise soothsaying, A. xvi., 16
μαστίζω, to scourge, A. xxvi., 25
μεγαλεῖα, great things, i., 49; A. ii., 11
μελίσσιος, of honey, xxiv., 42
μεριστής, divider, xii., 14
μεσημβρία, south, A. viii., 26; xxii., 6
μεστόω, to fill, A. ii., 13
μεταβάλλομαι, to change one's mind, A. xxviii., 6
μετακαλέομαι, call for, A. vii., 14; x., 32; xx., 17; xxiv., 25
μεταπέμπω, send for, A. x., 5, 22, 29; xi., 13; xxiv., 24, 26; xxv., 3
μετεωρίζομαι, to be of doubtful mind, xii., 29
μετοικίζω, to remove the dwelling-place, A. vii., 4, 43
μετρίως, moderately, A. xx., 12
μηδαμῶς, by no means, not so, A. x., 14; xi., 8
μίσθιος, hired, salaried, xv., 17, 19
μίσθωμα, hired house, A. xxviii., 30
μνᾶ, pound, mina, xix., 13, 16, 18, 20, 24, 25
μόγις, hardly, ix., 39
μοσχοποιέω, to make a calf, A. vii., 41

ναύκληρος, ship-owner, A. xxvii., 11
ναῦς, ship, A. xxvii., 41
νεανίας, young man, A. vii., 58; xx., 9; xxiii., 17, 18, 22
νεοσσός, young (especially of birds), ii., 24
νεωκόρος, temple-sweeper, xix., 35
νησίον, island, A. xxvii., 16
νοσσιά, brood, xiii., 34

ὀγδοήκοντα, fourscore, ii., 37; xvi., 7
ὁδεύω, to journey, x., 33
ὁδοιπορέω, to go on one's journey, A. x., 9
ὀδυνάομαι, to be sorrowful, ii., 48; xvi., 24, 25; A. xx., 38

ὀθόνη, sheet, A. x., 11; xi., 5
οἴκημα, cell, A. xii., 7
οἰκονομέω, to be a steward, xvi., 2
ὀκνέω, to delay, A. ix., 38
ὁλοκληρία, perfect soundness, A. iii., 16
ὄμβρος, shower, xii., 54
ὁμιλέω, talk together, commune, xxiv., 14, 15; A. xx., 11; xxiv., 26
ὁμότεχνος, of the same craft, A. xviii., 3
ὄνειδος, reproach, i., 25
ὁπότε, when, vi., 3
ὀπτάνομαι, to be seen, A. i., 3
ὀπτός, broiled, xxiv., 42
ὀργυιά, fathom, A. xxvii., 28
ὀρεινός, hilly, mountainous, i., 39, 65
ὀρθρίζω, to rise early, xxi., 38
ὁροθεσία, boundary, A. xvii., 26
οὐρανόθεν, from heaven, A. xiv., 17; xxvi., 13
οὐσία, substance, property, xv., 12, 13
ὀφρύς, brow, iv., 29
ὀχλοποιέω, gather a company, A. xvii., 5

παθητός, destined to suffer, A. xxvi., 23
παμπληθεί, all at once, xxiii., 18
πανδοχεῖον, inn, x., 34
πανδοχεύς, host, x., 35
πανοικί, with all one's house, A. xvi., 34
πάντη, always, A. xxiv., 3
παραβιάζομαι, constrain, xxiv., 29; A. xvi., 15
παράδοξος, strange, v., 26
παραθεωρέω, neglect, A. vi., 1
παραινέω, admonish, A. xxvii., 9, 22
παρακαθίζω, sit by, x., 39
παρακαλύπτω, to hide, ix., 45
παραλέγομαι, to sail near by, A. xxvii., 8, 13
παράλιος, near or by the sea, vi., 17
παρανομέω, to transgress law, A. xxiii., 3
παραπλέω, to sail by, A. xx., 16
παράσημος, sign or emblem, A. xxviii., 11
παρατείνω, continue, prolong, A. xx., 7
παρατήρησις, observation, xvii., 20
παρατυγχάνω, fall in with, meet, A. xvii., 17
παραχειμασία, wintering near or at, A. xxvii., 12
παρενοχλέω, trouble, A. xv., 19
παρθενία, virginity, ii., 36
παροίχομαι, to pass away, A. xiv., 16
παροτρύνω, stir up, A. xiii., 50
πατρῷος, of the fathers, A. xxii., 3; xxiv., 14; xxviii., 17
πεδινός, plain, vi., 17
πεζεύω, to go afoot, A. xx., 13
πειράω, attempt, A. ix., 26; xxvi., 21
πενιχρός, poor, xxi., 2
πεντεκαιδέκατος, fifteenth, iii., 1
περιάπτω, kindle, xxii., 55
περιαστράπτω, shine round about, A. ix., 3; xxii., 6
περικρατής, master (of the boat), A. xxvii., 16
περικρύπτω, hide, i., 24
περικυκλόω, compass round, xix., 43
περιλάμπω, shine round about, ii., 9; A. xxvi., 13
περιμένω, wait for, A. i., 4
πέριξ, round about, A. v., 16
περιοικέω, dwell round about, i., 65
περίοικος, neighbor, i., 58
περιοχή, place, contents of a passage (of scripture), A. viii., 32
περιῤῥήγνυμι, rend off, A. xvi., 22

περισπάομαι, to be cumbered, x., 40
περιτρέπω, pervert, A. xxvi., 24
πήγανον, rue, xi., 42
πιέζω, press down, vi., 38
πίμπραμαι, to be inflamed or swollen, A. xxviii., 6
πινακίδιον, writing-tablet, i., 63
πλέω, to sail, viii., 23; A. xxi., 3; xxvii., 2, 6, 24
πλημμύρα, flood, vi., 48
πλόος, sailing, voyage, A. xxi., 7; xxvii., 9, 10
πολιτάρχης, ruler of the city, A. xvii., 6, 8
πολίτης, citizen, xv., 15; xix., 14; A. xxi., 39
πολλαπλασίων, manifold more, xviii., 30
πορφυρόπωλις, seller of purple, A. xvi., 14
πραγματεύομαι, to trade, xix., 13
πράκτωρ, officer, exactor, xii., 58
πρεσβεία, embassy, xiv., 32; xix., 14
πρηνής, headlong, A. i., 18
προβάλλω, put forward, xxi., 30; A. xix., 33
προκηρύσσω, preach before (time), A. iii., 20; xiii., 24
προμελετάω, meditate beforehand, xxi., 14
προοράω, see before, A. ii., 25; xxi., 29
προπορεύομαι, go before, i., 76; A. vii., 40
προσαναβαίνω, go up, xiv., 10
προσαναλίσκω, spend, viii., 43
προσαπειλέομαι, threaten farther, A. iv., 21
προσδαπανάω, spend more, x., 35
προσδέομαι, to need, xvii., 25
προσδοκία, expectation, xxi., 26; A. xii., 11
προσεάω, permit, A. xxvii., 7
προσεργάζομαι, gain, xix., 16
προσκληρόομαι, consort with, A. xvii., 4
προσλαλέω, speak to, A. xiii., 43; xxviii., 20
πρόσπεινος, very hungry, A. x., 10
προσπήγνυμι, crucify, A. ii., 23
προσποιέομαι, make as though, xxiv., 28
προσρήγνυμι, beat vehemently upon, vi., 48, 49
προσφάτως, lately, A. xviii., 2
προσψαύω, touch, xi., 46
προσωπολήμπτης, respecter of persons, A. x., 34
προτάσσομαι, be appointed beforehand, A. xvii., 26
προτείνω, bind, A. xxii., 25
προτρέπομαι, exhort, A. xviii., 27
προϋπάρχω, to be beforetime, xxiii., 12; A. viii., 9
προφέρω, bring forth, vi., 45
προχειρίζομαι, choose, appoint, A. xxii., 14; xxvi., 16
προχειροτονέομαι, to be chosen before, A. x., 41
πρώρα, prow, A. xxvii., 30, 41
πρωτοστάτης, ringleader, A. xxiv., 5
πτοέομαι, to be terrified, xxi., 9; xxiv., 37
πτύσσω, to roll together (a parchment), iv., 20
πυρά, fire, A. xxviii., 2, 3

ῥαβδοῦχος, serjeant, A. xvi., 35, 38
ῥᾳδιούργημα, crime, villany, A. xviii., 14
ῥᾳδιουργία, villany, mischief, A. xiii., 10
ῥῆγμα, ruin, vi., 49
ῥήτωρ, orator, A. xxiv., 1
ῥώννυμαι, farewell, A. xv., 29; xxiii., 30

σάλος, swell of the sea, billows, xxi., 25
σανίς, board, A. xxvii., 44
σεβαστός, Augustan, A. xxvii., 1
σικάριος, assassin, A. xxi., 38
σίκερα, strong drink, i., 15
σιμικίνθιον, apron, A. xix., 12
σινιάζω, sift, xxii., 31
σιτομέτριον, portion of meat, xii., 42
σκάπτω, dig, vi., 48; xiii., 8; xvi., 3
σκάφη, boat, A. xxvii., 16, 30, 32
σκευή, tackling, A. xxvii., 19
σκηνοποιός, tent-maker, A. xviii., 3
σκιρτάω, leap, frisk, i., 41, 44; vi., 23
σκληροτράχηλος, stiff-necked, A. vii., 51
σκῦλα, spoils, xi., 22
σορός, bier, vii., 14
σπαργανόω, wrap in swaddling-clothes, ii., 7, 12
σπερμολόγος, babbler, A. xvii., 18
στέμμα, garland, A. xiv., 13
στερεόω, to strengthen, A. iii., 7, 16; xvi., 5
στιγμή, moment (of time), iv., 5
στρατηγός, captain, magistrate, xxii., 4, 52; A. iv., 1; v., 24, 26; xvi., 20–38
στρατία, host, ii., 13; A. vii., 42
στρατοπεδάρχης, captain of the guard, A. xxviii., 16
στρατόπεδον, army, xxi., 20
συγγένεια, kindred, i., 61; A. vii., 3, 14
συγγενίς, kinswoman, i., 36
συγκαλύπτομαι, to be covered, xii., 2
συγκαταβαίνω, to go down with, A. xxv., 5
συγκατατίθεμαι, to consent, xxiii., 51
συγκαταψηφίζομαι, to be numbered with, A. i., 26
συγκινέω, stir up, A. vi., 12
συγκομίζω, carry away (for burial), A. viii., 2
συγκύπτω, to be bent together, xiii., 11
συγκυρία, chance, coincidence, x., 31
συγχέω, stir up, A. xxi., 27
συγχύνω, confound or confuse, A. ii., 6; ix., 22; xix., 32; xxi., 31
σύγχυσις, confusion, A. xix., 29
συζήτησις, disputation, A. xv., 2, 7; xxviii., 29
συκάμινος, sycamine, xvii., 6
συκομωραία, sycamore, xix., 4
συκοφαντέω, accuse falsely, iii., 14; xix., 8
συλλογίζομαι, to reason together, xx., 5
συμβάλλω, to put together in mind, ponder, confer, encounter, meet, help, ii., 19; xiv., 31; A. iv., 15; xvii., 18; xviii., 27; xx., 14
συμπάρειμι, to be present with, A. xxv., 24
συμπεριλαμβάνω, embrace, A. xx., 10
συμπίνω, drink with, A. x., 41
συμπίπτω, fall in, vi., 49
συμπληρόω, fill; of time, to come fully, viii., 23; ix., 51; A. ii., 1
συμφύομαι, spring up with, viii., 7
συμφωνία, music, xv., 25
συμψηφίζω, count, or reckon up, A. xix., 19
συναθροίζω, gather together, xxiv., 33; A. xii., 12; xix., 25
συναλίζομαι, to be assembled together, A. i., 4
συναρπάζω, catch, viii., 29; A. vi., 12; xix., 29; xxvii., 15
συνδρομή, a running together, concourse, A. xxi., 30
σύνειμι, to be with, x., 18; A. xxii., 11

σύνειμι (*εἶμι, to go*), to be gathered together, viii., 4
συνελαύνω, set at one, A. vii., 26
συνέπομαι, accompany, A. xx., 4
συνεφίστημι, assail together, A. xvi., 22
συνθρύπτω, break, A. xxi., 13
συνοδεύω, journey with, A. ix., 7
συνοδία, company (of travellers), ii., 44
συνομιλέω, talk with, A. x., 27
συνομορέω, to border together, to adjoin, A. xviii., 7
συντόμως, concisely, A. xxiv., 4
σύντροφος, brought up with, A. xiii., 1
συντυγχάνω, to come to, or at, viii., 19
συνωμοσία, conspiracy, A. xxiii., 13
σύρτις, quicksand, A. xxvii., 17
συσπαράσσω, to tear, ix., 42
συστρέφω, gather, A. xxviii., 3
συστροφή, concourse, A. xix., 40; xxiii., 12
σφάγιον, victim, slain beast, A. vii., 42
σφοδρῶς, exceedingly, A. xxvii., 18
σφυρόν, ankle-bone, A. iii., 7
σχολή, school, A. xix., 9

τακτός, set, appointed, A. xii., 21
ταννῦν, now, A. iv., 29; v., 38; xvii., 30; xx., 32; xxvii., 22
τάραχος, stir, A. xii., 18; xix., 23
τάχιστα, with all speed, A. xvii., 5
τεκμήριον, proof, A. i., 3
τελεσφορέω, bring fruit to perfection, viii., 14
τεσσαρακονταετής, period of forty years, A. vii., 23
τεσσαρεσκαιδέκατος, fourteenth, A. xxvii., 27, 33
τετράδιον, quaternion, A. xii., 4
τετραπλόος, fourfold, xix., 8
τετραρχέω, to be tetrarch, iii., 1
τιμωρέω, punish, A. xxii., 5; xxvi., 11
τοῖχος, wall, A. xxiii., 3
τραῦμα, wound, x., 34
τραυματίζω, to wound, xx., 12; A. xix., 16
τραχύς, rough, iii., 5; A. xxvii., 29
τρῆμα, eye (of a needle), xviii., 25
τρίστεγον, third loft, A. xx., 9
τρισχίλιοι, three thousand, A. ii., 41
τροφοφορέω, to bear as a nursing father, A. xiii., 18
τρυγών, turtle-dove, ii., 24
τυφωνικός, tempestuous, whirling, A. xxvii., 14

ὑγρός, moist, fresh, green, xxiii., 31
ὑδρωπικός, a dropsical person, xiv., 2
ὑπερείδω, overlook, A. xvii., 30
ὑπερεκχύνομαι, run over, vi., 38
ὑπερῷον, upper room, A. i., 13; ix., 37, 39; xx., 8
ὑπηρετέω, serve, minister, A. xiii., 36; xx., 34; xxiv., 23
ὑποβάλλω, suborn, A. vi., 11
ὑποζώννυμι, undergird, A. xxvii., 17
ὑποκρίνομαι, feign, xx., 20
ὑπολαμβάνω, suppose, answer, receive, vii., 43; x., 30; A. i., 9; ii., 15
ὑπονοέω, think, suppose, A. xiii., 25; xxv., 18; xxvii., 27
ὑποπλέω, sail under, A. xxvii., 4, 7
ὑποπνέω, blow softly, A. xxvii., 13
ὑποστρώννυμι, spread, xix., 36
ὑποτρέχω, run under, A. xxvii., 16
ὑποχωρέω, withdraw, v., 16; ix., 10

φαντασία, pomp, A. xxv., 23
φάραγξ, valley, iii., 5
φάσις, tidings, A. xxi., 31

φάτνη, manger, ii., 7, 12, 16; xiii., 15
φιλανθρώπως, courteously, A. xxvii., 3
φιλονεικία, strife, xxii., 24
φιλόσοφος, philosopher, A. xvii., 18
φιλοφρόνως, courteously, A. xxviii., 7
φόβητρον, a terror, fearful sight, xxi., 11
φόρτος, lading, A. xxvii., 10
φρονίμως, wisely, xvi., 8
φρυάσσω, rage, A. iv., 25
φρύγανον, stick, A. xxviii., 3
φυλακίζω, imprison, A. xxii., 19
φύλαξ, keeper, A. v., 23; xii., 6, 19

χάραξ, trench, xix., 43
χάσμα, gulf, x., 26
χειμάζομαι, to be tempest-tossed, A. xxvii., 18
χειραγωγέω, lead by the hand, A. ix., 8; xxii., 11
χειραγωγός, one leading by the hand, A. xiii., 11
χλευάζω, mock, A. xvii., 32
χορός, dancing, xv., 25
χόρτασμα, sustenance, A. vii., 11
χράω, lend, xi., 5
χρεωφειλέτης, debtor, vii., 41; xvi., 5
χρονοτριβέω, spend time, A. xx., 16
χρώς, body, skin, A. xix., 12
χῶρος, northwest, A. xxvii., 12

ψώχω, to rub, vi., 1

ὠνέομαι, to buy, A. vii., 16
ᾠόν, egg, xi., 12

INTRODUCTION TO THE EPISTLES OF JAMES, PETER, AND JUDE.

The name "catholic" is applied to the epistle of James, the two epistles of Peter, the three of John, and the epistle of Jude. The term is variously explained, some regarding it as equivalent to *canonical*, others as opposed to *heretical*, and as applied to writings which agree with the doctrines of the universal church. Others, again, suppose that this group of epistles was so designated, in order to distinguish it from the two other groups formed by the Gospels and Acts, and the Pauline epistles, as a *general* collection of the writings of other apostles.

The better explanation is that they are called "catholic," or *general*, because addressed to no particular church or individual, but to a number of scattered churches or people (see 1 Pet. i. 1, and James i. 1). In this sense the term does not strictly apply to the second and third epistles of John, which are addressed to individuals, and includes them only when regarded in the light of appendices to the first epistle. We speak in this Introduction of the epistles of James, Peter, and Jude only, reserving remarks on the epistles of John for the general introduction to the Johannine writings, in the second volume.

THE EPISTLE OF JAMES.

According to the oldest arrangement of the New Testament, the epistle of James stands first in order of all the apostolical epistles. The most competent critics generally agree in designating as its author James, the president of the church at Jerusalem, and known as the *Lord's brother*.

"No doubt," says Dean Stanley, "if we look at James' influence and authority from the more general point of view, whether of the whole Jewish Christian world or of the whole Gentile Christian world, it sinks into nothing before the majesty of Peter and Paul;" but within the circle of the purely Palestinian Christians, and in Jerusalem, James is the chief representative of the Christian society. The later traditions of the Jewish Christians invest him with a priestly sanctity. His austerities and devotions are described in extravagant terms. He is said to have kneeled until his knees were as hard as the knees of camels, and to have been constant in prayer in the temple. He went barefoot, and practised abstinence from wine, and wore the long hair, the linen ephod, and the unshorn beard of the Nazarites, and even abstained from washing. He was known as "The Just." The people vied with each other to touch the hem of his garment; and he is reputed to have called down rain in the drought, after the manner of Elijah. His chair was preserved as a relic until the fourth century, and a pillar in the valley of Jehoshaphat marked the spot where he fell.

The account of his martyrdom is given by Eusebius from the lost work of Hegesippus, by Josephus, and in the Clementine Recognitions. In Hegesippus and the Recognitions, the story is dramatic and deeply tinged with romance. The narrative of the former "is," says Dr. Schaff, "an overdrawn picture of the middle of the second century, colored by Judaizing traits, which may have been derived from 'the Ascents of James' and other apocryphal sources." It is, substantially, as follows: Having been asked, "What is the gate of Jesus?" he replied that he was the Saviour; from which some believed that Jesus is the Christ. The Jews and Scribes and Pharisees, becoming alarmed, came to James, and besought him to restrain the people from going after Jesus, to persuade against him all that came to the Passover, and, with this view, to stand on the pinnacle of the temple, where he might be seen and heard by all the people. They accordingly placed him there, and said, "O Just One, to whom we all give heed, inasnuch as the people is gone astray after Jesus who is crucified, tell us what is the gate of Jesus?" He answered, with a loud voice, "Why ask ye me concerning Jesus, the Son of man? He sits in heaven, on the right hand of the mighty power, and he is also about to come in the clouds of heaven." Many being convinced, and saying, "Hosanna to the Son of David!" the Scribes and Pharisees said, "We have done ill in furnishing so great a testimony to Jesus. Let us go and cast him down." They went up then and threw him down, and as he was not killed by the fall they began to stone him. And he, turning round, knelt and said, "I beseech thee, Lord God and Father, forgive them, for they know not what they do." But while they were thus stoning him, one of the priests, of the sons of Rechab, cried, saying, "Stop! what do ye? The Just One prays for you;" and one of them, one of the fullers, took the club with which he used to press the cloths, and struck it on the head of the Just One. And so he bore witness, and they buried him on the place by the temple.

The epistle was probably written from Jerusalem, where James would be likely to become acquainted with the condition of the Jews, through those who came up at the feasts. Certain allusions in the epistle go to confirm this. The comparison of the double-minded man to a wave of the sea (i. 6), and the picture of the ships (iii. 4), might well be written by one dwelling near the sea and familiar with it. The illustrations in iii. 11, 12—the figs, the oil, the wine, the salt and bitter springs—are furnished by Palestine, as are the drought (v. 17, 18), the former and the latter rain (v. 7), and the hot, parching wind (i. 11), for which the name *καύσων* was specially known in Palestine.

The epistle is written from a Jewish stand-point. "Christianity appears in it, not as a new dispensation, but as a development and perfection of the old. The Christian's highest honor is not that he is a member of the universal church, but that he is the genuine type of the ancient Israelite. It reveals no new principle of spiritual life, such as those which were to turn the world upside down in the teaching of Paul or of John, but only that pure and perfect morality which was the true fulfilment of the law" (Stanley). Twice only the name of Christ occurs (i. 1; ii. 1); the word "gospel" not at all; and there is no allusion to Redemption, Incarnation, Resurrection, or Ascension. The rules of morality which he lays down are enforced by Jewish rather than by Christian motives and sanctions. The violation of the "royal law" is menaced with the sentence of the law (ii. 8, 13); and uncharitable judgment is deprecated on the ground of the law's condemnation, and not as alien to the spirit of Christ.

At the same time, the very legalism of the epistle is the outgrowth of the Sermon on the Mount, the language of which it reflects more than any other book of the New Testament. It meets the formalism, the fatalism, the hypocrisy, the arrogance, insolence, and oppression engendered by the sharp social distinctions of the age, with a teaching conceived in the spirit, and often expressed in the forms of the Great Teacher's moral code. "The epistle," says Dr. Scott, "strikes the ear from beginning to end as an echo of the oral teaching of our Lord. There is scarcely a thought in it which cannot be traced to Christ's personal teaching. If John has lain on the Saviour's bosom, James has sat at his feet."

The following correspondences may be noted:

MATTHEW.	JAMES.
v. 3.	i. 9; ii. 5.
v. 4.	iv. 9.
v. 7, 9.	ii. 13; iii. 17.
v. 8.	iv. 8.
v. 9.	iii. 18.
v. 11, 12.	i. 2; v. 10, 11.
v. 19.	i. 19 seq., 25; ii. 10, 11.
v. 22.	i. 20.
v. 27.	ii. 10, 11.
v. 34 seq.	v. 12.
v. 48.	i. 4.
vi. 15.	ii. 13.
vi. 19.	v. 2 seq.
vi. 24.	iv. 4.
vi. 25.	iv. 13–16.
vii. 1 seq.	iii. 1; iv. 11 seq.

MATTHEW.	JAMES.
vii. 2.	ii. 13.
vii. 7, 11.	i. 5, 17.
vii. 8.	iv. 3.
vii. 12.	ii. 8.
vii. 16.	iii. 12.
vii. 21–26.	i. 22; ii. 14; v. 7–9.

The style and diction of the epistle are strongly marked. Links connecting them with the historic individuality of the writer, which are so numerous in the case of Peter, are almost entirely wanting. The expression, "Hearken, my beloved brethren" (ii. 5), suggests the similar phrase, Acts xv. 13; and the ordinary Greek greeting, χαίρειν, *hail* (Acts xv. 23), is repeated in Jas. i. 1; the only two places where it occurs in a Christian epistle. The purity of the Greek, and its comparative freedom from Hebraisms, are difficult to account for in a writer who had passed his life in Jerusalem. The style is sententious and antithetic; the thoughts not linked in logical connection, but massed in groups of short sentences, like the proverbial sayings of the Jews; with which class of literature the writer was evidently familiar. His utterance glows with the fervor of his spirit; it is rapid, exclamatory, graphic, abrupt, sometimes poetical in form, and moving with a rhythmical cadence. "It combines pure and eloquent and rhythmical Greek with Hebrew intensity of expression."

THE EPISTLES OF PETER.

The life and character of the apostle Peter are familiar to all readers of the Gospels and Acts. It has already been shown in the Introduction to the Gospel of Mark how the style and diction of that gospel exhibit the influence of Peter, and how the characteristics which appear in the Acts, in those scenes in which Peter was the only or the principal actor, reappear in the second gospel. If these epistles are from his pen, we may therefore expect to find in them traces of the keen-sightedness, the ready application of what is observed, and the impulsiveness and promptness which appear in the other two books, always allowing for the difference between a narrative and a hortatory style.

It has been observed that "the sight, and what it should do and reap, fills a great space in Peter's letters." Accordingly, we read that God's salvation is ready to be *revealed* in the last time (1, i. 5); the angels desire to *look into* the mysteries of the gospel (1, i. 12); Christ was *manifested* at the end of the times (1, i. 20); the Gentiles shall *behold* your good works (1, ii. 12); unbelieving husbands shall be convinced by *beholding* the chaste behavior of their wives (1, iii. 2); the apostle was a *witness* of Christ's sufferings (1, v. 1), and an *eye-witness* of his majesty (2, i. 16); the elders must exercise *oversight* of the flock (1, v. 2). Similarly he speaks of the day of *visitation*, or, lit., *overlooking* (1, ii. 12); Christ is the *bishop*, lit., *overseer*, of souls (1, ii. 25); he who lacks Christian graces is *blind, seeing only what is near* (2, i. 9); Lot was vexed at *seeing* the wickedness of his neighbors (2, ii. 8); the wicked have *eyes* full of adultery (2, ii. 14).

Equally apparent is his readiness to apply what he sees and hears. "Not one thought," says Canon Cook, "connected with the mystery of salvation is presented without an instant and emphatic reference to what a Christian ought to feel, and what he ought to do. No place in the spiritual temple is so humble that he who holds it has not before him the loftiest sphere of spiritual action and thought. Injunctions which touch the heart most powerfully are impressed upon us as we contemplate the eternal glory, the manifestations of Christ's love." Thus we have sanctification of the spirit *unto obedience* (1, i. 2); be holy in *living* (1, i. 15). The first epistle abounds in exhortations to personal religion (ii. 10–18; iii. 1–16; iv. 1–11; v. 1–9). Christian graces shall make believers to be neither *idle* nor *unfruitful* (2, i. 8); they shall not fall if they *do* these things (2, i. 10); he exhorts to holy *living* and *godliness* (2, iii. 11).

It is in such pointed and practical exhortations as these that the prompt and energetic character of the apostle reappears. Dr. Davidson observes that the writer is "zealous, but mild, earnest, but not fervid;" a statement which is adapted to provoke a smile from one who has felt the nervous grip of the first epistle, and which becomes palpably absurd if we admit, as of course Dr. Davidson does not, the authenticity of the second. The "mild tone" assuredly is not dominant there; but, in any event, it would be strange if the letters did not show traces of the mellowing of years, and of the ripening of the spirit of Christ in this once passionate and headstrong disciple. The second chapter of the second epistle is no feeble reminder of the Peter who smote off the ear of Malchus.

The graphic and picturesque character of these letters is notable. In the two epistles, containing eight chapters, the longest of which consists of but twenty-five verses, there are one hundred and nineteen words which occur nowhere else in the New Testament. Picture-words abound, such as *ὠρυόμενος*, *roaring* (1, v. 8); *ὁπλίσασθε*, *arm yourselves* (1, iv. 1); *ἐπικάλυμμα*, *cloke* (1, ii. 16); *φιμοῦν*, *put to silence*, lit., *muzzle* (1, ii. 15); *σκολιός*, *froward*, lit., *awry* or *twisted* (1, ii. 18); *ἐκτενῶς*, *fervently*, lit., *on the stretch* (1, i. 22); *ἀπόθεσις*, *putting off* (2, i. 14); *ἔξοδος*, *decease* (2, i. 15); *διαυγάζειν*, *dawn* (2, i. 19); *αὐχμηρὸς*, *dark* or *dry* (2, i. 19); *ἐπίλυσις*, *interpretation*, lit., *untying* (2, i. 20); *στρεβλοῦσιν*, *wrest*, as with a windlass (2, iii. 16), and many others.

The same graphic character appears in what may be styled *reminiscent* words or phrases, in which the former personal experience of the writer is mirrored. Thus, *gird yourselves* with humility (1, v. 5, see note there) recalls the picture of the Lord girded with a towel and washing the disciples' feet. *To look into* (1, i. 12) expresses *a stooping down* to gaze intently, and carries us back to the visit of Peter and John to the sepulchre on the morning of the resurrection, when they *stooped down* and looked into the tomb. In *feed* the flock (Rev., *tend*, 1, v. 2) is reflected Christ's charge to Peter at the lake. The recurrence of the word *ἀπροσωπολήμπτως*, *without respect of persons* (1, i. 17), used in a kindred form by Peter, Acts x. 34, would seem to indicate that the scene in the house of Cornelius was present to his mind; and *be watchful* (1, v. 8) may have been suggested by the remembrance of his own drowsiness in Gethsemane, and of Christ's exhortation to watch. So, too, it is interesting to read the words *buffeted* (1, ii. 20), *the tree* (τὸ ξύλον, an unusual word, used by him, Acts v. 30 ; x. 39), and *stripe* or *weal* (1, ii. 24), in the light of the gospel narratives of Christ's sufferings. Christ had called Simon *a rock*, and a little later *a stumbling-block*. Peter combines both words into one phrase, *a rock of offence* (1, ii. 8). A very striking instance appears in the reference to the Transfiguration (2, i. 17, 18), where he uses the peculiar word ἔξοδος, *decease ;* lit., *going out*, which occurs in Luke ix. 31, and also in Heb. xi. 22. Compare, also, *tabernacle*, in 2, i. 13, 14, with *let us make three tabernacles*.

Both epistles are pervaded with an Old-Testament atmosphere. The testimony of Old-Testament prophecy, teaching, and history is emphasized (1, i. 10–12 ; iii. 5, 6, 20 ; 2, i. 19–21 ; ii. 1, 4–8, 15, 16 ; iii. 2, 5, 6). Old-Testament quotations and references are brought into the text, though the introductory formulas, *because it is written*, and *wherefore it is contained in scripture*, do not occur in the second epistle ; and the interweaving, as of familiar expressions, is not so conspicuous there as in the first epistle (see 1, i. 16, 24, 25 ; ii. 6, 7, 9, 10, 23, 24 ; iii. 6, 10, 14 ; iv. 8, 18 ; v. 5, 7 ; 2, i. 19–21 ; ii. 5, 6, 7, 15, 21 ; iii. 5, 6, 8, 13). The church of Christ is represented as the church of Israel perfected and spiritualized (1, ii. 4–10) ; the exhortation to holiness (1, i. 15, 16) is given in the language of Lev. xi. 44 ; Christ is described (1, ii. 6) in the terms of Isaiah xxviii. 16, and Ps. cxviii. 22 ; and the prophetic utterance of Isaiah concerning the servant of Jehovah (lii. 13–liii. 12) reappears in 1, ii. 23, 24.

The epistles are evidently the work of a Jew. We find, as we might expect, the writer illustrating his positions from Jewish history and tradition, as in his references to Noah, Sarah, Balaam, and his use of the word ῥαντισμὸς, *sprinkling* (1, i. 2), a peculiarly Levitical term. He shows how the spirit of Christ dwelt in the Old-Testament prophets, and how Christians are a royal priesthood.

The resemblance, both in ideas and expressions, to passages in the epistles of Paul and James is marked, especially in the first epistle. It will be instructive to compare the following :

James.	1 Peter.
i. 2, 3.	i. 6, 7.
i. 10, 11.	i. 24.
i. 18.	i. 23.
iv. 6, 10.	v. 5, 6.
v. 20.	iv. 8.

Paul.	1 Peter.
Rom. xii. 2.	i. 14.
Rom. iv. 24.	i. 21.
Rom. xii. 1.	ii. 5.
Rom. ix. 33.	ii. 6–8.
Rom. ix. 25, 26.	ii. 10.
Rom. xiii. 1–4.	ii. 13, 14.
Gal. v. 13.	ii. 16.
Rom. vi. 18.	ii. 24.
Rom. xii. 17.	iii. 9.
Rom. xii. 6, 7.	iv. 10, 11.
Rom. viii. 18.	v. i.
Rom. ii. 7, 10.	i. 7.
Rom. viii. 17.	iv. 13.
Rom. xii. 13.	iv. 9.
Rom. xiii. 13.	iv. 3.
Rom. xiii. 14.	iv. 1.
1 Thess. v. 6.	v. 8.
1 Cor. xvi. 20.	v. 14.

Nor are such resemblances wanting in the second epistle, though they are resemblances in tone, subject, and spirit, rather than verbal. It is in this epistle that Peter designates Paul's writings as scripture (iii. 16). Compare

Paul.	2 Peter.
Rom. i. 28; iii. 20.	i. 2.
1 Tim. i. 4; iv. 7.	i. 16.
1 Tim. vi. 5; Tit. i. 11.	ii. 3.
1 Cor. x. 29; Gal. v. 13.	ii. 19.
Rom. ii. 4; ix. 22.	iii. 15.
Gal. ii. 4.	ii. 1.

Into the much-vexed question of the authenticity of the second epistle we are not called upon to enter. The point of differences of style between the two epistles is a fair one. There are such differences, and very decided ones, though perhaps they are no more and no greater than can be explained by diversity of subject and circumstances, and the difference in the author's age. Some of the expressions peculiar to the second epistle are—*granting things which pertain unto life and godliness* (i. 3); *precious and exceeding great* (i. 4); *adding all diligence*, and *supply virtue* (i. 5); *an entrance richly supplied* (i. 11); *receiving forgetfulness* (i. 9); *sects of perdition* (ii. 1); *cast down to Tartarus* (ii. 4); *the world compacted out of water and by means of water* (iii. 5), etc.

But, while allowing for these differences, and recognizing the weakness of the external evidence for the authenticity of the epistle, the internal evidence of style and tone seems to us to outweigh the differences, and to show that both epistles were from the same hand. There is the same picturesqueness of diction, and a similar fertility of unusual words. Of the one hundred and twenty words which occur only in the writings of Peter, fifty-seven are peculiar to the second epistle; and, what is still more noteworthy, only one of these words, ἀπόθεσις, *putting off*, is common to the two epistles—a fact which tells very strongly against the hypothesis of a forgery. That hypothesis, it may be observed, is in the highest degree improbable. The Christian earnestness, the protest against deception, the tender and adoring reminiscence of Christ, the emphasis upon the person and doctrine of the Lord Jesus which mark this epistle, imply a moral standard quite inconsistent with the perpetration of a deliberate forgery.

Comparisons of expressions in this epistle with those used or inspired by Peter in the Acts of the Apostles exhibit a close correspondence; and a correspondence, which, however, must not be too strongly pressed, appears on a comparison with certain passages in the gospels. Thus the verb δωρέομαι, *to give*, occurs only in Mark xv. 45, and 2 Pet. i. 3, 4 (see Introduction to Mark, on the relations between Mark and Peter); and the recurrence of the words *exodus*, or *decease*, and *tabernacle* in the same connection (2 Pet. i. 13–15, 17, 18) is very striking from the pen of one who, at the Transfiguration, heard the heavenly visitants conversing of Christ's *decease*, and who proposed to build *tabernacles* for their abode. The repeated use of the word στηρίζω, *stablish*, and its derivatives (i. 12; iii. 17; ii. 14; iii. 16) is also suggestive, in view of the admonition of Jesus to Peter by the same word—*strengthen* thy brethren (Luke xxii. 32).

There is the same retrospective character in both epistles. In both the writer teaches that prophecy does not carry its own interpretation; in both he alludes to the small number saved from the flood; both have the same sentiments on the nature and right use of Christian liberty, and on the value of prophecy; in both ἀρετή, *virtue*, is attributed to God, a use of the word occurring nowhere else in the New Testament.

The style of both epistles is vigorous rather than elegant, strong, and sometimes rough, the work of a plain, practical man, and of an observer rather than a reasoner, whose thoughts do not follow each other in logical sequence. The fervid spirit of the writer appears in his habit of massing epithets, and repeating his thoughts in nearly the same words and forms (see, for instance, 1 Pet. i. 4; ii. 4, 11; i. 19; ii. 9. Also, i. 7, and iv. 12; i. 13, and iv. 7, v. 8; i. 14, and ii. 11, iv. 2; ii. 15, and iii. 1, 16; ii. 19, and iii. 14, iv. 14. 2 Pet. i. 4, 8, 17; ii. 10, 11, 12-15; iii. 15). Professor Ezra Abbot has brought out some remarkable correspondences between this epistle and the writings of Josephus, and maintains that the author of the letter is largely dependent upon the Jewish historian (*Expositor*, 2d series, iii., 49). The second epistle of Peter cannot be studied apart from

THE EPISTLE OF JUDE.

This brief letter is assigned to the Judas of Matt. xiii. 55, one of the brethren of Jesus, and of James, the author of the catholic epistle. It is a hotly debated question whether Peter's second letter or Jude's epistle is the earlier, and, consequently, which writer drew upon the other. It is quite evident, either that the one used the other's epistle or that both drew from a common source. A satisfactory decision is impossible in the present state of the evidence. The matter which is common to the two epistles, besides various scattered resemblances, is principally in Jude 3–18; 2 Pet. 1–5; ii. 1–18 (see Ezra Abbot, *Expositor*, 2d series, iii., 139).

Besides the resemblance to Second Peter, the epistle is marked by its apocryphal references, especially to the Book of Enoch (see notes on 9, 14). In style it is terse and picturesque. "It is Greek as learned by a foreigner, and partly from books, and it is mixed up with Hebrew phrases." It contains at least fifteen words not found elsewhere in the New Testament. Dean Alford says: "It is an impassioned invective, in which the writer heaps epithet on epithet, and image on image, and returns again and again to the licentious apostates against whom he warns the church, as though all language were insufficient to give an adequate idea of their profligacy, and of his own abhorrence of their perversion of the grace and doctrines of the Gospel."

THE FIRST GENERAL EPISTLE OF PETER.

CHAPTER I.

1. **Peter** (*Πέτρος*). See on Matt. xvi. 18. As Paul in his letters does not call himself by his original name of Saul, so Peter calls himself, not Simon, but Peter, the name most significant and precious both to himself and to his readers, because bestowed by his Lord. In the opening of the second epistle he uses both names.

An apostle. Of all the catholic epistles, Peter's alone puts forward his apostleship in the introduction. He is addressing churches with which he had no immediate connection, and which were distinctively Pauline. Hence he appeals to his apostleship in explanation of his writing to them, and as his warrant for taking Paul's place.

To the strangers—elect (ver. 2, *ἐκλεκτοῖς παρεπιδήμοις*). The Rev., properly, joins the two words, *elect who are sojourners*, instead of continuing *elect* with *according to the foreknowledge*, etc., as A. V.

Elect. Regarding all whom he addressed as subjects of saving grace. The term corresponds to the Old-Testament title of Jehovah's people: Isa. lxv. 9, 15, 22; Ps. cv. 43. Compare Matt. xx. 16; xxii. 14; Rom. viii. 33.

Sojourners (*παρεπιδήμοις*). Persons sojourning for a brief season in a foreign country. Though applied primarily to

Hebrews scattered throughout the world (Gen. xxiii. 4; Ps. xxxix. 12), it has here a wider, spiritual sense, contemplating Christians as having their citizenship in heaven. Compare Heb. xi. 13. The preposition παρά, in composition, implies a sense of *transitoriness*, as of one who passes *by* to something beyond.

Scattered (διασπορᾶς). Lit., *of the dispersion;* from διασπείρω, *to scatter* or *spread abroad;* σπείρω meaning, originally, *to sow.* The term was a familiar one for the whole body of Jews outside the Holy Land, scattered among the heathen.

2. **According to** (κατὰ). In virtue of; in accordance with.

Foreknowledge (πρόγνωσιν). Only here and Acts ii. 23, in Peter's sermon at Pentecost. He is distinguishing there between *foreknowledge* and *determinate counsel.*

The Father. Implying that the relation contemplated by the divine foreknowledge is a new relation of *sonship.*

In sanctification (ἐν ἁγιασμῷ). Compare 2 Thess. ii. 13. The spiritual state *in* which the being elected to salvation is realized. The word is peculiarly Pauline, occurring eight times in Paul's epistles, and besides only here and Heb. xii. 14.

Unto obedience (εἰς). Note the three prepositions: *according to* (κατά) the foreknowledge; *in* (ἐν) sanctification; *unto* (εἰς) obedience. The *ground*, *sphere*, and *end* of spiritual sanctification.

Sprinkling (ῥαντισμὸν). Here in a passive sense—*the being sprinkled.* Properly, the ritualistic act of sprinkling blood or water. See Num. xix. 19, 21. Compare Heb. ix. 13; xii. 24; Num. xix. 9, 13, where the water in which were the ashes of the red heifer is called ὕδωρ ῥαντισμοῦ, *water of sprinkling* (Septuagint), which the A. V. and Rev. Old Testament render *water of separation.* The word and its kindred verb occur only in Hebrews and Peter.

Jesus Christ. The foreknowledge of *the Father*, the sanctification of *the Spirit*, the obedience and sprinkling of the blood of Jesus Christ *the Son*. The Father *foreknowing*, the Son *atoning*, the Spirit applying the Son's work in *sanctifying*. "The mystery of the Trinity and the economy of our salvation are intimated in this verse" (Bengel).

Grace and peace (*χάρις—εἰρήνη*). Pauline terms. See Rom. i. 7. The salutation is peculiar by the addition of *be multiplied*, which occurs 2 Pet. i. 2; Jude 2, and nowhere else in the salutations of the epistles. It is found, however, in the Septuagint, Dan. iv. 1 (Sept. iii. 31), and vi. 25. Professor Salmond observes: "If the Babylon from which Peter writes can be taken to be the literal Babylon (see on v. 13), it might be interesting to recall the epistles introduced by salutations so similar to Peter's, which were written from the same capital by two kings, Nebuchadnezzar and Darius, of two great dynasties, and addressed to all their provinces."

3. **Blessed** (*εὐλογητὸς*). *εὖ, well, λόγος, a word. Well-spoken-of; praised; honored.* Used in the New Testament of God only. The kindred verb is applied to human beings, as to Mary (Luke i. 28): "*Blessed* (*εὐλογημένη*) art thou." Compare the different word for *blessed* in Matt. v. 3, etc. (*μακάριοι*), and see notes there. The style of this doxological phrase is Pauline. Compare 2 Cor. i. 3; Eph. i. 3.

Hath begotten us again (*ἀναγεννήσας ἡμᾶς*). The verb is used by Peter only, and by him only here and ver. 23. It is in the aorist tense, and should be rendered, as Rev., *begat;* because regeneration is regarded as a definite historical act accomplished once for all, or possibly because Peter regards the historical act of Christ's resurrection as virtually effecting the regeneration. The latter sentiment would be Pauline, since Paul is wont to speak of Christians as dying and rising with Christ. Rom. vii. 4; vi. 8–11.

Lively (*ζῶσαν*). Better, as Rev., literally rendering the participle, *living:* a favorite word with Peter. See i. 23; ii. 4, 5, 24; iv. 5, 6; and compare Acts ix. 41, where Peter is the prominent actor; and x. 42, where he is the speaker.

Hope (ἐλπίδα). Peter is fond of this word also (see i. 13, 21; iii. 5, 15), which, in classical Greek, has the general signification of *expectancy,* relating to evil as well as to good. Thus Plato speaks of living *in evil hope* ("Republic," i., 330); i.e., in the apprehension of evil; and Thucydides, of the *hope of evils to come;* i.e., the expectation or apprehension. In the New Testament the word always relates to a future good.

4. **An inheritance** (κληρονομίαν). A Pauline word, from κλῆρος, *a lot,* and νέμομαι, *to distribute among themselves.* Hence an inheritance is originally a portion which one receives by lot in a general distribution. In the New Testament the idea of *chance* attaching to the lot is eliminated. It is the portion or heritage which one receives by virtue of birth or by special gift. So of the vineyard seized by the wicked husbandmen: "Let us seize on his inheritance" (Matt. xxi. 38); of Abraham in Canaan: "God gave him none *inheritance*" (Acts vii. 5); "an eternal *inheritance*" (Heb. ix. 15).

Incorruptible, undefiled, and that fadeth not away. Note Peter's characteristic multiplication of epithets. *Incorruptible* (ἄφθαρτον). From ἀ, *not,* and φθείρω, *to destroy* or *corrupt. Undefiled* (ἀμίαντον). From ἀ, *not,* and μιαίνω, *to defile,* though the verb means especially to defile by *staining,* as with color; while μολύνω, also translated *defile* (1 Cor. viii. 7), is *to besmirch,* as with mire. We might render *unstained,* though the word is not used with any conscious reference to its etymology. *That fadeth not away* (ἀμάραντον). Used by Peter only, and but once. From ἀ, *not,* and μαραίνομαι, *to wither.* The loveliness of the heavenly inheritance is described as exempt from the blight which attaches to earthly bloom. As between ἄφθαρτον, *incorruptible,* and ἀμάραντον, *unwithering,* the former emphasizes the indestructibility of *substance,* and the latter of *grace* and *beauty.* The latter adjective appears in the familiar botanical name *amaranth*. It will be observed that all of these three epithets are compounded with the negative particle *ἀ*, *not*. Archbishop Trench aptly remarks that "it is a remarkable testimony to the reign of sin, and therefore of imperfection, of decay, of death throughout this whole fallen world, that as often as we desire to set forth the glory, purity, and perfection of that other, higher world toward which we strive, we are almost inevitably compelled to do this by the aid of negatives; by the denying to that higher order of things the leading features and characteristics of this." Compare Apoc. xxi. 1, 4, 22, 23, 27; xxii. 3, 5.

Reserved (τετηρημένην). Lit., *which has been reserved*, a perfect participle, indicating the inheritance as one reserved through God's care for his own from the beginning down to the present. *Laid up and kept* is the idea. The verb signifies *keeping* as the result of *guarding*. Thus in John xvii. 11, Christ says, "*keep* (τήρησον) those whom thou hast given me;" in ver. 12, "I *kept* them" (ἐτήρουν); *i.e.*, preserved by guarding them. "Those whom thou gavest me I *guarded* (ἐφύλαξα)." So Rev., which preserves the distinction. Similarly, John xiv. 15, "*keep* (τηρήσατε) my commandments;" *preserve* them unbroken by careful watching. So Peter was delivered to the soldiers to *guard* him (φυλάσσειν), but he was *kept* (ἐτηρεῖτο) in prison (Acts xii. 4, 51). Compare Col. i. 5, where a different word is used: ἀποκειμένην, lit., *laid away*.

For you (εἰς). The use of this preposition, instead of the simpler dative, is graphic: *with reference to* you; with you as its direct object.

5. **Kept** (φρουρουμένους). A military term. Lit., *garrisoned*. Rev., *guarded*. Compare 2 Cor. xi. 32, and the beautiful metaphorical use of the word at Philip. iv. 7, "shall *guard* your hearts." The present participle indicates something *in progress*, *a continuous process of protection*. Hence, lit., *who are being guarded*. "The inheritance is *kept*; the heirs are *guarded*" (Bengel).

By (ἐν) the power; **through** (διὰ) faith; **unto** (εἰς) salvation. *By*, indicating the efficient cause; *through*, the secondary agency; *unto*, the result.

Salvation. Note the frequent occurrence of this word, vv. 9, 10.

Ready (ἑτοίμην). Stronger than *about to be*, or *destined to be*, implying a state of waiting or preparedness, and thus harmonizing with *reserved.*

6. **Ye greatly rejoice** (ἀγαλλιᾶσθε). The word is always employed in the New Testament for *great* or *lively* joy. See Matt. v. 12; Luke i. 47; x. 21.

For a season (ὀλίγον). More literally and correctly, as Rev., *for a little while.* Compare ch. v. 10. The word is used nowhere else in the New Testament in this sense.

In heaviness (λυπηθέντες). Lit., *having been grieved.* Rev., *ye have been put to grief.*

Through (ἐν). But Rev., better, *in;* the preposition not being instrumental, but indicating the *sphere* or *environment* in which the grief operates.

Manifold (ποικίλοις). Literally the word means *variegated.* It is used to describe the skin of a leopard, the different-colored veinings of marble, or an embroidered robe; and thence passes into the meaning of *changeful*, *diversified*, applied to the changing months or the variations of a strain of music. Peter employs it again, ch. iv. 10, of the grace of God, and James of temptations, as here (i. 2). Compare πολυποίκιλος, *manifold*, in Eph. iii. 10, applied to the wisdom of God. The word gives a vivid picture of the *diversity* of the trials, emphasizing this idea rather than that of their *number*, which is left to be inferred.

Temptations (πειρασμοῖς). Better, *trials*, as in margin of

Rev., since the word includes more than direct solicitation to evil. It embraces all that goes to furnish a *test* of character. Compare Jas. i. 2.

7. **Trial** (δοκίμιον). Only here and Jas. i. 3. Rev., *proof*. The word means a *test*. As the means of proof, however, is not only the touchstone itself, but the trace of the metal left upon it, the sense here is the *result* of the contact of faith with trial, and hence the *verification* of faith. The expression is equivalent to *your approved faith*. Compare Rom. ii. 7, 10.

Than of gold. Omit the *of*, and read *than gold*. The comparison is between the approved faith and the gold; not between the faith and the *proof* of the gold.

Though it be tried (δοκιμαζομένου). Kindred with δοκίμιον, *proof*, and better rendered by Rev., *proved*. The verb is used in classical Greek of assaying or testing metals, and means, generally, *to approve* or *sanction upon test*. It is radically akin to δέχεσθαι, *to receive*, and hence implies a proof with a view to determine whether a thing be worthy to be received. Compare 1 Cor. iii. 13; Gal. vi. 4; 1 John iv. 1. It thus differs from πειράζειν, *to try* or *tempt* (see on πειρασμοῖς, ver. 6), in that that verb indicates simply a putting to proof to discover what good or evil is in a person; and from the fact that such scrutiny so often develops the existence and energy of evil, the word acquired a predominant sense of putting to the proof with the design or hope of breaking down the subject under the proof—in other words, of *temptation* in the ordinary sense. Hence Satan is called ὁ πειράζων, *the tempter*, Matt. iv. 3; 1 Thess. iii. 5. See on Matt. vi. 13. Archbishop Trench observes that "δοκιμάζειν could not be used of Satan, since he never proves that he may approve, nor tests that he may accept."

Might be found (εὑρεθῇ). In accord with the preceding expressions, and indicating discovery as the result of scrutiny.

Praise and glory and honor. Such is the order of the best texts, and so Rev. *Glory* and *honor* often occur together in the New Testament, as Rom. ii. 7, 10; 1 Tim. i. 17. Only here with *praise.* Compare *spirit of glory*, ch. iv. 14.

8. **Full of glory** (δεδοξασμένῃ). Lit., *glorified*, as Rev., in margin.

Receiving (κομιζόμενοι). The verb originally means *to take care of* or *provide for;* thence *to receive hospitably* or *entertain; to bring home with a view to entertaining* or *taking care of.* Hence, *to carry away so as to preserve, to save, rescue,* and so to carry away *as a prize or booty.* Generally, *to receive* or *acquire.* Paul uses it of receiving the awards of judgment (2 Cor. v. 10; Eph. vi. 8; Col. iii. 25). In Hebrews it is used of receiving the promise (x. 36; xi. 39), and of Abraham receiving back Isaac (xi. 19). Peter uses it thrice, and in each case of receiving the rewards of righteousness or of iniquity. See ch. v. 4; 2 Pet. ii. 13.

10. **Have inquired and searched diligently** (ἐξεζήτησαν—ἐξηρεύνησαν). Rev., properly, renders the aorists *sought and searched diligently.* The ἐξ in composition has the force of *out*, searched *out*, and is rendered by *diligently.*

Sought. Used of Esau's seeking carefully for a place of repentance, in Heb. xii. 17.

Searched. Used nowhere else in the New Testament. Compare Septuagint, 1 Sam. xxiii. 23, of Saul's searching out David.

11. **Did signify** (ἐδήλου). Imperfect tense: better, *was declaring*, all along through the prophetic age, in successive prophets. See the same verb in 1 Cor. iii. 13; 2 Pet. i. 14.

When it testified beforehand (προμαρτυρόμενον). Only here in New Testament.

Of Christ (εἰς Χριστὸν). Lit., *unto Christ.* So Rev., in margin. The sufferings *destined for* Christ, as in ver. 10 he speaks of the grace, εἰς ὑμᾶς, *unto you;* i.e., destined to come unto you. Peter was especially concerned to show that the sufferings of Christ were in fulfilment of prophecy, because it was a subject of dispute with the Jews whether the Christ was to suffer (Acts iii. 18; xxvi. 22, 23).

The glory (τὰς δόξας). Rev., correctly, *the glories.* The plural is used to indicate the successive steps of his glorification; the glory of his resurrection and ascension, of the last judgment, and of the kingdom of heaven.

12. **Did minister** (διηκόνουν). Imperfect tense, *were ministering.* See on Mark ix. 35. The term is applicable to any kind of service, official or not. Compare 2 Cor. iii. 3.

Desire (ἐπιθυμοῦσιν). The word commonly denotes *intense* desire. It is used by Christ in expressing his wish to eat the passover (Luke xxii. 15); of the prodigal's desire to satisfy his hunger with the husks (Luke xv. 16); and of the flesh lusting against the spirit (Gal. v. 17).

To look into (παρακύψαι). A very graphic word, meaning *to stoop sideways* (παρά). Used by Aristophanes to picture the attitude of a bad harp-player. Here it portrays one stooping and stretching the neck to gaze on some wonderful sight. It occurs in Jas. i. 25, describing him who looks into the perfect law of liberty as into a mirror; and in Luke xxiv. 12; John xx. 5, 11, of Peter and John and Mary *stooping* and looking into the empty tomb. Possibly the memory of this incident unconsciously suggested the word to Peter. The phrase illustrates Peter's habitual emphasis upon the testimony of *sight* (see Introduction). Bengel acutely notes the hint in παρά, *beside,* that the angels contemplate the work of salvation *from without,* as spectators and not as participants. Compare Heb. ii. 16; Eph. iii. 10.

13. **Gird up** (ἀναζωσάμενοι). Lit., *having girded up.* Used here only. The metaphor is suggested by the girding up of

the loose eastern robes preparatory to running or other exertion. Perhaps recalling the words of Christ, Luke xii. 35. Christ's call is a call to active service. There is a fitness in the figure as addressed to *sojourners* and *pilgrims* (ch. i. 1; ii. 11), who must be always ready to move.

Mind (διανοίας). See on Mark xii. 30.

Be sober (νήφοντες). Lit., *being sober.* Primarily, in a physical sense, as opposed to excess in drink, but passing into the general sense of *self-control* and *equanimity.*

Hope to the end (τελείως ἐλπίσατε). Better, as Rev., *set your hope perfectly:* wholly and unchangeably; without doubt or despondency.

That is to be brought (τὴν φερομένην). Lit., which is *being brought*, as Rev., in margin. The object of hope is already on the way.

14. **Obedient children** (τέκνα ὑπακοῆς). Literally, and more correctly, as Rev., *children of obedience.* See on Mark iii. 17. The Christian is represented as related to the motive principle of his life as a child to a parent.

Fashioning yourselves (συσχηματιζόμενοι). See on Matt. xvii. 2; and compare Rom. xii. 2, the only other passage where the word occurs. As σχῆμα is the outward, changeable *fashion*, as contrasted with what is *intrinsic*, the word really carries a warning against conformity to something changeful, and therefore illusory.

15. **As he which hath called you is holy** (κατὰ τὸν καλέσαντα ὑμᾶς ἅγιον). *As* of the A. V. is *according to*, or *after the pattern of;* and *holy* is to be taken as a personal name; the *which hath called* being added for definition, and in order to strengthen the exhortation. Render, therefore, *after the pattern of the Holy One who called you.* So, nearly, Rev., in margin. A similar construction occurs 2 Pet. ii. 1: *the Lord that bought them.*

Conversation (*ἀναστροφῇ*). A favorite word with Peter; used eight times in the two epistles. From ἀνά, *up*, and στρέφω, *to turn*. The process of development in the meaning of the word is interesting. 1. A turning upside down. 2. A turning about or wheeling. 3. Turning about in a place, going back and forth there about one's business; and so, 4, one's mode of life or conduct. This is precisely the idea in the word *conversation* (Lat., *conversare, to turn round*) which was used when the A. V. was made, as the common term for *general deportment* or *behavior*, and was, therefore, a correct rendering of ἀναστροφή. So Latimer ("Sermons"): "We are not bound to follow the *conversations* or doings of the saints." And Shakspeare, 2 Hen. IV., v., 5:

> "But all are banished till their *conversation*
> Appear more wise and modest to the world."

Our later limitation of the meaning to the interchange of talk makes it expedient to change the rendering, as Rev., to *manner of living*.

17. **If ye call on the Father—judgeth.** More correctly, Rev., *If ye call on him as Father;* the point being that God is to be invoked, not only as Father, but as Judge.

Without respect of persons (*ἀπροσωπολήμπτως*). Here only. Peter, however, uses προσωπολήμπτης, *a respecter of persons*, Acts x. 34, which whole passage should be compared with this. Paul and James also use the kindred word προσωποληψία, *respect of persons*. See Rom. ii. 11; Jas. ii. 1. James has the verb προσωποληπτέω, *to have respect of persons*. The constituents of the compound word, πρόσωπον, *the countenance*, and λαμβάνω, *to receive*, are found in Gal. ii. 6; and the word is the Old-Testament formula *to accept* or *to raise the face* of another; opposed to *making the countenance fall* (Job xxix. 24; Gen. iv. 5). Hence, *to receive kindly*, or *look favorably* upon one (Gen. xix. 21; xxxii. 20, etc.). In the Old Testament it is, as Bishop Lightfoot observes, "a neutral expression involving no subsidiary notion of partiality, and is much oftener found in a good than in a bad sense. When it becomes an independent Greek phrase, however, the bad sense attaches to it, owing to the secondary meaning of πρόσωπον, *a mask;* so that πρόσωπον λαμβάνειν signifies to regard the *external circumstances* of a man, his rank, wealth, etc., as opposed to his real, intrinsic character."

Sojourning (παροικίας). Compare *sojourners*, ver. 1.

18. **Ye were redeemed** (ἐλυτρώθητε). The verb occurs only in two other passages, Luke xxiv. 21; Tit. ii. 14. It carries the idea of a ransom-*price* (λύτρον, from λύω, *to loose*).

With silver or gold (ἀργυρίῳ ἢ χρυσίῳ). Lit., with silver or gold *money;* the words meaning, respectively, *a small coin* of silver or of gold.

Conversation. Rev., *manner of life.* See on ver. 15.

Received by tradition from your fathers (πατροπαραδότου). A clumsy translation; improved by Rev., *handed down from your fathers.* The word is peculiar to Peter.

19. **But with the precious blood of Christ.** The word Χριστοῦ, *of Christ*, stands at the end of the sentence, and is emphatic. Render, as Rev., *with precious blood as of a lamb*, etc., *even the blood of Christ.*

Lamb. Peculiarly appropriate from Peter. See John i. 35–42. The reference is to a *sacrificial* lamb.

Without blemish (ἀμώμου). Representing the Old-Testament phrase for absence of physical defect (Exod. xii. 5; Lev. xxii. 20. Compare Heb. ix. 14).

Without spot (ἀσπίλου). Compare 1 Tim. vi. 14; Jas. i. 27; 2 Pet. iii. 14. In each case in a moral sense.

20. **Foreordained** (προεγνωσμένου). Lit., and better, *foreknown*, as Rev.

Manifested (φανερωθέντος). Observe the difference in tense. *Foreknown* is the perfect participle, *has been known from all eternity down to the present:* "in reference to the place held and *continuing to be held* by Christ in the divine mind" (Salmond). *Manifested* is the aorist participle, pointing to a definite act at a given time.

In these last times (ἐπ' ἐσχάτου τῶν χρόνων). Lit., as Rev., *at the end of the times.*

21. **Which raised.** Compare Rom. iv. 24.

That your faith and hope might be in God. Some render, *that your faith should also be hope toward God.*

22. **Purified** (ἡγνικότες). The Septuagint translation of the Old-Testament technical term for the purification of the people and priests (Josh. iii. 5; 1 Chron. xv. 12; 1 Sam. xvi. 5). Also, of the separation from wine and strong drink by the Nazarite (Num. vi. 2–6). In this ceremonial sense, John xi. 55; Acts xxi. 24, 26; xxiv. 18. In the moral sense, as here, Jas. iv. 8; 1 John iii. 3. Compare καθαρίσας, *purifying*, Acts xv. 9.

Obeying (ὑπακοῇ). Rev., *obedience.* A peculiarly New Testament term unknown in classical Greek. In the Septuagint only 2 Sam. xxii. 36; rendered in A. V. *gentleness.* Rev., *condescension*, in margin.

Unfeigned (ἀνυπόκριτον). 'Α, *not*, ὑποκριτής, *actor.* The latter word is from ὑποκρίνεσθαι, *to answer* on the stage, and hence *to play a part* or *to act.* A hypocrite is, therefore, an *actor.*

With a pure heart (ἐκ καθαρᾶς καρδίας). The best texts reject καθαρᾶς, *pure.* Render, therefore, as Rev., *from the heart.*

Fervently (ἐκτενῶς). Used by Peter only, and only in this passage. He uses the kindred adjective ἐκτενής, *without ceasing*, in Acts xii. 5, where the narrative probably came from him, and also at ch. iv. 8; "*fervent* charity." The words are compounded with the verb τείνω, to stretch, and signify *intense strain;* feeling *on the rack.*

23. **Being born again** (ἀναγεγεννημένοι). Rev., *having been begotten again.* Compare Jas. i. 18.

Of (ἐκ) seed—**by** (διά) the word. Note the difference in the prepositions; the former denoting the *origin* or *source* of life, the latter the *medium* through which it imparts itself to the nature.

Word of God (λόγου Θεοῦ). The gospel of Christ. Compare ver. 25, and Peter's words, Acts x. 36. Also, Eph. i. 13; Col. i. 5; Jas. i. 18. Not the *personal* Word, as the term is employed by John. Nevertheless, the connection and relation of the personal with the revealed word is distinctly recognized. "In the New Testament we trace a gradual ascent from (*a*) the *concrete message* as conveyed to man by personal agency through (*b*) *the Word*, the revelation of God to man which the message embodies, forming, as it were, its life and soul, to (*c*) THE WORD, who, being God, not only reveals but imparts himself to us, and is formed in us thereby" (Scott, on Jas. i. 18, "Speaker's Commentary").

Seed (σπορᾶς). Nowhere else in the New Testament. Primarily, the *sowing* of seed.

24. **Of man.** Following the reading ἀνθρώπου, in the Septuagint, Isa. xl. 6, which Peter quotes here. But the best texts read αὐτῆς, *of it*, or, as Rev., *thereof.*

Withereth (ἐξηράνθη). Literally, the writer puts it as in a narrative of some quick and startling event, by the use of the aorist tense: *withered was the grass.* Similarly, *the flower fell* (ἐξέπεσεν). Lit., fell *off*, the force of ἐκ.

25. **Word of the Lord** (*ῥῆμα κυρίου*). Compare ver. 23, and note that *ῥῆμα* is used for *word*, instead of λόγος; and **Κύριος**, *Lord*, instead of **Θεός**, *God*, which is the reading of the Hebrew, and of most copies of the Septuagint. The substitution indicates that Peter identifies Jesus with God. No very satisfactory reason can be given for the change from λόγος to *ῥῆμα*. It may be due to the Greek translation, which Peter follows.

CHAPTER II.

1. **All** (*πᾶσαν—πάντα*). Lit., *every*, or *all manner of*.

Evil-speaking (*καταλαλιάς*). Lit., *speakings against*. A rare word. Only here and 2 Cor. xii. 20.

2. **New-born** (*ἀρτιγέννητα*). Peculiar to Peter, and only in this passage. Lit., born but *just now* (*ἄρτι*).

Babes (*βρέφη*). The word signifying peculiarly a child *at birth*, or of tender years. See Luke xviii. 15; Acts vii. 19. Of the infant Jesus, Luke ii. 12, 16. Here marking the recency of Christian life in the converts addressed.

Desire (*ἐπιποθήσατε*). The compound is intensive; *earnestly* desire. So Rev., *long for*. Compare Philip. ii. 26.

The sincere milk of the word (*τὸ λογικὸν ἄδολον γάλα*). The A. V. has rendered **λογικὸν**, *of the word;* but wrongly. It describes the quality of the *milk* as *spiritual* or *rational*, as opposed to *literal* and *ceremonial*. In the only other place where it occurs (Rom. xii. 1) it is rendered *reasonable;* which Rev. gives here in margin.

Sincere (*ἄδολον*) is another epithet of the *milk*. Lit., *without guile*, *unadulterated*. Compare *guile* in ver. 1. Laying aside guile, desire the *guileless* milk, etc. Hence Rev. renders the whole passage, *Long for the spiritual milk which is without guile*.

That ye may grow thereby. The best texts add, *unto salvation.*

3. **Ye have tasted** (ἐγεύσασθε). Aorist tense. More literally, *ye tasted.* "A taste excites the appetite" (Bengel). Compare *long for*, ver. 2, and Ps. xxxiv. 8.

Gracious (χρηστὸς). Actively benignant, "as distinguished from other adjectives which describe goodness on the side of its *sterling worth* and its *gentleness*" (Salmond). See on Matt. xi. 30.

4. **Coming** (προσερχόμενοι). Indicating a *close* (πρός) and an *habitual* (present participle) approach and an intimate association.

A living stone (λίθον ζῶντα). Omit *as unto.* So Rev. The words are in apposition with *whom* (Christ). Compare Peter's use of the same word, *stone*, in Acts iv. 11, and Matt. xxi. 42. It is not the word which Christ uses as a personal name for Peter (Πέτρος); so that it is not necessary to infer that Peter was thinking of his own new name.

Disallowed (ἀποδεδοκιμασμένον). Rev., *rejected.* See on the simple verb, ch. i. 7. The word indicates rejection *after trial.*

Of God (παρὰ Θεῷ). *Of* in the A. V. is equivalent to *by;* but παρά has a stronger sense, implying the absolute power of decisive choice which is *with* God. Render, as Rev., *with God;* i.e., God being judge; and compare Matt. xix. 26; Rom. ii. 11.

Precious (ἔντιμον). At ch. i. 19 (*precious* blood) another word is used (τίμιος), denoting *essential* preciousness. The word here indicates the preciousness as *recognized* or *held in honor.*

5. **Living stones—built up—a spiritual house.** It seems as though Peter must have had in mind the conception em-

bodied in Christ's commission to him, of a building erected upon a rock. The metaphor of a house built of living stones is violent, and sufficiently characteristic of Peter; yet it pictures, in a very striking way, the union of *stability*, *growth*, and *activity* in the ideal church. Note the transition from *babes growing* (ver. 2) to *stones built up*. But, as Salmond remarks, "In Paul we have even bolder instances of apparent confusion of metaphors, as when, in one breath, he represents believers as at once *walking*, *rooted*, and *built up* in Christ (Col. ii. 6, 7).

To offer up (ἀνενέγκαι). The usual Old-Testament (Septuagint) term for offering of sacrifice. Lit., *to bring up* to the altar. Compare Heb. xiii. 15. The force of ἀνά, *up*, appears in the fact of the altar being *raised*. The word is often used of carrying from a lower to a higher place. Thus Matt. xvii. 1; Luke xxiv. 51. In this sense ver. 24 of this chapter is suggestive, where it is said that Christ *bare* (ἀνήνεγκεν) our sins: *carried them up* to the cross. See note there.

6. **It is contained** (περιέχει). From περί, *round about*, and ἔχω, *to hold*. Hence, *to contain* or *comprehend*. So Luke v. 9, *he was astonished* (θάμβος αὐτὸν περιέσχεν); lit., *astonishment held him encompassed*. Also, Acts xxiii. 25, "He wrote a letter *after this manner* (περιέχουσαν τὸν τύπον τοῦτον); lit., *containing this form*. The verb here is impersonal. The kindred word περιοχή occurs only in Acts viii. 32, rendered *place*; i.e., the passage of scripture: either the *contents* of the passage or the section of the book *circumscribed* or *marked off*.

In the scripture (ἐν γραφῇ). The best texts reject the article. *Γραφή* means a *passage* of scripture. See on Mark xii. 10. Hence Rev., *in scripture*; margin, *in a scripture*.

Behold I lay, etc. See Rom. ix. 33.

Precious. See on ver. 4.

7. **He is precious** (ἡ τιμή). Wrong. Render, as Rev., *For you therefore which believe is the preciousness* (*honor*, in margin).

Is made the head of the corner (ἐγενήθη εἰς κεφαλὴν γωνίας). Rev., correctly, "*was* made." The preposition εἰς, *unto*, carrying the idea of *coming unto* the place of honor, is not rendered in A. V. or Rev. Lit., it would be, *was made or became unto the head*, etc.

9. **Generation** (γένος). Better, Rev., *race:* a body with a common life and descent.

Nation (ἔθνος). **People** (λαὸς). The distinction between these three words cannot be closely pressed. *Race* emphasizes the idea of *descent; nation*, of *community*. *Λαὸς*, *people*, occurring very often in the Septuagint, is used there mostly of the Israelites, the chosen people. The same use is also frequent in the New Testament; but it is employed in a more general sense, as by Luke ii. 10. It would seem that this idea, however, in its metaphorical and Christian application, the *chosen Israel* of God, directed Peter's choice of the word, since he adds, *a people for God's own possession.*

Peculiar (εἰς περιποίησιν). Lit., *a people for acquisition.* Rev., *a people for God's own possession.* Wyc., *a people of purchasing.* Cranmer, *a people which are won.* The word occurs 1 Thess. v. 9, rendered *obtaining* (Rev.); Eph. i. 14, *God's own possession* (Rev.). See Isa. xliii. 21 (Sept.), where the kindred verb occurs: "This people have I *formed for myself* (περιεποιησάμην).

Shew forth (ἐξαγγείλητε). Only here in New Testament. *Proclaim, tell abroad.*

The praises (τὰς ἀρετὰς). Lit., *the virtues.* So Rev., *excellencies.* The word occurs Isa. xliii. 21 (Sept., see above), and is rendered *praise.* See, also, Isa. xlii. 12 (Sept.), "Declare his *praise* (ἀρετὰς) in the islands."

10. **People** (λαὸς). See on ver. 9, and note the choice of the term here. *A people of God.* Compare Rom. ix. 25, 26.

11. **Beloved** (ἀγαπητοί). A favorite term with Peter, occurring eight times in the epistles. See the phrase, *our beloved Barnabas and Paul*, Acts xv. 25, in the letter sent by the council at Jerusalem to the Gentile Christians, the account of which, doubtless, came from Peter. Compare *our beloved brother Paul*, 2 Pet. iii. 15.

Strangers (παροίκους). Rev., *sojourners*. Compare ch. i. 17, "the time of your *sojourning* (παροικίας)."

Which (αἵτινες). The compound pronoun denotes a class, *of that kind which*, classifying all fleshly desires in one category.

12. **Conversation.** Rev., *behavior*. See on ch. i. 15.

Whereas (ἐν ᾧ). Rev., correctly, *wherein*; in the matter in which.

They speak against (καταλαλοῦσιν). Compare *evil-speakings*, ver. 1, and Acts xxviii. 22.

Which they shall behold (ἐποπτεύοντες). Rev., *beholding*. Used by Peter only, here and ch. iii. 2. The kindred noun ἐπόπτης, *an eye-witness*, occurs only at 2 Pet. i. 16. It is a technical word, meaning one who was admitted to the highest degree of initiation in the Eleusinian mysteries. Here it conveys the idea of *personal witness*; behold *with their own eyes*.

Evil-doers (κακοποιῶν). The word occurs four times in Peter, and nowhere else in the New Testament except John xviii. 30, where it is applied by the priests to Christ himself.

Visitation (ἐπισκοπῆς). The radical idea of the word is that of *observing* or *inspecting*. Hence ἐπίσκοπος, *an overseer* or *bishop*. *Visiting* grows naturally out of this, as *visitare* from *visere, to look at attentively*. See Introduction, on Peter's emphasis upon sight; and compare *behold*, in this verse. The "day of visitation" is the day of *looking upon*: "When God shall look upon these wanderers, as a pastor over his flock, and shall become the *overlooker* or *bishop* of their souls" (ver. 25, Lumby).

13. **Submit yourselves** (ὑποτάγητε). Rev., *be subject.* See Rom. xiii. 1 sq.

Ordinance of man (ἀνθρωπίνῃ κτίσει). Lit., *to every human creation* or *institution.* Rev., *creation,* in margin.

King. The emperor, styled *king* by Greek writers.

14. **Sent** (πεμπομένοις). The present participle. In the habit of being sent: sent from time to time.

By him. The king; not the Lord.

Punishment (ἐκδίκησιν). Not strong enough. Better, *vengeance,* as Rev. Compare Luke xviii. 7; Rom. xii. 19.

Them that do well (ἀγαθοποιῶν). Only here in New Testament.

15. **Put to silence** (φιμοῦν). A very graphic word, meaning *to muzzle* or *gag.* Compare 1 Cor. ix. 9; 1 Tim. v. 18. See on Matt. xxii. 12.

Ignorance (ἀγνωσίαν). In classical Greek it is an ignorance arising from not coming into contact with the person or thing to be known. It occurs only once again in the New Testament, 1 Cor. xv. 34. Here it signifies not *want of acquaintance,* but of *understanding;* a state of ignorance.

Of foolish men (τῶν ἀφρόνων ἀνθρώπων). Of *the* foolish men; the article referring to those just mentioned, who speak against them as evil-doers.

16. **Using** (ἔχοντες). Lit., *having* or *holding.*

Cloke (ἐπικάλυμμα). Only here in New Testament. Lit., *a veil*. The idea is that of using Christian freedom as a mask for ungodly license. Paul uses the kindred verb (Rom. iv. 7) of the covering of sins. On the sentiment, compare Gal. v. 13.

18. **Servants** (οἰκέται). *Household* servants. So Rev., in margin. Not a common term in the New Testament, occurring only in three other passages: Luke xvi. 13; Acts x. 7; Rom. xiv. 4. Some suppose that Peter intended to cover by it freedmen and other dependants in the household, or that he uses it with a conciliatory purpose, as presenting the slave in closer relation with the family.

Gentle (ἐπιεικέσιν). A common derivation of this word is from εἴκω, *to yield*. Hence the meaning, *mild*, *yielding*, *indulgent*. But the true derivation is from εἰκός, *reasonable;* and the word implies rather the *not being unduly rigorous:* "Wherein not strictness of legal right, but consideration for one another, is the rule of practice" (Alford). Compare Philip. iv. 5, where, for *moderation* (τὸ ἐπιεικὲς), Rev. gives *forbearance*, with *gentleness* in margin. According to Aristotle, the word stands in contrast with ἀκριβοδίκαιος, *one who is exactingly just*, as *one who is satisfied with less than his due*.

Froward (σκολιοῖς). Lit., *crooked*. See Luke iii. 5. Peter uses the word in Acts ii. 40 (*untoward*); and Paul, in Philip. ii. 15 (*crooked*). The word *froward* is Anglo-Saxon *fream-ward* or *from-ward*, the opposite of *to-ward*. (See *untoward*, above.) Thus Ben Jonson:

> "Those that are *froward* to an appetite;"

i.e., *averse*. Compare the phrases *to-God-ward* (2 Cor. iii. 4); *to-us-ward*.

19. **Conscience toward God** (συνείδησιν Θεοῦ). Rev., in margin, *conscience of God*. The idea is not *conscientiousness* in the ordinary sense, but *the conscious sense of one's relation to God;* his *consciousness of God*. Thus one suffers patiently,

not from a conscientious sense of duty, but from an inner consciousness of his relation to God as a son, and to Christ as a joint-heir, which involves his suffering with him no less than his being glorified with him.

20. **What glory** (ποῖον κλέος). Lit., *what kind of glory*. This word for *glory* occurs nowhere else in the New Testament.

Buffeted (κολαφιζόμενοι). See Matt. xxvi. 67: struck with the fist. This whole passage, vv. 19–24, bears the mark of Peter's memories of the scene of Christ's last sufferings (see Introduction)—the blows of the servants, the scorn of the high-priest, the silent submission of Jesus, the cross, the stripes.

21. **Leaving** (ὑπολιμπάνων). Only here in the New Testament.

An example (ὑπογραμμὸν). Only here in the New Testament. A graphic word, meaning *a copy* set by writing-masters for their pupils. Some explain it as a copy of characters *over* which the student is to *trace* the lines.

Follow (ἐπακολουθήσητε). Lit., *follow upon*. The compound verb implies *close* following. From *writers* and *painters*, the metaphor changes now to a *guide*.

22. **Found** (εὑρέθη). Stronger than the simple *was*, and indicating a guilelessness which had stood the test of *scrutiny*. Compare Matt. xxvi. 60; John xviii. 38; xix. 4, 6. Christ's sinlessness had also stood the test of Peter's intimacy.

23. **Reviled—again** (ἀντελοιδόρει). Only here in the New Testament.

Committed himself (παρεδίδου). But this gives a reflexive force to the verb which has no parallel. Commentators are divided, some supplying *his cause*, as Rev., in margin; others, *his judgment*; others, *his revilers*. Better, the *subject* of the contest—his *insults* and *injuries*. Salmond renders, *but left it to him*, etc.

Judgeth righteously. Compare *without respect of persons*, ch. i. 17.

24. **Bare** (ἀνήνεγκεν). See on ver. 5. Bare *up* to the cross, as to an altar, and offered himself thereon.

The tree (ξύλον). Lit., *wood*. Peter uses the same peculiar term for the cross, Acts v. 30; x. 39.

Being dead (ἀπογενόμενοι). Rev., more strictly, *having died*. Used here only in the New Testament. The rendering of the verb can be given only in a clumsy way, *having become off unto sins;* not *becoming separate* from sins, but having *ceased to exist* as regards them. Compare Rom. vi. 18.

Stripes (μώλωπι). Lit., *bruise*. So Rev., in margin. Only here in New Testament; meaning a *bloody wale* which arises under a blow. "Such a sight we feel sure, as we read this descriptive passage, St. Peter's eyes beheld on the body of his Master, and the flesh so dreadfully mangled made the disfigured form appear in his eyes like one single bruise" (Lumby).

25. **For ye were as sheep going astray** (ἦτε γὰρ ὡς πρόβατα πλανώμενοι); *i.e.*, as commonly understood, ye were like straying sheep. But the *ye were* should be construed with the participle *going astray*, the verb and the participle together denoting *habitual* action or condition. Render, as Rev., *ye were going astray like sheep*. See on Mark xii. 24.

Bishop. See on ver. 12.

CHAPTER III.

1. **Likewise** (ὁμοίως). Rev., *in like manner;* better, because *likewise* in popular speech has, wrongly, the sense of *also*. Peter means in like manner with *servants* (ch. ii. 18).

Be in subjection (ὑποτασσόμεναι). Lit., *being in subjection*, or *submitting yourselves;* the same word which is used of the submission of servants (ch. ii. 18).

Be won (κερδηθήσονται). Rev., *be gained.* The word used by Christ, Matt. xviii. 15: "*gained* thy brother."

2. **While they behold** (ἐποπτεύσαντες). See on ch. ii. 12.

Conversation. See on ch. i. 15. Rev., *behavior.*

Coupled with fear (ἐν φόβῳ). Lit., *in fear.*

3. **Of plaiting** (ἐμπλοκῆς). Only here in New Testament. Compare 1 Tim. ii. 9. The Roman women of the day were addicted to ridiculous extravagance in the adornment of the hair. Juvenal ("Satire," vi.) satirizes these customs. He says: "The attendants will vote on the dressing of the hair as if a question of reputation or of life were at stake, so great is the trouble she takes in quest of beauty; with so many tiers does she load, with so many continuous stories does she build up on high her head. She is tall as Andromache in front, behind she is shorter. You would think her another person." The hair was dyed, and secured with costly pins and with nets of gold thread. False hair and blond wigs were worn.

Putting on (ἐνδύσεως). Only here in New Testament. Female extravagance in dress in the days of the empire reached an alarming pitch.

4. **Meek** (πραέος). See on Matt. v. 5.

Of great price (πολυτελές). The word used to describe costly raiment, 1 Tim. ii. 9.

5. **Adorned** (ἐκόσμουν). Imperfect tense. *Were accustomed* to adorn.

6. **Amazement** (πτόησιν). Rev., *terror*. Compare the kindred verb πτοηθῆτε, *be terrified*, Luke xxi. 9; xxiv. 37; on which, see note. The word means *a scare*, or *nervous excitement*.

7. **According to knowledge.** With an intelligent recognition of the nature of the marriage relation.

The woman (τῷ γυναικείῳ). Not a noun, however, as would appear from the ordinary rendering, but an adjective, agreeing with σκεύει, *vessel*, as does also ἀσθενεστέρῳ, *weaker*. Both are attributes of *vessel; the female vessel as weaker*. So Rev., in margin.

Vessel (σκεύει). Compare 1 Thess. iv. 4. The primary idea of *vessel*, which is formed from the Latin *vasellum*, the diminutive of *vas*, a *vase*, is that of the receptacle which covers and contains; the case or protecting cover. Hence it is allied, etymologically, with *vest*, *vestment*, and *wear*. It is used in the New Testament (1) in the sense of a *cup* or *dish* (Luke viii. 16; John xix. 29; 2 Tim. ii. 20; Apoc. ii. 27; xviii. 12). (2) Of the man, as containing the divine energy, or as a subject of divine mercy or wrath, and hence becoming a divine instrument. Thus Paul is a *chosen vessel* to bear God's name (Acts ix. 15). Vessels *of wrath* (Rom. ix. 22); *of mercy* (Rom. ix. 23). So of the woman, as God's instrument, along with man, for his service in the family and in society. (3) Collectively, in the plural, of all the implements of any particular economy, as a house, or a ship. Matt. xii. 29, *goods;* Acts xxvii. 17, the *tackling* or *gear* of a ship.

Giving (ἀπονέμοντες). Only here in New Testament. The word means, literally, *to portion out*, and is appropriate to the husband as *controlling* what is to be meted out to the wife.

Hindered (ἐγκόπτεσθαι). So A. V. and Rev., and the best texts, and the majority of commentators. The word means, literally, *to knock in; make an incision into;* and hence, generally, *to hinder* or *thwart* (Gal. v. 7; 1 Thess. ii. 18). Some, however, read ἐκκόπτεσθαι, *to cut off* or *destroy*.

8. **Of one mind** (ὁμόφρονες). Rev., *like-minded*. Only here in New Testament. Compare Rom. xii. 16; xv. 5; Philip. ii. 2, etc. Indicating unity of thought and feeling. From ὁμός, *one and the same*, and φρήν, *the mind*.

Having compassion one of another (συμπαθεῖς). Only here in New Testament, though the kindred verb is found Heb. iv. 15; x. 34. The rendering is needlessly diffuse. Rev., much better, *compassionate; sympathetic*, in margin. Interchange of fellow-feeling in joy or sorrow. Our popular usage errs in limiting *sympathy* to sorrow.

Love as brethren (φιλάδελφοι). Rev., more strictly, *loving as brethren*. Only here in New Testament.

Pitiful (εὔσπλαγχνοι). Only here and Eph. iv. 32. Rev., better, *tender-hearted*. From εὖ, *well*, and σπλάγχνα, *the nobler entrails*, which are regarded as the seat of the affections, and hence equivalent to our popular use of *heart*. The original sense has given rise to the unfortunate translation *bowels* in the A. V., which occurs in its literal meaning only at Acts i. 18.

Courteous. The A. V. has here followed the reading of the Tex. Rec., φιλόφρονες. But the best texts read ταπεινόφρονες, *humble-minded*. So Rev. This occurs nowhere else in the New Testament, though the kindred noun ταπεινοφροσύνη, *humility*, is found often. See on ταπεινός, *lowly*, notes on Matt. xi. 29.

9. **Rendering evil,** etc. See Rom. xii. 17.

Blessing (εὐλογοῦντες). Not a noun governed by *rendering*, but a participle. Be not rendering evil, but *be blessing*.

10. **Will love** (θέλων ἀγαπᾶν). Not the future tense of *love*,

but the verb *to will*, with the infinitive: he that *desires* or *means to love.* Rev., *would love.*

11. **Eschew** (ἐκκλινάτω). The old word *eschew* is from the Norman *eschever*, *to shun* or *avoid.* It reappears in the German *scheuen*, to be *startled* or *afraid*, and in the English *shy*, and *to shy* (as a horse). The Greek word here occurs only twice elsewhere (Rom. iii. 12; xvi. 17), where Rev. renders *turn aside* and *turn away.* It is compounded of ἐκ, *out of*, and κλίνω, *to cause to bend* or *slope;* so that the picture in the word is of one *bending aside* from his course at the approach of evil. Rev., *turn away from.*

13. **Followers** (μιμηταὶ). Lit., *imitators.* But the best texts read ζηλωταὶ, *zealots.* So Rev., *zealous.*

14. **Blessed.** See on Matt. v. 3.

Be troubled (ταραχθῆτε). The word used of Herod's trouble (Matt. ii. 3); of the agitation of the pool of Bethesda (John v. 4); of Christ's troubled spirit (John xii. 27).

15. **Sanctify the Lord God.** The A. V. follows the Tex. Rec., reading τὸν Θεὸν, *God*, instead of τὸν Χριστὸν, *Christ*, which is the reading of the best texts. The article with *Christ* shows that κύριον, *Lord*, is to be taken predicatively. Render, therefore, as Rev., *sanctify Christ* (*the* Christ) *as Lord.*

Ready to give an answer (ἕτοιμοι πρὸς ἀπολογίαν). Lit., *ready for an answer. Answer* is our word *apology*, not in the popular sense of *excuse*, but in the more radical sense of *defence.* So it is translated Acts xxii. 1; Philip. i. 7, 16. *Clearing of yourselves*, 2 Cor. vii. 11.

Meekness. See on Matt. v. 5.

16. **Having a good conscience** (συνείδησιν ἔχοντες ἀγαθήν). The position of the adjective shows that it is used predica-

tively: *having a conscience good* or *unimpaired*. Compare Heb. xiii. 18, "We have a *good conscience* (καλὴν συνείδησιν)." Συνείδησις, *conscience*, does not occur in the gospels, unless John viii. 1–11 be admitted into the text. Nor is it a word familiar to classical Greek. It is compounded of σύν, *together with*, and εἰδέναι, *to know;* and its fundamental idea is *knowing together with one's self*. Hence it denotes the consciousness which one has within himself of his own conduct as related to moral obligation; which consciousness exercises a judicial function, determining what is right or wrong, approving or condemning, urging to performance or abstinence. Hence it is not merely intellectual consciousness directed at conduct, but moral consciousness contemplating *duty*, testifying to moral obligation, even where God is not known; and, where there is knowledge of God and acquaintance with him, inspired and directed by that fact. A man cannot be conscious of himself without knowing himself as a *moral* creature. Cremer accordingly defines the word as "the consciousness man has of himself in his relation to God, manifesting itself in the form of a self-testimony, the result of the action of the spirit in the heart." And further, "conscience is, essentially, determining of the self-consciousness by the spirit as the essential principle of life. In conscience man stands face to face with himself." Conscience is, therefore, a *law*. Thus Bishop Butler: "Conscience does not only offer itself to show us the way we should walk in, but it likewise carries its own authority with it, that it is our natural guide, the guide assigned us by the Author of our nature; it therefore belongs to our condition of being; it is our duty to walk in that path and follow this guide." And again, "That principle by which we survey, and either approve or disapprove our own heart, temper, and actions, is not only to be considered as what is, in its turn, to have some influence, which may be said of every passion, of the lowest appetites; but likewise as being superior; as from its very nature claiming superiority over all others; insomuch that you cannot form a notion of this faculty, conscience, without taking in *judgment, direction, superintendency*. This is a constituent part of the idea, that is, of the faculty itself; and to preside and govern, from the very economy and constitution of man, belongs to it. Had it strength as it had right; had it power as it had manifest authority, it would absolutely govern the world" (Sermons II. and III., "On Human Nature").

Conscience is a *faculty*. The mind may "possess reason and distinguish between the true and the false, and yet be incapable of distinguishing between virtue and vice. We are entitled, therefore, to hold that the drawing of moral distinctions is not comprehended in the simple exercise of the reason. The conscience, in short, is a different faculty of the mind from the mere understanding. We must hold it to be simple and unresolvable till we fall in with a successful decomposition of it into its elements. In the absence of any such decomposition we hold that there are no simpler elements in the human mind which will yield us the ideas of the morally good and evil, of moral obligation and guilt, of merit and demerit. Compound and decompound all other ideas as you please, associate them together as you may, they will never give us the ideas referred to, so peculiar and full of meaning, without a faculty implanted in the mind for this very purpose" (McCosh, "Divine Government, Physical and Moral").

Conscience is a *sentiment:* i.e., it contains and implies conscious emotions which arise on the discernment of an object as good or bad. The judgment formed by conscience awakens sensibility. When the judicial faculty pronounces a thing to be lovable, it awakens love. When it pronounces it to be noble or honorable, it awakens respect and admiration. When it pronounces it to be cruel or vile, it awakens disgust and abhorrence.

In scripture we are to view conscience, as Bishop Ellicott remarks, not in its abstract nature, but in its practical manifestations. Hence it may be *weak* (1 Cor. viii. 7, 12), unauthoritative, and awakening only the feeblest emotion. It may be *evil* or *defiled* (Heb. x. 22; Tit. i. 15), through consciousness of evil practice. It may be *seared* (1 Tim. iv. 2), branded by its own testimony to evil practice, hardened and insensible to the appeal of good. On the other hand, it may be *pure* (2 Tim. i. 3), unveiled, and giving honest and clear moral testimony. It may be *void of offence* (Acts xxiv. 16), unconscious of evil intent or act;

good, as here, or *honorable* (Heb. xiii. 18). The expression and the idea, in the full Christian sense, are foreign to the Old Testament, where the testimony to the character of moral action and character is borne by external revelation rather than by the inward moral consciousness.

Falsely accuse (ἐπηρεάζοντες). Compare Luke vi. 28; the only other passage where the word occurs, Matt. v. 44, being rejected from the best texts. The word means *to threaten abusively; to act despitefully*. Rev., *revile*.

17. **If the will of God be so** (εἰ θέλοι τὸ θέλημα τοῦ Θεοῦ). More literally, as Rev., preserving the play upon the word *will*, *if the will of God should so will*.

18. **The just for the unjust.** But the Greek without the article is more graphic: *just for unjust*.

In the flesh. The Greek omits the article. Read *in flesh*, the material form assumed in his incarnation.

In the spirit. Also without the article, *in spirit;* not as A. V., *by the Spirit*, meaning the Holy Ghost, but referring to his spiritual, incorporeal life. The words connect themselves with the death-cry on the cross: "Father, into thy hands I commend my spirit." Huther observes, "Flesh is that side of the man's being by which he belongs to earth, is therefore a creature of earth, and accordingly perishable like everything earthy. Spirit, on the other hand, is that side of his being according to which he belongs to a supernal sphere of being, and is therefore not merely a creature of earth, and is destined to an immortal existence."

Thus we must be careful and not understand *spirit* here of the Spirit of God, as distinguished from the *flesh* of Christ, but of the *spiritual nature* of Christ; "the higher spiritual nature which belonged to the integrity of his humanity" (Cook).

19. **By which** (ἐν ᾧ). Wrong. Rev., correctly, *in which:* in the spiritual form of life; in the disembodied spirit.

Went and preached (πορευθεὶς ἐκήρυξεν). The word *went*, employed as usual of a *personal* act; and *preached*, in its ordinary New-Testament sense of proclaiming the Gospel.

To the spirits (πνεύμασιν). As in Heb. xii. 23, of disembodied spirits, though the word ψυχαὶ, *souls*, is used elsewhere (Apoc. vi. 9; xx. 4).

In prison (ἐν φυλακῇ). Authorities differ, some explaining by 2 Pet. ii. 4; Jude 6; Apoc. xx. 7, as the final abode of the lost. Excepting in the last passage, the word occurs nowhere else in the New Testament in a metaphorical sense. It is often translated *watch* (Matt xiv. 25; Luke ii. 8); *hold* and *cage* (Apoc. xviii. 2). Others explain as *Hades*, the kingdom of the dead generally.

20. **In which** (εἰς ἣν). Lit., *into which*. A pregnant construction; *into which* they were gathered, and *in which* they were saved.

By water (διὰ). Rev., *through*. Some take this as instrumental, *by means of water*; others as local, *by passing through* the water, or being brought safely through the water into the ark. Rev., in margin, *were brought safely through water*.

21. **The like figure whereunto.** Following a rejected reading, ᾧ, *to which*; so that the literal rendering would be the *antitype to which*. Read ὃ ἀντίτυπον, *which, the antitype* or *as an antitype*; i.e., which *water*, being the antitype of that water of the flood, doth now save you, even baptism. Rev., *which, after a true likeness doth now*, etc. Ἀντίτυπον, *figure*, or antitype, is from ἀντί, *over against*, and τύπος, *a blow*. Hence, originally, *repelling a blow*: a blow against a blow; a counterblow. So of an *echo* or of the *reflection* of light; then a *correspondence*, as of a stamp to the die, as here. The word occurs only once elsewhere, Heb. ix. 24: "the *figures* of the true."

Putting away (ἀπόθεσις). Peculiar to Peter. Here and 2 Pet. i. 14.

Filth (ῥύπου). Only here in New Testament. In classical Greek signifying especially *dry* dirt, as on the person.

Answer (ἐπερώτημα). Only here in New Testament. In classical Greek the word means a *question* and nothing else. The meaning here is much disputed, and can hardly be settled satisfactorily. The rendering *answer* has no warrant. The meaning seems to be (as Alford), "the seeking after God of a good and pure conscience, which is the aim and end of the Christian baptismal life." So Lange: "The thing asked may be conceived as follows: 'How shall I rid myself of an evil conscience? Wilt thou, most holy God, again accept me, a sinner? Wilt thou, Lord Jesus, grant me the communion of thy death and life? Wilt thou, O Holy Spirit, assure me of grace and adoption, and dwell in my heart?' To these questions the triune Jehovah answers in baptism, 'Yea!' Now is laid the solid foundation for a good conscience. The conscience is not only purified from its guilt, but it receives new vital power by means of the resurrection of Jesus Christ."

This is the sense of ἐπερωτᾷν εἰς, in the only place where it occurs in scripture, 2 Sam. xi. 7 (Sept.): "David *asked of him* how Joab did (ἐπερώτησεν εἰς εἰρήνην Ἰωάβ)." Lit., *with reference to the peace of Joab*. Rev. renders, *the interrogation*, and puts *inquiry, appeal*, in margin.

22. **Gone into heaven.** Perhaps with the scene of the ascension in Peter's mind.

CHAPTER IV.

1. **Arm yourselves** (ὁπλίσασθε). Only here in New Testament. The thought is Pauline. See Rom. xiii. 12; 2 Cor. vi. 7; Eph. vi. 10, 17; 1 Thess. v. 8; Col. iii. 12.

Mind (ἔννοιαν). Only here and Heb. iv. 12. Literally the word means *thought*, and so some render it here. Rev. puts it in margin. The rendering *intent, resolution*, is very doubtful.

It seems rather to be the thought *as determining the resolution.* Since Christ has suffered in the flesh, be ye also willing to suffer in the flesh.

2. **Live** (βιῶσαι). Only here in New Testament.

The rest of the time (ἐπίλοιπον). Only here in New Testament.

3. **For the time past,** etc. Compare Rom. xiii. 13.

Us (ἡμῖν). The best texts omit.

Of our life (τοῦ βίου). The best texts omit.

Will (βούλημα, the better reading for θέλημα). *Desire, inclination.* See on Matt. i. 19.

When we walked (πεπορευμένους). Rev., rightly, *ye* walked. Construe with *to have wrought.* The time past may suffice for *you* to have wrought the desire, etc., *walking as ye have done;* the perfect participle having an inferential reference to a course of life now done with.

Lasciviousness (ἀσελγείαις). The following enumeration of vices is characteristic of Peter's style in its fulness and condensation. He enumerates six forms of sensuality, three personal and three social: (1) Ἀσελγείαις, *wantonness.* See on Mark vii. 22. Excesses of all kinds, with possibly an emphasis on sins of uncleanness. (2) Ἐπιθυμίαις, *lusts.* See on Mark iv. 19. Pointing especially to fleshly lusts, "the inner principles of licentiousness" (Cook). (3) Οἰνοφλυγίαις, *excess of wine.* Only here in New Testament. The kindred verb occurs in the Septuagint, Deut. xxi. 20; Isa. lvi. 12. From οἶνος, *wine,* and φλέω or φλύω, *to teem with abundance;* thence to *boil over* or *bubble up, overflow.* It is the *excessive, insatiate* desire for drink, from which comes the use of the word for the *indulgence* of the desire—*debauch.* So Rev., *wine-bibbings.* The remaining three are *revellings, banquetings,* and *idolatries.*

Revellings (κώμοις). The word originally signifies merely a *merry-making;* most probably a *village* festival, from κώμη, a *village.* In the cities such entertainments grew into carouses, in which the party of revellers paraded the streets with torches, singing, dancing, and all kinds of frolics. These revels also entered into religious observances, especially in the worship of Bacchus, Demeter, and the Idaean Zeus in Crete. The fanatic and orgiastic rites of Egypt, Asia Minor, and Thrace became engrafted on the old religion. Socrates, in the introduction to "The Republic," pictures himself as having gone down to the Piraeus to see the celebration of the festival of Bendis, the Thracian Artemis (Diana); and as being told by one of his companions that, in the evening, there is to be a torch-race with horses in honor of the goddess. The rites grew furious and ecstatic. "Crowds of women, clothed with fawns' skins, and bearing the sanctified thyrsus (a staff wreathed with vine-leaves) flocked to the solitudes of Parnassus, Kithaeron, or Taygetus during the consecrated triennial period, and abandoned themselves to demonstrations of frantic excitement, with dancing and clamorous invocation of the god. They were said to tear animals limb from limb, to devour the raw flesh, and to cut themselves without feeling the wound. The men yielded to a similar impulse by noisy revels in the streets, sounding the cymbals and tambourine, and carrying the image of the god in procession" (Grote, "History of Greece"). Peter, in his introduction, addresses the sojourners in Galatia, where the Phrygian worship of Cybele, the great mother of the gods, prevailed, with its wild orgies and hideous mutilations. Lucretius thus describes the rites:

> "With vigorous hand the clamorous drum they rouse,
> And wake the sounding cymbal; the hoarse horn
> Pours forth its threatening music, and the pipe,
> With Phrygian airs distracts the maddening mind,
> While arms of blood the fierce enthusiasts wield
> To fright the unrighteous crowds, and bend profound
> Their impious souls before the power divine.
> Thus moves the pompous idol through the streets,
> Scattering mute blessings, while the throngs devout
> Strew, in return, their silver and their brass,

Loading the paths with presents, and o'ershade
The heavenly form ; and all th' attending train,
With dulcet sprays of roses, pluckt profuse,
A band select before them, by the Greeks
Curetes called, from Phrygian parents sprung,
Sport with fantastic chains, the measured dance
Weaving infuriate, charmed with human blood,
And madly shaking their tremendous crests."

De Rerum Natura, ii., 618–631.

Banquetings (πότοις). Lit., *drinking-bouts.* Rev., *carousings.*

Abominable (ἀθεμίτοις). Only here, and by Peter in Acts x. 28. More literally, *unlawful*, emphasizing the idolatries as violations of divine law.

4. **Run not with them.** "In a troop" (Bengel); like a band of revellers. See above. Compare Ovid's description of the Bacchic rites :

" Lo, Bacchus comes ! and with the festive cries
Resound the fields ; and mixed in headlong rout,
Men, matrons, maids, paupers, and nobles proud,
To the mysterious rites are borne along."

Metamorphoses, iii., 528–530.

Excess (ἀνάχυσιν). Only here in New Testament. Lit., *pouring forth.* Rev. has *flood* in margin. The word is used in classical Greek of the *tides* which fill the hollows.

Riot (ἀσωτίας). From ἀ, *not*, and σώζω, *to save.* Lit., *unsavingness*, prodigality, wastefulness; and thence of squandering on one's own debased appetites, whence it takes the sense of *dissoluteness* or *profligacy*. In Luke xv. 13, the kindred adverb ἀσώτως is used. The prodigal is described as *scattering* his substance, to which is added, *living wastefully* (ζῶν ἀσώτως). Compare Eph. v. 18; Tit. i. 6.

5. **That is ready** (ἑτοίμως ἔχοντι). Lit., *having himself in readiness;* there at God's right hand in heaven, whither he has

gone (ch. iii. 22). Implying, also, a *near* judgment. Compare ver. 7.

7. **Is at hand** (ἤγγικεν). Lit., *has come near.* The word constantly used of the coming of Christ and his kingdom. See Matt. iii. 2; Mark i. 15; Luke x. 9; Heb. x. 25.

Be ye sober (σωφρονήσατε). The word is from σῶς, *sound*, and φρήν, *the mind.* Therefore, as Rev., *be ye of sound mind.* Compare Mark v. 15.

Watch (νήψατε). See on ch. i. 13. The A. V. has followed the Vulgate, *vigilate* (*watch*). Rev. is better: *be sober.*

Unto prayer (εἰς προσευχάς). Lit., *prayers.* The plural is used designedly: prayers of all kinds, private or public. Tynd. renders, *Be ye discreet and sober, that ye may be apt to prayers.* Compare Eph. vi. 18, "with *every kind* of prayer, and watching *thereunto.*"

8. **Fervent** (ἐκτενῆ). See, on the kindred adverb *fervently*, notes on ch. i. 22.

Love covereth, etc. Compare Jas. v. 20; Prov. x. 12.

9. **Using hospitality.** Compare Rom. xiii. 13.

10. **A gift** (χάρισμα). Originally, something *freely* given: a gift of *grace* (χάρις). Used in New Testament (*a*) of *a blessing of God graciously bestowed*, as upon sinners (Rom. v. 15, 16; xi. 29); (*b*) of *a gracious divine endowment:* an extraordinary gift of the Holy Spirit dwelling and working in a special manner in the individual (1 Tim. iv. 14; 2 Tim. i. 6; Rom. xii. 6, 8). So here.

Manifold. See on ch. i. 6.

11. **Oracles** (λόγια). In classical Greek, of the oracular re

sponses of heathen deities. Here, divine utterances or revelations. Compare Acts vii. 38; Rom. iii. 2; Heb. v. 12.

Giveth (χορηγεῖ). Only here and 2 Cor. ix. 10. Peter uses the compound ἐπιχορηγέω, *furnish*, in 2 Pet. i. 5; which see.

12. **Think it not strange** (μὴ ξενίζεσθε). *I.e.*, alien from you and your condition as Christians. Compare v. 4.

Fiery trial (πυρώσει). The word means *burning*. In Prov. xxvii. 21 (Sept.), it is rendered *furnace*. In Ps. lxv. (Sept.), lxvi. (A. V.), we read, "Thou, O God, hast proved us: thou hast *smelted* us, as silver is *smelted*." Compare Zech. xiii. 9.

Which is to try you (ὑμῖν γινομένῃ). The A. V. thus makes the trial a thing of *the future*; mistranslating the Greek present participle, *which is taking place*. This participle, therefore, represents the trial as *actually in progress*. The Rev. does not give this force by its *which cometh upon you*.

To try you (πρὸς πειρασμὸν). Lit., *for trial* or probation.

Strange thing (ξένου). Compare *think it not strange*, above.

Happened (συμβαίνοντος). Again the present participle. Better, perhaps, *were happening*; by chance, instead of with the definite purpose indicated by "taking place *with a view to probation*." See above.

13. **Inasmuch as ye are partakers.** Compare Rom. viii. 17.

Be glad with exceeding joy (χαρῆτε ἀγαλλιώμενοι). Lit., *ye may rejoice exulting*. See on ch. i. 6.

14. **The spirit of glory and of God** (τὸ τῆς δόξης καὶ τὸ τοῦ Θεοῦ πνεῦμα). Lit., *the spirit of glory and that of God*. The repetition of the article identifies the spirit of God with the spirit of glory: the spirit of glory, and *therefore* the spirit of

God: who is none other than the spirit of God himself. Hence Rev., better, *the spirit of glory and the spirit of God.*

Resteth (ἀναπαύεται). Compare Isa. xi. 2; Luke x. 6; Num. xi. 25, 26; Mark vi. 31; Matt. xxvi. 45; Apoc. xiv. 13. Also, Matt. xi. 28, where the word is used in the active voice, *to give rest* or refreshment.

15. **A busybody in other men's matters** (ἀλλοτριοεπίσκοπος). Only here in New Testament. Lit., *the overseer of another's matters.* One who usurps authority in matters not within his province. Rev., *meddler.* Compare Luke xii. 13, 14; 1 Thess. iv. 11; 2 Thess. iii. 11. It may refer to the officious interference of Christians in the affairs of their Gentile neighbors, through excess of zeal to conform them to the Christian standard.

16. **A Christian.** Only three times in the New Testament, and never as a name used by Christians themselves, but as a nickname or a term of reproach. See on Acts xi. 26. Hence Peter's idea is, if any man suffer from the contumely of those who contemptuously style him *Christian.*

19. **Commit** (παρατιθέσθωσαν). Give in charge as a deposit. Compare Luke xii. 48; Acts xx. 32; 1 Tim. i. 18. The word is used by Christ in commending his soul to God (Luke xxiii. 46).

Well-doing (ἀγαθοποιΐᾳ). Only here in New Testament. Compare ch. ii. 14. The surrender to God is to be coupled with the active practice of good.

CHAPTER V.

1. **Also an elder** (συμπρεσβύτερος). Only here in New Testament. Better, as Rev., *fellow-elder.* The expression is decisive against the primacy of Peter.

Witness (μάρτυς). The word is used in the New Testament to denote (*a*) a *spectator* or *eye-witness* (Acts x. 39; vi. 13). (*b*) One who *testifies* to what he has seen (Acts i. 8; v. 32). (*c*) In the forensic sense, a *witness in court* (Matt. xxvi. 65; Mark xiv. 63). (*d*) One who vindicates his testimony by suffering: a *martyr* (Acts xxii. 20; Heb. xii. 1; Apoc. ii. 13; xvii. 6). The first three meanings run into each other. The eye-witness, as a spectator, is always such with a view to giving testimony. Hence this expression of Peter cannot be limited to the mere fact of his having *seen* what he preached; especially since, when he wishes to emphasize this fact, he employs another word, ἐπόπτης (2 Pet. i. 16). Therefore he speaks of himself as a witness, especially in the sense of being called to testify of what he has seen.

Partaker (κοινωνός). This use of the word, expressing a present realization of something not yet attained, occurs in no other writer in the New Testament. See on 2 Pet. i. 4.

2. **Feed** (ποιμάνατε). Better, Rev., *tend*, since the verb denotes all that is included in the office of a shepherd—guiding, guarding, folding, no less than feeding, which latter is expressed by βόσκω. There is, doubtless, a reminiscence in the word of Christ's charge to Peter (John xxi. 15–17). Both words are used there: "*Feed* (βόσκε) my lambs" (ver. 15); "*tend* (ποίμαινε) my sheep" (ver. 16); "*feed* (βόσκε) my sheep" (ver. 17). The A. V. obliterates the distinction by rendering all three *feed*. Bengel rightly remarks, "Feeding is part of tending." See on Matt. ii. 6.

Taking the oversight. The best texts omit. Rev. retains.

By constraint (ἀναγκαστῶς). Only here in New Testament.

Willingly (ἑκουσίως). Only here and Heb. x. 26.

For filthy lucre (αἰσχροκερδῶς). From αἰσχρός, *disgraceful*, and κέρδος, *gain*. Only here in New Testament. The word *filthy* is intended to convey the idea which lies in αἰσχρός, *base* or *dishonorable;* becoming such if it is made the motive of the minister's service. Compare 2 Cor. xii. 14.

Willingly (προθύμως). Not strong enough. The word is compounded of πρό, *forward*, and θυμός, *heart* or *spirit*. Hence Rev., *with a ready mind;* a forward spirit; denoting not mere *willingness*, but *zeal*. Only here in New Testament. Compare the kindred adjective πρόθυμος, *ready* (Rom. i. 15; Matt. xxvi. 41; Mark xiv. 38), and the kindred noun προθυμία, *readiness* (2 Cor. viii. 11, 12, 19; ix. 2).

3. **As lording it** (κατακυριεύοντες). See Matt. xx. 25; Acts xix. 16. Other words are used for the exercise of *legitimate* authority in the church: προΐσταμαι, *to be over* (1 Thess. v. 12; 1 Tim. v. 17); ποιμαίνω, as ver. 2, *tend*. But this carries the idea of *high-handed* rule.

Heritage (κλήρων). Plural. Κλῆρος means *a lot*. See on *inheritance*, ch. i. 4. From the kindred adjective κληρικός comes the English *cleric*, contracted into *clerk*, which in ecclesiastical writings originally signified a minister; either as being chosen *by lot* like Matthias, or as being the lot or inheritance of God. Hence Wycliffe translates the passage, "neither as having lordship in *the clergie*." As in the Middle Ages the clergy were almost the only persons who could write, the word *clerk* came to have one of its common modern meanings. The word here, though its interpretation is somewhat disputed, seems to refer to the several *congregations*—the *lots* or *charges* assigned to the elders. Compare προσεκληρώθησαν, *were added as disciples;* A. V., *consorted with* (Acts xvii. 4). Rev. renders *charge*. Why not *charges?*

Examples (τύποι). Peter uses three different terms for a *pattern* or *model:* ὑπογραμμός, *a writing-copy* (ch. ii. 21); ὑπόδειγμα, for which classical writers prefer παράδειγμα, *an architect's plan* or *a sculptor's or painter's model* (2 Pet. ii. 6); τύπος (see on ch. iii. 21), of which our word *type* is nearly a transcript. The word primarily means the impression left by a stroke (τύπτω, *to strike*). Thus John xx. 25, "the *print* of the nails." Used of the stamp on coin; the impression of any engraving or hewn work of art; a monument or statue; the *figures* of the tabernacle of Moloch and of the star Remphan (Acts vii. 43). Generally, an *image* or *form*, always with a statement of the object; and hence the kindred meaning of a *pattern* or *model*. See Acts xxiii. 25; Rom. v. 14; Philip. iii. 17; Heb. viii. 5.

4. **The chief Shepherd** (ἀρχιποίμενος). Only here in New Testament. In harmony with ver. 2. "The last thing Peter could have dreamed of as possible would be its misapplication to himself or his so-called successors" (Cook). Compare Heb. xiii. 20, *great Shepherd;* and John x. 11, 14, *good Shepherd.* Also, Ezek. xxxiv. 15, 16, 23.

Ye shall receive. See on *receiving*, 1 Pet. i. 9.

Crown (στέφανον). From στέφω, *to put round, encircle.* It is the crown of victory in the games; of military valor; the marriage wreath, or the festal garland, woven of leaves or made of gold in imitation of leaves. Thus it is distinguished from the *royal* crown, which is διάδημα, of which *diadem* is a transcript. In Paul, στέφανος is always used of the *conqueror's* crown, not of the *king's* (1 Cor. ix. 24–26; 2 Tim. ii. 5). Though it is urged that Peter would not have employed a reference to the crown of the victors in the games, because of the abhorrence of the Palestinian Jews for heathen spectacles, yet the reference to the crown of leaves seems to be determined by the epithet *unfading*, as compared with garlands of earthly leaves. The crown of thorns woven for Jesus is called στέφανος, with reference rather to its being *twined* than to its being a caricature of a kingly crown.

5. **Be clothed with humility** (τὴν ταπεινοφροσύνην ἐγκομβώσασθε). The last word is a very peculiar one, occurring only here. It is derived from κόμβος, a *roll, band,* or *girth:*

a *knot* or *roll* of cloth, made in tying or tucking up any part of the dress. The kindred word ἐγκόμβωμα, from which the verb is directly formed, means a *slave's apron*, under which the loose garments were girt up. Compare Horace's "puer alte cinctus," *a slave girt high*. Hence the figure carries an exhortation to put on humility as a *working virtue* employed in *ministry*. This is apparent from the evident reminiscence of that scene in which Peter figured so prominently—the washing of the disciples' feet by the Lord, when he *girded himself* with a towel as a servant, and gave them the lesson of ministry both by word and act. Bengel paraphrases, "Put on and wrap yourselves about with humility, so that the covering of humility cannot possibly be stripped from you."

Resisteth (ἀντιτάσσεται). A strong and graphic word. Lit., *setteth himself in array against*, as one draws out a host for battle. Pride calls out God's armies. No wonder, therefore, that it "goeth before destruction."

The proud (ὑπερηφάνοις). See on *pride*, Mark vii. 22. Compare Jas. iv. 6.

To the humble. See on Matt. xi. 29.

6. **Mighty hand** (κραταιὰν χεῖρα). A phrase found nowhere else in the New Testament, but occurring in the Septuagint, Ex. iii. 19; Deut. iii. 24; Job xxx. 21. The adjective κραταιὰν, *mighty*, is, moreover, used only here. Compare Luke i. 51, 52.

7. **Casting** (ἐπιῤῥίψαντες). The aorist participle denoting an act once for all; throwing the whole life with its care on him.

All your care (πᾶσαν τήν μέριμναν). *The whole of* your care. "Not every anxiety as it arises, for none will arise if this transferrence has been effectually made." *Care.* See on Matt. vi. 25, *take no thought*. Rev., rightly, *anxiety*.

He careth (μέλει). Meaning the *watchful* care of interest and affection. The sixth and seventh verses should be taken together: *Humble yourselves* and *cast all your anxiety*. Pride is at the root of most of our anxiety. To human pride it is humiliating to cast everything upon another and be cared for. See Jas. iv. 6, 7.

8. **Be sober** (νήψατε). See on ch. iv. 7.

Be vigilant (γρηγορήσατε). Rev., *be watchful*. See on Mark xiii. 35; and 1 Thess. v. 6, where both verbs occur: *watch* and *be sober*. A reminiscence of the scene in Gethsemane: *Could ye not watch with me?* (Matt. xxvi. 40, 41).

Adversary (ὁ αντίδικος). The article points to a well-known adversary. From ἀντί, *against*, and δίκη, *a lawsuit*. Strictly, an adversary in a lawsuit. Here an adversary in general. Compare Zech. iii. 1–5. Only here, in New Testament, of Satan.

The devil. See on Matt. iv. 1.

Roaring (ὠρυόμενος). Only here in New Testament. The word conveys somewhat of the sense by the sound (*oruomenos*). It denotes especially the howl of a beast in fierce hunger.

Lion. Augustine says, "Christ is called 'a lion' (Apoc. v. 5) because of his courage: the devil, because of his ferocity. The one lion comes to conquer, the other to hurt." Seven Hebrew words are used for this animal; six to describe his movements and four to describe his roar. He is mentioned in the Bible about one hundred and thirty times. In Job iv. 10, 11, five different words are used for him. In Judges xiv. 5; Ps. xxi. 13; ciii. 21 (Sept.), the same word as here is used for the roaring of the lion as a translation of the Hebrew word for *the thunder* in Job xxxvii. 4.

Walketh about (περιπατεῖ). Compare Job i. 7; ii. 2. This word gave name to that sect of Greek philosophers known as *Peripatetics*, because they walked about while teaching or disputing. "St. Peter calls Satan *the Peripatetic*" (Cox, on Job). The Arabs call him *the Busy One*. It was to Peter that Christ said, "Satan hath desired to have you," etc. (Luke xxii. 31).

Devour (καταπίῃ). Lit., *swallow down*. See on Matt. xxiii 24.

9. **Resist** (ἀντίστητε). The Rev., very judiciously, substitutes *withstand; resist* having been already used in ver. 5 for ἀντιτάσσεται. *Withstand* is, moreover, the more accurate rendering; as the verb means rather *to be firm against onset* than *to strive* against it. *With* in *withstand* is the Saxon *wid, against*, which appears in the German *wider*.

Steadfast (στερεοὶ). Compare 2 Tim. ii. 19; and the kindred verb στερεόω, *to strengthen* (Acts iii. 7, 16; xvi. 5). Paul, in Col. ii. 5, uses a cognate noun, στερέωμα, evidently as a military metaphor: "Beholding your *order* (τάξιν, compare ἀντιτάσσεται, ver. 5) and your *solid front* or *close phalanx*" (στερέωμα). It might be difficult to find, on the whole, a better rendering than *steadfast*, yet it falls a little short of the meaning. *Steadfast* is Anglo-Saxon, *stede, a place*, and *faest, fast;* and hence means *firm in its place;* but στερεοὶ conveys also the sense of *compactness, compact solidity*, and is appropriate, since a number of individuals are addressed and exhorted to withstand the onset of Satan as one compacted body. Στερεός implies solidity *in the very mass and body of the thing itself;* steadfastness, mere holding of place. A rock is στερεός, *firm, solid;* but a flexible weed with its tough roots resisting all efforts to pull it up, may be *steadfast*. The exhortation is appropriate from Peter, the Rock.

The same afflictions (τὰ αὐτὰ τῶν παθημάτων). Rev., better, *sufferings*. A very peculiar construction, occurring nowhere else in the New Testament. Lit., *the same things of sufferings*, emphasizing the idea of *identity*.

Are accomplished (ἐπιτελεῖσθαι). More correctly, *are being accomplished*. The present infinitive denotes something *in process* of accomplishment.

Brethren (ἀδελφότητι). Lit., *brotherhood.* Only here and ch. ii. 17.

10. **Who hath called us** (ὁ καλέσας ἡμᾶς). But the tense is the aorist, and the true reading is ὑμᾶς, *you*, instead of *us.* Render, therefore, as Rev., *who called you;* before the foundation of the world. See Rom. viii. 29, 30, and compare *unto his eternal glory* and *them he also glorified.*

By Christ Jesus (ἐν Χριστῷ Ἰησοῦ). The best texts omit *Jesus.* So Rev., which also renders, better, *in* Christ, denoting the *sphere* or *element* in which the calling and its results take place: "Christ as the life, head, and very principle of all existence to the Christian" (Cook).

Awhile (ὀλίγον). Rev., more literally, *a little while.* See on ch. i. 6.

Make you perfect, etc. The Tex. Rec. makes this and the three following verbs in the optative mood, expressing a *wish.* So the A. V. But the best texts make them all indicative future, and thus convert the wish or prayer into an assurance. Thus, then,

Shall himself perfect (αὐτὸς καταρτίσει). The A. V. overlooks the αὐτὸς, *himself*, which is very significant as indicating God's *personal* interest and energy in the work of confirming his children.

Shall perfect. Rev. reads *restore*, in margin. The root of this word appears in ἄρω or ἀραρίσκω, *to fit* or *join together.* So ἄρθρον means a *joint.* The radical notion of the verb is, therefore, *adjustment*—the putting of all the parts into right relation and connection. We find it used of mending the nets (Matt. iv. 21), and of restoring an erring brother (Gal. vi. 1); of framing the body and the worlds (Heb. x. 5; xi. 3); of the union of members in the church (1 Cor. i. 10; 2 Cor. xiii. 11). Out of this comes the general sense of *perfecting* (Matt. xxi 16; Luke vi. 40; 1 Thess. iii. 10).

Shall stablish (στηρίξει). The word is akin at the root to *στερεός*, *steadfast* (ver. 9), and is the very word used by Christ in his exhortation to Peter, "*strengthen* thy brethren" (Luke xxii. 32). Possibly there is a reminiscence of this in Peter's use of the word here. Compare 1 Thess. iii. 13; 2 Thess. ii. 17; Jas. v. 8; Apoc. iii. 2.

Shall strengthen (σθενώσει). Only here in New Testament. Compare Eph. iii. 16.

Shall settle (θεμελιώσει). Omitted by some texts, and by Rev. From θεμέλιος, a *foundation*. The radical notion of the word is, therefore, *to ground securely*. It occurs in Matt. vii. 25, of the house *founded* on a rock; in Heb. i. 10, of laying the foundations of the earth. In Eph. iii. 18, it is joined with *rooted*. The massing of these expressions, unconnected by conjunctions, indicates strong feeling. Bengel thus sums up the whole: "Shall *perfect*, that no *defect* remain in you: shall *stablish*, that nothing may *shake* you: shall *strengthen*, that you may overcome every adverse force. A saying worthy of Peter. He is strengthening his brethren."

12. **Silvanus.** Probably the companion of Paul known in the Acts as *Silas* (xv. 22, 27, 32, 34, 40, etc.), and called *Silvanus* by Paul in 2 Cor. i. 19; 1 Thess. i. 1; 2 Thess. i. 1.

A faithful brother. *Brother* has the definite article, *the* faithful brother, designating him as one well known for his fidelity. Rev. renders *our*, with *the* in margin.

Unto you. Construe, not as A. V., *a brother unto you*, but *I have written unto you*. So Rev.

As I suppose (ὡς λογίζομαι). Too feeble, since the verb denotes a *settled persuasion* or *assurance*. See Rom. iii. 28, "we *conclude*" or *reckon*, as the result of our reasoning. Compare Rom. viii. 18; Heb. xi. 19. Rev., *as I account him*.

I have written (ἔγραψα). Lit., *I wrote.* An example of what is known as the *epistolary aorist.* The writer regards the time of writing as his correspondent will do when he shall have received the letter. We say in a letter, *I write.* Paul, writing to Philemon, says ἀνέπεμψα, *I sent;* since to Philemon the act of sending would be already past. Therefore in using this form of expression Peter does not refer to the second epistle, nor to another now lost, but to the present epistle.

Briefly (δι' ὀλίγων). Lit., *through few* (words). Compare Heb. xiii. 22, where the expression is διὰ βραχέων, *through brief words.*

Testifying (ἐπιμαρτυρῶν). Only here in New Testament. See on ver. 1.

Wherein ye stand (εἰς ἣν ἑστήκατε). The best texts read στῆτε, imperative. So Rev., *stand ye fast therein.* Lit., "*into* which stand," the preposition with the verb having the pregnant force of entering *into* and standing fast *in.*

13. **The church.** The word is not in the Greek, but is supplied with the feminine definite article ἡ. There is, however, a difference of opinion as to the meaning of this feminine article. Some suppose a reference to Peter's own wife; others, to some prominent Christian woman in the church. Compare 2 John 1. The majority of interpreters, however, refer it to the church.

Babylon. Some understand in a figurative sense, as meaning Rome; others, literally, of Babylon on the Euphrates. In favor of the former view are the drift of ancient opinion and the Roman Catholic interpreters, with Luther and several noted modern expositors, as Ewald and Hoffmann. This, too, is the view of Canon Cook in the "Speaker's Commentary." In favor of the literal interpretation are the weighty names of Alford, Huther, Calvin, Neander, Weiss, and Reuss. Professor Salmond, in his admirable commentary on this epistle, has so forcibly summed up the testimony that we cannot do better than to give his comment entire: "In favor of this allegorical interpretation it is urged that there are other occurrences of *Babylon* in the New Testament as a mystical name for Rome (Apoc. xiv. 8; xviii. 2, 10); that it is in the highest degree unlikely that Peter should have made the Assyrian Babylon his residence or missionary centre, especially in view of a statement by Josephus indicating that the Emperor Claudius had expelled the Jews from that city and neighborhood; and that tradition connects Peter with Rome, but not with Babylon. The fact, however, that the word is mystically used in a mystical book like the Apocalypse—a book, too, which is steeped in the spirit and terminology of the Old Testament—is no argument for the mystical use of the word in writings of a different type. The allegorical interpretation becomes still less likely when it is observed that other geographical designations in this epistle (ch. i. 1) have undoubtedly the literal meaning. The tradition itself, too, is uncertain. The statement in Josephus does not bear all that it is made to bear. There is no reason to suppose that, at the time when this epistle was written, the city of Rome was currently known among Christians as Babylon. On the contrary, wherever it is mentioned in the New Testament, with the single exception of the Apocalypse (and even there it is distinguished as 'Babylon, *the great*'), it gets its usual name, Rome. So far, too, from the Assyrian Babylon being practically in a deserted state at this date, there is very good ground for believing that the Jewish population (not to speak of the heathen) of the city and vicinity was very considerable. For these and other reasons a succession of distinguished interpreters and historians, from Erasmus and Calvin, on to Neander, Weiss, Reuss, Huther, etc., have rightly held by the literal sense."

Marcus. Rev., *Mark.* John Mark, the author of the gospel. See Introduction to Mark, on his relations to Peter.

My son. Probably in a spiritual sense, though some, as Bengel, think that Peter's own son is referred to.

14. **Kiss of charity.** Compare 1 Cor. xvi. 20.

THE SECOND GENERAL EPISTLE OF PETER.

CHAPTER I

1. **Simon Peter.** Note the addition of *Simon*, and see on 1 Pet. i. 1. The best-attested orthography is *Symeon*, which is the form of his name in Acts xv. 14, where the account probably came from him. This also is the Hebraic form of the name found in the Septuagint, Gen. xxix. 33, and elsewhere. Compare Apoc. vii. 7; Luke ii. 25, 34; iii. 30; Acts xiii. 1. The combined name, Simon Peter, is found Luke v. 8; John xiii. 6; xx. 2; xxi. 15, and elsewhere, though in these instances it is given as *Simon;* Symeon occurring only in Acts xv. 14. While his name is given with greater familiarity than in the first epistle, his official title, *servant and apostle*, is fuller. This combination, servant and apostle, occurs in no other apostolic salutation. The nearest approach to it is Tit. i. 1.

Of Jesus Christ. The word *Christ* never occurs in the second epistle without *Jesus;* and only in this instance without some predicate, such as *Lord*, *Saviour*.

To them that have obtained (τοῖς λαχοῦσιν). Lit., obtained *by lot*. So Luke i. 9; John xix. 24. In the sense which it has here it is used by Peter (Acts i. 17) of Judas, who had *obtained* part of this ministry. In this sense it occurs only in that passage and here.

Like precious (ἰσότιμον). Only here in New Testament. The word should be written *like-precious*. Compare *precious* in 1 Pet. i. 7, 19; ii. 4, 6, 7. Not the same in measure to all, but having an equal value and honor to those who receive it, as admitting them to the same Christian privileges.

With us. Most probably the Jewish Christians, of whom Peter was one. Professor Salmond remarks, "There is much to show how alien it was to primitive Christian thought to regard Gentile Christians as occupying in grace the self-same platform with Christians gathered out of the ancient church of God." See Acts xi. 17; xv. 9–11.

Saviour. Frequently applied to Christ in this epistle, but never in the first.

2. **In the knowledge** (ἐν ἐπιγνώσει). The compound expressing *full* knowledge, and so common in Paul's writings.

Our Lord (κυρίου ἡμῶν). The word *Lord* in the second epistle is always used of God, unless *Christ* or *Saviour* is added.

3. **Hath granted** (δεδωρημένης). This is the only word which Peter and Mark *alone* have in common in the New Testament; a somewhat singular fact in view of their intimate relations, and of the impress of Peter upon Mark's gospel: yet it tells very strongly against the theory of a forgery of this epistle. The word is stronger than the simple δίδωμι, *to give*, meaning *to grant* or *bestow* as a *gift*. Compare Mark xv. 45.

Godliness (εὐσέβειαν). Used only by Peter (Acts iii. 12), and in the Pastoral Epistles. It is from εὐ, *well*, and σέβομαι, *to worship*, so that the radical idea is *worship rightly directed*. Worship, however, is to be understood in its etymological sense, *worth-ship*, or reverence paid to worth, whether in God or man. So Wycliffe's rendering of Matt. vi. 2, "that they be *worshipped* of men;" and "*worship* thy father and thy mother," Matt. xix. 19. In classical Greek the word is not confined to religion, but means also *piety* in the fulfilment of human relations, like the Latin *pietas*. Even in classical Greek, however, it is a standing word for *piety* in the religious sense, showing itself in right reverence; and is opposed to δυσσέβεια, *ungodliness*, and ἀνοσιότης, *profaneness*. "The recognition of dependence upon the gods, the confession of human dependence, the tribute of homage which man renders in the certainty that he needs their favor—all this is εὐσέβεια, manifest in conduct and conversation, in sacrifice and prayer" (Nägelsbach, cited by Cremer). This definition may be almost literally transferred to the Christian word. It embraces the confession of the one living and true God, and life corresponding to this knowledge. See on ver. 2.

Called (καλέσαντος). Also used of the divine invitation, 1 Pet. ii. 9, 21; iii. 9; v. 10.

To glory and virtue (ἰδίᾳ δόξῃ καὶ ἀρετῇ). Lit., and properly, *by his own glory and virtue*, though some read διὰ δόξης καὶ ἀρετῆς, *through glory and virtue*. Rev. adopts the former. The meaning is much the same in either case.

His own (ἰδίᾳ). Of frequent occurrence in Peter, and not necessarily with an emphatic force, since the adjective is sometimes used merely as a possessive pronoun, and mostly so in Peter (1 Pet. iii. 1, 5; 2 Pet. ii. 16, 22, etc.).

Virtue. See on 1 Pet. ii. 9. Used by Peter only, with the exception of Philip. iv. 8. The original classical sense of the word had no special moral import, but denoted excellence of any kind—bravery, rank, nobility; also, excellence of land, animals, things, classes of persons. Paul seems to avoid the term, using it only once.

On *glory* and *virtue* Bengel says, "the former indicates his *natural*, the latter his *moral*, attributes."

4. **Whereby** (δι' ὧν). Lit., *through which;* viz., his glory

and virtue. Note the three occurrences of διά, *through*, in vv. 3, 4.

Are given (δεδώρηται). Middle voice; not passive, as A. V. Hence Rev., correctly, *he hath granted.* See on ver. 3.

Exceeding great and precious promises. Rev., *his* exceeding great, etc., by way of rendering the definite article, τὰ.

Precious (τίμια). The word occurs fourteen times in the New Testament. In eight instances it is used of material things, as stones, fruit, wood. In Peter it occurs three times: 1 Pet. i. 7, of tried faith; 1 Pet. i. 19, of the blood of Christ; and here, of God's promises.

Promises (ἐπαγγέλματα). Only in this epistle. In classical Greek the distinction is made between ἐπαγγέλματα, promises *voluntarily* or *spontaneously* made, and ὑποσχέσεις, promises made *in response to a petition.*

Might be partakers (γένησθε κοινωνοὶ). Rev., more correctly, *may become*, conveying the idea of a *growth.* See note on κοινωνὸς, *partaker*, 1 Pet. v. 1; and compare Heb. xii. 10.

Having escaped (ἀποφυγόντες). Only in this epistle. To escape *by flight.*

Through lust (ἐν ἐπιθυμίᾳ). Rev. renders *by* lust, as the *instrument* of the corruption. Others, *in* lust, as the *sphere* of the corruption, or as that in which it is grounded.

5. **Beside this** (αὐτὸ τοῦτο). Wrong. Render, *for this very cause*, as Rev. Lit., *this very thing.* Just as τί, *what?* has come to mean *why?* So the strengthened demonstrative acquires the meaning of *wherefore, for this very cause.*

Giving all diligence (σπουδὴν πᾶσαν παρεισενέγκαντες) The verb occurs only here in New Testament, and means, literally, *to bring in by the side of: adding* your diligence to the divine promises. So Rev., *adding on your part.*

Add to your faith, etc. The A. V. is entirely wrong. The verb rendered *add* (ἐπιχορηγήσατε) is derived from χορός, a *chorus,* such as was employed in the representation of the Greek tragedies. The verb originally means *to bear the expense of a chorus,* which was done by a person selected by the state, who was obliged to defray all the expenses of training and maintenance. In the New Testament the word has lost this technical sense, and is used in the general sense of *supplying* or *providing.* The verb is used by Paul (2 Cor. ix. 10; Gal. iii. 5; Col. ii. 19), and is rendered *minister* (A. V.), *supply* (Rev.); and the simple verb χορηγέω, *minister,* occurs 1 Pet. iv. 11; 2 Cor. ix. 10. Here the Rev., properly, renders *supply.*

To your faith (ἐν τῇ πίστει). The A. V. exhorts *to add* one virtue to another; but the Greek, *to develop one virtue in the exercise of another:* "an increase by growth, not by external junction; each new grace springing out of, attempting, and perfecting the other." Render, therefore, as Rev. *In your faith supply virtue, and in your virtue knowledge,* etc.

Virtue. See on ver. 3, and 1 Pet. ii. 9. Not in the sense of moral excellence, but of the *energy* which Christians are to exhibit, as God exerts his energy upon them. As God calls us by his own *virtue* (ver. 3), so Christians are to exhibit *virtue* or *energy* in the exercise of their faith, translating it into vigorous action.

6. **Temperance** (ἐγκρατεία). Self-control; holding the passions and desires in hand. See 1 Cor. ix. 25.

Patience (ὑπομονήν). Lit., *remaining behind* or *staying,* from μένω, *to wait.* Not merely endurance of the inevitable, for Christ could have relieved himself of his sufferings (Heb. xii. 2, 3; compare Matt. xxvi. 53); but the heroic, brave patience with which a Christian not only *bears* but *contends.*

Speaking of Christ's patience, Barrow remarks, "Neither was it out of a stupid insensibility or stubborn resolution that he did thus behave himself; for he had a most vigorous sense of all those grievances, and a strong (natural) aversation from undergoing them; . . . but from a perfect submission to the divine will, and entire command over his passions, an excessive charity toward mankind, this patient and meek behavior did spring." The same writer defines patience as follows: "That virtue which qualifieth us to bear all conditions and all events, by God's disposal incident to us, with such apprehensions and persuasions of mind, such dispositions and affections of heart, such external deportment and practices of life as God requireth and good reason directeth (Sermon XLII., "On Patience").

Godliness. See on ver. 3. The quality is never ascribed to God.

Brotherly kindness (φιλαδελφίαν). Rev. renders, literally, *love of the brethren.*

Charity (ἀγάπην). There seems at first an infelicity in the rendering of the Rev., *in your love of the brethren love.* But this is only apparent. In the former word Peter contemplates Christian fellow-believers as naturally and properly holding the first place in our affections (compare Gal. vi. 10, "*Especially* unto them which *are of the household of faith*"). But he follows this with the broader affection which should characterize Christians, and which Paul lauds in 1 Cor. xiii., the *love of men as men.* It may be remarked here that the entire rejection by the Rev. of *charity* as the rendering of ἀγάπη is wholesome and defensible. *Charity* has acquired two peculiar meanings, both of which are indeed included or implied in *love,* but neither of which expresses more than a single phase of love —*tolerance* and *beneficence.* The A. V. in the great majority of cases translates *love;* always in the Gospels, and mostly elsewhere. There is no more reason for saying "*charity* suffereth long," than for saying, "the *charity* of God is shed abroad in our hearts," or "God is *charity.*"

8. **Be in you** (ὑπάρχοντα). Rev., *are yours;* following the sense of *possession* which legitimately belongs to the verb; as Matt. xix. 21, *that thou hast;* 1 Cor. xiii. 3, *goods.* In the sense of *being* the verb is stronger than the simple εἶναι, *to be;* denoting being which is *from the beginning,* and therefore attaching to a person as a proper characteristic; something *belonging* to him, and so running into the idea of *rightful possession* as above.

Barren (ἀργοὺς). From ἀ, *not,* and ἔργον, *work.* Hence, more correctly, as Rev., *idle.* Compare "*idle* word" (Matt. xii. 36); "standing *idle*" (Matt. xx. 3, 6); also, 1 Tim. v. 13. The tautology, *barren* and *unfruitful,* is thus avoided.

In the knowledge (εἰς). Rev., more correctly, *unto.* The idea is not idleness *in* the knowledge, but idleness in pressing on and developing *toward* and finally *reaching* the knowledge. With this agrees the compound ἐπίγνωσιν, the *constantly increasing* and finally *full* knowledge.

9. **But** (γὰρ). Wrong. Render as Rev., *for.*

He that lacketh these things (ᾧ μὴ πάρεστιν ταῦτα). Lit., *to whom these things are not present.* Note that a different word is used here from that in ver. 8, *are yours,* to convey the idea of possession. Instead of speaking of the gifts as *belonging* to the Christian by habitual, settled possession, he denotes them now as merely *present* with him.

Blind (τυφλός). Illustrating Peter's emphasis on *sight* as a medium of instruction. See Introduction.

And cannot see afar off (μυωπάζων). Only here in New Testament. From μύω, *to close,* and ὤψ, *the eye.* Closing or contracting the eyes like short-sighted people. Hence, *to be short-sighted.* The participle *being short-sighted* is added to the adjective *blind,* defining it; as if he had said, *is blind,* that is, *short-sighted* spiritually; seeing only things present and not heavenly things. Compare John ix. 41. Rev. renders, *seeing only what is near.*

And hath forgotten (λήθην λαβὼν). Lit., *having taken forgetfulness.* A unique expression, the noun occurring only here in the New Testament. Compare a similar phrase, 2 Tim. i. 5, ὑπόμνησιν λαβὼν, *having taken remembrance:* A. V., *when I call to remembrance:* Rev., *having been reminded of.* Some expositors find in the expression a suggestion of a *voluntary acceptance* of a darkened condition. This is doubtful, however. Lumby thinks that it marks the advanced years of the writer, since he adds to failure of sight the failure of *memory*, that faculty on which the aged dwell more than on sight.

That he was purged (τοῦ καθαρισμοῦ). Rev., more literally, *the cleansing.*

10. **The rather** (μᾶλλον). The adverb belongs rather with the verb *give diligence.* Render, as Rev., *give the more diligence.*

Brethren (ἀδελφοί). The only instance of this form of address in Peter, who commonly uses *beloved.*

Fall (πταίσητε). Lit., *stumble*, and so Rev. Compare Jas. iii. 2.

11. **Shall be ministered abundantly** (πλουσίως ἐπιχορηγηθήσεται). On the verb see ver. 5. Rev., *shall be richly supplied.* We are to furnish in our faith: the reward shall be furnished unto us. *Richly*, indicating the fulness of future blessedness. Professor Salmond observes that it is the reverse of "saved, yet so as by fire" (1 Cor. iii. 15).

Everlasting kingdom (αἰώνιον βασιλείαν). In the first epistle, Peter designated the believer's future as an *inheritance;* here he calls it a *kingdom.* *Eternal*, as Rev., is better than *everlasting*, since the word includes more than duration of time.

12. **I will not be negligent.** The A. V. follows the reading οὐκ ἀμελήσω, which it renders correctly. The better reading, however, is μελλήσω, *I intend*, or, as often in classical Greek, with a sense of *certainty*—I shall *be sure*, which Rev. adopts, rendering *I shall be ready*. The formula occurs in but one other passage, Matt. xxiv. 6, where it is translated by the simple future, *ye shall hear*, with an implied sense, *as ye surely will hear*.

Ye know (εἰδότας). Lit., *knowing*. Compare 1 Pet. i. 18.

Established (ἐστηριγμένους). See on 1 Pet. v. 10. Perhaps the exhortation, "*strengthen* thy brethren," may account for his repeated use of this word and its derivatives. Thus, *unstable* (ἀστήρικτοι); *steadfastness* (στηριγμοῦ), 2 Pet. iii. 16, 17.

In the present truth (ἐν τῇ παρούσῃ ἀληθείᾳ). *I.e.*, the truth which is present with you through the instruction of your teachers; not the truth at present under consideration. See on ver. 9; and compare the same phrase in Col. i. 6, rendered, *is come unto you*.

13. **Tabernacle** (σκηνώματι). A figurative expression for *the body*, used also by Paul, 2 Cor. v. 1, 4, though he employs the shorter kindred word σκῆνος. Peter also has the same mixture of metaphors which Paul employs in that passage, viz., *building* and *clothing*. See next verse. Peter's use of *tabernacle* is significant in connection with his words at the transfiguration, "Let us make three *tabernacles* (Matt. xvii. 4). The word, as well as the entire phrase, carries the idea of *brief duration*—a frail *tent*, erected for a night. Compare ver. 14.

To stir you up by putting you in remembrance (διεγείρειν ὑμᾶς ἐν ὑπομνήσει). Lit., *to stir you up in reminding*. See the same phrase in ch. iii. 1.

14. **Shortly I must put off this my tabernacle** (ταχινή ἐστιν ἡ ἀπόθεσις τοῦ σκηνώματός μου). Lit., *quick is the put-*

ting off of my tabernacle. Rev., *the putting off of my tabernacle cometh swiftly.* Possibly in allusion to his advanced age. *Putting off* is a metaphor, from putting off a garment. So Paul, 2 Cor. v. 3, 4, being *clothed, unclothed, clothed upon.* The word occurs, also, 1 Pet. iii. 21, and is used by Peter only. *Cometh swiftly*, implying the speedy approach of death; though others understand it of the *quick, violent* death which Christ prophesied he should die. "Even as our Lord Jesus Christ hath showed me." See John xxi. 18, 19. Compare, also, John xiii. 36, and note the word *follow* in both passages. "Peter had now learnt the full force of Christ's sayings, and to what end the following of Jesus was to bring him" (Lumby).

Hath shewed (ἐδήλωσεν). But the tense is the aorist, pointing back to a definite act at a past time (John xxi. 18). Hence, *shewed me*, or, as Rev., *signified.* Compare 1 Pet. i. 11, *did signify.*

15. **Ye may be able** (ἔχειν ὑμᾶς). Lit., *that you may have it.* A similar use of *have*, in the sense of *to be able*, occurs Mark xiv. 8. The same meaning is also foreshadowed in Matt. xviii. 25, *had not to pay;* and John viii. 6, *have to accuse.*

Decease (ἔξοδον). *Exodus* is a literal transcript of the word, and is the term used by Luke in his account of the transfiguration. "They spake of his *decease.*" It occurs only once elsewhere, Heb. xi. 22, in the literal sense, the *departing* or *exodus* of the children of Israel. "It is at least remarkable," says Dean Alford, "that, with the recollection of the scene on the mount of transfiguration floating in his mind, the apostle should use so close together the words which were there also associated, *tabernacle* and *decease.* The coincidence should not be forgotten in treating of the question of the genuineness of the epistle."

Call to remembrance (μνήμην ποιεῖσθαι). The phrase occurs nowhere else in the New Testament. In classical Greek, *to make mention of.* An analogous expression is found, Rom. i

9, μνείαν ποιοῦμαι, *I make mention.* See, also, Eph. i. 16; 1 Thess. i. 2; Philem. 4. Some render it thus here, as expressing Peter's desire to make it possible for his readers to report these things to others. Rev., *to call these things to remembrance.*

16. **We have not followed** (οὐ ἐξακολουθήσαντες). A strong compound, used only here and ch. ii. 2, 15. The ἐξ gives the force of following *out; in pursuance of; closely.*

Cunningly devised (σεσοφισμένοις). Only here and 2 Tim. iii. 15, in which latter passage it has a good sense, *to make thee wise.* Here, in a bad sense, *artfully framed* by human *cleverness* (σοφία). Compare *feigned words,* ch. ii. 3.

Fables (μύθοις). This word, which occurs only here and in the Pastoral Epistles, is transcribed in the word *myth.* The reference here may be to the Jewish myths, rabbinical embellishments of Old-Testament history; or to the heathen myths about the descent of the gods to earth, which might be suggested by his remembrance of the transfiguration; or to the Gnostic speculations about *aeons* or emanations, which rose from the eternal abyss, the source of all spiritual existence, and were named *Mind, Wisdom, Power, Truth,* etc.

Coming (παρουσίαν). Or *presence.* Compare ch. iii. 4. Another word, ἀποκάλυψις, *revelation,* is used in 1 Pet. i. 7, 13; iv. 13, to describe the appearing of Christ.

Eye-witnesses (ἐπόπται). See on *behold,* 1 Pet. ii. 12. Only here in New Testament. Compare the different word in Luke i. 2, αὐτόπται, *eye-witnesses.*

Majesty (μεγαλειότητος). Used in only two passages besides this: Luke ix. 43, of the *mighty power* (Rev., *majesty*) of God, as manifested in the healing of the epileptic child; and Acts xix. 27, of the *magnificence* of Diana.

17. **When there came** (ἐνεχθείσης). Lit., *having been borne.* Compare *come* (Rev., ver. 18); *moved* (ver. 21); and *rushing* wind, lit., a wind *borne along* (Acts ii. 2).

From (ὑπὸ). Lit., *by.*

Excellent (μεγαλοπρεποῦς). Or *sublime.* Only here in New Testament. In Septuagint (Deut. xxxiii. 26), as an epithet of God, *excellency.* The phrase *excellent glory* refers to the bright cloud which overshadowed the company on the transfiguration mount, like the shekinah above the mercy-seat.

18. **Voice** (φωνὴν). Note the same word in the account of Pentecost (Acts. ii. 6), where the A. V. obscures the meaning by rendering, *when this was noised abroad;* whereas it should be *when this voice was heard.*

Which came (ἐνεχθεῖσαν). Lit., *having been borne.* See on ver. 17. Rev., *This voice we ourselves* (ἡμεῖς, *we,* emphatic) *heard come* (better, *borne*) *out of heaven.*

Holy mount. It is scarcely necessary to notice Davidson's remark that this expression points to a time when superstitious reverence for places had sprung up in Palestine. "Of all places to which special sanctity would be ascribed by Christ's followers, surely that would be the first to be so marked where the most solemn testimony was given to the divinity of Jesus. To the Jewish Christian this would rank with Sinai, and no name would be more fitly applied to it than that which had so constantly been given to a place on which God first revealed himself in his glory. The 'holy mount of God' (Ezek. xxviii. 14) would now receive another application, and he would see little of the true continuity of God's revelation who did not connect readily the old and the new covenants, and give to the place where the glory of Christ was most eminently shown forth the same name which was applied so oft to Sinai" (Lumby).

19. **We have also a more sure word of prophecy** (καὶ ἔχομεν βεβαιότερον τὸν προφητικὸν λόγον). The A. V is wrong,

since *more sure* is used predicatively, and *word* has the definite article. We may explain either (*a*) as Rev., *we have the word of prophecy made more sure*, i.e., we are better certified than before as to the prophetic word by reason of this voice; or (*b*) we have the word of prophecy as a surer confirmation of God's truth than what we ourselves saw, *i.e.*, Old-Testament testimony is more convincing than even the voice heard at the transfiguration. The latter seems to accord better with the words which follow. "To appreciate this we must put ourselves somewhat in the place of those for whom St. Peter wrote. The New Testament, as we have it, was to them non-existent. Therefore we can readily understand how the long line of prophetic scriptures, fulfilled in so many ways in the life of Jesus, would be a mightier form of evidence than the narrative of one single event in Peter's life" (Lumby). "Peter knew a sounder basis for faith than that of signs and wonders. He had seen our Lord Jesus Christ receive honor and glory from God the Father in the holy mount; he had been dazzled and carried out of himself by visions and voices from heaven; but, nevertheless, even when his memory and heart are throbbing with recollections of that sublime scene, he says, 'we have something surer still in the prophetic word.' . . . It was not the miracles of Christ by which he came to know Jesus, but the word of Christ as interpreted by the spirit of Christ" (Samuel Cox).

Unto a light (λύχνῳ). More correctly, as Rev., a *lamp*.

In a dark place (*ἐν αὐχμηρῷ τόπῳ*). A peculiar expression. Lit., a *dry* place. Only here in New Testament. Rev. gives *squalid*, in margin. Aristotle opposes it to *bright* or *glistering*. It is a subtle association of the idea of darkness with squalor, dryness, and general neglect.

Dawn (*διαυγάσῃ*). Only here in New Testament. Compare the different word in Matt. xxviii. 1, and Luke xxiii. 54, *ἐπιφώσκω*. The verb is compounded of *διά*, *through*, and *αὐγή*, *sunlight*, thus carrying the picture of light *breaking through* the gloom.

The day-star (φωσφόρος). Of which our word *phosphorus* is a transcript. Lit., *light-bearer*, like *Lucifer*, from *lux*, *light*, and *fero*, *to bear*. See Aeschylus, "Agamemnon," 245.

20. **Is** (γίνεται). More literally, *arises* or *originates*.

Private (ἰδίας). See on ver. 3. *His own*. Rev., *special*, in margin.

Interpretation (ἐπιλύσεως). Only here in New Testament. Compare the cognate verb *expounded* (Mark iv. 34) and *determined* (Acts xix. 39). The usual word is ἑρμηνεία (1 Cor. xii. 10; xiv. 26). Literally, it means *loosening*, *untying*, as of *hard knots* of scripture.

21. **Came** (ἠνέχθη). Lit., *was borne* or *brought*. See on vv. 17, 18.

Holy men of God (ἅγιοι θεοῦ ἄνθρωποι). The best texts omit *holy*, and read ἀπὸ θεοῦ, *from God*. Render, as Rev., *men spake from God*.

Moved (φερόμενοι). The same verb as *came*. Lit., *being borne along*. It seems to be a favorite word with Peter, occurring six times in the two epistles.

CHAPTER II.

1. **But.** Introducing a contrast with those who spake by the Holy Ghost (ch. i. 21).

There were (ἐγένοντο). Rev., better, *there arose*.

There shall be. Note that Peter speaks of them as *future*, and Jude (ver. 4) as *present*.

False teachers (ψευδοδιδάσκαλοι). Only here in New Testament.

Who (οἵτινες). Of that *kind* or *class* which, etc.

Privily shall bring in (παρεισάξουσιν). Only here in New Testament. The kindred adjective occurs Gal. ii. 4, "false brethren *privily brought in*" (παρεισάκτους). The metaphor is of *spies* or *traitors* introducing themselves into an enemy's camp. Compare Jude 4, *crept in unawares*. The verb means, literally, *to bring* (ἄγειν) *into* (εἰς) *by the side of* (παρά).

Damnable heresies (αἱρέσεις ἀπωλείας). Lit., *heresies of destruction*. Rev., *destructive heresies*. *Heresy* is a transcript of αἵρεσις, the primary meaning of which is *choice;* so that a heresy is, strictly, the choice of an opinion contrary to that usually received; thence transferred to the body of those who profess such opinions, and therefore a *sect*. So Rev., in margin, *sects of perdition*. Commonly in this sense in the New Testament (Acts v. 17; xv. 5; xxviii. 22), though the Rev. has an odd variety in its marginal renderings. See Acts. xxiv. 14; 1 Cor. xi. 19; Gal. v. 20. The rendering *heretical doctrines* seems to agree better with the context; false teachers bringing in *sects* is awkward.

Denying. A significant word from Peter.

The Lord (δεσπότην). In most cases in the New Testament the word is rendered *master*, the Rev. changing *lord* to *master* in every case but two—Luke ii. 29; Acts iv. 24; and in both instances putting *master* in margin, and reserving *lord* for the rendering of κύριος. In three of these instances the word is used in direct address to God; and it may be asked why the Rev. changes *Lord* to *Master* in the text of Apoc. vi. 10, and retains *Lord* in Luke ii. 29; Acts iv. 24. In five out of the ten occurrences of the word in the New Testament it means *master of the household*. Originally, it indicates *absolute*, *unrestricted* authority, so that the Greeks refused the title to any but the gods. In the New Testament δεσπότης and κύριος are used interchangeably of God, and of masters of servants.

Swift (ταχινὴν). Used by Peter only. See on ch. i. 14.

2. **Shall follow.** See on ch. i. 16.

Pernicious ways (ἀπωλείαις). The true reading is ἀσελγείαις, *lascivious doings.* So Rev. See on 1 Pet. iv. 3. The use of the plural is rare. Compare Jude 4.

3. **Through covetousness** (ἐν πλεονεξίᾳ). Lit., *in* covetousness; denoting the element or sphere in which the evil is wrought.

Feigned (πλαστοῖς). Only here in New Testament. From πλάσσω, *to mould,* as in clay or wax. The idea is, therefore, of words moulded at will to suit their vain imaginations.

Make merchandise (ἐμπορεύσονται). Only here and Jas. iv. 13. Compare Jude 16, *for the sake of advantage;* their glory being in having a multitude of followers.

Judgment (κρίμα). Rev., *sentence.* So, commonly, in New Testament; the *process* or *act* of judging being expressed by κρίσις.

Of a long time (ἔκπαλαι). Rev., better, *from of old,* bringing out thus more sharply the force of ἐκ. Only here and ch. iii. 5. Construe with *lingereth.*

Lingereth (ἀργεῖ). Only here in New Testament. Compare on the kindred adjective *idle,* ch. i. 8. There is a graphic picture in the sentence. The judgment is not *idle.* It is "represented as a living thing, awake and expectant. Long ago that judgment started on its destroying path, and the fate of sinning angels, and the deluge, and the overthrow of Sodom and Gomorrah were but incidental illustrations of its power; nor has it ever since lingered. . . . It advances still, strong and vigilant as when first it sprang from the bosom of God, and will not fail to reach the mark to which it was pointed from of old" (Salmond and Lillie).

Damnation (ἀπώλεια). More literally, Rev., *destruction*. The word occurs three times in vv. 1-3.

Slumbereth (νυστάζει). See on Matt. xxv. 5, the only other passage where it occurs.

4. **The angels.** No article. *Angels.* So Rev. Compare Jude 6.

Cast them down to hell (ταρταρώσας). Only here in New Testament. From Τάρταρος, *Tartarus*. It is strange to find Peter using this Pagan term, which represents the Greek hell, though treated here not as equivalent to *Gehenna*, but as the place of detention until the judgment.

Chains of darkness (σειραῖς ζόφου). Σειρά is a *cord* or *band*, sometimes of metal. Compare Septuagint, Prov. v. 22; Wisd. of Sol. xvii. 2, 18. The best texts, however, substitute σιροῖς or σειροῖς, *pits* or *caverns*. Σιρός originally is a place for storing corn. Rev., *pits* of darkness.

Of darkness (ζόφου). Peculiar to Peter and Jude. Originally of the gloom of the nether world, So Homer:

> "These halls are full
> Of shadows hastening down to Erebus
> Amid the *gloom* (ὑπὸ ζόφον)."
>
> *Odyssey*, xx., 355.

When Ulysses meets his mother in the shades, she says to him:

> "How didst thou come, my child, a living man,
> Into this place of darkness? (ὑπὸ ζόφον)."
>
> *Odyssey*, xi., 155.

Compare Jude 13. So Milton:

> "Here their prison ordained
> In utter darkness, and their portion set
> As far removed from God and light of heaven
> As from the centre thrice to the utmost pole."
>
> *Paradise Lost*, i., 71-74.

And Dante:

> "That air forever black."
> *Inferno*, iii., 329.

> "Upon the verge I found me
> Of the abysmal valley dolorous
> That gathers thunder of infinite ululations.
> Obscure, profound it was, and nebulous,
> So that by fixing on its depths my sight
> Nothing whatever I discerned therein."
> *Inferno*, iv., 7, 12.

> "I came unto a place mute of all light."
> *Inferno*, v., 28.

To be reserved (τηρουμένους). Lit., *being reserved.* See on 1 Pet. i. 4, "*reserved* in heaven."

5. **Saved** (ἐφύλαξεν). Rev., *preserved.* See on 1 Pet. i. 4, and compare "the Lord *shut him in*" (Gen. vii. 16).

Noah the eighth person. So the A. V., literally. Rev. is more perspicuous however: *Noah with seven others.* Compare 1 Pet. iii. 20.

A preacher (κήρυκα). Lit., a *herald.* Compare the kindred verb κηρύσσω, *to preach*, everywhere in New Testament. The word *herald* is beautifully suggestive, at many points, of the office of a gospel minister. In the Homeric age the herald partook of the character of an ambassador. He summoned the assembly and kept order in it, and had charge of arrangements at sacrifices and festivals. The office of the heralds was sacred, and their persons inviolable; hence they were employed to bear messages between enemies. The symbol of their office was the herald's staff, or *caduceus*, borne by Mercury, the herald-god. This was originally an olive-branch with fillets, which were afterward formed into snakes, according to the legend that Mercury found two snakes fighting and separated them with his wand, from which circumstance they were used as an emblem of peace. Plato ("Laws," xii., 941) thus speaks of the fidelity entailed by the office: "If any herald or ambassador carry a false message to any other city, or bring back a false message from the city to which he is sent, or be proved to have brought back, whether from friends or enemies, in his capacity of herald or ambassador, what they have never said—let him be indicted for having offended, contrary to the law, in the sacred office and appointment of Hermes and Zeus, and let there be a penalty fixed which he shall suffer or pay if he be convicted." In later times, their position as messengers between nations at war was emphasized. In Herodotus (i., 21), the word *herald* is used as synonymous with *apostle*. "Alyattes sent a *herald* (κήρυκα) to Miletus in hopes of concluding a truce, etc. The *herald* (ἀπόστολος) went on his way to Miletus." A priestly house at Athens bore the name of κήρυκες, *heralds*.

Bringing in (ἐπάξας). The verb may be said to be used by Peter only. Besides this passage and ver. 1, it occurs only at Acts v. 28, where Luke probably received the account from Peter as the principal actor: "ye intend to *bring upon us* (ἐπαγαγεῖν) this man's blood."

6. **Turning into ashes** (τεφρώσας). Only here in New Testament.

Having made them an example (ὑπόδειγμα τεθεικώς). Compare 1 Pet. ii. 21. The word for *example* is condemned as unclassical by the Attic grammarians, and παράδειγμα is substituted, which means, properly, *a sculptor's or a painter's model*, or *an architect's plan*.

7. **Just** (δίκαιον). Occurring three times in vv. 7, 8.

Vexed (καταπονούμενον). Only here and Acts vii. 24. Κατά gives the force of worn *down*. So Rev., *sore distressed*.

With the filthy conversation of the wicked (ὑπὸ τῆς τῶν ἀθέσμων ἐν ἀσελγείᾳ ἀναστροφῆς). Lit., *by the behavior of the lawless in wantonness*. Rev., *the lascivious life of the wicked*.

Life or *behavior* (ἀναστροφῆς). See on 1 Pet. i. 15. *Wicked* (ἀθέσμων), lit., *lawless.* Only here and ch. iii. 17. *Wantonness* (ἀσελγείᾳ), see on Mark vii. 22.

8. **Dwelling** (ἐγκατοικῶν). Only here in New Testament. Dwelling, and therefore suffering continually, from day to day.

In seeing (βλέμματι). Only here in New Testament. Usually of the *look* of a man from *without*, through which the vexation comes to the *soul.* "Vexed his righteous *soul.*"

Vexed (ἐβασανίζεν). See on Matt. iv. 24, *torments.* The original sense is to *test by touchstone* or *by torture.* See on *toiling*, Mark vi. 48. Rev. gives *tormented*, in margin.

Unlawful (ἀνόμοις). Rev., *lawless.* Only here in New Testament with *things.* In all other cases it is applied to *persons.*

9. **Godly** (εὐσεβεῖς). Used by Peter only. Compare Acts x. 2, 7. The reading at Acts xxii. 12, is εὐλαβής, *devout.* See on ch. i. 3.

Temptation (πειρασμοῦ). See on 1 Pet. i. 6.

To reserve (τηρεῖν). See on 1 Pet. i. 4. Rev., *keep*, is not an improvement.

To be punished (κολαζομένους). Only here and Acts iv. 21, where the narrative probably came from Peter. The participle here is, lit., *being punished*, and therefore the A. V. is wrong. Rev., rightly, *under punishment.* Compare Matt. xxv. 46.

10. **Go after the flesh.** Compare Jude 7.

Of uncleanness (μιασμοῦ). Only here in New Testament. See on *defilements*, ver. 20. Compare Jude 8.

Despise government. Rev., *dominion.* Compare Jude 8.

Presumptuous (τολμηταὶ). Only here in New Testament. Lit., *darers*. Rev., *daring*.

Self-willed (αὐθάδεις). Only here and Tit. i. 7. From αὐτός, *self*, and ἥδομαι, *to delight in*. Therefore a *self-loving* spirit.

They tremble (τρέμουσιν). Compare Mark v. 33. An uncommon word in the New Testament. Luke viii. 47; Acts ix. 6.

Dignities (δόξας). Lit., *glories*. Compare Jude 8. Probably angelic powers: note the reference to the angels immediately following, as in Jude 9 to Michael. They defy the spiritual powers though knowing their might.

11. **Power and might** (ἰσχύϊ καὶ δυνάμει). Rev., *might and power*. The radical idea of ἰσχύς, *might*, is that of *indwelling* strength, especially as *embodied:* might which inheres in physical powers organized and working under individual direction, as an army: which appears in the *resistance* of physical organisms, as the earth, against which one dashes himself in vain: which dwells in persons or things, and gives them influence or value: which resides in laws or punishments to make them irresistible. This sense comes out clearly in the New Testament in the use of the word and of its cognates. Thus, "Love the Lord thy God with all thy *strength*" (Mark xii. 30): "according to the working of his *mighty power*" (Eph. i. 19). So the kindred adjective ἰσχυρός. "A *strong* man" (Matt. xii. 29): a *mighty* famine (Luke xv. 14): his letters are *powerful* (2 Cor. x. 10): a *strong* consolation (Heb. vi. 18): a *mighty* angel (Apoc. xviii. 21). Also the verb ἰσχύω. "It is *good* for nothing" (Matt. v. 13): "shall not be *able*" (Luke xiii. 24): "I *can* do all things" (Philip. iv. 13): "*availeth* much" (Jas. v. 16).

Δύναμις is rather *ability, faculty:* not necessarily *manifest*, as ἰσχύς: power residing in one by nature. Thus *ability* (Matt. xxv. 15): *virtue* (Mark v. 30): *power* (Luke xxiv. 29; Acts i. 8; 1 Cor. ii. 4): "*strength* of sin" (1 Cor. xv. 56). So of *moral* vigor. "Strengthened with *might* in the *inner* man" (Eph.

iii. 16): "with all *might* (Col. i. 11). It is, however, mostly power *in action*, as in the frequent use of δυνάμεις for *miracles*, *mighty works*, they being exhibitions of divine virtue. Thus "*power* unto salvation" (Rom. i. 16): the kingdom coming *in power*" (Mark ix. 1): God himself called *power*—"the right hand of *the power*" (Matt. xxvi. 64), and so in classical Greek used to denote the *magistrates* or *authorities*. Also of the *angelic* powers (Eph. i. 21; Rom. viii. 38; 1 Pet. iii. 22). Generally, then, it may be said that while both words include the idea of manifestation or of power in action, ἰσχύς emphasizes the *outward*, physical manifestations, and δύναμις the *inward*, spiritual or moral virtue. Plato ("Protagoras," 350) draws the distinction thus: "I should not have admitted that the *able* (δυνατοὺς) are *strong* (ἰσχυροὺς), though I have admitted that the strong are able. For there is a difference between *ability* (δύναμιν) and *strength* (ἰσχύν). The former is given by knowledge as well as by madness or rage; but strength comes from nature and a healthy state of the body. Aristotle ("Rhet.," i., 5) says "*strength* (ἰσχὺς) is the power of moving another as one wills; and that other is to be moved either by drawing or pushing or carrying or pressing or compressing; so that the *strong* (ὁ ἰσχυρὸς) is strong for all or for some of these things."

Railing judgment. Compare Jude 9; Zech. iii. 1, 2.

12. **As natural brute beasts made to be taken and destroyed.** This massing of epithets is characteristic of Peter. *Natural* (φυσικὰ), Rev., *mere animals*, should be construed with *made*, or as Rev., *born* (γεγεννημένα). *Brute* (ἄλογα), lit., *unreasoning* or *irrational*. Rev., *without reason*. Compare Acts xxv. 27. *Beasts* (ζῶα). Lit., *living creatures*, from ζάω, *to live*. More general and inclusive than *beasts*, since it denotes strictly all creatures that live, including man. Plato even applies it to God himself. Hence Rev., properly, *creatures*. *To be taken and destroyed* (εἰς ἅλωσιν καὶ φθοράν). Lit., *for capture and destruction*. *Destruction* twice in this verse, and with a cognate verb. Render the whole, as Rev., *But these, as creatures without reason, born mere animals to be taken and destroyed.*

Speak evil (βλασφημοῦντες). Participle. Rev., rightly, *railing*. Compare vv. 10, 11.

And shall utterly perish in their own corruption (ἐν τῇ φθορᾷ αὐτῶν καὶ φθαρήσονται). There is a play upon the words, which the Rev. reproduces by rendering, "shall in their *destroying* surely be *destroyed*." The *and*, which in the A. V. connects this and the preceding sentence, is rather to be taken with *shall be destroyed*, as emphasizing it, and should be rendered, as Rev., *surely*, or as others, *even* or *also*. Compare on the whole verse Jude 10.

13. **And shall receive** (κομιούμενοι). Lit., *being about* or *destined to receive*. See on 1 Pet. i. 9, and compare 1 Pet. v. 4. Some good texts read ἀδικούμενοι, *suffering wrong*. So Rev., *suffering wrong as the hire of wrong-doing*.

Reward of unrighteousness (μισθὸν ἀδικίας). *Μισθὸς* is *hire*, and so is rendered in Rev. Compare Matt. xx. 8; Luke x. 7; John iv. 36. It also has in classical Greek the general sense of *reward*, and so very often in the New Testament, in passages where hire or wages would be inappropriate. Thus Matt. v. 12; vi. 1; x. 41. *Hire* would seem to be better here, because of the reference to Balaam in ver. 15, where the word occurs again and requires that rendering. The phrase μισθός ἀδικίας, *reward or wages of iniquity*, occurs only here and in Peter's speech concerning Judas (Acts i. 18), where the Rev. retains the rendering of the A. V., *reward of iniquity*. It would have been better to render *wages of iniquity* in both places. *Iniquity* and *unrighteousness* are used in English almost synonymously; though, etymologically, *iniquity* emphasizes the idea of *injustice* (*inaequus*), while *unrighteousness* (non-rightness) is more general, implying *all* deviation from right, whether involving another's interests or not. This distinction is not, however, observed in the Rev., where the rendering of ἀδικία, and of the kindred adjective ἄδικος, varies unaccountably, if not capriciously, between *unrighteous* and *unjust*.

As they that count it pleasure to riot (ἡδονὴν ἡγούμενοι τρυφήν). The *as* of the A. V. is needless. The discourse proceeds from ver. 13 by a series of participles, as far as *following* (ver. 15). Literally the passage runs, *counting riot a pleasure.*

Riot (τρυφήν). Meaning rather *daintiness, delicacy, luxuriousness.* Even the Rev. *revel* is almost too strong. Compare Luke vii. 25, the only other passage where the word occurs, and where the Rev. retains the A. V., *live delicately.* So, also, Rev. substitutes, in Jas. v. 5, *lived delicately* for *lived in pleasure.*

In the daytime. Compare Peter's words Acts ii. 15; also, 1 Thess. v. 7.

Spots (σπίλοι). Only here and Eph. v. 27. Compare the kindred participle *spotted* (Jude 23), and *defileth* (Jas. iii. 6).

Blemishes (μῶμοι). Only here in New Testament. The negatives of the two terms *spots* and *blemishes* occur at 1 Pet. i. 19.

Sporting themselves (ἐντρυφῶντες). From τρυφή, *luxuriousness.* See on *riot.* Rev., *revelling.*

With their own deceivings (ἐν ταῖς ἀπάταις αὑτῶν). The Rev., however, follows another reading, which occurs in the parallel passage Jude 12: ἀγάπαις, *love-feasts,* the public banquets instituted by the early Christians, and connected with the celebration of the Lord's Supper. Rev. renders *revelling in their love-feasts,* though the American Committee insist on *deceivings.* On the abuses at these feasts, see 1 Cor. xi. 20–22. For αὑτῶν, their *own,* the best texts read αὐτῶν, *their.*

While they feast with you (συνευωχούμενοι). The word originally conveys the idea of *sumptuous* feasting, and is appropriate in view of the fact to which Peter alludes, that these sensualists converted the love-feast into a revel. Compare Paul's words, 1 Cor. xi. 21, "one is hungry and another *drunken.*" This seems to favor the reading ἀγάπαις. The word occurs only here and Jude 12.

14. **Eyes.** Another illustration of Peter's emphasis on *sight.* It is the instrument of evil no less than of good. Compare Matt. v. 28.

Adultery (μοιχαλίδος). Lit., *an adulteress,* but used as an adjective Matt. xii. 39; xvi. 4.

That cannot cease (ἀκαταπαύστους). Only here, in New Testament. Compare *hath ceased* (1 Pet. iv. 1).

Beguiling (δελεάζοντες). Only here, ver. 18, and Jas. i. 14. From δέλεαρ, *a bait.* An appropriate word from Peter the fisherman. Rev., *enticing.*

Unstable (ἀστηρίκτους). A compound of the word at 1 Pet. v. 10, *stablish.* See note there, and on 2 Pet. i. 12.

An heart they have exercised (καρδίαν γεγυμνασμένην ἔχοντες). The A. V. is awkward. Better, Rev., *having a heart exercised. Exercised* is the word used for *gymnastic* training, from which *gymnastic* is derived.

With covetous practices. The A. V. follows the old reading, πλεονεξίαις. The best texts read πλεονεξίας, *covetousness.* Rev., therefore, rightly, *in covetousness.*

Cursed children (κατάρας τέκνα). Lit., *children of cursing;* and so Rev. See on Mark iii. 17, and 1 Pet. i. 14.

15. **Right** (εὐθεῖαν). Lit., *straight,* which is the radical meaning of *right.*

Are gone astray (ἐπλανήθησαν). See on Mark xii. 24.

Following (ἐξακολουθήσαντες). See on ch. i. 16; ii. 2. Compare Jude 11.

The way. Note the frequent occurrence of the word *way* in the story of Balaam (Num. xxii.), and Peter's use of the same phrase, as here, *the right ways* of the Lord, in Acts xiii. 10.

Bosor. Rev. gives *Beor*, the Old Testament form of the name.

Wages of unrighteousness. See on ver. 13.

16. **Was rebuked** (ἔλεγξιν ἔσχεν). Lit., *had a rebuke.* The word for *rebuke* only here in New Testament.

For his iniquity (ἰδίας παρανομίας). Rev., *his own transgression. His own*, see on ch. i. 3. *Transgression*, from παρά, *contrary to*, and νόμος, *law.* Only here in New Testament. Compare the kindred verb παρανομέω, also occurring but once, Acts xxiii. 3, where see note on *contrary to the law.*

The dumb ass. Inserting an article not in the text, and omitted by Rev.

Ass (ὑποζύγιον). Lit., *beast of burden.* An animal subjected to the *yoke.* From ὑπό, *beneath*, and ζυγόν, a *yoke.* See on Matt xxi. 5.

Speaking (φθεγξάμενον). The verb is found in Peter only, here and ver. 18, and in Acts iv. 18, a Petrine narrative. It is well chosen, however. The verb denotes the utterance of a sound or voice, not only by man, but by any animal having lungs. Hence, not only of men's articulate cries, such as a battle-shout, but of the neigh of the horse, the scream of the eagle, the croak of the raven. It is also applied to sounds made by inanimate things, such as thunder, a trumpet, a lyre, the ring of an earthen vessel, showing whether it is cracked or not. Schmidt ("Synonymik") says that it does not indicate any physical capability on the part of the man, but describes the sound only from the hearer's stand-point. In view of this general sense of the verb, the propriety is apparent of the defining phrase, *with man's voice.*

Forbad (ἐκώλυσεν). Rather, *hindered*, or, as Rev., *stayed*. Compare Acts viii. 36; Rom. i. 13, Rev.

Madness (παραφρονίαν). Only here in New Testament. But compare the kindred verb παραφρονέω (2 Cor. xi. 23), in the phrase, "*I speak as a fool.*" From παρά, *beside*, and φρήν, *the mind;* and so equivalent to the phrase, *beside one's self.*

17. **Wells** (πηγαὶ). Better, as Rev., *springs;* yet the Rev. has retained *well* at John iv. 14, where the change would have given more vividness to Christ's metaphor, which is that of an ever upleaping, living *fountain.*

Without water. As so often in the East, where the verdure excites the traveller's hope of water. Compare Jer. ii. 13, and the contrast presented in Isa. lviii. 11; Prov. x. 11; xiii. 14.

Clouds. The A. V. has followed the Tex. Rec., νεφέλαι, as in Jude 12. The correct reading is ὁμίχλαι, *mists*, found only here in New Testament. So Rev.

With a tempest (ὑπὸ λαίλαπος). Rev., *by a storm.* The word occurs only twice elsewhere—Mark iv. 37; Luke vii. 23—in the parallel accounts of the storm on the lake, which Jesus calmed by his word. There on the lake Peter was at home, as well as with the Lord on that occasion; and the peculiar word describing a *whirlwind*—one of those sudden storms so frequent on that lake (see note on the word, Mark iv. 37)—would be the first to occur to him. Compare Paul's similar figure, Eph. iv. 14.

Blackness (ζόφος). See on ver. 4, and compare Jude 13.

Of darkness (τοῦ σκότους). Lit., *the* darkness, denoting a well-understood doom.

Is reserved (τετήρηται). Lit., *hath been reserved*, as Rev. See on 1 Pet. i. 4; 2 Pet. ii. 4.

Forever. The best texts omit.

18. **When they speak** (φθεγγόμενοι). Rev., better, *uttering*. See on ver. 16.

Great swelling (ὑπέρογκα). Only here and Jude 16. The word means *of excessive bulk*. It accords well with the peculiar word *uttering*, since it denotes a kind of speech full of high-sounding verbosity without substance. Φθεγγόμενοι, *uttering*, is significantly applied alike to Balaam's beast and to these empty declaimers.

Entice. See ver. 14.

Were clean escaped. The A. V. follows the Tex. Rec., ὄντως ἀποφυγόντας; ὄντως meaning *really*, *actually*, as Luke xxiv. 34; and the participle being the aorist, and so meaning *were escaped*. But the best texts all read ὀλίγως, *in a little degree*, or *just*, or *scarcely*; and ἀποφεύγοντας, the present participle, *are escaping*; and denoting those who are in the early stage of their escape from error, and are not safe from it and confirmed in the truth. Hence, Rev., correctly, *who are just escaping*. Ὀλίγως, only here.

19. **Is overcome** (ἥττηται). Lit., *is worsted*; from ἥσσων, *inferior*. Only here, ver. 20, and 2 Cor. xii. 13.

Brought into bondage (δεδούλωται). *Enslaved*. Compare Rom. vi. 16.

20. **Pollutions** (μιάσματα). Only here in New Testament. Compare ver. 10. The word is transcribed in *miasma*.

Entangled (ἐμπλακέντες). Only here and 2 Tim. ii. 4. The same metaphor occurs in Aeschylus ("Prometheus"): "For not on a sudden or in ignorance will ye be *entangled* (ἐμπλεχθήσεσθε) by your folly in an impervious net of Ate (*destruction*)."

22. **According to the true proverb** (τὸ τῆς ἀληθοῦς παροιμίας). Lit., *that of the true proverb*, or *the matter of* the pro-

verb. For a similar construction see Matt. xxi. 21, *that of the fig-tree;* Matt. viii. 33, *the things of those possessed.* On *proverb*, see notes on Matt. xiii. 3.

Vomit (ἐξέραμα). Only here in New Testament.

Wallowing (κυλισμὸν). Only here in New Testament.

Mire (βορβόρου). Only here in New Testament. This use of *dogs* and *swine* together recalls Matt. vii. 6.

CHAPTER III.

1. **Beloved.** Occurring four times in this chapter.

Second—I write. An incidental testimony to the authorship of the second epistle.

Pure minds (εἰλικρινῆ διάνοιαν). The latter word is singular, not plural. Hence, as Rev., *mind.* The word rendered *pure* is often explained *tested by the sunlight;* but this is very doubtful, since εἵλη, to which this meaning is traced, means the *heat*, and not the *light* of the sun. Others derive it from the root of the verb εἱλίσσω, *to roll*, and explain it as that which is *separated* or *sifted* by *rolling*, as in a sieve. In favor of this etymology is its association in classical Greek with different words meaning *unmixed.* The word occurs only here and Philip. i. 10. The kindred noun εἰλικρίνεια, *sincerity*, is found 1 Cor. v. 8; 2 Cor. i. 12; ii. 17. Rev., here, *sincere.*

Mind (διάνοιαν). Compare 1 Pet. i. 13; and see on Mark xii. 30.

3. **Scoffers walking** (ἐμπαῖκται πορευόμενοι). This is the reading followed by A. V. But the later texts have added ἐμπαιγμονῇ, *in mockery*, occurring only here, though a kindred word for *mockings* (ἐμπαιγμῶν) is found Heb. xi. 36. This

addition gives a play upon the words; and so Rev., "*Mockers* shall come with *mockery*, walking," etc.

4. **From the beginning of the creation** (ἀπ' ἀρχῆς κτίσεως). Not a common phrase. It occurs only Mark x. 6; xiii. 19; Apoc. iii. 14.

Fell asleep (ἐκοιμήθησαν). A literal and correct translation of the word, which occurs frequently in the New Testament, but only here in Peter. Some have supposed that the peculiarly Christian sense of the word is emphasized *ironically* by these mockers. It is used, however, in classical Greek to denote *death*. The difference between the pagan and the Christian usage lies in the fact that, in the latter, it was defined by the hope of the resurrection, and therefore was used *literally* of a sleep, which, though long, was to have an awaking. See on Acts vii. 60.

5. **This they willingly are ignorant of** (λανθάνει αὐτοὺς τοῦτο θέλοντας). Lit., *this escapes them of their own will*. Rev., *this they wilfully forget*.

The heavens were. But the Greek has no article. Render, *there were heavens*. So, too, not *the* earth, but *an* earth, as Rev.

Standing (συνεστῶσα). Incorrect; for the word is, literally, *standing together*; i.e., *compacted* or *formed*. Compare Col. i. 17, *consist*. Rev., *compacted*.

Out of the water. Again no article. Render *out of water*; denoting not the *position* of the earth, but the *material* or mediating element in the creation; the waters being gathered together in one place, and the dry land appearing. Or, possibly, with reference to the original liquid condition of the earth—*without form and void*.

In the water (δι' ὕδατος). Omit the article. *Διά* has its usual sense here, not as Rev., *amidst*, but *by means of*. Bengel:

"The water served that the earth should consist." Expositors are much divided as to the meaning. This is the view of Huther, Salmond, and, substantially, Alford.

6. **The world that then was** (ὁ τότε κόσμος). Lit., *the then world.* The word for *world* is literally *order*, and denotes the perfect system of the material universe.

Being overflowed (κατακλυσθεὶς). Only here in New Testament. *Cataclysm* is derived from it.

7. **The heavens—which now are** (οἱ νῦν οὐρανοὶ). A construction similar to *the then world* (ver. 6). The *now* heavens, or the *present* heavens.

Kept in store (τεθησαυρισμένοι). Rev., *stored up.* Lit., *treasured up.* The same word which is used in Luke xii. 21, *layeth up treasure.* Sometimes with the kindred noun θησαυροὺς, *treasures*, as Matt. vi. 19; lit., *treasure treasures.*

Unto fire. Some construe this with *treasured up;* as Rev., *stored up for fire;* others with *reserved*, as A. V.; others again give the sense *stored with fire*, indicating that the agent for the final destruction is already prepared.

9. **Is not slack** (οὐ βραδύνει). Only here and 1 Tim. iii. 15. The word is literally *to delay* or *loiter.* So Septuagint, Gen. xliii. 10, "except we *had lingered.*" Alford's rendering, *is not tardy*, would be an improvement. The word implies, besides *delay*, the idea of lateness with reference to an appointed time.

Come (χωρῆσαι). Move on, or advance to.

10. **The day of the Lord.** Compare the same phrase in Peter's sermon, Acts ii. 20. It occurs only in these two passages and 1 Thess. v. 2. See 1 Cor. i. 8; 2 Cor. i. 14.

As a thief. Omit *in the night.* Compare Matt. xxiv. 43; 1 Thess. v. 2, 4; Apoc. iii. 3; xvi. 15.

45

With a great noise (ῥοιζηδὸν). An adverb peculiar to Peter, and occurring only here. It is a word in which the sound suggests the sense (*rhoizedon*); and the kindred noun, ῥοῖζος, is used in classical Greek of the whistling of an arrow; the sound of a shepherd's pipe; the rush of wings; the plash of water; the hissing of a serpent; and the sound of filing.

The elements (στοιχεῖα). Derived from στοῖχος, *a row*, and meaning originally *one of a row* or *series*; hence a *component* or *element*. The name for the letters of the alphabet, as being set in rows. Applied to the four elements—fire, air, earth, water; and in later times to the planets and signs of the zodiac. It is used in an ethical sense in other passages; as in Gal. iv. 3, "*elements* or *rudiments* of the world." Also of elementary teaching, such as the law, which was fitted for an earlier stage in the world's history; and of the first principles of religious knowledge among men. In Col. ii. 8, of formal ordinances. Compare Heb. v. 12. The kindred verb στοιχέω, *to walk*, carries the idea of *keeping in line*, according to the radical sense. Thus, walk *according to rule* (Gal. vi. 16); *walkest orderly* (Acts xxi. 24). So, too, the compound συστοιχέω, only in Gal. iv. 25, *answereth to*, lit., *belongs to the same row or column with*. The Greek grammarians called the categories of letters arranged according to the organs of speech συστοιχίαι. Here the word is of course used in a physical sense, meaning *the parts* of which this system of things is composed. Some take it as meaning the heavenly bodies, but the term is too late and technical in that sense. Compare Matt. xxiv. 29, *the powers of the heaven*.

Shall melt (λυθήσονται). More literally, as Rev., *shall be dissolved*.

With fervent heat (καυσούμενα). Lit., *being scorched up*.

11. **To be dissolved** (λυομένων). So Rev. But the participle is present; and the idea is rather, *are in process of dissolution*. The world and all therein is essentially transitory.

Ought ye **to be** (ὑπάρχειν). See on ch. i. 8.

Conversation (ἀναστροφαῖς). See on 1 Pet. i. 15. Rev., *living.*

Godliness (εὐσεβείαις). See on ch. i. 3. Both words are plural; *holy livings* and *godlinesses.*

12. **Looking for** (προσδοκῶντας). The same verb as in Luke i. 21, of *waiting* for Zacharias. Cornelius *waited* (Acts x. 24); the cripple *expecting* to receive something (Acts iii. 5).

Hasting unto (σπεύδοντας). Wrong. Rev., *earnestly desiring*, for which there is authority. I am inclined to adopt, with Alford, Huther, Salmond, and Trench, the transitive meaning, *hastening on;* i.e., "causing the day of the Lord to come more quickly by helping to fulfil those conditions without which it cannot come; that day being no day inexorably fixed, but one the arrival of which it is free to the church to hasten on by faith and by prayer" (Trench, on "The Authorized Version of the New Testament"). See Matt. xxiv. 14: the gospel shall be preached in the whole world, "and *then* shall the end come." Compare the words of Peter, Acts iii. 19: "Repent and be converted," etc., "*that so* there may come seasons of refreshing" (so Rev., rightly); and the prayer, "Thy kingdom come." Salmond quotes a rabbinical saying, "If thou keepest this precept thou hastenest the day of Messiah." This meaning is given in margin of Rev.

Wherein (δι' ἣν). Wrong. Rev., correctly, *by reason of which.*

Melt (τήκεται). Literal. Stronger than the word in vv. 10, 11. Not only the *resolving*, but the *wasting away* of nature. Only here in New Testament.

13. **We look for.** The same verb as in ver. 12. It occurs three times in 12–14.

New (καινοὺς). See on Matt. xxvi. 29.

14. **Without spot and blameless.** See on ch. ii. 13.

16. **Hard to be understood** (*δυσνόητα*). Only here in New Testament.

They that are unlearned and unstable (*οἱ ἀμαθεῖς καὶ ἀστήρικτοι*). Both words are peculiar to Peter. On the latter, see on ch. ii. 14.

Wrest (*στρεβλοῦσιν*). Only here in New Testament. Meaning, originally, *to hoist with a windlass or screw;* to twist or dislocate the limbs on a rack. It is a singularly graphic word applied to the perversion of scripture.

The other scriptures (*τὰς λοιπὰς γραφὰς*). Showing that Paul's epistles were ranked as scripture. See on Mark xii. 10.

17. **Being led away** (*συναπαχθέντες*). Better, Rev., *carried away.* It is the word used by Paul of Barnabas, when he dissembled with Peter at Antioch. "Barnabas was *carried away* with their dissimulation" (Gal. ii. 13).

Of the wicked (*ἀθέσμων*). See on ch. ii. 7.

Fall from (*ἐκπέσητε*). Lit., "fall *out of.*" Compare Gal. v. 4.

Steadfastness (*στηριγμοῦ*). Only here in New Testament. See on ch. i. 12.

LIST OF GREEK WORDS USED BY PETER ONLY.

ἀγαθοποιΐα, well-doing, 1, iv., 19
ἀγαθοποιός, a well-doer, 1, ii., 14
ἀδελφότης, brotherhood, 1, ii., 17; v., 9
ἄδολος, without guile, 1, ii., 2
ἄθεσμος, wicked, 2, ii., 7; iii., 17
αἰσχροκερδῶς, for filthy lucre, 1, v., 2
ἀκατάπαστος, that cannot cease, 2, ii., 14.
ἀλλοτριοεπίσκοπος, a busy-body in other men's matters, 1, iv., 15
ἅλωσις, capture, 2, ii., 12
ἀμαθής, unlearned, 2, iii., 16
ἀμάραντινος, unfading, 1, v., 4
ἀμαράντος, unfading, 1, i., 4
ἀμώμητος, blameless, 2. iii., 14
ἀναγεννάω, to beget again, 1, i., 3, 23
ἀναγκαστῶς, by constraint, 1, v., 2
ἀναζώννυμι, gird up, 1, i., 13
ἀνάχυσις, excess, 1, iv., 4
ἀνεκλάλητος, unspeakable, 1, i., 8
ἀντιλοιδορέω, to revile again, 1, ii., 23
ἀπογίνομαι, to be dead, 1, ii., 24
ἀπόθεσις, putting away, 1, iii., 21; 2, i., 14
ἀπονέμω, assign, impart, 1, iii., 7
ἀποφεύγω, to escape, 2, i., 4; ii., 18, 20
ἀπροσωπολήμπτως, without respect of persons, 1, i., 17
ἀργέω, linger, 2, ii., 3
ἀρτιγέννητος, new-born, 1, ii., 2
ἀρχιποίμην, chief shepherd, 1, v., 4
ἀστήρικτος, unsteadfast, 2, ii., 14; iii., 16
αὐχμηρός, dry, dark, 2, i., 19
βιόω, live, 1, iv., 2
βλέμμα, seeing, 2, ii., 8
βόρβορος, mire, 2, ii., 22
βραδυτής, slackness, 2, iii., 9
γυναικεῖος, female (adj.), 1, iii., 7
διαυγάζω, to dawn, 2, i., 19
δυσνόητος, hard to be understood, 2, iii., 16
ἐγκατοικέω, dwell among, 2, ii., 8
ἐγκομβόομαι, gird, 1, v., 5
ἑκάστοτε, always, 2, i., 15
ἔκπαλαι, from of old, 2, ii., 3; iii., 5
ἐκτενής, intense, 1, iv., 8
ἔλεγξις, rebuke, 2, ii., 16
ἐμπαιγμονή, mockery, 2, iii., 3
ἐμπλοκή, plaiting, 1, iii., 3
ἔνδυσις, putting on, 1, iii., 3
ἐντρυφάω, revel, 2, ii., 13
ἐξακολουθέω, follow (out), 2, i., 16; ii., 2, 15
ἐξέραμα, vomit, 2, ii., 22
ἐξερευνάω, search diligently, 1, i., 10
ἐπάγγελμα, promise, 2, i., 4; iii., 13
ἐπερώτημα, inquiry, appeal, 1, iii., 21
ἐπικάλυμμα, cloke, 1, ii., 16
ἐπίλοιπος, remaining, 1, iv., 2
ἐπίλυσις, interpretation, 2, i., 20
ἐπιμαρτυρέω, testify, 1, v., 12
ἐπόπτης, eye-witness, 2, i., 16
ἐποπτεύω, behold, 1, ii., 12; iii., 2
ἱεράτευμα, priesthood, 1, ii., 5, 9

ἰσότιμος, like-precious, 2, i., 1
κατακλύζομαι, to be overflowed, 2, iii., 6
καυσόω, to burn with intense heat, 2, iii., 10, 12
κλέος, glory, 1, ii., 20
κραταιός, mighty, 1, v., 6
κτιστής, creator, 1, iv., 19
κυλισμός, wallowing, 2, ii., 22
λήθη, forgetfulness, 2, i., 9
μεγαλοπρεπής, excellent, 2, i., 17
μίασμα, μιασμός, } defilement, 2, ii., 20; ii., 10
μνήμη, remembrance, 2, i., 15
μυωπάζω, to be shortsighted, 2, i., 9
μώλωψ, stripe, weal, 1, ii., 24
μῶμος, blemish, 2, ii., 13
οἰνοφλυγία, wine-bibbing, 1, iv., 3
ὀλίγως, but a little, just, 2, ii., 18
ὁμίχλη, mist, 2, ii., 17
ὁμόφρων, like-minded, 1, iii., 8
ὁπλίζομαι, arm one's self, 1, iv., 1
παρανομία, transgression, 2, ii., 16
παραφρονία, madness, 2, ii., 16
παρεισάγω, bring in privily, 2, ii., 1
παρεισφέρω, add, 2, i., 5
πατροπαράδοτος, handed down from the fathers, 1, i., 18
περίθεσις, wearing, 1, iii., 3
πλαστός, feigned, 2, ii., 3
πότος, carousing, 1, iv., 3
προθύμως, willingly, 1, v., 2
προμαρτύρομαι, testify beforehand, 1, i., 11
πτόησις, terror, 1, iii., 6
ῥοιζηδόν, with a great noise, 2, iii., 10
ῥύπος, filth, 1, iii., 21
σθενόω, strengthen, 1, v., 10
σειρός, a pit, 2, ii., 4
σπορά, seed, 1, i., 23
στηριγμός, steadfastness, 2, iii., 17
στρεβλόω, wrest, 2, iii., 16
συμπαθής, compassionate, 1, iii., 8
συμπρεσβύτερος, fellow-elder, 1, v., 1
συνεκλεκτός, elected together, 1, v., 13
συνοικέω, dwell with, 1, iii., 7
ταπεινόφρων, humble-minded, 1, iii., 8
ταρταρόω, cast down to hell, 2, ii., 4
ταχινός, quick, swift, 2, i., 14; ii., 1
τελείως, perfectly, 1, i., 13
τεφρόω, turn to ashes, 2, ii., 6
τήκομαι, melt, 2, iii., 12
τοιόσδε, such, 2, i., 17
τολμητής, daring, 2, ii., 10
ὑπογραμμός, example, 1, ii., 21
ὑποζύγιον, beast of burden, 2, ii., 16
ὑπολιμπάνω, leave, 1, ii., 21
ὗς, sow, 2, ii., 22
φιλάδελφος, loving as a brother, 1, iii., 8
φωσφόρος, day-star, 2, i., 19
ψευδοδιδάσκαλος, false teacher, 2, ii., 1
ὠρύομαι, roar, 1, v., 8

Of these, fifty-five are peculiar to the second epistle, and only one, ἀπόθεσις, *putting off*, is common to the two epistles.

THE EPISTLE OF JUDE.

---

1. **Jude.** Rev., *Judas.* One of the brethren of Jesus; not the brother of James the Apostle, the son of Alphaeus, but of James the superintendent of the church at Jerusalem. He is named among the brethren of the Lord. Matt. xiii. 55; Mark vi. 3.

Servant. He does not call himself an apostle, as Paul and Peter in their introductions, and seems to distinguish himself from the apostles in vv. 17, 18: "The apostles of our Lord Jesus Christ, how that *they* said," etc. We are told that Christ's brethren did not believe on him (John vii. 5); and in Acts i. the brethren of Jesus (ver. 14) are mentioned in a way which seems to separate them from the apostles. Δοῦλος, *bond-servant,* occurs in the introductions to Romans, Philippians, Titus, James, and 2 Peter.

Brother of James. That Jude does not allude to his relationship to the Lord may be explained by the fact that the natural relationship in his mind would be subordinate to the spiritual (see Luke xi. 27, 28), and that such a designation would, as Dean Alford remarks, "have been in harmony with those later and superstitious feelings with which the next and following ages regarded the Lord's earthly relatives." He would shrink from emphasizing a distinction to which none of the other disciples or apostles could have a claim, the more so because of his former unbelief in Christ's authority and mission. It is noticeable that James likewise avoids such a designation.

Kept. See on 1 Pet. i. 4. Compare John xvii. 6, 12.

In Jesus Christ (Ἰησοῦ Χριστῷ). The simple dative without preposition. Therefore *for* Jesus Christ; by the Father to whom Christ committed them (John xvii. 11). Compare 1 Thess. v. 23; Philip. i. 6, 10.

Called (κλητοῖς). At the end of the verse, for emphasis.

2. **Love.** Peculiar to Jude in salutation.

3. **Beloved.** Occurring at the beginning of an epistle only here and 3 John 2.

When I gave all diligence (πᾶσαν σπουδὴν ποιούμενος). Lit., *making all diligence;* the phrase found only here. In Heb. vi. 11, we find "*shew* diligence" (ἐνδείκνυσθαι); and in 2 Pet. i. 5, "*adding* diligence." See note there.

The common salvation. The best texts add ἡμῶν, *of us.* So Rev., "*our* common salvation."

It was needful (ἀνάγκην ἔσχον). Lit., *I had necessity.* Alford, *I found it necessary.* Rev., *I was constrained.*

Earnestly contend (ἐπαγωνίζεσθαι). Only here in New Testament.

The faith. The sum of what Christians believe. See on Acts vi. 7.

Once (ἅπαξ). Not *formerly,* but *once for all.* So Rev., "No other faith will be given," says Bengel.

4. With the whole verse compare 2 Pet. ii. 1.

Crept in unawares (παρεισέδυσαν). Rev., *privily.* See on 2 Pet. ii. 1. The verb means *to get in by the side* (παρά), to slip in by a side-door. Only here in New Testament.

Ordained (προγεγραμμένοι). The meaning is in dispute. The word occurs four times in New Testament. In two of these instances πρό has clearly the temporal sense *before* (Rom. xv. 4; Eph. iii. 3). In Gal. iii. 1, it is taken by some in the sense of *openly*, *publicly* (see note there). It seems better, on the whole, to take it here in the temporal sense, and to render *written of beforehand*, i.e., in prophecy as referred to in vv. 14, 15. So the American Rev.

Lasciviousness. See on 1 Pet. iv. 3.

Lord God. *God* is omitted in the best texts. On *Lord* (δεσπότην), see on 2 Pet. ii. 1.

5. **Ye once knew** (εἰδότας ἅπαξ). Entirely wrong. The participle is to be rendered as present, and the *once* is not *formerly*, but *once for all*, as ver. 3. So Rev., rightly, *though ye know all things once for all.*

6. **First estate** (ἀρχὴν). The word originally signifies *beginning*, and so frequently in New Testament, mostly in the Gospels, Acts, Hebrews, Catholic Epistles, and Apocalypse. From this comes a secondary meaning of *sovereignty*, *dominion*, *magistracy*, as being the *beginning* or *first place of power*. So mostly by Paul, as *principalities* (Rom. viii. 38); *rule* (1 Cor. xv. 24). Compare Luke xii. 11, *magistrates;* Rev., *rulers;* and Luke xx. 20, *power*. Rev., *rule*. A peculiar use of the word occurs at Acts x. 11, "the sheet knit at the four *corners* (ἀρχαῖς);" the corners being the *beginnings* of the sheet. In this passage the A. V. has adopted the first meaning, *beginning*, in its rendering *first estate*. Rev. adopts the second, rendering *principality*. The Jews regarded the angels as having dominion over earthly creatures; and the angels are often spoken of in the New Testament as ἀρχαί, *principalities;* as Rom. viii. 38; Eph. i. 21; so that this term would be appropriate to designate their dignity, which they forsook.

Habitation (οἰκητήριον). Only here and 2 Cor. v. 2.

Everlasting (ἀϊδίοις). Only here and Rom. i. 20. For a longer form ἀείδιος, from ἀεί, *always*.

Under darkness (ὕπο ζόφον). *Under* carries the sense of the darkness brooding *over* the fallen spirits. On *darkness*, see on 2 Pet. ii. 4. Compare Hesiod:

> "There the Titanian gods, to murky gloom
> Condemned by will of cloud-collecting Jove,
> Lie hid in region foul."
>
> *Theogony*, v., 729.

7. **The cities about them.** Admah and Zeboim. Deut xxix. 23; Hos. xi. 8.

Giving themselves over to fornication (ἐκπορνεύσασαι). Rev., more strictly, *having given*, etc. Only here in New Testament. The force of ἐκ is *out and out;* giving themselves up *utterly*. See on *followed*, 2 Pet. i. 16.

Going after (ἀπελθοῦσαι ὀπίσω). The aorist participle. Rev., *having gone*. The phrase occurs Mark i. 20; James and John leaving their father and *going after* Jesus. "The world is *gone after* him" (John xii. 19). Here metaphorical. The force of ἀπό is *away;* turning away from purity, and going after strange flesh.

Strange flesh. Compare 2 Pet. ii. 10; and see Rom. i. 27; Lev. xviii. 22, 23. Also Jowett's introduction to Plato's "Symposium;" Plato's "Laws," viii., 836, 841; Döllinger, "The Gentile and the Jew," Darnell's trans., ii., 238 sq.

Are set forth (πρόκεινται). The verb means, literally, to *lie exposed*. Used of meats on the table ready for the guests; of a corpse laid out for burial; of a question under discussion. Thus the corruption and punishment of the cities of the plain are *laid out* in plain sight.

As an example (δεῖγμα). Only here in New Testament. From δείκνυμι, *to display* or *exhibit;* something, therefore, which is held up to view as a warning.

Suffering the vengeance of eternal fire (*πυρὸς αἰωνίου δίκην ὑπέχουσαι*). Rev., rightly, substitutes *punishment* for *vengeance*, since δίκη carries the underlying idea of *right* or *justice*, which is not necessarily implied in *vengeance*. Some of the best modern expositors render *are set forth as an example of eternal fire, suffering punishment*. This meaning seems, on the whole, more natural, though the Greek construction favors the others, since *eternal fire* is the standing term for the finally condemned in the last judgment, and could hardly be correctly said of Sodom and Gomorrah. Those cities are most truly an *example* of eternal fire. "A destruction so utter and so permanent as theirs has been, is the nearest approach that can be found in this world to the destruction which awaits those who are kept under darkness to the judgment of the great day" (Lumby). *Suffering* (ὑπέχουσαι). Only here in New Testament. The participle is present, indicating that they are suffering to this day the punishment which came upon them in Lot's time. The verb means, literally, to *hold under;* thence *to uphold* or *support*, and so *to suffer* or *undergo*.

8. **Yet** (μέντοι). Not rendered by A. V., but expressing that though they have these fearful examples before them, *yet* they persist in their sin.

Dominion—dignities (κυριότητα—δόξας). It is not easy to determine the exact meaning of these two terms. **Κυριότης**, *dominion*, occurs in three other passages, Eph. i. 21; Col. i. 16; 2 Pet. ii. 10. In the first two, and probably in the third, the reference is to angelic dignities. Some explain this passage and the one in Peter, of *evil* angels. In Colossians the term is used with *thrones*, *principalities*, and *powers*, with reference to the orders of the celestial hierarchy as conceived by Gnostic teachers, and with a view to exalt Christ above all these. *Glories* or *dignities* is used in this concrete sense only here and at 2 Pet. ii. 10.

9. **Michael the archangel.** Here we strike a peculiarity of this epistle which caused its authority to be impugned in very

early times, viz., the apparent citations of apocryphal writings. The passages are vv. 9, 14, 15. This reference to Michael was said by Origen to be founded on a Jewish work called "The Assumption of Moses," the first part of which was lately found in an old Latin translation at Milan; and this is the view of Davidson, so far at least as the words "the Lord rebuke thee" are concerned. Others refer it to Zech. iii. 1; but there is nothing there about Moses' body, or Michael, or a dispute about the body. Others, again, to a rabbinical comment on Deut. xxxiv. 6, where Michael is said to have been made guardian of Moses' grave. Doubtless Jude was referring to some accepted story or tradition, probably based on Deut. xxxiv. 6. For a similar reference to tradition compare 2 Tim. iii. 8; Acts vii. 22.

Michael. Angels are described in scripture as forming a society with different orders and dignities. This conception is developed in the books written during and after the exile, especially Daniel and Zechariah. Michael (*Who is like God?*) is one of the seven archangels, and was regarded as the special protector of the Hebrew nation. He is mentioned three times in the Old Testament (Dan. x. 13, 21; xii. 1), and twice in the New Testament (Jude 9; Apoc. xii. 7). He is adored as a saint in the Romish Church. For legends, see Mrs. Jameson, "Sacred and Legendary Art," i., 94 sq.

A railing accusation (*κρίσιν βλασφημίας*). Lit., *a judgment of railing;* a sentence savoring of impugning his dignity. Michael remembered the high estate from which he fell, and left his sentence to God.

10. Compare 2 Pet. ii. 12.

They know not (*οὐκ οἴδασιν*). Mental comprehension and knowledge, and referring to the whole range of invisible things; while the other verb in this verse, also translated by A. V. *know* (*ἐπίστανται*, originally of *skill in handicraft*), refers to palpable things; objects of sense; the circumstances of sensual enjoyment. Rev. marks the distinction by rendering the latter verb *understand.*

Naturally (φυσικῶς). Only here in New Testament. Compare φυσικὰ, *natural,* 2 Pet. ii. 12.

11. **Woe** (οὐαὶ). Often used by our Lord, but never elsewhere except here and in the Apocalypse. The expression in 1 Cor. ix. 16 is different. There the word is not used as an imprecation, but almost as a noun: " *Woe* is unto me." So Hos. ix. 12 (Sept.).

Ran greedily (ἐξεχύθησαν). Lit., *were poured out.* Rev., *ran riotously.* A strong expression, indicating a reckless, abandoned devotion of the energies, like the Latin *effundi.* So Tacitus says of Maecenas, " he was *given up* to love for Bathyllus ; " lit., *poured out into love.*

After. Better, as Rev., *in ;* as, " *in* the way of Cain." The error was their sphere of action. Similarly,

In the gainsaying (τῇ ἀντιλογίᾳ). In the practice of gainsaying like Korah's. 'Αντιλογία is from ἀντί, *against,* and λέγω, *to speak.* Hence, literally, *contradiction. Gainsay* is a literal translation, being compounded of the Anglo-Saxon *gegn,* which reappears in the German *gegen, against,* and *say.*

Korah. Who spake against Moses (Num. xvi. 3). The water which Moses brought from the rock at Kadesh was called the water of *Meribah* (*Strife*), or, in Septuagint, ὕδωρ ἀντιλογίας, *the water of contradiction.*

12. **Spots** (σπιλάδες). Only here in New Testament. So rendered in A. V., because understood as kindred to σπῖλοι (2 Pet. ii. 13); but rightly, as Rev., *hidden rocks.* So Homer, (" Odyssey," iii., 298), " the waves dashed the ship against the *rocks* (σπιλάδεσσιν)." See on *deceivings,* 2 Pet. ii. 13. These men were no longer mere *blots,* but elements of danger and wreck.

When they feast with you. See on 2 Pet. ii. 13.

Feeding (ποιμαίνοντες). See on 1 Pet. v. 2. Lit., *shepherding themselves;* and so Rev., *shepherds that feed themselves;* further their own schemes and lusts instead of tending the flock of God. Compare Isa. lvi. 11.

Without fear (ἀφόβως). Of such judgments as visited Ananias and Sapphira. Possibly, as Lumby suggests, implying a rebuke to the Christian congregations for having suffered such practices.

Clouds without water. Compare 2 Pet. ii. 17, *springs without water.* As clouds which seem to be charged with refreshing showers, but are *borne past* (παραφερόμεναι) and yield no rain.

Whose fruit withereth (φθινοπωρινὰ). From φθίνω or φθίω, *to waste away, pine,* and ὀπώρα, *autumn.* Hence, literally, *pertaining to the late autumn,* and rightly rendered by Rev., *autumn* (trees). The A. V. is entirely wrong. Wyc., *harvest trees.* Tynd., *trees without fruit at gathering-time.*

Twice dead. Not only the *apparent* death of winter, but a *real* death; so that it only remains to pluck them up by the roots.

13. **Raging** (ἄγρια). Rev., *wild,* which is better, as implying *quality* rather than *act.* Waves, by nature *untamed.* The *act* or *expression* of the nature is given by the next word.

Foaming out (ἐπαφρίζοντα). Only here in New Testament. Compare Isa. lvii. 20.

Shame (αἰσχύνας). Lit., *shames* or *disgraces.*

Wandering stars. Compare 2 Pet. ii. 17. Possibly referring to comets, which shine a while and then pass into darkness. "They belong not to the system: they stray at random and without law, and must at last be severed from the lights which rule while they are ruled" (Lumby).

Blackness (ζόφος). See on 2 Pet. ii. 4.

Of darkness (τοῦ σκότους). Lit., "*the* darkness," the article pointing back to the darkness already mentioned, ver. 6.

14. **Enoch prophesied.** This is the second of the apocryphal passages referred to in notes on ver. 9. It is quoted from the apocryphal book of Enoch, directly, or from a tradition based upon it. The passage in Enoch is as follows: "Behold he comes with ten thousands of his saints, to execute judgment upon them, and to destroy the wicked, and to strive (at law) with all the carnal for everything which the sinful and ungodly have done and committed against him." The Book of Enoch, which was known to the fathers of the second century, was lost for some centuries with the exception of a few fragments, and was found entire in a copy of the Ethiopic Bible, in 1773, by Bruce. It became known to modern students through a translation from this into English by Archbishop Lawrence, in 1821. It was probably written in Hebrew. It consists of revelations purporting to have been given to Enoch and Noah, and its object is to vindicate the ways of divine providence, to set forth the retribution reserved for sinners, angelic or human, and "to repeat in every form the great principle that the world—natural, moral, and spiritual—is under the immediate government of God." Besides an introduction it embraces five parts: 1. A narrative of the fall of the angels, and of a tour of Enoch in company with an angel through heaven and earth, and of the mysteries seen by him. 2. Parables concerning the kingdom of God, the Messiah, and the Messianic future. 3. Astronomical and physical matter; attempting to reduce the images of the Old Testament to a physical system. 4. Two visions, representing symbolically the history of the world to the Messianic completion. 5. Exhortations of Enoch to Methuselah and his descendants. The book shows no Christian influence,

is highly moral in tone, and imitates the Old Testament myths.

With ten thousands of his saints (*ἐν ἁγίαις μυριάσιν*). Lit., *in* or *among holy myriads*. Compare Deut. xxxiii. 2; Zech. xiv. 5.

Ungodly (*ἀσεβεῖς*)—**ungodly deeds** (*ἔργων ἀσεβείας*, lit., *works of ungodliness*) which they have **ungodly committed** (*ἠσέβησαν*), and of all their hard speeches which **ungodly** (*ἀσεβεῖς*) **sinners,** etc. The evident play upon the word *ungodly* can be rendered but clumsily into English. Rev., translates, *All the ungodly, of all their works of ungodliness which they have ungodly wrought, and of all the hard things which ungodly sinners have spoken against him.* The words *ungodly sinners* are placed in an unusual position, at the end of the sentence, for emphasis; ungodliness being the key-note of the writer's thought.

Hard (*τῶν σκληρῶν*). *Speeches* is supplied. Lit., *hard things.* So Rev. The *railing, gainsaying;* the *profane and vain babblings* (2 Tim. ii. 16). Compare John vi. 60, *a hard saying,* where the word means not *abusive* but *difficult.* In Jas. iii. 4, *rough,* used of the *winds.* In Acts xxvi. 14, of Saul of Tarsus; "*hard* to kick against the pricks."

16. **Murmurers** (*γογγυσταὶ*). Only here in New Testament. Doubtless, originally, with some adaptation of sound to sense, *gongustai.* It is used of the cooing of doves.

Complainers (*μεμψίμοιροι*). From *μέμφομαι, to find fault with,* and *μοῖρα,* a *part or lot.* Lit., *blamers of their lot.*

Great swelling words. See on 2 Pet. ii. 18.

Having men's persons in admiration (*θαυμάζοντες πρόσωπα*). The Rev., *shewing respect of persons,* is neater, but the A. V. more literal: *admiring the countenances.* Compare Gen

xix. 21, Sept., "I have *accepted* thee:" lit., *have admired thy face.*

Because of advantage. See 2 Pet. ii. 3, 14.

Beloved. Compare ver. 3.

18. **Mockers.** See on 2 Pet. iii. 3.

Ungodly lusts (*ἐπιθυμίας τῶν ἀσεβειῶν*). Lit., *lusts of ungodlinesses.*

19. **Separate themselves** (*ἀποδιορίζοντες*). Only here in New Testament. *Themselves* is unnecessary. Better, as Rev., *make separations;* i.e., cause divisions in the church. The verb is compounded with *ἀπό*, *away;* *διά*, *through;* *ὅρος*, *a boundary line.* Of those who draw a *line through* the church and set *off* one part from another.

Sensual (*ψυχικοί*). See on Mark xii. 30. As *ψυχή* denotes life in the distinctness of individual existence, "the centre of the personal being, the *I* of each individual," so this adjective derived from it denotes what pertains to man as man, the *natural* personality as distinguished from the *renewed* man. So 1 Cor. ii. 14; xv. 44. The rendering *sensual*, here and Jas. iii. 15, is inferential: *sensual* because *natural* and *unrenewed* In contrast with this is

The spirit. The higher spiritual life. So the adjective *πνευματικός*, *spiritual*, is everywhere in the New Testament opposed to *ψυχικός*, *natural.* See 1 Cor. xv. 44, 46.

22. **And of some have compassion, making a difference.** This follows the reading, *καὶ οὓς μὲν ἐλεεῖτε* (*ἐλεᾶτε*) *διακρινόμενοι.* The best texts, however, read *διακρινομένους*, which would require, "On some have mercy *who are in doubt.* So Rev. Others, again, for *ἐλεεῖτε*, *have mercy*, read *ἐλέγχετε*, *reprove*, and render *διακρινομένους*, *who are contentious:* "Som

who are contentious rebuke." The Rev. rendering better suits what follows.

23. **Snatching them out of the fire.** The writer has in mind Zech. iii. 2, *a brand plucked from the burning.* Compare Amos. iv. 11.

With fear (ἐν φόβῳ). Lit., *in fear;* i.e., of the contagion of sin while we are rescuing them.

Spotted (ἐσπιλωμένον). Only here and Jas. iii. 6. See on 2 Pet. ii. 13.

24. **To keep you from falling** (φυλάξαι ὑμᾶς ἀπταίστους). Lit., "to keep you *without stumbling.* Only here in New Testament. See the kindred word *offend.* Rev., *stumble,* Jas. ii. 10; iii. 2.

Exceeding joy (ἀγαλλιάσει). See on 1 Pet. i. 6.

25. **Both now and ever** (καὶ νῦν καὶ εἰς πάντας τοὺς αἰῶνας). Lit., *both now and unto all the ages.* The best texts add πρὸ παντὸς τοῦ αἰῶνος, *before all time.*

LIST OF GREEK WORDS USED BY JUDE ONLY.

ἀποδιορίζω, to separate, 19
ἄπταιστος, without falling, 24
γογγυστής, murmurer, 16
δεῖγμα, example, 7
ἐκπορνεύω, to give over to fornication, 7
ἐνυπνιάζω, to dream, 8
ἐπαγωνίζομαι, earnestly contend, 3
ἐπαφρίζω, to foam out, 13
μεμψίμοιρος, complainer, 16
παρεισδύω, to creep in unawares, 4
πλανήτης, a wanderer, 13
σπιλάς, rock, 12
ὑπέχω, to suffer, undergo, 7
φθινοπωρινός, autumnal, 12
φυσικῶς, naturally, 10

THE GENERAL EPISTLE OF JAMES.

CHAPTER I.

1. **Jesus Christ.** Only here and in ch. ii. 1; nowhere in the speeches of James (Acts xv. 14, 15; xxi. 20 sq.). Had he used Jesus' name it might have been supposed to arise from vanity, because he was the Lord's brother. In all the addresses of epistles the full name, Jesus Christ, is given.

Servant (δοῦλος). Properly, *hired* servant. Compare Philip. i. 1; Jude 1.

That are scattered abroad (ἐν τῇ διασπορᾷ). Lit., *in the dispersion;* on which see on 1 Pet i. 1. Rev., *which are of the dispersion.*

Greeting (χαίρειν). Lit., *rejoice.* The ordinary Greek salutation, *hail! welcome!* Also used at parting: *joy be with you.* Compare the same expression in the letter from the church at Jerusalem, Acts xv. 23; one of the very few peculiarities of style which connect this epistle with the James of the Acts. It does not occur in the address of any other of the Apostolic Epistles.

2. **All joy** (πᾶσαν χαρὰν). *Joy* follows up the *rejoice* of the greeting. The *all* has the sense of *wholly.* Count it a thing *wholly joyful,* without admixture of sorrow. Perhaps, as Bengel suggests, the *all* applies to *all* kinds of temptations.

When (ὅταν). Lit., *whenever:* better, because it implies that temptation may be expected all along the Christian course.

Ye fall into (περιπέσητε). The preposition περί, *around,* suggests falling into something which *surrounds.* Thus Thucydides, speaking of the plague at Athens, says, "The Athenians, having fallen into (περιπεσόντες) such affliction, were *pressed* by it."

Divers (ποικίλοις). Rev., *manifold.* See on 1 Pet. i. 6.

Temptations (πειρασμοῖς). In the general sense of *trials.* See on Matt. vi. 13; 1 Pet. i. 6.

3. **Trying** (δοκίμιον). Rev., *proof;* but the American Revisers insist on *proving,* and rightly. See on 1 Pet. i. 7.

Worketh (κατεργάζεται). The compound verb with κατά, *down through,* indicates *accomplishment.* The proving will work successfully and thoroughly. This harmonizes with a *perfect work,* ver. 4.

Patience (ὑπομονήν). See on 2 Pet. i. 6, and Jas. v. 7.

4. **Perfect work** (ἔργον τέλειον). "This is followed by a perfect man. The man himself is characterized from his condition and work" (Bengel). *Work* (ἔργον) is the word with which κατεργάζεται, *worketh,* is compounded. It is the accomplished *result* of patience in moral purification and ennobling. Compare *work of faith,* 1 Thess. i. 3.

Perfect and entire (τέλειοι καὶ ὁλόκληροι). The two words express different shades of thought. Τέλειοι, *perfect,* from τέλος, *fulfilment* or *completion* (*perfect,* from *perfectus, per factus, made throughout*), denotes that which has reached its maturity or fulfilled the *end* contemplated. Ὁλόκληροι, from ὅλος, *entire,* and κλῆρος, a *lot* or *allotment;* that which has all which properly belongs to it; its *entire allotment,* and is, therefore, intact in all its parts. Thus Peter (Acts iii. 16) says of the restored cripple, "faith has given him this *perfect soundness* (ὁλοκληρίαν). Compare the familiar phrase, *an accomplished man.* Note, also, James' repetition of the key-words of his discourse, *rejoice, joy, patience, perfect.*

Wanting nothing (ἐν μηδενὶ λειπόμενοι). Rev., more literally, *lacking in nothing.* Note James' characteristic corroboration of a positive statement by a negative clause: *entire, lacking in nothing; God that giveth* and *upbraideth not; in faith, nothing doubting.* The conditional negative μηδενὶ, *nothing,* is used, rather than the absolute negative οὐδενὶ, as implying nothing which *may be supposed;* no *possible* thing.

5. **But.** Omitted in A. V. In pursuing this perfection you will find yourselves lacking in wisdom. One may say, "I know not how to become perfect;" *but,* if any man, etc.

Lack. Note the repetition.

Of God that giveth (τοῦ διδόντος Θεοῦ). The Greek puts it so that *giving* is emphasized as an attribute of God. Lit., "Ask of *the giving God,*" or of "God the giver."

Liberally (ἁπλῶς). Only here in New Testament. Literally the word means *simply,* and this accords with the following negative clause, *upbraiding not.* It is *pure, simple* giving of good, without admixture of evil or bitterness. Compare Rom. xii. 8, where a kindred noun is used: "He that giveth let him do it *with simplicity* (ἐν ἁπλότητι)." Compare, also, Prov. x. 22. Men often complicate and mar their giving with reproach, or by an assumption of superiority.

6. **Doubting** (διακρινόμενος). Compare Matt. xxi. 21. Not equivalent to *unbelief,* but expressing the hesitation which balances between faith and unbelief, and inclines toward the latter. This idea is brought out in the next sentence.

A wave (κλύδωνι). Rev., *surge*. Only here and Luke viii. 24; though the kindred verb occurs at Eph. iv. 14. The word is admirably chosen, as by a writer who lived near the sea and was familiar with its aspects. The general distinction between this and the more common κῦμα, *wave*, is that κλύδων describes the long *ridges* of water as they are propelled in horizontal lines over the vast surface of the sea; while κῦμα denotes the pointed masses which toss themselves up from these under the action of the wind. Hence the word κλύδων here is explained, and the picture completed by what follows: *a billow* or *surge*, driven by the wind in lines, and *tossed* into *waves*. Both here and in the passage in Luke the word is used in connection with the wind. It emphasizes the idea of *extension*, while the other word throws forward the idea of concentrating into a crest at a given point. Hence, in the figure, the emphasis falls on the *tossing;* not only moving before the impulse of the wind, but not even moving in regular lines; tossed into rising and falling peaks.

Driven by the wind (ἀνεμιζομένῳ). Only here in New Testament.

Tossed (ῥιπιζομένῳ). Only here in New Testament. From ῥιπίς, a *fan*. Anyone who has watched the great ocean-swell throwing itself up into pointed waves, the tops of which are caught by the wind and fanned off into spray, will appreciate the vividness of the figure.

7. **That man** (ἐκεῖνος). Emphatic, and with a slightly contemptuous force.

Anything, *i.e.*, which he asks for.

8. **A double-minded man is unstable,** etc. The A. V. puts this as an independent apophthegm, which is wrong. The sentence is a comment and enlargement upon *that man*. "Let not that man think," etc., "a double-minded man, unstable in all his ways." So Rev.

Double-minded (δίψυχος). Peculiar to James, here and ch. iv. 8. Not *deceitful*, but *dubious* and *undecided*.

Unstable (ἀκατάστατος). Only here in New Testament. The kindred ἀκαταστασία, *confusion*, is found ch. iii. 16, and elsewhere.

9. **But.** Omitted in A. V. Introducing a contrast with the double-minded.

The brother of low degree (ὁ ἀδελφὸς ὁ ταπεινὸς). Lit., *the brother, the lowly one.* Not in the higher Christian sense of ταπεινὸς (see on Matt. xi. 29), but, rather, *poor* and *afflicted*, as contrasted with *rich.*

Rejoice (καυχάσθω). Not strong enough. It is, rather, *boast.* So Rev., *glory.* Compare Rom. v. 3; Philip. iii. 3.

In that he is exalted (ἐν τῷ ὕψει αὐτοῦ). Lit., *in his exaltation.* Rev., *in his high estate.*

10. **In that he is made low** (ἐν τῇ ταπεινώσει αὐτοῦ). A form of expression similar to the preceding. Lit., *in his humiliation.* Both the A. V. and Rev. preserve the kinship between ταπεινὸς and ταπεινώσει, by the word *low.*

Flower (ἄνθος). Only here, ver. 11, and 1 Pet. i. 24.

11. **For the sun is no sooner risen,** etc. (ἀνέτειλεν γὰρ ὁ ἥλιος). By the use of the aorist tense James graphically throws his illustration into the narrative form: "For the sun *arose* —and *withered*," etc.

With a burning heat (τῷ καύσωνι). Rev., *with the scorching wind.* The article denotes something familiar; and the reference may be to the scorching east-wind (Job i. 19, Sept.; Ezek. xvii. 10), which withers vegetation. Some of the best authorities, however, prefer the rendering of the A. V.

Falleth (ἐξέπεσεν). Aorist tense. Lit., *fell off*.

The grace of the fashion (εὐπρέπεια τοῦ προσώπου). Lit., *the beauty of its face or appearance*. *Εὐπρέπεια* only here in New Testament.

Fade away (μαρανθήσεται). See on 1 Pet. i. 4.

Ways (πορείαις). Rev., *goings*. Only here and Luke xiii. 22. His goings to and fro in acquiring riches.

12. **Is tried** (δόκιμος γενόμενος). Lit., *having become approved*. See on *trial*, 1 Pet. i. 7. The meaning is not, as the A. V. suggests, *when his trial is finished*, but when he has *been approved by trial*. Rev., rightly, *when he hath been approved*.

The crown (στέφανον). See on 1 Pet. v. 4.

Of life (τῆς ζωῆς). Lit., *the* life: the article pointing to the well-known eternal life. The figure is not that of the *athlete's* crown, for an image from the Grecian games, which the Jews despised, would be foreign to James' thought and displeasing to his readers. Rather the *kingly* crown, the proper word for which is διάδημα, *diadem*. In Ps. xx. 3 (Sept.), στέφανος is used of the *royal* crown. In Zech. vi. 11, 14, the reference seems to be to a priestly crown, forming part of the high-priest's mitre.

13. **Of God** (ἀπὸ Θεοῦ). Lit., *from God*. Not *by* God, as the direct agent, but by agency proceeding *from* God. Compare Matt. iv. 1, where the direct agency, "*by* the spirit," "*by* the devil," is expressed by *ὑπό*.

Cannot be tempted (ἀπείραστος ἐστι). Lit., *is incapable of being tempted*. But some of the best expositors render *is unversed in evil things*, as better according both with the usage of the word and with the context, since the question is not of

God's being tempted, but of God's tempting. Rev. gives this in margin. Ἀπείραστος only here in New Testament.

Neither tempteth he (πειράζει δὲ αὐτὸς). The A. V. fails to render αὐτὸς: "*He himself* tempteth no man." So Rev.

14. **Drawn away** (ἐξελκόμενος). Only here in New Testament. This and the following word are metaphors from hunting and fishing. *Drawn away*, as beasts are enticed from a safecovert into a place beset with snares. Note the present participle, as indicating the *progress* of the temptation: "is *being drawn* away."

Enticed (δελεαζόμενος). As a fish with bait. Also the present participle. See on 2 Pet. ii. 14.

15. **The lust.** Note the article, omitted in A. V. The peculiar lust of his own.

Hath conceived (συλλαβοῦσα). Lit., *having conceived.*

Bringeth forth (τίκτει). Metaphor of the mother. Rev., *beareth.*

When it is finished (ἀποτελεσθεῖσα). Better, Rev., *when it is full grown.* Not when the course of a sinful life is completed; but when sin has reached its full development.

Bringeth forth (ἀποκύει). A different verb from the preceding, *bringeth forth.* Rev. has rendered τίκτει, *beareth*, in order to avoid the repetition of *bringeth forth.* The verb is used by James only, here and at ver. 18. The image is interpreted in two ways. Either (1) Sin, figured as female, is already pregnant with death, and, when full grown, bringeth forth death (so Rev., and the majority of commentators). "The harlot, Lust, draws away and entices the man. The guilty union is committed by the will embracing the temptress: the consequence is that she beareth sin. . . . Then *the* sin, that particular sin, when grown up, herself, as if all along pregnant with it, bringeth forth death" (Alford). Or (2) Sin, figured as male, when it has reached maturity, becomes the *begetter* of death. So the Vulgate, *generat*, and Wyc., *gendereth*. I am inclined to prefer this, since the other seems somewhat forced. It has the high endorsement of Bishop Lightfoot. There is a suggestive parallel passage in the "Agamemnon" of Aeschylus, 751–771:

> "There is a saying old,
> Uttered in ancient days,
> That human bliss, full grown,
> Genders, and dies not childless:
> And, for the coming race,
> Springs woe insatiate from prosperity.
> But I alone
> Cherish within my breast another thought.
> The impious deed
> Begets a numerous brood alike in kind;
> While households ruled by right inflexible
> Blossom with offspring fair.
> Insolence old
> In men depraved begetteth insolence,
> Which springs afresh from time to time
> As comes the day of doom, and fresh creates
> In Ate's dismal halls
> Fierce wrath from light,
> Unhallowed Daring, fiend invincible,
> Unconquered, with its parents' likeness stamped."

The magnificent passage in Milton's "Paradise Lost," ii., 760–801, is elaborated from these verses of James.

17. The first words of this verse form a hexameter line, thus:

Πᾶσα δό|σις ἀγα|θὴ καὶ| πᾶν δῶ|ρημα τέ|λειον.

Such verses, or parts of verses, occur occasionally in the New Testament. Sometimes they are quotations from the Greek poets; sometimes the writer's words unconsciously fall into metrical form. Poetical quotations are confined to Paul, Acts xvii. 28; 1 Cor. xv. 33; Tit. i. 12.

Every good gift and every perfect gift (see Greek above). The statement that these gifts are from God is in pursuance of the idea that God does not tempt men to evil. The gifts of God are contrasted with the evil springing from man's lust. Two words are used for *gift*. *Δόσις* occurs only here and Philip. iv. 15; there in an active sense; but here passive, as in Prov. xxi. 14 (Sept.). *Δώρημα* is found Rom. v. 16. It enlarges slightly upon the other word in emphasizing the gift as *free, large, full*; an idea which is further developed in ver. 18, *of his own will*. The Rev., rather awkwardly, endeavors to bring out the distinction by the word *boon*, for which the American Revisers insist on retaining *gift*. *Boon* originally means *a petition*; *favor* being a secondary and later sense, as of something given in response to a petition. The word is of Scandinavian origin, and the meaning *favor* seems to indicate a confusion with the Latin *bonus*, good; French, *bon*.

Perfect. Enlarges upon *good*, bringing out more distinctly the *moral* quality of the gift.

And cometh down (*καταβαῖνον*). A present participle, to be construed with *ἄνωθεν ἐστιν*, *is from above*. Lit., *is coming down from above*. As usual, this union of the participle with the finite verb denotes something *habitual*. Render, *descendeth from above*. Compare ch. iii. 15.

Father of lights (*τοῦ πατρὸς τῶν φώτων*). Lit., *the* lights, by which are meant the heavenly bodies. Compare Ps. cxxxv. 7 (Sept.); and Jer. iv. 23 (Sept.). God is called "the Father of the lights," as being their creator and maintainer. Compare Job xxxviii. 28; Ps. viii. 3; Amos v. 8.

Is no variableness (*ἔνι*). Abbreviated from *ἔνεστι*, *is in*. Stronger than the simple *is*, and denoting *inherence* or *indwelling*. Rev., *can be*.

Variableness (*παραλλαγή*). Better, Rev., *variation*. The word is not used, as some suppose, in a technical, astronomical sense, which James' readers would not have understood, but in the simple sense of *change* in the degree or intensity of light, such as is manifested by the heavenly bodies. Compare Plato, "Republic," vii., 530: "Will he (the astronomer) not think that the heaven and the things in heaven are framed by the Creator in the most perfect manner? But when he reflects that the proportions of night and day, or of both, to the month, or of the month to the year, or of the other stars to these and to one another, are of the visible and material, he will never fall into the error of supposing that they are eternal and liable to no deviation (οὐδὲν παραλλάττειν)—that would be monstrous."

Shadow of turning (τροπῆς ἀποσκίασμα). This is popularly understood to mean that there is in God not the faintest *hint* or *shade* of change, like the phrase, a *shadow of suspicion*. But the Greek has no such idiom, and that is not James' meaning. Rev., rightly, renders, *shadow that is cast by turning;* referring still to the heavenly orbs, which cast shadows in their revolution, as when the moon turns her dark side to us, or the sun is eclipsed by the body of the moon.

18. **Begat** (ἀπεκύησεν). Rev., *brought forth.* See on ver. 15, and compare 1 John iii. 9; 1 Pet. i. 23.

A kind of first-fruits (ἀπαρχήν τινα). *A kind of* indicates the figurative nature of the term. The figure is taken from the requirement of the Jewish law that the first-born of men and cattle, and the first growth of fruits and grain should be consecrated to the Lord. The point of the illustration is that Christians, like first-fruits, should be consecrated to God. The expression "first-fruits" is common in the New Testament. See Rom. viii. 23; xvi. 5; 1 Cor. xv. 20, 23; Apoc. xiv. 4.

19. **Wherefore.** The A. V. follows the reading ὥστε. But the correct reading is ἴστε, *ye know*, and so Rev. Others render it as imperative, *know ye*, as calling attention to what follows.

21. **Filthiness** (ῥυπαρίαν). Only here in New Testament, but James uses the kindred adjective (ch. ii. 2), "*vile* raiment."

Ῥύπος, *filth*, occurs in 1 Pet. iii. 21—on which see notes; and the verb ῥυπόω, *to be filthy*, is found in Apoc. xxii. 11.

Superfluity of naughtiness (περισσείαν κακίας). A translation which may be commended to the attention of indiscriminate panegyrists of the A. V. *Περισσεία* is an unclassical word, and occurs in three other New-Testament passages—Rom. v. 17; 2 Cor. viii. 2; x. 15. In all these it is rendered *abundance*, both by A. V. and Rev. There seems to be no need of departing from this meaning here, as Rev., *overflowing*. The sense is *abounding* or *abundant wickedness*. For *naughtiness* Rev. gives *wickedness*, as in 1 Pet. ii. 1, 16, where it changes *malice* to *wickedness*. It is mostly rendered *malice* in both A. V. and Rev. In this passage, as in the two from Peter, Rev. gives *malice*, in margin. *Malice* is an adequate translation, the word denoting a malevolent disposition toward one's neighbor. Hence it is not a general term for moral evil, but a special form of vice. Compare *the wrath of man*, ver. 20. *Naughtiness* has acquired a petty sense in popular usage, as of the mischievous pranks of children, which renders it out of the question here.

With meekness (ἐν πραΰτητι). Lit., "*in* meekness;" opposed to malice.

Engrafted (ἔμφυτον). Only here in New Testament. Better, and more literally, as Rev., *implanted*. It marks a characteristic of the word of truth (ver. 18). It is *implanted;* divinely *given*, in contrast with something acquired by study. Compare Matt. xiii. 19, "the word of the kingdom—*sown* in his heart." *Grafted* or *graffed* is expressed by a peculiar word, employed by Paul only, ἐγκεντρίζω, from κέντρον, a *sharp point*, thus emphasizing the fact of the *incision* required in grafting. See Rom. xi. 17, 19, 23, 24.

Which is able to save (τὸν δυνάμενον σῶσαι). Compare Rom. i. 16, "the *power* of God unto *salvation*."

22. **Hearers** (ἀκροαταὶ). Used by James only.

Deceiving (παραλογιζόμενοι). From παρά, *beside, contrary to*, and λογίζομαι, *to reckon*, and hence *to conclude by reasoning*. The deception referred to is, therefore, that into which one betrays himself by false reasoning—reasoning *beside* the truth.

23. **Beholding** (κατανοοῦντι). With the notion of *attentively* considering (κατά, *down into*, or *through*; compare εἰς, *into*, ver. 25). Compare Luke xii. 24, 27; Heb. iii. 1. So that the contrast is not between a *hasty* look and a *careful* contemplation (ver. 25, *looketh*). It is not mere careless hearing of the word which James rebukes, but the neglect to carry into practice what is heard. One may be an attentive and critical hearer of the word, yet not a doer.

His natural face (τὸ πρόσωπον τῆς γενέσεως). Lit., *the countenance of his birth;* the face he was born with.

In a glass (ἐν ἐσόπτρῳ). Better, Rev., *a mirror;* a *metallic* mirror. The word occurs only here and 1 Cor. xiii. 12.

24. **He beholdeth** (κατενόησεν). The aorist tense, throwing the sentence into a lively, narrative form: *he beheld himself* and *forgot.* Compare ver. 11.

25. **Whoso looketh** (ὁ παρακύψας). Rev., more strictly, *he that looketh.* See on 1 Pet. i. 12. The verb is used of one who stoops *sideways* (παρά) to look attentively. The mirror is conceived as placed on a table or on the ground. Bengel quotes Wisdom of Sirach xiv. 23: "He that prieth in at her (Wisdom's) windows shall also hearken at her doors." Coleridge remarks: "A more happy or forcible word could not have been chosen to express the nature and ultimate object of reflection, and to enforce the necessity of it, in order to discover the living fountain and spring-head of the evidence of the Christian faith in the believer himself, and at the same time to point out the seat and region where alone it is to be found" ("Aphorisms").

Into (εἰς). Denoting the penetration of the look into the very essence of the law.

The perfect law of liberty (νόμον τέλειον τὸν τῆς ἐλευθερίας). Lit., *the perfect law, the law of liberty.* So Rev. The law of liberty is added as defining the perfect law.

Continueth therein. Better, Rev., *so continueth;* i.e., continues looking.

Forgetful hearer (ἀκροατὴς ἐπιλησμονῆς). The latter word only here in New Testament. Lit., *a hearer of forgetfulness;* whom forgetfulness characterizes. Rev., very happily, *a hearer that forgetteth;* a rendering which gives the proper sense of forgetfulness *as a characteristic* better than A. V., *a forgetful hearer.*

Doer of the work. Lit., *of work,* as the noun has no article. Rev., *a doer that worketh.*

In his deed (ἐν τῇ ποιήσει αὐτοῦ). More correctly, as Rev., *in his doing.* Only here in New Testament. The preposition ἐν (*in*) marks the inner connection between doing and blessedness. "The life of obedience is the element wherein the blessedness is found and consists" (Alford).

26. **Seem to be** (δοκεῖ). Rev., correctly, *thinketh himself to be.* A man can scarcely *seem* to be religious, when, as Trench observes, "his religious pretensions are belied and refuted by the allowance of an unbridled tongue."

Religious (θρῆσκος). Only here in New Testament, and nowhere in classical Greek. The kindred noun θρησκεία, *religion,* occurs Acts xxvi. 5; Col. ii. 18; Jas. i. 26, 27; and means the *ceremonial service* of religion. Herodotus (ii., 37) uses it of various observances practised by the Egyptian priests, such as wearing linen, circumcision, shaving, etc. The derivation is uncertain. Θρέομαι, *to mutter forms of prayer,* has been suggested, as the followers of Wycliffe were called *Lollards,* from the old Dutch *lullen* or *lollen, to sing.* Hence the adjective here refers to a zealous and diligent performance of religious services.

Bridleth (χαλιναγωγῶν). Used by James only. See ch. iii. 2. Lit., *to guide with a bridle.* So Plato, "Laws," 701: "I think that the argument ought to be pulled up from time to time, and not to be allowed to run away, but held with bit and bridle."

27. **Undefiled** (ἀμίαντος). See on 1 Pet. i. 4. The two adjectives, *pure* and *undefiled*, present the positive and negative sides of purity.

To visit (ἐπισκέπτεσθαι). See on Matt. xxv. 36. James strikes a downright blow here at ministry by proxy, or by mere gifts of money. Pure and undefiled religion demands *personal contact* with the world's sorrow: to *visit* the afflicted, and to visit them *in their affliction.* "The rich man, prodigal of money, which is to him of little value, but altogether incapable of devoting any personal attention to the object of his alms, often injures society by his donations; but this is rarely the case with that far nobler charity which makes men familiar with the haunts of wretchedness, and follows the object of its care through all the phases of his life" (Lecky, "History of European Morals," ii., 98).

To keep (τηρεῖν). See on 1 Pet. i. 4.

Unspotted (ἄσπιλον). See on 1 Pet. i. 19.

CHAPTER II.

1. **Have** (ἔχετε). Rev., *hold*, not in the sense of *hold fast, cleave to*, but of *possessing, occupying*, and *practising*, as a matter of habit. Thus we say that a man *holds* his property by a certain tenure. A rented estate is a *holding.* So of an opinion, or set of opinions, with which one is publicly identified. We say that he *holds* thus and so.

With respect of persons (ἐν προσωποληψίαις). From **πρόσωπον**, *the countenance*, and **λαμβάνω**, *to receive. To re-*

ceive the countenance is a Hebrew phrase. Thus Levit. xix. 15 (Sept.): *Οὐ λήψῃ πρόσωπον πτωχοῦ: Thou shalt not respect the person* (*receive the countenance*) *of the poor.* Compare Luke xx. 21; Rom. ii. 11; and Jude 16.

The Lord of glory. Compare 1 Cor. ii. 8; Acts vii. 2; Eph. i. 17.

2. **Assembly** (*συναγωγὴν*). The word *synagogue* is a transcript of this. From *σύν*, *together*, and *ἄγω*, *to bring*. Hence, literally, *a gathering* or *congregation*, in which sense the word is common in the Septuagint, not only of assemblies for worship, but of gatherings for other public purposes. From the meeting itself the transition is easy to the *place* of meeting, the synagogue; and in this sense the term is used throughout the New Testament, with the following exceptions: In Acts xiii. 43, it is rendered *congregation* by the A. V., though Rev. gives *synagogue;* and in Apoc. ii. 9; iii. 9, the unbelieving Jews, as a body, are called *synagogue of Satan.* As a designation of a distinctively Jewish assembly or place of worship it was more sharply emphasized by the adoption of the word *ἐκκλησία*, *ecclesia*, to denote the Christian church. In this passage alone the word is distinctly applied to a Christian assembly or place of worship. The simplest explanation appears to be that the word designates the *place* of meeting for the Christian body, James using the word most familiar to the Jewish Christians; an explanation which receives countenance from the fact that, as Huther observes, "the Jewish Christians regarded themselves as still an integral part of the Jewish nation, as the chosen people of God." As such a portion they had their special synagogue. From Acts vi. 9, we learn that there were numerous synagogues in Jerusalem, representing different bodies, such as the descendants of Jewish freedmen at Rome, and the Alexandrian or Hellenistic Jews. Among these would be the synagogue of the Christians, and such would be the case in all large cities where the dispersed Jews congregated. Alford quotes a phrase from the "Testaments of the Twelve Patriarchs:" *the synagogue of the Gentiles.* Compare Heb. x. 25, "the *assembling together* (*ἐπισυναγωγὴν*) of yourselves."

With a gold ring (χρυσοδακτύλιος). Only here in New Testament. Not a man wearing a single gold ring (as A. V. and Rev.), which would not attract attention in an assembly where most persons wore a ring, but *a gold-ringed man*, having his hands conspicuously loaded with rings and jewels. The ring was regarded as an indispensable article of a Hebrew's attire, since it contained his signet; and the name of the ring, *tabbath*, was derived from a root signifying *to impress a seal*. It was a proverbial expression for a most valued object. See Isa. xxii. 24; Hag. ii. 23. The Greeks and Romans wore them in great profusion. Hannibal, after the battle of Cannae, sent as a trophy to Carthage, three bushels of gold rings from the fingers of the Roman knights slain in battle. To wear rings on the right hand was regarded as a mark of effeminacy; but they were worn profusely on the left. Martial says of one Charinus that he wore six on each finger, and never laid them aside, either at night or when bathing. The fops had rings of different sizes for summer and winter. Aristophanes distinguishes between the populace and those who wear rings, and in his comedy of "The Clouds" uses the formidable word σφραγιδονυχαργοκομῆται, *lazy, long-haired fops, with rings and well-trimmed nails*. Demosthenes was so conspicuous for this kind of ornament that, at a time of public disaster, it was stigmatized as unbecoming vanity. Frequent mention is made of their enormous cost. They were of gold and silver, sometimes of both; sometimes of iron inlaid with gold. The possible beauty of these latter will be appreciated by those who have seen the elegant gold and iron jewellery made at Toledo, in Spain. Sometimes they were of amber, ivory, or porcelain. The practice of wearing rings was adopted by the early Christians. Many of their rings were adorned with the symbols of the faith—the cross, the anchor, the monogram of Christ, etc. Among the rings found in the catacombs are some with a key, and some with both a key and a seal, for both locking and sealing a casket.

Goodly apparel (ἐσθῆτι λαμπρᾷ). Lit., *bright* or *shining clothes*. Rev., *fine clothing*.

Vile (ῥυπαρᾷ). Compare ch. i. 21; and see on 1 Pet. iii. 21.

3. **Ye have respect** (ἐπιβλέψητε). Lit., *ye look upon*, with the idea of respectful consideration; *ye regard*. Compare Luke i. 48; ix. 38.

In a good place (καλῶς). Lit., *honorably;* in a seat of honor.

Under. Not literally *underneath*, but down on the ground beside. Compare Matt. xxiii. 6, on the fondness of the Jews for the chief places in the synagogue.

4. **Are ye not partial in yourselves?** (οὐ διεκρίθητε ἐν ἑαυτοῖς). Wrong. The constant sense of the verb in the New Testament is *doubt*, except Acts xi. 2; Jude 9, where it means *dispute*. Compare ch. i. 6. The meaning here is, therefore, that, in making a distinction between the rich and the poor, they expressed a doubt concerning the faith which they professed, and which abolished such distinctions. Hence, Rev., rightly, *Are ye not divided in your own mind?*

Judges of evil thoughts (κριταὶ διαλογισμῶν πονηρῶν). Better, as Rev., "judges *with* evil thoughts." The form of expression is the same as in Luke xviii. 6, κριτὴς τῆς ἀδικίας, *the judge of injustice*, i.e., the unjust judge. So Jas. i. 25, *a hearer of forgetfulness*. The word *thoughts* is, rather, *reasonings*. See on *deceiving yourselves* (ch. i. 22). Compare Luke v. 21. Their evil *processes* of thought lead to these unjust discriminations.

5. **Hearken, my beloved brethren.** Alford cites this phrase as one of the very few links which connect this epistle with the speech of James in Acts xv. 13.

The poor of this world (τοὺς πτωχοὺς τοῦ κόσμου). But the correct reading is τῷ κόσμῳ, *to the world;* and the expression is to be explained in the same way as ἀστεῖος τῷ Θεῷ, *fair unto God*, Acts vii. 20, and δυνατὰ τῷ Θεῷ, *mighty through* (Rev., *before*) *God*, 2 Cor. x. 4. So Rev., *poor as to the world*, in the world's esteem. *Poor*, see on Matt. v. 3.

Rich in faith. The Rev., properly, inserts *to be*, since the words are not in apposition with *poor*, but express the object for which God has chosen them. Faith is not the *quality* in which they are to be rich, but the *sphere* or *element;* rich in their position as believers. "Not the *measure* of faith, in virtue of which one man is richer than another, is before the writer's mind, but the *substance* of the faith, by virtue of which *every* believer is rich" (Wiesinger, cited by Alford).

6. **Despised** (ἠτιμάσατε). Not strong enough. They had *manifested* their contempt; had *done* despite to them. Rev., correctly, *dishonored*. From the use of the aorist tense, *ye dishonored*, which the A. V. and Rev. render as a perfect, *ye have dishonored*, the reference would appear to be to a specific act like that described in vv. 2, 3.

Oppress (καταδυναστεύουσιν). Only here and Acts x. 38. The preposition κατά, *against*, implies a power exercised for *harm*. Compare *being lords over*, 1 Pet. v. 3, and *exercise dominion*, Matt. xx. 25, both compounded with this preposition.

Draw (ἕλκουσιν). Not strong enough. The word implies *violence*. Hence, better, as Rev., *drag*. Compare Livy's phrase, "*a lictoribus trahi*, to be dragged by the lictors to judgment;" Acts viii. 3, of Saul *haling* or *hauling* men and women to prison; and Luke xii. 58.

Judgment-seats (κριτήρια). Only here and 1 Cor. vi. 24.

7. **They** (αὐτοὶ). Emphatic. "Is it not *they* who blaspheme?"

Worthy (καλὸν). Rev., better, because stronger, *honorable*. By this epithet the disgracefulness of the blasphemy is emphasized.

By the which ye are called (τὸ ἐπικληθὲν ἐφ' ὑμᾶς). Lit., *which is called upon you;* the name of Christ, invoked in baptism. The phrase is an Old-Testament one. See Deut. xxviii. 10, where the Septuagint reads *that the name of the Lord has been called upon thee.* Also, 2 Chron. vii. 14; Isa. iv. 1. Compare Acts xv. 17.

8. **Fulfil the royal law** (νόμον τελεῖτε βασιλικὸν). The phrase occurs only here and Rom. ii. 27. Τελεῖν, *fulfil,* is stronger than the more common word τηρεῖν, *observe* or *keep,* which appears in ver. 10. Compare, also, Matt. xix. 17; xxiii. 3; John xiv. 15, etc. James here speaks of a *single* commandment, the proper word for which is ἐντολή, while νόμος is the *body* of commandments. It is appropriate here, however, since this special commandment sums up the entire law. See Rom. xiii. 10; Gal. v. 14. It is the *royal* law; the king of all laws.

The phrase *royal law* is of Roman origin (*lex regia*). In the kingly period of Roman history it did not signify a law promulgated by the absolute authority of the king, but a law passed by a popular assembly under the presidency of the king. In later times the term was applied to all laws the origin of which was attributed to the time of the kings. Gradually the term came to represent less of the popular will, and to include all the rights and powers which the Roman people had formerly possessed, so that the emperor became what formerly the people had been, sovereign. "It was not," says Gibbon, "before the ideas and even the language of the Romans had been corrupted, that a royal law (*lex regia*) and an irrevocable gift of the people were created. . . . The pleasure of the emperor, according to Justinian, has the vigor and effect of law, since the Roman people, by the royal law, have transferred to their prince the full extent of their own power and sovereignty. The will of a single man, of a child, perhaps, was allowed to prevail over the wisdom of ages and the inclinations of millions; and the degenerate Greeks were proud to declare that in his hands alone the arbitrary exercise of legislation could be safely deposited" ("Decline and Fall," ch. xliv.).

9. **Ye have respect to persons** (προσωπολημπτεῖτε). Only here in New Testament. See on ver. 1.

Ye commit sin (ἁμαρτίαν ἐργάζεσθε). Lit., "*work* sin." Compare Matt. vii. 23; Acts x. 35; Heb. xi. 33. The phrase is rather stronger than the more common ἁμαρτίαν ποιεῖν, *to do sin*, John viii. 34; Jas. v. 15; 1 Pet. ii. 22. The position of *sin* is emphatic: "it is *sin* that ye are working."

And are convinced (ἐλεγχόμενοι). Rather, as Rev., *convicted*. The word, which is variously rendered in A. V. *tell a fault, reprove, rebuke, convince*, while it carries the idea of *rebuke*, implies also a rebuke which produces a *conviction* of the error or sin. See on John viii. 46. Compare John iii. 20; viii. 9; 1 Cor. xiv. 24, 25.

10. **Keep** (τηρήσῃ). See on ver. 8.

Offend (πταίσῃ). Lit., as Rev., *stumble*.

He is guilty (γέγονεν ἔνοχος). Lit., *he is become guilty*. Ἔνοχος, *guilty*, is, strictly, *holden; within the condemning power of*. Compare Matt. xxvi. 66; Mark iii. 29; 1 Cor. xi. 27. Huther cites a Talmudic parallel: "But if he perform all, but omit one, he is guilty of every single one."

11. **A transgressor** (παραβάτης). From παρά, *beyond*, and βαίνω, *to go*. A transgressor, therefore, is one who *goes beyond the line*. So, also, *trespass*, which is *transpass*, from the Latin *trans, across*, and *passus, a step*. A similar word occurs in Homer, ὑπερβασία, a *transgression* or *trespass*, from ὑπέρ, *over*, and βαίνω, *to go*.

12. **So.** With reference to what follows, *speak* and *do*.

13. **He shall have judgment without mercy that hath shewed no mercy** (ἡ γὰρ κρίσις ἀνίλεως τῷ μὴ ποιήσαντι

ἔλεος). Lit., as Rev., *judgment is without mercy to him that hath shewed no mercy.* Both A. V. and Rev. omit the article "*the* judgment," that, namely, which is coming. *Hath shewed*, or, lit., *shewed* (aorist tense). The writer puts himself at the stand-point of the judgment, and looks backward.

Rejoiceth (κατακαυχᾶται). The simple verb **καυχάομαι** means *to speak loud, to be loud-tongued;* hence, *to boast.* Better, therefore, as Rev., *glorieth.* Judgment and mercy are personified. While judgment threatens condemnation, mercy interposes and prevails over judgment. "Mercy is clothed with the divine glory, and stands by the throne of God. When we are in danger of being condemned, she rises up and pleads for us, and covers us with her defence, and enfolds us with her wings" (Chrysostom, cited by Gloag).

14. **What doth it profit?** (τί τὸ ὄφελος). Lit., *what is the profit?* Ὄφελος, *profit*, only here, ver. 16, and 1 Cor. xv. 32.

15. **Be** (ὑπάρχωσιν). The distinction between this word and the simple εἶναι, *to be*, is very subtle. The verb ὑπάρχω originally means *to make a beginning;* hence, *to begin* or *to come into being;* and, though used substantially as a synonym of εἶναι, of a thing actually existing and at hand, it has a backward look to an antecedent condition which has been protracted into the present. Thus we might paraphrase here, "If a brother or sister, having been in a destitute condition, be found by you in that condition." ***Εἶναι***, on the other hand, would simply state the present fact of destitution. See on 2 Pet. i. 8.

Destitute (λειπόμενοι). Lit., *left behind;* and hence *lacking*, as Rev. Compare ch. i. 4, 5. This usage of the word occurs in James only.

Daily (ἐφημέρου). Only here in New Testament.

16. **Depart in peace** (ὑπάγετε ἐν εἰρήνῃ). Compare **ὕπαγε** or πορεύου εἰς εἰρηνήν, *go into peace*, Mark v. 34; Luke vii. 50.

Be filled (χορτάζεσθε). See on Matt. v. 6.

Those things which are needful (τὰ ἐπιτήδεια). Only here in New Testament.

17. **Being alone** (καθ' ἑαυτήν). Wrong. Rev., correctly, *in itself*. The phrase belongs to *dead*. It is dead, not merely in reference to something else, but absolutely.

18. **Without** (χωρὶς). Rev., more literally, *apart from*.

And I will shew thee, etc. The Rev. brings out the antithesis more sharply by keeping more closely to the Greek order: *I by my works will shew*, etc.

19. **Tremble** (φρίσσουσιν). Only here in New Testament. It means, originally, *to be rough on the surface; to bristle*. Hence, used of the fields with ears of corn; of a line of battle bristling with shields and spears; of a silver or golden vessel rough with embossed gold. Aeschylus, describing a crowd holding up their hands to vote, says, *the air bristled with right hands*. Hence, of a horror which makes the hair stand on end and contracts the surface of the skin, making "goose-flesh." Rev., much better, *shudder*.

20. **Vain** (κενέ). Lit., *empty*, without spiritual life.

Dead (νεκρά). But the best texts read ἀργή, *idle;* as of money which yields no interest, or of land lying fallow.

21. **When he had offered** (ἀνενέγκας). Incorrect. For the participle states the *ground* of his justification. *By works* gives the *general* ground; *offered*, etc., the *specific* work. Compare Gen. xxii. 16, 17. Rev., correctly, *in that he offered*. The word ἀνενέγκας is, lit., *brought up to;* and means, not actually to offer up in sacrifice (though Isaac was *morally* sacrificed in Abraham's will), but *to bring to the altar as an offering* See on 1 Pet. ii. 5.

22. **Wrought with his works** (συνήργει τοῖς ἔργοις). There is a play on the words in the Greek: *worked with his works.*

23. **Was fulfilled** (ἐπληρώθη). Not was *confirmed*, which the word does not mean either in New-Testament or in classical usage, but *was actually and fully realized.* James here uses the formula which in the Old Testament is employed of the realizing of a former utterance. See 1 Kings ii. 27; 2 Chron. xxxvi. 22 (Sept.).

Imputed (ἐλογίσθη). Lit., as Rev., *reckoned.*

He was called the friend of God. The term, however, does not occur either in the Hebrew or Septuagint, though it is found in the A. V. and retained in Rev. Old Testament. In 2 Chron. xx. 7 (Sept.), *thy friend* is τῷ ἠγαπημένῳ σου, *thy beloved.* In Isa. xli. 8 (Sept.), *my friend* is ὃν ἠγάπησα, *whom I loved.* "The friend of God" is still the favorite title of Abraham among the Jews and Mohammedans.

25. **Rahab.** Also referred to in Heb. xi. 31, among the examples of faith. Dante places her in the third heaven:

"Thou fain wouldst know who is within this light
That here beside me thus is scintillating,
Even as a sunbeam in the limpid water.
Then know thou, that within there is at rest
Rahab, and being to our order joined,
With her in its supremest grade 'tis sealed.

. . . .

First of Christ's Triumph was she taken up.
Full meet it was to leave her in some heaven,
Even as a palm of the high victory
Which he acquired with one palm and the other,
Because she favored the first glorious deed
Of Joshua upon the Holy Land."

Paradise, ix., 112–125.

Rahab became the wife of Salmon, and the ancestress of Boaz, Jesse's grandfather. Some have supposed that Salmon was one of the spies whose life she saved. At any rate, she became the mother of the line of David and of Christ, and is so recorded in Matthew's genealogy of our Lord, in which only four women are named. There is a peculiar significance in this selection of Rahab with Abraham as an example of faith, by James the Lord's brother.

Sent them out (ἐκβαλοῦσα). Better, *thrust them forth*, implying haste and fear. Compare Mark i. 12; Luke iv. 29; Acts xvi. 37.

Another way. Than that by which they entered. Through the window. See Josh. ii. 15.

26. **Works** (τῶν ἔργων). Note the article: *the* works belonging or corresponding to faith; *its* works.

CHAPTER III.

1. **Masters** (διδάσκαλοι). Literally, and better, *teachers*, with a reference to the exhortation to be *slow to speak* (ch. i. 19). Compare 1 Cor. xiv. 26–34. James is warning against the too eager and general assumption of the privilege of teaching, which was not restricted to a particular class, but was exercised by believers generally.

2. **Offend** (πταίομεν). Lit., *stumble*, as Rev. Compare ch. ii. 10.

To bridle. See on ch. i. 26.

3. **Behold.** Following the old reading, ἴδε. All the best texts read εἰ δὲ, *now if*. So Rev.

Bits (χαλινοὺς). Only here and Apoc. xiv. 20. It may be rendered either *bit*, as A. V., or *bridle*, as Rev., but *bridle* is preferable because it corresponds with the verb *to bridle* (ver. 2) which is compounded with this noun.

Horses. The position in the sentence is emphatic.

We turn about (*μετάγομεν*). Used by James only.

4. **The ships.** See Introduction, on James' local allusions. Dean Howson observes that "there is more imagery drawn from mere natural phenomena in the one short epistle of James than in all St. Paul's epistles put together."

So great. As the ship which conveyed Paul to Malta, which contained two hundred and seventy-six persons (Acts xxvii. 37).

Fierce (*σκληρῶν*). More literally, and better, as Rev., *rough*. The word primarily means *hard*, *harsh*.

Helm (*πηδαλίου*). Better, *rudder*, as Rev. The rudder was an oar worked by a handle. Helm and rudder were thus one. The word occurs only here and Acts xxvii. 40.

The governor listeth (*ἡ ὁρμὴ τοῦ εὐθύνοντος βούλεται*). Lit., *the impulse or desire of the steersman wisheth*. Ὁρμὴ, *impulse*, only here and Acts xiv. 5, of an *assault*, *onset*.

The governor (*τοῦ εὐθύνοντος*). Rev., *steersman*. Lit., *of him who is guiding*. Only here and John i. 23. From *εὐθύς*, *straight*.

5. **Boasteth great things** (*μεγαλαυχεῖ*). The best texts separate the compound, and read *μεγάλα αὐχεῖ*, of course with the same meaning. *Αὐχεῖ*, *boasteth*, only here in New Testament.

How great a matter a little fire kindleth (*ἡλίκον πῦρ ἡλίκην ὕλην ἀνάπτει*). The word *ὕλη* (only here in New Testament) means *wood* or *a forest*, and hence the *matter* or *raw material* of which a thing is made. Later, it is used in the philosophical sense of *matter*—"the foundation of the manifold"—opposed to the intelligent or formative principle *νοῦς*, *mind.* The authorized version has taken the word in one of its secondary senses, hardly the philosophical sense it would seem; but any departure from the earlier sense was not only needless, but impaired the vividness of the figure, the familiar and natural image of a forest on fire. So Homer:

> "As when a fire
> Seizes a thick-grown forest, and the wind
> Drives it along in eddies, while the trunks
> Fall with the boughs amid devouring flames."
>
> *Iliad,* xi., 155.

Hence, Rev., rightly, "*Behold how much wood* or *how great a forest is kindled by how small a fire.*

This, too, is the rendering of the Vulgate: *quam magnam silvam.*

6. **World of iniquity** (*κόσμος τῆς ἀδικίας*). *Κόσμος*, primarily, means *order*, and is applied to the world or universe as an orderly system. A world of iniquity is an organism containing within itself all evil essence, which from it permeates the entire man. *World* is used in the same sense as in the latter part of Prov. xvii. 6 (Sept.), which is not given in the A. V. "The trusty hath the whole world of things, but the faithless not a groat."

Is the tongue (*καθίσταται*). This differs a little from the simple *is*, though it is not easy to render it accurately. The verb means *to appoint, establish, institute*, and is used of the tongue as having an appointed and definite place in a system (among our members). It might be rendered *hath its place.*

Defileth (*σπιλοῦσα*). Lit., *defiling.* Only here and Jude 23. See on 2 Pet. ii. 13.

Setteth on fire (*φλογίζουσα*). Lit., *setting on fire.* Only in this verse in New Testament.

The course of nature (*τροχὸν τῆς γενέσεως*). A very obscure passage. *Τροχός* (only here in New Testament), from τρέχω, *to run*, applies generally to anything round or circular which runs or rolls, as a wheel or sphere. Hence, often a *wheel*. Used of the circuit of fortifications and of circles or zones of land or sea. From the radical sense, *to run*, comes the meaning *course*, as the course of the sun; and from this a *place* for running, a *race-course*. Γενέσεως, rendered *nature*, means *origin*, *beginning*, *birth*, *manner of birth*, production, and is used by Plato for the *creation*, or the sum of created things. It also means a *race*, and a *generation* or *age*. In the New Testament it occurs but twice outside of this epistle, viz., at Matt. i. 1, "the book of the *generation* of Jesus Christ," where the meaning is *origin* or *birth*; the *birth-book* of Jesus Christ. The other passage is Matt. i. 18, according to the best texts, also meaning *birth*. In Jas. i. 23, as we have seen, πρόσωπον τῆς γενέσεως is *the face of his birth*. We may then safely translate τροχός by *wheel*; and as *birth* is the meaning of γένεσις in every New-Testament passage where it occurs, we may give it the preference here and render *the wheel of birth*—i.e., the wheel which is set in motion at birth and runs on to the close of life. It is thus a figurative description of human life. So Anacreon:

> "The chariot-wheel, like life, runs rolling round."

Tertullian says: "The whole *revolving wheel of existence* bears witness to the resurrection of the dead." The Rev., which gives *nature*, puts *birth* in margin. This revolving wheel is kindled by the tongue, and rolls on in destructive blaze. The image is justified by the fact. The tongue works the chief mischief, kindles the most baleful fires in the course of life.

7. **Kind** (φύσις). Wrong. James is not speaking of the relation between *individual* men and individual beasts, but of the relation between the *nature* of man and that of beasts, which may be different in different beasts. Hence, as Rev., in margin, *nature*.

Beasts (θηρίων). Quadrupeds. Not beasts generally, nor wild beasts only. In Acts xxviii. 4, 5, the word is used of the *viper* which fastened on Paul's hand. In Peter's vision (Acts x. 12; xi. 6) there is a different classification from the one here; quadrupeds being denoted by a specific term, τετράποδα, *four-footed creatures.* There θηρία includes fishes, which in this passage are classed as ἐναλίων, *things in the sea.*

By mankind (τῇ φύσει τῇ ἀνθρωπίνῃ). Rather, *by the nature of man*, φύσις, as before, denoting the generic character. Every *nature* of beasts is tamed by the *nature* of man. Compare the fine chorus in the "Antigone" of Sophocles, 343–352:

"The thoughtless tribe of birds,
The beasts that roam the fields,
The brood in sea-depths born,
He takes them all in nets,
Knotted in snaring mesh,
Man, wonderful in skill.
And by his subtle arts
He holds in sway the beasts
That roam the fields or tread the mountain's height;
And brings the binding yoke
Upon the neck of horse with shaggy mane,
Or bull on mountain crest,
Untamable in strength."

8. **No man** (οὐδεὶς ἀνθρώπων). A strong expression. Lit., *no one of men.*

Unruly (ἀκατάσχετον). Lit., *not to be held back.* The proper reading, however, is ἀκατάστατον, *unsettled.* See on καθίσταται, *hath its place*, ver. 6. Rev., correctly, *restless.*

Deadly (θανατηφόρου). Lit., *death-bearing*, or *-bringing.* Only here in New Testament.

Poison (ἰοῦ). Rendered *rust* at ch. v. 3; and found only in these two passages and in Rom. iii. 13, in the citation of Ps. cxl. 3.

9. **God, even the Father** (τὸν Θεὸν καὶ πατέρα). The proper reading is τὸν Κύριον, *the Lord*, and the καὶ, *and*, is simply con-

nective. Read, therefore, as Rev., *the Lord and Father*. This combination of terms for God is uncommon. See ch. i. 27.

Which. Not *who*, which would designate *personally* certain men; whereas James designates them generically.

11. **Doth a fountain,** etc. The interrogative particle, μήτι, which begins the sentence, expects a negative answer. Fountain has the article, "*the* fountain," generic. See Introduction, on James' local allusions. The Land of Promise was pictured to the Hebrew as a land of springs (Deut. viii. 7; xi. 11). "Palestine," says Dean Stanley, "was the only country where an Eastern could have been familiar with the language of the Psalmist: 'He sendeth the springs into the valleys which run among the mountains.' Those springs, too, however short-lived, are remarkable for their copiousness and beauty. Not only not in the East, but hardly in the West, can any fountains and sources of streams be seen, so clear, so full-grown even at their birth, as those which fall into the Jordan and its lakes throughout its whole course from north to south" ("Sinai and Palestine"). The Hebrew word for a fountain or spring is *áyin*, meaning *an eye*. "The spring," says the same author, "is the bright, open source, the *eye* of the landscape."*

Send forth (βρύει). An expressive word, found nowhere else in the New Testament, and denoting a *full, copious* discharge. Primarily it means *to be full to bursting;* and is used, therefore, of budding plants, teeming soil, etc., as in the charming picture of the sacred grove at the opening of the "Oedipus Coloneus" of Sophocles: "*full* (βρύων) of bay, olive, and vine." Hence, *to burst forth* or *gush*. Though generally intransitive, it is used transitively here.

Place (ὀπῆς). Rather, *opening* or *hole* in the earth or rock. Rev., *opening*. Compare *caves*, Heb. xi. 38. The word is pleasantly suggestive in connection with the image of the *eye* of the landscape. See above.

* See Scott's "Castle Dangerous," ch. i.

Sweet water and bitter. The readers of the epistle would recall the bitter waters of Marah (Exod. xv. 23), and the unwholesome spring at Jericho (2 Kings ii. 19–21).

12. **So can no fountain both yield salt water and fresh.** The best texts omit *so can no fountain*, and the *and* between *salt* and *fresh*. Thus the text reads, *οὔτε ἁλυκὸν γλυκὺ ποιῆσαι ὕδωρ*. Render, as Rev., *neither can salt water yield sweet*. Another of James' local allusions, *salt* waters. The Great Salt Sea was but sixteen miles from Jerusalem. Its shores were lined with salt-pits, to be filled when the spring freshets should raise the waters of the lake. A salt marsh also terminated the valley through which the Jordan flows from the Lake of Tiberias to the Dead Sea, and the adjoining plain was covered with salt streams and brackish springs. Warm springs impregnated with sulphur abound in the volcanic valley of the Jordan. *Ἁλυκὸν*, *salt*, occurs only here in the New Testament.

13. **Wise and endued with knowledge** (*σοφὸς καὶ ἐπιστήμων*). A rendering needlessly verbose, yet substantially correct. Probably no very nice distinction was intended by the writer. It is somewhat difficult to fix the precise sense of *σοφός*, since there is no uniformity in its usage in the New Testament. In classical Greek it primarily means *skilled in a handicraft* or *art*. Thence it runs into the sense of *clever*, in matters of common life, *worldly wise*. Then, in the hands of the philosophers, it acquires the sense of *learned in the sciences;* and, ironically, *abstruse*, *subtle*, *obscure*, like the English *cunning*, which originally meant *knowing* or *skilful*, and is often used in that sense in the English Bible (see Gen. xxv. 27; 1 Sam. xvi. 16).

In the New Testament *σοφός* is used—1. In the original classical sense, *skilled in handicraft* (1 Cor. iii. 10). 2. *Accomplished in letters, learned* (Rom. i. 14, 22; 1 Cor. i. 19, 26; iii. 18). So of the Jewish theologians and doctors (Matt. xi. 25), and of Christian teachers (Matt. xxiii. 34). 3. In a practical sense, of the practice of the law of piety and honesty; so Eph. v. 15, where it is joined with *walking circumspectly*, and 1 Cor. vi. 5, where it is represented as the quality adapted to adjust differences in the church. 4. In the higher, philosophical sense, of devising the best counsels and employing the best means to carry them out. So of God, Rom. xvi. 27; 1 Tim. i. 17; Jude 25; 1 Cor. i. 25. In this passage the word appears to be used in the sense of 3: *practical wisdom in pious living.*

'Επιστήμων occurs only here in the New Testament. In classical Greek it is often used like *σοφός*, in the sense of *skilled, versed;* and by the philosophers in the higher sense of *scientifically* versed, in which sense it is opposed by Plato to *δοξαστής*, a mere *conjecturer.* In this passage *σοφός* would seem to be the broader, more general, and perhaps more dignified term of the two, as denoting the *habit* or *quality*, while *ἐπιστήμων* indicates the special development and intelligent application of the quality to particular things. The Rev., *wise* and *understanding*, gives the distinction, on the whole, as nearly as is necessary.

Conversation (*ἀναστροφῆς*). See on 1 Pet. i. 15.

Meekness of wisdom. On *meekness*, see on Matt. v. 5. The meekness which is the proper attribute of wisdom.

> "Knowledge is proud that she has learned so much,
> Wisdom is humble that she knows no more."

14. **Envying** (*ζῆλον*). The word is used in the New Testament both in a bad and a good sense. For the latter, see John ii. 17; Rom. x. 2; 2 Cor. ix. 2. From it is our word *zeal*, which may be either good or bad, wise or foolish. The bad sense is predominant in the New Testament. See Acts v. 17; Rom. xiii. 13; Gal. v. 20, and here, where the bad sense is defined and emphasized by the epithet *bitter*. It is often joined with *ἔρις*, *strife*, as here with *ἐρίθεια*, *intriguing* or *faction*. The rendering *envying*, as A. V., more properly belongs to *φθόνος*, which is never used in a good sense. *Emulation* is the better general rendering, which does not necessarily include envy, but may be full of the spirit of self-devotion. Rev. renders *jealousy*.

Strife (ἐριθείαν). A wrong rendering, founded on the mistaken derivation from ἔρις, *strife*. It is derived from ἔριθος, a *hired servant*, and means, primarily, *labor for hire*. Compare Tobit ii. 11: *My wife did take women's work to do* (ἠριθεύετο). Thus it comes to be applied to those who serve in official positions for their own selfish interest, and who, to that end, promote *party spirit and faction*. So Rom. ii. 8: *them that are contentious* (ἐξ ἐριθείας), lit., of *faction*. Rev., *factious*. Also, 2 Cor. xii. 20. Rev., here, rightly, *faction*.

15. **Wisdom** (σοφία). See on σοφός, ver. 13.

From above. Compare ch. i. 17.

Sensual (ψυχική). See on Jude 19.

Devilish (δαιμονιώδης). Or *demoniacal*, according to the proper rendering of δαίμων (see on Matt. iv. 1). Only here in New Testament. Devilish, "such," says Bengel, "as even devils have." Compare ch. ii. 19.

16. **Confusion** (ἀκαταστασία). See on *restless*, ver. 8.

Evil (φαῦλον). An inadequate rendering, because it fails to bring out the particular phase of evil which is dominant in the word: *worthlessness, good-for-nothingness*. In classical Greek it has the meanings *slight, trivial, paltry*, which run into *bad*. In the New Testament it appears in this latest stage, and is set over against *good*. See John iii. 20; v. 29; Tit. ii. 8. Rev., *vile*, which, according to its etymology, Lat., *vilis*, follows the same process of development from *cheap*, or *paltry*, to *bad*.

17. **First.** Emphasizing its inner quality, *pure*, as distinguished from its outward expressions. The idea is not first *numerically*, but first *essentially*. The other qualities are secondary as outgrowths of this primary quality.

Gentle (ἐπιεικής). See on 1 Pet. ii. 18.

Easy to be intreated (εὐπειθής). Only here in New Testament.

Without partiality (ἀδιάκριτος). Only here in New Testament and very rare in classical Greek. Rev., without *variance* or *doubting*. See on ch. i. 6.

CHAPTER IV.

1. **Lusts** (ἡδονῶν). Lit., *pleasures*, as Rev. Properly, *sensual* pleasures. The sinful pleasures are the outgrowths of the lusts, ver. 2.

That war (στρατευομένων). The thought of wars and fightings is carried into the figurative description of the sensuality which arrays its forces and carries on its campaign in the members. The verb does not imply mere fighting, but all that is included in military service. A remarkable parallel occurs in Plato, "Phaedo," 66: "For whence come wars and fightings and factions? Whence but from the body and the lusts of the body?" Compare 1 Pet. ii. 11; Rom. vii. 23.

2. **Ye lust.** See on *desire*, 1 Pet. i. 12; Mark iv. 19.

Desire to have (ζηλοῦτε). Rev., *covet*, and *are jealous*, in margin. See on ch. iii. 14.

3. **Ye ask** (αἰτεῖτε). See on ἠρώτων, *besought*, Matt. xv. 23.

Amiss (κακῶς). Lit., *evilly*: with evil intent, as explained by the following sentence.

Consume it upon (δαπανήσητε ἐν). More correctly, as Rev., *spend it in*. The sense is not *lay out expense upon your pleasures*, but *spend in the exercise of; under the dominion of*.

4. **Ye adulterers** (μοιχοὶ). All the best texts omit.

Adulteresses (μοιχαλίδες). The feminine term is the general designation of all whom James here rebukes. The apostate members of the church are figuratively regarded as unfaithful spouses; according to the common Old-Testament figure, in which God is the *bridegroom* or *husband* to whom his people are wedded. See Jer. iii.; Hos. ii., iii., iv.; Isa. liv. 5; lxii. 4, 5. Also, Matt. xii. 39; 2 Cor. xi. 2; Apoc. xix. 7; xxi. 9.

Will be (βουληθῇ εἶναι). More correctly, as Rev., *would be.* Lit., *may have been minded to be.*

Is the enemy (καθίσταται). Thereby *constitutes* himself. Rev., *maketh himself.* See on ch. iii. 6.

5. **Do ye think** (δοκεῖτε). See on ch. i. 26.

The scripture (ἡ γραφὴ). See on Mark xii. 10. Properly, a *passage* of scripture.

In vain (κενῶς). Only here in New Testament.

6. **Resisteth.** See on 1 Pet. v. 5.

Proud. See on Mark vii. 22.

Humble. See on Matt. vii. 29.

7. **Submit yourselves** (ὑποτάγητε). Rev., *be subject.* The verb means *to place* or *arrange under;* as *resist* (ver. 6) is *to array against.* God sets himself in array against the proud; therefore, array yourselves under God, that ye may withstand the devil.

8. **Purify** (ἁγνίσατε). One of the three instances in the New Testament in which the word is not used of *ceremonial* purification. The others are 1 Pet. i. 22; 1 John iii. 3.

Double-minded (δίψυχοι). Compare ch. i. 8.

9. **Be afflicted** (ταλαιπωρήσατε). Only here in New Testament. The kindred noun ταλαιπωρία, *misery*, occurs ch. v. 1.

Mourn (πενθήσατε). Used of grief that is *manifested*. So mostly in New Testament, and very commonly joined, as here, with *weep*. So Mark xvi. 10; Luke vi. 25, etc. In the next sentence occurs the kindred noun πένθος, *mourning*, into which *laughter*, also something manifest, is to be changed.

Heaviness (κατήφειαν). Properly, a *casting down of the eyes*. Compare Luke xviii. 13. Only here in New Testament.

12. **There is one lawgiver** (εἷς ἐστὶν ὁ νομοθέτης). The A. V. fails to note the emphatic position of *one*. Better, Rev., *one only is the lawgiver*. Νομοθέτης, *lawgiver*, only here in New Testament.

But who art thou? (σὺ δὲ τίς εἶ). According to the Greek order: *but thou, who art thou?*

13. **Go to now** (ἄγε νῦν). *Go to* is an obsolete phrase, though retained in Rev. It is a formula for calling attention: *come now*.

Such a city (τήνδε τὴν πόλιν). More accurately, as Rev., *this city*.

Continue there a year (ποιήσομεν ἐκεῖ ἐνιαυτὸν). Lit., *we will make a year*. See, for the same form of expression, Acts xv. 33; xviii. 23; 2 Cor. xi. 25. Better, as Rev., *spend a year there*. (Compare the A. V., Acts xviii. 23, rightly retained by Rev.) The word ποιήσομεν implies more than mere *continuance;* rather, a *doing something* with the year.

And. The frequent use of the copulative gives a lively tone to the passage, expressive of the lightness and thoughtlessness of a careless spirit.

Buy and sell (ἐμπορευσόμεθα). Rev., more concisely, *trade.* Only here and 2 Pet. ii. 3.

14. **Whereas ye know not** (οἵτινες οὐκ ἐπίστασθε). The pronoun marking a class, *as being of those who know not.*

What shall be on the morrow (τὸ τῆς αὔριον). Lit., *the thing of the morrow.* The texts vary. Westcott and Hort read, *Ye know not what your life shall be on the morrow, for ye are a vapor:* thus throwing out the question.

What is your life? (ποία). Lit., *of what kind or nature.*

It is even a vapor (ἀτμὶς γάρ ἐστιν). But all the best texts read ἐστε, *ye are.* So Rev., which, however, retains the question, *what is your life?*

Appeareth—vanisheth. Both participles, *appearing, vanishing.*

And then (ἔπειτα καὶ). The καὶ placed after the adverb *then* is not *copulative*, but expresses that the vapor vanishes *even as* it appeared.

15. **For that ye ought to say** (ἀντὶ τοῦ λέγειν ὑμᾶς). Ver. 14 was parenthetical, so that at this point the thought is taken up from ver. 13: *Ye who say we will go*, etc.—*for that ye ought to say.* The rendering in margin of Rev. is simpler: *instead of your saying.*

16. **Ye rejoice** (καυχᾶσθε). Rev., *glory.* See on ch. ii. 13.

Boastings (ἀλαζονείαις). Only here and 1 John ii. 16. The kindred word ἀλαζών, *a boaster*, is derived from ἄλη, *a wandering* or *roaming;* hence, primarily, *a vagabond, a quack, a mountebank.* From the empty boasts of such concerning the cures and wonders they could perform, the word passed into the sense of *boaster.* One may boast *truthfully;* but ἀλαζονεία is *false* and *swaggering* boasting. Rev. renders *vauntings*, and rightly, since *vaunt* is from the Latin *vanus*, *empty*, and therefore expresses *idle* or *vain* boasting.

CHAPTER V.

1. **Go to.** See on ch. iv. 13.

Weep and howl (*κλαύσατε ὀλολύζοντες*). Lit., *weep, howling*. The latter is a descriptive word, *ol-ol-uz-o*. Only here in New Testament, and denoting a more demonstrative and passionate expression of grief than weeping.

Miseries (*ταλαιπωρίαις*). Only here and Rom. iii. 16. See on *be afflicted*, ch. iv. 9.

That shall come upon (*ἐπερχομέναις*). Present participle. More correctly, as Rev., *that are coming*.

2. **Are corrupted** (*σέσηπεν*). Only here in New Testament.

Are moth-eaten (*σητόβρωτα γέγονεν*). Lit., *have become moth-eaten*. Only here in New Testament, but compare *σκωληκόβρωτος*, *eaten of worms*, Acts xii. 23; and see Matt. vi. 19, 20.

3. **Is cankered** (*κατίωται*). Only here in New Testament, from *ἰός*, *rust*, as in the following sentence. Also *poison*, as ch. iii. 8. The preposition *κατά* indicates *thoroughness, completely* rusted.

Flesh (*τὰς σάρκας*). The noun is plural: the *fleshy parts* of the body. So Sept. (2 Kings ix. 36): "the *flesh* (*τὰς σάρκας*) of Jezebel." So Apoc. xix. 18.

4. **Reaped down** (*ἀμησάντων*). Only here in New Testament. The primary meaning is *to reap corn;* also in classical Greek of *mowing down in battle*. The secondary, which some

mistake for the primary sense, is *to gather*, as for harvest. Rev., *mowed.*

Fields (χώρας). The more general word, *place*, for ἀγρός, the ordinary word for a *field;* though the usage is warranted by classical Greek, and occurs Luke xii. 16; John iv. 35, the only two instances besides this in the New Testament. It implies a larger tract than ἀγρός, as is evident in all the New-Testament passages cited. In two cases it refers to a rich man's estates; and in John iv. 35, the Lord directs the attention of the disciples to a broad area or series of fields.

Crieth (κράζει). An inarticulate cry. Compare Gen. iv. 10.

Lord of Sabaoth. Lord of hosts. The only instance in which the phrase is used by a New-Testament writer. Rom. ix. 29, is quoted from Isa. i. 9.

5. **Ye have lived in pleasure** (ἐτρυφήσατε). Only here in New Testament. See on 2 Pet. ii. 13, on the kindred noun τρυφή, *riot* or *revel.* Rev., *ye have lived delicately.*

Been wanton (ἐσπαταλήσατε). Only here and 1 Tim. v. 6. Ἐτρυφήσατε denotes *dainty* living: this word, *luxurious* or *prodigal* living. Rev., *taken your pleasure*, is colorless, and is no improvement on the A. V.

As in a day of slaughter (ὡς ἐν ἡμέρᾳ σφαγῆς). All the best texts reject ὡς, *as.* The meaning of the passage is disputed. Some find the key to it in the words *last days* (ver. 3). The phrase *day of slaughter* is used for *a day of judgment*, Jer. xii. 3; xxv. 34 (Sept.). According to this, the meaning is, *the day of judgment*, at the supposed near coming of Christ. Others explain that these men are like beasts, which, on the very day of their slaughter, gorge themselves in unconscious security.

7. **Be patient** (μακροθυμήσατε). From μακρός, *long*, and θυμός, *soul* or *spirit*, but with the sense of strong passion,

stronger even than ὀργή, *anger*, as is maintained by Schmidt ("Synonymik"), who describes θυμός as a *tumultuous welling up of the whole spirit;* a mighty emotion which seizes and moves the whole inner man. Hence the restraint implied in μακροθυμία is most correctly expressed by *long-suffering*, which is its usual rendering in the New Testament. It is a patient holding out under trial; a long-protracted restraint of the soul from yielding to passion, especially the passion of *anger.* In the New Testament the word and its cognates are sometimes rendered by *patient* or *patience*, which conceals the distinction from ὑπομονή, uniformly rendered *patience*, and signifying *persistent endurance*, whether in action or suffering. As Trench observes, "ὑπομονή is *perseverantia* and *patientia* both in one." Thus Bishop Ellicott: "The brave patience with which the Christian contends against the various hindrances, persecutions, and temptations that befall him in his conflict with the inward and outward world." Ὑπομονή contains an element of *manliness.* Thus Plato joins it with the adverb ἀνδρικῶς, *in a manly way*, and contrasts it with ἀνάνδρως, *unmanly, cowardly.* Μακροθυμία is exercised toward *persons;* ὑπομονή, toward *things.* The former is ascribed to God as an attribute (Luke xviii. 7; 1 Pet. iii. 20; 2 Pet. iii. 9, 15), the latter never; for *the God of patience* (Rom. xv. 5) is the God who *imparts* patience to his children. "There can be no resistance to God nor burden upon him, the Almighty, from *things.* Therefore ὑπομονή cannot find place in him" (Trench). Rev. retains A. V., *be patient.* The thought links itself naturally with that in the preceding verse: *the righteous doth not resist.*

Therefore. Since things are so. Referring to the condition of things described in the previous passage.

Brethren. In contrast with the rich just addressed.

Waiteth (ἐκδέχεται). With expectation. Compare Matt. xiii. 30; Mark iv. 27.

The early and latter rain (ὑετὸν πρώιμον καὶ ὄψιμον). Both adjectives only here in New Testament. Ὑετὸν, *rain*, is rejected by all the best texts. The *early* rain fell in October, November, and December, and extended into January and February. These rains do not come suddenly, but by degrees, so that the farmer can sow his wheat or barley. The rains are mostly from the west or southwest (Luke xii. 54), continuing two or three days at a time, and falling mostly in the night. Then the wind shifts to the north or east, and fine weather ensues (Prov. xxv. 23). The *latter* rains, which are much lighter, fall in March and April. Rain in harvest was regarded as a miracle (1 Sam. xii. 16–18). See Introduction, on James' local allusions.

9. **Grudge not** (μὴ στενάζετε). Better, as Rev., *murmur not*. The verb means *to sigh* or *groan*.

Standeth before the doors. In the act of entering.

10. **Example** (ὑπόδειγμα). See on 2 Pet. ii. 6.

Of suffering affliction (κακοπαθείας). Only here in New Testament. The word does not mean the *endurance* of affliction, but *affliction itself*. Hence, Rev., rightly, *suffering*.

The prophets. Compare Matt. v. 12.

11. **Endure** (ὑπομένοντας). Present participle. But the later texts read ὑπομείναντας, the aorist participle, *which endured;* referring to the prophets in the past ages. So Rev. On *endured* and *patience*, see on ver. 7.

The end of the Lord (τὸ τέλος κυρίου). A peculiar expression. The happy conclusion to which God brought Job's trials.

Very pitiful and of tender mercy (πολυσπλαγχνός καὶ οἰκτίρμων). The former adjective only here in New Testament; the latter here and Luke vi. 36. Rev., *full of pity and merciful*. Πολυσπλαγχνός is from πολύς, *much*, and σπλάγχνα, *the* *nobler entrails*, used like our *heart*, as the seat of the emotions. Hence the term *bowels* in the A. V. (Philip. i. 8; Col. iii. 12, etc.). Compare εὔσπλαγχνοι, *tender-hearted*, Eph. iv. 32. The distinction between this and οἰκτίρμων, *merciful*, seems to be that the former denotes the *general quality* of compassion, while the latter emphasizes the sympathy called out by special cases, being the feeling which is moved to pain at another's suffering.

12. **Any other oath.** See the common formulas of swearing, Matt. v. 35, 36.

13. **Is afflicted** (κακοπαθεῖ). See on the kindred word κακοπάθεια, *suffering*, ver. 10. Only here and 2 Tim. ii. 3, 9; iv. 5.

Let him sing psalms (ψαλλέτω). The word means, primarily, *to pluck* or *twitch*. Hence of the sharp *twang* on a bowstring or harp-string, and so *to play upon a stringed instrument*. Our word *psalm*, derived from this, is, properly, a tune played upon a stringed instrument. The verb, however, is used in the New Testament of singing praise generally. See 1 Cor. xiv. 15; Rom. xv. 9.

15. **The sick** (τὸν κάμνοντα). Rev. gives, better, the participial force, *him that is sick*. The word originally means *to work*. Hence, "him that is *laboring under* disease."

And if he have committed sins (κἂν ἁμαρτίας ᾖ πεποιηκώς). The Greek gives a shade of meaning which can hardly be transferred neatly into English, representing not merely the *fact* that the man has sinned, but his *condition* as a sinner. Literally the words read, *if he be having committed sins;* i.e., *in a state of having committed*, and under the moral or physical consequences of transgression.

They shall be forgiven (ἀφεθήσεται). Better, Rev., "*it* shall be forgiven," supplying the *commission* as a subject. The verb means *to send forth* or *discharge*, and is the standard New-Testament word for *forgiving*. *Forgiveness* (ἄφεσις) is a *putting* or *sending away of sins*, with a consequent discharge of the sinner; thus differing from πάρεσις (Rom. iii. 25), which is a *passing by* of sin, a *pretermission* as distinguished from a *remission*. See, farther, on Rom. iii. 25.

16. **Confess** (ἐξομολογεῖσθε). The preposition ἐξ, *forth, out*, implies *full, frank, open* confession, and so in every case of its use in the New Testament. See on Matt. iii. 6.

Faults (παραπτώματα). See on Matt. vi. 14.

The effectual, fervent prayer of a righteous man availeth much (πολὺ ἰσχύει δέησις δικαίου ἐνεργουμένη). Lit., *much availeth* (ἰσχύει, *is strong*), *the prayer of a righteous man working or operating*. The rendering of the A. V., besides being unwarranted by the text, is almost a truism. An *effectual* prayer is a prayer that *avails*. The Rev. is at once more correct and more natural: *The supplication of a righteous man availeth much in its working.*

17. **A man** (ἄνθρωπος). The generic word; human like ourselves, this thought being emphasized by the succeeding epithet *of like passions*. See the same expression, Acts xiv. 15.

Of like passions (ὁμοιοπαθὴς). Only here and Acts xiv. 15. There is some danger of a misunderstanding of this rendering, from the limited and generally bad sense in which the word *passions* is popularly used. The meaning is rather of *like nature and constitution*. Rev. puts *nature* in margin, which would be better in the text.

He prayed fervently (προσευχῇ προσηύξατο). Lit., *he prayed with prayer*. See a similar mode of expression, Gen. ii. 17 (Sept.), *ye shall surely die* (θανάτῳ ἀποθανεῖσθε); lit., *ye shall die with death*. Compare Luke xxii. 15; John iii. 29; Acts iv. 17. The addition of the cognate noun gives intenseness to the verb.

Hide—sins. A familiar Hebrew phrase. See Ps. xxxii. 1; lxxxv. 2; Prov. x. 12.

LIST OF GREEK WORDS USED BY JAMES ONLY.

ἄγε, go to, iv., 13; v., 1
ἀδιάκριτος, without doubting, iii., 17
ἀκατάστατος, unstable, i., 18; iii., 8
ἁλυκός, salt, iii., 12
ἀμάω, reap down, v., 4
ἀνέλεος, unmerciful, ii., 13
ἀνεμίζω, to drive with the wind, i., 6
ἀπείραστος, that cannot be tempted, or unversed, i., 13
ἁπλῶς, liberally, simply, i., 5
ἀποκυέω, bring forth, beget, i., 15, 18
ἀποσκίασμα, shadow, i., 17
αὐχέω, to boast, iii., 5
ἀφυστερέω, to keep back by fraud, v., 4
βοή, cry, v., 4
βρύω, to send forth, iii., 11
γέλως, laughter, iv., 9
δίψυχος, double-minded, i., 8; iv., 8
εἴκω, to be like, i., 6, 23
ἔμφυτος, implanted, i., 21
ἐνάλιος, in the sea, iii., 7
ἐξέλκω, to draw away, i., 14
ἐπιλησμονή, forgetfulness, i., 25
ἐπιστήμων, knowing, iii., 13
ἐπιτήδειος, needful, ii., 16
ὁ εὐθύνων, steersman, iii., 4
εὐπειθής, easy to be intreated, iii., 17
εὐπρέπεια, grace, i., 11
ἐφήμερος, daily, ii., 15
θανατηφόρος, deadly, iii., 8
θρῆσκος, religious, i., 26
ἰός, poison, rust, iii., 8; v., 3
κακοπάθεια, suffering, v., 10
κατήφεια, heaviness, iv., 9
κατιόω, to canker, v., 3
κατοικίζω, to cause to dwell, iv., 5
κενῶς, in vain, iv., 5
μαραίνω, to fade, i., 11
μετάγω, to turn about, iii., 3, 4
νομοθέτης, lawgiver, iv., 12
ὀλολύζω, to howl, v., 1
ὄψιμος, latter, v., 7
παραλλαγή, variation, i., 17
πικρός, bitter, iii., 11, 14
ποίησις, doing, i., 25
πολύσπλαγχνος, full of pity, v., 11
προσωποληπτέω, to have respect to persons, ii., 9
πρώϊμος, early, v., 7
ῥιπίζω, toss, i., 6
ῥυπαρία, filthiness, i., 21
σήπω, to corrupt, v., 2
σητόβρωτος, moth-eaten, v., 2
ταλαιπωρέω, to be afflicted, iv., 9
ταχύς, swift, i., 19
τροπή, turning, i., 17
τροχός, wheel, iii., 6
τρυφάω, to live daintily, v., 5
ὕλη, wood, forest, iii., 5
φιλία, friendship, iv., 4
φλογίζω, to set on fire, iii., 6
φρίσσω, to shudder, ii., 19
χαλιναγωγέω, to bridle, i., 26; iii., 2
χρή, ought, iii., 10
χρυσοδακτύλιος, adorned with gold rings, ii., 2

ADDITIONAL NOTE.

After the sheets of the three Gospels and the Acts had been printed, a careful revision of the lists of words peculiar to individual writers, and further examination of the various readings, revealed a number of omissions and errors. The lists are corrected in the following additional tables.

I take this opportunity of expressing my great indebtedness to the careful and exhaustive lists in Dr. Joseph H. Thayer's admirable lexicon, recently published. I only wish that I could have had the benefit of it in the preparation of the entire volume.

MATTHEW.

STRIKE OUT

xiii., 48, from *ἀγγεῖον*: *ἐϑνικός, εὐδία, ϑρῆνος, κῆτος, μεῖζον, μύλων, νοσσιά, πυῤῥάζω.*

CHANGE

τυφόω to *τύφω*.

ADD

ἄγγος, vessel, xiii., 48
ἀμφίβληστρον, casting-net, iv., 18
ἐγκρύπτω, to hide in, xiii., 33
εἰδέα, aspect, xxviii., 3
ἐνϑυμέομαι, think, i., 20; ix., 4
Θεέ (vocative), O God, xxvii., 46
καταϑεματίζω, to curse vehemently, xxvi., 74
λαμβάνειν συμβούλιον, to take counsel, xxvii., 1, 7; xxviii., 12
ὀλιγοπιστία, little faith, xvii., 20
παρατιϑέναι παραβολήν, set forth a parable, xiii., 24, 31
πληροῦν τὸ ῥηϑέν, to fulfil what was spoken, i., 22; ii., 15, 17, 23, etc.
τοὔνομα, by name, xxvii., 57
φυγή, flight, xxiv., 20.

MARK.

STRIKE OUT

ἅλς, γαμίσκομαι, μεϑόρια, ὄμμα, προσεγγίζω, σκώληξ.

CHANGE

ἔννυχον to ἔννυχος : *neut.*, after ἐπιβάλλω, to *intrans.*

ADD

ἀλλαχοῦ, elsewhere, i., 38
ἀνακυλίω, roll back, xvi., 4
ἀτιμάω, treat with contempt, xii., 4
διαρπάζω, to spoil, iii., 27
εἶτεν, then, iv., 28
ἐκθαυμάζω, to wonder greatly, xii., 17
θαμβέω, to be astonished, i., 27; x., 24, 32
ὁδὸν ποιεῖν, to make a way, ii., 23
τρυμαλιά, eye of a needle, x. 25.

LUKE.

STRIKE OUT

ἀναγνωρίζομαι, ἀνθυπατεύω, δικαστής, ἑκατοντάρχης, ἐμπιπλάω, xiv., 14, from εἰσπηδάω; ἐνύπνιον, ἐπέκεινα, ἐπιπορεύομαι, ἐπίστασις, ζωογονέω, θεομαχέω, θραύω, κατακληροδοτέω, κατάλοιπος, κατασοφίζομαι, καταφρονητής, i., 49, from μεγαλεῖα; μελίσσιος, πλέω, πολίτης, πολλαπλασίων, xxiv., 33, from συναθροίζω; συσπαράσσω, τροφοφορέω, τρυγών, φόρτος, φρυάσσω.

CHANGE

ἀνάληψις to ἀνάλημψις; ἐφοράω to ἐπεῖδον; ἐξώθω to ἐξωθέω; ἐποκέλλω to ἐπικέλλω; εὐθυμότερον to εὔθυμως; χράω to κίχρημι; λακέω to λάσκω; παρακαθίζω to παρακαθέζομαι; συζήτησις to συνζήτησις; under σύνειμι, x., 18, to ix., 18; σφυρόν to σφυδρόν.

ADD

Ἀθηναῖος, Athenian, A. xvii., 21, 22
ἀθροίζω, to gather, xxiv., 33
αἶνος, praise, xviii., 43
ἀμφιά(έ)ζω, to clothe, xii., 28
ἀνάπηρος, crippled, xiv., 13, 21
ἀποδεκατεύω, pay tithes, xviii., 12
Ἄραψ, Arabian, A. ii., 11
Ἄρειος Πάγος, Mars' Hill, A. xvii., 19, 22
Ἀρεοπαγίτης, Areopagite, A. xvii., 34
Ἀσιανός, of Asia, A. xx., 4
Ἀσιάρχης, Asiarch, A. xix., 31
Αὔγουστος, Augustus, ii., 1
Βεροαῖος, Berean, A. xx., 4
Γαλατικός, Galatian, A. xvi., 6; xviii., 23

διαγγέλλω, proclaim, preach, ix., 60; A. xxi., 26
διακαθαίρω, cleanse thoroughly, iii., 17
Διόσκουροι, Castor and Pollux, A. xxviii., 11
ἔα, let alone, iv.,.34
ἐκπηδάω, A. xiv., 14
under ἐλαίων, xix., 29; xxi., 37
Ελαμίτης, Elamite, A. ii., 9
Ἑλληνιστής, Hellenist, A. vi., 1; ix., 29; xi., 20
ἐμφανής, manifest, A. x., 40
Ἐπικούριος, Epicurean, A. xvii., 18
ἐπιῤῥίπτω, to cast upon, xix., 35
εὖγε, well, well done, xix., 17
Εὐρακύλων, the wind Euraquilo, A. xxvii., 14
εὐφροσύνη, joy, A. ii., 28; xiv., 17
Ἐφέσιος, Ephesian, A. xix., 28, 34, 35; xxi., 29
ἡμιθανής, half-dead, x., 30
καταδίκη, condemnation, A. xxv., 15
κατεφίστημι, make insurrection, A. xviii., 12
κλινάριον, couch, A. v., 15
λαμπρότης, brightness, A. xxvi., 13
λαμπρῶς, brilliantly, sumptuously, xvi., 19
Λιβερτῖνος, pertaining to a freedman, A. vi., 9
Λυκαονιστί, in the language of Lycaonia, A. xiv., 11
παῖς(ἡ), maid, viii., 51, 54
πανταχῆ, everywhere, A. xxi., 28
παραβάλλω, arrive, A. xx., 15
παρεμβάλλω, to cast up, xix., 43
περαιτέρω, further, besides, A. xix., 39
πνικτός, strangled, A. xv., 20, 29; xxi., 25
πνοή, wind, breath, A. ii., 2; xvii., 25
προσκλίνω, lean to, incline, A. v., 36
πρώτως, first, A. xi., 26
Πύθων, Python, A. xvi., 16
Σιδώνιος, Sidonian, A. xii., 20
σιτευτός, fatted, xv., 23, 27, 30
σκωληκόβρωτος, eaten by worms, A. xii., 23
Στωϊκός, Stoic, A. xviii., 18
συμπαραγίνομαι, to come together, xxiii., 48
συναλλάσσω, to reconcile, A. vii., 26
συνεπιτίθημι, attack jointly, A. xxiv., 9
Σύρος, Syrian, iv., 27
τριετία, space of three years, A. xx., 31
φίλη(ἡ), female friend, xv., 9
Χαλδαῖος, A. vii., 4

INDEX OF ENGLISH WORDS.

(*Figures refer to the pages.*)

INDEX OF GREEK WORDS.

(*Figures refer to the pages.*)